The Transformation of
Southern Politics

THE

TRANSFORMATION

OF SOUTHERN

POLITICS

Social Change and Political
Consequence Since 1945

Jack Bass & Walter DeVries

Basic Books, Inc., Publishers

NEW YORK

Library of Congress Cataloging in Publication Data

Bass, Jack.
　The transformation of southern politics.

　Bibliography: p.
　Includes index.
　　1.　Southern States—Politics and government—
1951–　　　　2.　Southern States—Social conditions.
3.　Afro-Americans—Southern States—Politics
and suffrage.　I.　DeVries, Walter, joint author.
II.　Title.
F216.2.B39　　　320.9′75′04　　　75–36375
ISBN: 0–465–08695–0

Contents

Contents

Preface

V. O. KEY was prophetic when he wrote in *Southern Politics in State and Nation,* published in 1949, that "of books about the South there is no end." Virtually every book written since then on the subject of southern politics has used the classic work of Key and his collaborator, Alexander Heard, as a starting point. Key's political insights and analysis of the electoral process, as well as his appreciative ear for the telling anecdote and the pungent phrase, will make his work worth reading long after the facts and personalities he described have faded from memory.

The core of the research for Key's book consisted of field interviews throughout the 11 states of the old Confederacy—Alabama, Arkansas, Florida, Georgia, Louisiana, Mississippi, North Carolina, South Carolina, Tennessee, Texas, and Virginia—and analyses of voting returns, historical trends, and demographic data.

Our book was written in the belief that the changes in the South since Key completed his classic work were such that only a similar approach, using his basic methodology of extensive interviewing in all 11 states, could present a comprehensive political portrait of the region as it enters the last quarter of the twentieth century.

The first three chapters provide a background to and an overview of the transformation of southern politics, treat the Republican emergence, the development of a two-party system, and the effect of the "southern strategy"; and explain the development of black politics. They are followed by chapters on each of the 11 states, arranged in alphabetical order. Most of the state chapters include sections that deal specifically with Republican development and with black politics, supplementing the introductory chapters on those subjects. The next two chapters examine, in turn, the political impact of the South in Congress and in the nation and the role of organized labor. The final chapter draws conclusions and projects trends.

Key wrote in his preface: "The politics of the South is incredibly complex. Its variety, its nuances, its subtleties range across the political spectrum . . . the South is changing rapidly. He who writes about it runs the risk that change will occur before the presses stop." That statement remains true.

The full variety, nuances, and subtleties that range across the changing politics of the South are found in the 11 state chapters. The exotic flavor of Louisiana, where tales of corruption are relished as part of the state's political folklore, contrasts with the rhetoric of rectitude which still lingers in Virginia. The pitched ideological battles between conservatives and liberals in Texas are completely unlike the mildly conservative blandness of North Carolina politics. The politics of accommodation contrasts with the politics of resistance and confrontation, as South Carolina and Mississippi react differently to the emergence of blacks into the political process. Florida demonstrates the swiftness with which institutional reform can be followed by substantive innovation in state government. Tennessee stands alone in its development of a genuinely competitive two-party system that shows signs of enduring. Arkansas exhibits clearly defined periods of transition from conservative Democratic one-party dominance to racial reaction against social change, to Republican challenge, and finally to a return of one-party Democratic dominance, but one in which a spirit of progressive moderation has emerged. A similar transition in Georgia has been less sharply defined, with one-party Democratic political control, having shifted from rural dominance to a new political consensus that reflects the more sophisticated influence of Atlanta. Even in Alabama, where the presence of George Wallace has to a large extent frozen political development, the appearance of change is no less real, if more subtle, than elsewhere in the South.

The authors conducted more than 360 interviews with active and retired politicians—including governors, members of Congress, legislators, and other state and local officeholders—political party officials, journalists, labor leaders, academic observers, and others in all 11 states. The list of interviews includes more than 50 blacks. Almost all of the interviews were tape-recorded, and most of them were conducted jointly by the authors. In less than a dozen cases were the interviews "off the record," and extensive use is made in the text of direct quotes from what developed into a thematic oral history project. All the tapes, and the typescripts of almost 200 interviews that were transcribed, have been filed with the Southern Historical Collection at the University of North Carolina at Chapel Hill for future use.

In addition to the interviews, other primary research for this book consisted of election data analysis (in which the authors received able assistance from Arlon Kemple) and a nationwide survey conducted by De Vries and Associates. A private client authorized use of the data for this book, and special computer runs were made to analyze differences and similarities in perceptions and attitudes between southerners and nonsoutherners and between whites and blacks in the South.

The U.S. Bureau of the Census provided assistance in compiling demographic data and made a special computer run to determine the percentage of residents of each state in 1950 and 1970 who were born outside the 11-state region.

The project was funded by grants from the Ford Foundation and the Rockefeller Foundation, and a home base and research facilities were provided by the Institute of Policy Sciences and Public Affairs at Duke University. An additional grant from the Rockefeller Foundation to the Southern Oral History Program at the University of North Carolina provided funds for tape transcription.

The advice of George Esser, director of the Southern Regional Council, in the solicitation of support for the project was invaluable.

The authors are indebted to Katy Martin for administrative support and manuscript preparation.

All the state chapters and several of the additional chapters were examined by one or more readers to whom the authors are indebted for insights and editorial suggestions. The readers were not always in agreement with the views found in this book, and this acknowledgment includes an acceptance by the authors of sole responsibility for anything said in the following chapters. Among these readers were Ray Jenkins, Dale Enoch, Jim Ranchino, William Mansfield, Elston Roady, Jack Nelson, Bruce Galphin, James Chubbuck, Hodding Carter III, Lester Salamon, Howard Covington, Thad Beyle, Jon Buchan, Harry Lightsey, Jr., Carlanna Hendrick, John Seigenthaler, David Price, Richard Murray, James Latimer, Charles McDowell, Merle Black, and Reese Cleghorn.

The authors also are indebted to Jacqueline Hall, director of the Southern Oral History Program at the University of North Carolina at Chapel Hill, and her administrative assistant, Bill Finger, for services provided in transcribing tapes of interviews.

In addition to the encouragement and advice of Alexander Heard and the sharing of insights and sources by Neal Peirce in the formative stages of this project, many others contributed their support.

The constraints of time and resources prevented more than passing mention of such deserving topics as the role of the federal judiciary in shaping southern politics since 1950, the impact of the women's movement, and an analysis of campaign financing—all subjects worth at least a full chapter and perhaps a book by other investigators.

Jack Bass and Walter DeVries

The Transformation of
Southern Politics

Chapter

1

THE EMERGING SOUTH

Political Transformation

ANDREW YOUNG, a black congressman from Atlanta whose political career evolved from the civil rights movement, was speaking to a conference of southern black mayors meeting in South Carolina. "You know, we can't help but be people who believe in doing the impossible," Young said, "because we've already done so much of it. But we sure got a long, long way to go. It's like the old black preacher says: we ain't what we oughta be; we ain't what we're gonna be; but thank God we ain't what we was."

Young's statement captured the essence of political change for the whole South—white and black—since World War II. The central themes of that change have been the emergence of southern blacks into the mainstream of political participation and the development of the Republican Party and its challenge to a one-party political system—forces that are creating progressive tendencies among the region's Democrats. The political change has been shaped both by the region's distinctive and tragic past and by the unique social and economic transformation through which the South has recently emerged to confront, with a sense of guarded optimism, the long-neglected problems that are the legacy of its history.

Each southern state has a political character and style that are as distinctive as those of 11 brothers and sisters from a single family. The states are linked by a common history that includes a plantation tradition based on slavery; a latent politics of conflict that for decades was suppressed by a one-party system which removed most descendants of the slaves from significant political participation; and the experience, unique in America, of wartime defeat and devastation.

The Democratic allegiance of the "solid South" prior to 1948 had developed from reaction to the Reconstruction government imposed by Republicans after the Civil War. The old Whig attitudes reemerged with the Democratic one-party system that developed from the Compromise of 1877. That compromise ended Reconstruction in exchange for a Republican victory by a margin of one electoral vote in the disputed Hayes-Tilden presidential election, and it allowed the white South to determine the region's policy of race relations.

Many white yeoman farmers were reduced to the status of poor whites in the devastation after the Civil War, and tens of thousands of them in every state lost their land in the ensuing decades under the crop-lien system. Their protest led to the sometimes radical populist uprising in the 1880s and 1890s, in which coalitions with blacks developed in many of the southern states. The populists constituted a mass movement that sought to establish political competition along social and economic class lines. The agrarian populists in the South were crushed by Bourbon forces—the ultraconservative Democrats—and poor whites were left in economic competition with blacks.

By the end of the first decade of the 1900s, all of the southern states had adopted new constitutions and passed election laws—including literacy tests, poll taxes, and other devices—that had the effect of not only removing a large majority of blacks from effective political participation but also diminishing the political role of poor whites. Segregation laws physically separated the poor of both races, and the rhetoric of political demagogues massaged the psyches of the alienated poor whites by imparting to them a status based on the myth of white supremacy. The fundamentalist religions of the poor of both races focused on acceptance of their condition and the promise of a better life in the hereafter.

In these political developments of the postbellum era, V. O. Key in 1949 found four major institutional forces which suppressed the grievances of the poor in the region: (1) the one-party system, in which issues tended to be suppressed; (2) disfranchisement, which left conservative elements basically in control; (3) the exclusion of blacks as political participants but not as political objects; and (4) malapportionment of state legislatures, which concentrated power in the hands of rural conservatives. By the 1970s all four had crumbled.

In the quarter century after Key's book, parallel movements of people from the farms to the cities and from agriculture to industry were accompanied by the collapse of the South's traditional social structure, which was based on rigid racial segregation. Simultaneously, mass migration patterns were occurring in which blacks moved out of the re-

4

gion, and white professionals and managers began migrating in from outside the South. The transformation of social and economic modernization struck a shattering blow to the traditional way of life that for many whites manifested itself in a politics of protest. As the region adjusts to the changes brought by industrialization, urbanization, and development of a pluralistic social structure, the South is emerging into an era of consolidation in which its destiny blends with that of the rest of the United States and that should add vitality rather than disruption to the nation's political process.

The "solid South" cracked wide open in 1948, beginning a revolt of almost three decades against the national Democratic Party, whose leadership had come to realize that a regional system of racial discrimination could not be tolerated after American blacks had fought in World War II to preserve democratic institutions. President Harry S. Truman's early attitudes about race were shaped by the pro-Confederate tradition of the area of southern Missouri in which he grew up. But his own instincts about democratic principles and the rights of the oppressed coalesced with his grasp of political reality when his appeal to urban clusters of black voters in St. Louis and Kansas City helped him win election to the U.S. Senate in 1934.

In his first year and a half after succeeding Franklin D. Roosevelt as president, Truman supported the creation of a permanent Fair Employment Practices Commission (FEPC). But southern opposition in Congress was vigorous. Senator James O. Eastland declared the FEPC was sponsored by the Congress of Industrial Organizations (CIO), "a carpetbag organization that has come into the South and is attempting to destroy Southern institutions and Southern civilization." Although Truman continued to express support for the measure in 1946, he exerted little pressure on Congress to act. The nation's black leaders encouraged their followers that fall to support Republicans in off-year elections, and the GOP won control of Congress, temporarily costing southern Democrats their hold on committee chairmanships.

Facing the 1948 election, Truman perceived the political importance of large black voting blocs in tipping the electoral vote of the largest states. He also realized that failure to deal with blatant racial discrimination would assist Soviet propaganda efforts and damage the image of the United States among the new nations in the world, whose support would go either to the United States or to the Soviet Union in decisions affecting global politics. In addition, Truman faced political opposition on the left from former Vice-President Henry Wallace, an outspoken advocate of strong civil rights measures.

Truman created the President's Committee on Civil Rights and early in 1948 demanded that Congress act on four proposals that directly affected the South: a permanent FEPC, an antilynching law, an anti–poll tax measure, and the prohibition of discrimination in interstate transportation facilities.

Southern reaction ranged from the genteel Virginia rhetoric of Senator Harry Byrd, Sr., who claimed that the president's program constituted a "devastating broadside at the dignity of Southern traditions and institutions," to the ghoulish oratory of U.S. Representative John Bell Williams of Mississippi, who said the president "has seen fit to run a political dagger into our backs and now he is trying to drink our blood."

At the 1948 Democratic National Convention, the South unsuccessfully sought to weaken a moderate civil rights plank pushed by the administration. Instead, the convention voted 651½–581½ to substitute a stronger proposal, pushed by northern liberals (led by Minneapolis Mayor Hubert H. Humphrey), that urged Congress to pass civil rights laws which would prevent discrimination in voting and employment and would protect the civil liberties of all Americans.

The Mississippi delegation and half of the Alabama delegates walked out as a band played "Dixie." Among the Alabama delegates who refused to leave the convention was a young state legislator named George Corley Wallace. He joined the remaining southern delegates in voting 263–13 for Senator Richard Russell of Georgia over Truman, with all the president's support coming from North Carolina delegates.

Many of the southerners reconvened at Birmingham, organized the States' Rights Party—whose members were later called Dixiecrats—and nominated a slate of Governor Strom Thurmond of South Carolina for president and Governor Fielding Wright of Mississippi for vice president. Their objective was to capture the 127 electoral votes of the 11 southern states, throw the election into the House of Representatives—where each state would have one vote—and win concessions for the South.

Although Truman scored a political upset with his victory that fall—in which his large majority among blacks was decisive in the populous states of California, Illinois, and Ohio—Thurmond carried the Deep South states of South Carolina, Alabama, Louisiana, and Mississippi. In all of them, he ran as the Democratic Party candidate. In Georgia, where Truman retained the party label on the state ballot, Thurmond suffered his only loss in the Deep South.[1]

The "solid South" of the Democrats had ended. Dwight Eisenhower made Republican inroads in 1952 with victories in Virginia, Tennessee, Florida, and Texas. The southern revolt against the national Democratic Party continued into the 1970s. Arkansas was the last of the southern states to defect, first to George Wallace in 1968 and then to Richard Nixon in 1972.

1. For an excellent analysis of the forces affecting white politicians and black civil rights, see Monroe Lee Billington, *The Political South in the Twentieth Century* (New York: Scribner's, 1975), chap. 4.

The South was changing to a more urban and suburban society, with demands for new priorities in government services that ranged from schools, transportation, and recreational facilities to zoning, garbage collection, and sewage disposal. The Eisenhower Republicans in the South often included leadership from the professional and business elite and a reform element that perceived the need to develop a two-party system and to challenge entrenched Democratic statehouse and courthouse organizations that generally were unresponsive to the needs of a changing society. Beginning with the Goldwater movement in the early 1960s, however, the Republican Party in much of the South generally developed as a party of reaction, on both racial and economic issues.

William C. Havard pithily summarized what many perceptive analysts in the South have noted when he observed: "The Whig mentality certainly survives among those who have most affected the growth of the new urban—or suburban—Republicanism in the South. In reading the pronouncements of many southern financiers and businessmen and of the politicians from both parties who are attempting to translate business issue-orientations into public policy, one frequently feels that he has transmigrated into the McKinley era." [2]

SOCIAL REVOLUTION

Whenever the South has experienced rapid social change, it has invariably been imposed from outside. From abolitionists to civil rights "agitators," the enemy has been identified as those who commit "the unpardonable sin of bringing the South and its problems to the attention of the nation and the world." [3]

To help explain why President Nixon's popularity remained far greater in the South than elsewhere during the Watergate controversy that led to impeachment proceedings and the president's resignation, youthful Republican state Representative Richard Hines of South Carolina explained in December 1973: "We feel he's being beleaguered by the same people who have beleaguered us. We don't like him because we feel he's too much of a compromiser, but we feel for him." [4] At a regional Repub-

2. William C. Havard, *The Changing Politics of the South* (Baton Rouge: Louisiana State University Press, 1972), p. 25.
3. Charles O. Lerche, Jr., *The Uncertain South: Its Changing Patterns of Politics in Foreign Policy* (Chicago: Quadrangle, 1964), p. 243.
4. Interview with Richard Hines, December 7, 1973.

lican leadership conference in Atlanta at that time, one speaker attacked the "lying polls" for their reports of Nixon's sunken popularity; another attacked the news media for their reporting on Watergate and related problems; and a third blamed it all on a "Democrat-controlled Congress." For traditional white southerners, the enemy was familiar—the outside.

It was the outside that launched the black revolution, beginning with the Supreme Court ruling in *Smith* v. *Allwright* (1944) that the whites-only primary was unconstitutional. The Truman policies, including desegregation of the armed forces, further undermined the foundation of legally imposed segregation. But the beginning of what came to be known as the Second Reconstruction was the 1954 Supreme Court decision *Brown* v. *Board of Education*, which began the slow process of formal dismantlement of de jure segregation, which continued to crumble through subsequent court decisions. The final blows came with the Civil Rights Act of 1964 and the Voting Rights Act of 1965, landmark legislation of the administration of President Lyndon B. Johnson in response to the demands of the civil rights movement.

The National Association for the Advancement of Colored People (NAACP) had chapters throughout the South, and the independent NAACP Legal Defense and Education Fund fought major court battles. Direct confrontation began when Rosa Parks, a weary black woman, refused to move to the back of a bus in segregated Montgomery, Alabama, in 1955. A resulting boycott by blacks elevated a young, local Baptist minister, Dr. Martin Luther King, Jr., into leadership of what became the Southern Christian Leadership Conference (SCLC). He emerged as a charismatic national leader whose tactics—often confronting violence with nonviolence—were patterned after those of Indian nationalist Mohandas Gandhi, who led efforts to overthrow British rule in his country.

Other civil rights organizations in the 1960s included the Congress of Racial Equality (CORE) and the Student Nonviolent Coordinating Committee (SNCC). The civil rights movement used direct action methods to confront overt racism and discrimination. In 1963, Dr. King led some 250,000 people—a fourth of them white—in a march on Washington and from the steps of the Lincoln Memorial made his "I Have a Dream" speech. In it, he articulated the dream of full equality for blacks in America. Although violence continued awhile in the Deep South, and the Vietnam war and the growing controversy surrounding U.S. participation in it drained some of the energy that had gone into the civil rights movement, the legal framework was established from which rapid political change developed in the South.

The forces of change that coalesced in the civil rights movement coincided with the elevation to the presidency of a man from Texas, that part southern and part western state, who viewed the reconciliation of regional differences as a special challenge. If Lyndon Johnson was a wheeler-dealer senator who looked out for the moneyed interests in Texas and made a personal fortune of his own, he was also a man who had grown up poor and absorbed from his father the legacy of the populist movement that had its roots in Texas. As a young congressional aide in the 1930s, he had made a point of going to the Senate galleries to listen to the economic radicalism of Huey Long's speeches. His natural instincts for the underdog coincided with his national ambitions as Senate majority leader in the 1950s. His realization that political possibilities were limited for a southerner with a record against civil rights interacted with an awareness that only the listing from the Negro of political, legal, and economic inequality would release the South from its bondage to the past.

Historian Eric Goldman, who observed him within the White House, wrote of Johnson: "Although not a Southerner in basic ways, an important part of him belonged to Dixie. When that strain came to the fore he sounded like most members of a group who feel themselves misunderstood and abused. He became intensely introspective; he talked about the Southern mentality a great deal, poked into it, defended and attacked it, kept trying to explain it to others and perhaps to himself." [5]

Johnson believed there were only three ways to win the southerner over to accepting civil rights. The first was to give clear and firm support to that policy, directly to the southerner's face. "There are men down there," he said, "they may not like it, but at least they would like it straight." The second was to recognize the habits of thought in the South, including its love of the Constitution. Although many traditional southern politicians tend to interpret the Constitution as beginning and ending with the Tenth Amendment—which concerns states' rights—Johnson said after his 1964 campaign, ". . . I talked the Constitution, which happens to include equality for the Negro." The third and most basic method was to reaffirm the populist legacy—that millions of white southerners from farms and small towns had been denied government programs to enhance their economic opportunity because of politicians who catered to upper-class interests and used the fear of the Negro to divert attention from the real issues. [6]

Johnson put it all together in a New Orleans speech in 1964 that attracted little attention at the time. He declared to a ballroom crowded with people who were not generally in sympathy with the Civil Rights Act that had passed that summer: "Whatever your views are, we have a Constitution and we have got a Bill of Rights and we've got the law of the land. And two-thirds of the Democrats in the Senate voted for it, and three-fourths of the Republicans." He paused and his right hand

5. Eric F. Goldman, *The Tragedy of Lyndon Johnson* (New York: Alfred A. Knopf, 1969), p. 243.
6. Ibid., p. 244.

came up. "And I signed it, and I am going to enforce it, and I am going to observe it. . . . I'm not going to let them build up the hate and try to buy my people by appealing to their prejudice."

Then he told a story of a Texas senator born in another southern state who sat up late one night discussing the South's economic problems and "how we had been at the mercy of certain economic interests, and how they had exploited us. They had worked our women for five cents an hour, they had worked our men for a dollar a day, they had exploited our soil, they had let our resources go to waste, they had taken everything out of the ground they could and they had shipped it to other sections." He described how the old senator (he was referring to Joseph W. Bailey, born in Mississippi, who served as U.S. senator from Texas in the early twentieth century) talked about how the South could have a great future if it could look at and develop its resources, and how he wished his health would permit him to return to his native state ". . . and make them one more Democratic speech. I just feel like I've got one in me. Poor old state, they haven't heard a real Democratic speech in thirty years. All they ever hear at election time is nigra, nigra, nigra."

"The audience gasped," Goldman wrote. "President Johnson quickly finished his ad lib, and for a long few seconds the room was quiet. Then, starting here and there, applause came and people stood up. Tentatively, slowly, the handclapping built into a standing, shouting ovation from almost every man and woman in the hall. It went on, a tremendous roar, for fully five minutes. The nineteen hundred Louisiana Democrats knew they had heard truth, political skill, and audacity combined in one electric moment." [7]

One of Lyndon Johnson's major objectives as president was to help bring the South back into the national mainstream. The 1964 Civil Rights Act—which ended discrimination in public accommodations and employment and laid the foundation for effective school desegregation in the South—forced a change in traditions and customs. The Voting Rights Act of 1965 removed major obstacles to black voting in the most recalcitrant southern states and ensured access for blacks to political power.

Andrew Young, the Atlanta congressman, recalled almost a decade later how he and other civil rights workers returned five days after passage of the Civil Rights Act of 1964 to a motel in St. Augustine, Florida. Only a week earlier, waitresses had poured hot coffee on blacks seeking service in the restaurant, and the manager had poured acid on people attempting to use the swimming pool. "We went back to that same restaurant, and those people were just wonderful," Young recalled. "They were apologetic. They said, 'We were just afraid of losing our businesses. We didn't want to be the only ones to be integrated. But if everybody's got to do it, we've been ready for it a long time. We're so

7. Ibid., pp. 247–248.

glad the president signed this law and now we can be through these troubles.' " [8]

Passage of the Voting Rights Act of 1965 emerged from the violence at Selma, Alabama. That spring, most of the nation watched with horror the televised confrontation on Edmund Pettus Bridge, when mounted state troopers and a sheriff's posse waded into Negro marchers who refused an order to stop their march toward the state capital of Montgomery and to turn around. Troopers and possemen flailed with clubs and bullwhips and used tear gas and electric cattle prods to send bloodied Negroes fleeing. Some who had fallen were trampled.

John Lewis, a black Alabama farmer's son who was president of SNCC then and director of the Atlanta-based South-wide Voter Education Project in the 1970s, recalled what it was like that day, as the lawmen advanced toward the marchers that Lewis was leading. "I felt that we had to stand there, that you couldn't turn back. . . . For some strange reason I didn't believe the troopers would do what they did, but I felt that we had to stay there. . . . It was a frightening moment, really terrifying." [9] Lewis suffered a skull fracture from the blow of a billy club. Subsequently, a white Unitarian minister from Boston was fatally clubbed on a street in Selma, Dr. King led a second march, and a white Detroit mother who came to lend support to the demonstrators was shot to death by Ku Klux Klansmen.

But before that second march, Lyndon Johnson personally went before Congress to urge a domestic law—the first time a president had done so in 19 years—and closed a dramatic appeal for voting rights legislation with a forceful recital of the slogan of the civil rights movement, "And . . . we . . . shall . . . overcome."

In the next few years, the civil rights movement appeared to die, symbolized by the assassination of Dr. King in April 1968. The Vietnam war was creating divisiveness among traditional liberals and had diverted funds and attention from Johnson's Great Society programs to combat poverty. Black frustrations and disillusionment had burst into violent riots in some northern ghettoes. But in the South, black leadership shifted slowly and quietly from civil rights organizations to a developing cadre of elected officials.

The basic legal battle had been won. Looking back, Young and Lewis acknowledged that the Voting Rights Act of 1965 provided the basis for challenge to traditional power relationships in the South. Many white politicians in the South agreed.

The Voting Rights Act and its subsequent extensions, explained Governor Edwin Edwards of Louisiana, "provided the vehicle to register hundreds of thousands of blacks in the South, and that provided the

8. Interview with Andrew Young, January 31, 1974.
9. Interview with John Lewis, November 20, 1973.

catalyst for something far more important, black power at the polls—not only in electing huge numbers of black legislators, local officials, and now even some congressmen, but more important in making white politicians sensitive to their needs and desires. That, of course, has served to elevate the status of the black, not only the quality of his schools, but the quality of his roads, and sewer systems, and water systems, and housing conditions in which he was living." [10]

Although blacks had still not achieved political parity with whites by the mid-1970s, black registration in the South had climbed from roughly 2 million when the Voting Rights Act was passed in 1965 to more than 3.5 million. Blacks tended to form political coalitions with white Democrats, who were adjusting to changed circumstances, but a handful of successful Republican candidates—such as Linwood Holton in Virginia, Howard Baker in Tennessee, and Winthrop Rockefeller in Arkansas—have demonstrated that moderate Republicans who address themselves to issues meaningful to blacks can receive significant black support at the polls.

A wave of "New South" Democratic governors in the 1970s—men such as Dale Bumpers and David Pryor in Arkansas, Reubin Askew of Florida, Jimmy Carter and George Busbee of Georgia, John West of South Carolina, Edwards of Louisiana, William Waller of Mississippi—showed varying degrees of responsiveness to the interests of blacks, and also the interests of working-class whites. Although Askew in Florida spoke in favor of busing and West in South Carolina supported expansion of the food stamp program and took affirmative steps to overcome discrimination in state government, few of the new governors dealt openly with the problems that directly affected blacks and that segment of the population—white and black—with incomes below the poverty level. There *was* more emphasis on "people" programs, such as expansion of public kindergartens, prison reform, consumer and environmental programs, governmental reorganization, and an end to the divisive racial politics exemplified by Lester Maddox in Georgia and John Bell Williams in Mississippi. The new governors by and large were moderates, but not liberals—"liberal" remained a suspect political label in the South.

Veteran southern correspondent Roy Reed of the *New York Times* summarized these men as "virtually all respectable and socially acceptable. Most were elected with the votes of the poor as well as the middle class, but their campaigns were not pitched primarily to the poor. . . . None of the new leaders has made real headway in providing industrial jobs for the multitudes of poor people who still live in the black belts. None has found the answers to newer problems such as urban blight and the growing concentration of economic power in fewer hands." [11]

10. Interview with Edwin Edwards, September 25, 1973.
11. *New York Times*, September 27, 1974.

He cited three of them—Askew of Florida, Edwards of Louisiana, and Bumpers of Arkansas—for making inroads on the regressive state tax structures in the South that placed disproportionate burdens on those less able to pay. Askew pushed through the first state corporate income tax in Florida. Bumpers won an increase in the top rate for state income tax in Arkansas, making it more progressive and thus placing a greater burden on those more able to pay. Edwards won legislative approval to double the severance tax on oil and gas, removed the 2 percent sales tax on food, and led the fight for a new state constitution that would make it possible to increase corporate income taxes.

As Table 1–1 shows, southern states rely disproportionately on the sales tax, whose impact falls greatest on those with lower incomes. Only Virginia falls below the average for all states in both the dollar amount per $1,000 income and the percentage of state revenues derived from sales taxes.

REAPPORTIONMENT

Malapportioned state legislative and congressional districts, in which rural areas received disproportionate representation, served as one of the props for Bourbon domination in much of the South at the time Key wrote *Southern Politics*. Blacks and many poor whites were effectively disfranchised in the black belt and other areas. The same plantation interests and their banker-merchant-doctor-lawyer allies, who were Whig leaders before the Civil War, combined with urban commercial and financial interests to dominate state governments in the first half of the twentieth century. The corruption during Reconstruction—and the exaggerated tales about it afterward—were followed in much of the South by an attitude that a "good government" was one which kept taxes low. The result was inadequate funding for education, health, welfare, and other social services.

The Supreme Court's key reapportionment decisions, *Baker* v. *Carr* (1962) and the "one man, one vote" dictum that followed in *Reynolds* v. *Sims* (1964), meant greater representation for urban and suburban areas, the strongholds of the new Republicanism. This gave a boost to two-party development, but except for Tennessee and (to a lesser extent) Florida, Republican growth in southern legislatures has been slow. Not a single Republican won election to the Alabama legislature in 1974, despite a single-member district reapportionment plan.

Blacks as well as Republicans have fought for such plans, which cut down the size of electoral districts and thus make campaign costs lower, and recruitment of candidates easier; furthermore, districts with

13

TABLE 1-1

Sales Taxes, Southern States, 1972 *

	GENERAL AND SELECTIVE SALES TAXES PER $1,000 OF PERSONAL INCOME	PERCENTAGE OF STATE TAX COLLECTIONS
United States (average of all states)	$38.98	55.5
Alabama	53.35	68.9
Arkansas	49.45	64.7
Florida	55.12	76.3 †
Georgia	47.67	66.8
Louisiana	46.41	50.4
Mississippi	71.84	76.6
North Carolina	44.70	54.1
South Carolina	54.84	66.5
Tennessee	47.24	70.1
Texas	42.31	70.1
Virginia	32.85	50.8

* In addition to the general sales tax, this chart includes revenue from sales taxes on specific products (often called excise taxes), including gasoline, tobacco products, and alcoholic beverages.
† Because food is exempt from the sales tax in Florida, a good portion of the sales tax burden falls on tourists.
Source: U.S. Department of Commerce, *State Tax Collections in 1972*, as adapted by Eva Galambos, in *State and Local Taxes in the South, 1973* (Atlanta: Southern Regional Council, December 1973), p. 8.

homogeneous residential patterns are more likely to allow blacks and Republicans—both of them minorities in the South—to win elections. And reapportionment has invariably improved the chances of black candidates. The number of blacks in the Alabama legislature increased from three to 15 after single-member districts were adopted. The number of blacks increased from three to 13 in the South Carolina House of Representatives and from one to eight in the Louisiana House after single-member districts were adopted. Not until the Supreme Court required some urban area single-member districts in Mississippi in 1975 did that state elect more than a single black legislator. The Mississippi case represented an extension of the Voting Rights Act's restriction against laws that have the effect of diluting the black vote. By the mid-1970s black caucuses had been organized and were developing increased levels of political sophistication in most of southern legislatures.

Although the introduction of single-member districts has increased the number of black legislators in every case, single-member plans have also tended to bring disunity to urban legislative delegations that previously had been elected in countywide or other multiple-member districts. Because black voting blocs frequently had come to hold the balance of power in multimember districts, thus influencing an entire legislative delegation from an urban county, one can argue that black influence was as great or greater under such arrangements. On the other hand, the smaller number of blacks who won such elections were threatened with the loss of necessary white support if they became too outspoken on behalf of black interests.

DECLINE OF REGIONAL DIFFERENCES

Given the changes sweeping through the South, is it still a distinct American region? The question of the "vanishing South" has provided lively debate in print, at academic symposia, and for less formal gatherings in recent years.

In the early 1970s, veteran *Newsweek* Atlanta bureau chief Joseph B. Cumming, Jr. wittily reported to the readers of *Esquire* the news that "the South is over." [12] Almost simultaneously, sociologist John Shelton Reed concluded on the basis of a study of survey data compiled between 1955 and 1966 that "the people . . . remain 'distinctively southern'" and that "two institutions, the family and the church, are more powerful in the South" than in any other region.[13]

Historian George B. Tindall noted that the church in the South "serves as one of the chief instruments of ethnic solidarity; it has governed thought; and its Biblical strains reverberate in the rhetoric of the region." [14] Such a sweeping statement obviously includes political rhetoric, in which insightful politicians use Biblical references as a kind of shorthand to communicate with their constituency, and demagogues use religion for their personal advantage. The link between conservative religion and political conservatism in the South is itself worth a thorough study.

In his valedictory presidential address to the Southern Historical Association, Tindall declared that southern historians "have somehow felt the regional differences in their bones" and he suggested a "southern ethnicity" that joins black and white southerners who "share the bonds of a common heritage, indeed a common tragedy, and often speak a common language, however seldom they may acknowledge it." [15]

12. Joseph B. Cumming, Jr., "Been Down Home So Long It Looks Like Up to Me," *Esquire*, August 1971, p. 84.

13. John Shelton Reed, *The Enduring South: Subcultural Persistence in Mass Society*, Lexington Books, Washington (Lexington, Mass.: D.C. Heath, 1972), pp. 84–87.

14. George B. Tindall, "Beyond the Mainstream: The Ethnic Southerners," *Journal of Southern History*, 40 (February 1974): 16.

15. Ibid., pp. 12, 18.

But data from a De Vries and Associates national survey depicts two separate Souths—one white and one black—with significantly divergent attitudes and perceptions toward issues and institutions.[16] Even though black and white southerners share a common heritage and history, they have experienced it from different perspectives. For example, a statement that the United States should grant a full and unconditional amnesty to those who refused to fight in Vietnam for reasons of conscience found only slightly more agreement outside the South (38 percent) than in the South (34 percent). But the statement drew 28 percent agreement from white southerners and 48 percent agreement from black southerners—a divergence much greater than that between South and non-South overall.

The data confirmed that differences between the South and non-South are fading—the effect of such forces as network television, migration patterns, and urbanization—and that racial differences within the region were greater than any differences between southern whites and nonsoutherners.

As the South in the 1970s achieved a level of school integration greater than outside the region and began to develop a society perhaps more racially integrated than the non-South, regional differences based on racial attitudes among whites also began to fade. With the issue of busing, school integration became more a national than a regional problem. For example, the following table from the De Vries survey showed no significant difference between southern whites and the non-South on a busing question. Although there was little probing on the issue, the relatively high level of disenchantment with busing among southern blacks may reflect concern about the treatment their children receive in schools located in white neighborhoods. The fact that blacks expressed more than twice the amount of "strong disagreement" with the antibusing statement suggests that they believe far more strongly in integrated schools.

The survey did reveal significant regional differences in regard to religion. Southerners were more than three times as likely as nonsoutherners to be Baptists, and nonsoutherners almost three times as likely to be Catholics. Within the region, blacks were more than twice as likely as whites to be Baptists. Church attendance was higher among southerners, at least monthly for 85 percent of the blacks and 67 percent of the whites, compared with only 55 percent of the nonsoutherners. Southern blacks rated the church the most reliable institutional or personal source of information about important issues. Although southern whites

16. The data are taken from an in-depth national survey of 4,004 Americans, 18 and older, in November and December 1974. The study was conducted for a private client who agreed to release the data for this book. Tables from special computer runs can be found in Appendix C.

Busing: *"Instead of busing, more tax dollars should be spent to see that black schools are brought up to the highest educational levels."*

	SOUTH	NON-SOUTH	TOTAL	SOUTH WHITE	SOUTH BLACK
Strongly agree	57.4%	57.1%	57.1%	57.0%	58.9%
Mildly agree	16.8	22.0	20.8	19.0	10.4
TOTAL AGREE	74.2	79.1	77.9	76.0	69.3
Mildly Disagree	7.6%	6.8%	7.0%	7.1%	8.8%
Strongly Disagree	12.0	9.1	9.8	9.2	19.3
TOTAL DISAGREE	19.6	15.9	16.8	16.3	28.1
Not Sure	6.2%	5.0%	5.3%	7.7%	2.6%

and nonsoutherners both rated the church the most reliable institutional source, both groups gave higher ratings to "spouse" and "doctors."

For political information, all three subgroups rated television the most reliable and believable source, but the rating was significantly higher among southern blacks. Newspapers were rated a much closer second by southern whites and nonsoutherners.

The survey data also showed some issues on which white and black southerners differed more from nonsoutherners than from each other. For example, on a question designed to test levels of confidence in major American groups and institutions, white and black southerners gave almost identical (54.7 percent and 54.1 percent) responses of a "great deal of confidence" in the military. In contrast, only 39.3 percent of nonsoutherners expressed a "great deal of confidence" in the military. But given the consistent differences between southern whites and blacks on other issues, it is entirely possible that the two groups agree for different reasons, with whites holding more traditional concepts of patriotism and blacks perceiving greater and more equal opportunity in the armed forces.

On some issues, there was little difference of opinion. Despite the South's reputation for individualism and a tradition of violence, 75 percent of white southerners agreed with a statement that guns should be registered like cars, with a requirement that owners be tested in order to be able to use one. The level of agreement between nonsoutherners and black southerners was slightly higher. A series of questions to measure disaffection showed high levels of alienation with government in both the South and non-South, with somewhat higher levels among black than white southerners.

Some of the sharpest differences developed when respondents were asked which level of government—federal, state, or local—did the best job of handling its own responsibilities. By far the highest support for the federal government (39 percent) came from southern blacks, who knew firsthand the ability of the federal government to effect social change. Only 11 percent of southern whites and 14 percent of nonsoutherners selected the federal government as doing the best job. Both groups gave almost identical ratings of approval (38 percent) to local governments, which received only 16 percent approval from southern blacks. There was less varience in support for state governments—32 percent from southern whites, 27 percent from nonsoutherners, and 25 percent from southern blacks.

The collective experience among southern blacks of a struggle for survival perhaps accounts for significant differences in attitudes toward right-to-life issues, including population growth, capital punishment, abortion, and euthanasia.

Right-to-Life Issues
(figures represent percentage agreeing with statement)

	SOUTH	NON-SOUTH	TOTAL	SOUTH WHITE	SOUTH BLACK
"Unless we stop the growth of population soon, the world will not be able to feed or clothe its people."	62.8	67.2	66.2	68.4	45.6
"There ought to be a mandatory death penalty for any premeditated murder."	71.7	71.6	71.6	73.2	65.8
"Abortion should not be allowed under any circumstances."	26.3	22.8	23.6	22.4	35.6
"Doctors should be allowed by law to end the life of a person with an incurable disease if the patient and family request it."	47.6	57.2	54.9	51.8	35.0
"A child who is born deformed and who could never lead a normal life should be allowed to die."	26.0	32.4	30.9	29.2	17.5

Responses from southern blacks contrasted significantly with those of southern whites and nonsoutherners, with blacks in every case more sensitive to the sanctity of life. Responses of southern whites and nonsoutherners showed only slight differences.

The survey revealed a number of differences in political perceptions and behavior. Almost an identical proportion of southern whites (47 percent) and nonsoutherners (48 percent) identified themselves as Democrats. White southerners split their tickets (voted for candidates of both parties) at a significantly higher rate in 1974 legislative races (29 percent) than did either nonsoutherners (16 percent) or southern blacks

(18 percent). Although three of every four black southerners said they voted only for Democratic candidates for the legislature, fewer than two of every five whites (39 percent) in the South did so, compared with 45 percent of nonsoutherners. Only 16 percent of southern whites voted straight Republican, compared with 27 percent of nonsoutherners.

DEMOGRAPHIC CHANGES

Migration patterns, urbanization, the abandonment of the family farm, and a developing economy all represent forces for political change in the South.

In a widely heralded speech in 1971 at Chapel Hill, North Carolina, George H. Brown, then director of the Bureau of the Census, joined the New South chorus. He noted that "for the first time since the 1870s, the past decade has shown that more people moved into the South than out of it." But the Census Bureau's definition of the South includes Delaware, Maryland, and the District of Columbia—all of which have served as destination points for blacks leaving the South of the old Confederacy —as well as such non-Confederate border states as West Virginia, Kentucky, and Oklahoma. Although the 11 Old South states gained 666,000 people through inmigration in the 1960s, it was only because 1,326,000 newcomers swelled the population of Florida. All 11 states actually gained population, but in most cases only because of natural increase, and not by migration from other regions.

Although the ten states exclusive of Florida suffered a net loss of 660,000 people through migration, there was a net inmigration of whites into the region during the 1960s. Alabama was the only state in the South that registered a net outmigration among whites—a sharp contrast with the 1950s, when seven of the 11 states registered outmigrations of whites as well as blacks. All 11 states had some outmigration of blacks during the decade that ended in 1970, ranging from 4,000 in Texas to 279,000 in Mississippi, a total of almost 1.5 million in the region and only 10,000 fewer than the net loss through migration during the 1950s.

Although the Census Bureau began reporting in the early 1970s that increasing numbers of blacks were returning to the South, one cannot necessarily interpret such data as representing a turnabout. A black family that moves from the Carolinas to Baltimore or Washington, D.C., is not counted as outmigrating by the Census Bureau, but a black family that moves from Philadelphia or Newark to Washington or Baltimore is considered to be inmigrating to the South.

Nevertheless, there is no doubt that changed conditions in the South, resulting from federal laws and court decisions and local adjustments to them, definitely are making the region more attractive to expatriate blacks, many of them disenchanted with conditions in northern ghettoes. "I didn't see any reason to stay up there in that madhouse when all I found was just as much discrimination and poverty, and even more crime, than there is down here," said Freddie Lee Reese, a 32-year-old native of Montgomery, Alabama, after returning to his hometown to work as a building supervisor after several years in Chicago.[17]

The 1960s showed signs of reversing long-standing migration trends from the South, and the Census Bureau's official 1974 population projections showed that the reversal had accelerated. While the population for the non-South showed a 2.8 percent rate of increase between 1970 and 1974, the rate was 7.7 percent for the 11 states of the Old South. The growth rate was greatest in Florida, with 19.2 percent over those four years, but each of the 11 states grew at a faster rate than the average for the non-South.

In addition, comparisons of 1950 and 1970 census data show that nonurban and farm declines were greater for the South than the non-South and that the southern metropolitan areas made rapid gains. The number of farms declined 58 percent in the South between 1950 and 1970, compared with a 43.5 percent decline in the non-South. During the same period, the number of persons employed in agriculture declined 69.5 percent in the South, compared with a 55.1 percent decline in the non-South. In South Carolina, the number of farms fell from 139,364 to 39,559, and agricultural employment plummeted from 198,268 in 1950 to 39,778 in 1970. The nonurban share of the population fell 16.8 percent in the South for the same period, compared with a 7.2 percent falloff for the non-South. Meanwhile, the proportion of southerners living in metropolitan areas increased by 20.7 percent, more than double the increase among nonsoutherners. The South remained considerably less metropolitan (55.2 percent) than the non-South (73.0 percent), but the difference was declining.

The relative lack of educational opportunity in the South is reflected in the level of educational attainment of the region's adult population. The share of southerners 25 years and over with four years of high school increased from 24.9 percent in 1950 to 44.4 percent in 1970. In 1950 the South was 10.8 percent behind the non-South in percentage of adults with four years of high school, and it was still 10.4 percent behind in 1970.

17. B. Drummond Ayres, "Blacks Return to South in a Reverse Migration," *New York Times,* June 18, 1974, p. 49.

18. See Appendix D for tables showing state-by-state demographic changes.

TABLE 1–2

Per Capita Personal Income, South and Non-South, 1950–1974

	1950	% OF U.S. AVERAGE		1974	% OF U.S. AVERAGE	INCREASE IN % OF U.S. AVERAGE, 1950–1974
Non-South	$1,624		Non-South	$5,676		
United States	1,496		United States	5,448		
Texas	1,349	90.2	Florida	5,416	99.4	13.7
Florida	1,282	85.7	Virginia	5,339	98.0	15.9
Virginia	1,228	82.1	Texas	4,952	90.9	0.7
Louisiana	1,120	74.9				
			THE SOUTH	4,780	87.7	14.8
THE SOUTH	1,091	72.9				
			Georgia	4,751	87.2	18.1
North Carolina	1,037	69.3	North Carolina	4,665	85.6	16.3
Georgia	1,034	69.1	Tennessee	4,551	83.5	17.1
Tennessee	994	66.4	Louisiana	4,391	80.6	5.7
South Carolina	893	59.7	South Carolina	4,311	79.1	19.4
Alabama	880	58.8	Alabama	4,215	77.4	18.6
Arkansas	825	55.1	Arkansas	4,200	77.1	22.0
Mississippi	775	51.8	Mississippi	3,803	69.8	18.0

Source: Bureau of Labor Statistics, U.S. Department of Labor.

Although every state in the South remained below the national average in per capita personal income, regional gains between 1950 and 1974 serve as a striking indicator of economic transformation within the region. Per capita personal income in the South in 1950 was 72.9 percent of that for the United States as a whole; by 1974 it had climbed to 87.7 percent. As Table 1–2 shows, the gains were uneven, ranging from 0.7 percent in Texas to 22.0 percent in Arkansas.

Although differences between the South and the non-South are fading, lingering regional distinctions remain. The South's history differs not only in the experience of Civil War defeat and Reconstruction but also in the plantation tradition that preceded the Civil War. The South retains from that culture a strong sense of place. Furthermore, although the South is finally emerging from the decades of economic stagnation that followed the Civil War and Reconstruction, it has not escaped the legacy of a colonial economy in which capital from other parts of the country was invested in low-cost labor, cheap land and energy, and new markets.

The South remains different in many crucial ways. Its percentage of black population is almost three times that of the non-South, its white population is substantially more Anglo-Saxon and less Eastern European in its ancestry; and its religion is far more fundamentalist Protestant than the rest of the country. Despite economic and educational advances since World War II, the 1970 census revealed that almost one southerner in five still lived in poverty, almost twice the percentage for the non-South; that no state in the South matched the average per capita personal income for the non-South; and that no state in the South matched the median level of years of education for persons 25 years and older in the non-South. In addition, the South has greater inequality of income between the races. For the non-South the ratio of black to white median income in 1971 was 69 percent, compared with only 56 percent for the South.

A significant factor in the changing character of the white South is the number of nonnatives who have migrated to the region. A special analysis conducted by the Bureau of the Census for this book shows that the percentage of nonnatives in the South—that is, people who were born outside the 11 states of the region—more than doubled between 1950 and 1970, from 8.8 percent to 18.7 percent. Whereas only four of the 11 states in 1950 had more than 10 percent of their population born outside the region, only two of the states had less than 10 percent in 1970—and both of those, Alabama and Mississippi, had nonnative populations of more than 9 percent. More than one of every four Virginians and two of every five Floridians were born outside the South. Because the newcomers were disproportionately white in number, their impact on the collective attitudes and perceptions of the white South were greater than their percentage of the total population.[19]

Most of the newcomers migrated from areas of two-party political competition, and throughout the South thousands of them have become involved politically, adding an additional ingredient to the ferment of political change in the region.

19. See Appendix D for demographic tables and charts.

Chapter

2

TWO-PARTY POLITICS

The Republican Rise

THE DIXIECRAT movement in 1948 followed earlier signs of political ferment in the region and marked the end of the Democratic "solid South." Then, in the 1950s, the phenomenon of "presidential Republicanism" that Key had already detected intensified, as presidential voting patterns developed along economic lines. The cities in the South joined the traditional mountain Republicans as a source of potential GOP strength. What was missing, however, was leadership that wasn't tied to a past when to be a Republican in the South meant an opportunity to share in patronage if the party was in power in Washington, or to hob-nob every four years with the leadership of a national political party at a convention. Those in control enjoyed what they had, and they could stay in control by keeping their group small.

The absence of quality leadership was perceived at the beginning of the 1950s by Alexander Heard, who had been Key's collaborator and chief interviewer. In *A Two-Party South?*, Heard observed: "To a greater or lesser degree in every southern state there must be changes in the high command if the party is to grow."[1]

The emerging political climate was such that a dynamic and skillful leader could make much of a small beginning. An example was the case of J. Drake Edens Jr., a South Carolina food-chain heir who grew up in Columbia and "heard my daddy cuss the Democrats from about 1935 on." It was a rare background for a youth in South Carolina, where the pact of loyalty to the national Democratic Party in exchange for state

1. Alexander Heard, *A Two-Party South?* (Chapel Hill: University of North Carolina Press, 1962), p. 98.

23

control of racial policy was as strong as anywhere in the South. But by 1960 the state had supported native son Strom Thurmond in the Dixie-crat movement, had come within 5,000 votes of a majority for Dwight Eisenhower running with independent electors in 1952, and had re-mained Democratic in 1956 with only a plurality when independent electors competed with Eisenhower's Republican label.

Edens went to his first precinct meeting in 1960 and worked that year in the Nixon campaign, which fell less than 10,000 votes short of victory in the state. The next year he helped draft Charles Boineau, a local young business executive to run in a special election, and he won to become the first Republican to sit in the South Carolina legisla-ture in this century. A year later, Edens was campaign manager for journalist-author William D. Workman, who received a very respectable 43 percent of the vote as a Republican challenger to veteran U.S. Sena-tor Olin D. Johnston.

For the next three years, the financially independent Edens—an eco-nomic conservative and racial moderate—served as GOP state chairman and built the first genuine political party organization the state had seen. Ironically, his guide was a manual produced by the Committee on Po-litical Education (COPE) of the AFL–CIO. "I rode all over the state, went into towns that I never knew existed. . . . I think the toughest county I ever hit was Chester. I tried to set up a county organization and went back to some of the people who had worked for Workman. I remember one night we called an organizational meeting, and I think three people showed up. I stayed in that county for one or two days with one or two people who had the courage to go out and help me find other people. I went to Bess Reed's farm and then I went to a feed store, and this sort of thing, just to find people willing to declare themselves as Republicans. We had a party rule that required at least six people to organize a precinct, and you had to have at least three organized pre-cincts in the county. . . . I probably made a dozen trips into Chester County and finally put an organization together."[2]

The South Carolina story is worth special emphasis, in part because the kind of dynamic and skillful leadership that Edens furnished re-mains a rare commodity among southern Republicans. No other Deep South state has achieved a level of two-party development comparable to South Carolina's. The credit is by no means due solely or even pri-marily to any individual, but among knowledgeable South Carolinians it is generally conceded that the strength of the Republican organization throughout the state was such that Senator Thurmond—a man uncanny at detecting the shift of political winds—viewed it safe to formally switch party allegiance in 1964 and openly support his equally conservative Republican friend, Barry Goldwater of Arizona. Philosophically, Thur-

2. Interview with J. Drake Edens, February 13, 1974.

24

mond certainly had more in common with Republicans than with Democrats, but he was hardly an alien among the likes of such southern Democratic senators as James Eastland, John Stennis, Richard Russell, John McClellan, Herman Talmadge, and Harry Byrd. By the time Edens stepped down as state chairman in 1965, the presence of Thurmond had legitimatized the party as a viable political entity.

Although Republicans in the other southern states worked on party organization, many of them beginning before South Carolina's, there was and has been little effort made outside of urban areas. In Alabama, internal strife and an attempt to move to the right of George Wallace decimated the Republicans in 1966. Only in Tennessee among the states of the Outer South did two-party development proceed at a pace comparable to that of South Carolina. In Tennessee, the same emphasis and dedication on organizing in urban areas, when added to the already existing base of mountain Republicans, proved sufficient to make Republicans truly competitive.

The origins of the mountain Republicans can be traced directly to the Civil War. Thousands of independent yeoman farmers bitterly opposed secession and fought on the side of the Union, often against neighbors who supported the Confederacy. Violent reprisals left a legacy of loyalty to the Republican Party that continues to be reflected in electoral returns. Two congressional districts in east Tennessee continue to elect Republicans whose seats are among the safest the GOP has anywhere. The influence of the mountain Republicans is reflected clearly by the maps in Appendix A. Those traditional Republicans provided a basis for GOP development in Tennessee, Virginia, and North Carolina but exist in only a few scattered counties in other states, such as Winston in Alabama and a cluster of counties in northwestern Arkansas.

Much weaker sources of traditional Republican support are found in the "German" counties in Texas (an area that runs south from Austin and was settled in the 1850s by antislavery farmers from Germany) and in a few eastern North Carolina counties in which there was a Republican-Populist fusion in the 1890s and where traditional Republican loyalties remain.

In addition to such hereditary groups, Republicans in the South fit into four major categories, some of them overlapping. One group consists of migrants from other regions, usually business and professional families who moved into the South as part of the industrialization and economic expansion and brought their Republicanism with them. They contributed substantially to the leadership of southern Republicanism in the 1950s. In Florida they provided a base of support comparable to that of the mountain Republicans in Tennessee, North Carolina, and Virginia.

A larger group consists of urban and suburban middle- and upper-middle-class migrants from farms and small towns, native southerners who joined the middle class and who, often receiving poor public services, developed negative attitudes toward social programs and hostility toward government spending and taxing. Only after reapportionment did they receive a fair share of representation in local and state government and in Congress. This group is a major source of ticket splitters, who often determine elections in the South, as well as in the rest of the country.

A much smaller group of Republicans in the South consists of reformers who are interested primarily in building a two-party system. The final group, and a large one throughout the South, includes those who were attracted by the Goldwater candidacy in 1964, many of them ideologues who are conservative on racial and economic issues and who tend to be more interested in party purity—and they equate purity with conservatism—than party success.

The first major Republican breakthrough came in the 1952 presidential election. The new Republican leadership included some men of real ability, such as New Orleans attorney John Minor Wisdom, later a federal appeals court judge. Collectively they were young, moderate, urbane, racially tolerant, and intrigued by the organizational side of politics. With Eisenhower, a war hero, as their candidate in 1952, they carried Florida, Tennessee, Texas, and Virginia—all states in the Outer South—but failed to crack the strongly segregationist Deep South.

In the cities, they developed a special appeal, attracting young and ambitious newcomers who had migrated from the small towns and farms or from the North and who lacked connections with the established social elite of the southern cities. Rootless young couples throughout the South found in the Republican Party a pathway to social acceptance in their communities, and the new leadership skillfully tapped the energies of young executives and professionals and their capable and highly competitive wives. The national Republican Party's pledges of fiscal conservatism, limited government, and firm anti-Communism provided ideological comfort.[3]

In 1956, despite the school desegregation decision written by Eisenhower-appointed Chief Justice Earl Warren, the president held all the former Confederate states he had won in 1952 and added Louisiana.

Although Eisenhower barely penetrated the Deep South in terms of winning electoral votes, he made inroads based on two swelling sources of racial and economic discontent, adding "Black Belt" and urban support to the traditional Republican base in the mountains. In 157 "Black Belt" counties which were most sensitive to the racial issue—and the primary source of Thurmond's Dixiecrat strength in 1948—the level of Republican support in 1952 increased eight times over 1948, against a threefold rise in the whole South. Political analyst Samuel Lubell found

3. See David Broder and Stephen Hess, *The Republican Establishment* (New York: Harper and Row, 1967), chap. 10.

that Eisenhower's support in the southern cities and suburbs paralleled that of the rest of the country, with a clear division along economic lines among whites. In a study of 13 cities in both Deep South and Outer South, Lubell found 75 percent support for Eisenhower in upper-middle-class and silk-stocking precincts and 39 percent support in working-class white precincts. There was a direct relationship between income and the percentage of Republican support. In black precincts, the average support for Eisenhower was 12 percent, although it was 25 percent in Atlanta and more than 20 percent in three other cities—Miami, Tampa, and Augusta.[4]

In 1960, despite the use of federal troops at Little Rock three years earlier and Republican sponsorship of the first two civil rights bills since Reconstruction, Richard Nixon carried Florida, Tennessee, and Virginia. Texas swung back to the Democrats, who had native son Lyndon Johnson on the ticket, and Louisiana—with its heavy Catholic population in the south—returned to the Democratic column in support of John F. Kennedy. But some presidential electors from Alabama and all from Mississippi went to third-party candidates.

THE "SOUTHERN STRATEGY"

The origin of what became the Republican "southern strategy" was a speech in 1961 by Barry Goldwater in Atlanta. "We're not going to get the Negro vote as a bloc in 1964 and 1968, so we ought to go hunting where the ducks are," he declared. Goldwater then spelled it out, saying that school integration was "the responsibility of the states. I would not like to see my party assume it is the role of the federal government to enforce integration in the schools."

Between 1962 and mid-1964, the proportions of the vote received by conservative GOP candidates for governor or senator reached new highs in Alabama, South Carolina, and Louisiana, with the greatest strength coming from urban areas. The first Republican candidate for governor in Mississippi in this century, a moderate by Mississippi standards, won a respectable 38 percent of the vote in 1963, but the Mississippi GOP the next year adopted a platform stating that segregation is "absolutely essential to harmonious racial relations."

Republican leadership was shifting in the South. Sophisticated Alabama lawyer John Grenier, bright, tough-minded, and the equal of Drake

4. Samuel Lubell, *Revolt of the Moderates* (New York: Harper, 1956), pp. 179–184.

Edens as an organizer began in 1963 to organize Goldwater delegates throughout the South. In 1964 moderate leaders from the Eisenhower era lost control of party machinery throughout the South, and blacks were virtually read out of the party.

Goldwater voted against the 1964 Civil Rights Act and became the first Republican ever to sweep the Deep South, but he lost the rest of the country. The pattern of his vote resembled that of Strom Thurmond in 1948, and his support among mountain and urban Republicans in the South declined from the levels achieved by Eisenhower and Nixon. Nevertheless, of the 507 southern counties which Goldwater won, 233 had never gone Republican before. Lubell characterized the five Deep South states which Goldwater carried as "a measure of the depth of support for a separatist racial policy." [5]

A study by Bernard Cosman of Deep South delegates and alternates to the Republican National Convention in San Francisco that year produced a profile of deeply conservative elitists who viewed politics in strongly ideological terms. All but two of the 97 Deep South delegates voted for Goldwater on the first ballot, and all but seven of 278 southern delegates (a count that included Oklahoma and Kentucky) voted for Goldwater.

The Cosman survey found that the delegates and alternates were all white; 75 percent were male. Three-fourths of the delegates had been born in the former Confederate states, more than half within the state they represented. More than 90 percent had attended college, and almost one-fourth had undertaken work beyond the undergraduate level. They were concentrated in the professional, managerial and proprietary categories. In social terms, 67 percent identified themselves as middle class, and 31 percent as upper class. The latter figure stood in striking contrast to a study of the 1964 presidential election by the Survey Research Center at the University of Michigan, which found that only 1 percent of the American electorate identified themselves as upper class. The SRC study found that 39 percent identified themselves as middle class, and 56 percent as working class. Only 2 percent of the Deep South Republican delegates and alternates claimed to belong to the working class.

More than 90 percent of those in the Cosman study disagreed with the statement "The role of the political party is to reconcile different interests rather than take clear stands on issues." Only the two delegates who did not vote for Goldwater expressed strong agreement with the statement.

The ultraconservatism of the southern delegates was reflected in attitudes toward domestic issues. At least 90 percent opposed federal involvement in employment guarantees, medical care, public power and

5. Quoted in Broder and Hess, *Republican Establishment,* p. 340.

28

housing, aid to education, and school integration. There was slightly less agreement (82 percent) that the federal government should take no action concerning Negro voting rights.[6]

Although Goldwater carried all five of the Deep South states—Alabama, Mississippi, South Carolina, Georgia, and Louisiana—he lost Tennessee, Virginia, and Florida, all of which had been Republican since 1952. In Texas, every Republican on the ballot with him lost, except for one legislator. The Republicans gained seven Deep South congressmen, but lost two in Texas.

(The passage the next year of the Voting Rights Act spurred concerted black registration efforts in each of the states Goldwater carried, states in which between 62 and 93 percent of the voting age blacks were unregistered in 1964.)

Despite the election in the next decade of several moderate Republican governors, such as Winthrop Rockefeller in Arkansas, Linwood Holton in Virginia, Winfield Dunn in Tennessee, and James Holshouser in North Carolina, the Goldwater brand of conservatism was stamped clearly on the GOP in the South. Goldwater's strategy killed the chance for the Republican Party to assume a role of reform in the one-party South, and the GOP increasingly attracted the most reactionary elements of the region to the party. Not only did the Goldwater movement force out moderate leadership in many southern states, but a decade later pragmatic conservative and moderate Republicans throughout the South complained in interviews with the authors of problems created by John Birch Society members and other ideologues who had flocked to the party during the Goldwater movement. In Alabama, for example, a major target of the Birchers and like-minded allies on the far right was John Grenier, the strategist who had coordinated the Goldwater delegate drive in the South.

Under the leadership of Richard Nixon, the Republican "southern strategy" became more sophisticated. Perhaps it was best defined by Nixon's attorney general, John Mitchell, who once told a group of southerners, "Judge us not by what we say, but by what we do." Although Richard Nixon won applause from Mississippi Republicans in 1966 when he told them, "Republicans must not go prospecting for the fool's gold of racist votes," columnist Joseph Alsop wrote in 1967 that Nixon had won Barry Goldwater's approval because he had indicated to Goldwater that, if nominated, he would adopt the "southern strategy" that Goldwater invented and still favored.

Roy Reed, an Arkansas native and veteran *New York Times* reporter, views Nixon's first inaugural as marking the end of the federal government's role as civil rights advocate. "Within six months after Nixon

6. Bernard Cosman, ed., with Robert Huckshorn, *Republican Politics* (New York: Praeger, 1968), chap. 3.

had taken office," Reed declared, "I was in a federal courtroom in Jackson, Mississippi, to report that the NAACP Legal Defense and Education Fund and the Justice Department for the first time were on opposite sides of a desegregation case." [7]

The Justice Department effort failed when the Supreme Court in late 1969 ruled in *Alexander* v. *Holmes* that " 'all deliberate speed' for desegregation is no longer constitutionally permissible. . . . Every school district is to terminate dual school systems at once and to operate now and hereafter only unitary schools."

To prevent the issue from smoldering into the 1970 elections, the Nixon administration adopted a program in which a team of federal officials visited most of the southern states, spelled out the unpleasant truth, and appointed statewide committees of prominent citizens to help develop a climate of acceptance. Scores of school districts developed and implemented plans that involved mass transfer of students to accomplish levels of integration that exceeded those outside the South. After an initial wave of emotional protest by many whites that involved flight by some to quickly established private schools, the changed circumstances were quietly accepted.

Despite that example of what leadership could accomplish, Nixon soon extended the "southern strategy" into a national strategy when, as president, he challenged the Supreme Court ruling that busing, within limits, was among the tools that could be used to achieve desegregation of public schools. By using the pejorative term "forced busing" and distorting the Supreme Court decision in *Swann* v. *Mecklenburg*, in a nationally televised address in support of "neighborhood schools," Nixon helped create a climate in which the North could voice respectable opposition to busing, thus blocking the only means by which, in many cases, genuine school desegregation could be accomplished. Despite the strong emotional opposition and turmoil created in several southern cities by busing plans, a stable pattern of desegregated schools developed after several years in Charlotte, N.C., the school district involved in the *Swann* busing decision.

Harry Dent, who served as political aide in the White House under Nixon, defended the former president's position on busing on grounds that it would have been wrong "to ram down [people's] throats" an unpopular decision. Dent said that every poll he saw showed strong opposition to busing, and that the president's position was "in the best interest of the country," regardless of the Supreme Court's ruling. Dent acknowledged that much of the desegregation accomplished in the South during the Nixon administration had resulted from the momentum generated by civil rights enforcement officials of the previous administration, but he said that Nixon's "velvet glove" approach made it more

7. Interview with Roy Reed, January 12, 1974.

acceptable.[8] Critics charged Nixon with distorting the Supreme Court's position on busing and with failing to exercise moral leadership by urging obedience of the decision as the law of the land, a position taken under similar circumstances by a few southern governors, including Robert McNair of South Carolina and Reubin Askew of Florida.

Atlanta Constitution editors Reg Murphy and Hal Gulliver, in their book *The Southern Strategy*, had this reaction: "It was a cynical strategy, this catering in subtle ways to the segregationist leanings of white Southern voters—yet pretending with high rhetoric that the real aim was simply to treat the South fairly, to let it become part of the nation again." [9]

A broader analysis came from Senator George McGovern, who cited the Nixon administration's cutback on domestic social programs in a speech before the South Carolina legislature in his 1972 campaign for the Democratic presidential nomination. "What is this southern strategy?" McGovern asked. "It is this. It says to the South: Let the poor stay poor, let your economy trail the nation, forget about decent homes and medical care for all your people, choose officials who will oppose every effort to benefit the many at the expense of the few—and in return, we will try to overlook the rights of the black man, appoint a few southerners to high office, and lift your spirits by attacking the 'eastern establishment' whose bank accounts we are filling with your labor and your industry. It is a clever strategy. But it's not for the benefit of the people of the South. And it's not for the benefit of the American nation."

Although Nixon swept all 11 states in the South in 1972, his victory was more a reflection of the national rejection of McGovern than of any mass southern conversion to Republicanism. In fact, maturing Republican conservatives in the South have begun to question the validity of the "southern strategy" in a region that includes 3.5 million registered black voters. They have lost too many elections to Democrats who won because of black votes alienated from Republicans because of that strategy. Republican conservatives also perceive a change in attitudes among white southerners, many of whom are ticket-splitting moderates who are adapting to a desegregating society, whose children attend school with blacks, and who resent politicians who raise racial passions.

"If conservatism means an extension of personal freedom, less infringement on the part of government over a human life," said Senator William Brock of Tennessee, "that is something that sells very well in the South. But if you try to extend that into a repression of a particular segment of the community—more law and order over the black community,

8. Interview with Harry Dent, February 22, 1974.
9. Reg Murphy and Hal Gulliver, *The Southern Strategy* (New York: Scribner's, 1971), p. 4.

for example, or less economic opportunity for the black community—that philosophy is so unworkable that it not only is going to lose the black vote, which we don't have much of anyway, but it is going to drive off whites who simply cannot accept it." [10]

Gil Carmichael, the Mississippi Republican leader who the Nixon White House would not help in a challenge to Senator James Eastland in 1972, said, "After more than a decade of building a two-party system in the South, the true Republicans in the South are realists. They have to deal with the cold, political structure that they're in, and they regret very much that the president's advisers or the president himself chose this southern strategy." [11] Like Holton in Virginia and Rockefeller in Arkansas, Carmichael demonstrated, both in his 1972 race for the Senate and 1975 campaign for governor, that progressive Republicans can win some black support.

TWO-PARTY DEVELOPMENT

Since 1963 the greatest acceleration in the party development has occurred in South Carolina and Tennessee. South Carolina moved from a position as the most Democratic state in the South to rank behind only the three states that had a large base of traditional mountain Republicanism—Tennessee, Virginia, and North Carolina—and Florida, with its traditional base of migrant Republicans from the Midwest and Northeast. Through 1974, only Tennessee had achieved genuine two-party status, but all 11 states showed some movement in the direction of two-party competition.[12]

South Carolina has come more to resemble states of the Outer South than the Deep South. It is the only Deep South state that has elected a Republican U.S. senator (albeit one who switched as a Democratic incumbent), that failed to cast its electoral votes for George Wallace in 1968, and whose Democratic congressional delegation in 1975 unanimously voted for extension of the Voting Rights Act. In 1974 it also became the first of the Deep South states to elect a Republican governor.

10. Interview with William Brock, February 1, 1974.

11. Interview with Gil Carmichael, March 30, 1974.

12. To test their subjective judgment of the development of party competition within each state, the authors updated a mathematical formula devised in 1963 by Austin Ranney that objectively measures such development. The Ranney formula, which analyzes election returns and is outlined in detail in Appendix E, then was modified to take into account voting on congressional races. The results (see Appendix A) confirmed the impressions gained from field research.

The victory of James B. Edwards was something of a fluke (see Chapter 11), but regardless of how it was achieved, it was another step toward two-party development.

In Tennessee, Republicans in the early 1970s had elected both of the state's U.S. senators, five of the eight U.S. representatives, and governor; for one term, they managed to control the state House of Representatives—by one vote—the only southern state in this century in which Republicans have even come close to controlling either house of a state legislature. Although Democrats in 1974 regained the governor's office and two U.S. House seats and strengthened their legislative majorities, two-party competition remains a reality in Tennessee.

From 1962 to 1972, southern Republicans made steady gains in congressional and legislative seats (see Tables 2-1—2-4). However in 1974 the GOP suffered a massive setback, paralleling the national anti-Republican reaction to Watergate and a recession economy. After the 1974 elections, Republican strength in southern state legislatures fell to 1966 levels, with a net loss of 22 state senators and 60 state representatives, or about 30 percent of Republican legislative seats. They lost 40 legislative seats in North Carolina alone. In Congress, nine southern Republican incumbents lost House seats, but the party picked up two seats against Democratic newcomers. A net loss of seven U.S. House seats and one U.S. senator returned southern Republican strength in Congress to the level of 1970. The peak Republican strength was in 1972, when the GOP won 31 percent of southern seats in Congress and 16 percent in state legislatures.

The development of southern Republican strength generally has been from the top down, with greatest strength at the presidential level. Virginia is the only southern state in which one Republican has succeeded another in the governor's office. A measurement of the real weakness of Republican development in the South is that by 1975 the GOP had elected only two statewide officials, other than governor, in all 11 states: Public Service Commissioner Paula Hawkins in Florida in 1972 and Lieutenant Governor John Dalton in Virginia in 1973.

A major weakness is the failure in many states to challenge Democrats at all levels. As Heard wrote in 1952, the contest for office is the backbone of party politics, and the greatest stimulus to party growth lies in a continuous stream of serious candidates. But in Texas, for example, Republicans as recently as 1974 have failed to offer candidates for lieutenant governor and attorney general, the second and third most powerful state offices.

In Congress, a political realignment has been occurring since 1966 among newly elected southerners. The new Republicans tend to be ultraconservatives who vote "more Republican" than did nonsouthern Republicans, while the new Democrats are moving toward their national party

TABLE 2-1

State Senate Delegations by Party Affiliation, 1948–1974

AFTER ELECTIONS OF... OR AROUND	1948 D	1948 R	1950 D	1950 R	1952 D	1952 R	1954 D	1954 R	1956 D	1956 R	1958 D	1958 R	1960 D	1960 R	1962 D	1962 R	1964 D	1964 R	1966 D	1966 R	1968 D	1968 R	1970 D	1970 R	1972 D	1972 R	1974 D	1974 R
Ala.	35	0	35	0	35	0	35	0	35	0	35	0	35	0	35	0	35	0	34	1	34	1	35	1	33	0	35	0
Ark.	35	0	35	0	35	0	35	0	35	0	35	0	35	0	35	0	35	0	35	0	34	1	34	1	34	1	34	1
																									(1)			
Fla.	38	0	38	0	37	1	37	1	37	1	37	1	37	1	37	1	42	2	37	11	32	16	33	15	25	14	27	12
																	(1)											
Ga.	54	0	53	1	53	1	53	1	53	1	53	1	53	1	52	2	44	9	46	7	48	7	50	6	48	8	51	5
La.	39	0	39	0	39	0	39	0	39	0	39	0	39	0	39	0	39	0	39	0	39	0	38	1	38	1	38	1
* Miss.	49	0	49	0	49	0	49	0	49	0	49	0	49	0	49	0	52	0	51	1	52	0	49	3	50	2	50	2
N.C.	48	2	48	2	48	2	49	1	47	3	49	1	48	2	48	2	49	1	43	7	38	12	43	7	35	15	49	1
S.C.	46	0	46	0	46	0	46	0	46	0	46	0	46	0	46	0	46	0	44	6	47	3	43	3	43	3	43	3
	(1)																						(1)		(1)		(1)	
Tenn.	28	4	29	4	29	4	28	5	27	6	28	5	27	6	27	6	25	8	25	8	20	13	19	13	19	13	20	12
Texas	31	0	31	0	31	0	31	0	31	0	31	0	31	0	31	0	31	0	30	1	29	2	29	2	28	3	28	3
* Va.	37	3	38	2	38	2	38	2	37	3	37	3	38	2	38	2	37	3	36	4	34	6	33	7	33	7	35	5
TOTALS	440	9	441	9	440	10	440	10	436	14	439	11	438	12	437	13	435	23	420	46	407	61	406	59	386	67	410	45
Republicans	2%		2%		2%		2%		3%		2%		3%		3%		5%		10%		13%		13%		15%		10%	

* Elected previous year.
Source: U.S. Statistical Abstract; Book of the States.

(Independent)
Democrat   Republican

TABLE 2-2

State House Delegations by Party Affiliation, 1948–1974

	1948		1950		1952		1954		1956		1958		1960		1962		1964		1966		1968		1970		1972		1974	
	D	R	D	R	D	R	D	R	D	R	D	R	D	R	D	R	D	R	D	R	D	R	D	R	D	R	D	R
Ala.	105	1	105	1	105	1	106 (1)	0	106	0	106	0	106	0	104	2	104	2	106	0	106	0	104	2	104	2	105	0
Ark.	99	1	98	2	97	3	97	2	97 (1)	2	100	0	99	1	99	1	99	1	98	2	96	4	98	2	99	1	97	3
Fla.	95	0	92	3	90	5	89	6	89	6	92	3	88	7	90	5	102	10	91	26	77	42	81	38	78	42	86	34
Ga.	204	1	204	1	202	3	202	3	202	3	202	3	203	2	203	2	198	7	183	22	169	26	173	22	151	29	157	23
La.	100	0	100	0	100	0	100	0	101	0	101	0	101	0	101	0	103	2	103	2	105	0	104	1	101	4	101 (1)	4
* Miss	140	0	140	0	140	0	140	0	140	0	140	0	140	0	140	0	122	0	120	2	122	0	120 (1)	1	119 (1)	2	119 (1)	2
N.C.	107	13	111	9	106	14	110	10	107	13	116	4	105	15	99	21	106	14	94	26	91	29	96	24	85	35	111	9
S.C.	124	0	124	0	124	0	124	0	124	0	124	0	124	0	124	0	124	0	107	17	119	5	113	11	103	21	107 (1)	17
Tenn.	80	19	80	19	80	19	80	19	78	21	82	17	80	19	78	21	75	24	59	39	49	49	56	43	51	48	63	35
Texas	150	0	149	1	150	0	150	0	150	0	150	0	150	0	143	7	149	1	147	3	142	8	140 (1)	10	133 (15)	17	135	15
* Va.	94	6	93	7	91	7	96	4	94	6	94	6	96	4	96	4	89	11	88	11	85	15	76	24	65	20	66	19
TOTALS	1,298	41	1,296	43	1,285	52	1,294	44	1,288	51	1,307	33	1,292	48	1,277	63	1,271	72	1,196	150	1,161	178	1,161	177	1,089	221	1,147	161
Republicans	3%		3%		4%		3%		4%		2%		4%		5%		5%		11%		13%		13%		17%		12%	

* Elected previous year.
Source: *U.S. Statistical Abstract; Book of the States.*

(Independent)
Democrat Republican

TABLE 2–3

U.S. Senate Election Results by Party Affiliation, 1948–1974

	1948		1950		1952		1954		1956		1958		1960		1962		1964		1966		1968		1970		1972		1974	
	D	R	D	R	D	R	D	R	D	R	D	R	D	R	D	R	D	R	D	R	D	R	D	R	D	R	D	R
Ala.	2	0	2	0	2	0	2	0	2	0	2	0	2	0	2	0	2	0	2	0	2	0	2	0	2	0	2	0
Ark.	2	0	2	0	2	0	2	0	2	0	2	0	2	0	2	0	2	0	2	0	2	0	2	0	2	0	2	0
Fla.	2	0	2	0	2	0	2	0	2	0	2	0	2	0	2	0	2	0	2	0	1	1	1	1	1	1	2	0
Ga.	2	0	2	0	2	0	2	0	2	0	2	0	2	0	2	0	2	0	2	0	2	0	2	0	2	0	2	0
La.	2	0	2	0	2	0	2	0	2	0	2	0	2	0	2	0	2	0	2	0	2	0	2	0	2	0	2	0
Miss.	2	0	2	0	2	0	2	0	2	0	2	0	2	0	2	0	2	0	2	0	2	0	2	0	2	0	2	0
N.C.	2	0	2	0	2	0	2	0	2	0	2	0	2	0	2	0	2	0	2	0	2	0	2	0	1	1	1	1
S.C.	2	0	2	0	2	0	2[a]	0	2	0	2	0	2	0	2	0	1	1[c]	1	1	1	1	1	1	1	1	1	1
Tenn.	2	0	2	0	2	0	2	0	2	0	2	0	2	0	2	0	2	0	1	1	1	1	0	2	0	2	0	2
Texas	2	0	2	0	2	0	2	0	2	0	2	0	2	0	1	1[b]	1	1	1	1	1	1	1	1	1	1	1	1
Va.	2	0	2	0	2	0	2	0	2	0	2	0	2	0	2	0	2	0	2	0	2	0	2[d]	0	1	1	1	1
TOTALS	22	0	22	0	22	0	22	0	22	0	22	0	22	0	21	1	20	2	19	3	18	4	17	5	15	7	16	6
Republicans	0%		0%		0%		0%		0%		0%		0%		5%		9%		14%		18%		23%		32%		27%	

D–Democrat
R–Republican

[a] Strom Thurmond was elected as a write-in candidate, joined the Democratic caucus.
[b] John Tower chosen in 1961 special election.
[c] Strom Thurmond switched parties in 1964, reelected as Republican in 1966.
[d] Harry Byrd, Jr., reelected as Independent, readmitted to Democratic caucus.

TABLE 2-4

U.S. House Election Results by Party Affiliation, 1948-1974

	1948		1950		1952		1954		1956		1958		1960		1962		1964		1966		1968		1970		1972		1974	
	D	R	D	R	D	R	D	R	D	R	D	R	D	R	D	R	D	R	D	R	D	R	D	R	D	R	D	R
Ala.	9	0	9	0	9	0	9	0	9	0	9	0	9	0	8	0	3	5	5	3	5	3	5	3	4	3	4	3
Ark.	7	0	7	0	6	0	6	0	6	0	6	0	6	0	4	0	4	0	3	1	3	1	3	1	3	1	3	1
Fla.	6	0	6	0	8	0	7	1	7	1	7	1	7	1	10	2	10	2	9	3	9	3	9	3	11	4	10	5
Ga.	10	0	10	0	10	0	10	0	10	0	10	0	10	0	10	0	9	1	8	2	8	2	8	2	9	1	10	0
La.	8	0	8	0	8	0	8	0	8	0	8	0	8	0	8	0	8	0	8	0	8	0	8	0	7	1	6	2
Miss.	7	0	7	0	6	0	6	0	6	0	6	0	6	0	5	0	4	1	5	0	5	0	5	0	3	2	3	2
N.C.	12	0	12	0	11	1	11	1	11	1	11	1	11	1	9	2	9	2	8	3	7	4	7	4	7	4	9	2
S.C.	6	0	6	0	6	0	6	0	6	0	6	0	6	0	6	0	6	0	5	1[a]	5	1	5	1	4	2	5	1
Tenn.	8	2	8	2	7	2	7	2	7	2	7	2	7	2	6	3	6	3	5	4	5	4	5	4	3	5	5	3
Texas	21	0	21	0	22	0	21	1	21	1	21	1	21	1	21	2	23	0	21	2	20	3	20	3	20	4	21	3
Va.	9	0	9	0	7	3	8	2	8	2	8	2	8	2	8	2	8	2	6	4	5	5	4	6	3	7	5	5
TOTALS	103	2	103	2	100	6	99	7	99	7	99	7	99	7	95	11	90	16	83	23	80	26	79	27	74	34	81	27
Republicans	2%		2%		6%		7%		7%		7%		7%		10%		15%		22%		25%		25%		31%		25%	

D—Democrat
R—Republican
[a] Switched in 1965.

position in voting—so much so, that by 1975 two-thirds of the southern Democrats in the House voted to extend the Voting Rights Act, and two-thirds of the southern Republicans voted against it.

Party data is unavailable on Republican strength in municipal, county, and other local offices. Although Republican mayors in southern cities and towns no longer are considered oddities, the percentage of local offices held by Republicans is believed to be less than their strength in state legislatures.

In the late 1960s and early 1970s, southern Republicans emphasized political realignment and expended considerable energy in efforts to convert conservative Democratic officeholders, announcing with great fanfare each one that switched. As late as December 1973, a major southern Republican leadership conference, held in Atlanta, was built around the theme of "realignment."

In a number of cases, Democratic legislators and other officials who did switch were defeated when they sought reelection or ran for higher office. In 1974 a Republican legislator in Georgia switched to the Democratic Party, and another in Florida did the same thing in 1975, possibly signaling an end to the trend of party defections to the GOP.

THE DEMOCRATIC RESURGENCE

The crucial question posed by Key and Heard was whether the changes that they could see developing would shake the hold of conservative politicians and their backers on the Democratic Party. As Heard explained insightfully, a progressive Democratic Party in the region could develop only if conservatives provided Republicans with the financial resources, energy, and impetus to challenge the Democrats and "only if it proves increasingly difficult to divide the expected adherents of liberal factions by appeals to racial prejudice." [13]

Until 1970, objective analysts would have concluded that the conservative hold on the dominant Democratic Party had remained basically unchanged. With only a few exceptions, the civil rights turmoil that began in the late 1950s and lasted through the 1960s divided working-class whites and blacks and prevented their coming together for a meaningful political coalition. It delayed the neo-populist tendencies that in the late 1940s and early 1950s had resulted in the election of such New Deal–oriented figures as Governors James Folsom of Alabama, Kerr Scott of North Carolina, Sidney McMath of Arkansas, and Earl Long of Louisiana, and such senators as Albert Gore and Estes Kefauver of Ten-

13. Heard, *Two-Party South?*, p. 248.

nessee and (in their early years) Lister Hill and John Sparkman of Alabama.

But by 1975, trends that traced back to 1966, the first election year after passage of the Voting Rights Act, were becoming clearly visible. Voting patterns of newly elected southern Democrats in Congress began to deviate from those of older conservatives (see Chapter 15).

Popular vote patterns were also changing. In 1970, ten of the 12 South Carolina counties that had given pluralities to George Wallace in 1968 cast a majority of their gubernatorial votes for Lieutenant Governor John West, a racially moderate Democrat running against Representative Albert Watson, a Thurmond-backed Goldwater Republican who made his racial views clear by wearing a white tie throughout his campaign.

That same year, moderates Dale Bumpers in Arkansas and Reubin Askew in Florida regained Democratic control by defeating incumbent Republican governors. Bumpers first defeated former Governor Orval Faubus, hero of the segregationists, in the Democratic primary.

A year earlier, Republican Linwood Holton, an outspoken critic of racial bias, won enough support from both blacks and organized labor in Virginia to win the governor's office. That election brought the collapse of the Byrd-dominated Democratic organization, but by the mid-1970s a vigorous new Democratic Party was developing in Virginia, a state in which genuine populist Henry Howell won more than 49 percent of the vote in his unsuccessful 1973 race for governor.

Segregationist former Governor Jimmie Davis fared poorly in the gubernatorial race in Louisiana in 1971, the same year that two racial moderates—William Waller and Charles Sullivan—battled for the Democratic nomination for governor in Mississippi. In 1974, segregationist Governors Lester Maddox in Georgia and Faubus in Arkansas suffered one-sided Democratic primary defeats against moderates George Busbee and David Pryor, both of whom faced token Republican opposition. In Tennessee, Ray Blanton, who had echoed George Wallace in a Senate race and lost almost 40 percent of the black vote to Republican Howard Baker in 1972, ran as a mildly populist racial moderate to lead a rejuvenated Democratic Party back into the governor's office.

Although the defeats of liberal U.S. Senators Albert Gore of Tennessee and Ralph Yarborough of Texas in 1970 and moderate Senator William Spong of Virginia in 1972 reflect countercurrents, the races for governor throughout the South since 1969 reflect a decline in racial tensions, the essential element for development of liberal tendencies among southern Democrats. By 1975, political analyst David Broder of the *Washington Post*, one of the most perceptive of contemporary American political observers, found in his travels little difference between the attitudes of most state political leaders, southern and otherwise, except that those in the South were "perhaps a bit more progressive." [14]

14. Interview with David Broder, April 5, 1975.

Throughout the South, Republican Party development and electoral success have stimulated Democrats to develop stronger political organizations. Only in states where Republicans developed full-time state headquarters with paid staff involved in research, fundraising, and candidate recruitment and training did the Democrats begin to develop such organizations. Conversely, in Arkansas, where the Republican threat collapsed after the defeat of Winthrop Rockefeller in 1970 and his subsequent death, Democratic Party leaders say they do not want to develop a strong party organization because it is not needed.

As the South emerges from its most traumatic period of change and enters a period of consolidation, Republican response to the new order may determine the future rate of two-party development. The 1974 elections may represent only a temporary setback for Republican fortunes in the South, or they may mark the end of a period of steady gain. The forces of political change remain active, but the number one problem that always has plagued the GOP in the region—a scarcity of dynamic and skillful political leadership—remains. The post-Watergate era will test the maturity of Republican development in the South.

Chapter

3

BLACK POLITICS

From Object to Participant

> Whatever phase of the southern political process one seeks to understand, sooner or later the trail of inquiry leads to the Negro.
>
> —V. O. Key [1]

THE LAST SPEAKER at a 1974 presidential prayer breakfast in an oversized Washington hotel ballroom was U.S. Senator John Stennis of Mississippi. He offered a brief testimony of his belief in the power of prayer after his recovery from a gunshot wound the previous year. Then the courtly onetime judge routinely delivered a warm and gracious introduction to a freshman congressman from Georgia, who gave the benediction.

The congressman was Andrew Young, a black clergyman and once the chief strategist and top aide for civil rights leader Martin Luther King, Jr. and the Southern Christian Leadership Conference (SCLC).

Later in the day, Young was asked what he would have said if someone had told him 20 years earlier that he would be introduced in 1974 by a senator from Mississippi as a congressman from Georgia at a presidential prayer breakfast.

"I would have said they were crazy," Young replied, "I mean, that would have been 1954. That was before the Supreme Court decision. And we couldn't even vote very well in the South. It was not long after that that my younger brother came back to New Orleans from the

1. V. O. Key, Jr., *Southern Politics in State and Nation* (New York: Knopf/Vintage Books, 1949), p. 5.

Navy, where he'd been a lieutenant. He's a graduate of Harvard University's dental school. He passed the state dental examination and went around the corner in the courthouse to register to vote, and they told him he flunked the literacy test. That's what it was like in the South." [2]

In parts of the South it had been worse. When Andy Young accepted the pastorate of a church in Thomasville, Georgia, in 1955, one of his first acts was to organize a voter registration drive. Less than a decade earlier, a black man had tried to register, and in Young's words "he was lassoed on the courthouse steps, and tied to the back of a pickup truck, and dragged around the black community until he was dead. And then he was cut loose again in front of a jail. . . . Blacks knew they had to turn to politics to survive. Voting was understood very early in Georgia as a life and death issue." [3]

The brief scene at the prayer breakfast illustrates a number of themes that run through the development of black politics in the South since World War II. The Negro was no longer a political object but had become a political participant. By the mid-1970s the civil rights movement —the "death" of which had been widely reported in the late 1960s—had moved off the streets and into the voting booths, and thereby into city halls, state legislative chambers, and finally the halls of Congress. The prayer breakfast itself symbolized that part of the civil rights movement which was religious in quality and tone, for black churches throughout the South had served as headquarters for that phase of the civil rights revolution which dealt with overt discrimination and was climaxed by passage of the 1965 Voting Rights Act. The ease with which Stennis expressed genuine personal warmth in his introduction of Young also reflected a special quality found among southerners, based on personal interracial relationships that existed even when legal and social institutions were segregated by law and custom. This quality has allowed a remarkable adjustment to desegregation in the region.

Of course, racism has not disappeared in the South, but there has been a change—and a degree of acceptance as well as accommodation by white southerners—that few would have predicted a decade earlier. In the words of Samuel DuBois Cook, a black political scientist and student of southern culture: "The evidence of change, at least on the basic and ultimate level, is mixed, ambiguous, ambivalent, complex, and contradictory. There are grounds for optimism and pessimism, faith and doubt, celebration and tears. What is true of Southern culture in general is true of Southern politics in particular." [4]

2. Interview with Andrew Young, January 31, 1974.
3. Ibid.
4. Samuel DuBois Cook, "Southern Politics Since Brown v. Board of Education: A Note on Change and Continuity," paper delivered at a symposium on the changing South at Clemson University, November 1973.

The forces of change had been gradually building for decades, but in Cook's words, "Brown v. Board of Education, in 1954, was more than a landmark case in constitutional law and the quest for a free society. It triggered the Civil Rights Movement, massive resistance not only to public school desegregation but to all other forms of change in the racial *status quo* as well. The ultimate significance of Brown v. Board of Education is that it broke the legal, institutional, and constitutional back of segregation." [5]

A few months after the prayer breakfast in Washington, Young was the luncheon speaker at the Holiday Inn in Santee, South Carolina, for a conference of the Association of Southern Black Mayors. Meeting in Tuskegee the previous November, one day after George Wallace had crowned a black homecoming queen at the University of Alabama, the same group had heard Wallace proclaim, "We're all God's children. All God's children are equal."

Young talked about the evolution from protest to politics, the importance for black politicians to retain the moral imperative of the civil rights movement, and about "the politics of communication and coalition" as a means to achieve the objectives of social and economic justice. He described the changing coalitions that are fundamentally reshaping southern politics.

"A lot of people don't understand the civil rights movement," Young told the mayors. "They saw us marching and they saw the dogs and the fire hoses, and they thought civil rights must mean only confrontation. But I was in Birmingham every day for every demonstration. And I wore my blue jeans every morning for demonstrations, and every afternoon I put on my suit and went downtown and sat down with the Chamber of Commerce and tried logically to work out a solution to those problems. Now, had we not been doing the confrontation and the communication and coalition simultaneously, we might have still been there marching, because the whole purpose of confrontation was to get the attention of people with power and resources to make change. And once we got the attention and once we got the opportunity to sit down together, we had to have something to say.

"And what we found was that while in every community . . . there were people who were hostile, people who were filled with hate, people who were blind with racism—there were also in those same communities, sometimes working side by side with those same people, very decent, honorable, loving people who wanted to solve these problems and who had some of the same ideas and same ideals that we had. So we spent time in every city in which we worked, cultivating a new coalition. What demonstrations did was bring it out in the open and force people

5. Ibid.

to kind of take sides, and there were usually in every community some good white people who were willing to work with the black community because they knew the problems we were marching about were not black problems at all.

"They would be there if everybody in the town was white, and they'd be there if everybody in the town was polka-dot. They are the problems of small towns and cities that are similar to the small towns and cities all over America and all over the world, and the problems are going to have to be solved in many instances by developing patterns of communication which, I say, 'deracializes' them."

At the SCLC, Young rose to executive director and won the admiration of civil rights reporters as an outstanding strategist and skilled administrator, but he maintained a low profile. A year after King's death in 1968, it was Young who successfully negotiated an end to the 100-day hospital strike, in Charleston, South Carolina, the last great SCLC victory.

A New Orleans native who grew up in an integrated middle-class neighborhood, the son of a dentist father and a schoolteacher mother, Young attended segregated public schools and later Howard University and Hartford Theological Seminary. He worked for the National Council of Churches before joining Dr. King in 1961. Married and the father of four children, he is handsome and articulate, both idealistic and pragmatic, a skilled negotiator who learned early from church politics that "it takes a certain amount of artfulness just to get people together to do things they really want to do," a man of medium brown complexion who both identifies strongly with black aspirations and understands the complexities and frustrations of white southerners reacting to the future shock of rapid social change.

"Andy," an SCLC co-worker once said, "understands the cracker mind."

Young spoke to the mayors for 40 minutes, without notes, analyzing the state of black politics in the South and its role in shaping national political developments. He covered all the themes that run through the story of black political development in the South, and there is no one better equipped to articulate them.

He emphasized the need to apply the principles of coalition and communication: "Too often we thought of a coalition as something we went along with on somebody else's program. But when you are the mayor and seeking additional support for your ideas, it won't go very far in your community unless we find patterns of communication that build up trust among people who formerly were different and unless we begin to deracialize some of our conflicts and deal with them as problems of people that would be here, regardless of race, creed, or color."

Young spoke to the mayors the day after Congress had approved legislation to retain funds for economic opportunity programs despite Nixon administration objections. "Once we began to realize that poverty is not a racial problem, but a problem for the nation in which we live, then all of a sudden Congress began to take another look at it."

He spoke of the frustrations of black elected officials at a time of high aspirations. "For ten years we went around yelling 'Freedom Now'—and a lot of people translated that into having a black congressman, meaning we're going to have all of our freedom now, so on Monday morning they come to city hall and say, 'Where is it?'" There was appreciative laughter. "And somehow it's our job, and we have accepted the challenge in running for public office, to say that we are going to pull people together and help them to do the things that need doing in order for us to survive as a people and as a nation."

Young then switched to the language of practical politics. In the first month after his election to Congress, Young explained, he was visited by the presidents of Lockheed, the Coca-Cola Bottling Co., and Delta Airlines—the three largest corporations in his district—"and there was no reason to believe that I would be for them or do anything for them at all."

Within a month after he got on the House Banking Committee, "every bank in the district had me to lunch or to meet with the executives, or they came by. Now my voting record as far as the American Banking Association [is concerned] is zero. On 20 votes I voted against what they thought was right on every vote. But that doesn't stop them from calling me up every time there's a vote and letting me know what their point of view is. Nor does it stop me from helping them when they are having problems in the federal bureaucracy. Now they're not against me, not because I voted like they wanted me to vote, but because when it comes down to good government and congressional service, our office has serviced them as well or better than any congressman has ever done." Young added that "the same thing works in reverse. . . . Every southern congressman is a friend of mine. I don't care what his votes have been in the past."

He told of his first month in Congress, when the president of a black land-grant college wanted him to introduce an amendment to a bill in a subcommittee chaired by Representative Jamie Whitten of Mississippi. "You know, I made a career of fighting Jamie Whitten down in Mississippi," Young explained, "and I didn't know the way to the bathroom yet, and here he's the powerful congressman from Mississippi. But I had sense enough to go over and talk to him. And when I sat down and explained to him the reasonableness of this proposal, he said, 'Well you don't have to offer that as an amendment. We will work that into the bill in committee.'

"You know as well as I do," Young continued, "there's a southern style of doing things that likes to cooperate quietly because it doesn't get you in trouble, but they don't want to do anything publicly because they think the South is still like it was when they got elected. But gradually we're electing a new breed of southerner. And all across the South you will find the kind of people going to Congress as a result of your votes are people you can communicate with, that you can work with, and that are anxious to represent you.

"And when you need sewer money or money for rural development or money for any kind of program, the first man you should go to is your congressman, because he sees you as a potentially tremendous ally and also as a tremendous threat. Whether you realize your power or not, especially in Democratic areas, any time blacks don't go out and support the party, Republicans now will take over in the South, and those southern Democrats know that, and they know that they can't afford to alienate any of the emerging new black leadership, and they are anxious to serve the needs of your communities."

A glance at the voting records of southern Democrats elected to the House since 1966 shows what Young is talking about. A 1973 study by the Joint Center for Political Studies at Howard University showed that such new southern Democrats as Ray Thornton of Arkansas, Mendel Davis of South Carolina, Charles Rose of North Carolina, Walter Flowers of Alabama, Gillis Long and Lindy Boggs of Louisiana, and William Stuckey and Bo Ginn of Georgia—all from districts with 25 percent or more black population—voted 40 to 80 percent of the time with the congressional black caucus on a range of social, economic, and civil rights issues. The study also revealed that all but one of the eight southern Republicans in Congress from districts 25 percent or more black voted less than 10 percent of the time with the black caucus.[6]

To understand the potential of black politics in the practice of the art of the possible, we turn to Georgia, which in 1975 had more than a score of black legislators. The legislative black caucus established liaison with the congressional black caucus through Young and expanded its impact statewide through the more than 100 members of the Georgia Association of Black Elected Officials (GABEO—pronounced Gabby-O).

When the OEO extension bill in 1974 was lodged in the Equal Opportunities Subcommittee of the House Education and Labor Committee, which included veteran Democratic Representative Robert G. Stephens, Jr. of Georgia, black legislators in Georgia were called on for help. Working through GABEO, they swamped Stephens with letters from black elected officials in his district. He responded in a lithographed letter that he would "do all I can" to get the bill reported out and passed. Stephens expressed "regret that the number of letters I received on this matter prevents me from sending each one who wrote me a personal reply." GABEO President Edward McIntyre of Augusta, a county coun-

6. See Chapter 15 for congressional voting patterns.

cilman who resides in Stephens's district and who coordinated the letter-writing effort, said after receiving the form letter from the congressman, "Blacks are beginning to learn the political process and how you get things done. And we're using those tools and techniques that have been used by other people for years." [7]

In his speech to the mayors, Young talked about the changing attitudes of white politicians, in response to the increased level of black voter participation. "There are white congressmen who didn't feel they could vote decent [when I came to Washington], but it's amazing how well they're learning their lessons," Young said. "And it goes back to what Frederick Douglass said years ago. The struggle for freedom is a struggle to save black men's bodies and white men's souls.

"It used to be Southern politics was just 'nigger' politics, who could 'outnigger' the other—then you registered 10 to 15 percent in the community and folk would start saying 'Nigra,' and then you get 35 to 40 percent registered and it's amazing how quick they learned how to say 'Nee-grow,' and now that we've got 50, 60, 70 percent of the black votes registered in the South, everybody's proud to be associated with their black brothers and sisters."

By 1975, black voter registration in the 11 states of the old Confederacy totaled more than 3.5 million, a factor that had changed politics within the region and that could significantly affect the outcome of future "southern strategies" in presidential elections. In the seven states covered initially by the Voting Rights Act of 1965, black registration more than doubled, to 2.4 million, in the decade after the act was passed.

Black registration had begun to increase significantly in many southern states in the early 1960s, spurred by the Atlanta-based Voter Education Project, but it increased more sharply after passage of the Voting Rights Act. That act removed literacy requirements for six southern states and part of a seventh,* and the extension of the act later removed literacy qualifications for voting in all states.

A 1964 constitutional amendment had already eliminated the poll tax as a requirement for voting in federal elections, and a 1966 Supreme Court decision eliminated the poll tax for state elections. Although Key had found that the poll tax served more to disfranchise poor whites than blacks, he concluded in a chapter describing and analyzing the literacy test that it was "a fraud and nothing more," that it was applied chiefly to Negroes, and that "only in exceptional cases is the test administered fairly." [8]

Although the Voting Rights Act provided for federal registrars and

7. Interview with Edward McIntyre, April 22, 1975.
* Fully covered under the 1965 Voting Rights Act were Alabama, Georgia, Louisiana, Mississippi, South Carolina, and Virginia. Part of North Carolina was also covered. Texas was added in 1975, when the act was extended.
8. Key, *Southern Politics*, p. 576.

federal election observers, neither were used extensively. Much more significant was Section 5 of the act, which required that "any voting qualifications, or prerequisite to voting, or standard, practices, or procedure with respect to voting" in a covered jurisdiction must be cleared by the U.S. attorney general or the U.S. District Court for the District of Columbia for a determination that the change is not discriminatory "in purpose or effect" before it can be enforced. The provision's intent was to break the cycle of substituting new discriminatory laws and procedures whenever old ones were struck down. By the mid-1970s, Section 5 had been used to review changes affecting polling places, registration times and places, qualifications for office, schedules of elections, city boundaries, and even court-approved reapportionment plans. Congress knew that seemingly minor changes in electoral law could, in fact, serve to exclude minorities from participation or to minimize the effect of their participation.[9]

After Young had talked about the effect of black political participation, he moved to the theme of racial reconciliation. His speech came shortly after George Wallace had received endorsements from several elected black officials in Alabama, including two young mayors in the audience that heard Young. "I'm willing to forgive or forget the racial past of the South," Young said, "but I'm not willing to say that everybody that comes to the mourner's bench as a sinner can all of a sudden be the pastor of the church. [This indirect reference to Wallace drew laughter.]

"And what I want to say to the new breed of southern congressmen coming up, to the new breed of southern governors coming up, to the converted southern governors coming along [more laughter], you're welcome to the fold; we're always glad to have sinners coming in, but let's see what you can do to deliver, let's see what you can do to deliver goods and services, because it's no big thing anymore for somebody to call me brother. The thing I want to know is: are you going to feed my people? Are there going to be jobs and services and hospitals in my communities that are going to meet the needs of my people? Are there going to be cooperative strategies between statehouses, city halls, and county courthouses that begin to really promise not just a New South ideology, but a New South of economic growth and political development, where people really and truly don't just call each other brother, but where they live like brothers. Where if one brother lives in a brick house, the other doesn't have to live in a shack; he can at least have a smaller brick house, or cement block, at least have a roof over his head.

"So I'm looking not at what people say anymore, and I don't think any

9. The preclearance feature also served as a deterrent against passage of discriminatory laws, just as the provision for federal registrars spurred recalcitrant registrars in hard-core areas to act in good faith. See U.S. Commission on Civil Rights, *The Voting Act: Ten Years After* (Washington, D.C., 1975), p. 27.

of us ought to do that anymore, and people are not looking at what we say anymore; they're looking at politicians on what they are able to deliver."

The increased black vote that Young talked about resulted in more than just a change in rhetoric from white politicians. Many white politicians throughout the South reported to the authors that their experience in campaigning among blacks had sensitized their feelings and affected them personally as well as politically. State Senator Edgar Mouton, who speaks with the candor that is common among the Cajun French in Louisiana, described his experience when he made his first race for the state Senate in 1964 from Lafayette Parish:

"I was born and raised here and I had never shaken hands with a black person before I ran for office. We had black servants, and black people working for us, [but] the first time I shook hands was a traumatic thing. And sure enough, the first was named Mouton, a black Mouton. . . . But then once you got into it, and saw the very difficult times that the blacks have had, how they survived in our society with the burden that government put on them, it is unbelievable we didn't have a revolution before now. I got deeply involved in the poverty program, and I learned to greatly respect the feelings of the blacks. It is very difficult to understand what they have been through, unless you campaign among them for a while. You find more sensitivity among the white politicians for the black community than you do in the black community for the white politician. The white politician tends to become much more sensitive to the black community [than do whites in general].

"I didn't know much about blacks when I got started. I went to a meeting where I was the only white person there, and I made a five-minute, very general, simple talk, and said goodbye. They said 'Wait, we've got some questions.' I stayed there for three hours answering questions—would I appoint blacks to boards and so forth—and one man said, 'I have a question that I can't answer; if you can answer it, I'll vote for you.'

"I said, 'What is that?'

"He said, 'I have a boy who is seven years old, and we were driving down the road the other day and he saw a lineman working on a power line, and he said, 'Daddy, when I grow up I want to be a lineman like him.'

"Then he told me that, as I knew, the power company doesn't hire black people, and he asked me, 'Can you tell me how I can tell my son he can't be that lineman because he is black?' "

Mouton continued, "I couldn't give him an answer. It opened my eyes that this fellow had the same feelings for his son that I have for my daughters. When you think along those lines, as corny as it sounds, when you put yourself into a one-and-one human relationship, you can understand that if they get bitter and kind of hit us a little bit, you can't blame them."

Mouton said that white politicians generally, and especially those in the tolerant Cajun parishes of south Louisiana, have become more responsive to blacks for two reasons. "They certainly have to be responsive, knowing that if they get a label as antiblack and they have 15 percent black in their district, it would make a difference," he said. "Also, I think you will find that generally, especially in the south Louisiana politicians, they are becoming frankly more attentive to the needs of the blacks as a person." [10]

Mouton also contended that white legislators were more willing than blacks to take the initiative in making accommodations when dealing with legislators of the other race. Similarly, black legislators throughout the South, especially those who broke the color line in their states, told the authors that one of their first major tasks was to "educate" white politicians to the needs of blacks after decades of discrimination.

The number of black legislators in the South—which neared 100 in the 1975 elections—will continue to increase as more states adopt single-member legislative districts. In 1974 the number of black legislators elected in Alabama increased from three to 15, in the South Carolina House the increase was from three to 13; in both cases, the reason was a change to single-member districts. Altogether, the number of black elected officials in the 11 southern states grew from 72 in 1965, when the Voting Rights Act was passed, to 1,652 in 1975 (see Tables 3-1–3-3).

Like so much about the South since World War II, the progress in black political development suggested by statistics can blind the unwary to the problems that remain. Despite the tripling of elected black officials in the region between 1970 and 1975, blacks still comprised barely 2 percent of all elected officials in the region, although they represent nearly 20 percent of the voting-age population. The first black state Supreme Court judge was named in 1975, an appointment by Governor Reubin Askew of Florida, but no black had yet been named to the federal bench in the South. Although three blacks were among the region's 108 U.S. representatives, there were no elected black officials in any statewide office in the South.

Although most of the 66 black mayors in the South in 1975 represented small, black-majority communities, they also included the chief executives of two state capitals, Maynard Jackson of Atlanta and Clarence Lightner of Raleigh. The election of Lightner in 1973 was considered especially significant because the black voting-age population there was less than 25 percent, and his election demonstrated a recently developing attitude among southern whites that issues can be more im-

10. Interview with Edgar Mouton, January 13, 1974.

TABLE 3–1

Black Elected Officials, by State and Share of Total, 1970–1975

STATE	BLACK ELECTED OFFICIALS 1970	BLACK ELECTED OFFICIALS 1975	TOTAL ELECTED OFFICIALS 1975	BLACK SHARE OF TOTAL 1975	BLACK SHARE OF VOTING AGE POPULATION
Alabama	86	161	4,060	4.0%	23.0%
Arkansas	55	171	10,289	1.7	15.4
Florida	36	87	5,070	1.7	12.5
Georgia	40	168	7,226	2.3	22.9
Louisiana	64	237	4,761	5.0	26.6
Mississippi	81	192	4,761	4.0	31.4
North Carolina	62	194	5,504	3.5	19.4
South Carolina	38	132	3,078	4.3	26.3
Tennessee	38	96	7,877	1.2	13.9
Texas	29	150	23,038	0.7	11.3
Virginia	36	64	3,587	1.8	16.6
Totals	565	1,652	79,251	2.1	17.8 *

* This is the black percentage of total voting-age population in the 11 states of the South, and not a mean (average) of the percentages in each state.
Source: Adapted from tables compiled by Joint Center for Political Studies, Washington, D.C.

TABLE 3–2

Black Elected Officials, by State and Level of Office, 1975

	U.S. HOUSE	STATE HOUSE	STATE SENATE	MUNIC-IPAL	COUNTY	LAW ENFORCE-MENT	EDUCA-TION
Alabama	0	13	2	58	17	51	20
Arkansas	0	3	1	80	21	1	65
Florida	0	3	0	68	2	6	8
Georgia	1	19	2	89	12	8	37
Louisiana	0	8	1	69	45	34	80
Mississippi	0	1	0	82	29	41	39
North Carolina	0	4	2	125	12	5	46
South Carolina	0	13	0	56	22	15	26
Tennessee	1	9	2	27	43	6	8
Texas	1	9	0	60	1	9	70
Virginia	0	1	1	42	17	3	0
Totals	3	83	11	756	221	179	399

Source: Adapted from tables compiled by Joint Center for Political Studies, Washington, D.C.

TABLE 3–3

Black Share of Total Population and Voting-Age Population, by State, 1970

STATE	TOTAL POPULATION			VOTING-AGE POPULATION [*]		
	TOTAL	BLACK	BLACK SHARE OF TOTAL	TOTAL	BLACK	BLACK SHARE OF TOTAL
Alabama	3,444,165	903,467	26.2%	2,210,645	508,326	23.0%
Arkansas	1,923,295	352,445	18.3	1,268,285	195,522	15.4
Florida	6,789,443	1,041,651	15.3	4,680,402	584,293	12.5
Georgia	4,589,575	1,187,149	25.9	2,945,287	673,581	22.9
Louisiana	3,641,306	1,086,832	29.8	2,253,549	600,425	26.6
Mississippi	2,216,912	815,770	36.8	1,373,145	431,617	31.4
North Carolina	5,082,059	1,126,478	22.2	3,323,017	644,511	19.4
South Carolina	2,590,516	789,041	30.5	1,635,353	429,598	26.2
Tennessee	3,923,687	621,261	15.8	2,597,960	359,885	13.9
Texas	11,196,730	1,399,005	12.5	7,196,894	814,067	11.3
Virginia	4,648,494	861,368	18.5	3,059,214	508,995	16.6
Total South	50,046,182	10,184,467	20.4	32,543,751	5,750,820	17.7
Total Non-South	153,165,744	12,395,822	8.1	101,024,094	7,321,123	7.2
U.S. Total	203,211,926	22,580,289	11.1	133,567,845	13,071,943	9.8

[*] Voting-age population is the number of people 18 years and older.
Source: Adapted from Table 17, 1975 edition of *National Roster of Black Elected Officials*, compiled by the Joint Center for Political Studies, Washington, D.C. Population figures based on 1970 census.

portant than a candidate's race. Lightner received widespread white suburban support in an election in which growth policies and land use planning were major issues and in which his opponent was a white executive employed by downtown businessmen.

Lightner was in the audience as Young challenged the black mayors to provide a new kind of leadership in the South. Echoing sentiments expressed by Martin Luther King, Jr. shortly before his death, Young said, "I strangely think we're going to be able to deliver in the South, partly because we know our racist heritage, and there are still people in the North who aren't convinced that racism has infected them like a cancerous malignancy. We know what it is; we know it when we see it; we can identify it; we don't let it get in the way of our solving problems even when it exists. And because we may have an opportunity to deracialize and deal with some of the hard political and economic issues of our time, I think the direction of this nation is going to be determined by the direction that comes from the southern part of the United States."

At the same time, Young said that black politicians who "play the game," who go overboard to endorse a George Wallace or a Richard Nixon in exchange for federal and state grants for their districts, were failing to exercise moral leadership and thereby forfeiting a special kind of political opportunity.

"The kind of leadership that you bring is really a new phenomenon that nobody understands yet, a new breed of southern leadership that's never been there before, and that new breed of southern leadership creates the New South that the press has been talking about for a long time. People elected us because in one measure there was nobody else they could trust. Everybody else had had a chance to steal, and we were the only honest ones left, and the question is are we really honest, or is it that we just haven't had our chance yet to steal?"

He spoke of the "strong, moral people that look to us for leadership . . . the strong black women who worked and sweated and slaved to get us through school, who prayed for us when we were trying to go astray, who still are responsible for our election, for most of the money raised in our churches and most of the business done by our businesses.

"So we've got to keep our governments free of corruption. We've got to set a kind of example that we can look our children in the eyes and say we didn't have much to work with, but this is what we did. Now you proudly carry on and do what you can."

But despite the leadership qualities and impressive abilities displayed by such officials as Young and Representative Barbara Jordan of Texas, and the high-principled dedication of many black state legislators and other officials, there were also black officials with little integrity and limited sophistication. One black legislator in Alabama, who sought legislation to create a pari-mutuel betting commission in his home county with himself as commissioner at a five-figure salary, told a reporter for the *New York Times*, "Why should you expect black politicians to operate differently from white ones?"

The first black legislator in the South in the modern era, state Senator Leroy Johnson of Georgia, was defeated for reelection in 1974 after he was indicted for income tax evasion, thus ending a 12-year political career at the age of 46. Of the three black legislators initially elected in South Carolina, one subsequently was convicted for failure to file income tax returns and another was disbarred. Mayor Lightner of Raleigh failed to win reelection in 1975 after a series of separate criminal indictments that involved his wife and two of his children. These officials had made positive and valuable contributions, and there was a tragic quality in their downfall.

In interviewing more than 50 black political leaders throughout the South, the authors generally found a determined commitment toward humanistic concerns among those whose political involvement began during or before the civil rights movement, but a tendency towards less idealism and less regard for the morality of means and ends among younger black politicians.

State Senator Julian Bond of Georgia, a civil-rights activist before he entered politics, said that black politics has been "a tremendous success in winning elections and putting black faces in high places, but a failure in having an ideology that would make all the effort and suffering and sacrifice of the past meaningful." He added, "The trend I see is that too many of the newer black politicians are beginning to be mirror images of their white counterparts. For example, too many of the younger guys, you see them do something wrong—not illegal necessarily, but a little unethical or something—and they say in justification, 'White people have been doing this for years; it's our turn now.' My view is it's never your turn to do anything that is wrong; just because other people have done so is no reason for you to do it. Black politics hasn't been a success in developing unity [of purpose] among black politicians." [11]

A fact of the political process is that campaigns cost money, and the income level for southern blacks in the mid-1970s remained less than 60 percent of that for southern whites. The lack of financial resources in the black community has virtually forced black political leaders, whatever their motives, to depend on traditional white sources of financing. A major problem arises when a candidate who might best represent black interests lacks the financial resources of a more conservative opponent.

In Greensboro, North Carolina, whose black community is politically well organized, all candidates for office are interviewed by a committee, which then selects what is usually a bipartisan ticket for endorsement by the Voters League. Each black registered voter is mailed a copy of the endorsement. Before the mailing, receipts and bills for all expenses are compiled and prorated among the candidates, who are told, "This is the best investment you can make with your campaign funds." A president of the organization told the authors, "We haven't had anyone turn us down, but we have on occasion not required someone to pay if they can't afford it." [12]

"Buying" of support from local black leaders by white politicians has occurred or at least been attempted with undetermined frequency, but the authors heard consistent reports throughout the South that the ability of such "leaders" to deliver has diminished because of an increasingly sophisticated black electorate and the candidates' use of television, direct mail, community visits, and other means of direct communication with the voters. The impression from scores of interviews with knowledgeable black and white sources is that most of the money that passes hands is used for legitimate campaign purposes, such as postage, or for gasoline money and drivers to provide transportation on election day, but that misuse of such funds is not rare.

A further impression from such interviews is that group self-interest

11. Interview with Julian Bond, April 17, 1975.
12. Interview with Hermon Fox, December 20, 1973.

is a prime motivation among black political brokers in the South, most of whom support candidates on the basis of their commitment to meet the needs of the masses of blacks—and such candidates' ability to deliver on that commitment.

It should be remembered there are many places in the South where blacks voted long before the civil rights movement, that the black vote was often manipulated by white politicians, and that elements of this tradition remain alive. In their book on Negro political development in the South, Reese Cleghorn and Pat Watters discussed such manipulation in some detail. For example, they reported that in McIntosh County, Georgia, the sheriffs stayed in office for decades partly because of strong Negro support, which the sheriffs cultivated. As late as 1917, the county still had a Negro representative in the Georgia legislature, the last of his race there until 1962. Negroes constituted a majority of the population and half the electorate long before the Voting Rights Act. Georgia law permitted voting at 18 many years before Congress lowered the voting age nationally, and Negro students of legal age in the county seat of Darien were taken in groups to register. Their principal, who was black, was a member of the county board of registrars.

Cleghorn and Watters wrote:

> The Negroes' support of Sheriff Tom Poppell was a bitter pill for reform elements in McIntosh. This county was widely noted for its bizarre law enforcement practices, operation of tourist [speed] traps and toleration of criminal elements. The anti-Poppell forces, repeatedly defeated, maintained that the sheriff bought Negro support in part by a rural Georgia version of a city ward-heeling system: he named numerous Negro special deputies who, his opponents complained, were sometimes given *carte blanche* authority in law enforcement in their areas in exchange for their political support. Welfare rosters in McIntosh were unusually big in relation to population, with Negroes the most numerous beneficiaries. The sheriff's faction maintained a close identification with these benefits. But all of this was within a system of rigid segregation. Negroes held no full-time public offices before 1966, when one was elected to the County Commission, and what they received for their votes principally was toleration of small-time rackets such as illegal bars and the numbers game, relatively benign police treatment in general, and relatively easy dispensation of welfare funds, which largely are paid for by the state and federal governments.[13]

In 1974, reporter Jon Buchan of the *Charlotte Observer* reported on the activities in little Pageland, South Carolina, where People United Together (PUT) and a competing political organization among blacks adopted rival slates in the Democratic primary, in which three major candidates for governor were racial moderates. Only PUT organized car pools, and its candidate received more than three times the vote of his nearest competitor. Local political managers said the amounts of money spent were less than in the past and that outright vote buying was a

13. Pat Watters and Reese Cleghorn, *Climbing Jacob's Ladder* (New York: Harcourt, Brace and World/Harbinger, 1967), pp. 332–333.

fading practice—most of the cash was "hauling money" to get people to the polls. One 65-year-old veteran political manager said that although votes might still go for $3 or "a few drinks of likker" here and there, it was harder to influence blocs of voters than in the past. "With television and radio and new people in the mills, and everybody having cars, you can't tell until the last vote is counted," he said. "More people just vote on their own." [14]

Black leadership throughout the South talks of the need for blacks to provide their own sources of political funds in order to achieve full political independence. As blacks in the South become more affluent and more politically sophisticated, such resources may develop.

If southern blacks have basically won the right to equality in political participation, the larger battle of economic justice remains to be won. Martin Luther King, Jr. wrote:

> With . . . the Voting Rights Act one phase of development in the civil rights revolution came to an end. A new phase opened, but few observers realized it or were prepared for its implications. For the vast majority of white Americans, the past decade—the first phase—had been a struggle to treat the Negro with a degree of decency, not of equality. White America was ready to demand that the Negro should be spared the lash of brutality and coarse degradation, but it had never been truly committed to helping him out of poverty, exploitation or all forms of discrimination. . . . The real cost lies ahead. The stiffening of white resistance is the recognition of that fact. The discount education given Negroes will in the future have to be purchased at full price if quality education is to be realized. Jobs are harder and costlier to create than voting rolls. The eradication of slums housing millions is complex far beyond integrating buses and lunch counters.[15]

The implication of that challenge of the future as well as recognition of accomplishments of the past were recognized by Andy Young when he concluded his talk to the black mayors: "I look around here and I see faces that were in the jails of the South not long ago. It's always dramatic to go to Greene County [Alabama] where [William McKinley] Branch and [Thomas] Gilmore—I can remember them getting beat up on the courthouse steps—now one of them is the probate judge and the other one is the sheriff.

"You know we can't help but be people who believe in doing the impossible, because we've already done so much of it. But we sure got a long, long way to go. It's like the old black preacher says: We ain't what we oughta be; we ain't what we're gonna be; but thank God we ain't what we was." [16]

14. *Charlotte Observer*, July 22, 1974.

15. Martin Luther King, Jr., *Where Do We Go from Here: Chaos or Community?* (New York: Harper and Row, 1967), pp. 3–7.

16. The speech by Andrew Young was taped by the authors. Quotations came from the transcript.

Chapter

4

ALABAMA

The Wallace Freeze

WHATEVER his impact elsewhere, George Corley Wallace's dominance of Alabama politics has served to freeze the state's political development.

If Wallace has symbolized the resistance to black aspirations—an appeal to racism—his appeal goes deeper than that, touching the alienation of citizens who are frustrated by big government, big business, big labor, even big religion, and who find it difficult to adjust to the rapid change of a modern technological society.

Sitting in his wheelchair in the governor's office, Wallace talks of being more compassionate after his own near assassination, of having made "mistakes," and he projects himself as a "populist," a term quite respectable in Alabama and part of a tradition that nurtured the beginning of Wallace's political career.

But the record reveals more rhetoric than reality in Wallace's professed concern for the "little man." The vested interests—the "big mules" of Birmingham—have learned they have little to fear from Wallace. In 1974 the *Birmingham News*, voice of the establishment in Alabama's largest city, for the first time endorsed Wallace for reelection.

When Wallace lost the 1958 race for governor, he was a young country judge who had developed as a protege of genuine populist Jim Folsom. It was a contest in which Wallace was perceived as a moderate—and he vowed he would never again be "out-segged" (or "out-nigguhed," as his biographer Marshall Frady claims and Wallace denies).

In 1962 he was elected governor; his tax program included a plank against a sales tax increase. When the legislature scuttled Wallace's tax program and substituted a sales tax increase, his designated House speaker, Albert Brewer, recalls going to the governor's office and expressing sympathy, "because you'll have to veto it."

"Because of his pledge, I didn't see that he had any choice," Brewer later recalled. "He looked at me in silence for a moment and said, 'I'll just holler nigger and everybody will forget it.' And he did. And they did. I was 33 years old and speaker of the House and was never so disillusioned in my life." [1]

As governor, Wallace did little for the "little man." His legislative leaders who went to Congress tended to fit the mold of the old stereotype southern conservative, voting consistently with northern Republicans against social legislation. Yet economic liberalism has deep political roots in Alabama. There was a strong populist outgrowth of the Farmers Alliance, and it is generally conceded that in 1894 Reuben F. Kolb, the Farmers Alliance candidate for governor, was "counted out" in the conservative Black Belt through stuffed ballot boxes and other devices. Kolb, who received 47.5 percent of the vote in 1892, demanded state control over banks and railroads, an easing of credit, regulation of the crop lien system that bled sharecroppers and tenants, and an end to the convict lease system that provided labor for mines, steel foundries, and farms.

Liberalism reemerged in the late 1920s and 1930s when U.S. Senator Hugo Black regularly toured the state, educating the public about political realities, including the need to regulate the dominant economic institutions. As a Supreme Court justice, Black voted consistently to expand the basic American concepts of equality and justice to include southern Negroes and believed absolutely that the framers of the Constitution considered free speech "always the deadliest enemy of tyranny." Although Black became a pariah in Alabama in the 1950s and 1960s,[2] it was the New Deal–style populists from the northern half of the state who for more than 30 years dominated the Alabama congressional delegation. They took the obligatory stands against civil rights (in the 1970s, Senator John Sparkman said with a sigh of relief that the biggest change in Alabama politics since World War II was that "the Negro question is dead"),[3] but they devoted most of their energy to housing, hospital, and highway programs. For 22 years, until Lister Hill's retirement in early 1969, he and Sparkman served together in the U.S. Senate and provided leadership in major programs in education, public health and health research, housing, and other areas.

The change in the Alabama congressional delegation is reflected in the shift of its overall ratings by the liberal Americans for Democratic Action and the conservative Americans for Constitutional Action. In

1. Interview with Albert Brewer, July 9, 1974.
2. Black was honored at a testimonial dinner in Birmingham given by the Alabama bar; after he died, he was accorded other honors in his native state.
3. Interview with John Sparkman, January 31, 1974.

1963, the year Wallace was first inaugurated governor, the overall ADA rating was 34.1 and the ACA rating 27.4. By 1974, the liberal ADA rating was down to 12.8 and the conservative ACA rating was up to 65.6. Only Representative Robert Jones of northernmost Alabama and Senator Sparkman, whose populist ardor cooled considerably as Wallace inflamed the populace against the federal government, remain of the progressives. Jones in 1975 became chairman of the House Public Works Committee, but in 1976 he announced plans to retire.

The populist legacy in Alabama politics, however, is only part of a strong bifactional tradition that splits roughly along conservative and liberal lines. Examination of the Goldwater vote in 1964 showed a strong correlation with the Strom Thurmond Dixiecrat vote in Alabama in 1948, a reflection of both racial and economic conservatism and of a continuous struggle in that period between Democratic loyalists and states' righters.

In 1948, when national Democrat Jim Folsom was governor and Hill and Sparkman were senators, Alabama was the only state in which voters were unable to cast ballots for Harry Truman. There were other southern states in which Dixiecrats took over the machinery of the Democratic Party, but only in Alabama did electors for Truman fail to appear. Faced with a choice of Thurmond or Republican Thomas Dewey, 80 percent of the Alabama voters cast ballots for Thurmond, who was running "under the rooster" (i.e., as a Democrat) in Alabama.

Twelve years later there was a fierce competition between states' righters and loyalists for control of the slate of Democratic presidential electors. Democratic voters in Alabama choose presidential electors in a primary; in 1960, nominations went to the five loyalist electors and six unpledged (states' righters) who cast their ballots for Harry F. Byrd of Virginia.[4]

GEORGE   WALLACE   AND
THE   POLITICS   OF   RACE

Because George Wallace has so completely dominated Alabama politics since 1962, his career is worth examining in detail.

Wallace's father and grandfather served as county functionaries in

4. Author Neal Peirce has suggested that only five-elevenths of the Alabama Democratic vote in the 1960 presidential election should have been credited to John F. Kennedy and that six-elevenths should have been credited to Senator Byrd. The Peirce theory would erase the national popular vote lead of 118,559 for Kennedy and give the popular vote lead that year to Richard Nixon by roughly 58,000 votes. See Peirce, *The People's President* (New York: Simon and Schuster, 1968), pp. 102–104, 348–349.

Barbour County in the eastern Black Belt. Young Wallace served as a page in the state Senate, worked his way through college at the University of Alabama after his father's death, won the state Golden Gloves boxing championship as a bantamweight, graduated with a law degree in 1942, and married Lurleen Burns, a teenage dime-store clerk.

He served as a combat flight engineer in a B-29 bomber in World War II and was discharged with a small pension for partial disability for a psychoneurotic condition. In 1956 the Veterans Administration continued the 10 percent rating after reexamination resulted in a diagnosis of anxiety reaction.

After being appointed an assistant state attorney general, Wallace in 1946 was elected at age 27 to a four-year term in the legislature. He was reelected in 1950. At the 1948 Democratic national convention he served as an elected delegate and refused to join a majority of the Alabama delegation in a walkout over a civil rights plank. He was elected a circuit judge in 1952 and served that year as chairman of the southern delegation on the Platform Committee at the Democratic National Convention.

Arthur Shores, the senior black lawyer in Alabama who since 1968 has served on the Birmingham City Council and as mayor pro tem, recalls practicing in Wallace's court: "I've never been before a judge who was as cordial." [5]

As a legislator, Wallace was allied with Governor James E. Folsom, "the little man's big friend," a 6'8" giant who preached Jacksonian democracy and attempted to practice the populist traditions of northern Alabama, a region which voted against secession before the Civil War and which was settled by yeoman farmers whose sons later were reduced to sharecropper and tenant status. Big Jim wanted to tax the "big mules" of Birmingham, to provide highways and improved welfare benefits and educational opportunities. Folsom perceived that poor blacks and poor whites shared common interests.

Folsom understood that a malapportioned legislature dominated by whites in the Black Belt, where black voters were disfranchised, blocked real reform in taxation and social programs for Alabama. The legislature had not been reapportioned since adoption of the 1901 constitution, a document that Folsom charged in his 1946 campaign "was written by reactionaries in behalf of corporations." Attempts by Folsom to remove the poll tax and reapportion the legislature frightened conservatives not only because of the prospect of voting by Negroes but because these reforms would also mean voting by the "wrong sort" of whites.[6]

Folsom had vowed never to use the race issue—and he never did, even when it might have forestalled political defeat.[7] In 1949, during

5. Interview with Arthur Shores, July 17, 1974.
6. William Barnard, *Dixiecrats and Democrats* (Tuscaloosa: University of Alabama Press, 1974), p. 48.
7. Ibid., p. 15.

his first term as governor, Folsom declared in a Christmas message to the people of Alabama, "As long as the Negroes are held down by deprivation and lack of opportunity, the other poor people will be held down alongside them. Let's start talking fellowship and brotherly love, and doing unto others. And let's do more than talk about it; let's start living it."

Folsom was elected to a second term in 1954, and Circuit Judge George Wallace was his campaign manager in southern Alabama. When the legislature passed an "interposition" resolution "nullifying" the Supreme Court's school desegregation decision, Folsom called it "hogwash" and refused to sign it. He told a reporter in 1955, "I could never get excited about our colored brothers. They've been here 300 years, and I estimate they'll be here another 300 years or more. I'm not going to get my ulcers in an uproar. I find them to be good citizens. If they had been making a living for me like they have for the Black Belt, I'd be proud of them instead of kicking them and cussing them all of the time." [8]

Down the street in Montgomery from the state capitol on Goat Hill is a black Baptist church, and the young minister there—27-year-old Martin Luther King, Jr.—got a call in 1956 to meet with the governor after King became leader of the Montgomery bus boycott. Big Jim acknowledged to the young minister that his demands were reasonable enough and advised him that in politics you don't ask for crumbs, you ask for the whole loaf and hope to get at least half. One version has it that Folsom then told King, somewhat cryptically, to "read about Ghandi and don't fight back." [9] But King had already read about Ghandi, and he was off to lead a revolution.

Folsom then went too far. When flamboyant Representative Adam Clayton Powell of Harlem visited Montgomery, the governor's limousine greeted him at the airport, and Powell said afterward in a speech that the pair sipped scotch together at the governor's mansion. [10] It was all Folsom's enemies needed. Folsom failed a major test in 1957 when he did not prevent a mob from driving Arthurine Lucy, a black woman, from the University of Alabama campus when she enrolled there. In 1958, the last year of his second term as governor, a segregationist opponent defeated Folsom for the post of Democratic national committeeman.

To perceptive liberals in Alabama, Folsom was a "flawed masterpiece." [11] Folsom had generated massive public support as a candidate, but with a streak of truculent independence, obstinacy, suspicion, and

8. *Birmingham Post-Herald,* June 29, 1955.

9. Ray Jenkins, *New York Times,* May 4, 1974.

10. Folsom denied the story, emphasizing it was well known that he was a bourbon man who didn't drink scotch, and later insisted he only had a beer.

11. A quote attributed by Montgomery editor Ray Jenkins to Virginia Durr, a sister-in-law of Hugo Black, who agreed with the characterization. (Interview with Ray Jenkins, July 8, 1974.)

perhaps an inner uncertainty, he remained an outsider to the liberal faction, which should have been his natural ally, as well as to the conservatives who were his perennial and self-chosen enemies.[12]

By 1958, Alabama was becoming the focal point of the civil rights struggle, and resistance among whites became an emotional obsession. Wallace in fact ran very much as a segregationist in 1958; he had made a name for himself as a circuit judge with a promise to jail FBI agents and other federal officials if they attempted to gain access to court records for an investigation of alleged racial discrimination in voter registration. The man who "out-segged" him in the gubernatorial primary was Attorney General John Patterson, a 38-year-old crime fighter whose father had been murdered while cleaning up racketeering in Phoenix City. As attorney general, Patterson had outlawed the NAACP in Alabama.

Later Patterson, who was a Kennedy loyalist in 1960, became a Wallace ally and political confidante. He acknowledged that his own record on race had effectively ended his political career (he ran unsuccessfully for chief justice of the state Supreme Court in 1970 after losing in 1966 to Lurleen Wallace for governor). He fretted about whether the national Democratic Party was leading George Wallace down the primrose path —courting him until the 1976 convention, only to drop him when it would be too late to launch an effective third-party campaign.

In 1962 nobody "out-segged" Wallace. The violence of his defiant rhetoric set the tone that made Alabama for the next four years a battleground in the civil rights struggle. Wallace pledged in his 1963 inaugural address, "In the name of the greatest people that have ever trod this earth, I draw the line in the dust and toss the gauntlet before the feet of tyranny, and I say: Segregation now—segregation tomorrow—segregation forever."

Six months later he symbolized his defiance of the federal courts by literally standing in the schoolhouse door to block admission of two black students at the University of Alabama. President Kennedy quickly federalized the Alabama National Guard, and the students were admitted a few hours later. Then, when a federal court first ordered black students admitted to an all-white public school at Tuskegee, Wallace sent state troopers to surround the school and prevent it from opening. Wallace simultaneously encouraged efforts to establish a white private school.

Allen Parker, a local bank president in Tuskegee and native rural white Alabamian who believed that each individual had a responsibility to adjust to changing conditions, tried to enroll his children in the public school and subsequently served as a leader in biracial city and then

12. Barnard, *Dixiecrats and Democrats,* p. 127.

county governments that were in transition toward black dominance. His reward came when Wallace directed that state deposits be withdrawn from the bank.

To put Wallace's action in better perspective, one can look at other states in 1963. In Georgia, Governor Carl Sanders, counseling racial moderation and compliance with the law, blocked an effort to have Wallace address the legislature. At almost the same time Wallace was declaring his "segregation forever" speech in Montgomery, outgoing Governor Ernest F. (Fritz) Hollings in South Carolina told the legislature there: "As we meet, South Carolina is running out of courts. If and when every legal remedy has been exhausted, this General Assembly must make clear South Carolina's choice, a government of laws rather than a government of men. As determined as we are, we of today must realize the lesson of one hundred years ago, and move on for the good of South Carolina and our United States. This should be done with dignity. It must be done with law and order." A few days later, with quiet dignity, Harvey Gantt entered Clemson University as the first black to break the racial barrier at a previously all-white educational facility in South Carolina. State police provided security.

In Alabama, Wallace chose instead to exploit the passions of prejudice. It was during his first administration that a church in Birmingham was bombed and four young black girls killed, that busloads of freedom riders were assaulted for challenging segregation, that Martin Luther King was jailed and fire hoses used on his followers, that several civil rights workers were murdered, and that law enforcement officers whipped and beat black marchers at Selma, Alabama.

All America watched the violent drama unfold on television. The Selma incident led directly to the Voting Rights Act of 1965, and it was violence in Alabama and elsewhere that led Congress to enact the 1964 Civil Rights Act—two laws that since have transformed the South.

Perhaps the South and the nation required a George Wallace somewhere to serve as a catharsis by giving vivid expression to racism and bringing it to national consciousness, to vent the pent-up emotions of the mass of southern whites, who within a decade would be accepting the beginnings of a desegregated society.

Wallace emerged as a national political figure in the 1964 Democratic primaries, but he faced the formidable problem of maintaining his state power base. Unable to succeed himself as governor, Wallace decided to run his wife, Lurleen, in 1966 after Ryan deGraffenried, a popular state senator from Tuscaloosa and a moderate, died in an airplane crash while campaigning for the office. A victory for Lurleen meant that George would still run the show, and to the mass of Alabamians he was a hero against the outside forces that beleaguered them. As her husband's surrogate, Lurleen Wallace won easily in the Democratic primary, then led the Democratic ticket to a crushing defeat of what was becoming a serious challenge by Alabama Republicans, a defeat from which the state GOP has yet to recover.

Roughly 100,000 Alabamians came out to cheer Governor Lurleen at her inaugural and took home programs entitled "Two Governors, One Cause." She promised "as a wife and mother" to fight federal orders for school desegregation, calling them "an effort to gain control of the hearts and minds of our children." They heard Governor George declare "Alabama is where freedom lives and works. That is why the words 'Alabama' and 'freedom' have come to have the same meaning." Mrs. Wallace, a shy woman who died of cancer in 1968, was popular with the voters and made contributions of her own by increasing funds for mental health and development of state parks.

Although George Wallace received 71 percent of the vote in Alabama in his 1968 third-party try for president, Alabama was clearly adjusting to changing social conditions. The business establishment in Birmingham had joined with moderates to establish a new form of city government and to overthrow the racist political leadership. As elsewhere in the South, it had become apparent that bad race relations was bad for business. Arthur Shores, the black political leader and lawyer whose house had twice been bombed, was appointed to fill a vacancy on the city council. Black political awareness was developing throughout the state, and dramatic increases in black voter registration as a result of the Voting Rights Act also stimulated increased white voter registration.

After Lieutenant Governor Albert Brewer succeeded Governor Lurleen Wallace upon her death, he made a deliberate effort to lower his state's national profile by taking a low-key approach to racial matters and concentrating on economic development. Wallace made both public and private pledges not to run against Brewer in 1970, and Brewer supported Wallace in his third-party 1968 presidential campaign, in which Wallace carried five states with 46 electoral votes.

Despite his pledges not to run against Brewer in 1970, Wallace needed a base for the 1972 presidential election campaign. Perhaps more importantly, the record shows that Wallace is a man for whom political campaigning is almost a compulsion. As Marshall Frady wrote ". . . there seems to lurk a secret, desperate suspicion that facing him, aside from and beyond his political existence, is nothingness—an empty, terrible white blank. It's as if, when the time finally arrives for him to cease to be a politician, he will simply cease to be." [13]

Here's the record of what Ray Jenkins, the astute editor of the *Alabama Journal* in Montgomery, calls "Wallace's insatiable yearning to hear the roar of the crowd":

13. Marshall Frady, *Wallace* (New York: World Publishing Co./Meridian, 1970), p. 21.

¶ In 1958 he made his first race for governor and lost.
¶ In 1960, he did not run for any office, a year which associates would refer to (until 1972, the year of the shooting) as the low point of his life.
¶ In 1962 he ran for governor and won.
¶ In 1964 he ran in presidential primaries and drew national attention for his respectable showing in Maryland, Wisconsin, and Indiana.
¶ In 1966 he ran his wife, Lurleen, for governor, and she won.
¶ In 1968 he ran a third-party campaign for president and got on the ballot in all 50 states.
¶ In 1970 he ran for governor and won after a runoff.
¶ In 1972 he entered 15 Democratic presidential primaries, winning six of them, including Michigan and Maryland in the North.[14]
¶ In 1974 he ran for governor and won overwhelmingly.
¶ In 1976 he entered Democratic presidential primaries, but defeats by Jimmy Carter in Florida and North Carolina eliminated Wallace as a significant national figure.

In the 1970 race for governor, Wallace trailed Brewer in the first primary. The combination of a successful registration drive by Wallace forces and the revival of racial rhetoric, which he muted in the first primary, turned the tide. The following advertisement from the 1970 runoff, which appeared in the Montgomery newspapers, speaks for itself.

IF YOU WANT TO SAVE
Alabama As We Know Alabama
Remember!
The Bloc Vote (Negroes And Their
White Friends) Nearly Nominated
Gov. Brewer On May 5th. This
Black and White
Social-Political Alliance
MUST NOT DOMINATE
THE PEOPLE OF ALABAMA!
This Spotted Alliance Must Be Defeated!
This May Be Your Last Chance.
VOTE RIGHT—
VOTE WALLACE

After his narrow victory in 1970, Wallace made peace with many of his enemies. One of the first signs of the "new Wallace" image came in his tax package in 1971, which included taxes on utilities and the truck-

14. Even after Wallace was shot the day before the Maryland primary in May 1972 and while his recovery remained uncertain, there was an attempt that August to get him on the ballot again as a candidate of the American Independent Party. The effort failed in part because of the lack of credibility of Tom Turnipseed, Wallace's 1968 campaign manager, with AIP leaders. Turnipseed, who in July had discussed possible political work with Nixon campaign aides John Mitchell and Harry Dent, later insisted that his efforts to get Wallace on the ballot were backed by Cornelia Wallace, the governor s second wife, that she thought even a limited campaign would boost her husband's spirits, and that George Wallace would have accepted a genuine draft. (Interviews with Turnipseed and others.)

ing industry and got away from direct consumer taxes. Other new revenues came from requiring banks for the first time to pay interest on state deposits. (In 1973, however, a bill aimed at moderate tax reform never even got a hearing from an administration-dominated committee.)

In part, the 1971 tax package was intended to heal the rift between Wallace and organized labor, a fairly strong force in Alabama. In 1968, state AFL–CIO President Barney Weeks and others compiled a "Wallace Labor Record" that was printed in local labor publications throughout the country, to the detriment of his presidential campaign. Weeks, who has been state AFL–CIO president since 1957, was allied through 1970 with liberal elements against Wallace, in the face of strong opposition from many pro-Wallace union members.

One Sunday afternoon in 1971, Weeks got a telephone call about the tax bill from Wallace's labor coordinator. After Weeks expressed support for the tax package, he was coaxed to call Wallace at home and promise lobbying help in passing it. Weeks recalls, "I told him why I called, that we were going to help him. He said, 'Oh, you've made my day. It just seemed like nobody was going to help me. You just call me any time, day or night, don't make any difference if I'm at the office or at home. Don't you hesitate.' It was just like old home week, and from that day on he's been just full of cooperation." [15]

Whether it was the close race in 1970, the reaction to labor's opposition in 1968, or national ambitions in the future, Weeks isn't sure—but the fact is that Wallace cooperated in passing improved workmen's compensation and unemployment benefits, including elimination of a one-week waiting period for unemployment insurance eligibility. When Weeks sought funds to establish a university-based center for labor education and research at the University of Alabama at Birmingham, Wallace readily agreed to provide the money. The center, the only one of its kind in the South, conducts workshops and training sessions for union personnel on a variety of issues and offers courses on contract negotiation, mediation, and other matters. Wallace later agreed to fund an expansion of the center's activities. In addition, Wallace began appointing union representatives to state boards and commissions for the first time. And Wallace turned consistently to Weeks and the AFL–CIO State Labor Council for recommendations on such appointments.

Among Alabamians, it was Wallace's fighting style even more than his stand on issues that aroused admiration. A statewide poll by the Montgomery newspapers in 1971 showed that one-fourth of the public admired Wallace because, in the words of a 49-year-old Birmingham man who disapproved of Wallace's record as governor, "I like his willingness to speak his mind." More than three times as many Alabama residents admired Wallace for standing up for his beliefs than respected his conduct in office.

15. Interview with Barney Weeks, November 25, 1974.

A majority of Alabama citizens that year opposed a 1972 presidential campaign for Wallace. The single reason cited most often was expressed by a 27-year-old Selma man who said "He's simply not qualified." The same man also expressed admiration for Wallace's willingness to "stand up for what he thinks is right."

Majority support for a presidential campaign came only from rural residents and those 65 and over. Northern Alabama residents opposed the presidential race 53 percent to 32 percent, but southern Alabama favored it 43 percent to 36.5 percent. Wallace's weakest support came from young people and suburban residents. Only in the 18–29 age category did a majority disapprove of his handling of the job as governor, and by 56–37 percent the young people opposed a 1972 presidential campaign.

"THE SHOOTING" AND ITS AFTERMATH

In 1972, Wallace was a truly national figure. His jibes at the "pointy-headed bureaucrats" and the "intellectuals who look down their noses at you" appealed not only to the "white backlash" but also to the growing sense of alienation, resentment against war protesters, and frustrations of powerlessness expressed by blue-collar workers and others in public opinion polls.

Furthermore, Wallace fully understood the fundamentalist Protestant outlook that dominates much of the South and serves as a force for right-wing politics. His message to the masses is religious as well as racial, and few issues reflect this more than the school prayer controversy. In a 1972 presidential campaign speech, Wallace declared:

> Public school prayer has been nearly nonexistent for the past eight years. What has happened in those eight years? Crime, especially juvenile crime, has risen at a most alarming rate. Eight years ago, drug abuse in schools was almost unheard of; today it is an epidemic. Our nation's moral fabric has been rotting away—as evidenced by the hard-core pornographic filth that now flourishes on our newsstands and in our theaters. This may be coincidence, but I don't think so.

The argument was illogical, but his masterful manipulation of an inflammatory and emotional issue was typical.

Wallace was on the eve of his greatest national triumph—twin victories in the Maryland and Michigan presidential primaries—then he was shot four times at a political rally in Laurel, Maryland, on May 15. The assassination attempt resulted in permanent paralysis below the waist and a painful battle for his life. There was a series of serious operations, periods of depression marked by crying spells, and continuous therapy.

67

Wallace calls the attack "the shooting," not softening it with any euphemism; his recovery was such that by 1974 he could campaign vigorously, give a strong delivery to a 40-minute speech, and learn to live with constant pain. One Wallace intimate said the governor had learned that a sure way to get rid of a visitor who had overextended his time was simply to clutch his side and grimace.

Wallace enhanced his "fighting spirit" image by his battle with death, and his physical condition generated additional sympathy. An April 1973 poll by the Montgomery newspapers showed a 75–13 percent favorable response to a question about whether a governor should get an immediate lifetime pension if he is disabled while in office (the 1975 legislature passed such a pension bill), and 64 percent thought Wallace would be a good choice for governor again in 1974.

The shooting and its aftermath led to an enhanced national image of respectability for Wallace. By mid-1974 a Louis Harris poll showed the nation viewed Wallace, by 61 to 17 percent, as "a man of high integrity." The month he was shot in 1972, a narrow plurality of only 40–35 percent held that view.

The invitations pouring in from individuals and groups outside the South who would have shunned him earlier are a source of great satisfaction to Wallace, one of the first things he talks about to visiting strangers. Visits of homage to Wallace and his Alabama, such as that by Senator Edward Kennedy in 1973 (to present a "spirit of America" award to Wallace) and President Nixon in 1974 (to declare Alabama "the conscience of America") are cited with satisfaction by Wallace as evidence of his national acceptance.

Wallace used the Kennedy visit to reinforce his relations with organized labor. The governor spotted Barney Weeks in the crowd and had the labor leader join the dignitaries on the grandstand. In 1974 the AFL–CIO endorsed Wallace for the first time, and black members on the State Labor Council raised no objection. One of them told Weeks, however, that he wanted Wallace to know that blacks were looking for more appointments to decision-making bodies.

With his eye on 1976, Wallace in his 1974 reelection campaign directed his efforts at three specific aims: (1) to win big, which even without campaigning would be easy enough, (2) to demonstrate by a vigorous campaign that his physical condition was no handicap; and (3) to win with black support, demonstrating a new image to improve his national standing.

On a November weekend in 1973, Wallace crowned a black homecoming queen at the University of Alabama and then addressed a South-wide conference of black mayors at Tuskegee. There he received a standing ovation and told them, "We're all God's children. All God's children are equal." [16] And a few weeks before his 1975 inaugural, Wal-

16. *Newsweek*, December 3, 1973, p. 38.

lace quietly visited Martin Luther King's old church, spoke from the pulpit, and was wheeled out while the congregation sang "Battle Hymn of the Republic."

To youthful black mayors such as Johnny Ford of Tuskegee and A. J. (Jay) Cooper of Pritchard, endorsements of Wallace represent no more than practical politics. "I want to get things done for my city, and playing politics is one of the most effective ways of doing it," said Ford, a Democrat who supported Richard Nixon and saw a payoff in federal funds and projects for Tuskegee.[17]

John Lewis, the black native of Alabama whose skull was fractured in the altercation at Selma in 1965, returned there nine years later as director of the Atlanta-based Voter Education Project to express concern about black endorsements and support for Wallace. "Too many people have died. Too many people have suffered for us to sell our vote for 30 pieces of silver, for an opportunity just to sit in the state capitol or visit the governor's mansion," Lewis said.[18]

Wallace paraded the endorsements of such mayors as Ford, Cooper, and other black elected officials, and national news media in some cases reported as much as 30 percent black support for Wallace. However, an analysis of selected black precincts by the editor of a Negro newspaper in Birmingham (whose publisher in 1975 was named by Wallace as his first black cabinet member) showed only 7 percent of the black vote for Wallace in the 1974 Democratic primary. For example, the combined totals of the almost all-black Hill School and Washington School precincts gave Wallace 170 votes to 2,013 for little-known state Senator Gene McLain, and 255 for three other candidates. A statewide analysis of black precincts done for a state official showed 12 percent. Apparently, despite Wallace's gestures and endorsements, at least 88 percent of the blacks in Alabama still voted against George Wallace in 1974.

Although Wallace led the balloting in 66 of the 67 counties, he lost Macon (Tuskegee) to McLain despite Mayor Ford's endorsement, and he won by a plurality in the Black Belt counties of Perry and Bullock. In two large urban counties, both with strong black political organizations, Wallace won with only a plurality in Montgomery and a majority of only 5,000 in Jefferson (Birmingham), where 129,000 votes were cast. In Montgomery, whose aggressive newspapers had exposed many shortcomings in the Wallace administration, McLain ran well in many middle- and upper-income white precincts.

There is divided opinion about whether Wallace really has changed because of his own brush with death or merely recognizes new political realities and is shifting with the wind. Wallace himself says, "I do know that when you get shot and face death and almost die that you do understand the frailty of human life. And it makes you more compassionate

17. Ibid.
18. *New York Times,* April 25, 1974.

toward those who suffer. . . . Black ministers prayed for me in Alabama just like white ministers prayed for me. And they were upset, too, about my being shot. And I appreciate that very much because I probably got as many prayers from black churches as white churches. And I won't say that that changed my attitude, because my attitude never was anti [black]. Because that's contrary to my religious upbringing. But I suppose that I can better sympathize with the plight of anybody that happens to be unfortunate better than I used to. . . . The black people all over the country have had a tougher time economically. Everybody knows that." [19]

Alabama Democratic Conference President Joe Reed, who came out of the civil rights movement and is an avowed political enemy of Wallace, says of him, "I think deep down George Wallace is a racist, deep in his heart. As the political climate changes, I think basically he will adjust because he understands, too, there are certain realities that—just like I understand the reality that I can't be elected governor of Alabama because I'm black—he sees that he cannot continue to find a place in history as a racist. So now an effort is being made to minimize that. He feels that he needs blacks generally and Alabama blacks in particular to say that this guy's all right now." [20]

Wallace contends that his programs to provide trade and technical schools with free transportation, to provide free textbooks, and to develop the state industrially have all helped blacks as well as whites. And Wallace promised after his reelection in 1974 to follow the lead of governors in every other southern state by appointing more blacks to decision-making positions and hiring blacks in the executive office. Wallace's apparent opposition to the death penalty, although unspoken, delayed reenactment of capital punishment in Alabama, after a 1973 Supreme Court decision held existing statutes unconstitutional.

Although Wallace received 64 percent of the vote in the Democratic primary, the 36 percent given McLain and lesser candidates suggests that a solid core of anti-Wallace vote remains in Alabama. The major complaint of thoughtful critics in Alabama is Wallace's disinterest in the mechanics of government.

Editor Ray Jenkins related a story told by a state senator, a sophisticated legislator who was close to Wallace, about a meeting in the governor's office. "We had a $110 million bond issue that we were trying to get through the legislature," the senator explained, "and we had everybody, all of Wallace's people down there, all the legislative leaders and what have you, and we were holding a strategy session on how to get this $110 million bond issue passed. We were talking about spending a $110 million of the taxpayers' money, and I looked around and the gov-

19. Interview with George Wallace, July 15, 1974.
20. Interview with Joe Reed, July 10, 1974.

ernor of this state was gone. I looked all around and there he was standing over by the window looking out the window eating a Baby Ruth."

Jenkins continued, "So he doesn't care about things like this. He is bored by it. But at the same time, he's so smart; Wallace is about ten notches in intelligence above most governors I have ever known. He has got a keen memory, one which works very quickly, a mind that has an instinct for making the right decisions quickly, and just by half doing it, he could make things run pretty well, but he is not what you would call a good administrator at all, not by a long shot." [21]

After the editorial board of the *Anniston Star* spent two hours with Wallace in an interview during the 1974 campaign, the newspaper said in an unenthusiastic endorsement of challenger McLain, "His strong point and the overriding issue in this campaign is that he would actually BE governor." Wallace's physical disability did not bother the *Star;* nor was it entirely the amount of time Wallace spends out of state in his presidential campaigns.

> When you talk to [Wallace] about making state government more effective, about putting budget and management people in his office to make sure the bureaucracy does a better job for the people, he loses interest. The discomfort of his wounds seems to seize him, and a mist comes over his eyes, but only when you talk about actually governing.
> When the conversation turns to politics, the fire returns. He is the evangelist-politician; the farmer's son needling the pompous and arrogant; the littlest kid on the block whipping the neighborhood bully. All he wants is one perpetual campaign and the record shows it.[22]

STATE OF THE STATE

Although Alabama is by no means unique in the South in inflating its industrial expansion, the degree of exaggeration practiced by Wallace is unusual. After a fish fry was held at the beginning of 1974 to announce the previous year's figures, the *Alabama Journal* editorialized that "baloney might have been more appropriate for the occasion."

Editorial page editor Ray Jenkins had been doing some double-checking. Earlier he had found that in 1971 only 6,000 more people were working in Alabama factories than a year earlier, despite claims by Wallace's Alabama Development Office of 20,920 new jobs. Although Wallace cited ADO figures to show more than 42,000 new jobs for 1973, statistics of the U.S. Department of Labor revealed only 5,900 new manufacturing

21. Interview with Ray Jenkins, February 5, 1974.
22. *Anniston Star*, May 5, 1974.

jobs that year for the state. When Wallace replied that it takes awhile for the full benefits of industrialization to be felt, the *Journal* pointed out that although the ADO claimed 252,951 industrial jobs from new and expanded industry over a ten-year period, only 89,200 such jobs had been filled. Between 1960 and 1973, while Wallace dominated Alabama, the growth rate in nonagricultural employment was 45.9 percent, less than any other state in the South. During the same period, Arkansas and South Carolina moved ahead of Alabama in per capita personal income.

On the positive side, the Tennessee Valley Authority, which in the 1930s ended the annual spring flooding of small towns and farm country and began to provide cheap electricity and water transportation, has since helped bring almost $2 billion in heavy industry to towns along the Tennessee River in northern Alabama. The $500 million Tennessee-Tombigbee Canal, on which work began in 1972, will link the Tennessee River with the Warrior-Tombigbee waterway that meanders 463 miles from Birmingham to Mobile. It could make Mobile a port to rival New Orleans and will open up underdeveloped areas of the state for economic growth.

But despite some past progress and future potential, Alabama in the 1970s ranked 49th in the nation in per capita income—behind only Mississippi—15.7 percent of its housing lacked adequate plumbing, and a casual ride through the rural countryside of the Black Belt revealed the desperate poverty from which hundreds of thousands of black Alabamians in recent decades have migrated in search of a better life.

Although Wallace is often compared with Huey Long as a dominant southern political figure who achieved a national following, the Louisiana Kingfish's record on social issues reflects both far greater concern with making government provide services for people and a far greater willingness to tax those most able to pay.

In Alabama, Wallace achieved political success by keeping the masses of people happy with rhetoric and his position on emotional issues and by keeping the special interests happy with his substantive program. It is the formula that won political success for Eugene Talmadge in Georgia rather than that of Huey Long. Robert Vance, the veteran state Democratic Party chairman in Alabama, said of Wallace, "I may be wrong about this and I might not be fair to him, but I don't recall his ever having taken a position on something just because it was right." [23]

A major distinction between Wallace and Long is that Long included *all* the poor in those he professed to represent, whereas the most downtrodden of all in Alabama—the blacks—served as Wallace's political scapegoats in campaign after campaign.

23. Interview with Robert Vance, July 16, 1974.

Long battled the special interests that had controlled Louisiana, and he increased their taxes to pay for roads, hospitals, schools, and free textbooks. Wallace, too, speaks glowingly of the "hallmark" of his administration, the system of 29 trade schools and 18 junior colleges, with free bus transportation available in all areas of the state to any Alabama youth. But higher education officials in the state complain that the junior colleges are mediocre at best, were located for political purposes, and serve more as high school extensions than as parallels to four-year colleges. These officials contend that graduates who enter at the junior level in the state's higher education system are often ill prepared.

The junior college system evolved almost as a casual afterthought; it was Wallace's response to a suggestion by Rankin Fite, a master legislator who retired in 1974, that a junior college be established in his district because the people there needed something. Wallace agreed to the idea, but asked, "why not make it statewide?" The system was financed by adding 2 cents tax on each can of beer. Developed with little planning or provision for staffing, the system compares unfavorably with similar postsecondary programs in Florida and the Carolinas, which were established in an orderly manner and based on population trends rather than political influence.

Few states can match the regressive nature of the Alabama tax structure. The 4 percent state sales tax includes food and drugs, and local government bodies can in some localities impose as much as an additional 3 percent in sales taxes. Only the intervention of the federal courts has compelled the state to enforce equalization in property tax assessment, one of a number of areas where the federal courts in Alabama have taken charge because of the failure of the state government to assume its responsibilities. Some land was assessed for as little as 2–10 cents an acre.

The reason for these low assessments was that Wallace went along with the Farm Bureau, the voice of large landowners and politically one of the most powerful special interest groups in Alabama, in providing for assessment of farm land on the basis of use rather than value. One effect was to make subsidized land speculators out of large farmers and corporate landowners, especially those near metropolitan areas. Wallace also agreed to freeze corporate and personal income taxes in the state constitution at 5 percent, a low ceiling even for the South.

Although Wallace points to heavy debt spending for ports and highways, road building in Alabama remains based more on political influence than traffic analysis. And if education expenditures have increased under Wallace, and free textbooks now are provided statewide, Alabama still ranks at the bottom in per capita spending for elementary and secondary education and is among the most backward states in the South in terms of public kindergarten development.

Pierre Pelham, a Harvard Law School graduate from Mobile who served as Wallace's floor leader in the Senate for 1970–1974, insisted that Wallace's expressions of concern for the plight of the unfortunate were genuine but conceded that Wallace had little interest in day-to-day administration of government. An unknown citizen in the state who calls the governor's office with a complaint likely will get priority for a return call from the governor more often than would his Senate floor leader, said Pelham, a commentary both on Wallace as master politician and disinterested administrator.

PARTY POLITICS

Although Wallace's brother Gerald, a powerful influence in the administration, has been involved in financial payoffs from purchases and contracts with the highway department and other transactions with state agencies, George Wallace himself is a man whose reputation even among political enemies in Alabama is one of personal honesty. He had little known personal wealth.

During his years of dominance, Wallace developed a statewide organization with "Wallace coordinators" in every county, individuals who not only met together during campaigns, but might also gather with top Wallace aides during the governor's tenure in office. Whether or not he served as a county functionary, the local coordinator often became a conduit for patronage and other favors. But unlike the Long machine in Louisiana, the organization seldom was mobilized for other candidates.

Wallace suffered an embarrassing setback in 1974 when his attempt to win back control of the state Democratic Party failed. Robert Vance, a forceful Birmingham lawyer, had won the party chairmanship in 1966, and the Alabama Democratic Party had subsequently dropped the slogan "White Supremacy for the Right" from its rooster symbol on election day ballots. Progressive in outlook and pragmatic in approach, Vance opened the party to blacks and retained loyal ties to the national Democratic Party organization.

An attempt was made to dump Vance at the 1974 state convention, with 24-year-old Michael Griffin, Wallace's top political aide, and others directing the effort. "There's no way in hell they can beat us," Griffin told a reporter before the election. With that kind of assurance, Wallace himself attended the convention to be on hand for another small moment of glory. But Vance coolly presided, declared that a voice vote favored a secret ballot, and the vote turned out 66–51 in Vance's favor.

That evening at a Birmingham bar, a delegate was heard to remark, "If I was Wallace, I'd buy me a new crowd." [24]

Vance had earned Wallace's wrath at the 1972 Democratic National Convention by casting his presidential vote for former North Carolina Governor Terry Sanford, who had lost his home state primary to Wallace. In the interest of party harmony, Vance agreed at the 1974 state convention that he would support the candidate in 1976 who "the people of the state want," which Wallace proclaimed as a pledge of support to him.

In his own way, U.S. Senator James B. Allen, former lieutenant governor under Wallace and successor to Lister Hill, is considered a master politician equal to Wallace among home folks, and his popularity in polls is consistently higher than Wallace's. Every year, Allen goes into each county on an "eat, meet, and greet" tour that includes a Dutch-treat meal to which the influential are invited but which any citizen can attend. Allen then returns to Washington and mirrors the views of the folks at home.

The number of blacks attending the Allen functions is increasing, and Allen is a successful example of the conservative Dixie Democrat who gets black votes by being a Democrat and white votes by voting conservative. Insofar as state Democratic Party matters are concerned, Allen works closely with Vance and the state party organization. "He's been helpful to the party . . . one of the most accommodating people you'll ever want to meet on political party matters," says Vance. "I disagree with him on a great many votes. But as a human being he's just a great guy." [25]

GOVERNMENT INSTITUTIONS

Institutionally, the office of governor in Alabama is one of the strongest in the country, in part because the legislature is so weak. By tradition, the governor chooses the speaker of the House, and through him influences committee assignments and selection of chairman. Also by tradition, the lieutenant governor allows the governor to select the chairman and majority of members to the two major committees in the Senate. (Lieutenant Governor Jere Beasley broke that tradition in 1975.)

Although the legislature once was notorious for its domination by

24. Editorial, *Alabama Journal*, June 18, 1974.
25. Interview with Robert Vance, July 16, 1974.

special interests and was ranked 50th in the nation by the 1971 study of the Citizens Conference on State Legislatures, reapportionment and especially the single-member district plan implemented in 1974 have given new life to that body.

The "one man, one vote" decision in *Reynolds* v. *Sims* was an Alabama case, and the initial result was to break the stranglehold that white conservatives in the Black Belt had held for half a century over any major progressive legislation. For six decades the legislature had refused to carry out the reapportionment mandated every ten years by the state constitution.

In the late 1950s, the 2,057 white voters of Lowndes County, whose 80 percent majority black population was totally disfranchised by the poll tax and the threat of intimidation, had their own senator—the same as the 130,000 registered voters of Jefferson County. Although Jefferson County increased its representation from six house seats and a senator to 20 representatives and seven senators after court-ordered reapportionment in 1965, all but seven came from high-income white neighborhoods of Birmingham and its suburbs until the single-member district plan came into effect. Both black senators—the first since Reconstruction—and seven of the 13 black representatives elected in 1974 came from Jefferson County.

Almost half of the 140-member legislature (35 senators and 105 representatives) who were elected to four-year terms in 1974 were under 40 years old. It is a more diverse group than ever before and may serve as an incubator for future leadership in the state—but not, as we shall see, for Republicans.

Whether reapportionment will free the legislature from domination by special interests remains to be seen. The Farm Bureau, a powerful lobby when Key wrote *Southern Politics,* remains a powerful political force that continues to be allied with the "big mules" in Birmingham. U.S. Steel maintains a low profile but is reported to work effectively through Associated Industries and the state Chamber of Commerce, both of which represent business interests and combats efforts by the state attorney general's office in pollution control and consumer protection. Utilities continue to exert influence for the status quo, but South Central Bell has moved to correct discriminatory hiring practices.

BLACK POLITICS

Compared with other states in the South, Alabama blacks are perhaps as well organized as any, but factionalism and the overpowering presence of Wallace have lessened their impact. Although black third-party efforts, such as the indigenous Black Panther political movement in the Black Belt and the success of the National Democratic Party of Alabama (NDPA) in tiny Greene and a few other counties, have attracted more national attention, the most influential black group in the state is the Alabama Democratic Conference (ADC). The ADC evolved during the period when the NAACP was outlawed in Alabama.

The showdown between the NDPA and the ADC came in 1972. The ADC supported Senator John Sparkman, and it was black support that allowed Sparkman to avoid a runoff in the Democratic primary. In the general election, veteran civil rights leader John LaFlore of Mobile ran as the NDPA nominee and fully expected solid black support. He wound up with only 3 percent of the vote, however, as blacks voted 6–1 in support of Sparkman, the ADC-endorsed candidate.

The presence of NDPA allowed blacks to get on the ballot in the 1960s in counties where the regular Democrats had blocked them, and the NDPA presence helped spark reform of the state Democratic Party. But after Vance opened up the party to blacks, the ADC began to function as a black caucus within the Democratic Party. Conference President Joe Reed became vice-chairman for minority affairs of the state Democratic Party.

The major threat to the ADC's role as the major political voice for Alabama blacks no longer comes from the NDPA and its chairman, Dr. John Cashin of Huntsville, but from elected black officials. The 15 black legislators form the basis for an effective black caucus. Whether they, the black mayors, and other elected officials get together to form an effective statewide organization will depend on whether factionalism and leadership rivalries can be overcome.

One of the state's most perceptive white politicians said of black leadership in the state: "They're getting to be jealous of each other and they're fighting and they're being for or against a candidate or an issue a lot of times not on the basis of the merits or how it stands to benefit blacks, but on whether or not one of their rivals is in closer to that man than they are. And if it keeps on and really splinters, then people who really have got these hopes for the South—they're going to be in trouble. I'm afraid it's headed that way. Now, of course, once you get equality of opportunity, then it will be good for them to be like that." Another observed more succinctly, "Let's face it: our niggers are acting like white folks."

The first wave of black leadership in Alabama came out of the churches. Next came the middle-class professionals. New leadership is coming out of the labor movement: four A. Philip Randolph Institutes in Alabama have helped develop political leadership among black union members.

Noteworthy development of local black leadership came in Birmingham, where Police Commissioner Eugene (Bull) Connor and his police dogs and fire hoses once made international headlines in attacks on civil rights workers. That city's leadership finally reacted to Connor's tactics in 1962, worked with blacks and organized labor to change the city's form of government, and launched Operation New Birmingham—something of a model of broad-based community response to long-standing social problems.

The 1968 appointment of Arthur Shores to a city council was followed by the movement of younger black leaders into political prominence. Mayor George Seibels, a moderate Republican, supplied leadership and an ample measure of boosterism, but by the mid-1970s there were reports that the city's leadership was becoming stagnant and complaints that it was living on its laurels.

REPUBLICANS

Republican Party development in Alabama peaked in 1966, a year that proved devastating to the GOP, and has declined steadily since then.

Not a single Republican won election to the 1974 legislature, even though single-member districts were supposed to help Republicans as well as blacks win election. Republicans had counted on holding their two incumbents and electing another ten or so in 1974, but both incumbents lost, as voters seemed to heed George Wallace's call for voting a straight Democratic ticket. Yet the three Republican congressmen easily won reelection, apparently on the basis of personality. Only one had more than token opposition.

Republicans won five congressional seats in the 1964 Goldwater landslide in Alabama, and the most dramatic political development of the next decade was the rise and then almost complete collapse of the Republican Party in the next two years. In Alabama, Republican development was tied to the politics of race, and George Wallace was to prove that they could not compete with him on that issue.

From a handful of traditional Republican counties in the Appalachian foothills, Republican voting strength developed in the urban centers and Black Belt counties in presidential voting from 1952 to 1964. In the two decades before 1952, no Republican presidential candidate had received as much as 20 percent of the vote in Alabama. But the Eisenhower nomination and his visit to Birmingham that year brought new life to the Republican Party. The Eisenhower ticket received 35 percent of the vote in 1952 and 39.4 percent in 1956. In 1960 the Nixon-Lodge ticket received 41.7 percent.

A year later, Jim Martin, an unknown Republican who proved to be a colorful and effective campaigner, barely missed an upset victory over venerable Senator Lister Hill. The use of federal troops to suppress a riot that fall on the campus of the University of Mississippi had whipped segregationist sentiment to a frenzy. Martin used such code words for segregation as "states' rights," and Hill became the scapegoat for "that government in Washington." Wallace didn't help Hill by appearing on the same platform with him and attacking the federal government.

Martin received 49.1 percent of the vote, and he polled 54.8 percent in the Black Belt, a gain of 18.1 percentage points over Nixon's 1960 showing there. This compared with a gain of only 4.3 percent in the metropolitan areas and no gain in the traditional Republican counties. The GOP now attracted the support of white voters most deeply concerned about segregation.

In 1964, Goldwater swept the state with 69.5 percent. The greatest Republican increase came from lower income whites in the cities and from the Black Belt counties, where few Negroes were registered. In that same election, Martin and four other Republicans won congressional seats, and the GOP appeared on its way to making Alabama a competitive two-party state.

As seen by John Grenier, a Birmingham lawyer who served as Republican Party national executive director in 1964, Goldwater's candidacy did three things for the Republican Party in the South. First, it extended Republican support to the Black Belt areas that stretch from Tidewater, Virginia, to east Texas. Second, his defeat of the eastern establishment and its allies in the Republican Party allowed the southerners to join westerners as participants in party leadership. And third, it created a viable cadre of leadership throughout the southern Republican Party.[25]

Nowhere was this more true than in Alabama. Republicans established a state headquarters in Birmingham with a paid staff. Efforts during the next two years focused on recruiting more than 100 candidates for the legislature, with prospects of capturing a third of the seats and establishing what Grenier called "a permanent taproot" of Republicanism. The party raised campaign funds and took aim in 1966 on Sparkman's Senate seat and possibly the governor's office.

Even though Wallace could not succeed himself, Grenier believed the governor's office was out of reach for the Republicans. But he felt that Sparkman was vulnerable, especially with Martin as the candidate. Otherwise, he felt Martin should hold onto his seat in Congress. Grenier himself was willing to run for governor, with the idea that he could lend direction to the ticket, absorb a loss, and perhaps lay the base for a

25. Interview with John Grenier, July 1974.

future statewide race. But a year before the election, he found Martin interested and determined to run for governor. Even after deGraffenried's death and the entry of Lurleen Wallace in the governor's race, Grenier found Martin still determined to run for governor.

By the time she won a majority in the first primary, running as a surrogate for her husband, Grenier had announced his own candidacy for the Senate and refused overtures that he step aside for Martin, who had suddenly changed his mind. Martin's critical comments about Mrs. Wallace in the campaign backfired, and he finished with 31 percent of the vote; in the Black Belt his percentage fell to 24 percent. Grenier finished with 40 percent, and the Republicans lost two of their five congressional seats. The GOP also won only one legislative seat. It was a disaster from which they still have not recovered. In 1974, Republicans expected to elect at least 10–20 legislators under the new single-member system. Instead, they elected none, losing even their two incumbents.

With Wallace on the ballot as a presidential candidate in 1968, Richard Nixon received only 14 percent of the vote, the worst Republican presidential showing in Alabama since Alf Landon in 1936. Against McGovern in 1972, Nixon carried the state with 74 percent. But Montgomery contractor Winton (Red) Blount, who returned home from his Nixon cabinet job as postmaster general to run against Sparkman, won only 33 percent of the vote. It was clear Alabama voters had become sophisticated at ticket splitting.

While some Republicans criticized Blount for an inept campaign, he recalls that he was campaigning as a Nixon-Blount candidate, "the guy who could do things for Alabama with Nixon," and that Sparkman in early September released a letter from the White House saying that he was a great statesman and that Nixon could use him back in the Senate. Two weeks later, the White House ostentatiously sent a presidential plane to Alabama to pick up Sparkman to go back to Washington for a routine vote. And in October, White House Press Secretary Ron Ziegler was asked at a briefing, "Does the President support Red Blount?" And Blount recalls Ziegler answering, "Well, he doesn't oppose him." When the reporter came back and said, "Well, that wasn't the question. Does he support Red Blount?" Ziegler replied, "Well, I've answered your question." Blount also recalls that when Vice-President Spiro Agnew came down to say he was supporting his friend Red Blount, he added that he wasn't campaigning against John Sparkman.

When Blount was asked if he felt a sense of betrayal after his service in Nixon's cabinet, he replied, "Oh, I wouldn't put it that way. I mean politics is a pretty tough game, and I'm a grown boy." [26]

Blount's story was typical of White House politics in the Nixon administration when it came to a choice between party building in the

26. Interview with Winton Blount, July 10, 1974.

South or offending a senior Democratic incumbent with a friendly voting record. Because Wallace was perceived as a threat to Nixon, $400,000 was funneled from the White House to the Brewer campaign in the 1970 Democratic gubernatorial primary, and Postmaster General Blount and Vice-President Agnew both had complimentary things to say about Brewer in that campaign. After the $400,000 contribution was disclosed during the Senate Watergate hearings, Blount declined to comment on his possible involvement in channeling the $400,000, the same position he took in an interview with the authors. Brewer professed ignorance of the contribution.

Alabama's three Republican congressmen, all Goldwater conservatives elected before they were 40, appear solidly entrenched. The best known, Representative W. Jack Edwards of Mobile, won respect in Washington that was reflected in his narrow (85–82) defeat as vice-chairman of the House Republican Conference in 1970. He later won election as secretary of the conference.

Internally, the Republican party in Alabama split into warring factions after 1966, with Grenier a leading representative of the moderate wing against a more ideological wing that included members of the John Birch Society and "Dixiecrats" who had left the Democratic Party because it had become too liberal on social issues.

As long as Wallace continues to dominate Alabama politics, Republican chances of political recovery appear virtually nonexistent. In 1974 the more practical Republican leaders sought to avoid a direct challenge to Wallace because it was futile. They believed that Republicans might have a chance at other offices, but a small group insisted the party had a duty to run a candidate for governor. He finished with 15 percent of the vote. Not only was the GOP wiped out in the legislature, but it also missed what many felt was a chance in the race for lieutenant governor if Wallace had gone unchallenged.

CATALYST FOR CHANGE

Despite its relative political stagnation, Alabama has undergone fundamental social and political changes. The catalyst for change has come primarily through the federal judiciary.

In Alabama, U.S. District Judge Frank M. Johnson, Jr.'s bold application of the law to correct long-standing practices of social injustice made more impact on the daily lives of Alabamians than the stewardship of George Wallace in the governor's office. The two men were classmates at the University of Alabama Law School, but Johnson was a lifelong Republican from the "free state" of Winston County, where local citizens gathered in a mass meeting after Alabama seceded from the Union and passed a resolution to secede from Alabama. Johnson grew up in the tradition of Jacksonian Republicanism, in an area where families traced their ancestry from men who fought with Andrew Jackson and were dedicated to the Union and who became Republican when that was the party of Unionism.

At 37, Johnson was appointed as the youngest judge on the federal bench by President Eisenhower in 1955. Many of the most far-reaching federal court decisions in Alabama, including the "one man, one vote" dictum, resulted from Johnson's teaming up with Richard T. Rives, a member of the Fifth Circuit Court of Appeals whose office is in the same building in Montgomery as Johnson's. Rives, a Truman appointee, was a major ally in the 1940s of Lister Hill and John Sparkman and a leader of the Democratic loyalists in their fight against the Dixiecrats.

The source of conservative political power in Alabama for decades had rested with the restricted electorate and a malapportioned legislature. There had been no reapportionment since the 1901 constitution, which had disfranchised blacks and many poor whites with a cumulative poll tax, a list of more than 30 disqualifying crimes, and a literacy requirement that included "interpretation" of a section of the U.S. Constitution. The number of Negroes registered in 14 Black Belt counties dropped from 78,311 in 1900 to 1,081 three years later.

The precursor of the Supreme Court's landmark reapportionment decision was *Gomillion* v. *Lightfoot,* a case brought after the boundaries of Tuskegee in Macon County were gerrymandered by the legislature to prevent the overwhelming black majority from gaining political control. Based on the earlier Supreme Court decision that reapportionment was a "political thicket" to be avoided, Judge Johnson ruled against the Negro plaintiffs.

But the Supreme Court ruled that the plaintiffs had standing if the motive was discrimination on the basis of race, and the case was returned to Judge Johnson to make that determination. "Of course, there wasn't any question but that the motive was to disenfranchise blacks insofar as the municipality of Tuskegee was concerned," Johnson recalled much later. "I so found and held. But that was the forerunner of your reapportionment case. It had the effect of saying there's no political thicket in which the federal courts shouldn't get involved in." [27] Without saying so specifically, the Supreme Court extended that principle in *Baker* v. *Carr,* the seminal reapportionment case from Tennessee.

Johnson and Wallace have personalized the opposite forces that have clashed in Alabama, beginning in 1957 when Judge Johnson won in a

27. Interview with Frank M. Johnson, Jr., July 10, 1974.

confrontation with Wallace, then an obscure state judge who had threatened to jail any federal agent who came into his jurisdiction to examine voter registration records under the 1957 Civil Rights Act. Wallace backed down after Johnson threatened to cite him for contempt.

A look at Johnson's record confirms not only his major role in affecting social change in Alabama but also his effect on public policy in the state, a role nearly as central as that of Wallace on electoral politics. Johnson joined Rives to extend the principle of the 1954 school decision to a nonschool area, the Montgomery bus system, thus ending the boycott led by the Reverend Martin Luther King, Jr., speeding the desegregation of all public facilities, and indirectly launching King's leadership role in the civil rights movement. Johnson issued the order which gave black Alabamians and their northern allies the right to march from Selma to Montgomery to protest discrimination in voter registration procedures, a march which led to the crucial confrontation on the Edmund Pettus Bridge.

Johnson presided as trial judge of the three Ku Klux Klansmen convicted by an all-white jury for civil rights violations in the murder of Viola Liuzzo, a Detroit housewife who had joined the Selma march. He issued landmark decisions affirming the rights of students to express their views and to hear the views of others in campus appearances. He and Judge Rives served on the three-judge court which abolished the Alabama poll tax, handed down the nation's first statewide school desegregation order in *Lee* v. *Macon,* and extended the reapportionment decision to the single-member district plan that came into effect in 1974 and resulted in the substantial increase in black legislators.

Judge Johnson emphasized that although court decisions may result in social change, they are not made for that purpose. "When you have a voting rights case and you find that there's been a pattern in practice of discrimination against the blacks in registering to vote, you don't register the blacks to vote so that they can gain political power in Macon County or Lowndes or Sumter or Perry. You are faced with some legal issues, and if they are entitled to relief you give them relief and you order that they be registered. Now the effect of their registering and voting and electing a sheriff and other county officials is something that the court's not concerned with, and has no interest in it. . . . The role federal judges have played in the South has been one of effecting resultantly a social change. And there's no question about it. But that wasn't the motive and it wasn't the purpose and it wasn't the intent." [28]

The activism of the federal judiciary also has stimulated change in the state courts. Chief Justice Howell Heflin of the Alabama Supreme Court, elected in 1970 over a segregationist, former Governor Patterson, has implemented much of the court reform he fought for as president of the

28. Interview with Frank M. Johnson, Jr., July 10, 1974.

state bar association. Heflin believes that newer and younger state Supreme Court justices in Alabama and other states "are more people-minded. . . . I think now there is a feeling that human rights should be looked upon more so than property rights." [29]

Johnson believes there's "not any question" that Alabama has undergone a genuine transformation in terms of people's attitudes on race. "I think that's an area in which we've made more progress than they've made in the northern states. People in the South and people in this state are basically law-abiding people. They love their country, love their flag. They're patriotic. They answer the call when it's necessary and always have. And I think they'll continue to do it. And they have accepted decisions that a lot of people thought they would never accept. They've tolerated and accepted social changes that some people thought they would never accept. They've done it, in the main, with good grace and without rancor. There are exceptions to that, and the newspapers always play those up. Which is news. I'm not critical of it, but they do. But by and large there's been an acceptance of the social change that these decisions have brought about that I would have never thought possible."

As an example of what he means by acceptance, Johnson cited his observations at lunch in a Montgomery restaurant. "You have whites and blacks eating together. They're not doing that because of the law. Because the law doesn't require that they sit at the same table. The law doesn't require that they carry on an animated conversation during their lunch." [30]

In addition to the reapportionment and statewide school desegregation decisions, Johnson has issued orders that in effect gave his court jurisdiction over the state mental health program, property tax assessment, hiring practices that had discriminated against blacks in the highway patrol, and the state penal system—each time to overcome inequities when the state failed to act. In the future, this brand of judicial activism may leave an additional imprint in ending discriminatory practices in employment and housing.

To Wallace, such action amounts to judicial tyranny. For example, he talks about the court's action on reapportionment, "They don't pass on the constitutionality of the plan, they go down there and draw it up and put it into law. They legislate it. That's exactly what Thomas Jefferson said was going to happen someday. And that's what we oppose. That's what people in the country oppose. Every time they issue a court order they obey it. Next year that's not good enough. Another court order. Hundreds of little children go to this school this year, that school next, the next year to another school. You're right. The federal courts have

29. Interview with Howell Heflin, July 9, 1974.
30. Interview with Frank M. Johnson, Jr., July 1974.

had more impact on the people's rights and prerogatives than has the legislature of the state and the governor of the state." [31]

But Alabama's progressive and dynamic attorney general, Bill Baxley, looks at it differently. "We holler about the federal courts having too much power," Baxley said, "but if you have states' rights, you also have to have states' responsibilities. The state refused to face up to its responsibilities time and again. We abdicated our power." [32]

Baxley was elected in 1970 as a 29-year-old reformer who espoused equality for all and defeated an entrenched incumbent who resorted to the politics of race. Baxley not only cracked down on Birmingham's industrial polluters, fought official corruption, and battled for consumer interests, but he also hired young Ivy League law school graduates, named a black lawyer to head a division in his office, and within four years had four black lawyers on his staff.

On the walls of his office hang portraits of Franklin D. Roosevelt, Harry S. Truman, Abraham Lincoln, Lyndon Johnson, and John F. Kennedy, and there's also a photograph of Jim Folsom. A plaque in Baxley's office is adorned with this quotation from Dante: "The hottest places in hell are reserved for those who, in a time of crisis, maintain their neutrality."

Baxley believes that one reason race became the issue it did in Alabama and elsewhere in the South "is because good, decent officeholders were afraid to do their bit on educating the people. I think that weakness on the part of good men allowed race to reach the proportions that it did. Not just in the South but nationwide." [33]

Despite the difference in image, style, and rhetoric between himself and Wallace, Baxley reported that in his four years as attorney general "there couldn't have been anybody nicer and more cooperative to me in my office as he's been. There's no way any governor could have done more for this office than he's done. I haven't asked for anything we didn't get." After a pause, Baxley added, "Why, I don't know." [34]

There is a widespread belief among politically informed Alabamians that the Democratic gubernatorial primary in 1978 will be between Baxley and Jere Beasley, the youthful lieutenant governor who represents the old politics. Other speculation is that Cornelia Wallace—a niece of Jim Folsom—may run for governor; but if so, she is far more independent than the first Mrs. Wallace. A Baxley victory could trigger a major Republican effort to rally conservatives behind someone like Blount, a man of undoubted executive ability and generally a moderate on the race issue.

31. Interview with George Wallace, July 1974.
32. Peirce, p. 239.
33. Interview with Bill Baxley, July 9, 1974.
34. Ibid.

Although Wallace faded as a national figure in 1976, if his health remains good he may well run for Sparkman's Senate seat in 1978, when Sparkman will turn 79. As a senator, Wallace would have the opportunity to play to the national press—the same opportunity that Huey Long grabbed in the 1930s when he had national ambitions.

As the consummate politician, Wallace read correctly the implications of the 1970 election results: that the Alabama electorate was changing, that there was more talk about "bad national publicity" (a code phrase used by moderates), and that the racial rhetoric was losing some of its effectiveness. Thus, Wallace began to make peace with organized labor, ended his badgering of unfriendly newspapers, muted his racial rhetoric, and made overtures to the established business leadership in the state. The change began before he was shot, but much of it went unnoticed until 1974.

There is no doubt that Alabama has changed and that Wallace has responded to that change. As long as George Wallace remains active, his political future and that of the state will remain intertwined.

Chapter

5

ARKANSAS

Emergence of Moderation

IN ARKANSAS the South meets the West, and geography helps shape political developments that flow from a heritage of conflicting values and forces.

The flat delta country that borders Mississippi and Tennessee on the east takes on the characteristics of the Deep South. The southern border extends westward across the top of Louisiana until it juts into east Texas. The land becomes more hilly and the tradition changes as one moves to the western border with Oklahoma and north to the boundary that connects with Missouri. A few counties in the northwest hold a remnant of mountain Republicanism that dates back to Union loyalty in the Civil War.

The state has a distinctly rural flavor. Centrally located Little Rock is the only city with more than 100,000 population, and the two competing newspapers there, the liberal *Gazette* and the conservative *Democrat*, both have circulation and political influence that extend statewide.

Historically, Arkansas rejected secession until after the fall of Fort Sumter, but then fought with the Confederacy and afterward shared the experience of Reconstruction. The state voted Democratic in every presidential election until 1968, when George Wallace won with a plurality, and never voted for a Republican presidential candidate until the Nixon landslide in 1972. This is a record of Democratic allegiance unmatched by any other state.

In the 1880s and 1890s, Arkansas was a hotbed of populism and the organizational base for the Agricultural Wheel, an energetic organization with a radical streak that spread briefly to other states and bears a resemblance to the grassroots Arkansas Community Organizations for

Reform Now (ACORN), which has protested "discriminatory" utility rates and has been involved in other issues in the 1970s. Populism in Arkansas demonstrated the clearest record of racial liberalism in any southern state. The People's Party platform took an official stand in behalf of the poor and "downtrodden, regardless of race." [1]

At the beginning of this century, Arkansas suffered the bitter political cleavage of hill country and Little Rock against the lowlands when neo-Populist Jeff Davis served three terms as governor. Although no governor until Orval Faubus again succeeded in serving more than two terms (four years), V. O. Key remarked of Davis that "his war against the corporations, like those of his contemporaries in other states, ended in futility."

Davis was followed by four decades of political consensus, during which the conservatives controlled the state without serious challenge and social issues remained submerged. Key suggested that the reduction of a majority of the state's farm operatives to tenant status by the mid-1930s helped explain the death of agrarian radicalism in Arkansas and the rest of the South. He wrote: "The reduction of a free and independent (though mortgaged) yeomanry to the status of sharecroppers, too poor to pay a poll tax and too depressed to have hope, may underlie the disappearance of most of the fire from southern politics." [2]

That fire flared briefly in 1932 when Huey Long stormed the state on behalf of Hattie Carraway, "this little woman" who had served out the last year of the term of her deceased husband and sought a full term on her own. She wasn't given a chance against four prominent opponents, but Long in seven days delivered 39 speeches, traveled 2,100 miles, addressed approximately 200,000 people, and aroused into a full fury the resentment felt vaguely by the farmers, welding their feelings into a genuine class protest. Long declared, "We're all here to pull a lot of potbellied politicians off a little woman's neck." Mrs. Carraway had voted with Long in the Senate on a proposal to limit any individual to $1 million annual income, and Long railed against the Wall Street millionaires who controlled the Congress, telling it what laws to pass and not to pass. They were like men running a restaurant: "They've got a set of Republican waiters on one side and a set of Democratic waiters on the other side, but no matter which set of waiters brings you the dish, the legislative grub is all prepared in the same Wall Street kitchen." Mrs. Carraway carried 29 of the 31 counties in which Long spoke and became the first woman ever elected to a six-year Senate term. [3]

1. Lawrence C. Goodwyn, *Democratic Promise: The Populist Movement in America* (New York: Oxford University Press, 1976), chap. 5.
2. V. O. Key, *Southern Politics in State and Nation* (New York: Knopf/Vintage, 1949), p. 185.
3. T. Harry Williams, *Huey Long* (New York: Bantam, 1971), pp. 613–623.

THREE MEN, THREE ERAS

Poverty that was more severe among whites than in any state wore down the spirit of protest. Thus it was that Winthrop Rockefeller, a scion of all that Wall Street represented, found a "mass inferiority complex" when he moved to Arkansas in 1953 to start his own new life. After compiling a heroic combat record in World War II, he lived as a playboy for a stormy period that ended in a $6 million divorce settlement with his wife, Bobo. He came to Arkansas at the urging of an old army friend. In developing the $10 million complex that is WinRock Farms at Petit Jean Mountain, Rockefeller discovered that men would drive from miles around looking for work. Thus he directed his energies first toward industrial development and then toward politics.

When V. O. Key described Arkansas as a state with "pure one-party politics," conservatives dominated the Democratic structure of government. Rockefeller, more than any other person, played the key transitional role in turning Arkansas around, politically and economically, but Republican development receded with his defeat in 1970 and subsequent death. Despite a $10 million investment by Rockefeller to develop his own and the Republican Party's political fortunes, one-party Democrat dominance has returned to Arkansas, but with dominant figures who are moderate, young, and progressive. Just as Rockefeller dominated the transitional period, Orval Faubus symbolized an era of racial reaction that preceded Rockefeller, and Dale Bumpers personifies the emerging politics of progressive moderation.

Rockefeller estimated before his death that he invested more than $35 million in Arkansas, including $5 million for philanthropic causes and $10 million for political activities, including four campaigns for governor and the building of a Republican Party.

The start of his involvement in the public affairs of Arkansas came as chairman of the Arkansas Industrial Development Corporation, to which he was appointed by Governor Orval Faubus in 1955. In the next eight years, more than 600 new industrial plants came to Arkansas; many of them were small, but it was the beginning of industrialization. Aided by a powerful congressional delegation, especially Senator John McClellan, Rockefeller as governor continued to concentrate on getting plants located in rural areas, near the people who needed jobs. By the late 1960s he was saying there had been "a whole about-face in people's attitudes here."

A flamboyant and sentimental multimillionaire who served as a catalyst for modernization during a pair of two-year terms, Rockefeller replaced Faubus in 1966 after building an unprecedented Republican coalition fueled by blacks and moderate Democrats.

Meanwhile, Faubus, an Ozark populist who became an international symbol of racism, during 12 years as governor developed firm control over a closed Democratic Party and dominated the government of his state. He rocketed to political invincibility in 1957 with his defiance of a federal court order to integrate Central High in Little Rock. That act pushed President Eisenhower into sending federal troops to Little Rock to enforce the federal court order and launched a decade of rabble-rousing racial rhetoric among Deep South politicians.

Faubus was an unlikely candidate for such a role. He had emerged from Madison County in the Ozarks with a liberal image that was reflected in the editorials he wrote for a weekly newspaper. As a youth, he had tagged along while his hardscrabble farmer father made socialist speeches in Madison and adjoining counties. It was as administrative assistant to liberal Governor Sid McMath, who led the G.I. reform movement after World War II which sought to clean up widespread political corruption, that Faubus gained his first exposure to statewide politics.

After his first election as governor in 1954, Faubus expanded the Democratic State Committee to add six Negroes. As governor, he won a $22 million tax increase to improve education funding, began the industrial development program, and created the Children's Colony in Arkansas, a model institution for the mentally retarded.

The story is told of an aged father in overalls who came to the governor's office, asked to see Faubus, and explained that his boy had been sent to the state prison farm for a petty theft case but was needed back home. The farmer explained he was just too old to farm his crops. After a few moments of silence, the old man said he guessed there was nothing that could be done and turned to leave, but Faubus stopped him and explained, "I'm just trying to decide whether I should send a state trooper for him now or take you home to the mansion with me to spend the night, and we'll go for him in the morning." The old man spent the night at the mansion.

One explanation of the Faubus reputation for "being close to the people" and "knowing what the people think" derived from his private use of polling. He was one of the first governors to use public opinion research in developing his governmental programs. Faubus would take a program to the legislature, such as a tax increase for teacher's pay, secure in the knowledge that there was widespread public support for the idea despite legislative protests that the people wouldn't stand for a tax increase.

When Faubus ran for the usual second term in 1956, fiery young segregationist Jim Johnson, a former state senator who later was elected to the state Supreme Court, accused the governor of being "soft" on integration and declared his first act as governor would be to replace with whites the six Negroes Faubus had appointed to the Democratic State Committee. Faubus won 58 percent of the vote against Johnson and three lesser candidates. The race issue had begun to surface, but it was not yet ripe.

School integration was making quiet progress in Arkansas by 1957, with most of the state-supported colleges admitting black students and ten school districts desegregating in areas where few blacks lived. Two school board candidates in Little Rock who endorsed a gradual desegregation plan were elected in March over two opponents of the plan. But the entire Arkansas congressional delegation the year before had signed the Southern Manifesto, which declared that the Supreme Court, "with no legal basis for their action, undertook to exercise their naked judicial power and substituted their personal and political ideas for the established law of the land." The fact that Senator J. William Fulbright of Arkansas signed that manifesto and Senator Lyndon Johnson of Texas did not was later given as an explanation why Johnson was acceptable to John F. Kennedy as a running mate in 1960 but Fulbright was unacceptable as his secretary of state.

A week before school was scheduled to open for the 1957 fall term, Faubus made an unexpected appearance to support a group seeking a temporary injunction against integration at Central High. He expressed fear of mob violence and bloodshed if the integration order were carried out, but a federal court the next day set aside the state court injunction. Faubus called out the National Guard "to keep the peace." They turned away nine black students who attempted to enter Central High under court order.

Faubus insisted he acted to prevent mob violence, but no mob appeared, and editor Harry Ashmore of the *Arkansas Gazette* accused Faubus of "manufacturing" a threat of violence. Ashmore considered Faubus a weak man who failed to exert responsible leadership in a crisis. Winthrop Rockefeller later said in an interview with author Neal Peirce that he had spent two-and-a-half hours with Faubus before his intervention. "I reasoned with him, argued with him, almost pled with him" not to intervene, telling him "the local situation was none of his business," Rockefeller said. He also insisted that Faubus told him, "I'm sorry, but I'm already committed. I'm going to run for a third term, and if I don't do this, Jim Johnson and Bruce Bennett [both segregationist politicians] will tear me to shreds." [4]

Almost 17 years later, Faubus's eyes would light up and he would become animated when he discussed these events, as if they had hap-

4. Neal Peirce, *The Deep South States of America* (New York: W. W. Norton, 1974), p. 132.

pened only a week before. Faubus still insisted that massive violence would have resulted if he hadn't acted. He spoke of FBI reports that were never released which he said would substantiate his story that the threat of violence was real, and he expressed pride that no lives were lost in Arkansas because of civil rights violence. He spoke of "illegal" court orders, and he blamed the *Gazette* for stirring emotions by attempting to portray Little Rock as an impending model for desegregation throughout the South when the public considered the court order illegal.

Faubus blamed federal authorities and the Eisenhower administration for putting him on the spot in a politically explosive situation. Faubus declared, "They could sit back and issue a court order that was going to cause literally hell and destroy many people, economically and politically. And they would just sit back and fold their hands and let somebody else reap the storm. Well, hell, it was their storm. A bunch of goddamn cowards for not coming in in the beginning and saying, 'This is a federal court order. We're going to have federal authorities here to see to it that it's obeyed and enforced.' Then I wouldn't have been involved." [5]

The details of the Central High School confrontation are complex, but the governor's actions pushed President Eisenhower into sending federal troops to Little Rock to enforce the federal court order. The troops remained until the end of the 1957–1958 school year, and Faubus reaped a political harvest. His defiance at Little Rock propelled him to four more two-year terms as governor. His strongest support shifted from the populist-oriented hill country to the delta flatlands of the east. These were the counties with the heaviest black population, but where voting was controlled by whites.

Sid McMath later said, "The last man I would have expected to have called out the National Guard in defiance of federal court orders was Orval Faubus." McMath, who never accepted the Faubus version, took the position that even if it was reasonably accurate, Faubus as governor "should have used the National Guard to protect the children, instead of blocking their entry; his actions gave encouragement to the racist rabble-rousers, and slowed down industrial development in the state."

Jim Johnson came to complain ruefully, "He used my nickel and hit the jackpot." In the June 1958 primary, Faubus carried all 75 counties and received 69 percent of the vote against two legitimate candidates. After his smashing victory, Faubus called a special session of the legislature and won authority to close down high schools in Little Rock, which he did in the fall, action that subsequently was endorsed by a public referendum. In the routine integration of public facilities in contemporary Little Rock, that period of frenzied emotionalism seems

5. Interview with Orval Faubus, June 14, 1974.

like ancient history. But at the end of 1958, a Gallup poll showed Faubus as one of the ten most admired men in the world.

Faubus easily won reelection in 1960, but McMath finished second in a field of six in 1962. Faubus missed being forced into a runoff by less than 6,500 votes, an indication of creeping disenchantment. By then he had become, according to the *Gazette,* "the darling of the East Arkansas planters—the heirs of the men who had chased populism into the hills and dared Orval Faubus's ancestors to bring it out. Eventually, men of money all over the state fell into line behind the agricultural wealth, until today, there is evidence that Mr. Faubus draws as heavy support from the financial community as any governor in recent history." [6]

The man considered most influential of all was W. R. (Witt) Stephens, chairman of the board and president of the Arkansas-Louisiana Gas Co. (Arkla), at times a legislator himself, and the uncle of Fourth District Representative Ray Thornton. During the 1950s, the state Public Service Commission approved three yearly rate increases averaging $3.2 million for Arkla, many of whose officers served on boards of the state's largest banks, which during the Faubus era held millions in state funds that were deposited without interest.

Stephens, who never got beyond the eighth grade, is the kind of self-educated, wealthy, behind-the-scenes manipulator found in politics throughout the South. Rockefeller in his interview with Neal Peirce described Stephens as a charming, skilled, amoral businessman-politician who controlled much of the political process of the state through money and sheer skill and who had 17 of the state's 35 senators on his payroll through retainers or other devices. Stephens later praised Rockefeller for turning the state around on the race issue.

In 1964, when Winthrop Rockefeller, who had given financial support and encouragement to Republicans in the past, jumped into the race against Faubus, moderate white Democrats organized as "Independents for Rockefeller." As a Republican, Rockefeller received 43 percent of the vote, but Faubus received 84 percent of the black vote, in part because Rockefeller waffled on the Civil Rights Act of 1964 and Faubus endorsed the Johnson-Humphrey ticket against Barry Goldwater.

Faubus retired undefeated, but Jim Johnson left the state Supreme Court and won the Democratic nomination for governor in 1966. His segregationist rhetoric was more strident than that of Faubus, and the Faubus wing of the party—the courthouse Democrats—backed another candidate. Rockefeller was elected in 1966 and again in 1968, putting together a coalition of Republicans, moderate Democrats, and blacks.

There were never more than five Republicans in the legislature when Rockefeller was governor. The local problems of a rural legislator were not things Winthrop Rockefeller could relate to. At the suggestion of an

6. *Arkansas Gazette,* April 1, 1962.

aide, Rockefeller once invited the legislators and their wives to WinRock Farms, his $10 million showplace cattle farm and residence. When the legislators left, they took more than $3,000 in linens and other souvenirs from his guest house, including a Steuben glass egg. Rockefeller was furious.[7]

Although he failed to win approval for his tax reform and government reorganization proposals and the voters turned down a new state constitution during his tenure, Rockefeller created a climate for change, an end to the old way of doing things, and he introduced modern management techniques into Arkansas state government. But after two terms, bickering with the legislature and public awareness of a drinking problem cost Rockefeller much of his popularity, and polls indicated that any moderate Democrat would beat him.

Dale Bumpers emerged as a political phenomenon. In his native Charleston, a town of less than 2,000 population in the foothills of the Ouachita Mountains, Bumpers was the only practicing attorney. He served as school board chairman, taught Sunday school, and directed the choir at the Methodist Church. He once had run for the state legislature—and lost.

A 200-pound, six-footer who believes that political leadership consists of "doing what you think is right," Bumpers put together $90,000 of personal and family assets and decided to make the race in 1970. He hired DeLoss Walker of Memphis, a highly successful campaign consultant described by one neutral colleague as "probably a decent technician with a nose for a good candidate."

In 1970, Bumpers was one of seven candidates seeking a runoff spot against Faubus, who at age 60 was seeking a comeback. The others included Attorney General Joe Purcell and former House Speaker Hayes McClerkin—both moderates. Bumpers staged a media blitz two weeks before the election, when polls showed him with less than 10 percent of the vote. Bumpers managed to edge Purcell by less than 5,000 votes for second place. Faubus by this time had become a man who polarized the electorate, and less than a majority supported him. When Bumpers easily defeated Faubus with 57 percent of the vote in the runoff, the Democratic Party in ten years had moved from a conservative, closed, tightly-knit operation to a moderate, decentralized, fragmented, independent, and open organization. With that election, Rockefeller and the Republicans were doomed to defeat.[8]

Bumpers had caught the eye of Senator Fulbright, among others. One eyewitness said that when Bumpers ran out of money in the general election campaign against Rockefeller, Fulbright personally got on the

7. Confidential interview with a former Rockefeller aide.
8. Jim Ranchino, *Faubus to Bumpers: Arkansas Votes, 1960–1970* (Arkadelphia, Ark.: Action Research, Inc., 1972), p. 68.

telephone and raised $10,000 to keep the television going, one reason for the extreme bitterness among Fulbright's staff when Bumpers ran against and defeated Fulbright four years later.

With a candidate like Bumpers, the moderate Democrats who had supported Rockefeller in the past now flocked back to their party. The margin for Bumpers was two-to-one despite a campaign by Rockefeller that cost almost $3 million. Bumpers received 62 percent of the vote, Rockefeller 32 percent, and Walter Carruth of the American Independent Party 6 percent. Carruth's weak showing destroyed the myth that the Wallace vote in Arkansas was a cohesive force in state politics.

As governor, Democrat Bumpers was personally effective with the legislature and achieved some of the reforms that had eluded Rockefeller. Bumpers implemented a governmental reorganization plan that consolidated 65 state agencies into 13, with department heads forming a cabinet directly responsible to the governor. In the governor's mansion, Bumpers kept in his office a small framed copy of the well-known quote from Edmund Burke: "The only thing necessary for the triumph of evil is that good men do nothing."

In his fourth year as governor, a poll showed Bumpers with a 91 percent approval rating among voters. The afternoon that Bumpers announced his candidacy against Senator Fulbright, an opinion survey showed Bumpers with 60 percent of the vote and Fulbright with only 27 percent. Despite overwhelming support for Fulbright among county officials and a majority of state legislators, Bumpers swept the state with 65 percent of the vote.

Fulbright, an aloof intellectual and aristocrat who generated pride among Arkansans that one of them was smart enough to win respect in Washington for his brains, served 30 years in the U.S. Senate. As chairman for 15 years of the Senate Foreign Relations Committee, which under his leadership became the leading forum for opposition to the Vietnam war and for a reduction of American commitments abroad, he helped shape American foreign policy during the third quarter of the 20th century.

Bumpers has never openly attacked an opponent in a campaign, and one veteran observer called him a "high road" candidate. "Ask the toughest questions and he takes the high road." It's a style Arkansas voters obviously like. Earl Epple of Prescott wrote in a letter to the editor of the pro-Fulbright *Arkansas Gazette* after the 1974 primary, "We were undecided for awhile until the Senator started his arrogant and most holier than thou attitude and thinking that he was indispensable."

In Arkansas, Bumpers is perceived as that state's most likely candidate for national office since Senator Joseph Robinson ran for vice-president with Al Smith in 1928. After the 1974 elections, *Time* magazine projected Bumpers, with his soft-spoken effectiveness and winning smile, as perhaps the most promising new political figure to emerge nationally from the South.

Like Faubus and Fulbright, Bumpers comes from the hills, the northwestern part of Arkansas settled by yeoman farmers inclined toward political independence and populism. Arkansas native Roy Reed wrote in the *New York Times,* after the defeat of Fulbright in 1974:

Mr. Bumpers is branded as a hill man as soon as he opens his mouth. His drawl is almost Western. He pronounces the letter "r" with a firmness that would make a Delta man shudder. . . .

Only a handful of blacks live in northwest Arkansas. Mr. Bumpers had dealt neither with blacks nor with Delta whites until he became Governor. He came to that office with the racial tolerance of the mountain people, but without the experience of day-to-day interracial dealings that Delta folk have.

His response to racial problems has been to try to incorporate them into a general populist philosophy. In his campaigns, he has appealed to low-income people. He speaks a language that factory workers and hardscrabble farmers can understand.

He talks of inflation not in theory and statistics but in anecdotes. The problems become drama in everyday life as he tells his audience of men who confide to him that they could not make it financially if they did not "moonlight" or if their wives did not work.

When he talks of the soaring price of gasoline and the profits of the big oil companies, there is passion in his voice, as if his blood remembered the ancestral poverty of the hills.

"This country must never again place [itself] in the position of being cowed and bended by the Arab sheiks who control that production," he told his campaign audiences this spring. "But more importantly, our future must never be placed in the hands of eight or ten major oil companies in the world."

The Bumpers administration drew a mixed reaction from black political leaders. "He keeps a black aide in the basement and he made less black appointments than Rockefeller," complained state Senator Jerry Jewell, a former state NAACP president, at the end of Bumpers's last term as governor. But black state Representative Henry Wilkins III believed Bumpers was sensitive to "human needs" and that his sensitivity to blacks would increase, in part because of substantial black support he received against Fulbright.

The subdued style of Bumpers in approaching problems as governor prompted a standing joke in Little Rock that if you asked Dale Bumpers if he was wishy-washy, he would reply, "Maybe I am and maybe I'm not." Bumpers denies the accusation, contending that he does not commit himself on an issue until he has to, because that "gives me the opportunity to study it until the last minute to make sure that I'm making the right decision. . . . If it's a decision that needs to be made and procrastination hurts, I make that decision." [9] Bold leadership that helps shape public opinion is not one of his characteristics.

9. Interview with Dale Bumpers, June 14, 1974.

Although Bumpers was attacked by Fulbright for refusal to debate and is criticized for failing to take specific positions on issues, one astute practitioner of the "new politics" in Arkansas noted: "In this state, the voters don't expect you to say with too much particularity what you mean to do, and *their* solutions to the problems become 'throw the rascals out, down with seniority, new faces, etc.,' but underneath the issues are moving. Bumpers' sloganeering 'stands,' such as 'Inflation Is Eating the Heart Out of America,' 'The Big Oil Lobby Has Too Much Power in Washington,' reflect a keen perception of the importance of the issues to the voters, as well as their *inability* (or unwillingness) to focus sharply on them or to demand precise programmatic stands on them."

POLITICS AFTER BUMPERS

After the Bumpers administration, Arkansas chose David Pryor as governor in 1974 in a race that apparently was the last hurrah for Faubus, who received only 35 percent of the vote and now had the smell of a loser. His old friend Witt Stephens and even Sheriff Marlin Hawkins, the political boss of Conway County and one of the last remnants of a machine organization that could still deliver the votes, were backing Pryor.

After Stephens and a group of other men of wealth met in a hotel room with Pryor in Little Rock, they effectively dried up political funds for other candidates. Pryor said the group supported him over Faubus because they "realized his day was over, and they know themselves that their day is about over," that Faubus attended the meeting seeking their support and then criticized Pryor for accepting it after Faubus was rejected. Pryor later said that if other candidates "were bluffed out, I can't believe it. . . . I would sure hope I had a much broader base of support than the few men in that room that particular day."

Pryor was 31 when he won election to Congress in 1966. As a congressman, he worked anonymously in a nursing home for several weeks because he was disturbed about treatment of the elderly. When he was denied creation of a subcommittee to investigate the institutions—which were thriving on Medicare payments—Pryor rented three trailers and set up a volunteer staff on Capitol Hill to investigate. His voting record in Congress was progressive, and at the 1968 Democratic national convention he served on the Credentials Committee and voted against seating the regular all-white delegation from Mississippi.

Pryor, who was criticized in a 1972 U.S. Senate campaign against

John McClellan because of heavy labor support, said his major goal as governor was to get divergent groups of people—labor and management, black and white, rural and urban—"to realize how many things they have in common rather than to exploit the differences they have." [10]

An admirer of Bumpers, Pryor shares the Bumpers philosophy of selective growth through attraction of high-paying industry. Like Bumpers, he hopes to keep Arkansas in tune with the national Democratic Party—and vice versa. However, Pryor suffered a major setback his first year in office when the state Supreme Court declared unconstitutional a bill Pryor had pushed to establish a constitutional convention to which the governor would appoint a majority of the delegates.

McClellan, the state's senior senator and perhaps the last of the old Arkansas conservatives, received 52 percent of the vote in a runoff against Pryor in 1972. At 76, McClellan proved a tough campaigner who managed to put together the courthouse machine, used money effectively among blacks, attacked Pryor's financial support from organized labor, and put together a winning organization.

McClellan also is the last of a congressional delegation once loaded with seniority and power. As chairman of the Senate Appropriations Committee, McClellan teamed up with House Ways and Means Chairman Wilbur Mills to look out for Arkansas at pork barrel time. The McClellan-Kerr Arkansas River Navigation System, a hugely expensive project that has opened Little Rock and Tulsa, Oklahoma, to the sea, memorialized the senator's name while he was still in the Senate.

McClellan plays little active role in the internal politics of the state. In alliance with Bumpers, he worked to name his 1972 campaign aide Craig Campbell as state Democratic Party executive director, despite protests from party regulars who objected that Campbell had voted for Richard Nixon over George McGovern.

When McClellan's term expires in 1978, he will be 82, and there will be plenty of candidates, with Pryor, dynamic young Attorney General Jim Guy Tucker, and one or two congressmen all very much interested.

At one time perhaps the most powerful member of the House of Representatives, Wilbur Mills shaped the nation's tax structure and many of its laws. In 1975, however, he relinquished the chairmanship of Ways and Means and the power that went with that post after an admission of alcoholism. Mills already had gotten into some political trouble back home after disclosure of legally questionable contributions from the milk and beer industries in his abortive 1972 presidential campaign. His trouble intensified in 1974. Not only did Republican opponent Judy Petty attack him for having "one foot in sour milk and the other in stale beer," but there was a widely publicized incident

10. Interview with David Pryor, June 13, 1974.

that involved Mills with drinking, a fistfight, and an auto accident while in the company of a stripper friend known as the "Argentine Firecracker."

Mills went home sheepishly, got audiences laughing with him about his predicament, and campaigned vigorously to win reelection with 59 percent of the vote. A waggish student at Hendrix College even altered the construction sign of the Wilbur D. Mills Center for the Study of Social Science to read "Wilbur D. Milks Center for the Study of the Dairy Sciences and A-Go-Go." The laughter stopped when Mills appeared after the election on the stage of a Boston burlesque house holding hands with his companion of the earlier incident. A Harvard Law School graduate who had earned a reputation as one of the hardest-working congressmen during his 36 years in Washington, Mills later admitted that he suffered from alcoholism, which caused temporary "blackouts from time to time—periods during which I have no knowledge of what I was doing . . . they explain some of my recent activities." He said he would remain in Congress and would conquer his disease by "total abstinence," but in 1976 announced plans to retire.

STATE GOVERNMENT

Although the Arkansas legislature remains a basically weak branch of government, it adopted a number of reforms in the early 1970s to strengthen its role and performance. After voters in 1970 rejected a new state constitution that would have provided annual sessions, removed the $1,200 salary limitation, provided for open committee meetings and recorded votes, and other reforms, the legislature appropriated funds for a study by the Eagleton Institute of Politics at Rutgers of Arkansas legislative procedure and performance. Most of its recommendations were adopted.

As a result, legislative committees now have been sharply curtailed, with ten parallel committees in the House and Senate. They meet jointly as interim committees when the legislature is not in session to study Arkansans' major problems and concerns. Legislative oversight of state agencies has been expanded to include line-item budgeting and performance, as well as fiscal audits. Committee meetings are now open, with recorded roll calls. For Arkansas, the changes represent major legislative reform, but the legislature remains limited to biennial meetings except for special sessions called by the governor.

To measure legislative quality is difficult, but the consensus of political observers interviewed in Arkansas is that reapportionment has brought an influx of urban legislators who tend to be less parochial in outlook than their predecessors.

A prime example of the effect of reapportionment is the case of Paul Van Dalsem of rural Perry County, who for years had been a dominant and domineering figure in the state House, a man described by Arkansas historian Richard E. Yates as "possessed of a bullhorn voice, an irascible temper, and a disposition to start unseemly legislative brawls." In a speech to an all-male Little Rock civic club in 1963, Van Dalsem said of women in politics, especially some Little Rock women who had lobbied in the recent session of the legislature, "They're frustrated. We don't have any of these university women in Perry County, but I'll tell you what we do up there when one of our women starts poking around in something she doesn't know anything about: We get her an extra milk cow. If that don't work, we give her a little more garden to tend to. And then if that's not enough, we get her pregnant and keep her barefoot."

Two years later, reapportionment threw rural Perry County into the same legislative district with Pulaski (Little Rock). Women there, some of whom removed their shoes before entering the polling places, responded to Van Dalsem's wit by sending him into political retirement.[11]

Another sign of improved legislative standards was the action taken by the state Senate in 1974 to expel veteran Senator Guy H. (Mutt) Jones after he was convicted of income tax evasion. Jones challenged the action, but lost in the state Supreme Court.

Arkansas was the last of the southern states to elect black legislators this century, three representatives and a senator in 1972.

BLACK POLITICS

Despite the lack of an effective statewide black political organization, there were more than 150 elected black officials in Arkansas in the mid-1970s, and an elected black officials association appeared to be in the offing.

Although Arkansas historically had its full share of Jim Crow laws, it was more tolerant than its Deep South neighbors in permitting blacks to vote. In practice, this often meant that dominant whites in the plantation counties could buy poll tax receipts and thereby control the votes of their sharecroppers and tenants, white as well as black.

11. Richard E. Yates in William C. Havard, *The Changing Politics of the South* (Baton Rouge: Louisiana State University Press, 1972), p. 25.

When precinct studies revealed that Orval Faubus had received 84 percent of the black vote in 1964 against Winthrop Rockefeller—who personally shared his family's philanthropic and philosophical commitments to equality for Negroes—Rockefeller's response was his usual one to political problems. He poured money into black registration drives, hired black organizers, financed car pools and drivers to get out the vote, and was outspoken on his views toward equal treatment for blacks. In 1966, Rockefeller won with 71 percent of the black vote, enough to furnish the margin of victory over Democrat Jim Johnson, a vitriolic segregationist who still managed to get 29 percent of the black vote, mostly from machine counties in the east.

By 1968, Rockefeller not only had financed a tight organization in the black community, but he had also demonstrated his commitment to open the doors of government by appointing a black as state director of antipoverty programs and by standing with blacks on the state capitol steps to sing "We Shall Overcome" after the assassination of Martin Luther King, Jr. Rockefeller received 91 percent of the black vote in 1968, and seemed to be converting many to Republicanism, at least on the state level, with most blacks participating that year in the Republican primary.

But Arkansas blacks also developed sufficient political sophistication to split their tickets. Democrat Hubert Humphrey won overwhelming support among blacks in Arkansas in 1968, and Democratic Senator J. William Fulbright won 70 percent of the black vote against Republican Charles Bernard. In fact, there had been a deal between Fulbright and Rockefeller. Fulbright's people refrained from supporting Democrat Marion Crank in the governor's race, and Bernard's name was dropped from the Rockefeller car pool list that went to blacks. Bernard received 41 percent of the vote against Fulbright. Had Bernard, a moderate, received the same 90 percent black vote that Rockefeller received, he would have defeated Fulbright, who had voted consistently against civil rights legislation as a member of the southern bloc in Congress. On the other hand, Fulbright's votes for progressive social legislation won support among blacks.

Rockefeller still held onto 88 percent of the black vote in his unsuccessful 1970 campaign against Bumpers. Although there was nothing cynical in Rockefeller's use of money to develop black political support, others viewed it as "buying" the black vote. In his narrow victory in 1972, Senator John McClellan poured money into the black community; many rural black "leaders" in the east, who had taken money from Rockefeller and delivered the vote, did the same for conservative McClellan against Pryor, his progressive challenger.

State Representative Henry Wilkins III, a black political science professor from Pine Bluff, sharply criticized such practices in Fulbright's

1974 race. "This concept of purchasing black votes is about as old as certain candidates' long tenure in the Senate," Wilkins said in 1974, in an appeal to his constituents to reject the attempt to "sell the votes of black Arkansans." [12]

After a report that Fulbright's campaign committee used M. J. Probst, a white lawyer in Little Rock, to direct efforts to recruit and pay black poll watchers and drivers, a black aide to Fulbright, the Rev. Benjamin S. Grinage, said he was "incensed" by the action. He declared the hiring of a white for such work "continues to perpetuate the thinking that blacks cannot come to any decision or involve themselves in a campaign without white direction." Although Grinage first objected both to the appointment of a white man and to the hiring of professional black campaign workers, he modified his position by saying, "I see nothing wrong with spending money in the black community, because they do it in the white community." But he complained that when money is spent among white groups in a campaign, "you call that working with them. When you do it with blacks, you call it buying the black vote." Although Grinage declared his loyalty to Fulbright at a press conference less than a week before the election, and expressed hope the senator would be reelected, he said "it wouldn't be the end of the world if he wasn't." [13]

Bumpers, a man who always takes the high road on a controversial issue, called it "demeaning" for supporters of Fulbright to seek to "buy" the black vote in Arkansas. "I still don't think the black vote can be bought, and I think it's demeaning to try," he said. [14]

Fulbright's campaign expenditure report shows that he spent $965,000 and that Probst received $43,000, and the black Independent Voters League of Arkansas $18,000. Other sums were paid to individual blacks, many of whom had previously worked for Rockefeller.

After the election, in which Bumpers won 58 percent of the black vote, Wilkins said most of the abuses involved a group of black preachers in eastern Arkansas. "Every two years they would say, 'We can deliver the black vote for X number of dollars.' And in 1972, McClellan employed this group. This time they didn't carry the black vote, and Fulbright lost by about two-to-one. So I don't think they're going to be viable any more. . . . I think Mr. Bumpers has demonstrated that you didn't have to have money to win."

Wilkins said he doubted if more than 35 percent of the money spent by Fulbright and McClellan constituted "legitimate Election Day expenses. Most is hip pocket money, and I think their performance this time demonstrates that." Wilkins estimated that about a third of the

12. *Washington Post*, May 26, 1974.
13. *Arkansas Democrat*, May 24, 1974.
14. *Memphis Commercial-Appeal*, May 16, 1974.

black ministers involved in politics do it for the money, and about two-thirds "honestly seek to improve the lot of their parishioners." Wilkins insisted that blacks must raise their own money and make their own decisions in supporting candidates.[15]

In their unity, blacks made the difference in the two elections won by Winthrop Rockefeller. But with the death of Rockefeller and the development of the Nixon "southern strategy," blacks realized there was little to gain in an alliance with conservative Republicans. The Bumpers victory over Rockefeller in 1970 proved that moderates could elect a governor without them. The absence of recognized statewide leadership further weakened black political impact in the state.

If black legislators succeed in achieving the development of an effective statewide black political organization that can overcome local factionalism, Arkansas blacks may become a cohesive political force. In the rural areas, ministers tend to retain major political roles, but in urban areas organized labor is training and organizing a new black leadership, and organized labor in Arkansas is more effective politically than in most southern states.

ORGANIZED LABOR

The return of blacks to the Democratic Party, together with an unusually effective political contribution by organized labor, strengthens the forces of political moderation.

Major credit for labor's strength is given state AFL–CIO President and COPE Director Bill Becker, an Illinois native with astute political instinct. Becker, who has been in Arkansas since 1949, moved into the top labor job in 1964. Among veteran labor leaders in the South, only Victor Bussie in Louisiana commands as much respect from state political leaders as does Becker.

One reflection of labor's influence is the state's unemployment compensation law: in 1971, Arkansas became only the third state in the nation to provide an escalator clause. Unemployment insurance provides two-thirds of the average weekly wage in the state, an unusually favorable percentage.

Organized labor not only is perceived by politically knowledgeable Arkansans as "a moving force," but it has also projected an image far more acceptable to the public than in most southern states. A 1974 poll showed that 30 percent of Arkansas voters view an endorsement by

15. Interview with Henry Wilkins III, June 16, 1974.

organized labor "more favorable" for a candidate and 19 percent as "less favorable." The remaining 51 percent see "no difference." By comparison, an endorsement by the liberal *Arkansas Gazette* was viewed "more favorable" by 21 percent and "less favorable" by 17 percent, and an endorsement by the conservative *Arkansas Democrat* was rated by 20–6 as "more favorable." The best endorsement of all for a politician was the blessing of Senator John McClellan, rated 41 percent "more favorable" and only 10 percent "less favorable."

REPUBLICANS

By the mid-1970s, the Republican Party was a faction-ridden organization that still maintained a large state headquarters building in downtown Little Rock, published a monthly party newspaper, supported a paid staff, and could claim one congressman and a quartet of state legislators as their major officeholders.

The last major Republican symbol, Representative John Paul Hammerschmidt—who was elected on Rockefeller's coattails in 1966—narrowly won reelection in 1974 with 51.5 percent of the vote against Bill Clinton, a 27-year-old Rhodes scholar and University of Arkansas law professor who had served as George McGovern's Texas field director in 1972. Clinton, a handsome and personable native of the district, put together a strong, broad-based organization and campaigned tirelessly for what had come to be viewed as a safe Republican seat.

Hammerschmidt, a onetime Republican state chairman and prosperous businessman who got along well with congressional Democrats from his state and earned a reputation for providing prompt and effective action on constituent requests, had been reelected in 1972 with 77 percent of the vote. His district includes the traditionally Republican mountain counties in the northwest.

The collapse of the Republican Party in Arkansas really preceded the 1974 elections. In 1974 the GOP actually doubled its representation in the legislature, going from a token two seats to a token four—three in the House and one in the Senate. But the three GOP contenders for statewide office received the smallest percentage of the statewide vote in the last eight elections.

Perhaps of even more significance, the total vote cast in the 1974 Democratic primary exceeded that in the general election for the first time since 1962, an indication that Arkansas voters no longer perceived the Republicans as genuine challengers.

Some Republicans are counting on Winthrop Paul Rockefeller, the son and heir of Winthrop Rockefeller, to become active and again provide the excitement and resources to stimulate new life for the party. After the death of his father in 1973, 24-year-old Win Paul wrote in a letter to the party newspaper, "I know how not only the Republican Party in general, but the survival and progress of the two party system in our Arkansas was very dear to Dad's heart. I can only hope, in time, to be able to show it as close to ours." The younger Rockefeller took a year off to study animal husbandry and agriculture and has told associates he wants to make a record of his own before becoming politically active. In the 1980s the name of Rockefeller may again become a political force in Arkansas.

The Republican Party, crippled by the death of its patron and the loss of its alliance with the blacks, can continue to function in the role of a watchdog party. But until and unless another strong personality develops, Republican chances for dominance appear dim. Nevertheless, continued urbanization and economic growth should enable the Republicans to remain viable as an alternative if the Democrats drift from moderation.

TRENDS

In terms of party organization and structure, the Democratic Party in Arkansas is perhaps the weakest in the South. Bumpers took little interest in party building, and one top party official said he would oppose building a strong Democratic Party organization as long as Republicans are so weak.

Although there is no party registration in Arkansas, polls in the 1970s consistently showed that less than 20 percent of the electorate considered themselves Republicans, and more than 55 percent considered themselves Democrats. Polls also showed that less than 20 percent of the electorate were "strong segregationists," a reflection of racial moderation that translates into a progressive outlook on other issues that were long submerged by race. A majority consider themselves at least mildly integrationist in outlook, a profound change from the late 1950s and early 1960s that reflects the effects of integration, education, and, to some extent, increased black political participation.

In addition, polls show that Arkansans, like citizens elsewhere, now get most of their political information from television, and it was the development of the mass media and the civil rights movement that provoked the emotional response and extreme reaction that broke through the veneer of consensus which for so long had dominated Arkansas politics. It was television more than any other factor that made the race issue emerge, at least temporarily, as an issue more important than personality.[16]

In 1968, Arkansas voters elected Republican Winthrop Rockefeller as governor, chose Democrat J. William Fulbright as senator, and gave a 28 percent plurality to American Independent George Wallace for president. As disparate as the choices appear, there was a common "antiestablishment" trend—Rockefeller at the state level against the entrenched Democratic organization, Fulbright in his opposition to President Johnson and the war in Vietnam, and Wallace in his appeal to voters alienated from the national two-party leadership. To political scientist Jim Ranchino, "Arkansas voters were at their best in 1968. They were discerning and well aware of the choices available. They voted their independence and their individualism." [17]

Although Arkansas voters have demonstrated a willingness to cross party lines to express themselves, traditional voting habits remain an important clue in predicting voter behavior. No state has been more traditionally Democratic than Arkansas. If Arkansans remain comfortable in their new mold of moderation, Arkansas appears the southern state most likely to return to loyal support of Democrats in national elections, provided the party nominates candidates who are not perceived as extreme.

16. James B. Bonds, "Pure One-Party Politics—Revisited," Unpublished paper filed at the Arkansas Institute of Politics and Government, Little Rock, January 1974, p. 3.

17. Ranchino, *Faubus to Bumpers*, p. 65.

Chapter

6

FLORIDA

Government in the Sunshine

IN the 1950s a persistent young state representative from Dade County (Miami) got a bill passed by the House and persuaded veteran state Senator Charley Johns to set a hearing before his Senate committee. On the afternoon of the hearing, the representative showed up 45 minutes early and at the request of Johns gave a detailed explanation of the bill.

At the appointed time, the senator looked at his watch and said, "It's time for the meeting." He walked to the committee room, declared a quorum was present by proxy, and asked the representative to explain his bill. "You mean the whole thing?" he asked, having just explained it.

"Why, yes, the committee needs to know about it."

So the young man went through the whole thing again. The chairman then asked if anyone else wanted to speak—and of course, nobody else was there except the secretary. The chairman moved to report the bill favorably and said, "The secretary will call the roll." And after each name was called, Johns leaned over and said, "No, by proxy," until the secretary finally called out "and Mr. Chairman."

"You know," Johns declared, "that's a damn good bill. Mark me yes." And with that, he got up and adjourned the meeting.

The story, still told in Tallahassee, is a classic symbol of the days of the "Pork Chop gang," [1] a band of small county senators who dominated state policy and who in turn were dominated by special interests.

Of the lobbyists, none was so powerful as Edward Ball, brother-in-law and confidant of the late Alfred I. du Pont. From 1935 on, Ball managed the du Pont estate, whose assets included control of the Florida East

1. A name first penned by newsman Don Clendenin, later editor of the *Tampa Tribune*.

Coast Railway, 30 banks in the Florida National Banks group, and the St. Joe Paper Co., which owns more than a million acres of timberland in Florida. The estate prospered, in part because of Ball's talents at persuading the legislative leaders of the Pork Chop era of the wisdom of his views on matters affecting taxation and state regulation of business.

The legislature had virtually no staff, its members had no offices, the more than 200 state agencies and departments operated with little oversight, and a handful of dominant oldtimers allowed new legislators to participate in ceremonial rituals but shared little in the way of decisions on policy. Population was a minor factor in the formulas that sent revenues from gasoline taxes, racetracks, and other sources back to the counties. There were 38 senators, and no county had more than one. The small counties consistently got the best cut of the hog.

"When a senator represented a county with 2,500 people, and was elected by maybe as little as 400 of those people, he tended to be extremely conservative and took care of getting jobs for the few," explained Allen Morris, the venerable clerk of the Florida House, an author and former newsman who was interviewed for V. O. Key's book in 1948. "He couldn't see paying schoolteachers a great deal because the local teacher was the wife of the mailman or the butcher, so their combined salaries, of which he would be aware, would be quite large. And he knew that she wasn't going to move away because of the salary. She was caught up in it. So they represented their constituency as they saw it, and the constituency was happy with it. They didn't care what the metropolitan newspapers said about them. The *Tribune* had possibly a circulation of five in that senator's district. They probably didn't sell a single copy in the county of the president of the Senate. The only way that he ever knew what the paper said about him was that somebody sent him a clipping." [2]

There were younger men, independent and ambitious, who had come out of World War II and gone to college and wanted to get things moving, but they were blocked. Meanwhile, people were flooding into the state, making Florida a melting pot for the southeastern half of the United States. They brought new views and political attitudes.

STATE OF THE STATE

In every decade since 1900, the percentage increase in Florida's population has never been less than double that of the nation. The rapid influx of population makes Florida different from the rest of the South.

2. Interview with Allen Morris, May 16, 1974.

The sense of place, kinship, tradition, and ties to the land are lacking outside the Panhandle, the northern strip of Florida that extends down from southern Georgia and Alabama and shares their political and social traditions. The Panhandle remains strongly Democratic and racially conservative, with a populist tradition, much like eastern North Carolina, but with some liberal bastions in university communities. The Panhandle gave strong support to liberal Claude Pepper in his losing Senate race in 1950 and voted overwhelmingly for George Wallace in 1968 for president and in 1972 in the state's presidential primary. The area least affected by inmigration, it served as the center for the Pork Choppers.

Great urban areas developed in Dade (Miami), Broward (Fort Lauderdale), Pinellas (St. Petersburg), and Hillsborough (Tampa) counties; but the Pork Choppers weren't really aware of them or their problems because of the counties they represented. In Jefferson, Liberty, and Gadsden Counties, there was no growth. By 1960, less than 15 percent of the population could elect a majority in either house of the legislature.

Of the nearly 3 million migrants to Florida between 1950 and 1970, 94 percent have located in the southern half of the state, below the "frostproof" line that runs east-west roughly through Ocala.[3] Despite a state population of 6.8 million in 1970, Florida had no city with a population as large as 550,000. Florida's population is concentrated in a vast suburbia of trailer parks, modest residential developments and apartments, and high-rise condominiums and exclusive subdivisions. The result has been to make Florida unlike any other Southern state politically. The "uncrystallized social structure" of Florida, which is less fixed than other southern states by family or community attachments, was summarized by Key:

> In politics loyalties have not been built up, traditional habits of action with respect to local personages, leaders, parties, and issues have not been acquired. Social Structure, to use a phrase of perhaps ambiguous meaning, has not taken on definite form in the sense of well-recognized and obeyed centers of political leadership and of power. Flux, fluidity, uncertainty in human relations are the rule. Whether it can be proved, there is plausibly a relation between a diverse, recently transplanted population and mutable politics.[4]

Barely a third of Florida's total population are natives of the state, and a routine item in biographical sketches in the legislative manual is the year in which the legislator moved to Florida.

3. *Economic Report of the Governor* (Tallahassee, 1974), p. 30.
4. V. O. Key, *Southern Politics in State and Nation* (New York: Knopf/Vintage Books, 1949), p. 86.

GOVERNMENTAL REFORM

The buildup of urban counties whose problems went unnoticed by state government built pressure that brought political upheaval after "one man, one vote" reapportionment in 1967. Government in Florida was transformed almost overnight into a system far ahead of any other in the South in terms of its responsiveness to specific issues and its institutional ability to respond.

Several things happened simultaneously in the late 1960s. Reapportionment shifted control of the legislature to the long-ignored urban areas and at the same time made possible the entry of a significant Republican minority into the legislature. Republican Governor Claude Kirk's flamboyance and unpredictability further unsettled the status quo, forcing the legislature to assume a stronger leadership role. An aggressive press operating under Florida's "government in the sunshine" law brought openness and accountability to government and served as a catalyst for reform. Vigorous young leaders, many of them trained in Florida Blue Key at the University of Florida, entered the legislature.

Finally, after decades of stagnation, the legislature began to grapple with the problems of a growing state. It produced a new constitution, restructured state government, reformed taxes, and passed innovative laws such as no-fault divorce and no-fault insurance. The 1971 report of the Citizens Conference on State Legislatures, *The Sometimes Governments,* ranked the Florida legislature fourth nationally, the only southern state ranked in the top 25. It ranked first in the nation in independence —a result of excellent staffing, ready access to its work by the press and public, the availability of information resources, and a public record of committee deliberations and actions, including roll-call votes. A well-staffed auditing bureau provides the means for oversight of state agencies.

A computer provides instant information on the status of every bill. Legislative facilities in the modernistic new state capitol will include a closed-circuit television network in the senate that will allow each member to examine amendments offered on the floor on pending legislation.

Although political theorists tend to oppose rotating leadership in the legislature, the system in Florida produced an outstanding series of leaders in the reform era. The House speaker and Senate president are all-powerful for their two years. They appoint all committees and name their chairmen. The rotation system allows any really bright and capable new member to aspire to a leadership position in a few years and helps attract such people to run. The concentration of power in the presiding officers is such that they could quickly become entrenched dictators if the rotation tradition were removed.

After he took office in 1975, Speaker Don Tucker proposed an end to the rotating system, but with a provision that one-third of the House membership could petition for election by secret ballot of a new speaker. If approved, the change would allow Tucker to serve a second term and provide a base for a possible race for governor in 1978.

Citizen politics in Florida has developed into a highly competitive amateur sport, with a high turnover of concerned and talented young people. During the reform period, the legislature was marked by the lack of partisanship and lack of ideology in grappling with issues.

Political observers in the state express concern whether the leadership will continue to renew itself. Even at $12,000 annual salaries, among the highest in the South, the legislature is losing the leadership that transformed the state; many legislators are lawyers of sufficient ability to easily make $75,000 or more in private practice. The Citizens Conference recommended legislative salaries in the $20,000–30,000 range for Florida because of the state's size and the growing complexity of its problems.

Many of the leaders dropping out of active politics in the state talk about the pressure and demands, and of being "burned out" after six or eight years. "We've become so expert and so staffed and so computerized that we have taken on more of a load than the human equation can stand," said Mallory Horne during his last year as president of the state Senate, after a 20-year legislative career. "The whole idea is to deliberate, and the atmosphere is not good for that. Then, you take the other thing, where 15 or 20 percent do 90 percent of the work, and you are really killing those guys. They are walking around glassy-eyed the last three weeks of a session. They really look sick." [5]

Horne was an unsuccessful candidate for the U.S. Senate in 1974, one of four Democratic candidates who had served in the Florida Senate, a body whose graduates include Governor Reubin Askew and U.S. Senators Lawton Chiles and Richard Stone.

A novel feature of state government in Florida is the elected cabinet. Although the new constitution and executive reorganization reduced the cabinet's authority, each of the six elected officials—secretary of state, attorney general, comptroller, treasurer, commissioner of agriculture, and commissioner of education—has a major department to administer. In addition, the cabinet sits with the governor to oversee half a dozen major departments.

Until the new constitution provided a second term for the governor, the members of the cabinet usually ran for and won reelection and exercised much of the real power in Florida.

The scandal-free tradition of the cabinet was upset in 1973 and 1974 with press disclosures of questionable practices by three cabinet members that resulted in apparent personal gain from the use of their posi-

5. Interview with Mallory Horne, May 21, 1974.

tions. One resigned while under investigation, another was defeated for reelection, and a third resigned after he was indicted and subsequently impeached by the House. All three got into trouble over matters involving their departments, not general cabinet affairs.

Critics of the cabinet system contend it weakens a governor's ability to provide executive leadership, but defenders argue that the system prevents concentration of too much power in one office, provides for a more deliberative decision-making process, spreads responsibility, and forces into the open decisions on such matters as state land purchases and sales.

There is national significance in the renaissance of state government in Florida. Both in its efficiency and openness, it could serve as a model for government at the state and federal level. Senators Chiles and Stone are leading advocates in Washington for complete openness on non-security matters. No state matches Florida in experience with openness in government, and political leaders there understand that secrecy breeds suspicion and that public confidence derives from trust. The sunshine law is considered by Governor Askew to have had "the single biggest good effect upon government since I have been in politics." [6]

The Florida sunshine law was the first to stipulate that all meetings of public officials must be open, with penalties for violations. Decisions made at closed meetings are illegal. When city officials in St. Petersburg negotiated in executive session with union officials to end a garbage collectors' strike, a court held the contract invalid. Subsequent negotiations were conducted with the press present. Both sides got daily feedback. Impossible demands were dropped, and a settlement was quickly reached that drew support both from the public and the striking workers.

No state in the South and perhaps in the nation can match the capitol press corps in Tallahassee. There are more than 26 full-time journalists assigned, and collectively they are aggressive, talented, and dedicated. The *St. Petersburg Times*, which devotes several pages of coverage a day when the legislature is in session, sends copies to each member that are delivered before breakfast. Its traditional in-depth reporting and investigative coverage of state government is a model of excellence that may be unmatched in the country.

Although the larger *Miami Herald* maintains an outstanding bureau in Tallahassee and participates with the *St. Petersburg Times* in a joint news service, the *Herald* did not until the mid-1970s devote comparable space to legislative news and provide front-page display. Other newspapers and the wire services also put more manpower into coverage of state government in Florida than comparable media in other states. This not only results in a better-informed public but also tends to stimulate

6. Interview with Reubin Askew, July 8, 1974.

action by the legislature. A legislator with a new idea knows publicity is available.

Even after the sunshine law was passed, the Florida Senate continued its practice of executive sessions until four reporters refused to leave one day and had to be physically removed. The episode was so unsettling to the Senate that it has not met in secret since, despite constitutional authority to do so.

Former Representative Marshall Harris of Miami, a legislative reformer, believes the press in Tallahassee is the key to setting ethical standards. "Our press is excellent," he said, "They are a good investigating press corps, and they just rip the hell out of anybody that gets out of line. . . . That's all you really need, basically, to keep a legislature honest, is a good press corps and a couple of people who set an example within the legislature. That will raise the tone of your legislature faster than any law you pass." [7]

In addition to the sunshine law, Florida pioneered in its "Who Gave It—Who Got It" law on campaign contributions. Florida statutes now set stiff ethical standards, stipulate requirements for financial disclosure by public officials and candidates, and limit campaign spending. The result is that Florida, although second only to Texas in size and population among southern states, has perhaps the least expensive political campaigns of any state in the South.

The 1970 law on campaign expenditures limits any candidate for governor or U.S. senator to $350,000 in the primaries and a like amount in the general election. For other statewide officials, the limit in each category is $250,000. The limit is $75,000 in each category for the U.S. House, and $25,000 for legislative, county, and city offices. No individual may give more than $3,000 for statewide, $2,000 for congressional, or $1,000 for local races.

The "Who Gave It—Who Got It" campaign finance law dates back to a 1951 crusade by the *St. Petersburg Times*. Interest in the law began after the 1950 Senate primary between George Smathers and Claude Pepper, when word spread they had each spent far more than the $100,000 they claimed. Then came the Kefauver Crime Committee hearings and the revelation that three men had met in a Jacksonville hotel room to split the $450,000 cost of the 1948 gubernatorial campaign of Fuller Warren. One was W. H. Johnston, a racetrack operator with connections to the Al Capone mob; the second was C. V. Griffin, one of Florida's most prosperous citrus growers (an industry that looks to state government for favorable treatment); and the third was multimillionaire Louis E. Wolfson, who would later serve nine months in jail for a stock registration violation. [8]

7. Interview with Marshall Harris, May 17, 1974.
8. Neal Peirce, *The Deep South States of America* (New York: W. W. Norton, 1974), p. 459.

The *St. Petersburg Times* has not been alone in its vigilance on campaign spending. In 1972, Tallahassee Bureau Chief William Mansfield of the *Miami Herald* directed a six-month effort to analyze and codify information in campaign contributions to each legislator. The result was a series of articles concluding that at least $1 of every $2 collected came from lobbyists or special interest groups and that the law was "so riddled with loopholes and so lacking in enforcement . . . that it often punishes the honest, who properly report, while rewarding the dishonest, who do not."[9] Laws setting up enforcement machinery passed the legislature after publication of the series.

The *Herald* bureau broke further new ground in legislative reporting near the end of the 1973 session when it reported the status of several items of special interest legislation, together with voting records of key legislative committees and the amounts each committee member received in campaign contributions from the affected industry. The following story by Bruce Giles provides an example:

> Shipping lines would be exempt from nearly $1.5 million in sales taxes they now pay on ship repairs under a bill pending in the Senate. . . .
> Sen. Bruce Smathers (D., Jacksonville), one of the sponsors of the proposal, received at least $1,240 from one ship repair facility, Jacksonville Shipyards. Senate President Mallory Horne received $1,000 in campaign contributions from the same company.
> Shipping interests contributed at least $2,265 to the 11 Ways and Means Committee members who voted for the measure. The four who voted against it received none.
> Members voting for the measure and their shipping contributions include: W. D. Childers (D., Pensacola), $100; William Gillespie (D., New Smyrna Beach), none; Warren Henderson (R., Sarasota), none; David Lane (R., Fort Lauderdale), $100; Julian Lane (D., Tampa), $525; Ken Plante (R., Oviedo), none; Ralph Poston (D., Miami), $100; Smathers, $1,240; Russel Sykes (R., West Palm Beach), none; Alan Trask (D., Fort Meade), $100; John Ware (R., St. Petersburg), $100.[10]

The earlier articles provided a rare public look into who pays the tab for campaign financing and revealed that 449 candidates for the 160-member legislature received $3.8 million (an average of about $8,500 apiece) for the 1972 primary and general election campaigns. A similar study after the 1974 elections disclosed even more lobbyist money, but far fewer reporting violations.

Senator Dempsey Barron, the conservative and able dean of the Florida Senate whose election as Senate president in 1975 prompted speculation about a possible return of the Pork Chop days, candidly discussed his view of the need for lawmakers to accept campaign contributions

9. William Mansfield and Bruce Giles, *Miami Herald*, Reprint Section (1973), p. 1.

10. Bruce Giles, "Now's the Time Special Interests, Lobbyists Make Their Move," *Miami Herald*, May 29, 1973, p. 15-A.

from lobbyists and special interests: "The first time I ran for office—it seems like 100 years ago, but it was really only 16—somebody sent me some money I didn't like. It was money I felt had some interests attached to it. So I returned it. I was very innocent and unknowledgeable about the true world of politics. But I came over to Tallahassee, young and idealistic, and I found out something, which is: No matter how idealistic you are, you can't do anything unless you're here. And that takes money." [11]

Florida already has a form of public subsidy for political parties. The state absorbs the cost of party primaries but collects filing fees from candidates which then are passed on to the candidate's party. Democrats get more money because they field more candidates, and the filing fees help pay the cost of a well-staffed state headquarters in Tallahassee. The Republicans, who were first to develop a headquarters and staff that provide research and other assistance to candidates at all levels, traditionally refund the filing fee to the candidate for campaign expenses. Membership dues and fundraising dinners pay their party costs. Not until Askew became governor did the Democrats in Florida take on the semblance of an organized political party.

PROFILE OF THE VOTER

In contrast with the traditional mountain Republicans who provided the core strength for party growth in Virginia, North Carolina, and Tennessee, the Republican base in Florida came from northern migrants who brought their Republicanism with them. But although Republican core strength derives from the migrants, it is a mistake to assume they are virtually all northern or overwhelmingly Republican. The survey for the Comparative State Elections Project showed that slightly more than a third of the Florida migrants came from other southern states. Most of them were younger people from neighboring Alabama and Georgia who were looking for economic opportunity rather than retirement in the sunshine. Between 1965 and 1970, their average age was 25.4 years, nine years younger than migrants from states that do not border on Florida. The southern migrants reflect their Democratic heritage, and 59 percent identified themselves as Democrats ("strong" or "not very strong"), compared with only 6 percent Republican identification.

Among the northern migrants, 37 percent identified themselves as Republicans and 31 percent as Democrats. Of those who grew up in

11. *Miami Herald*, Reprint Section, p. 2.

Florida, 63 percent identified as Democrats, 10 percent as Republicans, and the remainder as independents. Of the total Florida sample, 22 percent identified as Republicans and 49 percent as Democrats, almost identical to the total sample for the border South.[12]

Among voters over 65, there was 41 percent Republican identification and 42 percent Democratic, a reflection of the higher average age of northern migrants. Between 1965 and 1970, 40.2 percent of the net migration into Florida came from people 60 years of age or older. Migration is a two-way street, and although those leaving the state were fewer, they were also younger. The average age of the 641,000 out-migrants between 1965 and 1970 was 25.5, compared with 33 for the 1,215,000 inmigrants.[13]

Although newcomers continue to flow into the state (the rate of annual growth for the first four years of the 1970s was 4.8 percent, compared with 3.7 percent in the 1960s [14]), the roots of many of the migrants are deep enough to permit a developing awareness of political issues. Those issues at the state level center around growth and such growth-related problems as transportation, pollution, and protection and conservation of the environment.

A 1974 statewide survey concluded in regard to attitudes toward growth and development, "The difference in the way of thinking about this broad issue today from 10 years ago is that a majority of voters are presently willing to place some legal restrictions on growth and development. Three fourths of the voters say they would be willing to have government buy land along the Florida coast to preserve it from development. Three-fourths of the voters say they would be willing to and limit the actual number of people who move in." [15]

Two-thirds agreed that "growth and development here in Florida have hurt much of our environment beyond repair." Sixty percent felt that *more* state money should be spent on environment and conservation programs. The same survey also showed a desire for more attention to social programs, including such items as aid to the elderly and health care, as well as a general desire for better human relations.

The major concerns about overdevelopment, transportation, and pollution set Florida apart from the other southern states. Because there appear to be no quick solutions, these concerns are likely to remain major issues for some time in Florida politics.

Political pollster Patrick Caddell, president of Cambridge Survey Research, is a native of Florida and has polled extensively in his home

12. *Presidential Choices in the Nation and the States, 1968,* Institute for Research in Social Science, University of North Carolina at Chapel Hill, 1973, pp. 334–335.

13. *Economic Report of the Governor,* p. 85.

14. Ibid., p. 28.

15. William R. Hamilton and Associates, unpublished survey.

state. Caddell reports that the Florida voter "is concerned with the future and his children who must live in it. More often than not he would describe himself as a conservative even while supporting mostly progressive programs. He is humane in a tough sort of way. Basically well-motivated, the Florida elector is by no way close-minded. Even on the racial problem there has been a significant movement. His acceptance of racial integration and his support of basic civil rights are admirable efforts at change." [16]

REPUBLICANS

Modern Republican development in Florida began after World War II, and there was steady growth until the party hit a peak in the late 1960s. The real builder of the Republican Party was William C. Cramer. In 1950, two years after graduation from Harvard Law School, Cramer took over the party structure in Pinellas County, built an organization that elected Republicans to a majority of local offices in the St. Petersburg area, unsuccessfully ran for Congress in 1952, and two years later became the first Republican congressman from Florida since 1875. He remained a major figure in state party development and strategy and became national committeeman.

As early as 1948, Thomas Dewey had carried Pinellas (St. Petersburg), Sarasota, Palm Beach, Broward (Fort Lauderdale), and Orange (Orlando) counties and received a third of the statewide vote. Dixiecrat Strom Thurmond had received another 16 percent, and it was clear that Florida voters were ready to revolt against the Democratic Party at the presidential level.

From 1952 to 1972, presidential Republicanism became well established in Florida. Core Republican strength showed up in what Professor Manning Dauer has described as an urban horseshoe, with one leg beginning at Fort Lauderdale and Palm Beach, running up the east coast to Daytona Beach, then inland to Orlando and curving to St. Petersburg on the west coast and descending to Fort Meyers and Naples. The party developed a solid political organization in those areas. Partly as a result, Dwight Eisenhower carried the state twice and Richard Nixon three times for the Republicans. Only Barry Goldwater in 1964, who appeared to threaten Social Security, was rejected.

In 1966 and 1968, Republicans won the governor's office and a U.S. Senate seat. The standard explanation was that the Democrats had

16. Interview with Patrick Caddell, February 12, 1975.

nominated candidates who were too liberal, Miami Mayor Robert King High for governor in 1966 and former Governor Leroy Collins for senator in 1968. Collins was a racial moderate and progressive governor during six years of a tense transitional period; he had later served as President Johnson's community relations director and had negotiated with Martin Luther King, Jr. during the Selma crisis.

Republican Claude Kirk, an insurance executive who helped lead a "Democrats for Nixon" move in 1960 and ran unsuccessfully for the Senate in 1964 on the GOP ticket, was elected governor. Congressman Ed Gurney, a handsome New England native with a rigidly conservative voting record, went to the Senate after dubbing Collins "liberal Leroy." Gurney's supporters distributed pictures of Collins walking beside King at Selma.

The Kirk years represented a period of dynamic change. He entered office the same year that reapportionment resulted in a jump in Republican legislators from 12 to 59. It was a period in which Republican minority leader Don Reed, an able and enlightened conservative, worked closely with progressive Democratic liberals such as House Speaker Richard Pettigrew of Miami to push through reforms that modernized both the procedure and substance of the legislative process. "The one thing we were always able to do was, especially when he was speaker and when we were involved in reorganization, if there was an issue that we just couldn't resolve, we would just take it out on the floor and whoever won, won," Reed explained.[17]

Kirk helped create a climate for change in much the same way that Winthrop Rockefeller did in Arkansas. He fought with the elected cabinet and created an exciting atmosphere with his politics of confrontation, flow of creative ideas, and personal flamboyance. He fought to get a new constitution and brought fresh faces into state government, many of them appointments of high quality.

Although Kirk shattered the traditional way of doing things, he eventually made enough political blunders and engaged in sufficient personal excesses and displays of arrogance that in the end he became "a man whose flamboyance seemed to have degenerated into assininity."[18] He is remembered for lavish parties at the governor's mansion, for jetting around the country at state Republican Party expense, and for hiring a Madison Avenue firm with state funds to promote himself for the 1968 vice-presidential nomination. When teachers went on strike, he went on a visit to Disneyland. He vetoed a needed legislative pay increase after committing his support to it, then tried to make political capital out of the veto.

17. Interview with Don Reed, May 23, 1974.
18. Michael Barone, Grant Ujifusa, and Douglas Matthews, *The Almanac of American Politics—1976* (New York: E. P. Dutton, 1975), p. 160.

When the state Republican Party quit paying his bills, he put part of his staff to work on lavish fundraising. Neal Peirce relates how a 1969 state audit of the governor's office disclosed controversial expenditures, including overpayments for travel and spending without statutory authority for flowers, credit cards, Christmas cards, and food. Some $1–3 million in "campaign funds" were collected by Kirk in his first three years in office. A court forced disclosure of official records of a $500-a-year "Governor's Club," which showed receipts of $420,680 between April 1968 and January 1970. The 233 contributors to the fund included 47 who received Kirk appointments to state boards, committees, and commissions, 18 who were liquor licensees, 31 architect-engineers (most with state contracts), and 20 construction contractors eligible for state road projects.[19]

When the party quit paying to promote his vice-presidential ambitions, Kirk developed a "them against us" form of political paranoia. Reed, who believes that Kirk "probably did more for the state of Florida, knowingly or unknowingly, than any governor has ever done," recalled a visit to the governor's mansion and Kirk drawing his finger across the carpet on the floor and "telling me I was either with him or with Murfin [the competent Republican State Chairman Bill Murfin], and if I was with Murfin, I was obviously against him . . . He felt that he was king and that was that."[20] Reed responded with a few expletives and stalked out.

But the act that destroyed Kirk's public standing beyond repair was his takeover of the Manatee school system in 1970 in the face of court-ordered school desegregation that involved busing. Kirk suspended the school board, took over the running of the schools, and actually closed them. Then he went to Washington and postured about states' rights. His defiance ended quickly when a federal judge ordered a contempt citation and threatened the governor with a $10,000-a-day fine, and Kirk's foolishness was fully exposed.

Although Republicans clearly have established a challenging position in Florida and have become dominant in presidential elections since 1950, Tables 6–1 and 6–2 suggest Republican growth reached a plateau in the late 1960s. Although the Republican percentage of total registration has climbed sharply, there has been no weakening of Democratic numerical superiority. In the legislature, Republicans have been unable to move beyond the 35 percent they achieved in 1967.

---

19. Peirce, *Deep South States,* pp. 449–450.
20. Interview with Don Reed, May 23, 1974.

TABLE 6–1

Registration of Republicans and Democrats, 1960–1974

	DEMOCRATS			REPUBLICANS			OTHER
	TOTAL	WHITE	BLACK	TOTAL	WHITE	BLACK	TOTAL
1960	1,656,023	1,488,557 (89.9%)	167,466 (10.1%)	338,340	322,726 (95.4%)	15,614 (4.6%)	22,223
1968	2,090,787	1,796,138 (85.9%)	294,649 (14.1%)	619,062	605,619 (97.8%)	13,443 (2.2%)	55,467
1974	2,438,580	2,095,439 (85.0%)	343,141 (14.1%)	1,035,510	1,023,096 (98.8%)	12,414 (1.2%)	147,166

	TOTAL REGISTRATION	DEMOCRATS	REPUBLICANS	OTHER	DEMOCRATIC MAJORITY *
1960	2,016,903	1,656,340 (82.1%)	338,340 (16.8%)	22,223 (1.2%)	1,318,000
1968	2,765,316	2,090,787 (75.6%)	619,062 (22.4%)	55,467 (2.2%)	1,471,725
1974	3,621,256	2,438,580 (67.3%)	1,035,510 (28.6%)	147,166 (4.1%)	1,415,484

* Difference between number of registered Democrats and registered Republicans.
Source: Division of Elections, Department of State, Tallahassee, Fla.

TWO-PARTY POLITICS

The Kirk victory in 1966 over Robert King High represented a Republican breakthrough, but in reality it was a personal triumph based on a brilliant campaign developed for Kirk, aided by High's blunders.[21]

In 1964, Florida Democrats had foreseen the possibility that a Republican gubernatorial candidate might ride in on a presidential candidate's coattails and had succeeded in changing to off-year elections. Incumbent Governor Haydon Burns served a two-year term, then lost in 1966 in a primary runoff in which High projected himself as the champion of underdogs running against the special interests. The second primary was bitter, with Burns's integrity impugned and High branded a racial liberal. Governor Burns and his supporters moved behind Kirk, supplying money and manpower. Kirk already had a professional consultant, who put together the first modern media campaign in Florida. Nevertheless, a late summer poll showed High clearly ahead.

21. Patrick H. Caddell, *Florida Politics: The Myth and the Reality*, senior honors thesis, Harvard University, May 1969. This study makes a thorough analysis of the 1966 and 1968 elections.

TABLE 6–2

Republicans and Democrats in the Florida Legislature

YEAR	CHAMBER	DEMOCRATS	REPUBLICANS	REPUBLICAN PERCENTAGES	
1965	Senate	42	2	5	
	House	102	10	9	7.7
1967	Senate	28	20	42	
	House	80	39	33	35.3
1969	Senate	32	16	33	
	House	78	41	35	34.2
1971	Senate	32	16	33	
	House	81	38	32	32.3
1973	Senate	25	14	36	
	House	77	43	36	35.8
1975	Senate	27	12	31	
	House	86	34	28	28.9

* Percentages of seats held by major parties.
Source: Clerk of the House of Representatives, Tallahassee, Fla.

Having fought the professional politicians in the primary, High wooed the "courthouse gangs" and courted the special interests in the general election. "The hero of the 'little man' was suddenly exposed as a typical politician, and High suffered for it." [22] Instead of following his campaign manager's advice to concentrate in the 11 large urban counties that comprise 75 percent of the population—his area of strength—High instead opted for the rural areas, where he had done poorly in the primary. His campaign manager withdrew, and his organization crumbled.

The race issue was strongest in the rural areas. High made no inroads there with his pro–civil rights record, but Kirk took full advantage of the opportunity left by High's neglect of the urban areas. Kirk won with 53 percent of the vote, while Republican candidates for attorney general and treasurer were overwhelmed. However, Kirk's victory made people think in terms of a two-party system, and the Republican Party came to life. A new reapportionment ordered after Kirk took office gave Republicans enough seats in the legislature to sustain a veto.

When Kirk's popularity began to dive, Murfin led forces in the Republican Party that routed the governor in a battle for control of the party organization. Party people were trained, candidate seminars were held, and voter registration drives were conducted—all in preparation for 1968. Meanwhile, the Democrats did little or nothing.

Leroy Collins, who had served six years as governor (1954–1960), was attempting a political comeback in the 1968 race for the U.S. Senate. Until Askew, Collins was the only modern Florida governor to receive out-of-state recognition for ability and leadership qualities. Although his efforts were unsuccessful, he had attempted as governor to reapportion

22. Ibid., p. 27.

the legislature. His deep commitment to racial justice provided Florida with unusual leadership during the early years of the civil rights movement, but concern with racial issues created an emotional atmosphere in the legislature that stymied many of his reform efforts. Collins later accepted a request from President Lyndon Johnson to head the Community Relations Service, a conciliation agency created under the 1964 Civil Rights Act. At one point, as on-the-scene mediator during the civil rights march at Selma in 1965, Collins walked beside Martin Luther King, Jr., seeking his reaction to a tactical proposal from the Alabama governor's office. In a photograph he appeared to be marching *with* King, and the photo was used against him in rural areas during the 1968 Senate race.

The polls had shown Collins to be quite popular, but he failed to get a majority in the first primary. He won the runoff by only 3,000 votes against Attorney General Earl Faircloth, who used Collins's racial liberalism against him. Observers concluded that Collins lacked the powerful popular support the polls had shown, but Caddell's later analysis demonstrated that a key factor in the primary was the low turnout among Collins supporters. While 58 percent of the registered Democrats had turned out in the 1966 primary, the 1968 race was less exciting and attracted only 45 percent. But the dropoff was greatest where Collins was strongest, in the urban areas of peninsular Florida. The Panhandle, where Collins was disliked because of his racial moderation in the 1950s and 1960s, contributed more than 40 percent of the total vote in 1968, compared with only 31 percent in 1966. Dade County voted 66 percent for Collins, but turnout there dropped from 53 percent in 1966 to 32 percent. The figures were similar in other urban areas where Collins was strong, and Caddell projected that Collins would have received 60 percent of the vote had there been no falloff or had the falloff been evenly distributed. Some analysts attribute the falloff in the Collins strongholds to his failure to meet the racial smears head on; that is, by reacting defensively instead of saying he favored racial justice and was proud of it, Collins failed to energize his traditional supporters.

Most political writers assumed at the time that Collins was a sure loser in the general election. Sources of funds dried up, and little help was available from Democratic officeholders. Yet as late as September, Collins held a clear lead over Edward Gurney in private polls. But like Kirk, Gurney also brought in a skilled professional campaign manager. Striking billboards showed the handsome Gurney in a turned-up raincoat, with such slogans as "It's time for law and order." Dramatic 30-second and one-minute TV spots began to saturate the state in late September. One opened with an unkempt, obvious criminal type going before a judge, who lets him off some heinous criminal charge on a legal technicality. The concerned visage of Gurney appeared, and in an indignant tone he said, "It's time to treat criminals like criminals."

While the ultraconservative Gurney was projecting a dynamic image as a fighter, a man of action, an effective leader, Collins was running 30-minute televised documentaries that people were not watching. Collins fell 13 points in less than two months, and Gurney won a landslide 56 percent victory. A post-election survey revealed that television was the major factor in voters switching to Gurney. For the most part, people voted for Gurney because they liked the image he presented, an image that wasn't that of a conservative, but rather of a progressive defender of the common man. It was a new use of media in Florida, and it was devastatingly effective.

Republicans ran stronger at all levels in 1968, but Caddell's post-election survey disclosed that 58 percent of the voters still leaned toward or expressed a preference for the Democratic Party, compared with 29 percent Republican and 13 percent independent. But in terms of voting behavior below the presidential level, the results were 41 percent Democratic, 34 percent Republican, and 25 percent independent (these split their ballots about equally on state Supreme Court and other races).

By this time, Kirk was receiving a negative rating on performance, but Caddell's poll showed a 54 percent favorable rating for the Republican Party, compared with a disastrous 25 percent for the Democrats. The most common expressions about the Democratic Party were: "It's old," "Hasn't changed," "Got us into this mess," "Old and dying," "Corrupt," "Unresponsive," "Old leaders," and "Not vigorous." In contrast, the Republican Party drew such responses as: "It's young," "It's growing," "Has good people," "Trying to do something good." What emerged was a picture of a Democratic-oriented electorate in rebellion against an old, stagnant party dominated by tired politicians. In contrast, the Republicans emerged as young, dynamic, and progressive.[23]

After the elections of Kirk and Gurney, it became something of an article of faith that "Florida is basically a conservative state" or, as Kirk's campaign manager added, "basically a Republican conservative state."

When Caddell's postelection survey probed issues, it found Florida voters anything but "conservative." For example, 64 percent favored more federal aid to education and another 23 percent favored the same level. Seventy-nine percent supported programs of slum clearance and urban renewal, and 83 percent supported medicare. Forty-six percent of whites supported progress made in racial integration, and 57 percent of whites favored more or the same level of civil rights programs. The Job Corps received 84 percent approval.

"As long as the electorate perceives the Democratic Party as old, corrupt and complacent, then it will not hesitate to support Republican

23. Ibid., pp. 19–54.

candidates," Caddell concluded. "However, the potential support appears great for a revigorated [Democratic] Party representing a progressive Democracy." [24]

In 1970, veteran U.S. Senator Spessard Holland retired, and Representative Cramer, the real "Mr. Republican" in Florida, announced for the seat. But Kirk and Gurney viewed Cramer as a rival for party supremacy, and they led efforts to persuade U.S. Appeals Court Judge G. Harrold Carswell to announce for the seat after Carswell's nomination for the U.S. Supreme Court had been rejected. The result was a divisive and bitter Republican primary, with Cramer the winner over the politically inept Carswell.

Meanwhile, the Democrats were finally rejecting the old guard. Two obscure but progressive state senators, 42-year-old Reubin Askew and 40-year-old Lawton Chiles, emerged as winners in the primary for governor and senator respectively.

Askew was a state senator from Pensacola with 12 years in the legislature; he was known in Tallahassee "as the kind of guy who would work 14 hours a day on complex issues such as tax legislation." One veteran journalist went to him and urged him not to run, since he had "no chance" of winning and was too valuable in the Senate. But "Reubin Who?" campaigned for tax reform and a tax on corporate income, and he made a complete public financial disclosure and returned campaign contributions he felt were tied too closely to special interests. A nondrinking, nonsmoking Presbyterian elder who takes religion and government seriously, Askew would ask, "Isn't it time for some seriousness in the governor's office?"

Chiles, who had Senator Holland's support, undertook a 10,000-mile walking tour of the state, a novel gimmick that attracted widespread coverage and convinced voters that he "cared." One night in Miami, a television commentator contrasted a rally for Chiles at a Colonel Sanders fried chicken picnic with a swank black-tie, $1,000-a-plate dinner for Cramer. The voters got the message.

The two Democrats won decisively, Askew with 57 percent of the vote against Kirk and Chiles with 54 percent (a 130,000-vote margin) over Cramer. It was an election that brought renewal to the Democratic Party, which under Askew's direction developed a professional staff that worked on party organization, candidate recruitment, and some semblance of party unity, which was further enhanced when the new state constitution established the post of lieutenant governor and provided that candidates for governor and lieutenant governor run as a ticket, both in the primary and the general election. This was a new concept for the South, and it helps ensure continuity of party and policy in the event of succession.

24. Ibid., p. 60.

When Askew's first lieutenant governor, Tom Adams, was censored by the Senate because he used the services of the state employees for personal benefit, Askew stripped him of his duties as head of the Department of Commerce. For his second term running mate, Askew chose state Sen. Jim Williams, a man whose strength was characterized by Mallory Horne: "You could put a whole governor and the cabinet and every newspaper in the state on him and he'd get up to fight tomorrow. He's like a burrowing nematode; you might slow him down, but you are not going to stop him." Askew appointed Williams head of the Department of Administration, which handles budget, planning and personnel.

Although most statewide Democratic candidates still develop their own campaign organizations, Key's description of Florida as "every man for himself" has been modified. Askew and Chiles reinforced each other in 1970 and coordinated their separate campaigns. The development of party organization structures provide more cohesion than ever before in Florida. And in 1974, there was at least the appearance of unity among the Democrats.

Richard Stone, the first Jewish U.S. senator from the South, was a surprise winner in 1974. He had been elected to the Cabinet as Secretary of State in 1970. A rather bland political figure, Stone barely made the Democratic runoff against central Florida Representative Bill Gunter, the favorite, with Stone edging out fellow Dade Countian Richard Pettigrew. But Gunter's forces relaxed, and there was a falloff that ranged from 15 to 40 percent in central Florida. Stone campaigned vigorously and effectively in the Panhandle, playing his harmonica. Dade County turned out strong, and Stone scored an upset.

The incumbent, Senator Gurney, had fallen on hard times. He retired in the face of Federal and state grand jury investigations involving $300,000 in unreported campaign funds and alleged kickbacks for federal housing contracts in connection with fundraising in his behalf. A businessman, Jack Eckerd, defeated state Public Utilities Commissioner Paula Hawkins in the primary, and many Republicans contend that he would have retained Gurney's Senate seat for the GOP had not third-party candidate John Grady, a convincingly articulate physician who is a member of the John Birch Society, received 15 percent of the vote, to 44 percent for Stone and 41 percent for Eckerd.

Thus, by 1975 the Democrats once again held the governorship and both Senate seats. Before intra-party strife set in, the Republicans had shown what they could do: in Broward County (Fort Lauderdale), Republicans in the late 1960s organized the precincts, knocked on doors, recruited candidates and helped raise money for them, and took over virtually every office in the courthouse and won the congressional seat. They also forced Democrats to organize a genuine political party, which has begun to make the county competitive again. But Broward is an exception, and weak party organization tends to remain the rule for Republicans in Florida. The Republicans still operate on the premise that Florida is a "conservative" state.

As for the Democrats, they continue to reflect a heritage of no-party politics. "Our party vestiges were just like an old soldier group," said Lawton Chiles, "They went to meetings and fought, they never knocked on a door, they never passed out a piece of literature, they never solicited a vote. It was just a thing that you put on your uniform and went out and fought among each other." [25]

THE ASKEW ERA

Over the last decade, most southern governors have seethed privately over George Wallace, but few have dared to cross him in public. One exception was the late Winthrop Rockefeller, who at the 1968 Southern Governors Conference at Charleston called Wallace a "demagogue." Wallace, who just happened to be in Charleston revving up his presidential campaign, came by the Francis Marion Hotel to pay his respects. He told the press he just couldn't understand Governor Rockefeller. "Our folks always bought plenty of kerosene from his folks."

Of all the political figures in the South today, Reubin Askew stands in sharpest contrast with Wallace. Both basically appeal to the same alienated voter, Wallace with the politics of fear and Askew with the politics of trust. For that reason, as well as for his dominance of Florida state government, it is worthwhile to take a closer look at Askew's personal and political style.

Askew contends that a key to his success in Florida was that he challenged all the special-interest sacred cows at once. Once inaugurated, he fought tradition and exposed powerful lobbyists, who long had operated as a "shadow government" in Florida, to win the three-fourths vote in the legislature required for a special referendum on a corporate income tax. Askew campaigned statewide, and voters overwhelmingly passed the constitutional amendment.

The 5 percent corporate income tax produced more than $145 million in revenue in its second year. Other tax reform measures included repeal of the sales tax on household utilities ($30.3 million) and on apartment rent ($13.1 million). Food and medicine already were exempt from taxation.

Among the New South governors who emerged in the early 1970s, none surpass Askew either in programmatic achievements or in exercising

25. Interview with Lawton Chiles, January 30, 1974.

leadership to meet the challenges of a new social order. Nothing dramatizes the latter better than Askew's handling of the busing question, an issue exploited by politicians north and south, including occupants of the White House. Few political leaders at any level have been as forthright as Askew on that emotional issue.

At the University of Florida summer commencement in August 1971, a year in which desegregation plans involving busing were being implemented across Florida, Askew said this:

> We're learning that racial discrimination and democracy are incompatible. . . . Perhaps the most crucial September in the long and remarkable history of our public schools will be upon us in a matter of days. How sad it will be if the emotions of the hours become the legacy of a generation. Our schools must be maintained. Our children must be allowed to learn. And our laws must be respected and observed. I think that most Floridians understand this and will act responsibly in September.
>
> But those who know the value of our public school system and the danger of allowing it to collapse through lack of support have no right merely to sit around and hope. You graduates, faculty, and parents here tonight come from virtually every county in Florida. Most of you are products of public education. You have the ability and the opportunity to encourage reason and calm in your own communities in the days ahead. I sincerely hope you will do so. You have the ability and the opportunity to seek the broad community desegregation and cooperation which ultimately will make busing unnecessary. I sincerely hope that you will do that as well. For busing certainly is an artificial and inadequate instrument of change. Nobody really wants it—not you, not me, not the people, not the school boards—not even the courts. Yet the law demands, and rightly so, that we put an end to segregation in our society.
>
> We must demonstrate good faith in doing just that. We must demonstrate a greater willingness to initiate meaningful steps in this area. We must stop *inviting*, by our own intransigence, devices which are repugnant to us. In this way and in this way only, will we stop massive busing once and for all. Only in this way will we put the divisive and self-defeating issue of race behind us once and for all. And only in this way can we redirect our energies to our real quest—that of providing an equal opportunity for quality education to all of our children.

Later that year, he told the Florida PTA state conference:

> We cannot achieve equal opportunity in education by passing laws or constitutional amendments against busing—they could deny us what I believe is the highest destiny of the American people. That destiny, of course, is to achieve a society in which all races, all creeds, and all religions have learned not only to live with their differences—but to *thrive* upon them. No other civilization has learned to do that. But we can. And we must.

In 1972, when Republican legislators forced onto the ballot a referendum on whether voters favored a federal constitutional amendment to prohibit "forced busing and guarantee the right of each student to attend the appropriate public school near his home," Askew worked to get a second question on the ballot: "Do you favor providing an equal opportunity for quality education for all children regardless of race, creed, color or place of residence and oppose a return to a dual system of public schools?" Although 74 percent of the voters favored the antibusing amendment, 79 percent favored equal education and opposed a return to segregated schools. The question not only defused the busing issue but was also significant in reflecting the acceptance of desegregation in a state whose laws had once required segregation and where real desegregation had begun only a few years earlier. Askew's popularity actually increased after his stand on busing, and polls showed that people respected him for standing up for his beliefs even when they disagreed with him.

Askew's commitment to racial equality stems in large part from a deep personal religious commitment. "I think that your faith has to be at the center of your life and from it must emanate all of your decisions. . . . I think that my faith would go much more into my fundamental feeling about the race question per se, rather than just a question of busing. It was a very controversial position that I took, and I think it largely reflects my feeling, . . . which my faith is a part of, that God meant all of us to have a chance." [26]

Askew's "populist" orientation flows out of his childhood, described by *New York Times* reporter Jon Nordheimer:

> He was the last of six children born to an itinerant carpenter with a sixth grade education who left the family when the future Governor was born: "I never saw him except once, when I was about 10 years old, under very unpleasant circumstances." . . . His childhood memories of Oklahoma are few, but there are some:
> The unemployed men and their grim-faced women, the battered old cars loaded with the family and all its possessions, headed for California or anywhere, just to get out of there. His mother works as a waitress and later in a W.P.A. sewing room. In 1937, when he is 8 years old, she moves her brood to Pensacola, where she was raised, and takes a job as a maid in the San Carlos Hotel, a white-bleached commercial hotel on Garden Street. His first job is to go door-to-door in his neighborhood, a working-class section, and take orders for pies and cakes his mother bakes at night.
> "Mother taught us to hold our heads high and work." [27]

Allen Morris recalled that Askew first came to his attention when he was elected to the House and returned a copy of the *Florida Handbook*, a standard reference work which Morris writes and updates and which a lobbyist had sent to all members. "He is the only person, so far as I know, who ever has returned one," said Morris. "He just didn't think that it was the right thing to do to accept gifts." [28]

In Askew's first term as governor, Florida not only achieved tax reform but also moved ahead in the fields of criminal justice, education, and new approaches to environmental problems. The legislature passed the broad-

26. Interview with Reubin Askew, July 8, 1974.
27. Jon Nordheimer, "Florida's 'Supersquare'—A Man to Watch," *New York Times Magazine*, March 5, 1972, p. 52.
28. Interview with Allen Morris, May 16, 1974.

est no-fault auto insurance law in the country, as well as no-fault divorce. The court system was overhauled, and the system of electing judges was replaced by one in which a judicial review commission sends up three recommendations to the governor for each vacancy. The neglected penal system began to get attention, with a new emphasis on rehabilitation, development of a system of community correctional centers, and moves to end job discrimination against ex-convicts.

Blacks for the first time moved into government at every level of responsibility, including superior court judges, professional licensing and examining board members, and members of the state Board of Regents. In 1975, Askew appointed a black man to the Florida Supreme Court, the first Negro in this century named to a top state court in the South. Blacks were also named to head the state's Department of Community Affairs and the state division of the Office of Economic Opportunity. Near the end of his first term, one of the three black legislators praised Askew for his overall performance but complained that the governor never had called in the three of them to discuss problems facing the 15 percent of the Florida population that is black. The legislator also criticized Askew's failure to implement an affirmative action program to hire more blacks in state agenices.

During Askew's first term, Florida passed the pioneering Environmental Land and Water Management Act, which set up mechanisms through which developments of various kinds could be controlled at all governmental levels, and procedures by which certain lands could be declared environmentally endangered. A $240 million bond issue was approved for the public acquisition of environmentally endangered and recreation lands. The legislature also approved the Water Resources Act, the Comprehensive Planning Act, the Land Conservation Act, the Big Cypress legislation, and the Power Plant Siting Act. The new laws reflected and engendered a new concern in state government for harmonizing economic development, social concerns, and environmental conservation in public policy.

Election laws and their enforcement were strengthened. An Ethics Commission was created, and the first steps toward requiring full public financial disclosure by candidates, elected officials, and major appointees were taken. Reforms in school financing resulted in the state's bearing a greater share of the costs. Home rule for county and city governments was fully implemented. Workmen's compensation benefits were increased, and coverage expanded.

Of course, Askew is not without his critics. The overall quality of a number of his appointments came under criticism, together with what one veteran capital newsman described as a tendency by Askew to assume that those he appoints are as purely motivated as he is. Some former state Senate colleagues contend he became almost recriminatory when someone challenged his ideas after he acquired power, but one of those critics added, "The name 'Askew' has become symbolic with fairness and honesty, and for the most part, he has been that." [29] A Tallahassee newsman known as a cynic was asked by the authors to explain Askew's popularity. He pondered the question a moment, then blurted out, "He's just got this charisma of integrity."

Bidding for a second term, Askew received a remarkable 69 percent of the vote in the 1974 Democratic primary against 3 opponents, and he won by a landslide 62 percent in the general election against Jerry Thomas, a former Democratic president of the state Senate who had switched to the Republican Party.

Before his second term began, Askew looked ahead and said, "With the growth facing Florida, management of that growth is really going to transcend almost anything else. . . . The greater challenge may not be so much in terms of (new) legislation, but making work what is on the books."

Askew believes "that one of the fundamental responsibilities of people in public service is to have a willingness to lead and not simply just to respond." [30] As unremarkable and reasonable as such a position may sound, the politician who believes and practices it is rare. "I have an expression that 'I haven't lost a thing in politics.' And by that, I mean that I don't have to be in it. It is very much a part of my life, but if I really don't believe that I'm making a contribution and being honest with the people whose trust they have placed in me, then I really shouldn't be there." [31]

In 1974, a week after Lester Maddox lost a runoff election in his bid to regain the Georgia governorship, Askew accepted the new chairmanship of the Southern Governors Conference and declared forcefully in the presence of Governor George Wallace of Alabama: "Let it be recorded that in 1974 a clear and final message went out which said that the people of the South were too busy and concerned about serious problems to be preoccupied with and diverted by a political issue of the dark past. If we are to be preoccupied, let it be with the issues that are important and crucial to the well-being of the people we serve." [32]

Askew has shunned any act which might suggest that he has national ambitions. Although Askew keynoted the 1972 Democratic National Convention, he sent word to George McGovern that he was not interested in the vice-presidential nomination. Subsequently, he turned down invitations to meet with the editorial boards of the *Washington Post* and the *New York Times*. Close friends say his wife doesn't want him to run, and that his expressions of disinterest are absolutely sincere.

29. Interview with Mallory Horne, May 20, 1974.
30. Interview with Reubin Askew, July 8, 1974.
31. Ibid.
32. Ferrel Guillory, *Raleigh News & Observer*, September 15, 1974.

One close associate said in 1975, "Only one thing could make Reubin Askew run for president, and that's if he felt a genuine call from the Lord." [33] Earlier, Askew had said, "Running for office was something I knew I had to do. I have never tried to hide that desire. I feel God has plans for the world and men. If I had any talent, I had to use it for public service." [34]

Whatever Askew's political future, he stands out as a figure who marks a turning point in Florida politics.

His first administration achieved an impressive record of substantive reform that followed the procedural reform of the previous four years. Askew provided leadership to implement programs that culminated the efforts of a group of talented and action-oriented young legislators who flocked to Tallahassee after reapportionment with what one of them called a belief "that maybe government could work."

CONGRESS

Florida's 15-member House delegation reflects the state's political diversity. They split roughly into one-third conservative Republicans from the central part of the state, one-third moderate-to-liberal Democrats from the Miami and Tampa areas, and one-third conservative-to-moderate Democrats, mostly from northern Florida but including several carefully drawn districts in the central part of the state.

From the time of Claude Pepper's defeat in 1950 to the election of Lawton Chiles in 1970, the record of Florida senators was one of almost unbroken devotion to conservative interests. However, Spessard Holland, who as governor in 1937 led the fight that abolished the poll tax, in the 1960s did help pass a U.S. constitutional amendment to eliminate it everywhere. The Senate record of George Smathers, before he retired in 1968 for a more lucrative position as a Washington lobbyist, was less distinguished. Chiles in his first term won seats on the appropriations, budget, and Democratic steering committees—a major achievement for a first-term senator.

The fact that Florida in 1974 ranked seventh in defense spending in part reflects the role of First District Representative Robert L. F. (Bob) Sikes, a Panhandle Democrat whose district includes massive Elgin Air Force Base and the Naval Air complex around Pensacola. The dean of the Florida delegation, Sikes was first elected in 1940 and serves as chair-

33. Confidential interview with the authors.
34. Nordheimer, "Florida's 'Supersquare,' " p. 57.

man of the Military Construction Subcommittee of the House Appropriations Committee. Paul Rogers, another conservative Democrat, is a major influence on the nation's health policy as chairman of the House Commerce Committee's Subcommittee on Public Health. Nevertheless, Florida's congressional delegation has been less than a major force in Washington.

The grand old man of Florida politics is Claude Pepper, a New Deal liberal who supported civil rights and who refused to compromise his principles. In 1950, after 14 years in the Senate, he lost to Smathers's racist, red-baiting campaign. It was Smathers, a Democrat, who introduced his friend Charles G. (Bebe) Rebozo to fellow U.S. Representative Richard Nixon of California. And it was Nixon who in 1950 picked up the "red" Pepper slogan from Smathers and transferred it to the "pink lady" attack on Senator Helen Gahagan Douglas that helped defeat her. Pepper, who would have become chairman of the Senate Foreign Relations Committee in two years had he been reelected, returned to Washington in 1962 as a 62-year-old congressman from Miami.

In the twilight of his career, Pepper looked back without regrets. "I grew more liberal as I grew older, the opposite of most up here. I don't know just why, except that I just saw what the colossal problems and needs of the people were in so many areas—education, health, job training, housing, and all the things that have to do with the amenities of life. And I didn't know any potential aid equivalent to the United States government.

"People thought that I fought for things that I thought were right for the country. So, you always have the problem as to whether you ever fight for anything. You know, if you are ever going to have a battle, you've got to have somebody that's got to be up front. Now, they may not last through the battle, but somebody has to be a part of the advance. And I reckon that I just had to pay the price of losing what could have been a long Senate career, because I did have some convictions and principles. Maybe I was foolish enough to try and stand by them. I don't know. But taking it all in all, I will let the record stand as it is. And I suspect that if I had it all to do over again, I would do exactly what I did before." [35]

ORGANIZED LABOR

Few observers assess organized labor or its leaders to be strong in Florida. Legislative leaders seeking to improve conditions for farm laborers have found little help coming from organized labor. The 1974 legis-

35. Interview with Claude Pepper, February 1, 1975.

lature passed a collective bargaining act for public employees, but one House leader said, "Organized labor could never have passed a collective bargaining bill for public employees but for the fact that the Supreme Court of the state of Florida said, '[if] you don't, fellows, we're going to.' They appointed a committee that set guidelines so prolabor that a bill passed the legislature, but it wasn't because organized labor was able to wield any force in the Florida legislature. It has a large group from the two major urban areas, Tampa and Miami, who relate to liberal causes in general and thus tend to be on the side of organized labor." [36]

Labor interests in Florida tend to be focused narrowly on such matters as workmen's compensation and unemployment insurance. There is no state labor newspaper. Not only was Florida the first southern state to enact right-to-work legislation, but the state Supreme Court has also ruled unconstitutional the agency shop, where employees with union representation do not have to join the union but do have to pay a proportion of dues for services rendered by the union. Florida also has no minimum wage law. The decision to put workmen's compensation on a formula basis resulted because agreement was reached between labor leaders and lobbyists for Associated Industries, which basically represents industrial management in Florida.

Nevertheless, because of the change in the law governing public employees and because of agitation among the rank-and-file for more aggressive leadership, the political value of labor's endorsement has increased. The manpower labor has available at election time is an especially important asset in Florida because of the 1970 law setting strict limits on campaign expenditures.

MINORITIES

Like Texas, Florida has both black and Spanish-speaking minorities. Roughly 15 percent of the state's population in 1970 was black and 7 percent Latin; the Latins include Cubans and a lesser number of Puerto Ricans.

Miami has become "little Cuba" to refugees who left that country after it went Communist under Fidel Castro. The Florida Cuban community is largely professional and middle class, Republican oriented in large part because of the anti-Castro stance of the Nixon administration and the Bay of Pigs fiasco under the Kennedy administration. In addition, the Nixon administration provided substantial economic aid to the Miami Cubans.

36. Confidential interview with a Dade County legislator, May 1974.

Tampa is the center of an older Cuban community, settled originally by cigar workers. The Cuban population in Tampa tends to be almost solidly Democratic. Miami and Dade County elected their first Spanish-surname officials in the early 1970s, including Miami Mayor Maurice Ferré, and all were Democrats. Richard Stone's fluency in Spanish proved an asset in his 1974 U.S. Senate campaign.

By the mid-1970s, a majority of new voters among the Miami Cubans continued to register as Republicans, but the Democratic percentage was increasing steadily. The college-age children of Cuban refugees in Miami are reported to register to vote at a rate higher than native-born Americans.

A knowledgeable Cuban Democrat complained that Democrats at the state and local level, including Askew, have done little more than pay lip service to the Cubans in Miami, whereas the Republicans have been far more aggressive in courting Cubans and helping with their problems. Economically, the Cuban community in Miami is dynamic and entrepreneurial, and within a decade may well be the dominant economic group in Dade County. Some recent Republican victories in traditionally Democratic Dade have resulted in part from Cuban support.

If the Cubans are not united politically, they are not necessarily divided. "What we are is pluralistic," explained José Angueira, a lawyer and political science instructor who writes a Spanish-language newspaper column in Miami. "In other words, you won't see the Cuban community fighting with each other. We have our minor squabbles and so on, but it's not the type of thing that the community is split right down the middle. . . . It's in our character to be like that, very individualistic. You may be a friend of mine, you may be a leader and what have you, and I have a great deal of respect for you and so on, but if you press a little bit hard, if you push a little bit hard, I'm going to tell you to go jump in the lake." [37]

Cubans have demonstrated a willingness to support black candidates in Miami, but a Cuban-black political coalition appears no better than a long-term possibility, although it is discussed by political leaders in both communities.

Unlike the Cubans, Florida blacks are solidly Democratic. Although 33 percent of the 48,157 registered blacks in 1946 were Republicans, only 3.5 percent of the 355,555 registered blacks in 1975 were Republican. Numerically, black Republicans actually declined in that period, from 15,877 to 12,414. Blacks in 1975 comprised roughly 10 percent of the total registered vote.

Florida politicians seeking black votes began by going through the back door of the black church. This gradually changed, to the point where Askew and Chiles openly courted black votes in the 1970 election. "We

37. Interview with José Angueira, May 23, 1974.

said we were doing it, we appeared with blacks, and because Florida has changed, you might say that we were able to do that," Chiles said.[38]

Although race baiting was never a popular political sport in Florida and resistance to civil rights melted after passage of the 1964 Civil Rights Act, race remains a covert political issue. Black state Representative Gwen Cherry, a onetime president of the National Women's Political Caucus who considers black priorities even more important than women's, says the code words include "busing," "get all those lazy shiftless people and make them work," and "we've got to take all the crime off the streets."

There is no single, strong statewide black political organization, although several politically oriented black groups exist. Efforts to form a statewide association of black elected officials in the early 1970s were less than successful. "We really aren't as organized as we should be," said Representative Cherry, "and I think that one of the reasons may be that we didn't have it as hard as some of the other areas." [39]

38. Interview with Lawton Chiles, January 30, 1974.
39. Interview with Gwen Cherry, May 31, 1974.

Chapter

7

GEORGIA

The Politics of Consensus

ACROSS the span of a half century, an understanding of the politics of Georgia begins with the name Talmadge. Like fellow U.S. Senators Harry Byrd, Jr. of Virginia and Russell Long of Louisiana, Herman Talmadge's political success rests in the accident of birth. But political power in the United States is a legacy that father can hand to son only if the son has the skills and ambition to win a following of his own.

THE TALMADGE LEGACY

Between 1926 and 1946, Eugene Talmadge ran in every statewide Democratic primary but one. Three times he was elected commissioner of agriculture and four times governor in a state labeled "Rule of the Rustics" by V. O. Key. The elder Talmadge failed in two bids for the U.S. Senate. Like the Longs and the anti-Longs in Louisiana, Georgia's one-party politics in that period revolved around the Talmadge organization and its Democratic opponents. But unlike Huey Long, who fought the corporations and believed in an activist government, providing services like free textbooks and medical care to the poor of his state, Gene Talmadge captured support of Georgia's poverty-stricken rural whites primarily through racist appeals. At the same time, he won the approval of the Atlanta financial and business elite with a conservative outlook on government, low taxes, few government services, and even opposition to the New Deal.

Talmadge personified the politics of protest for poor rural whites frustrated by a system that had taken their land and relegated them to the status of tenants and share-croppers and who had been taught that their white skin gave them the only sense of status they possessed. He snapped his red galluses and rabble-roused about white supremacy. It was a legacy handed down from Tom Watson, a genuine Populist leader who failed in the 1890's in an attempt to build a successful biracial political party. Watson later turned with fury on the Negro and added Jews and Catholics as objects of hate. He left a legacy of strident racism whose residue continues to linger in Georgia.

Herman Talmadge emerged on the political scene when his father became fatally ill after winning the 1946 Democratic primary for governor. The elder Talmadge actually lost the popular election by 16,000 votes to James V. Carmichael, but won on the county-unit system, which had long ensured rural domination. Among the campaign activities of the younger Talmadge that year was an appearance as featured speaker at a barbecue birthday dinner for the grand dragon of the Ku Klux Klan. There he warned of the danger of allowing "ignorant Nigras" to vote, and asked, "Why should Nigras butt in and tell white people who should be elected in a white primary?" This was the year the U.S. Supreme Court overturned the white primary.

Under a technicality in Georgia state law, Herman Talmadge actually took over occupancy of the governor's office by armed force for 67 days after his father's death, but the Georgia Supreme Court ruled against him. He was elected as governor in his own right in 1948 for two years and in 1950 was narrowly reelected to a four-year term. His racist oratory had cemented his appeal to the rustics, and he won the loyalty of the business elite by calling in their tax experts to write a regressive package of consumer taxes to finance a progressive spending program. He imposed a 3 percent sales tax and spent more on education than in the previous history of the state, recognizing that the existing separate but unequal school system would never hold up regardless of how the Supreme Court ruled on school segregation. The state built 13,000 miles of new highways, began its modern drive for new industry, and appropriated funds for such neglected areas as mental health and agricultural research. Unlike his father, Herman Talmadge was a modernizing influence as governor.

By law a governor cannot succeed himself in Georgia, and since Eugene Talmadge no former governor has returned to office after an absence, although many have tried.

In 1956, with Herman Talmadge out of office, the powerful men of finance who dominated the back rooms of Georgia politics decided that

Senator Walter George had become insufficiently interested in promoting the affairs of Georgia in the nation's capital. In the twilight of a long career in Washington, George had developed a global outlook and surrendered the chairmanship of the Senate Finance Committee to head the Foreign Relations Committee. Moreover, his conservatism had mellowed.

Herman Talmadge, with the potential for developing seniority and power, was picked as the next senator, and polls indicated he would win. George, in his 70s, was ready to fight, but then learned that campaign funds had been cut off. The story has been reported that Robert Woodruff, the Coca-Cola chairman and golfing buddy of President Eisenhower, conferred with the president on a visit to the Augusta National Golf Club. Eisenhower subsequently spoke to Senator George, who after 33 years in the Senate announced simply that, "for good and sufficient reasons which I will not elaborate on at this time," he was dropping out of the race.

Woodruff was then in his 66th year. Almost two decades later, one of the state's most influential figures said of him, "He was the only man in Atlanta who could snap his fingers and everybody would genuflect." [1] (Woodruff gave away millions of dollars for civic improvements. When the Atlanta leadership divided over whether to fete Martin Luther King, Jr. for winning the Nobel Peace Prize, Woodruff said there should be no question about it; a dinner for Dr. King would be held. And it was.)

Roy Harris, the crusty and shrewd Augusta segregationist who was a power in Georgia politics for almost a half century and who organized Democrats for Goldwater in 1964 and managed George Wallace's successful 1968 presidential campaign in Georgia, said that Coca-Cola's influence flowed from the fact that it was not regulated and it "didn't mind spending money on politics." He also cited the interlocking directorships between Coca-Cola, the Georgia banks, and other corporate interests.[2]

One reason the power structure in Georgia could afford to dump George was the influence in Washington of Senator Richard B. Russell, who was president pro tem of the Senate and chairman of the Appropriations Committee when he died in 1971. Previously he served as chairman of the Armed Services Committee. Russell was elected to the Senate in 1933, before he was 40. He had already served as governor, and he defeated Eugene Talmadge in the 1936 Democratic primary for the Senate. As unofficial leader of the southern Democrats in the Senate, the patrician Russell directed determined opposition to civil rights legislation in the 1950s and 1960s. Russell never married, saying a politician needed to be totally committed to his work. He read the *Congressional Record* daily from cover to cover.

Russell's advocacy of military preparedness began in the 1930s. In those

1. Mills B. Lane, Jr., quoted in the *Atlanta Constitution*, March 23, 1975.
2. Interview with Roy Harris, April 22, 1974.

days such a position was unusual. Later he worked closely with fellow Georgian Carl Vinson, who served 50 years in Congress and was chairman of the House Armed Services Committee when he retired in 1964. Largely because of their influence, 15 military installations that employ more than 40,000 people are located in Georgia. Together with the Lockheed plant in Marietta, the single largest nongovernmental employer in the state, they contribute roughly $2 billion annually to the state's economy.

Elected to the Senate in 1956 and reelected in 1962, Talmadge by 1966 had grown tired of Washington. An opening developed for governor, and he expressed interest in returning home to make the race. The business elite passed the word quickly and clearly that they wanted him in Washington where he could do them more good. Talmadge decided to remain in the Senate. There his strong advocacy of support for Israel won Talmadge acceptance in the liberal Jewish communities in Atlanta and Savannah.

His 1966 acceptance of an invitation to address the Hungry Club, a luncheon group of Atlanta's Negro establishment, marked a further broadening of Talmadge's coalition. He told his Hungry Club audience that "all candidates are going to solicit the votes of all Georgia citizens." When a questioner asked why he had changed, since five or six years earlier he would not have spoken there, Talmadge drew appreciative laughter when he retorted, "Five or six years ago, you didn't invite me."

In the 1950s, Talmadge had presided over the selection of his gubernatorial successors: Marvin Griffin, his lieutenant governor and an ardent segregationist whose administration was marked by scandal and corruption; and Ernest Vandiver, lieutenant governor under Griffin and by marriage a nephew of Senator Russell. Since then, Talmadge has backed off from an open role in Democratic primary elections, but indirectly "Talmadge's people" at home often seem to unite behind one candidate or another. He campaigned actively in 1972 for Sam Nunn in the U.S. Senate race against Republican Fletcher Thompson. As chairman of the Senate Agriculture Committee, Talmadge effectively argued to rural Georgians that his chairmanship would be in jeopardy if Republicans won control of the Senate in what clearly would be a Nixon landslide in the presidential election that year. Thompson's defeat also ended any threat of a serious Republican challenge to Talmadge in 1974.

With the advent of television in the 1950s, Talmadge easily made the transition from "hot" stump oratory to the "cool" new medium. He later explained, "I use a calm, deliberate, rational, reasonable approach on TV. The viewer sitting in the quiet comfort of his home is not subject to the emotional hysteria of the stump." [3] With his incisive questioning as a

3. Neal Peirce, *The Deep South States of America* (New York: W. W. Norton, 1974), p. 315.

member of the 1973 Senate Watergate Committee, he demonstrated the modern Talmadge style to the nation as well.

Herman Talmadge understood and responded to the changes of modernization that were transforming Georgia. From a demagogue on the race issue to a cool, consensus-seeking political pragmatist, Talmadge bridges the gap between the old and the new. In fact, he is the only remaining Deep South Democrat who entered the Senate between December 1948 and November 1966. He is among the last of the political masters who dominated Congress for decades, and he also serves as elder statesman to the new breed of southern Democrat in the Senate—men who arrived during and after the civil rights revolution.

POLITICS OF TRANSITION

Marvin Griffin and Ernest Vandiver, who succeeded Herman Talmadge as governor, marked a period of transition away from rural traditionalism. Both represented the Talmadge faction, but Vandiver also was forced to face the reality of social change. He had campaigned in 1958 on the slogan that "no, not one" black would enter Georgia's white schools, and in 1960 he was involved in serious talks about closing the public schools rather than integrating them. But he accepted the inevitable and kept the University of Georgia open in 1961 when the first black students were admitted under court order. Vandiver warned the legislature that some integration was inevitable and that unless Georgia faced up to it, the issue "like a cancerous growth will devour progress—consuming all in its path—pitting friend against friend—demoralizing all that is good—stifling the economic growth of the state." A lesson already learned by Atlanta thus was taught to the entire state: racial strife was bad for business.

Griffin, a skillful orator less willing than Vandiver to "surrender" on segregation, sought a comeback in the 1962 race for governor. The corruption of the Griffin administration had been exposed by Pulitzer Prize-winning reporter Jack Nelson of the *Atlanta Constitution*, later to become the Washington Bureau Chief of the *Los Angeles Times*. The charges led to prosecution of Griffin's brother during the Vandiver administration. The corruption in the Griffin administration was such, Nelson recalled, that after the *Constitution* began running stories, "we got so many tips and calls that we had to ignore anything that involved less than a cabinet official or involved less than $100,000." [4]

In 1962, Griffin was defeated by Carl Sanders, president pro tem of the

4. Interview with Jack Nelson, April 22, 1975.

state Senate, a city resident of Augusta, and a business-oriented progressive on the race issue who paid lip service to segregation. As a Senate leader, Sanders had provided strong and often lonely leadership against efforts to close the public schools in the face of integration, during a period in which the issue was highly charged. As governor, Sanders blocked an invitation of the legislature to Alabama Governor George Wallace after Wallace openly defied desegregation efforts in his home state. It was an act for which Sanders later paid a heavy political price.

Sanders first announced for lieutenant governor. He then moved into the governor's race at the urging of anti-Griffin forces who lacked a strong candidate around whom they could rally, after the incumbent lieutenant governor suffered a "heart attack" and withdrew. Sanders not only won 58 percent of the popular vote against Griffin but also won a majority of the counties. Although Griffin ran strongest in rural areas, Sanders significantly received more than 60 percent of the vote in Talmadge's home county. A few years later, the Sanders-Griffin race was being casually discussed in Talmadge's office in Washington on a day "Miss Mitt," Herman Talmadge's mother and Eugene Talmadge's widow, was present. She remarked, "Oh, I knew Griffin wouldn't win. Herman wasn't going to let him." [5]

Talmadge had quietly passed the word to rural leaders in his organization, which boosted Sanders in the rural areas and helped his landslide victory. Griffin's record of graft and racism at a time of expanding black participation—together with the prospect of political revenge against the "outs" in a Griffin administration—apparently made him unacceptable both to political leaders and to the electorate.

In 1966, Republicans mounted their first major challenge in state politics. They nominated Howard (Bo) Callaway, who in 1964 had become Georgia's first Republican congressman since Reconstruction. That year, Georgia was one of the six states Barry Goldwater carried as a presidential candidate, the first time since Reconstruction that Georgia failed to vote Democratic in a presidential election. Callaway, a capable West Point graduate with inherited wealth from textiles and other interests, had formerly been active in the Talmadge faction of the Democratic Party.

After Vandiver withdrew his candidacy for health reasons and Talmadge quickly backed away from the gubernatorial race under pressure from financial supporters, the contestants in the 1966 Democratic primary were the liberal former Governor Ellis Arnall, Lester Maddox, unknown state Senator Jimmy Carter, and others. Maddox three times had run unsuccessfully for public office. In two attempts to become mayor of Atlanta, he had established himself as a defiant segregationist with a flair for attracting publicity. In 1962 he made a runoff in a race for lieutenant

5. Story related by Remer Tyson, former political editor of the *Atlanta Constitution,* who heard the remark by Mrs. Talmadge. (Interview, April 22, 1975.)

governor and received almost 45 percent of the vote. In the race, Maddox helped engineer a plan in which the Ku Klux Klan made a last-minute endorsement of his opponent, an attempt to hurt the opponent with blacks and "respectable" whites; Maddox carried most of the counties in which the special *Ku Klux Klan News* was distributed.[6]

He actively supported the Democrats for Goldwater organization in 1964 and was a leader in pressing for the invitation for Wallace that year to address the legislature, which Governor Sanders had called into special session to write a new state constitution. During the height of the crisis in Selma the following spring, Maddox picketed the federal courthouse in Atlanta. He marched with one sign, "Treason is the reason," then swapped it for another, "Down with Johnson, Justice Department, socialism and communism—Up with Wallace, free enterprise, capitalism, liberty, private property rights, America."

Arnall both misjudged the temper of the electorate and failed to adjust to the campaign style of the 1960s. Political analyst Bruce Galphin later wrote of Arnall: "He was a disaster on TV, coming across as a country bumpkin with old-fashioned ideas—the exact opposite of the true Arnall. The oratorical style that had wowed 'em when he beat ol' Gene Talmadge sounded like a parody on TV."[7]

Callaway, a Goldwater conservative who voted in Congress against aid to education, Medicare, civil rights, minimum wage, and urban aid bills, was unopposed as the Republican nominee. In his campaign for governor, he drove around in a Cadillac with a bumper sticker that said "I fight poverty—I work."

Although Arnall led the first primary, it was with less than 30 percent of the vote, and Maddox—with support from some Republicans who viewed him as a less formidable opponent—won handily in the runoff with 54.3 percent of the vote. Against Maddox, Callaway won almost solid support from the business elite, but he failed to make even symbolic moves to attract blacks or liberals. As a result, a write-in campaign for Arnall developed.

The *Atlanta Journal* endorsed Callaway, but Eugene Patterson, editor of the *Atlanta Constitution*, demurred, despite pressure from some of the most influential men of the state and the private views of his company's management. In a lengthy editorial that ran three full columns of type, he concluded:

> Is it wise for this newspaper to risk endorsing a weak Lester Maddox, a man whom it considers to be grossly unqualified, in the hope that four years of sure humiliation would at last cauterize the wound of racism in Georgia and send a shamed state forever recoiling from the blight of demagoguery,

6. Bruce Galphin, *The Riddle of Lester Maddox* (Atlanta: Camelot, 1968), pp. 44–45.

7. Ibid., p. 110.

as it recoiled for eight years after Marvin Griffin's governorship? Could such a sacrifice of four years be borne? We cannot advocate that it be risked.

Yet is it a wise course to risk endorsing Callaway, a strong man who we fear has the power and the connections to fasten a wrong idea—Goldwaterism—on this state not for four years but perhaps—the figure is his—20 years to come? We cannot in honesty advocate that either.

Nor can we give newspaper endorsement to the write-in movement for Ellis Arnall. The write-in option is an entirely legal and proper course for individuals to take if they so desire. But we regard that as a uniquely individual judgement, and not something for a newspaper either to institutionalize and urge upon the people as if it were a formal candidacy, or to oppose as if it were not the individual's right.

Thus The Constitution, in conscience, cannot recommend either nominee. . . .

The official final returns gave Callaway 453,665 votes, Maddox 450,626, and Arnall 52,831.

The Georgia state constitution provides that if no candidate receives a majority, the legislature must choose a governor from the two leading living contenders. A three-judge federal court ruled the section invalid, maintaining that a decision in the legislature would dilute the votes of the people. But the U.S. Supreme Court reversed the lower court and ruled 5–4 that nothing in the federal Constitution "either expressly or impliedly [sic] dictates the method a state must use to select its governor." Thus, Maddox won in the legislature, 182–66, with ten black legislators and one white abstaining despite a ruling from the presiding lieutenant governor that all must vote.

As governor, Maddox at first attempted to shed his extremist image. He brought in some competent professional staff personnel, declared in his inaugural that there would be "no place in Georgia . . . for those who advocate extremism or violence," made a few progressive moves in penal and welfare matters, and instituted a "Little People's Day" to allow anyone to visit the governor. He appointed several blacks to state boards and commissions. But Maddox soon reverted to his right-wing positions, and most of his more able staff members departed. He gave little direction to state government, but achieved a popular antiestablishment image.

The most enduring legacy of the Maddox administration is the increased independence of the legislature. Previously, the governor handpicked the speaker of the House, and a telephone beside the speaker provided a direct line to the governor's office while the House was in session. Because the legislature organized before Maddox took office, an independent speaker was elected, Representative George L. Smith, who after his death was remembered fondly as a skillful political master who orchestrated the House. His successor, onetime Maddox floor leader Tom Murphy, a hot-tempered, small-town north Georgian with a populist streak, retained the independence the House had achieved, and Murphy is likely to remain a force in Georgia politics for years.

The Maddox primary victory prompted U.S. Representative Charles Weltner, a liberal Democrat who had voted for the 1964 Civil Rights Act, to withdraw as a candidate for reelection in 1966 because of an oath that he support the Democratic nominee for governor. Republican Fletcher Thompson won the congressional seat, and Weltner failed in later attempts to come back politically. Although he won a degree of admiration for his act of conscience, many voters apparently judged that Weltner's action reflected a lack of political maturity.

THE RISE OF CONSENSUS

In 1970, Jimmy Carter tagged former Governor Sanders as the candidate of the Atlanta business establishment, ran a tireless campaign that actually began after his 1966 defeat, and went after the rural and small-town Maddox-Wallace vote. He told the state that Sanders's discourtesy to Wallace "broke down the relations of Georgia and Alabama" and was quoted on election eve as saying that Maddox was "the essence of the Democratic Party . . . he has compassion for the ordinary man. I'm proud to be on the ticket with him." *

Sanders, poor at birth, was an immaculate dresser, and the nickname of "cuff links Carl" stuck. Carter's disclosure of six-figure legal fees for Sanders from the Georgia Power Co. helped create the image of a man whose wealth had suddenly increased after leaving office.

Despite his campaign appeal to Wallace-Maddox voters, Carter also took his campaign to blacks in rural and small-town areas and received strong support among them. Atlanta's more politically sophisticated blacks backed Sanders.

Carter fell just short of a majority in the first primary, which included seven minor candidates, then won a landslide 59.4 percent of the vote in the runoff, sweeping the rural counties and winning smaller majorities in ten of the 12 most populous counties, losing only Fulton (Atlanta) and Richmond (Augusta, Sanders's hometown) among the urban counties.

In his inaugural speech, he told the people of Georgia: "I say to you quite frankly that the time for racial discrimination is over. . . . No poor, rural, weak, or black person should ever have to bear the additional burden of being deprived of the opportunity of an education, a job, or simple justice."

As governor, Carter proved to be a creative innovator, although some

* Unable to succeed himself as governor, Maddox ran successfully for the lieutenant governorship.

critics contended he often thought little of ideas that didn't originate with him. As lieutenant governor, a position of power in Georgia through the appointment of Senate committees and chairmen, Maddox quickly became a constant critic and obstructionist and the tool of a few shrewd, rural traditionalist Senate leaders.

Because Atlanta was the regional center for national media representatives, Carter was projected nationally as the principal spokesman for the group of "New South" moderates elected in 1970, which also included Reubin Askew of Florida, Dale Bumpers in Arkansas, and John West in South Carolina. Some of his fellow southern governors privately considered Carter all too eager to become the center of attention.

Like the other new southern governors, Carter acted symbolically and substantively on racial matters. He created a biracial commission to deal with problems of discrimination, made substantive appointments of blacks, designated a black highway patrolman among the four who served as his driver and security, and made the decision to hang a portrait of Martin Luther King, Jr. in the capitol. Maddox denounced the portrait hanging and charged that the slain civil rights leader and Nobel Peace Prize winner "did more to spread the cause of communism and socialism than any Georgian ever to live." [8]

The idea for the King portrait originated with Rita Samuels, a young black woman on Carter's staff who coordinated his biracial commission. Portraits of two other black Georgians were also selected—Henry McNeal Turner, a politically active minister and educator in the Reconstruction era, and educator Lucy C. Laney—but Dr. King's was the first, and the final decision was Carter's. Mrs. Samuels recalled that she had visited the capitol as a sixth-grade student and there was nothing she could relate to. The King portrait is important, she said, because "black kids should be able to see something, not only that they can identify with, but something that they recognize. And I guarantee you that nine kids out of ten, both black and white, would recognize Martin Luther King's portrait before they would any other portrait in the capitol." [9]

One progressive-minded legislator described Carter as "a good governor. He's wanted to do many things that have needed doing, and he's got some of them done. . . . Somebody said his greatest difficulty was that he was brought up in the Navy, and he thinks that he's commander of a submarine, and you give the orders and everything falls into line. Of course, a government or party doesn't work like that, but I think he has moved the state along in some ways that are well overdue." [10]

Perhaps his biggest achievement as governor was reorganization of the 300 state agencies into 22 departments, although his Human Resources

8. *Atlanta Constitution,* January 5, 1974.
9. Interview with Rita Samuels, April 30, 1974.
10. Interview with Grace Hamilton, May 1, 1974.

Department, a catchall agency with 30,000 employees in welfare, public and mental health, mental retardation, and juvenile problems, became a center of controversy and was further restructured after Carter left office. Carter also accomplished reorganization of the state's judicial system, a matter that had been debated for decades. He instituted a "zero budget" concept in which each agency annually was forced for the first time to justify every worker and program and state its priorities. He also required bidding for the first time by banks that held state funds, a move that resulted in higher interest on idle funds.

Few men in politics—or any other field—drive themselves as hard as Carter, a highly disciplined man whose image is softened by a boyish face with blue eyes, an easy, toothy smile, and a campaign style that projects vigor and a self-effacing sincerity.

When Carter was launching his campaign for the Democratic 1976 presidential nomination at the Kansas City "mini-convention" at the end of 1974, he was escorted by black Representative Andrew Young of Atlanta. Young called Carter "an authentic voice" of the South who empathizes with the poor of both races and said, "He deserves a look from the liberal community." [11] As governor, Carter usually had breakfast once a week with state AFL–CIO President Herb Mabry, in part a reflection of his perception of a developing political role for organized labor.

Roy Harris, the segregationist political leader whom Carter removed from the state Board of Regents when he named prominent blacks to the board, later declared of Carter, "I've known intimately every governor since 1912, and he's next to the sorriest." He called Carter a hypocrite. "His platform was 'I'm just like George Wallace and Lester Maddox.' . . . That's the way he got elected. And he turns out to be the most liberal governor in the South."

If Maddox served as a carping critic from one direction, Carter as governor was also the target of continuous criticism from the *Atlanta Constitution*, which had strongly supported Sanders in 1970. Carter had responded by ripping into the Atlanta newspapers. The son of Jack Tarver, the president of Atlanta Newspapers, Inc., was a lawyer in the Sanders law firm. At the same time, Carter's campaign manager and choice for Democratic state chairman was Atlanta lawyer Charles Kirbo, a soft-spoken boyhood playmate of Tarver's in the south Georgia town of Bainbridge. Kirbo's law firm did considerable legal work for Cox Enterprises, the parent company of the newspapers.

Kirbo characterized the constant sniping as "all personal," in part stemming from a letter sent by a top Carter aide, during the heat of the campaign, to Reg Murphy, then editor of the *Constitution*, that called Murphy "a kept bastard." Kirbo said Carter didn't know about the letter until two weeks after it was sent. "It's not just the letter, it's a lot of little

11. *New Republic*, April 12, 1975, p. 17.

things," Kirbo said.[12] The letter writer later was appointed by Carter to the Georgia Supreme Court. Murphy, who opposed Carter's reorganization plan, found little about Carter to praise, either in performance or personality. Kirbo called the situation "all very unfortunate," contending that Carter as governor represented the progressive outlook that the *Constitution* for so long had espoused.

Carter, an imaginative innovator, was succeeded by George Busbee, a skilled political technician and tactician who served 18 years in the House, the last ones as majority leader. Busbee survived a field of 12 for a runoff spot against Maddox in 1974, a year that reflected a further moderation of the Georgia electorate's attitude toward the race issue.

A year before the election, polls showed Maddox with solid support from little more than a third of the electorate, including about 25 percent of the blacks. One black official explained that many blacks looked upon Maddox as "honest" in expressing his racial views, while they doubted the sincerity of many "moderate" white politicians, and that Maddox had made some black appointments as governor and showed a sense of compassion toward the unfortunate. But when Maddox attacked the martyred King, whose photograph often hangs beside a picture of Jesus in the homes of blacks throughout the South, his grassroots support among black Georgians fell.

Strength for Maddox was greatest among white blue-collar workers with less than a high school education and among those 65 and older. Maddox was perceived as being sincere in his religious views and as being personally honest. But a precampaign poll taken by Tim Ryles, a political scientist who helped direct Busbee's campaign and later joined his staff, showed that a majority of Georgians (53 percent) disagreed with the statement "Lester Maddox makes me proud to live in Georgia," while 51 percent agreed with the statement "Lester Maddox spends too much time showing off." 27 percent "strongly" agreed with the second statement, and only 11 percent "strongly" disagreed.

Although Maddox led in the first primary with 36.1 percent of the vote, compared with 20.8 percent for Busbee, he had little residual support among the other candidates. Busbee won a landslide 59.9 percent runoff victory. In the 12 urban counties that contain half of the state's population, Busbee trounced Maddox, 298,045 to 121,077, or 71.1 percent. They split almost evenly in the remaining 147 counties, with Busbee receiving 50.5 percent of the vote. Busbee, who had served as the governor's handpicked floor leader during the Sanders administration, received his major financial support from the Sanders faction of the party. In his campaign, he directed his appeal at blacks and those whites with a high school but not a college education.

Carter's candidate was Bert Lance, a small-town banker and lay church

12. Interview with Charles Kirbo, May 1, 1974.

leader who had served as Carter's director of transportation. Lance drew heavy support among affluent whites, and Maddox's strength was concentrated among whites with less than a high-school education, especially among voters 65 and older. Busbee drew strong support from elected black officials, but Lance was the choice of upper and middle-class black leadership in Atlanta. Although Lance led the voting in black precincts throughout Atlanta, Busbee ran ahead among blacks in Savannah and other cities and in small towns and rural areas.

The repudiation of Maddox made it clear that the politics of race are not sufficient to win elections any longer in Georgia. Maddox shared the same deep beliefs in religious fundamentalism and racial separation as thousands of frustrated white Georgians alienated by rapid social and cultural change. He had become the symbol of resistance to racial change in the early 1960s, when he brandished ax handles to prevent blacks from eating at his Pickrick restaurant. But he proved inept at and ill prepared for political leadership. By the mid-1970s he was for most Georgians an embarrassment, a social and cultural anachronism.

In his inaugural address, Busbee said, "The political processes which led to this inauguration proclaim that Georgia has met the challenge of political maturity. The politics of race has gone with the wind."

Busbee entered the governor's office with a reputation for hard work and the pragmatism that comes from 18 years as a legislator, of being practical enough to know what he can pass and what he cannot. But the Georgia legislature, like many in the South, exists in an atmosphere in which casual conflict of interest is routine. It was not considered unusual when Busbee as House majority leader accepted an appointment to the board of directors of the Citizens and Southern Bank office in Albany, his hometown. In 1973 he was a sponsor of a bill to give banks such as C&S, the largest and perhaps most politically active bank in Georgia, expanded powers to buy up small-town banks.

One Georgia political writer questioned the virtue of Busbee's legislative background and wrote: "Those who know the Georgia general assembly could argue that the 'practicality' it teaches is simply a habit of compromising the needs of the people with the wishes of the affluent and the powerful." [13]

The judgment is perhaps overly harsh because political issues are seldom so clear. Key members of Busbee's staff included a lawyer-lobbyist from the Sanders law firm and a trucking millionaire from Busbee's hometown, and the voices of the powerful could expect sympathetic ears. But it was former Governor Sanders who also arranged and participated in a meeting in which Mayor Maynard Jackson and other Atlanta civic leaders discussed the city's problems, as Busbee listened cooperatively

13. Howell Raines, in a profile of Busbee in the *Washington Post*, February 9, 1975, p. B3.

and responded with support of the motel and hotel sales tax, an issue that had been kicking around for years.

"There is a very strong feeling throughout the state that Atlanta is the capital city and the way it goes is the way Georgia goes," Governor Busbee declared in 1975. He explained that rural as well as urban legislators now vote for MARTA (Atlanta's mass transit system), the planned World Congress Center, and measures such as the motel-hotel tax. "The rural-urban split in the legislature is almost nonexistent," Busbee said.[14]

Busbee is the epitome of the consensus politics which Georgia has developed. A racial moderate who in the legislature worked with organized labor in removing a one-week waiting period before eligibility for unemployment compensation, Busbee as a legislative leader in 1973 also helped sponsor a $50 million property tax rebate bill which brought $1.4 million in tax credits to Georgia Power alone. He stressed "unity" in his inaugural address and presented a mildly progressive program with no new taxes but some tax shifts that caused no frowns in corporate executive suites.

When Georgians talk of political reform, a name often mentioned is that of Zell Miller, the former executive director of the state Democratic Party who as lieutenant governor under Busbee insisted on open meetings in the Senate, urged limits on campaign spending, and pushed for genuine tax reform.

More representative of the mainstream of Georgia politics is junior U.S. Senator Sam Nunn, who was 34 when he was elected in 1972. Reg Murphy, then *Constitution* editor and formerly its chief political writer, said that Nunn's election "was an honest expression of what the people were looking for. A fellow who is relatively conservative, who is articulate, who is, they think, a square shooter, who is a new, fresh face, and who they anticipate is bright enough to make things work. He probably comes as close as any they've had in a long time to symbolize what Georgia politics is all about.[15]

Nunn's campaign included use of the race issue among whites, but blacks who knew him in the legislature look upon Nunn as a closet moderate. "I served with him for four years on the Judiciary Committee in the House," black state Representative Bobby Hill of Savannah said, "and I know him personally and know him to be what his public image would reflect. . . . I know that when we close the door and get in a smoke-filled room that we can count on him. And I also know that he's got to win for us to [benefit]. And so I understand that." [16]

Herman Talmadge, Jimmy Carter, George Busbee, and Sam Nunn all symbolize the consensus politics that dominates the contemporary Geor-

14. Interview with George Busbee, April 11, 1975.
15. Interview with Reg Murphy, April 30, 1974.
16. Interview with Bobby Hill, May 3, 1974.

gia Democratic Party, which survived an unsuccessful Republican challenge in the late 1960s and which today retains one-party dominance of
state government.

Basically, the Democratic coalition consists of blacks, courthouse Democrats who have learned the benefits of black allegiance to the Democratic
party, a developing role for organized labor, rural whites with a Democratic heritage who remain suspicious of urban Republicans and their
country club image, a few white urban liberals, and the top echelon of the
business and financial community, who tend to view Georgia Republicans
as somewhat unstable political amateurs. The self-interest of the business
elite merges with blacks and working-class whites in the broad quest for
modernization and economic development.

This quest for development is most evident in Atlanta, where "white
people of good will" allied with blacks in the 1950s and 1960s, when
Atlanta was known as the city "too busy to hate." While cities such as
Birmingham were paralyzed by the impact of social change, Atlanta
moved ahead. The city became the regional center for the nation's giant
corporations and federal agencies and then developed into the international headquarters for the South. Atlanta International Airport became
the second busiest in the nation.

Atlanta has come to represent urban growth in the South. It was the
heart of the civil rights movement in the 1960s and of black political
development in the late 1960s and 1970s. Atlanta became the first state
capital to elect a black mayor, one who followed a Jewish mayor. Much
of the rural antagonism toward Atlanta, the symbol of all that is urban,
has melted as the city and its suburbs have absorbed tens of thousands
of rural and small-town Georgians.

Although dominance of public policy by business interests prevails
throughout the South, Georgia is unique in its concentration of the business elite in the capital city. Atlanta is headquarters for Coca-Cola, the
largest banks, and most of the other major financial and corporate interests in the state. Tied in closely and serving as political brokers and con-
duits for campaign funds are several of the city's prestige law firms, the
most conspicuous being that of former Governor Carl Sanders.

The plutocracy's confidence in its fundamental control over public
policy allows it comfortably to grant small concessions to organized labor
or to blacks, a concept of enlightened self-interest that continues to accept
progressive government programs while quietly insisting on a tax system
that does not disturb corporate profits.

However, the 1975 efforts by Lieutenant Governor Zell Miller to expose
what he termed the "cruel hoax" of a so-called tax reform bill in the legislature suggests that the issue may come alive. Miller was successful in
helping kill one version of a property tax relief bill whose benefits would
have gone almost exclusively to large landowners, corporations, and those

who owned homes valued at more than \$25,000. Nevertheless, he was unsuccessful in winning acceptance of a top-to-bottom revision of the tax laws. A \$35 million tax relief package that passed was less blatant than the one exposed by Miller, but the corporate interests had little to be unhappy about.

The consensus extends even to Georgia's press. The *Atlanta Constitution* once stood out as a voice of conscience and well-reasoned criticism and as an organ of aggressive political reportage. A leader of the business elite recalled the civil rights movement: "When the trouble started in Mississippi and Alabama, the Atlanta papers were full of news stories. [Ralph] McGill was cussed everywhere. The mood of the town was if the newspapers would keep their damn mouths shut, this thing would go away. But when it came, the town met it with a different attitude. Instead of the newspaper provoking anything, they conditioned the populace to meet this thing." [17]

Once recognized nationally for their regional leadership under such editors as McGill and Eugene Patterson, the Atlanta newspapers have come to reflect their management's policy of parsimony. Much of the bite has disappeared from the editorial pages. Despite a few dedicated professional veterans, their writing staffs have become noted principally for the large numbers of able journalists who have left.

The company that owns the newspapers in Augusta, Savannah, and Athens is even more of a countinghouse operation. The Knight-Ridder newspapers in Macon and Columbus are more promising, but their influence is limited. Television reporting of politics and government is undistinguished.

The decline of the Atlanta newspapers leaves Georgia without an eminent critical voice to assess public policy. The capitol press corps in Atlanta is among the weaker in the South.

BLACK POLITICS

A fundamental change in Georgia politics occurred when the county-unit system died. Under the old county-unit system, each county had no fewer than two unit votes and no more than six. The eight largest counties each had six, the next 30 each had four, and the remaining 121 each had two unit votes. The county-unit system, a legacy from the method of representation by parishes during the colonial period and a Democratic Party rule after the Reconstruction era, was frozen into state law in 1917

17. Mills B. Lane, Jr., quoted in the *Atlanta Constitution*, March 23, 1975.

and insured continued rural domination. The system also bred corruption. Many small counties were controlled by "courthouse crowds" whose manipulation and sometimes simple falsification of vote totals would swing unit votes from one candidate to another.

A suit challenging the county-unit system was filed in Georgia immediately after the Supreme Court in 1962 entered its "political thicket" of reapportionment in *Baker* v. *Carr*. By then, the distortion of democratic principles was reflected by the fact that one vote in tiny Echols County was worth 99 in Fulton (Atlanta), a pattern duplicated with only slightly less exaggeration in many rural counties.

The end of the county-unit system meant a new type of campaigning for statewide office, with candidates going after the popular vote rather than concentrating their efforts on cultivating rural political chieftains. Legislative reapportionment followed, giving the cities a full share in state government and opening participation to urban blacks and Republicans.

Reapportionment of the state Senate in 1962 increased the number of senators elected in Fulton County from one to seven. One of those elected was Leroy Johnson, the first Negro in almost half a century to serve in a Deep South legislature. Three years later, eight blacks were elected to a reapportioned House, and six of them were still serving a decade after, providing a sophisticated cadre of political veterans who had become skilled at legislative infighting.

By 1975 the number of black legislators had increased to 20 in the House and two in the Senate. Two blacks served as committee chairmen in the House. A black caucus provides the black legislators with information about various committee activities and an opportunity to discuss legislative matters, but the caucus itself takes no position on issues.

When Julian Bond was elected to the House with the first group of blacks, he was refused a seat because of his endorsement of a resolution by the Student Nonviolent Coordinating Committee (SNCC) that strongly condemned the military draft and the U.S. military involvement in Vietnam. He was admitted only after the U.S. Supreme Court ruled that his First Amendment rights had been violated. George Busbee was among the House members who voted (184–12) against seating Bond; but by 1974, Bond and fellow Representative Ben Brown, a contemporary who as black caucus president was perhaps the most influential of the black legislators, stumped the state on behalf of Busbee. They had found him to be fair as a House majority leader and consistently helpful in providing support at crucial times for progressive legislation. After he moved to the Senate in 1975, Bond found himself fully accepted, with "none of the hostility" that he felt had lingered in the House.[18]

Andrew Young became the first Deep South black congressman after his election in 1972. Young represents a majority white district and he

18. Interview with Julian Bond, April 17, 1975.

quickly established himself as a man of quiet candor and unusual ability and popularity.

During his days with the Southern Christian Leadership Conference, Young displayed an uncanny knack for negotiating with local white power structures throughout the South.

More than a year after his election, Young was in Atlanta and saw a beefy-faced white man driving a pickup truck that contained a gun rack stop his vehicle, get out, and come toward him. Young later said he was afraid the man was going to attack him. Instead, he came over, shook hands, and said, "I just wanted you to know that you and Lester Maddox are the only two people I'm voting for this year." [19]

Young received 26 percent of the white vote and 98 percent of the black vote to win in 1972. In his congressional district, he outpolled Democratic presidential nominee George McGovern in every white precinct.

Young's election also is instructive on the subtle barriers black candidates have faced. In 1970 he won the Democratic nomination but lost the general election by 20,000 votes to incumbent Republican Fletcher Thompson in a district then 69 percent white in registration. By 1972 the Georgia legislature had been forced to reapportion the state's congressional districts to reflect the 1970 census. The new Fifth District boundaries excluded Young's residence by two blocks and moved the largely black west side of Atlanta out of the district. Formal objections to the Justice Department, which under the 1965 Voting Rights Act must review election law changes in Georgia to determine if there is a "racially discriminatory purpose or effect," resulted in an objection by the U.S. attorney general on the basis of the gerrymander and dilution of the black vote.

The legislature redrew the plan, and the new boundaries included Young's residence in a district in which 38 percent of the registered voters were black, a 7 percentage point increase over 1970. Young won with 53 percent of the vote after a skillfully executed, sophisticated campaign aimed at maximizing black turnout and targeting white precincts with characteristics favorable to his candidacy. When the plan was redrawn, a member of the reapportionment committee in the House was veteran Representative Grace Hamilton, a longtime leader in Atlanta community affairs who quietly insisted to the speaker that she be appointed to provide black representation on the committee. "We were concentrating on getting a viable district," she later explained,[20] and her presence helped ensure fairness in setting new boundaries.

Although no black legislators yet serve from rural counties, the legislative black caucus serves as the nucleus for the Georgia Association of Black Elected Officials (GABEO), whose meetings provide a forum for

19. Interview with Reg Murphy, April 30, 1974.
20. Interview with Grace Hamilton, April 29, 1974.

political issues and an informal occasion to discuss the qualities of candidates for statewide office. GABEO makes no endorsements.

Although the sophistication of black politics in Georgia is unmatched in the South, there is no common philosophy that binds black officeholders. Blacks in the legislature in 1975 ranged from a law-and-order former policeman who espoused capital punishment to Hosea Williams, a civil-rights activist and self-styled populist who battled both the white and black economic elites and concentrated on organizing the poor.

One of the most prominent black politicians in Georgia is Mayor Maynard Jackson, and the question of whether he can successfully govern Atlanta remains a major issue. An articulate young lawyer who won a small measure of support from low-income whites when he ran against Herman Talmadge for the Senate in 1968, Jackson was elected vice-mayor the following year and mayor in 1973, with substantial support from white business leaders. Jackson defeated incumbent Sam Massell, who had defeated the business establishment four years earlier with a coalition of blacks and lower-income whites. In 1973, however, Massell, who is Jewish, made an openly racist appeal against Jackson.

Jackson inherited problems that include white flight, rising crime, ghetto poverty, and related ills of a modern city, and he compounded them by isolating himself behind an overprotective staff, by making questionable appointments to several key positions, and by unnecessarily alienating many of his white supporters. Within a year of Jackson's election, black legislators from the Atlanta area, who had worked diligently to broaden the legislation that expanded the authority of Atlanta's mayor, complained they had difficulty getting in to see Jackson. Although heavy criticism followed the naming of a former college friend as Commissioner of Public Safety, a black lawyer with little background in law enforcement, it subsided when the crime rate dropped months later.

After George Busbee announced for governor in 1974, it took six weeks for him to get an appointment with Mayor Jackson. The following year, Busbee provided full support to win legislative approval of a motel-hotel sales tax to boost Atlanta revenues and promised to support any consensus that might be reached in regard to merger of city and county, a move needed for orderly planning and efficient administration of a rapidly growing metropolitan area. Atlanta had become a city in which blacks controlled the political power and whites the economic power. Merger would give the city a white majority again.

Atlanta, the boom city of the South in the 1960s, was characterized by a series of articles in the *Atlanta Constitution* in 1975 as "a city in crisis." The headline over the first story in the series read: "A decade of prosperity and goodwill has faded. . . . This Is a City in Crisis." However, some of Jackson's establishment white supporters urged critics to give the mayor time, contending he had the ability to grow with the job.

154

REPUBLICANS

In presidential politics, the revolt against the national Democratic Party developed more slowly in Georgia than in other states of the Deep South. In 1948 Dixiecrat Strom Thurmond failed to get on the ballot as the official nominee of the Democratic Party, as he did in neighboring Alabama and South Carolina, and Harry Truman carried the state. Republican percentages in presidential elections increased from 18.3 in 1948 to 37.4 for Richard Nixon in 1960, but not until the Goldwater movement of 1964 did Georgia move out of the Democratic column in presidential elections. George Wallace carried the state in 1968 as a third-party candidate, and Nixon received only 30.4 percent, less than he did in 1960. In 1972, Nixon took 75 percent of the vote.

In state and local elections, the Republican Party in Georgia demonstrated a strong base of urban support in the mid-1960s. Despite the setback of Callaway's defeat in the governor's race, the GOP elected two Atlanta area congressmen in 1966.

The Republicans' promise was such that five of the state's constitutional officers dramatically switched from the Democratic Party to join the GOP in 1968 in reaction to the events of the National Democratic Convention in Chicago. That chaotic affair involved extensive violence between police and antiwar demonstrators and a Credentials Committee victory for a delegation led by black Representatives Julian Bond and Ben Brown, who had challenged the handpicked Maddox delegation. Comptroller General Jimmy Bentley, a former aide and well-known associate of Senator Talmadge, joined the state treasurer, commissioner of agriculture, and two members of the state Public Service Commission in making the switch. Such a crossover of major officials was on a scale unprecedented in the South.

Bentley saw in the move "an opportunity to pull together the middle-of-the-road people, and people to the right of center in the state and build a real solid political structure." But instead of a warm welcome from the Republicans, the converts found a large measure of resentment from Republican regulars. "I was visited by a substantial delegation of Republicans," Bentley later recalled, "who were somewhat indignant because we had not consulted the Republican leadership before we joined the Republican Party."[21]

When Bentley ran for the GOP nomination for governor, an endorsement from Callaway provoked the criticism from other Republican officials that Callaway was trying to dominate the party. There was continued resentment of Bentley as a newcomer, and the election results

21. Interview with Jimmy Bentley, April 29, 1974.

demonstrated that the GOP was in fact an urban phenomenon whose nominating primary appealed to few voters in nonurban counties. Bentley lost to an Atlanta television newscaster who was unable to add to the urban base in the general election. None of Bentley's colleagues who switched won elective office again, although one of the former office-holders received an appointment as undersecretary of agriculture from the Nixon administration. Although many Republican elected officials in the state supported him, Bentley concluded that too many Georgia Republicans were more interested in what he called "Kamikaze" politics than in building a successful, broad-based political party.[22]

The defeat of Fletcher Thompson by Nunn in the U.S. Senate race in 1972, the year of Nixon's landslide vote in Georgia, was another blow to Republicanism in the state. The events of Watergate further weakened the Republicans, and their candidate for governor in 1974, law-and-order Macon Mayor Ronnie Thompson, received only 30 percent of the vote.

The failure of the Republicans to organize beyond their city and suburban base is reflected in the returns in Republican primaries. Even with the well-known Bentley in the race in 1970, there were fewer than 100 Republican votes in 99 counties and fewer than ten votes in eight counties. The total Republican primary vote that year was 107,555, barely one-eighth the Democratic primary turnout of 798,660. Only ten counties recorded fewer than 1,000 votes in the Democratic primary, and none as few as 500. In the 1972 Republican senatorial primary, 82 counties recorded fewer than ten votes, and none were recorded in 28 of them. The total Republican primary vote dropped to 78,418.

In the 1974 race for governor, 46 counties recorded ten votes or fewer in the Republican primary, 11 of them with no recorded votes. The total Republican vote dropped to 48,022, divided among five candidates. Ronnie Thompson received 19,691, or 41 percent, in the first primary, and he received 22,211 in the runoff, in which the turnout was even smaller. He had also filed as a candidate in the Democratic primary, where his numerical total of 23,933 was actually higher than the number he received in either Republican primary, although it was only 2.3 percent of the total Democratic primary vote. J. B. Stoner, a racist lawyer whose tirades against Negroes, Jews, and Catholics have caused Maddox to walk off a platform, received more votes (73,449) in 1974 while running a weak fourth (9 percent) in the Democratic primary for lieutenant governor than the total number cast in the Republican primary for governor.

Reapportionment allowed Republicans to gain a foothold in the legislature. By 1966 they had expanded their base there to 29 seats in both houses, but there was little subsequent growth. In 1974, they lost five of their 29 seats in the House, including one from an incumbent who

22. Ibid.

switched to the Democrats—a striking reversal for the modern South, where almost all recent party switches have been from Democrat to Republican—and two of their seven Senate seats.

They also lost their last congressional seat with the defeat of Ben Blackburn, a Nixon loyalist to the end and an ultraconservative who had held what appeared to be a safely Republican seat in the DeKalb County suburbs of Atlanta. He lost to Elliott Levitas, a liberal Jewish legislator who had practiced law with Ellis Arnall.

In the legislature, Republicans got effective leadership from House Minority Leader Michael Egan, a Harvard Law graduate and one of the few remaining Republican activists who entered the party in the 1950s. With the Democratic Party at that time dominated by segregationists, a moderate reform element moved into the GOP, but the group lost control after the Goldwater movement. Egan was one of the few white legislators who voted to seat Julian Bond in 1966, and in 1968 he was one of two delegates from the South who supported then Governor Nelson Rockefeller of New York at the Republican National Convention.

Compared with other Deep South GOP organizations, Georgia Republicans placed greater than average emphasis on building the party from the bottom up. In the 1960s a reform group won control of city government in Columbus, the state's second-largest city, and a black Republican was elected to the city council there, one of the few black Republican elected officials in the South. Although the party remains narrowly conservative in ideology and country club in image, a few progressives such as Egan and John Savage, the unsuccessful GOP candidate for lieutenant governor in 1974, argue for a broader appeal.

Nevertheless, the failure of Callaway to win in 1966 was costly to the GOP, and its record of defeat since then has left the state firmly in Democratic hands.

Chapter

8

LOUISIANA

Legacy of the Longs

> People in Louisiana have an ambivalent
> attitude about corruption. On the one hand,
> we deplore it. On the other hand, we
> brag about it.
>
> —T. Harry Williams [1]

DURING Earl Long's last campaign for governor in 1955, a state senator delivered a $25,000 campaign contribution from an association of theater owners who wanted repeal of an admissions tax.

After Long's election, the senator approached the governor to confirm his support for a repeal measure. Long declared he not only would not support the bill but would veto it if it passed, since the state needed the money.

"But governor, what will I tell them?" asked the distressed senator.

Long replied, "Tell them I lied."

The story is a favorite in Louisiana, and a judge who tells it explains that what really upset the senator was that it cost him a $25,000 lobbying fee. "What it means," the judge explained, "is that a bribe is an illegal contract and that Earl Long felt no obligation."

If Huey and Earl Long connived and bought or broke other men, they themselves were not for sale. "Earl didn't take a dime that didn't belong to him. I'm convinced of that," says Adrian LaBorde, an Alexandria newspaper editor who for decades has written a daily political column and has been close to every major political figure in the state. "He and I

1. Interview with T. Harry Williams, January 10, 1974.

didn't get along worth a damn. He was a boor and everything else, but as far as dishonest, no. Earl, if he did do something . . . get something under the table, it was to help somebody else, not to help Earl Long. That was one of his weaknesses. He was probably the most honest of the Longs." [2] There are persistent reports that Earl Long as governor kept a little black book that showed who was taking what from whom, and that he cracked down when things got out of hand.

Louisiana politics remain an exotic mixture of the populist philosophy, reawakened and perpetuated by the Longs; racism whose intensity peaked in the 1960s; the cultural clash between the fun-loving tolerant Cajuns of French-Catholic ancestry in the south and the moralistic, Anglo-Saxon Baptists of the North, who share the values of neighboring Mississippi; a black electorate that is growing stronger and more sophisticated; and the spicy urban culture of New Orleans and its suburbs. Add to that a remarkable labor leader who exerts major influence in state policy, and a unique, business-funded research organization that plays an activist role in pushing governmental reform. The final ingredients are a multi-factional Democratic Party that retains one-party domination and the stirrings of a Republican Party that perhaps is the most underdeveloped in the South.

In 1971, a black-white populist coalition for the first time elected a governor, Congressman Edwin Edwards, a proud Cajun despite his Welsh name and the state's first French-speaking Catholic official in this century. Spillover candidates from that governor's race were elected in 1972 to a U.S. Senate seat and two seats in the U.S. House.

Traditionally, the accepted political mores in Louisiana are based on a distinction between "legal graft"—that which does not come from tax money—and outright fraud and corruption. The explanation given most frequently for the tolerant attitude is what is termed the "Latin influence." This includes the early settlement of the area by the Spanish, but primarily refers to the more than 1 million Louisianans of French descent, most of them Cajuns—a corruption of the word "Acadians." After the French in Nova Scotia refused to pledge allegiance to the British after the French and Indian War in the 1760s, some 15,000 of them migrated to the Louisiana Territory (then controlled by France) and settled down as farmers in the bayou country, a land of haunting beauty dominated by moss-draped hardwood swamps.

Traditionally, the Cajuns are known for their candor and tolerance, which extends to race, gambling, alcohol, casual sex, and political corruption—as long as it's not too much. Steal a little, but don't get greedy. There's no dishonor in admitting a little graft as long as it involves only a cut from a fee or commission or special favors for political supporters, and doesn't involve direct theft of tax money.

2. Interview with Adrian LaBorde, January 12, 1974.

A veteran sheriff in one of the Cajun parishes, whose nickname "Cat" was derived from the string of cathouses he operated, was questioned by a television newsman from New Orleans a few years ago about the prostitution in his parish. The sheriff replied he saw nothing to get excited about, that he didn't consider it harmful "for a man to get a little piece of 'strange' from time to time." [3]

Corruption in Louisiana did not begin with Huey Long. Long's biographer, Professor T. Harry Williams, says that Louisiana was one of only two southern states in which there was a great deal of corruption during Reconstruction: "I always suspected the carpetbaggers were learners down here. They didn't bring it with them; they were taking lessons." [4] And there are some who say the state is no more corrupt than others— that it's just talked about more and isn't as hidden. But there is no question of a traditional public tolerance for political corruption and a record of exposure on a scale perhaps grander than anywhere else in the United States.

"Extortion, bribery, peculation, thievery, are not rare in the annals of politics, but in the scale, variety, and thoroughness of its operations the Long gang established, after the death of the Kingfish, a record unparalleled in our times," wrote V. O. Key. "Millions of dollars found their way more or less directly to his political heirs and followers." [5]

While Huey Long doubtless contributed to the atmosphere of political corruption, and while his dictatorial control of the state in the early 1930s corrupted the democratic process, the other side of his legacy is the influence of populism on him and the resulting "conviction that poverty and squalor were evils that were not inevitable and that government had an obligation to combat these evils." [6] As Key noted:

> He kept faith with his people and they with him. He gave them something and the corporations paid for it. . . . He is not to be dismissed as a mere rabble-rouser or as the leader of a gang of boodlers. Nor can he be described by convenient label: fascist, communist. He brought to his career a streak of genius, yet in his programs and tactics he was as indigenous to Louisiana as pine trees and petroleum. . . .
>
> In the maintenance of its power and in the execution of its program, the Long organization used all the techniques of reward and reprisal that political organizations have employed from time immemorial: patronage, in all its forms, deprivation of perquisites, economic pressure, political coercion in one form or another, and now and then outright thuggery. Beyond these short-range tactics, Long commanded the intense loyalties of a substantial

3. Related by Jerry Doty, political consultant and authority on Louisiana political ecology. (Interview, January 16, 1974).

4. Interview with T. Harry Williams, January 10, 1974.

5. V. O. Key, *Southern Politics in State and Nation* (New York: Knopf/Vintage, 1949), p. 156.

6. T. Harry Williams, "Huey, Lyndon, and Southern Radicalism," *Journal of American History* (Summer 1973):277.

proportion of the population. . . . The people came to believe that here was a man with a genuine concern for their welfare, not one of the gentlemanly do-nothing governors who had ruled the state for many decades.[7]

THE LONG TRADITION

Huey Long died of an assassin's bullet in 1935, but a statewide poll at the end of 1974 showed he still ranked first among voters as the best governor the state ever had. The 34-story state capitol in Baton Rouge, which Huey had built on a 27-acre tract in 1932 for a quarter of a million dollars, remains a dominant feature of the capital city's skyline. A larger-than-life statue of Huey dominates a landscaped garden on the capitol grounds.

There is much about Louisiana's state government and exotic politics that is unique, and many of the unique qualities stem from Huey, who once described himself as sui generis—one of a kind.

After World War II, Huey's brother Earl was twice elected governor and continued in state government the programs and philosophy Huey had begun at the start of the Depression. Under Huey, massive highway construction and free bridges had ended rural isolation; a system of charity hospitals provided health care for the poor; free textbooks for every child attacked an illiteracy problem that was the worst in the nation. The books went to children, not schools, thus including the French Catholics who attended parochial school. Huey's slogans of "Share the Wealth" and "Every Man a King" provoked national excitement during the Depression and pushed Franklin D. Roosevelt to the left at the end of his first term.

Unlike a George Wallace, whose record is strong on populist rhetoric and weak on performance, the Longs included blacks, the poorest of the poor, in their determination to help poor people. As a black newspaper editor in Louisiana expressed it, Huey was for the man "farthest down," and although the Negro was seldom mentioned in Huey's speeches, blacks were included in the "farthest down program." [8]

Earl Long—who was elected governor in 1947 and again in 1955—expanded programs and facilities for education, welfare, public health, transportation, and mental health. Huey had taxed the corporations, and they continue to pay higher taxes than in any other southern state, with most of the revenue coming from severance taxes on natural gas, oil, and sulfur.

7. Key, *Southern Politics*, pp. 157, 162.
8. *Shreveport Sun*, April 22, 1933, quoted in Williams, "Huey, Lyndon, and Southern Radicalism," 279.

Earl Long left office a discredited figure, in part because of corruption among his associates, but more by bizarre public behavior associated with mental illness during the last year or so of his life, resulting in part from what doctors described as a series of small strokes. Still, he won election to a congressional seat a few days before his death in 1960.

When northern reporters flocked down in the late 1950s to cover crazy Earl Long's escapades as governor, A. J. Liebling of the *New Yorker* perceived that the real story was Earl Long fighting to protect the rights of blacks. It was a period of the most emotional regional outpouring of reaction to civil rights—the era of massive resistance to desegregation, when even a state with the moderate image of Virginia closed its public schools.

Willie Rainach (pronounced Ray-nack), a rabid segregationist state senator and chairman of what amounted to an official segregation committee, was leading efforts to selectively enforce a statute that required voters to "interpret" the state constitution. Earl Long appeared before the legislature and in a rambling, sometimes almost incoherent speech he declared, "There ain't ten people looking at me, including myself, who, if properly approached or attacked, could properly qualify to vote." Rainach, who was wearing a broad necktie emblazoned with a Confederate flag and "who addressed a microphone with gestures appropriate to a mass meeting," pleaded with his colleagues not to let Long "sell Louisiana down the river."

Long, a master of ridicule, declared of Rainach: "After all this is over, he'll probably go up there to Summerfield, get up on his front porch, take off his shoes, wash his feet, look at the moon and get close to God." Then he shouted in Rainach's direction, "And when you *do*, you got to recognize that niggers is human beings!" And he pleaded, "To keep fine, honorable grayheaded men and women off the registration rolls, some of whom have been voting as much as 60 or 65 years—I plead with you in all candor." [9]

Earl knew that blacks supported Long programs, and it was practical politics as well as racial justice for which he waged a lonely battle. He lost the fight.

Where applied, the program of systematic removal worked. By the time of the 1959 governor's race, black registration from 1956 had declined in Ouachita Parish from 4,518 to 726, in Webster from 1,764 to 111, in Morehouse from 1,295 to 285, in East Feliciana from 1,349 to 70, in Washington from 1,783 to 241. In East Carroll, Madison, and West Feliciana Parishes, black registration remained unchanged—zero. The Justice Department brought suit, and federal judges later ordered the names restored to the books. (The effect of the Voting Rights Act of 1965 is reflected in 1974 registration figures, which showed 9,365 blacks regis-

9. A. J. Liebling, *The Earl of Louisiana* (Baton Rouge: Louisiana State University Press, 1970), pp. 30–31.

tered in Ouachita Parish, 5,097 in Webster, 4,006 in Morehouse, 5,067 in Washington, 3,756 in East Feliciana, 3,238 in East Carroll, 3,953 in Madison, and 2,136—a majority—in West Feliciana.)

Huey's son, Russell Long, elected in 1948 to the U.S. Senate when he was 30, is the youngest of the old breed of southern power brokers in Congress. Although his consistent efforts to increase Social Security benefits and fight to promote prosecution of price fixers in the drug industry stem from his father's heritage, it was Russell Long who as chairman of the Senate Finance Committee played the key role in killing the Family Assistance Plan of the Nixon administration, the first real attempt by the federal government to implement Huey's "share-the-wealth" ideas. FAP would have tripled the income of many destitute southerners.

Before his death, Huey shrewdly invested in the "Win or Lose" oil company—which never lost, as they say in Louisiana—and his son's wealth is estimated in excess of $100 million. Russell Long led the congressional battle to retain the depletion allowance for "independent" oil companies in 1975 after failing to keep it for all companies. He campaigned unsuccessfully for distant cousin Gillis Long for governor in 1963, and for the most part has stayed out of state politics ever since. Like Herman Talmadge in Georgia and Harry Byrd, Jr. in Virginia, two other senators who are heirs to a political dynasty but are capable men in their own right, Russell Long is politically secure at home.

Louisiana's other senator, J. Bennett Johnston, Jr., has political connections with the Long family: his father supported Earl Long and was rewarded by appointment as attorney to assist the inheritance tax collector, an office which until it was abolished was the most lucrative patronage position in state government.

A lawyer and a West Point graduate who as a state senator compiled a reputation for hard work and a record of reform in matters affecting government practices, Johnston grew up in a well-to-do family in Shreveport. He received 49.8 percent of the vote in a narrow loss to Edwin Edwards in the 1971 gubernatorial runoff. Johnston filed against incumbent Senator Allen Ellender the following year, and at age 40 fell into the Democratic nomination when Ellender died unexpectedly.

On national issues, Senator Johnston's early voting record is one of the more conservative among Democrats elected from the South in the last decade. He has bright prospects for a lengthy Senate career.

The voting record of Congressman Gillis Long, twice an unsuccessful candidate for governor, more closely reflects the political philosophy of his cousins Earl and Huey than that of Russell Long or Johnston. Gillis first was elected in 1962, two years after Earl's death, to the congressional seat Earl had won in 1960. At age 40, Gillis ran for governor in 1963 and lost much of the Long organization to John McKeithen, onetime House floor leader for Earl Long. The following year he lost his congressional seat to Speedy O. Long, another cousin who was a hard-line conservative. When Speedy retired eight years later, Gillis returned to Congress after another unsuccessful race for governor. His district was more than one-third black, and in 1973 he voted 78 percent of the time in support of the position of the Congressional Black Caucus on such domestic issues as continuation of legal services for the poor, minimum wage legislation, public service job program extension, and appropriations for community development. It was the highest level of support by any white member of Congress from the South.

Gillis Long retains broad-based support in his congressional district, in part a reflection of changing attitudes at home. Because governors are elected in off-year elections, a congressman can run without giving up his seat, and Long is young enough to try again in the future. Editor Adrian LaBorde in Alexandria, the major city in the district, considers the congressman "an awfully capable man." [10]

RACISM, POPULISM, AND REFORM

Racism and populism have alternated as the focus of Louisiana politics since Reconstruction. Until the rise of Huey Long, white Bourbon Democrats had ruled since the 1890s, when they used racist appeals to beat back the populist-oriented agrarian revolt, which in Louisiana had a sustained biracial character.

The intensity of response to racial issues in Louisiana surfaced clearly in 1948 when Strom Thurmond ran under the Democratic banner in the state and won with a 49 percent plurality. The only Democrats to carry Louisiana in a presidential election since World War II have been Adlai Stevenson in 1952, when he received strong support from the Longs and Alabama Senator John Sparkman was his running mate, and John F. Kennedy in 1960. In Louisiana, unlike the rest of the South, Kennedy's Catholicism was a political asset because roughly 45 percent of the whites are Catholic. A third-party, States' Rights ticket received only 21 percent of the 1960 vote, compared to 50 percent for Kennedy.

After Barry Goldwater won 57 percent of the Louisiana vote in 1964, the Comparative State Elections Project survey demonstrated that racial issues were central to his victory. Based on responses to specific questions on civil rights and economic issues, the survey developed two indexes, one for racism and the other for populism. Among voters ranked high and moderately high on the racism index, more than seven in ten voted for

10. Interview with Adrian LaBorde, January 12, 1974.

Goldwater, regardless of their rating on the populism index. Among voters who rated low on the racism index, 39 percent of those who were also low or moderate on the populism index voted for Goldwater. But among those both low on the racism index and high on populism, only 17 percent voted for Goldwater.[11]

Forty-nine percent of those who voted for Goldwater in 1964 voted for George Wallace in 1968.[12] Wallace won a 48 percent plurality as a third-party candidate in 1968, his rhetoric appealing to both racist and populist instincts. Although Democrat Hubert Humphrey finished second with 28 percent, he received less than 18 percent of the white vote. Despite the voting patterns, survey research showed a majority of whites in 1968 still considered themselves Democrats "when it comes to national politics." [13] Democratic identification declined steadily with increasing white family income.[14] The same survey also disclosed that 20 percent of the white Democrats considered Wallace a more loyal Democrat than Humphrey, and another 18 percent thought the two candidates were equal in party loyalty.[15]

The 1968 Wallace vote shifted solidly in 1972 to Richard Nixon. He won 70 percent of the vote in 1972 after receiving only 24 percent in 1968, a rejection by Wallace voters of George McGovern.

In state government, sentiment for reform ebbs and flows like the tide. Reaction to the graft associated with the Longs was reflected by a reform faction that tended to represent "good government" forces; these were often conservative, business-oriented candidates who believed the best way to stop graft was to cut government spending. A secondary reform element that has remained active through the years has supported social programs but sought to reform procedures and crack down on corruption.

Judge Robert Kennon, who served as governor between the two terms of Earl Long, represented the former group. Kennon was elected in the January 1953 primary, when the Long forces split. Earl Long had hand-picked Judge Carlos Spaht, but Russell Long backed Representative Hale Boggs. The Kennon administration is remembered for its lack of scandal and for a constitutional amendment requiring a two-thirds vote in each house of the legislature before taxes can be increased.

The leader of the reform forces after Kennon was New Orleans Mayor

11. Perry H. Howard, Maxwell E. McCombs, and David M. Kovenock, *Explaining the Vote: Presidential Choices in the Nation and the States, 1968*, Comparative State Elections Project, (Chapel Hill: Institute for Research in Social Sciences, University of North Carolina, 1973), p. 533.

12. Ibid., p. 594.

13. Ibid., p. 527.

14. Ibid., p. 528.

15. Ibid., p. 592.

deLesseps (Chep) Morrison ("ol' Della-soups" to Earl). A racial moderate whose New Orleans base was built around middle- and upper-income whites, he lost to populist Earl Long without a runoff in his first race for governor. He lost two other attempts after the race issue heated up.

Segregationist Jimmie Davis, the hillbilly singer who wrote the lyrics for "You Are My Sunshine" and served a term as governor before the first Earl Long administration, won in 1959, and John McKeithen ran as a segregationist four years later to defeat Morrison. Both times, Morrison led the first primary with 33.1 percent of the vote. Against Davis, he finished with 45.9 percent, and he received 47.8 percent against McKeithen.

Davis defeated the even more racist Rainach in the first primary, then picked up segregationist support in the runoff. As governor, Davis called five special sessions of the legislature to pass laws aimed at combating school desegregation. His defenders contend that his inflammatory rhetoric, which stirred emotions during a school desegregation crisis in New Orleans, was not a display of irresponsible leadership, as his critics charge, but rather provided an emotional outlet for the more violence-prone whites. Davis managed to accumulate considerable wealth, in part through movies and recordings. The traditional way of doing business with the state was not disturbed during his administrations.

Before running for governor, the mercurial McKeithen had served as Earl Long's floor leader in the House and then on the state Public Service Commission, the same office and the same district from which Huey Long had launched his career. McKeithen had cast a decisive vote against 10-cent coin telephone calls, and Louisiana is the last state in which one can make a nickel call from a coin-operated telephone.

After black precincts voted overwhelmingly in the first primary for Morrison, McKeithen's campaign cry was "he'p me," asking for help against the blacks and declaring himself a "100 percent segregationist." He also ran against the incumbent Davis administration, branding himself the "uncontrolled" candidate. He combined this reform image with that of a Long progressive, acknowledging his "guilt" in voting for tax increases as a Long floor leader in 1948, but pointing out the programs the taxes financed, such as free school lunches, old age pensions, and veterans' bonuses.[16]

Charlton Lyons, a wealthy Shreveport businessman and dedicated conservative, ran in 1963 as the state's first serious Republican candidate for governor and picked up almost 39 percent of the vote. He ran well in the Rainach strongholds and also picked up strong support among the south Louisiana supporters of Morrison—reflecting the traditional anti-

16. Perry H. Howard, "Louisiana: Resistance and Change," in William C. Havard, ed., *The Changing Politics of the South* (Baton Rouge: Louisiana State University Press, 1972), p. 564.

Long sentiment, the emergence of urban Republicanism that remains significant, opposition to McKeithen's use of the race issue, and resentment of Morrison's defeat.

Once elected, McKeithen quickly made political peace with Morrison, naming him director of a program to attract industry. Morrison died the following year in a plane crash.

McKeithen displayed dynamic leadership. He proved a super salesman in attracting new industry, and he exercised bold leadership during a period of tension between civil rights demonstrators and the Ku Klux Klan. He proved his ability to communicate with and understand both groups, declaring that blacks and whites would have to learn to get along together because neither group was leaving Louisiana. He also established a biracial commission at the state level to deal with the racial crisis, staffed it with a full-time counsel, and called out the National Guard to protect civil-rights marchers.

He passed a reform program that included a code of ethics and creation of a state ethics commission, a central purchasing system for the state, abandonment of the traditional system of investing millions of dollars of idle state funds in interest-free deposits with banks that had been campaign contributors, and new laws to promote industrial development. His popularity was such that in 1966 voters gave 70 percent approval to a constitutional amendment allowing a governor to succeed himself.

The death of Morrison and defeat of Gillis Long for reelection to Congress in 1964 had created a leadership vacuum, and McKeithen was assured of a second term. His popularity in New Orleans soared when he won voter approval for a gigantic domed stadium. Although the cost of the Superdome eventually rose to more than $160 million, compared with the original $35–40 million estimates, and despite criticism that the state had more pressing needs, the controversial structure had revitalized the central business district in downtown New Orleans long before the stadium's completion.

Camille Gravel, who had served as Democratic national committeeman and represented the forces of racial moderation during the heyday of the segregationists, explained that McKeithen never was antiblack and that his move to moderation was "a crass, political decision." "All he did was count votes," he claimed, as climbing black registration accelerated after the passage of the Voting Rights Act.

"Hell, I remember when we were trying to elect [state Senator Edwin] Edwards to Congress, McKeithen walking into the [governor's] mansion, and we had a meeting with him and some black people in the front room of the mansion; McKeithen then goes into a back room for a meeting with some leaders of the Klan. He was just a master politician. He just used whatever elements he could for whatever political purposes he could. Now Edwards is a different story. Edwards really in his heart, race means nothing to him. Never has. He really doesn't care. If you're black and doing your job or he likes you, he's got no problem. He's always been that way, as long as I've known him." [17]

Gravel explained that he and state AFL–CIO President Vic Bussie, a dynamic man who for 20 years has served as a key adviser to governors and as a major force in state politics, went to Washington to confer with then Vice-President Hubert Humphrey, who helped convince McKeithen to move when the governor hesitated to establish the Biracial Commission. "Humphrey is the one who said, 'You know, if you have aspirations you better get right on this thing.' We really plotted against McKeithen on that score." [18]

Regardless of the motivation, McKeithen's leadership gave a cue to local officials in dealing with racial matters. The former counsel to the Biracial Commission explained that after a Biracial Commission study disclosed that only ten blacks were employed by the Highway Department, the largest agency in state government, McKeithen attacked the problem of employment discrimination by calling in legislators, showing them current figures on black voter registration in their parishes, and telling them, "You sure could use some black employment in the Highway Department in your parish." Road work was a source of patronage, and it marked the beginning of the breakdown of employment discrimination in state government.[19]

McKeithen scored a massive victory in 1967, with 80 percent of the vote against token opposition from Representative John Rarick. The Republicans did not even run a candidate. But even as he was winning with tremendous popular support, discontent was spreading, and his second administration turned sour. In the summer of 1967 his successful industrial development program blew apart when industry began shutting down construction in the Baton Rouge area amid charges of widespread labor racketeering. McKeithen set up a Labor-Management Commission that for the next two years produced tales of cheating, shakedowns, violence, and duplicity by government officials. The Teamsters Union boss not only won special concessions for his union during a period of short labor supply, but also made deals for himself with contractors and suppliers. One such deal involved a conspiracy with a local businessman to form a local monopoly in concrete. One contractor reported that the price he paid for concrete in order to get labor peace was $3.45 a yard higher than the lowest bid.

It was an era when a plant manager who had recently moved to Baton Rouge called upon two local legislators to discuss a minor local bill in

17. Interview with Camille Gravel, January 14, 1974.
18. Ibid.
19. Related by John Martzell, former counsel to the Biracial Commission. (Interview, January 8, 1974.)

which he was interested. At their request, he agreed to give a party and was surprised to see scores of their friends—people he did not know. As the evening progressed, he finally cornered the legislators to discuss the matter of interest. One of them named the businessman who had the concrete monopoly and explained, "We both work for him and when he doesn't tell us how to vote, that's how we make our living." Reporter Bill Lynch of the New Orleans *States-Item,* perhaps the toughest investigative reporter in the state, swears the story is true: for a "fee" the legislators would get the bill passed.

The Labor-Management Commission also exposed three top state police officials. The state police superintendent and two top aides retired after it was revealed that their wives and daughters had been carried several years before on the payrolls of construction companies, listed in some instances as "male truck drivers." McKeithen ordered a new superintendent to clean up the department.

The attorney general's office took over prosecution, but after referral of almost 200 charges involving local law enforcement officers, none was ever convicted. The attorney general, Jack P. F. Gremillion, himself was indicted and later convicted of accepting a $10,000 fee in a different scandal.

When *Life* Magazine in 1967 ran a story on the widespread influence in Louisiana of organized crime chieftain Carlos Marcello of New Orleans, McKeithen denounced the magazine and led a delegation of prominent citizens to confer with the editors. When he returned to Baton Rouge, he made a televised public apology to the magazine and declared, "You've given us evidence here that we can go back to Louisiana with and clean up our state and we think put some people in the penitentiary. We can't wait to get back to Louisiana to do it."

Camille Gravel was named head of a special commission to investigate mob influence, but he resigned in disgust when the investigation halted after it began to focus on C. H. (Sammy) Downs, a key member of the McKeithen administration who kept a telephone in a locked box that allegedly linked Mafia figures directly with the governor's office. Apparently, only Downs had access to the telephone.

Three years later, *Life* issued a scathing second report, concluding that there was no evidence of personal involvement by McKeithen in any of Marcello's affairs, but reporting in detail the widespread influence still retained by Marcello, especially in the state Department of Revenue, which failed to prosecute a number of claims against Marcello's associates and enterprises. *Life* estimated a loss in state revenue of $100 million as a result of generally lax enforcement by the Department of Revenue.

Despite the tarnished image caused by the disclosures of corruption, McKeithen was one of a number of southern governors who took seriously the mention of his name by Vice-President Hubert Humphrey as a potential running mate for 1968. McKeithen introduced Humphrey at the state AFL–CIO convention that year with a glowing speech filled with praise for a man whose liberal, pro–civil rights record was less than popular with a majority of Louisiana residents. At the Democratic National Convention in Chicago, McKeithen pictured himself to Louisiana reporters as a major contender for the vice-presidency, but he received no serious consideration for the job after Humphrey's nomination. McKeithen then rushed back home to begin mending political fences and decided he could not support Humphrey for president, although he had endorsed him for the nomination before the Chicago convention.

McKeithen was discouraged and despondent, and he privately threatened to resign. Adrian LaBorde, the Alexandria editor, and his publisher, both of whom were close to McKeithen, were called by the governor's executive secretary to have breakfast at the mansion with McKeithen and try to convince him he would be making a mistake.

"We spent half a day there and told him that the worst thing that could happen to him and the state of Louisiana was for him to resign," LaBorde explained. "We talked him out of it."

LaBorde recalled McKeithen saying at the breakfast meeting, "I've had it up to here. I can't do anything with the legislature. The press is on me. The people don't believe in me any more. I'm going to turn it over to Taddy Aycock [the lieutenant governor]."

LaBorde thought McKeithen returned from the convention a "changed man," that he had really thought he would get the vice-presidential nomination, although nobody else seemed to share that belief. "He was having a bad press before that. And like I told him at this long breakfast meeting in the mansion, a lot of it was his fault. He overreacted to certain things. You're going to be criticized, I don't give a damn how good you are, and you've got to learn to take it. He overreacted. . . . McKeithen was convinced that the press in Louisiana was out to get him. But I didn't detect any real problem until after Chicago, when I found out he wanted to resign. And I thought it was a joke until I went down there and it wasn't a damned joke. He was just as serious as he could be." [20]

McKeithen had failed that year in an attempt to raise taxes, and he called a special session in the fall to try again. However, not until 1970, in the face of a threatened teachers' strike, did he win a tax increase. Also in 1970, McKeithen called another special session to deal with the school busing issue, which suddenly had become hot in Louisiana. His action was widely interpreted at the time as an effort to jump on the antibusing bandwagon and restore some of his lost popularity. But like Governor Claude Kirk in Florida, McKeithen failed in his attempt to exploit the issue. The special session produced a lot of rhetoric, but no effective legislation.

20. Interview with Adrian LaBorde, January 12, 1974.

Meanwhile, what came to be known as the legislative Mafia Investigating Committee looked into the *Life* allegations and uncovered a major scandal in the Revenue Department, finding that tens of thousands of citizens were not paying income taxes and that a number of businesses and industries were getting favored treatment either through design or incompetence. The committee investigations and hearings lasted more than a year, providing publicity that further eroded McKeithen's image.

Then, a federal grand jury investigating insurance commission kickbacks to public officials indicted McKeithen's commissioner of administration on charges of making a false statement. He was later acquitted, but the publicity hurt McKeithen. Sammy Downs, whom McKeithen had named public works director even after Downs was linked with Mafia figures while working in the governor's office, also was indicted by a grand jury in connection with $200,000 in commissions he received on voting machines purchased by the state. He was tried twice, with hung juries both times.

When U.S. Senator Allen Ellender died during the primary campaign, McKeithen jumped into the race as an independent in the general election against Bennett Johnston, but he polled only 23 percent of the vote, far behind Johnston's 55 percent.

Several years after leaving office, McKeithen said the investigations and trials had shown that his conduct was honest, despite the charges and allegations. He recalled when Earl Long had called him aside as an inexperienced 29-year-old legislator who had caught his eye, and told him: " 'I'm going to make you floor leader. Now, I want to give you a little advice. Watch out for that whiskey. It's ruined a lot of good men who had come here and had had a future. Leave women alone. You ever read over the vows a man takes when he gets married?' I said, 'Yes, sir.' 'Well, you leave them women alone. Don't take nobody's money. Keep yourself where you can look any son of a bitch in the eye.' "

McKeithen told the story with relish and said, "That's pretty good advice, isn't it? And when these young Republicans . . . young attorneys came in and started investigating around, I was in a position where I could look any son of a bitch in the eye."

McKeithen, a man who may enjoy politics too much to find contentment on the sidelines, said his ambition "really is just to have the respect and confidence of the bulk of the people in this state." [21]

The issue in the 1971 Democratic gubernatorial primary runoff was reform, and U.S. Representative Edwin Edwards and state Senator J. Bennett Johnston both ran as reform candidates. Edwards won by 4,488 votes in the closest election for governor in the state's history. Turnout statewide was 1,164,036. In the 22 parishes of Acadiana, or Cajun country, Edwards not only polled 68 percent of the vote but the turnout was

21. Interview with John McKeithen, January 12, 1974.

more than 5 percentage points greater than the statewide average. While only about one-fourth of the voting-age population (26.8 percent) reside in Acadiana, they constituted 31.5 percent of the registered voters and a full one-third (33.4 percent) of those who actually voted in the runoff. With a new ethnic pride reflected in bumper stickers that read "Cajun Power," 76.2 percent of the voters there turned out, compared with 71.1 percent statewide.

Edwards carried all 22 parishes in Acadiana, only one of 30 in north Louisiana, and two of the eight Florida parishes. Although he won only one of the four parishes in the New Orleans area, the vote there was extremely close, with Edwards receiving 49.2 percent of the vote. In the traditional manner, Edwards invested heavily in the traditional black political organizations in New Orleans, but Johnston appealed to a younger and less-known black leadership in the city and received a significant minority of the vote there. In the middle-class white suburbs of Jefferson County, Edwards received more than 49 percent of the vote, a division that reflected the reform campaigns run by both candidates. But elsewhere outside of Acadiana, the heaviest vote for Edwards came in parishes with heavy black populations.

Edwards had the support of organized labor and picked up enough urban working-class votes to go with his Cajun and black base. At the Istrouma High School polling place (Ward 1, Precinct 16) in Baton Rouge, a classic blue-collar white precinct that voted 64.4 percent for Wallace in 1968 and 73.5 percent for Nixon in 1972, Johnston led in the crowded first primary and Edwards ran third behind former Governor Jimmie Davis. In the runoff, Johnston won, 290–150, but Johnston added only 37 votes to his first primary total, while Edwards picked up 50 votes in the runoff. In the general election against Republican David Treen, Edwards increased his percentage from 34.1 in the runoff to 46.2, losing to Treen by 323–277. Statewide, Edwards received 57.8 percent of the vote against Treen, but only 47 percent of the white vote.

As governor, Edwards has proved to be a paradox. A skillful politician who has a first-rate mind, he caught the powerful oil and gas industry off balance by calling a special legislative session when the energy crisis first developed; the legislature roughly doubled the severance taxes on natural gas and oil, while removing the sales tax on food. Edwards won approval of a new constitution after five previous efforts had failed. He symbolically appointed a black female press secretary, and he installed a youthful management wizard who transformed the scandal-ridden Department of Revenue into an agency of model efficiency. Nevertheless, his administration has been tarnished by fiscal irregularities and by reports of his flamboyant personal life style.

Examined closely, the public record of Edwards's first term is one of achievement. The record includes a $54 million bond issue to construct a

49-school system of vocational-technical education; almost a threefold increase to $34.7 million for education of the handicapped; reductions in the much-abused patronage system, including abolition of the office of attorney to assist the inheritence tax collector, a post that reportedly was worth $100,000 annually in New Orleans; creation of a selection board for architects and engineers; abolition of insurance commissions, which for years had been paid under the table to legislators and friends of governors; establishment of a control system on highway expenditures to reduce the traditional power of the governor for "political" road-building favors to local officials; removal of the power to fill trial judge vacancies from the governor to the Supreme Court; approval of a 15-year, $107 million program for parks and recreation facilities; and the banning of pinball gambling machines. Perhaps the most significant reform came under Revenue Commissioner Joseph Traigle, a young management specialist handpicked by Edwards to clean up the Revenue Department. Traigle developed an image of efficiency and integrity in transforming that agency.

Edwards delivered on the major items in his 1971 platform—a constitutional convention, reorganization of the executive branch, and tax reform. In addition to a $300 million tax increase through increased taxes on natural gas and oil, Edwards achieved the elimination of the sales tax on food and medicine and restoration to individual taxpayers of a state income tax credit for federal income taxes, at a combined cost of roughly $110 million in individual tax relief. About $60 million of the net increase in revenues went for pay increases to teachers and state employees.

Some critics contended that the Edwards program put the state in an untenable long-range position, since gas and oil reserves are running out; thus, increased dependency on them may create grave problems in the future. Edwards's response is that "it is better to maximize the state's participation before they are depleted so the money can be used to build up our educational system, to build up our road system, to retire our state debt. . . . In other words, the better the financial picture of the state when that day does come, the easier it will be to accept the loss of revenue." [22]

The new constitution, which was written by a convention dominated by an atmosphere of political trade-offs, is permeated with extraneous and special-interest provisions, especially on matters of taxation. It places a limit on personal but not on corporate income taxes. The list of property tax exemptions ranges from boats and cars to a $30,000 homestead exemption—but no provision is made for renters. Because a $15,000 homestead exemption in the old constitution effectively eliminated taxes on 70 percent of the homes in the state, the beneficiaries of the additional relief are those in middle- and upper-income brackets. Other examples of special-interest provisions include one that allows the legislature to give

22. Interview with Edwin W. Edwards, January 16, 1974.

higher pay to state police and game wardens than to other civil service employees. Another provision increases from $200,000 to $500,000 the maximum annual rebate in severance taxes to the two dozen or so oil-rich parishes. The new constitution reserves exclusive use of the rebate to police juries (the parish governing board, equivalent to a county council), whereas the old constitution provided that a portion of the rebate would go to local education. Although the tax provisions guarantee that business and corporate interests will continue to pay a larger share of the property tax in Louisiana than in any other state, a ten-year tax exemption for new industry has been retained.

The homestead exemption, which goes to $50,000 for veterans and people over 65, in effect legalizes the traditional practices of many of the state's tax assessors, elected officials of considerable influence. None is more influential—or more controversial—than Lawrence Chehardy of Jefferson Parish, a man capable of raising several hundred thousand dollars for a favored candidate for governor and who believes homeowners should not pay taxes. His New Orleans suburban homeowners agree, regardless of the consequences to public services.

Chehardy campaigned extensively on New Orleans television in support of the new constitution in 1974, telling voters that rejection would mean higher taxes. Voters in the four New Orleans area parishes responded with a 103,371 margin in favor of the constitution, which in the other 60 parishes fell 5,000 short of a majority. The largest margin in favor, 51,372, came in Chehardy's Jefferson Parish stronghold. Chehardy's influence as a delegate at the constitutional convention was such that 113 other delegates signed a resolution paying him tribute because "his untiring efforts retained and increased the guardian angel of homestead exemptions and the barricade against higher income taxes in our document and delineated the distinction between mine and thine pertaining to our people and our government."

Although Edwards campaigned for the new constitution, in private he candidly acknowledged its deficiencies. "The constitution should say nothing at all about taxing except that the legislature is empowered to levy and collect taxes," he said. But he added: "There is no way in the world that I could get my way. . . . The last thing you ought to have in the constitution is how you assess property. You couldn't get nine people in this state to publicly take that position, but I can because it is not sound constitutional law." [23]

While Edwards received high marks for his official performance as governor, his personal habits and private finances tarnished the reform image. In a move that anywhere but Louisiana might have raised questions of propriety, Edwards appointed his wife Elaine to a temporary Senate vacancy after the death of Senator Ellender. When it was later

23. Ibid.

disclosed that she had lived in Washington at a Watergate apartment leased by a wealthy New Orleans architect, Edwards shrugged it off publicly as merely accepting a friend's offer of an unused facility. At the time, selection of architects for most public buildings in Louisiana required approval by the governor, and $15,000 campaign contributions in a governor's race by established architects were not unusual.

A handsome man who many women find attractive, Edwards received public attention with frequent trips to Las Vegas casinos, where he acknowledged losing as much as several thousand dollars on a visit. At the beginning of 1975, a reelection year, Edwards made public a New Year's resolution to stop his gambling. When a reporter asked if he would keep his resolution, Edwards smiled back, "The odds are eight to five."

Before his first term ended, Edwards came under investigation by the Internal Revenue Service, and there were widespread charges of "selling" offices because of the appointment of campaign contributors to a number of government positions.

Early in his administration, the governor's appointed chairman of the state Highway Commission and the governor's personal bodyguard launched a financial scheme, TEL Enterprises, in which Edwards held stock. They began buying banks and a hotel, and they announced plans for a 60-story One Edwards Square in Baton Rouge, similar to One Shell Square in Houston, with the implication that with the influence of the governor's office it would quickly be filled with renters.

Edwards took no action during a period of occasional news stories about TEL Enterprises activities, but Baton Rouge publisher Doug Manship then directed his staff to run a story a day on TEL Enterprises. A top reporter was assigned full-time, and the Associated Press picked up the story and gave it statewide coverage. Edwards put an end to his association with TEL Enterprises and fired his bodyguard, who then began to make allegations that political appointments had been "sold" to campaign contributors.

When veteran Secretary of State Wade O. Martin, who had served in that office for 30 years, announced in 1975 he would run against Edwards, Martin attacked the governor for the trips to Las Vegas. Martin declared that the governor had a lot of "cute" explanations, adding, "But after a while, people began to think a little bit and they thought that it's not so cute after all. . . . Kids get an example from a governor, and even the gambling people aren't so anxious to see their governor leaning over a crap table every few days." [24] Despite the controversy, Edwards won reelection with a landslide 61 percent of the vote, with Martin running a poor third.

One congressional observer of Edwards dismisses his personal habits as those of a "happy Frenchman," but knowledgeable political observers

24. *New Orleans Times-Picayune*, March 16, 1975, p. 34.

in the state who believe that Mafia Boss Marcello has ties with Las Vegas casinos worry about who pays the gambling bills and the implications of the answer to that question.

BLACK POLITICS

The constitution fashioned during Edwards's first term received overwhelming support among blacks, in large part because it included perhaps the strongest declaration of rights of any state constitution in the country. While there were reports of money changing hands to sway leaders of some black political organizations in New Orleans, the fact is that the new constitution provides state guarantees against discrimination in public accommodations, prohibits any laws that would discriminate on the basis of race or religion, establishes the right to counsel of an accused at every stage of criminal proceedings, guarantees the right of privacy, provides for automatic restoration of voting and citizenship rights to prisoners upon their release, and adds to the federal guarantee of equal protection of the laws a state guarantee as well. The new constitution also ensures black representation on the state Civil Service Commission and specifies a commitment to equal educational opportunity for all people.

State Representative Alphonse Jackson, a highly capable black legislator from Shreveport who was chairman of the Committee on a Declaration of Rights, was pleasantly surprised at achieving such a strong article. "It places, for the first time, strong emphasis on the rights of the individual over and against the rights of the state," he said.

Jackson praised Edwards for his accessibility to black groups and black meetings. "I think the man cares about this state," Jackson said, "Because he cares, I think he is aware of the fact that you can't have a large segment of the population of this state ill-housed, ill-clothed, ill-educated, and ill-fed. So his decisions are based on the fact that he has got to bring everybody along if the state is going to grow. I think he cares and I think he is sensitive to the problems."

"Louisiana," he continued, "is a vastly different place from what it was 15 years ago. Things are happening in this state. . . . We find in the [state] House of Representatives a great acceptance on the part of our colleagues. We don't have any problems socially." [25]

In Louisiana, as elsewhere in the South, the fact that blacks now register and vote in significant numbers not only means the election of congressmen like Gillis Long but also affects the voting behavior of entrenched conservatives.

25. Interview with Alphonse Jackson, January 16, 1974.

Few better examples exist than Otto Passman, who after his election in 1946 had run virtually unopposed until 1972 as a forthright conservative on economic and social issues and a critic of government spending. His primary opponent in 1972 received 39 percent of the vote, enough to encourage a serious challenge in a district almost 35 percent black. In 1973, Passman voted 39 percent with the Congressional Black Caucus, a higher percentage than any congressman from Alabama or Mississippi. Passman voted for higher minimum wage legislation, against greater restrictions on lobbying by poverty lawyers in the legal services program, and for more funds for bilingual education. He also voted to override a presidential veto of minimum wage extensions and against an amendment to prohibit issuance of food stamps to strikers.

Just how different Louisiana has become was demonstrated in a remarkable speech made in 1972 on the floor of the state House of Representatives by Risley Claiborne (Pappy) Triche. A country lawyer from the bayou town of Napoleonville in south Louisiana, he had led the fight in the early 1960s against school desegregation as floor leader for Governor Jimmie Davis.

Triche rose to speak in favor of two bills designed to protect racial minorities from employment discrimination. He candidly acknowledged that people would think, "Listen to that segregationist. Isn't that the guy who offered all the segregation bills in 1960 and fought the battle to preserve segregation in our public school system? The only reply I can make to that, gentlemen, is that yes, that occurred. And at that time in the state of development of the history of our state we thought that we were correct. And we now find that we were wrong."

Triche had retired in 1968 from the legislature, planning not to run again. "There's one thing that drove me back," he told his House colleagues, "And the thing that drove me back was I did not want to leave my children with the legacy that their daddy was a bigot and a racist. I am not a bigot and a racist. I want my family and my citizens and my friends and my constituents and the citizenry of this state to grow out of racism and bigotry. Let us join hands with all the people of this state, black and white, regardless of race, creed, or color, for the advancement and betterment of our state and nation."

What was remarkable about the speech was that unlike the George Wallaces and the Strom Thurmonds and the hundreds of lesser politicians who later rationalized that they really had always been fair-minded, or tried to explain that their actions had allowed time for people to adjust, Pappy Triche said, "we were wrong."

Alphonse Jackson was one of eight blacks, six of them from New Orleans, who were elected to the state House in 1972 after the state was reapportioned into single-member districts. Although there is no statewide formal black political organization, there is an informal network through which local black leaders communicate concerning statewide issues and candidates. Use of money to influence and get out the black vote is practiced to some degree in every southern state, but reports in Louisiana suggest that the sums involved, especially in New Orleans, may be greater than anywhere else, a reflection in part of the traditional political culture and the generally extravagant level of spending in Louisiana political campaigns.

In 1974, 42 of the 64 parishes had black populations of 25 percent or more. Eighty-five of the 92 black elected county officials resided in those parishes, 30 of them in the nine parishes with majority black populations.

Registration of both blacks and whites in the black-majority parishes is higher than the statewide average. White registration in those nine parishes in 1974 was 94.3 percent of the voting-age population, compared with 81.2 percent statewide. Black registration in those nine parishes was 73.4 percent, compared with 65.2 percent statewide. The white-black difference in registration rate was 21 percent in the majority black parishes, compared with 16 percent statewide.

Unlike South Carolina, where black registration rates tend to be significantly lower in counties with smaller percentages of black population, the registration rates for blacks in parishes with less than 25 percent black populations and those with 25–50 percent were almost the same.

Black registration in Orleans Parish (New Orleans), where a fourth of the black voting-age population resides, was 10.5 percent below the statewide average. But for New Orleans whites, who comprise a seventh of the total white population, registration was 23.2 percent below the statewide average.

Negro registration in New Orleans, which was 15 percent of the total in 1960, had increased to 38 percent by 1974, partly because of accelerated registration after passage of the 1965 Voting Rights Act and partly because of white flight from New Orleans to the suburbs after school desegregation was implemented in the early 1960s. Between 1960 and 1970 the white population in the city declined from 392,594 to 326,163, less than it had been in 1940. The black population increased from 234,931 in 1960 to 267,308 in 1970.

Beginning in 1946, New Orleans government was dominated by a reform machine called the Crescent City Democratic Association, led by deLesseps Morrison. Morrison and the CCDA dealt with a few Negro leaders, who at campaign time were given cash to spend as they saw fit. The two major black organizations in the 1950s were the Orleans Parish Progressive Voters League, formed by the Reverend A. L. Davis, and the Crescent City Independent Voters League, led by Clarence (Chink) Henry, president of the black shoremen's Local 1419.

As black registration rose sharply in the late 1960s, new organizations were formed. The Southern Organization for Unified Leadership (SOUL) emerged from the unsuccessful legislative campaigns of attorney Nils Douglas in the late 1960s and was centered in the Ninth Ward, home of one-fourth of the city's black population. A second major new black organization was the Community Organization for Urban Politics (COUP), centered in the Seventh Ward. Roughly a half dozen other organizations operated in other parts of the city.

SOUL acquired its reputation for strength in 1969. It helped Moon Landrieu roll up 90 percent of the black vote in his runoff victory for mayor. Landrieu successfully built a coalition of blacks and working-class whites and brought blacks in at all levels of municipal government. Gillis Long reportedly put more than $50,000 into SOUL for the first primary in the 1971 governor's race. Edwards contributed $60,000 in the runoff against Johnston, and COUP got $30,000 from Long in the first primary.[26]

The organizations have come under criticism for backing those candidates who promise immediate benefits to the organization, instead of utilizing the group's power for the general benefit of the black community. For example, SOUL in 1971 endorsed wealthy north Louisiana segregationist Jamar Adcock for lieutenant governor, despite his record, which was hardly problack.

The new organizations try to back winners, and as one observer noted, they expect to acquire power, which "brings patronage, board appointments, city hall jobs—first for the top level organization officials, and then, if there's something left over, for their constituents." [27] In 1973, Nils Douglas received a $20,000 legal retainer from the federally funded Family Health Foundation. His co-organizer of SOUL, Don Hubbard, became director of the agency at a salary of $39,500. An analysis by the Institute of Politics at Loyola in New Orleans suggested that SOUL endorsement might increase a candidate's margin by 15 percent or so, but where the candidates were well known in the black community, the influence fell off sharply. There is no evidence that SOUL increased turnout rates in its precincts.

The fragmentation and extreme materialism are distinct features of black organizations in New Orleans, but the black electorate there appears to be entering a new phase of political development and a new level of sophistication in which cues from an organization have less impact. Candidates have begun to communicate directly with black voters.

Regardless of how black voters divide among candidates in the Democratic primary in Louisiana, they vote solidly Democratic in general

26. Richard Murray and Arnold Vedlitz, *Political Organization in Deprived Communities* (Chicago: American Political Science Association, © 1974), pp. 34–35.

27. Ibid., p. 34, quoted from Jack Davis, "Faust Revisited: Is SOUL for Sale?" *New Orleans* (November 1973):40.

elections. One high-ranking state official explained that when blacks began voting in large numbers, many had limited education; with statewide use of voting machines, it was easier to teach them to pull the single master lever for the Democratic Party in general elections. Louisiana Republicans have provided little incentive for blacks to change their straight-ticket voting. As in South Carolina, political expediency helped encourage Louisiana Democrats to open the party to black participation.

REPUBLICANS

The days are long gone when a politician was identified as either a Long or anti-Long candidate, a distinction that produced bifactionalism in a one-party state. When Republicans began to challenge and win presidential elections in the 1950s, the traditionally anti-Long parishes (counties) were the first to go Republican.

Despite an obviously strong potential urban Republican base that is reflected in election returns, the Republican Party in Louisiana has failed to develop strong party leadership organization. The original growth of the party began in the 1950s under the leadership of New Orleans attorney John Minor Wisdom, who was appointed a federal judge by President Eisenhower and whose leadership capacity in the state GOP has since been unequaled.

Louisiana was the last southern state to elect Republicans to Congress during the modern era. The first, in 1972, was David Treen, a doctrinaire conservative. He was joined two years later by W. Henson Moore, a Baton Rouge attorney and racially moderate economic conservative, who won John Rarick's old seat after the incumbent right-winger lost in the primary to a more liberal television sports announcer.

Actually, it was the perseverance of Treen, who made three races for Congress and one for governor before being elected in 1972, that kept the party alive in the late 1960s. Even after reapportionment of the legislature into single-member districts, which in theory provides greater opportunity for Republicans as well as blacks, the GOP elected only four members, a number that should increase.

The GOP's organizational weakness is reflected by Comparative State Elections Project (CSEP) data, which show that in Louisiana only 19 percent of the respondents reported any contact by the Republican Party in 1968. This compared with a Deep South regional figure of 30 percent, and 64 percent nationally. Very little of the difficult, door-to-door precinct work that Republicans undertook in most other southern states was done in Louisiana.

Democrats, who in southern states tend to build a strong organization only after Republicans become challengers, contacted only 23 percent of the CSEP respondents in Louisiana, compared with 31 percent in the region and 62 percent nationally. The Wallace organization was relatively better off, contacting 16 percent in Louisiana, compared with a 20 percent Deep South standard and 15 percent nationally.[28]

Party morale also suffered when, in 1972, President Nixon supported Senator James Eastland in neighboring Mississippi over Republican challenger Gil Carmichael, one of the more attractive GOP candidates in the South. Treen later said it had a "demoralizing effect" among "staunch Republicans who believe in building the party." [29]

In 1975 there were only 47,500 registered Republicans, or 2.8 percent of the total registration.

A unique open-election law that went into effect in 1975 places all candidates on a single ballot; its effect is to minimize the role of party and to institutionalize the one-party status quo. The law provides that all candidates be listed on a single ballot by party designation—or independently, if a candidate so chooses. If no candidate receives a majority, there is a runoff between the two top contenders, even if they are both of the same party.

The Republicans ran no candidate for governor in 1975, when Edwards won reelection with 61 percent of the vote (without a runoff) against two serious opponents. The new law, promoted by Edwards, was advocated on the basis of "fairness": it wasn't fair for Democrats to fight through two politically bloody primaries and then face a fresh Republican opponent.

As Edwards demonstrated, the combination of the new election law and the concentration of power in the governor's office greatly increases the odds against an incumbent governor's losing a bid for a second term. Furthermore, by eliminating an assured general election ballot position for Republicans and thus further discouraging them from fielding candidates, the new election law cuts off the lifeblood of a developing minority party.

LABOR AND BUSINESS

The impact of personality on politics manifests itself in a unique way in Louisiana in two remarkable men, Victor Bussie and Edward Steimel, respectively the state president of the AFL–CIO and the executive director of the Louisiana Association of Business and Industry (LABI).

28. Howard, McCombs, and Kovenock, *Explaining the Vote,* p. 545.
29. Interview with David Treen, January 31, 1974.

It is no accident that Louisiana is the only state in the South without a right-to-work law. Former Governor McKeithen described Bussie as "a very effective, aggressive leader." Edwards, who was supported by labor, attributes the "tremendous effectiveness" of organized labor in the legislature directly to Bussie.

One reason for labor's effectiveness is a firm policy of supporting for reelection every legislator whose voting record they judge to be good, regardless of who runs against him. The support includes contributions averaging about $200, but far more important is the availability of volunteer workers and distribution of literature in working-class neighborhoods.

In addition to Bussie and his full-time staff of four AFL–CIO state officials, at least six other full-time lobbyists are brought in when the legislature is in session. At six o'clock every morning, Bussie directs a staff meeting that reviews all bills and their status. The staff attends sessions and committee meetings, but there is an ironclad rule not to wine and dine legislators.

Unlike most southern labor leaders, whose interests tend to be focused on such directly labor-related issues as workmen's compensation or unemployment benefits, Bussie explained, "We take the position in this state that we are not just interested in what affects labor; we are interested in anything that affects people. . . . We have taken the position that it is just as important to a man who has a retarded child to have a facility in this state to help him as it is for us to negotiate a substantial wage increase for him." [30]

In the process, Bussie has won allies and enhanced the image of organized labor. A New Orleans editor tells of a society matron who thinks Bussie is "the greatest man alive" because he played a key role in helping art patrons get legislation passed regarding an arts commission. Labor is represented on virtually every state board or commission, Bussie himself serving on roughly 20.

Bussie's critics maintain that his involvement in nonlabor issues often is cynically motivated and intended to build coalitions to broaden his power base. But in addition to his skill as a political infighter, Bussie is respected for his intelligence, grasp of issues, and courage for standing firm on unpopular issues.

He has been an ardent supporter of civil rights, and his house was dynamited in the early 1960s when he supported school integration. A fireman from Shreveport whose father was a railroad worker laid off for four years in the Depression, Bussie experienced discrimination as he grew up. "I am of French descent and consequently not totally white myself in the eyes of some people," he said. "That might have helped motivate my deep-rooted feeling that everybody ought to have an equal

30. Interview with Victor Bussie, January 14, 1974.

opportunity; I don't care who he is." [31] Alphonse Jackson said of Bussie, "Blacks consider him a friend."

A thoughtful, soft-spoken man who is large-boned and stands 6'4", Bussie has no desire to run for public office. "I've seen it ruin too many people," he said. "They have to compromise too much." [32]

Bussie's influence with governors is almost legendary. When Governor Earl Long's mental illness was diagnosed by a team of doctors who thought it essential to send him out of the state for treatment, Bussie was one of a handful of intimates called in to help make the physical transfer. It sparked a deep interest in mental health, and Bussie later became president of the state Mental Health Association and a director of the national organization.

A former aide to McKeithen recalled Bussie sitting behind the governor's desk one day in a conference that included McKeithen and others discussing a legislative matter. The telephone rang, and it was a legislative floor leader asking whether the bill in question should be brought to the floor. Bussie answered the phone and without conferring with the governor directed that the matter be delayed.

When Edwards was asked who were the dominant forces in political decision making, he replied, "There are none, except to some extent Victor Bussie." [33]

Respect for Bussie extends to Democratic politicians far beyond the boundaries of Louisiana. Speakers at the 1975 three-day state AFL–CIO convention included five announced or potential presidential candidates: Senators Henry Jackson of Washington, Birch Bayh of Indiana, Edmund Muskie of Maine, and Lloyd Bentsen of Texas, and Representative Morris Udall of Arizona. In addition, there were Governor Edwards, Revenue Commissioner Traigle, and U.S. Representative Andrew Young of Atlanta, a New Orleans native and the only black congressman from the Deep South. Such an all-star lineup at the state convention is typical and reflects the influence and respect that Bussie commands.

In every administration, there are issues on which Bussie and the governor vigorously disagree and periods in which he is out of favor. For more than two decades the same applied to Edward Steimel, who until 1975 was executive director of the Public Affairs Research Council of Louisiana, known as PAR.

PAR was created in 1951 by forces that basically had opposed the Longs and who saw the need for a reliable research organization to deal with public policy issues. Because the state had no research arm of its own, Steimel's influence was strengthened because he made PAR's serv-

31. Ibid.
32. Ibid.
33. Interview with Edwin W. Edwards, September 25, 1973.

ices available to governors and legislators. PAR's research has also been widely utilized by editorial writers throughout the state.

Steimel, an Arkansas native with a background in public relations and fundraising, shaped PAR into a business-oriented voice of enlightened self-interest that viewed public policy in broad terms. Bussie and the AFL–CIO held PAR membership, but ceased participating after Steimel was named by a federal court in 1971 to write a reapportionment plan for the Louisiana legislature. Bussie opposed the single-member district plan, which reduced labor influence in urban parishes, where a relatively small controlled voting bloc could be decisive for an entire slate of candidates running at large.

The fact that Steimel was so chosen reflected both the respect for PAR as a research organization and the influence of Steimel on matters of public policy. Not only did his single-member district plan enhance the opportunity for blacks and Republicans to get elected, but it also resulted in an overhaul of the legislature.

In 1971, PAR developed a list of 33 public issues acted on by the legislature, compiled the votes of all 144 legislators, and published it. Interest was such that 35,000 copies were printed and sold. "We ended up in political ads, editorials, and everything else," said Steimel, "and became the major reason for the defeat of nearly 60 percent of the legislature in 1971. The guys who got elected, those new 60, are quite aware we are going to do this again. They know we're going to make available to the public something to judge them on. And it reforms them. Maybe it is in terms of what we think reform is, but the public has to buy what we are doing." [34]

Although PAR sharply criticized the new state constitution because of its "antibusiness" tax provisions and Edwards attacked Steimel publicly as a "carpetbagger from Arkansas," PAR researched more than 20 specific proposals requested by Edwards in his first term, most of them leading to legislative proposals and action. Many of them altered tax collection procedures, and the improved efficiency produced roughly $10 million in increased revenue.

There have been times when Steimel and Bussie were allied on issues, such as the successful effort to create a state ethics commission and a lawsuit the AFL–CIO brought in federal court that attacked the property tax system. PAR provided research assistance for that suit. Bussie characterized Steimel as "basically a very fine and honorable man, and I mean that sincerely. He represents big business, and you have to take that into consideration when you look at their analyses of problems." [35]

For his part, Steimel contended that a major reason why Louisiana

34. Interview with Edward Steimel, January 14, 1974.
35. Interview with Victor Bussie, January 14, 1974.

ranked ahead of only Alabama in employment growth rate between 1960 and 1973 was the lack of a right-to-work law—which to business signified that organized labor had too much political influence in the state.

Like Bussie, Steimel does not hesitate to step into controversy, and even with PAR he acknowledged that he practiced "brinksmanship" on the question of lobbying, which PAR as a tax-exempt organization is not allowed to do. "We try to get our research into the minds of the decision-makers and to influence them," Steimel said. "We don't make any bones about it. That's what we're here for. We want to change things. We want . . . to do our best to change them without direct lobbying." [36]

After Steimel left in 1975 to direct the Louisiana Association of Business and Industry, PAR remained as a research organization. In his new role with LABI, Steimel was free to lobby. Financed by the major financial and industrial groups in the state, LABI began at once to contribute campaign funds in legislative races and set its sights on right-to-work legislation.

SUMMARY AND CONCLUSIONS

The exotic political climate of Louisiana reflects the state's unique cultural blend. Although the traditional populist sentiment that is the legacy of the Longs was strengthened by the emergence of blacks into full political participation, black factionalism developed to the extent that candidates for statewide office often were supported or opposed on the basis of a rival faction's attitude rather than the candidate's position on the issues.

Although the strength of organized labor in Louisiana is unmatched in the South and adds additional pressure for a government that taxes wealth and expends public services, the creation of LABI provides a counterforce.

The failure of the Republican Party to develop strong leadership and organization has retarded the development of two-party competition, despite significant Republican sentiment that shows up consistently in voting results in urban areas. However, the open-election law has had the effect of institutionalizing continued one-party domination.

Despite the recent flood tide of reform sentiment, the traditional public tolerance of petty graft and conflicts of interest, and the entrenched forces that profit by corrupting the political process, will remain as barriers to the goals of progressive reformers.

36. Interview with Edward Steimel, January 14, 1974.

Chapter

9

MISSISSIPPI

Out of the Past

IN THE ROTUNDA of the museum-piece capitol in Jackson there stands a life-sized statue of Theodore Gilmore Bilbo, an almost gnome-like figure with a hand reaching forward, the fingers spread apart and grasping upward. No state matches Mississippi in its contribution to racist political rhetoric, and until his death in 1947, Bilbo was the acknowledged master.

Robert Clark is a soft-spoken, strong-willed, and politically effective former rural schoolteacher who for eight years, until 1976, served as the lone black legislator in Mississippi in this century. With a deadpan expression, Clark tells the story of his entrance to the capitol after his first election—his first visit to the building.

"They told me to come in the south entrance. I didn't know why they wanted me to come in the south entrance, but somebody told me—it was because Senator Bilbo's statue faces the south, and they said that Jim Eastland had told them to have me come in that way. That Bilbo was going to stop me. And after he didn't stop me, I understand Jim Eastland got on the phone and called Bilbo and asked him why he didn't stop me and what was this all about. Bilbo said, 'Jim, when I left Mississippi I left it in your hands, best hands I thought I could find. I'm surprised that you're letting that nigger come in there.' And Jim Eastland told Bilbo, 'Well, Bilbo, when you left here we didn't have all these damn civil rights laws and longhairs and everything. We got them here now and, there isn't a damn thing I can do about it.' And Bilbo said, 'Yeh, Jim, we got some damn nigger firemen down here, and there isn't anything I can do about it either.' "[1]

1. Interview with Robert Clark, March 28, 1974.

More than a quarter century ago, V. O. Key wrote that "northerners, provincials that they are, regard the South as one large Mississippi. Southerners, with their eye for distinction, place Mississippi in a class by itself. . . . Every southern state finds some reason to fall back on the soul-satisfying exclamation, 'Thank God for Mississippi!' Yet Mississippi only manifests in accentuated form the darker political strains that run throughout the South." [2]

STATE OF THE STATE

The years have since proved just how perceptive an observer Professor Key was. Not until the late 1960s was there an end to the era of church bombings, murders, and beatings of civil rights leaders who urged fellow black Mississippians to register and vote. It was an era of Ku Klux Klan terror, of a closed society that would tolerate no dissent, when to speak out as a moderate was an act of courage.

Mississippi has been called "perhaps the most traditional . . . particularistic and underdeveloped state in the country" on political issues. [3] No state resisted change more or was as possessed as much by its past. However, the catharsis Mississippi underwent in the 1960s released the state psychologically. After his election in 1971, Governor William Waller adopted as an almost formal state slogan the phrase, "Mississippi—the State of Change." The transformation in Mississippi in recent years has been more swift than in any other state.

Resistance to racial change broke down in Mississippi after the 1970 midyear desegregation of its school system, within which some segregated classrooms can still be found. Despite opposition from the Nixon administration's Justice Department, the Supreme Court in the fall of 1969 ruled in *Alexander* v. *Holmes* that "'all deliberate speed' for desegregation is no longer constitutionally permissible. . . . Every school district is to terminate dual school systems at once." Almost overnight, desegregation became a fait accompli, and the acceptance of the new status quo by white Mississippians surprised virtually everyone. Although they overstate the situation, it is significant that by the mid-1970s many Mississippi politicians would proclaim to visitors, "We're the most integrated state in the country," and they would say it with pride.

2. V. O. Key, *Southern Politics in State and Nation* (New York: Vintage, 1949), p. 229.

3. Samuel G. Patterson, "The Political Cultures of the American States," *Journal of Politics* (February 1968): 197.

Beneath the surface, racial tensions remain. Yet more than a fourth of the registered voters now are black, and the beginnings of a desegregated society have brought freedom to thousands of moderate white Mississippians who had been stifled by the atmosphere of repression in the 1960s and the fear of economic reprisal and social ostracism.

The percentage of black population remains higher in Mississippi than any other state, nearly 37 percent in 1970. Mississippi has the second-largest proportion of rural population in the nation, and the highest in the South. Among its cities only Jackson has a population in excess of 50,000. Measured by any index, poverty remains more acute here than in any other state. These facts must be recognized to understand the state's politics.

The political character of Mississippi is in a state of flux and indecision. The potential for a genuine two-party system, with a competitive and somewhat moderate Republican Party shows some promise.

Because of their numbers, blacks possess the potential for greater influence in Mississippi than anywhere else in the South, but only if unity among splintered factions and development of effective coalitions can be achieved. The unmatched legacy of racial violence and economic reprisals means that fear is a greater factor than in other states in inhibiting black political participation, especially in many rural areas.

The shrewd domination of public policy exercised quietly by Senator James Eastland is unmatched in the South, but advancing age of the political old guard and the dynamics of change set limits on the endurance of that influence.

The forces of modernization are on the ascendency in Mississippi. The abundance of land and water and the presence of unexploited mineral resources provide a rich potential for development. Mechanization has ended the system of labor-intensive agriculture, which had produced a public policy aimed at preventing competition for labor, and there is systematic planning toward a balanced economy. Instrumental in this transformation has been the state's impressive Research and Development Center, which serves as a major institutional force for change, both in economic development and in helping the state's insular business establishment recognize that blacks as well as whites must be brought into the economic mainstream if Mississippi is to prosper. The Center has set a goal of raising per capita income in Mississippi to the national average by 1992. Director of the center is Dr. Kenneth Wagner, an independent and tough-minded individual who came to Mississippi from Georgia Tech and developed a broad-based systems approach to economic development, the real hope for the state.

By the mid-1970s the "R & D Center" was providing local leaders throughout Mississippi with enlightened and professional guidance and direction. The state was divided into ten planning and development districts, with goals for jobs for each county broken down by economic sector.

The act creating the R & D Center gave it semi-independent status under the aegis of the Board of Trustees of Institutions of Higher Learning, thus shielding it from direct political interference. The center is located in a modernistic, eight story building in the Jackson suburbs and is unmatched in the South, and perhaps the nation, as a research arm of state government.

Creation of industrial jobs secure from local economic pressures has long-range political implications, especially for blacks, many of whom have been inhibited from full political participation because of the fear of economic reprisals. But Mississippi pays a high cost for its new industry. In the 1960s, under Governor Ross Barnett's direction, the corporate income tax was reduced from 6 to 3 percent, provision was made to reduce corporate property tax assessments, a right-to-work provision was written into the constitution, and ten-year property tax exemptions were provided for new industry. The state already provided for issuance of state bonds to finance new industrial plants, with industry paying them off at low interest rates.

When Litton Industries negotiated to build a "shipyard of the future" at Pascagoula that would mean 12,000 high-paying industrial jobs, a unionized work force, and a tax-exempt $130 million bond issue by the state to be paid off over 30 years by Litton, Barnett's successor, Governor Paul Johnson, Jr., agreed and squelched public debate on the matter. When Litton threatened to withdraw if the matter became a political issue, Johnson in 1967 called in all seven candidates for governor and taped each of their promises to keep it out of politics.

As the state moves away from political and economic isolation, its horizons are expanding. Mississippi has long been handicapped by the loss of tens of thousands of its brightest and best-educated young people, who escaped to search for opportunity and greater freedom, or left because of conscience, or were driven out. The few really able people who remained or returned exhibit an awareness of the challenge, an almost somber acceptance of the burdens of leadership, an acknowledgment that the change that has already occurred merely provides the basis on which to begin the task of overcoming the state's dark legacy.

HISTORY

Mississippi's early settlers brought three basic philosophies with them. The yeoman small farmers who descended from middle Tennessee into the northeast hill country were products of frontier Jacksonian democracy and harbored doubts about slavery. From the Atlantic seaboard states of the Old South came a few ambitious sons of plantation aristocrats whose lands at home were becoming worn. Lured along with them, by the potential for quick wealth from rich bottom land and the acquisition of slave labor to raise cotton, were the far more numerous disciples of John C. Calhoun. They helped plant the seeds of Calhoun's race theories—that the presence of black slaves gave all whites an equality of superiority that provided the basis for a white democracy and, as a corollary, that the slaves were little more than draft animals.

The late-developing plantation society in the Delta—a fertile wedge of alluvial soil up to three counties wide that today stretches behind the Mississippi River levees more than 200 miles from Vicksburg north to Memphis—accepted in large part the gentlemanly aristocratic racism of the Virginia and South Carolina plantation owners, who viewed slaves as children who never grew up. This developed into a more paternalistic attitude which looked down on poor whites as inferiors as well.

In 1828 the Mississippi legislature declared that slavery was a "national evil," but the frontier spirit was quickly corrupted by the plantation system, which channeled the aspirations of yeoman farmers into the purchase of land and slaves and gave them social status on the basis of skin color. In addition to neutralizing frontier opposition to slavery and producing a landed aristocracy, the expanding plantation system in antebellum Mississippi prevented the development of an independent urban middle class capable of challenging the dominance of the landed upper classes.[4]

The Civil War was devastating. The fifth wealthiest state in the union in 1860, Mississippi plummeted to the bottom. The 1860 wealth included $218 million as the cash value of 437,000 slaves, a cash value that disappeared with the stroke of a pen when Abraham Lincoln signed the Emancipation Proclamation. Of 78,000 men sent to fight in the Civil War —more than Mississippi's total white male population between the ages of 18 and 45—only 28,000 returned, many with artificial limbs. Its cities lay in ashes, its cotton was confiscated as Confederate property, land values crashed, and nearly everyone's personal wealth was wiped out.

An example is the family of former Governor J. P. Coleman, Mississippi's relatively moderate leader of the 1950s and now a judge on the Fifth Circuit Court of Appeals in New Orleans, who continues to reside in Ackerman at the base of the Mississippi hill country. He grew up in the 16-room house of his grandfather's 2,000-acre farm, which had been worked by more than 100 slaves. "When the war was over, he plowed a mule the rest of his life just like his former slaves had done. I am the

4. For further development of this point and its effects on the subsequent development of Mississippi, see Lester M. Salamon, *Mississippi as a Developing Society* (Bloomington: Indiana University Press, forthcoming).

first of his descendants to get a college education; that's how deep he went in economically." [5]

The Reconstruction reformers equalized property assessments on the basis of market value, as they sought to eliminate inequities in a tax system in which influential landowners and compliant sheriffs had undervalued property and passed the tax burden on to small property owners. A century later, after blacks in 1973 won political control of Bolton, a town of less than 1,000 population 20 miles west of Jackson, one of the first acts of youthful Mayor Bennie Thompson and his all-black council was to order reassessment of property in the town. Although whites protested, they lost in court, and the property tax base for the town jumped from $400,000 to $1.4 million, and tax revenues increased from $8,000 to $26,000. With the additional revenue, the new governing body expanded services, purchased the town's first garbage truck, acquired a fire truck for the first time, tripled the size of the police force, and sent all the policemen to the state police academy in Jackson for professional training.

Although Reconstruction reforms also helped poor whites, who supported the Republican cause in significant numbers, the equal political status of blacks diminished the social status previously held by poor whites because of skin color. A conservative campaign of indoctrination on "status" rather than economic issues weaned away white support, but the significant fact remains that for a brief period thousands of whites worked closely with blacks in political conventions at all levels, and a degree of genuine social contact between the races was established.

But Reconstruction ended with a reign of terror in the rural areas. In county after county in 1875, small racial incidents provided excuses for the local Democratic clubs to mount their horses and scour the countryside, killing key black leaders as they went. The death toll reached the hundreds, and the number of wounded was much greater.[6]

The Mississippi Plan, which involved the systematic use of terror to restore white political supremacy, was exported to South Carolina a year later, and Reconstruction ended in the political deal that gave disputed electoral votes in the South to Republican Rutherford B. Hayes for his one-vote victory in the 1876 presidential election. Although black domination was over and black political participation fell sharply, as late as 1889 a convention of Mississippi Negroes nominated candidates for all state offices. That, combined with the efforts of Senator Henry Cabot Lodge of Massachusetts to provide for federal control of elections, mo-

5. Interview with J. P. Coleman, March 30, 1974. In the 1960s, it was the landowning descendants of former slaves who provided the nucleus of leadership in those rural counties that developed strong black political organizations. Most counties lacked enough self-sufficient black yeomen to fill that role.

6. Vernon Lane Wharton, *The Negro in Mississippi*, pp. 191–192, quoted in Salamon, *Mississippi as a Developing Society* (in press).

tivated whites to seek the total elimination of the Negro from public affairs.[7] At the time, blacks constituted almost 58 percent of the population.

The constitutional convention of 1890 effectively disfranchised blacks, as well as thousands of poor whites. To white Mississippi, such action was also required in order to end widespread election fraud. Virtually every account of Mississippi political history contains the remarkable speech at that convention by Judge J. J. Chrisman:

> It is no secret that there has not been a fair count in Mississippi since 1875, that we have been preserving the ascendency of the white people by revolutionary methods. In other words, we have been stuffing ballot boxes, committing perjury, and here and there in the state carrying the election by fraud and violence until the whole machinery for elections is about to rot down. No man can be in favor of perpetuating the election methods which have prevailed in Mississippi since 1875 who is not a moral idiot.[8]

With the federal government never blinking at the assault on the Fifteenth Amendment guarantee that the right to vote "shall not be denied or abridged . . . on account of race, color, or previous condition of servitude," the constitution Mississippi adopted in 1890 required payment of poll taxes, increased residency requirements, and required that all voters be able to understand and interpret the meaning of any section of the Constitution. It was a document of which U.S. Senator Bilbo half a century later boasted "that damn few white men and no niggers at all can explain." The effect was to completely disfranchise blacks and eliminate thousands of poor whites as voters.

Within 15 years, almost all of the former Confederate states had adopted new constitutions that contained franchise limitations similar to Mississippi's, thus formalizing a one-party white man's political system that would endure for almost a half a century. By the time the People's Party came to Mississippi in the 1890s, blacks already had been disfranchised, and the state did not experience the biracial character of the Populist movement that was felt throughout much of the South.

The ruling class that remained was so proud of its leadership against democracy that the state's *Official and Statistical Register* for 1904 listed among "Mississippi First's" the fact that:

> Mississippi was the first state in the Union to solve the problem of white supremacy in the South by lawful means. The Constitution of 1890 disfranchises the ignorant and vicious of both races, and places control of the State in the hands of the virtuous, intelligent citizens.

7. William F. Holmes, *The White Chief: James Kimble Vardaman* (Baton Rouge: Louisiana State University Press, 1970), p. 45.

8. *Jackson Daily Clarion Ledger,* September 11, 1890, quoted in A. D. Kirwan, *The Revolt of the Rednecks* (Lexington: University of Kentucky Press, 1959), pp. 60–64.

One of the Reconstruction reforms that later resulted in conservative white control of the state was legislative reapportionment on the basis of population, thus shifting power to the heavily black Delta counties. With blacks removed from the election process but counted for apportionment purposes, "black" counties—primarily from the Delta—elected 68 representatives to the state House with 44,500 white voters, while the "white" counties in the hills, with 71,000 white voters, elected only 52 representatives.

For half a century, political division between the Delta and the hills, or rather the philosophies those regions symbolized, dominated Mississippi politics. As Key wrote, "the delta planter and the redneck stride on, not as sharply defined geographic groups, but as states of mind formed long ago. . . . The mores, morals, and ways of life of the two groups differ —perhaps not so much as their preachers would have them believe, but enough to have political significance." [9] For years the sinful Delta planters joined the wicked Gulf Coast counties and the cities to vote wet against the prohibitionists in the hills. The Delta's pretensions of aristocracy contrasted with the neopopulist sentiment of the hills.

Under James K. Vardaman and Theodore Bilbo, the Populist doctrines of anticorporationism, the cause of the common man, and the demand for better services were combined with the most blatant racist rhetoric. Bilbo's followers, tenants and sharecroppers descended from a line of yeoman farmers who lost their land under crop lien laws to the furnishing merchant—who furnished supplies on credit secured by liens on the farmer's next year's crop and his land—were victims of national credit and agricultural policies that led first to the Populist revolt and later to the New Deal agricultural programs.

Although Bilbo was unmatched as a racial demagogue, in his two terms as governor (1916–1920 and 1928–1932) and later as senator he showed concern about fulfilling his campaign promises. He was a progressive on nonracial issues, voting down the line for Roosevelt's New Deal. Nevertheless, with the poverty that existed in Mississippi, there was little that the Vardaman and Bilbo brand of progressivism could achieve within the state. Another reason for its failure was that they worked only to improve the lot of poor whites, although until 1940 a majority of the state was black. They and other southern leaders who attempted to combine progressive programs with racism failed to realize that it was impossible to resolve the problems of a whole state while trying to suppress a substantial segment of the population. There was no basic difference between the Delta planter and Bilbo on the place of the Negro. The difference was one of style, an unspoken understanding by one and vulgar demagoguery by the other.

9. Key, *Southern Politics*, pp. 232–233.

When Mississippi launched its Balance Agriculture with Industry (BAWI) program in the late 1930s under a governor from the Delta, the result was an influx of low-paying, white-only industries that avoided the Delta and avoided competition for the Delta's labor force.

After World War II there was some promise of better communications between the races, although views on segregation were unchanged. In 1949, James Eastland's home area of Sunflower County had even established an interracial committee to investigate the appalling condition of Negro schools. Times were improving, and newspapers began to criticize the politicians who continued the Vardaman-Bilbo rhetoric of race hatred. Outside forces were moving that would transform the state's social order and lay the foundation for a new politics—but not without cost.

THE BATTLEGROUND

Mississippi served as the battleground for the South and the nation after the Supreme Court ruled in 1954 that school segregation must end. The initial reaction of many citizens was one of regretful acceptance. The Supreme Court allowed time for opinion to jell, but from Washington there was little leadership. President Eisenhower made a few cautious remarks which many construed to mean he wished the decision had not happened.

In his masterful narrative of this period in Mississippi, author Walter Lord wrote: "Into this vacuum roared a cyclone—an ardent band of white supremacists whose sense of purpose was matched only by their skill. They knew exactly what they wanted, and as past masters at the art of state politics, they knew exactly the chords to strike that would best arouse the average, frightened, isolated, white Mississippian." [10]

When the Court in 1955 issued a mild implementation decree that urged "all deliberate speed," it was taken in Mississippi for a sign of weakness. Senator Eastland set the tone when he told a cheering audience in 1955, "You are not required to obey any court which passes out such a ruling. In fact, you are obligated to defy it." By then, Citizens Councils had been organized in the Delta, the "responsible people" who would keep in touch and act together to stop any move toward desegregation. By the fall of 1954 the councils had boasted of 25,000 members and were spreading throughout the South. Blacks pushing for constitutional rights suffered economic reprisals, losing their credit and their jobs.

10. Walter Lord, *The Past That Would Not Die* (New York: Harper and Row, 1965), p. 61.

Greenville editor Hodding Carter watched the brewing storm and wrote a national magazine article about the Citizens Council that was headlined "A Wave of Terror Threatens the South." He was promptly censured by the state legislature for "selling out the state for Yankee gold" and formally declared a liar by a vote of 89–19 in the Mississippi House of Representatives. Carter learned of the resolution during a stopover on a raft trip down the Mississippi River. He promptly telephoned in a signed editorial, stating, "I herewith resolve by a vote of 1 to 0 that there are 89 liars in the State Legislature, beginning with Speaker Sillers and working way on down to Representative Eck Windham of Prentiss, a political loon whose name is fittingly made up of the words 'wind' and 'ham.' . . . I am hopeful that this fever, like the Ku Kluxism which rose from the same kind of infection, will run its course before too long a time. Meanwhile those 89 character mobbers can go to hell collectively or singly and wait there until I back down. They needn't plan on returning."

Men of such strength and character were rare, and the next decade was marked by determined resistance to change and by conflict that unleashed national forces of action and reaction. Among all institutions that helped shape opinion in Mississippi, the newspaper published and edited by Carter and later by his son, Hodding Carter III, stood almost alone as a voice of reason with the strength to survive. The state developed into a closed society in which dissent was ruthlessly suppressed.

At Yazoo City, where 53 local Negro citizens filed a petition seeking reorganization of the public schools on a "nondiscriminatory basis," all but six withdrew their names within three months when their credit was cut off by local stores and banks or they were dismissed from jobs and told they could only be rehired after withdrawing from the petition.

In Belzoni some 400 Negroes had registered to vote during 1953 and 1954, spurred by a black minister, the Reverend George Washington Lee. Systematically they were told to "go down to the courthouse and get your name off the books." Within weeks during the spring of 1955, more than 300 did strike off their names. In March, the Belzoni Citizens Council was reported to be behind a list of 94 registered voters being circulated to stores and banks. A black grocer still refused to take his name off the voting rolls—and soon lost his store. In May, Lee was shot to death in his car. A related murder followed a few months later.

By December 1955 the number of registered black voters in the state had fallen from 22,000 in 1952 to less than 12,000. Senator Eastland, who through the years would say in Washington that "there is no discrimination in Mississippi," declared in an address to the Citizens Councils Convention in Jackson on December 1, 1955: "The Supreme Court of the United States in the false name of law and justice has perpetrated a monstrous crime. . . . The antisegregation decisions are dishonest decisions. . . . The judges who rendered them violated their oaths of office. They have disgraced the high office which they hold. . . . There is no law that a free people must submit to a flagrant invasion of their personal liberty." Eastland already had declared that sociologists cited by the Supreme Court in the desegregation case were "agitators who are part and parcel of the Communist conspiracy to destroy our country."

To the poor whites in Mississippi, reared in a society that gave them status on the basis of skin color and taught that the black man was an inferior being, the message was clear. Desegregation was a Communist plot to "mongrelize the races." There was violence elsewhere in the South, but Mississippi became the nation's major battleground.

During this period, Governor Coleman shunned racial rhetoric and sought a moderate course of resistance, but he was succeeded in 1959 by Ross Barnett, the handpicked candidate of the Citizens Councils. His campaign song, "Roll with Ross," declared, "He's for segregation one hundred percent. He's not a mod-rate like some other gent." Barnett was an affluent attorney, a mild-mannered man with a clever cunning, in the guise of a country-style lawyer. He also had a simpleminded and sincere belief in segregation.

Had it not been a time of crisis, Barnett might have been remembered as a well-intentioned, harmless figure. He increased the already generous bounties Mississippi offered to business, aggressively sought new industry, and readily agreed to a suggestion by a pair of Jackson businessmen to authorize a study by a California-based consulting firm that would lead to creation of the Mississippi Research and Development Center, which by the 1970s would become a major institutional force for modernization. In Jackson, the story is still told of Barnett being asked at a press conference in 1960, his first year in office and a period when he was besieged by patronage requests, what he thought should be done about Quemoy and Matsu, the two tiny islands off the coast of China involved in an incident that had become an issue in the Kennedy-Nixon presidential campaign. Barnett appeared puzzled by the question, but tried his best to answer it, responding, "Maybe we could make them game wardens."

But these were not ordinary times. The executive director of the Citizens Council, William J. Simmons (who in 1974 would call off a press conference in Jackson when local black television newsmen showed up routinely), had begun preparing Barnett speeches. Citizens Council members were named to the State Sovereignty Commission, the official state segregation investigative committee, and a propaganda arm of the Citizens Council was given a $20,000 contribution from Sovereignty Commission funds and placed on a $5,000 monthly retainer. The Citizens Councils claimed 80,000 members in the state and were at the peak of their influence.

Meanwhile, the election of John F. Kennedy and his commitment to racial justice changed the character of the federal role. The Civil Rights Division of the Justice Department, virtually ignored by the Eisenhower administration, became a center of action. Burke Marshall, a taciturn young man known for patience and devastating powers of logic, at his confirmation hearing to head the division softly assured Senator Eastland about the role of the Justice Department in matters involving voting rights, "I would expect to file suits in some cases where the investigation started without a specific complaint." There had been no such activism under Eisenhower, despite congressional authorization.

Marshall fundamentally disagreed with the Eisenhower philosophy that laws cannot change the hearts of men. "But laws *can* change the hearts of men," he would say. As he saw it, the whole point of any law was to set desirable standards which might otherwise be ignored if people were left to do what they wanted. It was the law that set the climate that made change possible, he stressed, and just as important was its enforcement: "Knowledge that the law is going to be enforced is vital. Very often that knowledge alone makes conciliation possible." [11]

Critics later complained that the Justice Department, by its emphasis on civil suits and conciliation and a reluctance to press for criminal prosecutions, unintentionally projected an image of weakness that encouraged violence and intimidation against those engaged in voter registration and related activity. Such critics contended that the failure to provide federal protection for those exercising civil rights was a major factor in radicalizing elements of the civil rights movement.

Justice Department lawyers came to Mississippi and spent hundreds of painstaking hours slowly amassing evidence to assault the resistance of Mississippi to black voter registration. In Forrest County, for example, 300-pound voting registrar Theron Lynd by 1961 had managed in two years to find not a single Negro applicant qualified to register. Science teacher David Roberson, who was bound for Cornell on a National Science Foundation grant, in the spring of 1961 found himself interpreting Section 273 of the state constitution—a tangled, 155-word sentence specifying the procedure for adopting a constitutional amendment.

Here is Roberson's account of what happened to him that fall: September 28, Lynd convinced Roberson there wasn't enough time to try again that day to register . . . October 2, Lynd was out when Roberson came back . . . October 12, Roberson finally got his chance—only to learn, several days later, that he had failed. Why? Lynd just "walked out."

U.S. District Judge Harold Cox, Senator Eastland's good friend, agreed with the state's lawyers that before the federal government could see the registrar's records, it must back up its charges with fuller details—but this, of course, was exactly why the government needed the records. In short, the very information the court demanded was the same information it refused to let the government have.

11. Ibid., p. 119.

All this could have gone on forever—which was, of course, just what Mississippi wanted. For its basic strategy was the one that had worked in the days of Reconstruction: be stubborn enough, and the federal government would tire of the game. But the Justice Department effort to gather evidence was led by John Doar, a patient and persistent 30-year-old attorney who would explain, "You've just got to keep going back." It was the heart of his approach. He was as aware as anyone of Mississippi's reliance on the "Second Reconstruction"—the theory that it was really just like 1875 again, and that the federal government would go away if only the state held out long enough. And to Doar the answer was an emphatic demonstration that this simply was not so. Be patient, understanding—get to know the people and their problems—but above all, keep going back until the law is accepted.[12] (In 1974, Doar directed the impeachment inquiry against President Nixon for the House Judiciary Committee.)

The federal government also was chipping away at other areas, including desegregation of waiting room facilities at terminals engaged in interstate commerce, but the case that marked the beginning of the end for the policy of resistance was the entrance of James Meredith into the University of Mississippi, the first Negro to break the color line in education in the state. A 29-year-old Air Force veteran, Meredith decided on applying for admission to the University of Mississippi on the day John F. Kennedy was inaugurated president, stating in his letter to the college registrar, "I am an American-Mississippi-Negro citizen." Procedural changes were made in the admissions requirements, and after 11 months of delay and litigation, federal Judge Sidney Mize concluded the "overwhelming weight of the testimony is that the plaintiff was not denied admission because of his color or race."

A month later, the Fifth Circuit Court of Appeals declared, "This case was tried below and argued here in the eerie atmosphere of never-never land," and stressed that segregation in Mississippi schools and colleges was a "plain fact known to everyone." The litigation continued. Letters of recommendation which Meredith had gotten from five "responsible Negro citizens" in his hometown subsequently were withdrawn by four of them after an interview at the local bank with an assistant state attorney general before the local justice of the peace. They had misunderstood, they said—they thought Meredith only wanted a job, and now that his real intention was clear, they readily agreed to sign retractions, stating they could no longer certify to his good moral character.

University officials continued to testify that race was not a factor in denial of admission to Meredith and was never even discussed, that the fellow was simply a troublemaker. Judge Mize agreed. He noted that

12. Ibid., pp. 124–125.

although segregation was practiced before the Supreme Court decision, there was no longer a policy that kept qualified Negroes from entering the university.

In its reversal of Mize's order, the Fifth Circuit remarked, "This about-face policy, news of which may startle some people in Mississippi, could have been accomplished only by telepathic communications among the University's administrators." A year and a half after Meredith had first applied for admission, the Fifth Circuit directed Judge Mize to order his admission.

But Fifth Circuit Judge Ben Cameron of Meridian, who privately acknowledged his belief that he represented Mississippi, upset legal precedent when he issued a formal stay to suspend the circuit court's order, even though he himself had not sat on the case. The full court overruled, and Cameron again ordered a stay. The case seesawed back and forth until U.S. Supreme Court Justice Hugo Black, supported with a brief from the Justice Department, set aside Cameron's order on September 10 and ordered Meredith immediately admitted. Judge Mize acknowledged privately that Mississippi had run out of courts and expressed the opinion that the excitement would die down now that all legal remedies had been exhausted.

Elsewhere in the South, the federal judiciary tended to take the heat off elected officials by issuing desegregation orders, which the states would then appeal. In many cases there was a conscious, if unspoken, realization by the judges that the people in their state would accept more readily a decision of law handed down by a judge who was one of them. But in Mississippi, Eastland's power as chairman of the Senate Judiciary Committee—his approval was a political necessity for the appointment of judges in his state—may have made the difference. Judges in Mississippi have tended to join in the resistance to change, a practice that continues in the state. (In 1975, at a hearing on arguments for single-member legislative districts—which in other states, such as Louisiana, Alabama, Georgia, and South Carolina, had resulted in the election of substantially more blacks to the legislature—Circuit Court Judge Coleman rejected an effort to introduce such results as evidence. "What they have done in other states and so forth is really of no help," he said.)

Even though legal recourse had ended after the Supreme Court's order on Meredith, Barnett in an abject failure of leadership called forth the discredited theory of interposition. This doctrine, based on Calhoun's argument that a state might "interpose" its authority against the federal government (an issue that clearly had been settled by the Civil War), had already been disinterred and then discarded by the "massive resisters" in Virginia.

Nevertheless, on September 13, 1962, three days after Justice Black's order, Barnett went on statewide television and declared: "We will not surrender to the evil and illegal forces of tyranny. . . . We must either submit to the unlawful dictates of the federal government or stand up like men and tell them 'NEVER!' " He said he and other officials should be willing to go to jail "to keep faith with the people."

Five days later, the Justice Department formally entered the case for the first time. *Jackson Clarion-Ledger* columnist Tom Ethridge, in a typical display of his unrestrained rhetoric, declared in reference to Robert Kennedy, "Little Brother has evidently concluded that the South must be forced to abandon its customs and traditions in deference to 'world opinion'—especially that of Asiatic cow-worshippers and African semi-savages not far removed from cannibalism." It was a typical example of the type of leadership exercised by the state's largest newspaper during the era of turmoil.

In the next five days, Barnett engaged in more than 20 secret telephone conversations with Attorney General Kennedy and one with the president, promising to cooperate in a face-saving surrender. Meanwhile, instead of trying to appeal to reason, Barnett fed the emotional hysteria that gripped the state. After three attempts to enroll Meredith were called off at the last minute by Robert Kennedy at Barnett's insistence that the situation was too unstable, a transcript of one of the secret Barnett-Kennedy conversations eventually disclosed that Barnett insisted on having the federal marshals pull their guns and point them, after which he would step aside.

Robert Kennedy agreed to have the head marshal pull a gun; the remainder of a contingent of 25 or 30 marshals would have their hands on their guns and holsters, with an understanding that Barnett would ensure the preservation of law and order and see to it that no harm came to either the chief marshal or to Meredith.

> BARNETT: "Yes . . . hold just a minute, will you. Hello, General, I was under the impression that they were all going to pull their guns. This could be very embarrassing. We got a big crowd here and if one pulls his gun and we all turn, it would be very embarrassing. Isn't it possible to have them all pull their guns?"
>
> RFK: "I hate to have them all draw their guns, as I think it could create harsh feelings. Isn't it sufficient if I have one man draw his gun and the others keep their hands on their holsters?"
>
> BARNETT: "They must all draw their guns. Then they should all point their guns at us, and then we could step aside. This could be very embarrassing down here for us. It is necessary."

Kennedy agreed, after being assured that Mississippi forces would preserve law and order. An hour later, Barnett called for another postponement because of high tension among the sheriffs and other law enforcement people congregated around the entrance to Ole Miss. Kennedy contacted the marshals, then only 20 miles from the campus, to turn around again.

Two nights later, 40,000 people at an Ole Miss football game in Jackson insisted that Barnett, the hero of the hour, address them. The tension was electric, and Barnett declared hoarsely: "I love Mississippi; I love her people; I honor her customs." Highly respected, Jackson-based newsman W. F. (Bill) Minor reported: "Thousands of Confederate battle flags burst forth throughout the stadium, shimmering in the night like a forest fire running before the wind." The roar of the crowd drowned out the rest of Barnett's words.[13]

A former legislator who later became a constitutional officer recalled Barnett's vacillation and indecision. Once he even called on the legislature to create a state militia to fight the U.S. Army, an idea shot down at once by legislative leaders.[14]

Barnett's failure to exercise responsible leadership led directly to the confrontation the next night, when a full-scale riot involving thousands erupted after a federal marshal escorted Meredith to the campus. By the time Meredith enrolled the next morning, 160 federal marshals had been injured, 38 percent of those on hand. Twenty-eight of them had been shot. Two bystanders, one a French journalist, were dead. More than 6,000 U.S. Army troops went to the campus to join Mississippi National Guardsmen and help restore order. In a remarkable display of restraint, no shots were fired by federal forces, who used tear gas to control the rioters. In all, the federal government spent almost $5 million to ensure that the University of Mississippi complied with the law.

Official defiance was over in Mississippi, but the forces of terror had been unleashed. The "respectable" resistance of the Citizens Councils had failed. Enough unsophisticated and badly educated poor whites— the "rednecks"—believed what their leaders told them: they had to resist an illegal, Communist-inspired plan to destroy racial purity. Hatred and frustration were mixed with a confused sense of moral fervor among those who formed and joined the virulent White Knights of the Ku Klux Klan, the major perpetrators during the next few years of a statewide wave of violence and intimidation that sent feelings of revulsion through thousands of silent Mississippians.

The White Knights were organized after the election of Paul Johnson, Jr., lieutenant governor under Barnett, over Coleman. Johnson, who three times sought the governorship his father had held, joked that the NAACP (National Association for the Advancement of Colored People) stood for "Niggers, Alligators, Apes, Coons and Possums." A widely distributed leaflet depicted Johnson at Oxford, Mississippi, with his fist apparently raised against the chief U.S. marshal. (Later, it was reported to be one of a sequence of photographs in which Johnson was moving his arm down

13. W. F. (Bill) Minor, "From Bilbo to Booze," unpublished manuscript.
14. Confidential interview.

to shake hands.) Johnson accused Coleman, who had been host to John F. Kennedy in the governor's mansion and had supported him in 1956 for the vice-presidential nomination, of allowing the hated Kennedy to sleep in Bilbo's bed. But the assassination of Kennedy shocked Johnson, and in his inaugural speech in 1964 he included this phrase for his fellow Mississippians: "You and I are part of this world, whether we like it or not."

Johnson never condemned segregation, but he kept his mouth shut—enough to make him a moderate in Mississippi. Johnson called for federal help against the Klan, and the largest FBI office outside of Washington was established in Jackson, eventually to become suspect for having used extralegal methods to combat the Klan.

The White Knights were found responsible for the murder in 1964 of three civil rights workers near Philadelphia, Mississippi. In McComb, "almost nightly bombs were being set off at Negro homes and churches, blacks were being taken out and flogged, bullets ripped through windows. . . . The one thread of conscience, the lone link with civil sanity came from the newspaper voice of Editor Oliver Emmerich, then approaching his 70s. Eleven arrests eventually were made after Johnson sent in state patrol investigators and the FBI. Judge W. H. Watkins, Jr. accepted guilty pleas from all 11, and placed them on probation, but on condition that if there was any further bombing or racial terror in the community they would immediately be sent to prison. He in effect indicted the entire community and made it co-responsible for the good behavior of the 11. Significantly, the bombings stopped, the church burnings ended, and the community for the first time in months regained its self-respect." [15]

Emmerich editorialized: "Inescapably McComb problems are the problems of McComb people. And McComb people must solve them." He said the citizens who had shrugged off the "ugly record" of violence "inexorably must share in the responsibility for violence even though they may not have been near the scene of violence."

Although segregationist Representative John Bell Williams was elected governor in 1967 to succeed Johnson, it was significant that Barnett finished a poor fifth in an attempted comeback. Also significant is the fact that state Treasurer William Winter—a genuine political moderate—led the first primary. Williams campaigned as a martyr after he had been stripped of his 20 years' seniority for supporting Republican Barry Goldwater in 1964, a year in which Goldwater's vote against the Civil Rights Act was sufficient to win him 87 percent of the vote in Mississippi.

15. Minor, "From Bilbo to Booze," unpublished manuscript.

BLACK POLITICS

In no other southern state was white resistance to black political participation so total and so unrestrained as in Mississippi. Official Mississippi had lost none of its ingenuity or determination in thwarting blacks from registering to vote. The credo expressed by James K. Vardaman in 1907 remained an article of faith: "The Negro should never be trusted with the ballot. He is different from the white man. He is congenitally unqualified to exercise the most responsible duty of citizenship." [16]

The state constitution was amended in 1960 to require that a potential voter be "of good moral character," with local registrars making that determination. A 1962 statute required that local newspapers publish for at least two weeks the names of persons who had applied for registration, thus putting any black on clear notice that registration entailed the risk of white retaliation.

Although the South-wide Voter Education Project spent more money in Mississippi than in any other state, fewer than 4,000 new voters were registered in two years, a reflection of the level of intimidation, violence, and official obstruction. Mississippi had experienced five years of civil rights activity more intensive than anywhere else in the South by the time the Voting Rights Act of 1965 was passed, but only 6.7 percent of the black voting-age population was registered. This compared with 19.3 percent in Alabama, 27.4 percent in Georgia, 31.6 percent in Louisiana, and 37.3 percent in South Carolina. [17]

The 1963 assassination of moderate state NAACP Field Secretary Medgar Evers in Jackson marked a turning point. A bloody riot was narrowly averted when John Doar of the Justice Department moved from behind a line of armed Jackson police and strode forward to confront 500 angry blacks after the funeral procession. Doar raised both hands and shouted, "I am John Doar with the Justice Department. Go on home; this is not the way to win your rights. I know you are angry, but the way is through the courts." There were curses and murmurs of dissent, but the mob broke and melted away down the street. [18]

One response was the return to Mississippi of Charles Evers, Medgar's brother, a charismatic leader who organized boycotts and voter registration drives, won election as mayor of Fayette, and ran for governor in 1971. He ran against William Waller, the former district attorney who

16. James K. Vardaman, quoted by Len Holt, *The Summer That Didn't End* (New York, 1965), p. 311.
17. U.S. Civil Rights Commission, *The Voting Rights Act: Ten Years After,* January 1975, p. 43.
18. Minor, "From Bilbo to Booze," unpublished manuscript.

had twice prosecuted the accused slayer of Medgar Evers—getting a hung jury both times—and a man who became the first governor since James P. Coleman to declare himself a national Democrat.

In the fall of 1963, NAACP President Aaron Henry, a druggist from the Delta town of Clarksdale, and a white chaplain from black Tougaloo College ran for governor and lieutenant governor in an informal "Freedom Election." A remarkable turnout of 80,000 people voted, more than four times the number of blacks registered in the state.

The "Freedom Summer" of 1964 attracted hundreds of northern white college students to Mississippi, where they joined black students and lived with black families and worked for voter registration in an atmosphere of tension. Three civil rights workers, two of them northern whites and one a Mississippi black youth, were slain by Ku Klux Klansmen and buried in an earthen dam in Neshoba County. It was a crime that involved local law enforcement officers and shocked the country.

In 1964 a black challenge to the all-white Mississippi delegation at the Democratic National Convention in Atlantic City set off a national political reform movement. It directly led to Democratic Party guidelines that provided an expanded national role for blacks, women, and young people.

The Mississippi Freedom Democratic Party (MFDP) had been organized by a coalition of civil rights organizations. After being excluded from the regular Democratic meetings, they developed a parallel political structure, selecting delegates, holding precinct meetings, running county conventions in 35 of the 82 counties, and holding a state convention attended by 2,500 people. They elected forty-four delegates and twenty-two alternates to the Democratic national convention, sixty-two blacks and four whites.

Fannie Lou Hamer, a Sunflower County neighbor of Jim Eastland and th youngest of a sharecropper's 20 children, had been kicked off a plantation where she worked after trying to register to vote. She testified before a stunned Credentials Committee at Atlantic City and a national television audience about what happened after she and six other blacks were arrested in Winona after several of them sought service at the bus station lunch counter:

> They carried me into a room and there were two Negro boys in this room. The state highway patrolman gave them a long, wide blackjack and he told one of the boys, "Take this . . . and if you don't use it on her, you know what I'll use on you." I had to get over a bed flat on my stomach and that man beat me . . . that man beat me till he gave out. And by me screamin' it made a plainclothes man—he didn't have on nothin' like a uniform—he got so hot and worked up he just run there and started hittin' me on the back of my head. And I was trying to guard some of the licks with my hands and they just beat my hands till they turned blue.

The Credentials Committee struck a compromise that amounted to a significant political victory for the challengers. Reasoning that a legal party was one that complied with the law of the state it sought to represent, the committee recommended seating the "regular" delegation, provided they would sign a loyalty oath. (Only four signed; the rest walked out.) But the committee recommended amending the rules of the convention to provide that in the future a state must ensure that "all voters, regardless of race, color, creed or national origin, will have the opportunity to participate fully in party affairs." From that ruling developed the quota systems for blacks, women, and youth at the 1972 national convention and the affirmative action plans required of each state in 1976. The committee also offered the status of delegate-at-large to Aaron Henry and Ed King, his running mate in the 1963 Freedom Election, and extended a welcome to the other Freedom delegates as honored guests, a form of de facto recognition.

Liberals and national civil rights leaders who had helped guide and assist the challenge from the beginning urged acceptance, but a majority of the Freedom Democrats rejected the offer. The young college-educated leaders, becoming radicalized by experiences such as the one Mrs. Hamer described, believed in fighting for absolute goals without concession, and they viewed the compromise as a sellout. They also objected to the fact that the Committee had picked the two delegates, rather than allowing the delegates to exercise the forms of democracy they were attempting to teach at the grassroots level.

But Aaron Henry was not a radical. He believed that change for poor blacks in Mississippi could come only if they were helped by powerful allies, that coalitions were necessary to achieve change within a system, and that such change could be achieved. It was the radicals of the Student Nonviolent Coordinating Committee (SNCC) within the Mississippi Freedom Democratic Party who articulated the protest politics of what developed into the New Left of the late 1960s and early 1970s, a national movement whose focus shifted from civil rights to protest against the war in Vietnam.

In Mississippi, the Freedom Democratic Party continued to develop its organization at the grassroots level, and the ideological split between the moderates such as Henry and the young radicals from SNCC began to widen. The slogan of "Black Power," frightening to whites and little understood, began to be heard.

In 1965, Henry and other NAACP leaders joined with other moderate blacks, white liberals, and organized labor to develop a coalition with as broad a base as possible, in order to work for change within the system. The Freedom Democrats, who saw their position as one based on morality and justice, sought "to unite the entire Negro community into an independent, radically democratic organization so as to be able to act politically from a position of maximum strength." [19] Henry, Charles Evers, and other NAACP-oriented blacks feared that the "separatist" program of the Freedom Democrats would further polarize the state along racial lines, thereby jeopardizing the chances of building a broadly integrated party of loyal Democrats in Mississippi.

In fact, the existence of the more radical MFDP allowed a more moderate image for the new coalition group than would otherwise have been possible for a biracial political organization in Mississippi. In 1964 the MFDP had nominated four candidates to run for Congress in the June primary, but their petitions were refused by the Mississippi secretary of state. After a mock election in the fall, they organized national support and lobbied in Washington against the seating of the contested Mississippi congressmen, actually winning 149 votes for their position and thus posing a genuine threat to the Mississippi political establishment.

While the challenge to the congressional delegation was being considered, the Mississippians in Washington sent word home to Governor Johnson to straighten out the registration laws, and the governor provided leadership to rid the state constitution of its "read and understand" requirement for registration. The governor's floor leader told the House, "If you think this nation is going to permit us to continue to discriminate, you are living in a world of fantasy."

The attention being focused on the denial of the franchise to Mississippi blacks helped lead to the Voting Rights Act of 1965, which brought in federal registrars and suspended literacy requirements, and which took the steam out of the challenges. In Mississippi, the results were dramatic. From 6.7 percent prior to 1965, the percentage of black voting-age population that was registered rose to 59.8 percent by September 1967, the highest percentage at that time of any of the seven southern states covered by the Voting Rights Act.[20]

But unlike South Carolina, where even before the Voting Rights Act Democratic leaders had quietly begun to assimilate blacks into the system as a buffer against white defections to the Republican Party, the Mississippi leadership was too rigid to adjust.

In a battle between the competing groups challenging the Democratic structure in the state, the moderates won control of the organized Young Democrats, thus establishing a link to the national party. The moderate group was funded in part by the national AFL–CIO and aimed at building an organization entirely of loyal Democrats. State AFL–CIO

19. Lawrence Guyot, chairman of the Freedom Democratic Party, quoted in Marion Symington, "Challenge to Mississippi," unpublished history honors thesis, Harvard University, 1969. (Guyot was among those arrested and beaten in the Winona incident described by Mrs. Hamer.)

20. U.S. Civil Rights Commission, *Voting Rights Act: Ten Years After*, p. 43.

President Claude Ramsey, a native Mississippian who since his election as president in 1959 has been an outspoken opponent of the Klan and of Senator Eastland, brought in Charles Evers to help organize the first meeting. The initial meeting of 125 included Hodding Carter III, who would succeed his Pulitzer Prize-winning father as editor and publisher of the newspaper in Greenville and who would play a significant leadership role in the factional dispute.

By 1968, Evers had been elected mayor of Fayette and had helped in efforts that resulted in the election of 14 other black officials in the state. He was one of three blacks elected among 20 delegates by the district Democratic conventions. However, Governor John Bell Williams refused to allow any blacks among the additional group of 24 delegates and 12 alternates named by the state Democratic convention, a body of 800 delegates that included 42 blacks, the first to attend since 1890. Evers, who had suggested a minimum of ten blacks among the 44 delegates, withdrew in protest, declaring he would not be a pawn "to deny full representation" to his people.

Evidence of widespread irregularities at the meetings of the "regular" Democrats, where the moderates had sought to participate, were collected. Leaders of the Freedom Democrats recognized they had a common goal with the moderates in attempting to unseat the regulars, and the factions joined in a "loyalist" coalition that held conventions in 72 counties to elect their delegates.

Aaron Henry, always a political realist, had told a meeting of rural blacks that summer in Mississippi, "When you get right down to it, the challenge is not a question of right and wrong; it is a political question. If they think they can get more votes out of the country by supportin' us, then they'll support us. If they can get more from John Bell Williams, they'll support him." [21] The loyalists won an 85–10 vote on the Credentials Committee and were seated. Senator Eastland called the action "a political fraud." It was another step toward open biracial politics in Mississippi.

Governor Williams, whose intransigence amounted to a virtual dare to the Credentials Committee, did not bother to go to the convention, and he apparently believed his attitude would make him more popular among the segregationists at home. After Wallace's landslide victory in Mississippi in 1968, Williams said, "Mississippi's Democratic Party, as far as I am concerned, is no longer associated with the National Democratic Party."

By 1972 the "loyalist" faction headed by Aaron Henry and Charles Evers was recognized by the National Democratic Party, while the "regulars" dominated state government but were isolated from the national party. There had been a considerable thaw, however, and Governor

21. Symington, "Challenge to Mississippi," p. 88.

William L. Waller sought to lead a delegation to the national convention that would be recognized. Significantly, he won over AFL–CIO President Claude Ramsey. In some counties the loyalists and the regulars were the same people, and meetings of the regulars were far more open than before. But clashes became more pronounced as the delegate selection process advanced to the district and state level.

Unlike Williams, Waller battled for recognition, but his last-minute offer to the loyalists of 40 percent representation at all levels of party organization could not be guaranteed and was rejected by the loyalists. The Credentials Committee again decided that the loyalists had more closely followed the national party's guidelines for delegate selection.

Eastland, whose own power in Washington was jeopardized by the failure to unify the Democratic Party in Mississippi—he was accepted in the Democratic caucus by only a four-vote margin after the 1972 election—quietly encouraged subsequent resolution of the conflict. Eastland prefers to work unseen, through intermediaries, but in the spring of 1975, he personally called state Representative Stone Barefield, the House elections committee chairman and a supporter of George Wallace, and convinced him to allow a presidential preferential primary law go to Governor Waller, together with Barefield's preferred bill, which was geared for Wallace. Governor Waller vetoed the Barefield bill and signed into law one that in 1976 allowed the loyalists to make a decision whether to hold a presidential primary to elect delegates or to nominate at district conventions. A key intermediary in the negotiations was the chancery clerk in Eastland's Sunflower County. The action cleared the way for resolving the dispute between the regulars and the loyalists, thus removing a potential problem for Eastland in the Senate Democratic caucus in 1977.

Within the state, the 1971 elections, in which virtually all state and local officials were elected to four-year terms, had major implications for black politics. Charles Evers ran for governor as an independent candidate, but his questionable strategy and monopoly of outside funds for his own campaign were factors in the failure to achieve significant results. Of 309 black candidates, only 50 were elected, most of them to offices of little consequence, such as constable or justice of the peace. Twenty-eight of 29 legislative candidates lost, and incumbent Robert Clark barely retained his seat. All 14 candidates for sheriff lost. All ten candidates for chancery clerk, the top county administrative office, lost. All ten candidates for county superintendent of education lost. Of 74 candidates for supervisor—the powerful five-member board that governs each county—only eight were elected.

There was clear evidence of fraud in some counties, and the 1975 report of the U.S. Civil Rights Commission reported: "Acts of violence against blacks involved in the political process still occur often enough in Mississippi that the atmosphere of intimidation and fear has not yet cleared." [22] The report cited specific cases and concluded that fear remains a deterrent to black political participation in Mississippi.

The charismatic Evers opened his campaign for governor by urging blacks to vote for an avowed segregationist in the Democratic primary, suggesting that he (Evers) would have a chance of winning by picking up moderate white support. Evers then urged blacks to boycott the primary runoff between Waller and Lieutenant Governor Charles Sullivan, both of whom ran as racial moderates and both of whom promised to bring blacks into state government.

Aaron Henry, from Sullivan's hometown of Clarksdale, once had been prosecuted by Sullivan for "illegal" picketing during the days of demonstrations, but Henry later termed Sullivan as one of those whites who had "turned the corner" on race and had actively supported him. Other blacks were supporting Waller, who had vigorously prosecuted the accused killer of Medgar Evers. A heavy black vote in the runoff would have placed blacks in a stronger bargaining position with whomever won the election; thus, Evers's strategy of discouraging blacks from participating in the runoff was questionable.

Because of his national stature as a civil rights leader, Evers was able to raise funds from out-of-state sources, but little went to help local candidates. The heavy Evers television campaign, apparently prompted by a heady belief that he could win (he received 22 percent of the vote), helped mobilize white voters, who turned out in record numbers. Evers appeared on numerous occasions with members of an integrated striking woodworkers union, but a postelection analysis of six white precincts in Jackson showed he received less than 3.5 percent of the vote, and other black candidates received even less.

In rural areas, black voters who required assistance were required to announce their preferences orally to white election officials, many of whom were happy to allow a vote for Evers but brought at least subtle pressure against voting for local black officials.

The controversy over the Evers campaign strategy, together with his subsequent indictment on charges of income tax irregularities, somewhat dimmed his leadership role among Mississippi blacks. But the 1971 election provided blacks with additional experience in campaign techniques, raised their level of political sophistication, brought about a degree of reconciliation between the rival Freedom Democratic Party and NAACP factions, and offered a campaign for governor in which race was not an issue between the major candidates.

During eight years as the lone black in the Mississippi legislature (he was joined by three others after the 1975 elections), Robert Clark of Holmes County gained insights into state politics shared by no other black in Mississippi.

22. U.S. Civil Rights Commission, *Voting Rights Act: Ten Years After*, p. 174.

A former educator with a master's degree from Michigan State University, Clark was one of the indigenous leaders of the Mississippi Freedom Democratic Party, and Holmes has proved unique in actually implementing the MFDP philosophy of participatory grassroots democracy. Units of the party met regularly in 17 communities in the county, more than once a month in most. Monthly, a countywide meeting was held to discuss everything which was of interest in the black community. At the "countywide," major problems in the community are forwarded for action to the MFDP executive board. Whether the structure can adjust to changing circumstances remains to be seen, but as Clark says, it works.

Even before legislative salaries were raised from $7,000 annually to $12,400 beginning in 1976, Clark worked full-time as a legislator, serving almost as an unofficial governor to Mississippi blacks, who came to him from throughout the state with their problems. When Clark entered the legislature he found himself ostracized at social events, but those barriers gradually broke down, and as black participation at the polls increased, white politicians became more and more responsive. "Black folks have a hell of a lot more respect of the white politician than they know," said Clark. "They got power that they're not using."

When Clark first went to the legislature, there were times when he actually spoke against legislation he favored because he said it was the only way whites would vote for it. By 1974 the legislature had passed a strong consumer protection bill that was clearly perceived, although never publicly stated, to be of special benefit to blacks, who had long been victimized by unscrupulous business practices. "You don't see black or white anywhere in that bill," Clark said, "but every legislator here knows what that bill is saying. . . . It passed solely because blacks are voting. . . . Yes, there's a change in the legislature, because there's a change in the state."

Nothing so well illustrates the lack of a genuine Democratic Party organization in Mississippi as the experience of Clark, who served as chairman of both the loyalists and regulars in Holmes County but who runs for the legislature as an independent. "We don't have a party in Mississippi," he said, "really, we don't." [23] In 1975, Clark participated in the strategy committee of Gil Carmichael, the moderate Republican candidate for governor. During the Carmichael campaign, Clark told other blacks that a Republican victory would destroy old-guard control of the Democratic party.

23. Interview with Robert Clark, March 28, 1974.

THE POLITICS OF TRANSITION

Nothing reflects better the alienation of Mississippi voters and the non-party character of the state's politics than its presidential voting patterns.

Mississippi had been in the forefront of reaction to President Truman's civil rights initiatives in 1948, and Governor Fielding Wright ran for vice-president on Strom Thurmond's Dixiecrat ticket, which easily carried Mississippi. J. P. Coleman helped hold the state for the Democrats in 1952 and 1956 and barely lost it in 1960, when an independent slate pledged to Senator Harry Byrd of Virginia was elected, with the blessings of Ross Barnett.

The fact that the 87 percent vote for Goldwater was by no means a switch to Republicanism was demonstrated four years later when Richard Nixon received only 14 percent, as George Wallace won 63 percent in a three-way race. In 1972, however, Mississippians proved they understood Nixon's "southern strategy," and his 80 percent of the vote was highest in the nation.

At the state level, the election and administration of Governor William L. Waller in many ways represented a challenge to the political establishment and a transition to an as yet undefined political order.

Waller was elected in 1971 in a two-level campaign. One was the product of DeLoss Walker, the Memphis campaign technician, who in some cases reproduced almost word for word the advertising copy from the 1970 Dale Bumpers gubernatorial campaign in Arkansas, substituting Waller's name and photograph. It was Waller running against the establishment, "the Capitol Street gang" that included the banks, newspapers, and top business elite in Jackson. On a less visible level, Waller's campaign relied on the network of political operatives, county supervisors, and other local officials linked to Eastland. Waller was Eastland's choice, or so the story is told repeatedly in Mississippi, because he appeared to be the candidate most likely to beat Charlie Sullivan, who had committed the unpardonable sin: he had once been overheard at a social gathering to say he might someday challenge Jim Eastland for the Senate. Eastland's friends provided needed campaign funds, and at one dinner Bunker Hunt, a sometime business partner of Eastland and a son of H. L. Hunt, the late right-wing oil billionaire from Texas, was reportedly credited with being the campaign's largest single contributor.

Before being elected lieutenant governor, Sullivan had run for governor—like Waller, as a district attorney taking on the establishment—but now he was associated with the administration of John Bell Williams, whose performance was perhaps better than his image, especially in his ability to utilize his Washington experience to expand federal programs in Mississippi. Sullivan led the 1971 primary with 38 percent of the vote but lost in the runoff to Waller, who then swamped Charles Evers in the general election.

Waller brought innovation to the governor's office, holding weekly press conferences (at some he brought in agency heads and asked more questions than the press did) and making extensive annual legislative proposals. However, Waller developed little rapport with the legislature, which for the first time in more than 30 years began to override vetoes by a governor. And in Mississippi, more than in any other state, the legislature is supreme.

In Waller's words, "Legislators now draw up the budget, recommend it to themselves for approval, and then—through agencies such as the PEER [Performance Evaluation and Expenditure Review] Committee —they can tell the agency heads how to spend the money." [24] Waller also cited a study by political scientist Joseph Schlesinger in which, on an index comparing the formal powers of all 50 state governors, Mississippi ranked 50th.

Some of Waller's proposals reflected genuine populist instincts, including support for consumer protection and an end to the traditional practice of making interest-free state deposits in the large banks in Jackson. But a minor scandal developed when it was disclosed that new bank charters throughout the state were going to Waller cronies, with the governor himself often a stockholder, and that interest-free deposits were made in some of the new banks from funds excluded from the new provision requiring interest payments on most surplus state funds.

Waller's recommendations for a new state constitution and for a provision permitting a governor to succeed himself were ignored by the legislature. A major increase in teachers' salaries, taking Mississippi off the bottom in that statistic, occurred in the Waller administration, but was apparently more a result of effective lobbying by the Mississippi Education Association and the threat of a teachers' union than anything else. The legislature also funded a $600 million highway construction program recommended by Waller, but the program was actually authorized during the previous administration.

Waller did set a new tone and direction for the state by finally appointing blacks to state boards and agencies, but few of those appointed had been involved in any way with civil rights activity. When he named a black staff member to work on bringing blacks into state government, the governor revealed that his staffer's salary would be $6,000 a year, an indication of what kind of openings blacks might expect to find.

A 1974 study by the private Mississippi Council on Human Relations disclosed 44 state agencies and departments without a single black employee. Excluding those agencies that had records of hiring blacks for segregated programs and facilities, such as higher education and the

24. William Waller, speech to Mississippi Economic Council, February 4, 1975.

state's hospitals, the study found that blacks comprised less than 6 percent of the state work force. (In South Carolina, second to Mississippi in percentage of black population, blacks comprised 27 percent of total state employment and 30.5 percent of the population.) Despite the changed climate and the sloganeering, Waller failed to create a state biracial commission to deal with complaints of discrimination, leaving Mississippi and Alabama as the only Deep South states without such an agency. And Mississippi remained the only state without a compulsory school attendance law.

Another example of Waller's failure to match his rhetoric about change with action came in a 1974 schoolbook controversy. The conservative Mississippi Textbook Board refused to approve for use in the schools a new textbook, *Mississippi: Conflict and Change,* which was widely acclaimed by several notable regional historians and described as "historically accurate" by Waller's personal representative. The author of the only acceptable text began writing books for Mississippi public schools after Ross Barnett implemented a mandatory history course in 1962 with the caveat, "There is nothing so important as the molding of the hearts and minds of our young people." As part of the molding, Barnett attempted to purge the educational system of textbooks which did not condone the segregated way of life. Despite a personal plea from the authors of the new text, Waller declined to intervene in the controversy.

Waller received wide attention when he proclaimed Medgar Evers Day on the tenth anniversary of the slaying of the civil rights leader, but the governor did not attend the commemoration. Perceptive observers in Mississippi viewed the governor's proclamation as a move to balance his earlier approval of a work release arrangement for a former Klansman convicted in the murder of Vernon Dahmer, another former civil rights leader. Waller had served as defense lawyer for the convicted killer in his appeal before the state Supreme Court, and his approval of a program to allow the man freedom to work outside the prison had drawn criticism from blacks.

In summarizing Waller as a political leader, a press agent in the governor's office concluded an otherwise extravagant profile with a rather balanced assessment from the *Biloxi Daily Herald:* "While Bill Waller may not go down in the book as the shrewdest, most pragmatic politician the State has produced, . . . he should be applauded for his attentiveness to the broader needs of the State he governs."

In the 1975 elections, the old ways continued to change. Lieutenant Governor William Winter, once the liberal hope, had become a figurehead for the state Democratic establishment, and he suffered a landslide defeat in a revolt by the voters. Cliff Finch, a maverick challenger, won 58 percent of the vote for a one-sided victory in the Democratic primary and went on to turn back a surprisingly strong Republican challenge. Heavy support from a coalition of blacks and working-class whites provided Finch's margin of victory, and his response as governor will help shape the direction of politics in Mississippi.

A wealthy trial lawyer who had been a solid supporter of Ross Barnett as a legislator in the early 1960s, Finch developed an image as the workingman's candidate with his populist rhetoric and an attention-getting campaign that involved his spending one day a week working at such jobs as stamping prices on groceries, pumping gas, and driving a bulldozer. The lunchpail became his campaign symbol. The Eastland organization, which suffered a defeat in the primary when Winter lost, moved in behind Finch in the general election, and Finch promised after the election to resolve the dispute between the regulars and loyalists in the Democratic Party.

Another sign of change was the election of Evelyn Gandy as the first female lieutenant governor in the South. Although she had held minor office in the state for a number of years, her surprise victory against better-known opponents reflected another element of revolt against the old guard.

REPUBLICANS

More than most of the other Deep South Republican organizations, the GOP in Mississippi in recent years has demonstrated its willingness to go what veteran state Chairman Clark Reed calls "an extra mile" to get at least token black representation in the party. This reflects a sense of enlightened self-interest.

Reed has recruited some articulate, thoughtful young black professionals, allowed them active roles in party matters, and given them a fair share in patronage during Republican administrations. Reed served as top Republican for patronage matters during the Nixon administration, often competing with Eastland. Reed's long years of continuity as state chairman in a state without a Republican governor or senator and his chairmanship of the Association of Southern Republican State Chairmen placed him in a position of political influence unequaled by any other nonofficeholder in the South.

Typical of the active blacks are Eugene McLemore and Clell Ward, lawyers in Greenville, who contend that a strong two-party system will benefit blacks in Mississippi and that because there is a Republican Party, it should have black representation. In McLemore's words, "just by the mere fact that I am in the Republican Party and have been in some of the state-level decision-making, I've been able to moderate or change certain views." [25]

25. Interview with Eugene McLemore, April 2, 1974.

A "lily-white" group of Republicans wrested full party control in 1960 from the old "Black and Tan" element. Jackson businessman Rubel Phillips, a moderate, ran for governor in 1963 and again in 1967. He received 38 percent in the first race, but analysis indicated that he received basically the moderate vote that had supported losing Democrat J. P. Coleman in the Democratic primary against Paul Johnson's racist campaign. In 1967, when he received only 30 percent against John Bell Williams, Phillips said, "As long as they remain in Mississippi, the Negro and the white are bound together—even though they may live separate lives, in separate communities. They are bound together so closely that neither can rise significantly without lifting the other." His campaigns helped provide a basis for moderate support within the GOP.

The ultraconservative wing of the party was represented by Prentiss Walker, chicken farmer and chairman of the 1960 independent electors slate, who was elected to Congress in 1964 on the Goldwater sweep, as the only congressional candidate the Republicans fielded. Two years later he ran against Eastland, futilely claiming that Eastland wasn't a "true" conservative. Eastland got two-thirds of the vote, and four GOP congressional candidates lost that year.

The two Republican congressmen, Thad Cochran and Trent Lott, were elected in the Nixon sweep of 1972; Cochran actively campaigned for the black vote and subsequently hired a black aide. It was enough to win votes in a district with a 43 percent black population, but in Cochran's first year in Congress he voted only 2 percent of the time with positions taken by the Congressional Black Caucus, considerably less than any of the three Mississippi Democratic congressmen who also represented districts with more than 35 percent black population.

When James Meredith filed for the Republican nomination for the U.S. Senate against Eastland in 1972, his entry forced party regulars, who viewed the unpredictable Meredith as a threat to GOP congressional candidates, to recruit an active candidate. They came up with Gil Carmichael, an enlightened Meridian businessman and party activist who proved to be a dynamic campaigner.

The Nixon White House, recipient of many favors from Eastland, made it clear that it was supporting the senator, sending two cabinet members to Mississippi to appear with him. The White House directed that Carmichael be excluded from the platform at a rally in Jackson which Vice-President Spiro Agnew, then a hero in Mississippi, addressed on behalf of the GOP congressional candidates, Cochran and Lott. The episode clearly demonstrated the limited commitment of Nixon to effective party building in the South. Carmichael managed to win 42 percent of the major party vote, won substantial support from blacks, and laid the groundwork for his 1975 race for governor.

In that race, for the first time this century, Republicans made a serious challenge for the governorship, with Carmichael receiving 47 percent of the vote against Cliff Finch. Despite Carmichael's strength at the top of the ticket, Republicans gained only one state House seat in 1975.

Carmichael ran an issue-oriented campaign that called for a new state constitution, passage of the Equal Rights Amendment and handgun control legislation, a compulsory school attendance law, and other progressive measures. He introduced a new style to political campaigning in Mississippi: his disclosure of campaign contributions and their sources, as well as his personal financial records, broke new ground in openness. He conducted both regular press conferences and "people's press conferences," to which the public was invited to come and ask questions. He also developed the issues in an extensive media campaign.

A postelection survey indicated that two-thirds of Carmichael's votes came from people who had never before voted for a Republican candidate for governor. Finch's "workingman" image, combined with traditional Democratic voting habits and the support of such black leaders as Aaron Henry and Charles Evers, helped him carry 80 percent of the black vote. In the survey, only 6.1 percent of the voters identified themselves as Republicans, compared with 50.7 percent Democrats. Another 23.2 percent identified themselves as independent, and 20 percent either did not know or refused to say.

The major success for Republicans has been at the municipal level, where elections are held in the off-numbered year from state and county elections. Beginning with the election of nine of 20 candidates in 1965, Republicans have invariably elected more than 40 percent of the candidates they ran, winning 62 seats in 1973. They won the office of mayor in four of the 25 largest towns and cities in the state, including Meridian, the second-largest city. But in the legislature, they still held only five seats after the 1975 elections, three in the House and two in the Senate.

The Republicans run a well-financed state headquarters with a full-time paid staff and a budget in excess of $200,000. The party engages in candidate recruitment and support at all levels, in sharp contrast to the Democrats, who with their split personality in Mississippi lacked even a state headquarters in 1975 and who existed only as a frame of reference, not as a formal political party.

CONGRESS

In 1972, per capita federal spending in Mississippi amounted to $1,158, greater than for any state in the South except Virginia, where the figure was inflated by federal installations in the Washington suburbs.

Such federal largesse reflects the power and influence of the state's congressional delegation, especially Eastland and John Stennis in the Senate. But both men are in their 70s, part of a fading era in which the seniority system concentrated power in the hands of Democrats from a one-party South.

Eastland is viewed at home as the consummate politician, a man who reportedly once told a complaining staffer taking care of a problem for a demanding constituent, "a political debt is never paid off." Stennis, whose voting record against civil rights and social legislation matches Eastland's, never indulged in racist campaign rhetoric. The two maintained an "arrangement" on patronage matters, and Stennis developed the reputation of a "statesman." The two have worked together to bring in federal money.

In the House, the most influential remaining congressman is Jamie Whitten, elected in a special election in 1941 at the age of 31. As a ranking Democrat on the Appropriations Committee, Whitten wields considerable influence. At home he has proved to be one of those adaptable Democrats who shifted with changing times. One of those whose seats were challenged in 1964 for party disloyalty, Whitten at the Democratic mini-convention in Kansas City in December 1974 stood up in a loyalist-led caucus and praised the movement to build "a progressive Democratic Party in Mississippi." He also displayed backslapping camaraderie with Aaron Henry at a reception for Harold Ford, the newly elected black congressman from Memphis.

David Bowen, a native Mississippian educated at Harvard and Oxford as a political scientist, served as coordinator of state-federal programs under Governor John Bell Williams. Bowen worked to fully implement Lyndon Johnson's Great Society programs and also laid the groundwork for a successful congressional race in 1972, becoming the first mainstream national Democrat in Congress from Mississippi in more than a decade.

Whitten voted 27 percent of the time in support of the Congressional Black Caucus in 1973 roll calls, and Bowen gave 32 percent support to such programs. In contrast to Cochran, who opposed such measures, Whitten and Bowen voted to increase spending for farm loans, override a presidential veto of rural sewer grants, increase appropriations for the Department of Health, Education, and Welfare, extend Federal Housing Authority subsidy programs, provide emergency medical services, and increase funding for school lunches.

Mississippi's future political direction in large part likely will shape and be shaped by the replacements it chooses for the men who have represented the state in the U.S. Senate since the 1940s.

The two democratic factions came together in the delegate selection process for the National Convention in 1976, and a testimonial dinner for Senator Eastland attracted black leaders such as Charles Evers and Aaron Henry. Mississippi at last was shedding its past.

Chapter

10

NORTH CAROLINA

The Progressive Myth

AT THE END of the 1940s, V. O. Key described North Carolina as "the progressive plutocracy," a state that was the leader of what the South might become. A press more liberal than any other in the South, the traditional institutional strength of the University of North Carolina at Chapel Hill, a higher level of industrialization, and a history in which the plantation influence played a lesser role—all had contributed to the progressive image. "It has been the vogue to be progressive," Key wrote. "Willingness to accept new ideas, sense of community responsibility toward the Negro, feeling of common purpose, and relative prosperity have given North Carolina more sophisticated politics than exists in most southern states." [1]

Although Key believed the state would remain on its progressive course, he realized the balance was precarious: "The comfortable picture of the Tar Heel state as an area of progress, tolerance, and enlightenment is scotched most forcefully by North Carolinians themselves . . . They know that every liberation from every ancient taboo is bought or buttressed by shrewdness and hard work and endless patience. Yet they take pride in what they accomplish and seldom indulge in complacency that ignores work yet undone." [2]

North Carolina remains a plutocracy, but a complacency has replaced the "energetic and ambitious" mood that Key detected. Migrants to the state who are familiar with the progressive reputation tend to be struck by the reality they find. "The farther you get from North Carolina, the

1. V. O. Key, *Southern Politics in State and Nation* (New York: Vintage, 1949), p. 211.
2. Ibid., p. 206.

more progressive it looks," declared Ferrel Guillory, an astute observer who moved from New Orleans to become chief political writer for the *Raleigh News and Observer*.[3]

The progressive image the state projected in the late 1940s has evolved into a progressive myth that remains accepted as fact by much of the state's native leadership, despite ample evidence to the contrary. Although North Carolina has changed with the times, it is perhaps the least changed of the old Confederate states. Because of its moderation, it yielded more easily to the forces of change, but it missed the dynamic reaction to resistance that so swiftly transformed political and social development elsewhere in the South. Nor has it experienced the impact of urbanization as much as most other border South states have.

When Key wrote, the race issue was still suppressed in North Carolina, as it had been for 50 years through a process in which men of some distinction ran against each other "within the accepted framework," an unspoken code which barred the arousal of racial antagonisms. The Negro was given a degree of paternalistic protection and allowed marginal political participation. But once political appeals on race were unleashed, in the 1950 U.S. Senate race against Frank Porter Graham, they proved a powerful force, and the progressive momentum slowed.

That campaign is worth examining in some detail. As president of the University of North Carolina, Frank Graham had continued the tradition his father had established of making that institution the center for an unfettered examination of southern life and history and the shaper of the progressive spirit in the state. He had received an interim appointment to the U.S. Senate and was running for a full term. Key had characterized Graham as "by all odds the South's most prominent educator and versatile public servant" who stood in the "forefront of American progressivism." Graham neither smoked, nor drank, nor cussed—admirable attributes in moralistic North Carolina, the only state left in the South where liquor is not sold by the drink.

Graham received 49.1 percent of the vote in the first primary, falling 5,635 votes short of a clear majority over Willis Smith, who trailed by 53,000 votes. Smith was a former president of the American Bar Association and chairman of the Board of Trustees of Duke University. He hesitated to call for a runoff, doing so only a few hours before the deadline. The runoff followed the defeat in Florida of liberal Senator Claude Pepper by George Smathers in a racist, red-baiting campaign. And between the two primaries in North Carolina, the U.S. Supreme Court had ruled that Pullman dining cars could not be racially segregated and that the universities of Texas and Oklahoma would have to admit Negro students.

3. Interview with Ferrel Guillory, December 11, 1973.

Graham forces were confident of victory until the closing days of the election, when handbills flooded the state that screamed in oversized type:

"WHITE PEOPLE WAKE UP"

They declared that "Frank Graham Favors Mingling of the Races" and predicted dire consequences unless Willis Smith was elected senator. Graham had served on President Truman's Civil Rights Commission, and the last three days of the campaign were marked by advertisements in newspapers throughout the state proclaiming, "End of Racial Segregation Proposed" or "The South Under Attack." Radio spots hammered such messages as "Do you know that 28 percent of the North Carolina population is colored?" A mass whispering campaign intimated that the election of Graham would mean an end to racial segregation in the public schools.

Thousands of handbills were distributed throughout the state that pictured a Negro youth who, it was falsely alleged, Graham had appointed to West Point. (A Negro youth had placed as an alternate through competitive examinations.) In one tobacco-farming community, Graham took along the white youth who actually had received the appointment, an attempt to show how untrue the whole racial campaign was. When he finished speaking, Samuel Lubell reports, an angry murmur riffled through the crowd: "Why didn't he bring the nigger he appointed? Who was he trying to fool, showing us that white boy?"

In addition to the race issue, allegations were spread that Graham was a Communist sympathizer. Their force was such that a few years later, the South Carolina Senate voted to ban an appearance by Graham to speak at a state college for women because of his alleged Communist ties. The lone senator who voted against the ban was John C. West, who became that state's "New South" governor in 1971.

In North Carolina, Lubell reported, "the mob mood that was built up in the final days of the campaign was not unlike that preceding a lynching. In Wilmington a precinct worker telephoned the Graham manager and demanded hysterically, 'Come and take all your literature out of my house! My neighbors won't talk to me!' Graham stickers came off automobiles as people found it uncomfortable to say they were for him. In Raleigh an eight-year-old schoolboy, who spoke up for Graham, was beaten up as 'a nigger lover' by other children. A Durham election official, favorable to Graham, was awakened during the night by the jangling telephone. When his wife answered, she was asked, 'How would you like a little stewed nigger for breakfast?'"

In areas where open racial appeals would not be effective, Graham's support of New Deal–Fair Deal policies was used to appeal to economic interests, but the whispering campaign about school integration touched all areas. Lubell reported an interview in a suburban residential area in Greensboro, whose residents were ready to vote for Eisenhower as a Republican in 1952 but who had supported Graham because of his reputation as the South's most progressive educator:

> One worker for Willis Smith had written an eloquent campaign letter, picturing the threat to family security in inflationary policies which robbed savings of their value and which taxed away so much of one's earnings. She showed the letter to the wife of a doctor, who campaigned for Graham in the first primary. The doctor's wife read it and exclaimed, "That's a fine letter! It expresses my sentiments exactly."
>
> Then, as she turned to leave, the doctor's wife added, "You know I don't want my daughter to go to school with Negroes."

When the votes were counted, Smith was the winner. Eighteen eastern counties which Graham had won in the first primary, areas of heavy black population and susceptible to racial appeals, swung against him in the runoff. But in the cities, the major shift came from the economically conservative middle class. Lubell concluded, "The surprise in Graham's defeat was the revelation that the cry of 'nigger' could inflame even the well-educated, well-to-do middle class. . . . It was not only the bigots who turned against 'Doctor Frank' but many 'progressive' North Carolinians." [4] Lubell's precinct analysis showed that voting patterns for Smith in North Carolina and Smathers in Florida both paralleled the pattern of support for Dixiecrat and Republican presidential candidates in 1948, the combination of economically and racially conservative voters who were to form the nucleus of the emerging Republican Party in the South.

Pepper later recalled discussing the 1950 campaign with Graham. "Frank said that within a week or ten days after my election, a lot of that same crowd moved right up into North Carolina that had been working against me. He said, in ten days, they had made him out such a monster that his friends would hardly speak to him." [5]

In each election since then, race has seldom failed to emerge in at least one North Carolina campaign, either overtly or covertly. For example, in 1956, after North Carolina congressman Thurmond Chatham and Charles B. Deane refused to sign the "Southern Manifesto" that denounced the Supreme Court's school desegregation decisions, both were defeated for reelection. Although a third nonsigner, Harold Cooley, survived another ten years in office, the North Carolina congressional delegation's voting record since has been one of the most conservative in the South. In a ranking of southern "progressivism" using composite averages of Senate and House delegations from 1965–74, as measured by their

4. Samuel Lubell, *The Future of American Politics*, rev. ed. (New York: Doubleday Anchor, 1956), pp. 106–115.
5. Interview with Claude Pepper, February 1, 1974.

degree of opposition to *Congressional Quarterly*'s "conservative coalition" roll call votes and House votes on civil rights roll calls, North Carolina ranked behind only South Carolina and Mississippi in its conservative voting record in Congress.[6]

In the 1960s, the emergence of Dr. I. Beverly Lake as a political figure around whom the submerged racial issue could surface further demonstrated that the "progressive" image was less real than perceived. And the racial issue persisted into 1972, when television commentator Jesse Helms won election as the state's first Republican senator in this century. He campaigned as an antibusing candidate, although Helms would contend that blacks were as opposed to "forced busing" as whites. That same year, the voters repudiated former Governor Terry Sanford, who had remained a leader of the state Democratic Party's progressive wing, in a presidential primary against George Wallace.

STATE OF THE STATE

The social change that began in the late 1950s was less traumatic in North Carolina. Because the progressive reputation and the more moderate approach created an image that change was occurring, there was less pressure to change from both the federal government and the civil rights movement. "Pupil placement laws were so devastatingly effective as deterrents to integration that North Carolina managed to 'hold the line' with its moderate stance as successfully as a state like Virginia with its hardline position of 'massive resistance.'"[7]

"Because there were Terry Sanfords who handled desegregation problems in an astute fashion, North Carolina didn't get the attention, and the pressure was not brought to bear as greatly as on other Southern states," explains Howard Lee, the perceptive black mayor of Chapel Hill. "To be sure, there has been some change in North Carolina . . . but when you really look at the amount of actual progress that is being made in practically every category in this state, we're behind."[8]

In a 1973 "quality of life" study by the Midwest Research Institute that analyzed 100 different statistical measurements to determine a social-economic-political-environmental index, North Carolina ranked

6. Merle Black, "Nominal Democrats and Real Republicans: The Voting Behavior of North Carolina Congressmen," in Thad Beyle and Merle Black, eds., *Politics and Policy in North Carolina* (New York: MMS Press, 1975), p. 173.

7. August B. Cochran III, "Desegregating North Carolina's Schools," in ibid., p. 202.

8. Interview with Howard Lee, December 13, 1974.

46th among all the states and eighth among the 11 states of the Old Confederacy. Six years earlier, the institute had ranked North Carolina 40th in the nation and fourth among the southern states.

The 1973 study noted that the nonwhite infant death rate for North Carolina was higher than in any southern state except Mississippi. Only South Carolina and Mississippi had fewer telephones per 100 population. North Carolina had fewer lawyers per 100,000 population than any other southern state. Only three of the other southern states spent less per capita on welfare. Only three had a higher rate of Selective Service draftees fail the mental test. Only South Carolina and Arkansas at 10.5 had a lower level of median school years of education for persons 25 and older than North Carolina's 10.6. Only South Carolina had a lower percentage of voting-age population registered to vote. In addition, North Carolina ranked 49th in the nation in average hourly rate for manufacturing wages—and last in percentage of manufacturing work force who belonged to labor unions.

But these statistics are seldom mentioned in North Carolina, certainly not by politicians. With a few exceptions, such as the beginning of a kindergarten program by the state and the administration of limited health care programs by the University of North Carolina, the problems these statistics suggest get little attention from state government.

Neal Peirce cites a single statistic that tells much about the problems of eastern North Carolina: in 1972 it produced the nation's highest percentage of volunteers for the Army, a reflection of local prospects for employment and educational opportunity.

Although there is much talk within the state about urban growth, and considerable attention has been focused on the fast-growing metropolitan Piedmont Crescent that curves from Raleigh through Durham, Greensboro, and Winston-Salem to Charlotte, only 38 percent of the population in 1970 lived in metropolitan areas that contained a central city of 50,000 population or more, and 44 percent lived in places of less than 2,500 population. In the South, only Arkansas and Mississippi have populations that are less urban.

By 1970 the Piedmont was the fastest-growing region of the state, and 60 percent of the population lived there, three-fifths in the metropolitan areas. Another 31 percent lived in the east, where population has been stable, and about 9 percent in the mountains.

There are stirrings of change in the east, the beginnings of industry in the larger towns, the development of superfarms, and the first manifestations of dissatisfaction with the status quo, leading to a major union victory in 1974, when workers in Roanoke Rapids voted for representation by the Textile Workers Union of America. But the issue of a comprehensive plan of development for this region of more than a million and a half people is seldom raised.

The political battle easterners have fought in recent years has been whether to build a medical school at East Carolina University and thus add to the empire of Leo Jenkins, its politically ambitious chancellor. Jenkins contends that if doctors are trained in the east, more are likely to remain there and practice, a contention that runs counter to studies which show that doctors tend to settle in urban areas with greater economic opportunities and social amenities. The doctor shortage is very real, and the easterners won the battle to build a second medical school for the state. But what was never really debated was whether the same amount of funds could not have delivered health care services more effectively by financing clinics and hospital residency programs coordinated by the established medical school at the University of North Carolina at Chapel Hill.

Little apparent attention has been focused on the lack of economic development in eastern North Carolina, a tobacco-growing region of scrubby pine trees and declining population whose level of health care, educational attainment, and income pull down the overall statistics for the state. Nevertheless, when President Nixon in 1973 eliminated funds for the Coastal Plains Regional Development Commission, newly elected Republican Governor James E. Holshouser, Jr. declined to join the Democratic governors of South Carolina and Georgia, the other affected states, in criticizing the move. Of course, one may view eastern North Carolina as a rural preserve that should remain unchanged as part of the state's agricultural heritage—provided one is willing to ignore the poverty that in recent decades has forced the outmigration of tens of thousands of citizens, those who protest conditions by voting with their feet.

Despite these problems, native North Carolinians have a very strong attachment to their state. In the Comparative State Elections Project,[9] one question read, "All things considered, would you say that (your state) is the best state in which to live?" For the entire United States, 62.6 percent agreed. In North Carolina, a positive response came from 82.3 percent, higher than in any other state. Only 10.8 percent responded negatively, and 6.9 percent were "not sure." There was virtually no difference in the responses from the state's three regions, the east, the Piedmont, and the west. Merle Black at the University of North Carolina reports that natives with the most education were as enthusiastic about the state as those with the least formal education. He concluded: "Consequently the state appears to lack substantial numbers of well educated, 'home-bred' critics or individuals who dissent from the

9. This study and analysis of voting behavior was based on survey research involving more than 7,000 voters in 13 states, representing all regions of the country, after the 1968 presidential election. The study was coordinated and its reports published by the Institute for Research in Social Science, University of North Carolina at Chapel Hill, in 1974.

prevailing orthodoxy." The major dissenters were well-educated migrants to the state, only a third of whom found North Carolina the "best."

Across the nation, the survey found that the individuals most likely to approve of their state of current residence were the "natives"—the elderly, the residents of rural areas and urban locations outside metropolitan areas, the least educated, and the least wealthy. Within North Carolina, each of these types provides a greater degree of support for the state than do their counterparts in the nation as a whole. And Black found "a disproportionate size of such groups within the state."

Sociologist John Shelton Reed has noted the positive value of localism in the sense of "an appreciation of the qualities of one place as opposed to others," but he also noted the darker side, its rootedness in "limited experience and narrow horizons." [10] There is an obvious sense of well-being among North Carolina natives, who like southerners elsewhere have a strong sense of place, a sense of community. And in terms of climate, attractive scenery, and perhaps a somewhat lower cost of living than the nation as a whole, the state has some appealing qualities. But by objective standards, there is ample room for improvement.

Key argued that "ruling groups have so inveterate a habit of being wrong that the health of a democratic order demands that they be challenged and constantly compelled to prove their case." [11] And Black concluded: "The likelihood of such challenges occurring with regularity are dim indeed in a political system in which the natives believe that they are living in an ideal state. Yet without such challenges it will be difficult, if not impossible, for the state to alter substantially its relatively weak position on many 'objective' rankings of the states." [12]

Significantly, the CSEP findings for North Carolina disclosed no differences between blacks and whites. Black natives viewed the state as favorably as did the whites, but migrant blacks tended to be rather critical. And the more than 379,000 blacks who migrated out of North Carolina in the 1950s and 1960s apparently found some qualities lacking.

Although North Carolina has one of the most modern and impressive legislative buildings in America, those adjectives seldom are applied to the legislature itself, which in 1971 was ranked 47th by the Citizens Conference on State Legislatures. The *News and Observer* in 1974 commented:

> The State Legislative Building stands as one of the most outwardly handsome temples built to democracy in America. Its glistening marble, lush

10. John Shelton Reed, *The Enduring South* (Lexington, Mass., D. C. Heath, 1974), p. 35.

11. Key, *Southern Politics*, p. 310.

12. Merle Black, "Is North Carolina Really the 'Best' American State?" in Beyle and Black, eds., *Politics and Policy in North Carolina*, pp. 33–34.

carpets, resplendent brass and tinkling fountains could grace a Taj Mahal. But the marble is but a veneer glued to cinder block. And the proceedings echoing through the temple's chambers these past three months have been as democratic as the Cadillacs clustered in its basement.[13]

William L. Bondurant, a foundation executive who served 18 months as Governor James E. Holshouser's director of administration, said the legislature is where "provincial and partisan" political attitudes still dominate. But Bondurant added, "I had read reports about that, and the reports were not exaggerated. But what went unreported were the efforts of the people who were doing the right thing. There is a hard core of solid, good people in the legislature." [14] One veteran state House reporter said, "These guys are basically honest. There are conflicts of interest rather than corruption. For example, the Senate Banking Committee a few years ago had a majority of members who were board members of banks."

Until 1975, "good government," a term which in the South has come to mean government sympathetic to business interests, had become a byword in North Carolina, where it had come also to mean government free of corruption and scandal. However, the state's reputation for corruption-free government diminished a bit with the disclosure by a former Southern Bell executive of an illegal corporate political slush fund that had donated thousands of dollars to all the serious candidates for governor in 1972, including Holshouser, as well as to Lieutenant Governor James B. Hunt, Jr. The governor appoints members of the State Utilities Commission, the regulatory body for utilities; the lieutenant governor appoints Senate committees and their chairmen.

Investigation by the *Charlotte Observer*, which broke the story, subsequently disclosed a cozy relationship between Southern Bell and key legislators. For example, Southern Bell's lobbyist escorted several legislators on a deep-sea fishing trip in 1970 that cost $1,379 and was included as part of the company's business costs when it sought a $23.1 million rate increase that year. Former state Senator Gordon Allen, who made the trip when he was a member of the Senate Public Utilities Committee, said, "I see nothing sinister or evil in it."

The Southern Bell disclosure and subsequent stories that revealed how the major banks put together pools of campaign funds aroused a degree of nervousness in political circles in the state, touched off a major investigation into political activity by the state's utilities, and created an atmosphere from which a reform movement could emerge. But some politicians wondered why there was a furor; they considered it common knowledge that corporate interests dominated campaign financing in the state.

13. *Raleigh News and Observer*, April 14, 1974.
14. Quoted in *Raleigh News and Observer*, June 30, 1974.

Key had already written of governmental dominance for half a century by "an economic oligarchy . . . [whose] control has been achieved through the elevation to office of persons fundamentally in harmony with its viewpoints." [15] The state's banking laws are such that of the nation's 30 largest banks, the only two located in the Southeast, Wachovia and North Carolina National, are both in North Carolina. And another North Carolina bank, First Union, is among the next three largest in the Southeast.[16]

The local advisory boards of the bank branches reflect the local power structure. The giant tobacco companies, the textile and furniture manufacturers that dominate the state's low-wage industrial base, the insurance industry, and the electric power companies tend to be as satisfied as the bankers with state government.

DEMOCRATS

If the progressive spirit in North Carolina has become complacent in recent years, the heritage of the state reflects a deep-rooted respect for civil liberties. The state's colonial population included a heavy proportion of independent-minded and Calvinistic Scotch and Scotch-Irish immigrants, and North Carolina refused to ratify the U.S. Constitution until it included a Bill of Rights. Free Negroes had the right to vote under the state's first constitution in 1776. Although that right was taken away 60 years later by a 65–62 vote at the 1835 constitutional convention, free Negroes had been given citizenship status in 1776. This fact was overlooked by the U.S. Supreme Court in the *Dred Scott* case when it declared that free Negroes had not been citizens of any state when the U.S. Constitution was adopted.[17]

In 1860, North Carolina seceded only after Virginia's withdrawal from the Union had isolated the state, and only after the firing on Fort Sumter. North Carolina's slave population and number of plantations were fewer than those of any other southern state except Tennessee. It was a rural state, with no city of more than 10,000 population. In the mountains, many men remained Unionists, and their descendents, including Governor Holshouser, became hereditary Republicans.

15. Key, *Southern Politics*, p. 211.

16. *World Almanac, 1976* (N.Y., Cleveland: Newspaper Enterprise Assoc.), 1975. (Source: *The American Banker*).

17. North Carolina Advisory Committee to the U.S. Commission on Civil Rights, *Equal Protection of the Laws in North Carolina* (Washington, D.C.: U.S. Government Printing Office, 1962), p. 5.

The state's attitude toward civil liberties was manifested by Sam Ervin, whose U.S. Senate career began with a leading role in the inquiry that led to the downfall of Senator Joseph McCarthy and ended with his direction of the Watergate Committee and the downfall of Richard Nixon. Although much of Ervin's energy was spent in opposing civil rights legislation, his battles against attempts to encroach upon the Bill of Rights earned him a reputation as a civil libertarian.

When Ervin left the Senate at the beginning of 1975, he sent a newsletter to the people of North Carolina, telling them that the framers of the Constitution "knew that false opinions cannot possibly be dangerous to a country if truth is left free to combat error." And while he encouraged his constituents to "cling to the ancient landmarks of truth," he also told them to "be forever ready to test the soundness of new ideas."

It was after a Republican-Populist coalition that had the support of voting Negroes elected a governor in 1896 that North Carolina in 1900 adopted a literacy requirement for voting which resulted in disfranchisement of the majority of the Negro voters. (A grandfather clause protected most of the illiterate whites.) As in the rest of the South, the success of the various efforts to disfranchise blacks left the state firmly in control of the Democrats and resulted in one-party domination. But Governor Charles B. Aycock, who supported the literacy requirement, also fought for the general principle of public education and insisted that it must include the education of Negroes.

Between 1900 and 1968, the state voted Democratic in every presidential election except 1928. That year, U.S. Senator Furnifold Simmons, who since 1900 had dominated the Democratic organization in the state, endorsed Herbert Hoover against Al Smith and led a revolt against the national ticket. Two years later, the Democrats treated Simmons as an apostate and turned him out after five terms in the Senate. Only six of the 49 Republicans elected to the legislature in 1928 managed to survive the 1930 election. After the defeat of Senator Simmons, control of the Democratic Party shifted to the "Shelby dynasty." O. Max Gardner, a former maverick, was elected governor with Simmons's support in 1928; along with anti–New Deal Senator Josiah Bailey, Gardner dominated the state Democratic organization until after World War II.

Although the office of governor in North Carolina is weak institutionally—he cannot succeed himself, and North Carolina is the only state without a gubernatorial veto—the traditional strength of the Democratic Party, more united and cohesive than in most southern states, gave him status as the party leader. A succession of politically skillful governors exerted considerable influence with the legislature.

In 1948, Secretary of Agriculture Kerr Scott pulled an upset victory and launched a new era in North Carolina politics. Scott got the support of the "branch head boys," the rural people of North Carolina who were isolated by dirt roads and a lack of telephone and electric service. He is remembered as the governor "who got the state out of the mud." When Scott died in 1957, there were rural shopkeepers who closed their country stores upon hearing the news and placed wreathes on the door.

His son Robert Scott later became governor, and his brother Ralph Scott remains a power in the state Senate. Kerr Scott was one of those inner-directed men who possess an innate capacity for political leadership; he touched people and treated politics as a way to serve them. It was typical of his style that his appointment to the U.S. Senate of University of North Carolina President Frank Graham, for years one of the outstanding educators and voices of humanistic concern in the South, was announced almost casually at a dinner in Chapel Hill.

Ralph Scott recalled once asking his brother why he wanted to run for governor. " 'You're a layman,' I said. 'I can see where a lawyer would run; it gives him connections of one kind or another. But you can't get nothing out of it.' "

And he recalls his brother responding, " 'I want to go to Raleigh to represent those people that don't have any lobbyists down there. That's my main reason for wanting to go.' " [18]

In his battles to force utility monopolies to provide electric and telephone service to rural people, Scott called on I. Beverly Lake, a brilliant lawyer who later became a symbol of racist politics and who now sits on the state Supreme Court.

Scott's 1954 Senate campaign was managed by Terry Sanford, a leader of the Young Democrats—an organization then composed of bright and ambitious young men, many of them World War II veterans, who wanted to get North Carolina moving. Another man who cut his political teeth in the Scott campaign was Robert Morgan, who in 1960 managed Lake's campaign against Sanford and in 1974 resigned as attorney general to run successfully for the U.S. Senate seat vacated by the retirement of Sam Ervin.

North Carolina's last progressive era came in the administrations of Luther Hodges, Sr. and Sanford. Although moderate in comparison with those of other southern states, the pupil placement laws sponsored by the Hodges administration in the face of school desegregation basically amounted to a state scheme aimed at delay and evasion, providing for school closings and tuition grants to private schools. Hodges later defended the measures as "safety valve" legislation. But on the whole, in his seven years as governor—he stepped up from lieutenant governor in early 1953 upon the incumbent governor's death—the former business executive and Marshall Plan administrator surrounded himself with a

18. Interview with Ralph Scott, December 20, 1973.

capable, creative staff and focused attention on industrial diversification.

One proposal led to the creation of Research Triangle Park, a 5,000-acre project that provides corporate and government research units with access to nearby Duke University in Durham, North Carolina State University in Raleigh, and the University of North Carolina in Chapel Hill. By early 1975 there were 10,000 employees in Research Triangle Park, an annual payroll in excess of $120 million, and capital investment in buildings and equipment of more than $300 million. The Research Triangle Institute was created jointly by the three universities as a non-profit research facility for both government and business, and the three universities also participate in the operation of one of the largest computer centers in the world.

About half the total employment comes from IBM, one of a number of corporate research entities. The Environmental Protection Agency's major research unit, which was landed by North Carolina because of Sanford's influence with the Kennedy White House,[19] also is located at Research Triangle Park.

As secretary of commerce under President Kennedy, Hodges told the nation: "The forces that bar minorities from employment, decent housing, adequate educational facilities, and social benefits make a shocking contribution to slums and crime and disease. The real economic vigor our economy needs today is not possible as long as one segment of the population has these artificial limits on its freedom and earning power."[20]

Sanford was the last Democratic nominee for governor to campaign for the national presidential ticket when he actively supported the Kennedy-Johnson candidacy, which won in North Carolina. Sanford later thought he had made a mistake in not concentrating exclusively on his own race in a two-party contest.[21] Sanford paid lip service to segregation in his campaign for governor, but he emphasized that the state needed massive education and not massive resistance. He won the Democratic primary runoff with 56 percent of the vote against Lake, whose prosegregation campaign included sharp criticism of the Supreme Court and the NAACP. In November, Sanford received only 54 percent of the vote against Robert Gavin, a moderate who waged a progressive campaign calling for a $1-an-hour minimum wage, bond issues for highway construction, and civil service for all state employees, and who repeatedly mentioned North Carolina's low national economic and educational ranking.

19. Interview with Henry Hall Wilson, congressional liaison for the White House in the Kennedy administration (and formerly campaign office manager for Sanford), December 19, 1973.

20. North Carolina Advisory Committee, *Equal Protection*, p. 153.

21. Interview with Terry Sanford, December 3, 1973.

Sanford provided leadership that reflected the progressive spirit reported by Key. The Sanford administration made a frontal attack on long-neglected needs in education. It created a state system of community colleges and technical institutes that in the mid-1970s enrolled more than 50,000 students. Sanford also established the North Carolina Fund (financed primarily by the Ford Foundation), which sponsored experimental antipoverty programs that helped stimulate and set an example for national antipoverty legislation. He created a North Carolina School of the Arts and a Learning Institute to develop innovative educational programs. Industrial diversification received continued emphasis.

He also proved to be one of the most liberal governors in the South in dealing with the racial issue. Floyd McKissick, the first black ever to attend the University of North Carolina Law School and national head of the Congress of Racial Equality (CORE) when that organization was viewed as one of the more militant civil rights groups, recalls that when Sanford was governor, "We used to meet with him, have breakfast with him at the mansion. He called me in and said, 'Now look, I'm not opposed to the demonstrations. I just don't want violence. You demonstrate all you want; just recognize your limits.' I said, 'Well, we are going to demonstrate.' He said, 'Well, I'm going to set up a Good Neighbor Council in this state.'" [22]

Sanford's liberal position on race cost him support among whites, and opponents called him "Food Tax Terry" after his imposition of a regressive 3 percent sales tax on food to pay for educational programs. The food tax issue was raised against him in the 1972 presidential primary, although some observers felt it was raised by those who really opposed Sanford's racial policies but did not want to attack him directly on that issue.[23]

Early in 1975, when Sanford was president of Duke University and planning another presidential bid, he proposed that the sales tax on food be eliminated in North Carolina. Sanford said the food tax in 1961 "was absolutely essential" to fund the technical institutes, community colleges, and other educational programs, but critics of the tax in 1961 pointed out that there was no state tax at that time on tobacco and that an effort should have been made to seek other revenue sources. A former aide said a tax increase in 1961 perhaps could have been avoided if the state treasurer had not badly underestimated revenue forecasts.[24]

Like Hodges, Sanford developed a first-rate staff with vision—a characteristic which those close to the scene in North Carolina contend has since vanished from the governor's office. Sanford developed relevant

22. Interview with Floyd McKissick, December 6, 1973.
23. Interview with Ralph Scott, December 20, 1973.
24. Confidential interview with the authors.

issues and innovative programs, and he is perhaps the last North Carolina governor to make an active effort to educate the public politically. But he went out of office relatively unpopular, and later he said the one thing that with hindsight he would have done differently would have been to make a greater effort to explain to the public what he was doing and why it was important—just doing good things wasn't enough.[25]

Although Sanford developed a progressive coalition of young men, many of whom have remained politically active, no permanent organization was created that could win elections. In 1964, when U.S. District Judge L. Richardson Preyer resigned to run for governor as the candidate of the progressive wing, state Judge Dan Moore ran as a moderate-conservative, and Lake ran again as a conservative segregationist. The progressives hoped for a Preyer-Lake runoff in which Preyer would win enough of Moore's supporters for a majority. As expected, Preyer led in the first primary with 281,430 votes, but Moore was second with 257,872, to 217,172 for Lake. The Lake supporters in the runoff moved solidly to Moore. Robert Scott was elected lieutenant governor in his first race for political office.

Moore defeated Gavin by a larger margin than Sanford did, with 57 percent, but in 1968, Scott received less than 53 percent of the vote against conservative Republican Representative Jim Gardner.

The Moore and Scott administrations were less dynamic than the ones preceding them. Moore appointed Lake to the Supreme Court, but also quietly made significant increases in the number of blacks appointed to positions in state government. Scott broke through the resistance of the tobacco industry in North Carolina and succeeded in imposing the state's first cigarette tax. Perhaps his most significant achievement was the reorganization of higher education into a unified university system under one board of governors. He also pushed successfully for a $1.60 state minimum wage.

But Scott became the target of political attack from within his own party, and the 1972 campaign left the North Carolina Democrats temporarily leaderless. Hargrove (Skipper) Bowles had pulled an upset over Lieutenant Governor Pat Taylor in the Democratic primary, utilizing modern media techniques, something new to North Carolina. But after the primary, Bowles made remarks antagonistic to supporters of both Taylor and Governor Scott, and many Democrats blame the Bowles defeat by Holshouser in November on his failure to exercise party leadership after the primary. They attribute the low turnout in November in part to the county organizations' disinclination to work hard for Bowles. The old county political machines in North Carolina, as elsewhere, are casualties to the television era, but influence remains marginally significant, although far from dominant. Despite heavily contested battles

25. Interview with Terry Sanford, December 3, 1973.

for governor and the U.S. Senate, North Carolina was one of only two southern states that showed a numerical decline in voter turnout from 1968.

Since 1948, the more progressive element within the old bifactional Democratic Party has been dominant. Kerr Scott was the first of the insurgents to defeat the established conservative order. Senator B. Everett Jordan, who retired in 1972, was a Kerr Scott man as party chairman but later jumped into the Old Guard faction that descended from the "Shelby dynasty." Hodges, who succeeded to the governor's office, was somewhat independent of and acceptable to both groups. Sanford came out of the Scott campaigns.

The last of the Old Guard to win was Governor Moore in 1964. In 1968, the last vestiges of the Democratic Old Guard disappeared when Melville Broughton, Jr., son of a former governor, lost to Robert Scott in the Democratic primary and switched to the Republican Party, into which he disappeared from view. In 1972 both Taylor and Bowles came out of the Sanford wing, with Bowles an insurgent against the local organization veterans, who in the main supported the lieutenant governor.

New leadership emerged in 1974 from Robert Morgan and Lieutenant Governor Hunt, who began to play a more aggressive role. Morgan proved that he could unify the Democrats in 1974, a year in which Watergate and the recession made the Republican Party far less attractive. Significantly, Morgan appealed for support as a Democrat, and his billboards carried the party label. The billboards of Republican candidate William Stevens carried no party label.

Ferrel Guillory analyzed the campaign on the eve of the election:

> Morgan's obvious attempts were to bind together a Democratic coalition, including both blacks and liberals and Eastern conservatives. He has done so, it seems, by stressing the economic issues and by even having his campaign take on something of a populist tone. His criticism of the Ford administration's economic package has gotten most of the press attention lately, but Morgan's speeches also point to corporations paying a smaller percentage of income taxes than middle income families, too many wealthy individuals being allowed to get away with no taxes, and to his own modest six-room house in Harnett County, if it were on the housing market, being out of the reach of most potential home-buyers because of economic conditions.[26]

After his election in 1968, Morgan was one of the first state attorneys general in the South to take an activist role in consumer protection. He hired black lawyers for his staff and cultivated black political leaders. In his 1974 campaign he made a clear break with I. Beverly Lake. Morgan told an NAACP meeting in Charlotte that he managed Lake's 1960 campaign because Lake had been his professor in law school at

26. *Raleigh News and Observer,* November 3, 1974.

Wake Forest and had helped Morgan in his first political contest for Harnett County court clerk. "I think my entire public career before then [the 1960 campaign] and since then has been one of fairness to all people," Morgan said.

Lake then sent a letter withdrawing support from Morgan. Lake said he felt Morgan was apologizing for his role in the 1960 campaign when in fact, Lake said, Morgan had urged him to run and was in agreement with Lake's presentation of the race issue. In response, Morgan called it "immaterial" whether he agreed with Lake in 1960 and said, "We've all grown as the traditions and times changed." [27]

After the 1960 Lake campaign, Morgan had campaigned on behalf of Terry Sanford. "He introduced me, spoke for me, went to rallies I couldn't go to," Sanford recalled. "He carried the Lake forces back around to me, or I would have lost." [28]

Conservatives in the east accepted Morgan's position in 1974. John J. Burney of Wilmington, a former segregationist state senator, said they understood the need to appeal for a broader base, especially since the racial tensions of the 1960s had diminished. "He should appear before any group," Burney said. "The people in the east are not narrow-minded. They know you have to go before any group."

The pattern of the Wallace vote in 1968 and 1972 was similar to that of Lake in 1960 and 1964, and Republican Jesse Helms in his 1972 U.S. Senate campaign successfully put together a combination of Wallace-Lake voting patterns in the east and traditional Republican support from the Piedmont and the west. But the east returned to its solidly Democratic voting pattern in supporting Morgan in 1974.

Morgan, a man who enjoys the mechanics of politics, may play a major role in state Democratic politics in the future.

REPUBLICANS

It was from the traditional and hereditary mountain Republicans that the modern North Carolina GOP developed. Unlike the Deep South, where the Republicans won at the presidential level in what basically was a revolt against the Democratic Party, the Republicans built up from the local level in North Carolina, expanding into urban areas in the Piedmont, where younger voters were looking for a change from entrenched courthouse Democrats, and also attracting economic conservatives. Although they picked up adherents because of the race issue, this was much less a factor in North Carolina than in the Deep South.

27. *Raleigh News and Observer,* October 17, 1974.
28. Interview with Terry Sanford, December 3, 1973.

Since the 1940s, urban voting in North Carolina, as elsewhere in the South, has come more and more to reflect the same economic divisions as in cities elsewhere in the country. Republican support tends to grow as one goes up the economic scale.

The initial Republican breakthrough came in 1952, when Charles R. Jonas overcame Democratic gerrymandering efforts to win election to Congress from a district dominated by Charlotte. A hardworking, constituent-oriented fiscal conservative, Jonas subsequently proved unbeatable. He served 20 years until he retired in 1972 and was succeeded by another Republican, Jim Martin, a college chemistry professor.

Ten years after Jonas was elected, he was joined in Congress by James Broyhill, from the neighboring district in the Appalachian foothills. Jonas and Broyhill happen to be the sons of the two men who for 45 years represented North Carolina on the Republican National Committee. Broyhill ran for Congress when a candidate search committee on which he served could not find anyone else to run. A number of local Republicans already had been elected in counties in his district. He recalls that it was Republican sheriffs who appointed the first black deputies.

Broyhill believes the key to Republican development is "to show the people that we can be effective in running programs and administering programs and advocating solutions to problems . . . at the state level. And I think that we have to show that we're appealing to all people, not just whites, but blacks and whites. . . . Unfortunately, over the years, we have had too many candidates in some places that get 100 percent of the [black] vote against them." [29]

Broyhill is linked closely in philosophy with James Holshouser, who served six years as party chairman and as state House minority leader before his election to the governorship in 1972. As governor, Holshouser projected a moderate image by appointing blacks to several highly visible positions in his administration, and he worked closely with the state's bipartisan Women's Political Caucus in appointing women to positions in government and on boards and commissions. He also gave support to such black-oriented enterprises as Soul City, the new town project being coordinated by Floyd McKissick.

But there was little initiative in dealing with basic problems of low income and poverty, and Holshouser grew defensive after a conference on hunger in Chapel Hill pointed out that North Carolina had one of the poorest records of any state in dealing with that problem, and that more than a half million people in the state who were eligible for food stamps were not receiving them. At a press conference not long afterward, Holshouser said he thought local officials should handle the problem, and he declared, "From my own standpoint, I like to think that if

29. Interview with James Broyhill, January 30, 1974.

the statistics don't prove anything else, it is that a significant number of North Carolinians still have enough pride that they wouldn't be involved [in the food stamp program]." [30] Later, he endorsed expansion of the food stamp program, reasoning that it would produce more revenue for the state through the state sales tax on food.

Thus, although Holshouser appealed to the race consciousness of blacks, he didn't overcome the consciousness of the mass of blacks of being part of the lower economic class.

Once a minority party comes to power, it can build strength either by focusing its energies on the administration of government and the development of programs that touch people's lives, which involves the risk of opposition to change, or it can concentrate its energy and time building party organization. In its first two years, the Holshouser administration concentrated on the latter. This included a divisive fight over the party chairmanship in which eastern conservative Frank Rouse was deposed.

Rouse's fight wasn't so much with Holshouser as with his top aide and controversial political operative, Gene Anderson. Raleigh editor Claude Sitton, a former national editor of the New York Times, once referred to Anderson as "the Svengali in the governor's office" whose critics "believe with some reason that he is retained to feed non-issues to the Holshouser administration's friends and to destabilize any non-issues launched by its enemies." [31] And Democratic state Representative Claude DeBruhl referred to Anderson as the "staff Rasputin" in the governor's office.[32] Rouse describes Anderson in language that is even less kind. But a former key aide to Holshouser defended Anderson as "absolutely indispensable" because someone had to play the role of hatchet man in confronting an entrenched Democratic state bureaucracy.[33]

Although eastern North Carolina includes the heaviest concentration of blacks, it lacked the plantation characteristics of Black Belt regions of other southern states. There was a populist strain, and the east strongly supported the economic liberalism of the New Deal. In the 1948 Dixiecrat movement, Strom Thurmond's economic conservatism and anti–civil rights appeal generally drew its strongest support across the South from counties with high percentages of black population. But not in North Carolina, where his greatest strength came from the more urbanized Piedmont and from counties along the South Carolina border. Likewise, in 1964, eastern North Carolina gave less support to Barry Goldwater than did other regions in the urban South with large, heavily rural black populations.

30. James E. Holshouser, press conference, July 23, 1974.
31. Raleigh News and Observer, November 3, 1974.
32. Ibid., November 10, 1974.
33. Confidential interview with the authors.

Rouse, a contractor in Kinston and earthy son of a tobacco farmer, lost the GOP party chairmanship in 1973 to Holshouser's handpicked candidate. He says that "in the east, we're redneck people. Now to people in Mecklenburg County [Charlotte], 'redneck' means a guy is stupid. To me, 'redneck' means country, it means that he's rural, that he's extremely honest, that he's plainspoken and ultraconservative in that he's highly moral and an inherent Southern Baptist, and he's independent-minded." [34] Thus, the popularity of Helms in the east is not altogether so much what he says, but the honest and plainspoken way he says it.

Rouse believes that Goldwater failed to win the east because of the Democratic legacy since the Civil War and because voters in North Carolina register by party. "There was an obligation [to vote Democratic]. It was a thing of honor, something they take seriously." [35] Others recall that Goldwater came to Raleigh in 1964 and said he did not favor price supports on tobacco, more of which is grown in eastern North Carolina than anywhere else in the United States. It was consistent with his telling the old folks in Florida he did not like Social Security or his promise in Tennessee to sell the Tennessee Valley Authority.

Alexander Heard concluded that in 1948, "the pull of party loyalty—in these counties of traditionally greatest party loyalty—seemed to take precedence over fears stimulated by civil rights disturbance." [36] But by 1968, the "civil rights disturbance" was more pronounced, and there was open lack of support for the Democratic presidential candidate among state party leaders. Thus, eastern North Carolina became a Wallace stronghold, reacting to the rhetoric that combined racial conservatism and economic liberalism.

After the 1972 election, North Carolina appeared to be a genuine two-party state. The GOP candidate for governor since 1960 had averaged more than 47 percent of the vote, and the Republicans appeared to have established a competitive position. Their numbers in the legislature had increased steadily to 50 in 1972—35 in the 120-member House and 15 in the 50-member Senate. They held four of the state's 11 seats in the House. And they also elected a U.S. Senator, Jesse Helms, an ultraconservative who accused Richard Nixon of "appeasing Red China" after Nixon's presidential trip there. The conservatism of Helms represents a broad-based ideological commitment. He explained: "This government cannot survive if it continues this fiscal irresponsibility that has been practiced for a generation now. We have got to balance the budget. We have got to reduce government spending. We have got to remove the federal government from the lives of the people. The federal gov-

34. Interview with Frank Rouse, December 17, 1973.
35. Ibid.
36. Alexander Heard, *A Two Party South?* (Chapel Hill: University of North Carolina Press, 1952), p. 272.

ernment was never envisioned to be a provider, a welfare organization. . . . The federal government ought to be against price controls because they won't work, and the free market system is the only thing that is going to work. Minimum wages—this is a purely political device. Anybody who is honest with himself knows that every time you raise the minimum wage, either on the state or federal level, you do nothing but lop off thousands upon thousands of jobs and put these people out of work." [37]

In 1974, however, Republican candidates received less than 40 percent of the vote in the statewide races for U.S. senator and attorney general. Two incumbent U.S. representatives suffered upset losses, and Republicans lost 40 seats in the legislature, including 14 of their 15 seats in the Senate. These losses came after two years in which Governor Holshouser had focused his attention on party building and after he had actively campaigned for the party candidates.

Although the effects of Watergate and the recession hurt the Republicans here as elsewhere, the magnitude of the defeat was greater than in any other state. However one interprets the results, they certainly were no endorsement of the Republican administration in Raleigh.

A clear split developed in the Republican Party in 1974 between factions identified as the Holshouser-Broyhill wing and the conservative Helms wing. One factor in the split was the support given by Holshouser to state Representative William C. Stevens, a brother-in-law of Congressman Broyhill, for the Senate nomination, after Helms had been led to believe that Holshouser would accept state Senator Hamilton C. Horton for the nomination. Horton withdrew and claimed he had been "sandbagged" by Holshouser and Gene Anderson. Although Holshouser subsequently appointed Horton as chairman of the state Milk Commission in a show of harmony, Helms was clearly displeased. In 1974, he gave only token support in the east to Republican candidates, who fared poorly there.

Holshouser came into office when the state had a $265 million surplus and thus was able to fulfill his campaign promises to provide additional funds for public education, mental health, and state employees' compensation. He expanded the state kindergarten program but rejected a $190 million tax relief proposal. As governor, he reflected his lack of executive experience by a tendency to react to the proposals of others and to avoid exercising leadership. He said little or nothing on such controversial issues as liquor-by-the-drink, the death penalty, and no-fault insurance. As a Republican governor unable to succeed himself, with no veto and a Democratic-dominated legislature, Holshouser preferred to avoid conflict except on partisan issues. He offered little in the way of new direction for tackling basic problems in the state.

37. Interview with Jesse Helms, March 8, 1974.

A prime example was his administration's response to the state's economic dependence on low-wage industry. More than 60 percent of the manufacturing work force remains in textile, apparel, and furniture manufacturing. After state AFL–CIO President Wilbur Hobby in the fall of 1974 blew the whistle on the Raleigh Chamber of Commerce's active discouragement of a Xerox Corporation effort to locate a unionized plant near Raleigh, the *News and Observer* pointed out that the situation was another example of the way "low-wage industries and their allies who dominate the economy" oppose growth that threatens to bring labor unions or competition in the labor market. The Xerox plant would have paid $5 an hour, well above the $3.74 hourly rate then prevailing in the Raleigh area and more than double the $2.46 state average hourly rate. The Raleigh Chamber of Commerce simultaneously was promoting a Holshouser-backed referendum to provide state-backed revenue bond financing for industrial development, on the grounds that "North Carolina is presently unable to compete with neighboring states for blue-chip, high-wage industry."

The irony did not escape the *News and Observer*, which gave other examples and commented, "This pattern of local conniving to screen out desirable industry drew the attention of officials in the administration of Governor Bob Scott. They called it a major barrier to improving North Carolina's industrial mix. Their campaign to end the practice never got off the ground. The 'no-growth-if-it-hurts-us' forces saw to that." The editorial added that Holshouser had commissioned a Research Triangle study on the subject, which recommended that if the state was serious about improving the economy, it must intensify efforts to attract high-paying technical industries and discourage further textile industry growth. However, Holshouser's secretary of natural and economic resources indicated that action should be left to local government. The *News and Observer* concluded: "Nothing here indicates that the Holshouser administration is ready to fight the tiger." [38]

ORGANIZED LABOR

Although North Carolina has lagged behind all the other southern states in union activity, a fact not unrelated to its next-to-bottom standing in average manufacturing wages, state AFL–CIO President Wilbur Hobby is the only union leader in the South to have run for governor. "I really got involved in it because it didn't seem like we could get anybody to

38. *Raleigh News and Observer*, November 10, 1974.

discuss issues," Hobby explained of his 1972 race.[39] Hobby, who had worked in Henry Howell campaigns in Virginia, adopted Howell's slogan of "Keep the Big Boys Honest" and Howell's issue of taking the sales tax off food—an issue that state Senator McNeill Smith, one of the state's liberal hopes, picked up in the North Carolina legislature.

A onetime worker in a Durham cigarette factory, the heavyset Hobby is something less than the ideal media candidate. But he is no political novice. He spent several years as regional Committee on Political Education (COPE) director in the South before returning to his native North Carolina. Although he received only 7 percent of the vote in the governor's race in the 1972 Democratic primary, Hobby believes his race helped the unions. "I think people know there is a trade union movement in the state now. They know that it can talk about issues, that the big people in the utilities and the banks and the insurance companies run this state, and that it ought to be a people's government. And I think they know now that the unions are the champion of the little man." [40]

Hobby recalls that there was an active and successful coalition of labor, blacks, and liberals in Durham in the late 1940s, "but the race thing killed it." However, he points to Ku Klux Klan leader C. P. Ellis, who grew up with Hobby in Durham. Ellis confronted blacks on school desegregation in the early 1970s, then realized they had many of the same goals as whites and began organizing a biracial union among Duke University employees.

The successful union vote by 3,000 workers of the J. P. Stevens textile firm in Roanoke Rapids in 1974 may represent a breakthrough in North Carolina, but the union lost a later vote that year at another major textile chain when the economy went sour.

Hobby believes that integration of the work force in the textile industry will lead to greater union acceptance because blacks tend to welcome union representation and because white workers are accepting blacks as they come to know them better. "They've kept us apart, and they talked about blacks. And the only ones working there were sweeping the floor. We didn't know nothing about them, but now they're in our unions. We still have a little friction sometimes in the local unions but just the fact that they're meeting together. You can see coalitions forming, where a local union official who may have been a redneck realizes he's going to have to switch and have some black votes if he's going to win again." [41]

Hobby regularly invites Chapel Hill Mayor Howard Lee to speak to the state labor convention and to smaller groups. "I don't know if North Carolina is ready yet to elect a black lieutenant governor," Hobby said

39. Interview with Wilbur Hobby, December 18, 1973.
40. Ibid.
41. Ibid.

of Lee, "but he's extremely popular with our people who have been exposed to him." [42] With eight A. Philip Randolph chapters in the state, the AFL–CIO is actively engaged in political education among blacks and is developing higher levels of political sophistication and skills among black union members.

Politically, union activity tends to be most effective in Winston-Salem, Greensboro, and Durham, and AFL–CIO lobbying helped push through the legislature a $1.80-an-hour minimum wage law in 1973. In Winston-Salem, organized labor has supported a number of Republican candidates, and Holshouser appointed Republican-oriented union leader Cory Vance to the state Industrial Commission, which hears workmen's compensation cases.

But compared with states like Arkansas, Louisiana, Tennessee, and Texas, union membership in North Carolina is low and organized labor remains relatively weak. The legacy of bitter and bloody textile strikes in the 1920s and 1930s and repressive measures (often sanctioned by government) against union organizers in the 1950s have all contributed to labor weakness. And government policy still reflects the unspoken concern of business to discourage union growth.

In 1970, 15 percent of all textile workers in America were in North Carolina, and in 1975 textile hourly wages averaged $1.26, less than the national factory average or $50.40 weekly. But the idea of diversification has not been sold to many local officials.

BLACK POLITICS

V. O. Key quoted a northern Negro reporter who in 1947 visited North Carolina with a critical eye after hearing of the harmony that prevailed. The reporter concluded that North Carolina held promise to be a model in its race relations, "something of a living answer to the riddle of race."

When Howard Lee came to North Carolina to attend graduate school after being active in the civil rights movement in his native Georgia, it was at the end of the Sanford administration. He recalled his impression that the image of North Carolina among blacks elsewhere in the South was that "when you heard the name North Carolina you weren't thinking about the South, so you never took a real close look at it. It wasn't until I came here in 1964 that my attitude about North Carolina, about what was truly inside the boundaries of this state, changed. I came here thinking there was no other state in the South that was as racially

42. Ibid.

progressive as North Carolina. I did not know any difference until I got here . . . I think the relationship that existed here was a paternal relationship between blacks and whites and that those blacks in power aided in that relationship." [43]

Although limited black political participation has always been allowed in North Carolina, most of the activity was centered in the cities, especially Durham with its relatively large black middle class. Greensboro blacks developed a strong and effective organization in Guilford County in the 1960s. And Raleigh elected a black mayor in 1973 and Charlotte a black state senator in 1974.

In the rural east, where the black population is most heavily concentrated, black registration remained below that of the rest of the state. Not only was the region bypassed by the civil rights movement, but it was also a hotbed of Ku Klux Klan activity in the 1960s, and the Klan in North Carolina was larger and more virulent than in any state outside of Alabama and Mississippi during that period.

Compared to the rest of the Black Belt, the church was relatively weak in eastern North Carolina. Many of the ministers lived in easily accessible Durham or Raleigh, cities with long-standing middle-class black communities, and commuted on weekends; a number of ministers had more than one church. The morticians, another source of black leadership in the rural South, tended to operate relatively small establishments and were dependent on whites for financing. The relatively few black lawyers tended to shun politics because of the pressures that would rise against them in the local courts.

The election to the 1975 legislature of the first two black senators in this century brought to six the total number of blacks in both houses—fewer than in such border states as Tennessee and Texas and fewer than in any Deep South state except Mississippi.

The legislators recognize the need to develop a statewide black political organization, and there is movement in that direction. The quality of black legislators in North Carolina is high in terms of ability and leadership potential. Representative H. M. Michaux of Durham ran for attorney general in 1974 and was encouraged by the response he received. The nomination was made by the state Democratic Executive Committee for a special election to fill a vacancy created by the resignation of Robert Morgan to run for the U.S. Senate. It was the unity of the black caucus in the committee that provided the margin of victory on the sixth ballot for Rufus Edmiston, a 33-year-old lawyer who for ten years had served as a key staff aide to Senator Sam Ervin.

When Howard Lee ran for Congress in 1972 against veteran incumbent L. H. Fountain, Lee received 41 percent of the vote, and his three-

43. Interview with Howard Lee, December 13, 1973.

month campaign stimulated 18,000 blacks in the predominantly rural district to register for the first time. But one postelection analysis indicated that less than half of the registered blacks actually voted, and Lee attributed his defeat to the failure of blacks to vote and the lack of experienced black political leadership in the rural areas. In North Carolina as a whole, 72.2 percent of the whites and 54.4 percent of the blacks of voting age were registered at the end of 1974. This 17.8 percent difference compared with only an 0.5 percent difference in South Carolina.

Lee believes racial attitudes are changing rapidly and recalls a white peanut farmer he met during his congressional campaign who invited Lee to stay for dinner with the farmer, his wife, children, and mother-in-law. Lee ran for lieutenant governor in an attempt to "wake the sleeping black vote." He hoped to put together a coalition of working-class whites and blacks by taking strong positions on delivery of health care, tax reform, housing, job quality, and vocational education.[44]

Perhaps no political campaign better reflected changing attitudes on race than the 1973 mayor's race in Raleigh in which black City Councilman Clarence Lightner won support from a coalition of white suburbanites concerned about urban and suburban sprawl. In a city where less than 16 percent of the voters are black, Lightner defeated the director of the Raleigh Merchants Bureau. Lightner won 19–1 in black precincts and captured a majority in white suburban areas to receive 53 percent of the total vote. Although Lightner ran best in white areas heavily populated by recently arrived Research Triangle employees, he received a respectable 37 percent of the vote in East Raleigh, his weakest area.

WOMEN IN POLITICS

One area in which North Carolina does stand out in the South is the role of women in politics, the outgrowth of a strong, bipartisan North Carolina Women's Political Caucus (NCWPC). When the caucus organized in 1972, there were two women in the legislature. The number jumped to nine the next year and to 13 in 1975, more than in any other state legislature in the United States. Many other women won election as county commissioners.

More than a thousand women attended the first NCWPC meeting, which included as co-convenors the League of Women Voters, United

44. Interview with Howard Lee, December 13, 1973.

Church Women, the Federation of Women's Clubs, the National Organization of Women (NOW), the AFL–CIO, and the vice-chairwomen and national committeewomen of both political parties. The NCWPC encouraged women to run for office, staged workshops with professional political consultants, and provided advice and a written checklist on the nuts and bolts of conducting a political campaign. The caucus helped sensitize women to politics and began to break the psychological barriers that inhibit many women from running for public office.

On such women-related issues as restrictive credit laws and adequate day care centers there was agreement without regard to party. Holshouser pledged in his campaign to utilize more women in his administration, and he followed up by meeting with the caucus and utilizing of a talent bank they had compiled in making appointments of women to state boards and commissions.

"If we are more successful," said Martha McKay, organizer and first chairperson of the caucus, "one reason is the caucus from the beginning was in no way a fringe group. It was very clearly people who had been centrally involved in politics."

CONGRESS

Not only has the North Carolina delegation to Congress been one of the most conservative in its voting patterns, but it has also been among the least influential from the South. Since 1952, no North Carolina Democrat has served on any of the three major committees in the House—Rules, Appropriations, and Ways and Means—except for one term on Appropriations by former Representative Nick Galifianakis. Until Sam Ervin received national exposure as a civil libertarian in the Watergate hearings, there was little to distinguish the state's senators. Previously, Ervin had served as a solid member of the conservative bloc and was noted as a prominent strategist in opposition to civil rights legislation.

An exception to the overall conservative voting record is that of Representative L. Richardson Preyer, the defeated candidate for governor in 1964. Since his election to the House in 1968, Preyer has compiled a moderate-to-liberal voting record.

Seventh district Representative Charles G. Rose, elected in 1972 when he was 33, is a former member of the Terry Sanford law firm and in his first term showed signs of leadership among the new southern Democrats in Congress, who tend to vote more with the national party. Three other new Democrats elected in 1972 and 1974 showed similar tendencies.

Federal per capita spending in North Carolina was $815 in 1973, less

than in any other state in the South, an indication that the state's congressmen have not been very effective in funneling federal dollars into
projects at home.

VOTING TRENDS

The Comparative State Elections Project found that the highest percentage of Democratic identifiers in North Carolina, in sharp contrast
to other border South states, were those in the highest income bracket.
Of those with family incomes of $15,000 or more, 70 percent identified
as Democrats, compared with only 40 percent in Texas and 29 percent
in Florida. Also striking was the fact that the lower middle-income
group ($6,000–8,999) showed the highest Republican (25 percent),
highest independent (27 percent), and lowest Democratic (47 percent)
identification.[45] While local tradition is no doubt a factor, those findings
suggest that both workers and management understand well the role
the Democratic Party has played in North Carolina.

A major finding was that Republican Party identification lags behind
Republican voting all across North Carolina. "While a growing proportion of North Carolinians may be voting Republican farther down the
ballot than ever before, many of these voters have not yet made the
psychological break with the Democratic party which would enable
them to think of themselves as Republicans."[46]

In terms of self-perception, 60 percent of the North Carolina voters
in 1968 regarded themselves as Democrats, which matched voter identification for the Deep South rather than the border South. But the 21
percent Republican identification matched that for the border South
and is stronger than for the Deep South.

Urban middle- and upper middle-class voters in North Carolina are
likely to follow their northern counterparts in predominantly Republican
voting patterns, but whether they will identify themselves as Republicans or as independents who tend toward ticket splitting remains to be
seen.

A 1972 postelection survey disclosed that 17.6 percent of the registered Democrats voted straight Republican, while none of the registered
Republicans in the survey voted straight Democratic. The same survey
found the following characteristics more prevalent among ticket splitters:

45. David M. Kovenock, James W. Prothro and Associates, *Explaining the Vote:
Presidential Choices in the Nation and the States* (Chapel Hill, N.C.: Institute for
Research in Social Science), vol. II, pp. 331, 383, 429.

46. Thad Beyle and Peter Harkins, *Explaining the Vote* (Chapel Hill, N.C.:
Institute for Research in Social Science, 1973), vol. II, p. 384.

more formal education, lived in urban areas, were younger (21–39 years), professional, executives, salespersons, white collar and civil service, females and whites.[47] Total registration was 73.3 percent Democratic, 23 percent Republican, and 3.9 percent independent or no party.

Humphrey and Wallace voters in 1968 tended to agree in their views on the need for more jobs and better wages and government help for labor unions. But they differed in their views on racially tinged issues, such as open housing, government help for Negroes, cutting poverty program spending, and giving the police more authority.[48]

In his 1974 campaign for the U.S. Senate, Democrat Robert Morgan urged North Carolina voters to "return to the party of your fathers." The degree to which they responded supports a theory that the 1968 supporters of George Wallace in North Carolina were engaged in a temporary revolt against the dominant party, a revolt against an unpopular candidate and the party's national stance on the racial issue.[49] With another unpopular Democratic presidential candidate in 1972, the Wallace vote shifted solidly to Nixon, and the traditionally Democratic east voted for Helms, a familiar face and voice whose television editorials for years had attacked many of the same targets on which Wallace had focused.

The 36.8 percent straight Republican voting behavior found in the 1972 De Vries study matched almost identically the 37 percent vote received by William Stevens, the Republican candidate for the U.S. Senate in 1974. In the east, Stevens received only 31 percent, compared with 54 percent for Helms and 44 percent for Holshouser in 1972.

The 1974 election results project no clear trends for the state. The steady gradual increase in Republican percentage of the votes for governor from 1948 to 1972 suggest a solid, challenging two-party base despite the 1974 debacle. One study of voting patterns since 1948 shows that Republicans in North Carolina run consistently better in congressional and senatorial races in presidential election years. The analysts conclude that the highly involved electoral "core" which votes in every election tends to be more Democratic, but that the electoral "periphery" requiring the greater stimulation of a presidential election consistently has increased the Republican percentage.[50]

Except for Arkansas, which has two-year terms for governor, North Carolina is the only state in the South that elects its governor in presidential election years, a unique advantage for Republicans in the Tar Heel state. But the 1974 elections left in doubt whether Republicans can

47. De Vries & Associates, "North Carolina Statewide After-Election Survey."
48. Beyle and Harkins, p. 398.
49. Ibid.
50. Richard J. Trilling and Daniel F. Harkins, "The Growth of Party Competition in North Carolina, 1948 to 1974," in Beyle and Black, eds., *Politics and Policy in North Carolina*, p. 86.

regain a competitive position and destroyed Republican hopes for near-term dominance.

As in Virginia and Tennessee, North Carolina Democrats began to understand the necessity for building a stronger political party organization after the election of a Republican governor. The surprise upset of Republican Representative Wilmer (Vinegar Bend) Mizell in 1974 by politically unknown weekly newspaper publisher Steve Neal in part was attributed to the fact that Forsyth County (Winston-Salem) Democrats were better organized than ever before. County Democratic Chairman Wayne Corpening, a Wachovia Bank vice-president and former director of administration under Governor Dan Moore, developed a precinct system in which a telephone number for each precinct was published that would provide a ride, babysitter, etc., for any voter who called. There were a series of meetings for groups of party workers from half a dozen or so precincts at which Morgan or Edmiston and others would appear for a pep talk. Mizell had received 58 and 65 percent of the vote in the two previous elections, and the district had appeared to be safely Republican.

Short-run Republican recovery after the 1974 election disaster will depend on the record of the last half of the Holshouser administration, on whether moderate and conservative factions can unite, and on whether the party can develop quality candidates.

SUMMARY

The last decade has produced no leaders who have advocated a new approach or a new way of looking at problems. In terms of social and economic development, North Carolina—like Alabama under George Wallace—has not kept pace with the rest of the South. In recent North Carolina elections, the issues have been muted and based on racial attitudes rather than on programs that affect the masses. This may help account for the relatively low levels of turnout in recent elections.

Key's description of North Carolina as a "progressive plutocracy" was an apt one in the late 1940s. But when one compares indices of economic development, the level of participation and modernization of the political process, the relative neglect of long-standing social problems, the controlling oligarchy's perpetuation of "no-growth-if-it-hurts-us," two decades of a congressional delegation among the most conservative in the South, and the emergence of race as a significant political issue, what remains is a political plutocracy that lives with a progressive myth.

Chapter

11

SOUTH CAROLINA

The Changing Politics of Color

AT THE 1968 Democratic National Convention in Chicago, South Carolina's delegation sat impatiently after lunch waiting for a visit from Vice-President Hubert Humphrey, who was running more than an hour behind schedule.

In an impromptu move, the Reverend I. DeQuincey Newman rose slowly and suggested that the state's national committeeman, 80-year-old state Senator Edgar A. Brown, say a few words. Brown, for decades a political power in the state, had attended every national convention since 1924, and the suggestion drew hearty applause. For Newman, the veteran NAACP field secretary in South Carolina, this was his first national convention as a delegate since 1956—and it was the Republican convention he had attended that year.

After a few stories, Brown looked over at Newman, could not decide how to address him, and finally blurted out, "I.D., do they call you preacher or reverend?"

Newman replied gently, "Well, senator, in polite company, I couldn't say what. . . ."

Laughter filled the room, and a smiling Edgar Brown nodded his head up and down and declared, "Yes, I've been called some of that, too."

The smuggest smile in the room came from a state official who knew that one afternoon a couple of years earlier, Brown had to be physically restrained in his law office in Barnwell from going after Newman, who was leading a voter registration drive and a street demonstration against registration procedures in Barnwell County.

The ballroom incident between these onetime adversaries illustrates the politics of accommodation in the face of racial change. To understand the sweeping changes in the political role of blacks in the South, there is no better place to look than South Carolina.

Even before the Voting Rights Act of 1965, some white Democratic politicians in South Carolina perceived that a gradual assimilation of blacks into the system would strengthen either their own factional interests or the future interests of the Democratic Party against possible defections to the Republican Party. This meshed with the traditional aim of black political leadership in the state: to seek accommodation and develop change within the "system."

South Carolina remains second only to Mississippi in percentage of black population, with 30.5 percent in the 1970 census. There has been a steady decline since 1900 when the state was 58.4 percent Negro. The percentage was 42.9 in 1940, 38.8 in 1950, and 34.9 in 1960. Twelve of the state's 46 counties contained majority black populations in 1970, compared with 21 in 1950. While heavy outmigration of blacks continued in the 1960s, the migration pattern of whites reversed itself, with a net inmigration.

Between 1950 and 1970, the percentage of urban dwellers increased from 36.7 to 47.6. Each of the state's three sections has developed an urban center: Charleston and two adjoining counties in the coastal plains; a developing urban corridor stretching along I-20 from Florence through Columbia to Augusta, Georgia, in the Midlands; and the I-85 corridor that extends east and west from Greenville in the Piedmont. Only Columbia had a population in excess of 100,000, but the three major cities were centers of Standard Metropolitan Statistical Areas of roughly 250,000.

The heaviest population losses have occurred in counties with majority black populations. The 23 counties that lost population in the 1960s included 14 of the 15 that in 1960 had black majorities.

V. O. Key subtitled his chapter on South Carolina "The Politics of Color." In 1948, he wrote:

> South Carolina's preoccupation with the Negro stifles political conflict. Over offices there is conflict aplenty, but the race question muffles conflict over issues latent in the economy of South Carolina. Mill workers and plantation owners alike want to keep the Negro in his place. In part, issues are deliberately repressed, for, at least in the long run, concern with genuine issues would bring an end to the consensus by which the Negro is kept out of politics. One crowd or another would be tempted to seek his vote. . . .[1]

But the beginning of a new politics already had been ordained. In 1947, U.S. District Judge J. Waities Waring, a converted white supremacist and an eighth generation Charlestonian of impeccable connection, decreed in *Elmore* v. *Rice*, "South Carolina is the only State which now

1. V. O. Key, *Southern Politics in State and Nation* (New York: Vintage, 1949), p. 131.

conducts a primary election only for whites. . . . I cannot see where the skies will fall if South Carolina is put in the same class as these and other states."

In no state did the political role of blacks change so completely, so quickly, or with fewer jagged edges. Their quest has been what pioneer black legislator I. S. Leevy Johnson describes as "a mission to get blacks a bigger piece of the pie." [2] From 1947 onward, the drive by South Carolina blacks for full political participation has represented a major thrust in the politics of the state—intersecting, time and again, with the zigzag political career of Strom Thurmond, who personifies the changing politics of reaction.

From Dixiecrat candidate for president in 1948 to write-in winner for the U.S. Senate in 1954 to Republican conversion in 1964 to kingmaker for Richard Nixon in 1968 to open courtship of an expanded black electorate in 1972, Thurmond has been the dominant political figure during a quarter century of dramatic change. Thurmond personifies the white revolt against traditional loyalty to the national Democratic Party. He also symbolizes the searing individualism and rebellious attitude toward arbitrary authority that is deeply rooted in South Carolina history.

In 1972, a 51-year-old textile worker explained that he would vote for the 69-year-old Thurmond in his Senate reelection campaign because "he stands up for what he believes in, even if it's wrong." [3] Thurmond's 1972 turnabout on race came after the defeat in the 1970 election for governor of his protégé, Congressman Albert Watson, whose campaign was labeled "racist" even by some fellow Republicans. Watson lost to John C. West, one of a series of mildly progressive Democratic governors, who declared in his 1971 inaugural address, "The politics of race and divisiveness have been soundly repudiated in South Carolina."

If Senator Thurmond represents one side of the coin of change, the other is symbolized by Senator Ernest F. (Fritz) Hollings, who was the first of a series of four governors to both shape and reflect a changing Democratic party that tended to become progressive and moderate as it increasingly relied on black support.

Few states have a governor whose office is so weak institutionally, but Hollings began in 1959 to show that persuasion could be used to bend in a progressive direction the power structure centered around the rural barons—traditionalists of considerable ability—who controlled the powerful legislature. An example is the birth of South Carolina's widely acclaimed system of technical education colleges, which played a central role in the state's rapid industrial development.

To get a commitment of state funds for what at the time was a new concept being developed in neighboring North Carolina, Hollings spent

2. Interview with I. S. Leevy Johnson, March 3, 1975.
3. *Charlotte Observer*, October 29, 1972, p. 11D.

one evening over a fifth of bourbon coaxing, cajoling, and pleading his case with Edgar A. Brown, chairman of the Senate Finance Committee and the kingpin in the powerful Senate. The evening ended with an empty bottle, but also with an agreement in one handwritten paragraph that would establish the new law. Perhaps because of the bourbon, the two men forgot to include terms of service for members of the board that would direct the new agency. The initial appointees served permanently for more than a decade until the agency was merged into a new administrative body.

Beginning with the Hollings administration and extending for 16 years through Governors Donald Russell, Robert E. McNair, and John C. West, South Carolina politics has been transformed by new forces that left dead or dying the three dominant characteristics that had prevailed since Reconstruction. These were (1) one-party politics, designed to unify the white man against the Negro; (2) a policy and practice of excluding the Negro from effective political participation; and (3) a reaction to the waste, graft, and mismanagement of Reconstruction that had manifested itself as a reaction against all social legislation. The post-Reconstruction era left a legacy in which it was accepted as an article of faith among South Carolina political leaders that the least expensive government was the best government.

BACKGROUND

South Carolina was the state which mothered secession and whose troops fired, on Fort Sumter to ignite the Civil War. Although the state tends to be regarded as part of the Deep South, it is also one of the original 13 colonies, and more Revolutionary War battles were fought here than in any other state.

The colonial heritage makes it part of the Old South, and it moved into the era of post–World War II modernization sharing both the aristocratic manner and respect for good manners of Virginia and the racial unity of Mississippi. Before the Civil War, cotton had spread to the westernmost counties of the Appalachian foothills. The up-country yeoman farmers, many of them descendents of Scotch-Irish Calvinists who had migrated from Pennsylvania into the valleys of Virginia and then to the Carolinas in search of homesteads, yielded on racial matters to the low-country planters.

They and their lawyer-doctor-merchant class assumed leadership in public affairs as an extension and reflection of their station in life, a role analogous to their lay leadership of the Episcopal Church. To help quell sectional strife, the state capital was moved in 1786 from Charleston to Columbia, a planned city whose site was selected for its central location. Within two decades, the University of South Carolina was established there, in large part because the low-country political leaders wanted to ensure that future leaders from the populous up-country would be educated men and that their education would include instilling a proper appreciation of tidewater values.

Although South Carolina can claim its full share of post-Reconstruction racial demagogues, there also is a legacy of political sophistication from the antebellum period. In addition, the aristocratic tradition provided a racial framework in which paternalism prevailed, and in which the harsh reality of racial discrimination was covered at least by a veneer of good manners. The Bourbons who usually controlled South Carolina tended to despise poor whites as "trash" who were no less lowly than the Negroes. In the framework of aristocratic racism, the Negroes were viewed as children who never grew up.

The Agrarian movement of Pitchfork Ben Tillman in South Carolina in the 1890s lacked the radical economic programs of the Populist movement elsewhere in the South. The battles were more between the coarser rural gentry and the more genteel Bourbon men of commerce.

Unlike the deeper South, where even the poorest white could count his skin color as a badge of superiority, South Carolina valued stability as a higher social value than segregation and rejected extremist rhetoric. Once segregation crumbled, the social transformation followed with little violence.

From Reconstruction to the end of World War II, unity on the racial issue had resulted in unyielding loyalty to the national Democratic Party, based on the unspoken understanding of noninterference with the racial status quo. Thus, in 1929, when North Carolina revolted against the Democratic nomination of a Catholic wet and voted Republican, South Carolina voted 91.4 percent for Al Smith.

This unity was achieved only by smothering differences on national issues. Since the Democratic Party was the white party, the politics of issues did not develop in South Carolina. Key acknowledged that the "repression" of issues at the state level may have been the inevitable result of avoiding disagreement on national issues as much as deliberate policy by those in control.[4]

But forces were at work to develop a competitive party politics from which disagreement on racial matters would be followed by development of other issues.

4. Key, *Southern Politics*, p. 131n.

GROWTH OF TWO-PARTY COMPETITION

When John Gunther published *Inside U.S.A.* in 1948, he wrote of Strom Thurmond as "the liberal governor" of South Carolina, a man who sought industrial development, urged rent controls, and even broke tradition by appointing a black physician to a state advisory board.

Thurmond is a man with an acute political sense of shifts in public sentiment and a disposition for zealotry once he takes a position. The central issue in 1948 was civil rights—specifically, the proposals by President Truman and the Democratic platform to end discrimination in employment and elsewhere. Although such issues as support for state control of tidelands oil and alarm over alleged Communist influences in government were included in the States' Rights Party platform, Thurmond emerged as the segregationist symbol of the 1948 Dixiecrat movement.

Two months before accepting the Dixiecrat nomination, Thurmond told a gathering in Mississippi, "The leadership of the Democratic party may as well realize that the South's electoral votes are no longer in the bag for the Democratic nominee." Although Thurmond remained a nominal Democrat for another 16 years, he consistently maintained that the South's only weapon to gain concessions from the national party on civil rights was the threat of a bolt. When he accepted the Dixiecrat nomination in 1948, Thurmond declared, "There are not enough laws on the books of the nation, nor can there be enough laws, to break down segregation in the South." *

Although he received 72 percent of the vote in South Carolina in leading a psychological break from the national Democratic Party, Thurmond failed two years later to unseat incumbent Senator Olin D. Johnston in the Democratic primary. A onetime textile worker and former governor who 12 years later derailed Hollings in his first Senate race, Johnston tended to support Democratic social programs in Congress. Before his death, Johnston commented in 1964 about the increasing political role of blacks, "Their vote counts just as much as anybody else's."

Thurmond went on to achieve an unprecedented write-in victory in his bid for the U.S. Senate in 1954. What happened was that Senator Burnet Maybank died five days before the deadline for the Democratic Party to certify its nominee. Maybank had been unopposed, and the 46-member state Democratic Committee declared it was too late to hold a primary. Instead, they nominated Democratic National Committeeman Edgar Brown, the leader of the powerful state Senate—an exclusive

---

* Alec P. Lamis, "The Disruption of a Solidly Democratic State: Civil Rights and South Carolina Electoral Change, 1948–1972." *The Journal of Political Science* (Clemson, S.C.: South Carolina Political Science Association), in press.

club in which many of the committeemen also held membership. The action followed the narrow provisions of the law, but the major newspapers in the state viewed the decision with outrage and launched an editorial crusade claiming that the people had been denied the right to elect a new senator. The voters rebelled by writing in Thurmond's name.

James F. Byrnes, the state's most significant political figure in the 20th century—a member of both houses of Congress, Supreme Court justice, secretary of state, White House domestic chief in World War II—returned home as a revered figure upon whom was bestowed the honor of serving as governor after Thurmond. Byrnes had resigned after a year on the Supreme Court at the request of President Franklin D. Roosevelt. Byrnes later indicated a feeling of betrayal at what he perceived to be encouragement from Roosevelt to make what proved to be a humiliatingly unsuccessful attempt to gain the 1944 vice-presidential nomination, which would have meant the presidency when Roosevelt died a year later. Later, Byrnes was dropped from President Truman's cabinet. He returned home a quietly embittered man.

In a parallel to John C. Calhoun's defense of the dying institution of slavery after his national period, Byrnes returned home and became a defender of racial segregation. In his 1951 inaugural address, he urged a 3 percent sales tax "to provide for the races substantial equality in school facilities. We should do it because it is right. For me, that is sufficient reason. If any person wants an additional reason, I say it is wise."

Byrnes shocked Democratic loyalists when he supported Republican Dwight Eisenhower for president in 1952 and invited him to the state capitol for a campaign speech. Later, he supported Thurmond's write-in campaign and the Nixon and Goldwater presidential candidacies, contributing his prestige to the developing Republican Party in the state.*

Although Byrnes disapproved of the Supreme Court's 1954 school desegregation decision, he was perhaps the one man of sufficient stature in the South who might have been able to offer regional leadership toward acceptance rather than defiance. Instead, he joined with the critics of the Court.

Although Democratic presidential candidates carried South Carolina in 1952, 1956, and 1960, it was never with more than fifty-one percent of the vote. In 1964, Goldwater won with a 59 percent landslide victory, Thurmond switched to the Republican Party, and Congressman Watson—unopposed for reelection as a Democrat—openly joined Thurmond in the Goldwater campaign effort.

* Edgar Brown later blamed the defection of Byrnes to Thurmond in the 1954 write-in campaign on the fact that Brown, veteran national committeeman and a longtime personal and political friend of Byrnes, had been assigned the chore at the 1944 Democratic National Convention of informing Byrnes that he would not be the vice-presidential nominee. Brown told friends after his loss to Thurmond that Byrnes had never forgiven him and had mistakenly believed that Brown had participated in the decision to deny Byrnes the vice-presidential nomination.

Heading the Republican campaign effort was their state chairman, J. Drake Edens, Jr., heir to a chain foodstore fortune who possessed considerable drive and organizational ability. Methodically and persistently, he built a strong party organization, something the Democrats had never done. After House Democrats stripped Watson of his two years' seniority, he dramatically resigned and won reelection as a Republican with 70 percent of the vote.

With the development of Republican core strength, the state's Democratic establishment found it expedient to make overtures to blacks, who were coming to embrace the Democratic Party nationally for the same reasons that many whites were leaving it. Republicans had elected their first legislator since Reconstruction in a 1962 special election, and their candidate for the U.S. Senate that year received 43 percent of the vote. In 1966, with Thurmond at the head of the ticket, Republicans made their first major challenge in state politics. They won 17 seats in the 124-member state House of Representatives and six in the state Senate. Thurmond and Watson easily won reelection, and the Republican candidates for governor and lieutenant governor each received more than 41 percent of the vote. Republican Marshall Parker came within 11,000 votes of defeating former Governor Hollings for the U.S. Senate.

An analysis showed a steady decline in the traditional Democratic strength among working-class whites, a growing Republican allegiance among upper-income whites, and Democratic solidarity among blacks, whose solid support apparently provided the victory margin in 1966 for Governor McNair and Lieutenant Governor West. The vote in 99 working-class precincts averaged 58.5 percent for four statewide Democratic candidates in 1966. This was 7.2 percent above their statewide average, but the same precincts had provided a difference of 23 percent for John F. Kennedy in 1960 and Olin Johnston in 1962, and a difference of 18.4 percent for Lyndon Johnson in 1964 against Goldwater.

The 1966 elections set into motion trends that continue in South Carolina politics. They established a challenging position for the Republican Party and a base for two-party politics. The black vote, faced with a Thurmond-Watson segregationist image in the Republican Party, provided a solid, stable bloc of Democratic support. There have been several local elections in which Republican moderates challenged conservative Democrats and received substantial numbers of black votes, but the unyielding ideological conservatism on social issues and a lack of sensitivity to black aspirations has tended to drive blacks into the Democratic Party, which has welcomed them. Finally the 1966 returns reflected a basic economic split among urban white voters, a division that also has persisted.

Although Thurmond helped carry South Carolina for Nixon in 1968 with a plurality of 38 percent of the vote, the Republicans lost 17 of 25 seats in the legislature, a level of strength to which they have not since returned. In a rerun of their 1966 race, Parker lost by more than 150,000 votes to Hollings in a contest for a full six-year Senate term.

The level of party competition has remained rather stable since 1966. Republicans won 38.9 percent of the vote in contested congressional races in 1968, 37.4 percent in 1970, 39.6 percent in 1972, and 41.4 percent in 1974. The 1972 Republican percentage would have been higher, but their one incumbent congressman went unchallenged by the Democrats that year and his district was not included among the contested races.

Competitive races for governor have stimulated voter interest. The 1966 gubernatorial race attracted 439,842 voters, the highest ever to vote in South Carolina in any nonpresidential election. The turnout increased to 482,145 in 1970 and 523,199 in 1974. But when expressed as a percentage of voting-age population, the turnout was only 32.5 percent in 1966, 32.9 percent in 1970, and 32.0 percent in 1974.

The victory of James B. Edwards in 1974 over retired General William C. Westmoreland in the first state Republican primary reflected continued GOP growth. Edwards, who became South Carolina's first Republican governor since Reconstruction, is a well-intentioned oral surgeon who became politically active in 1964 after reading *The Conscience of a Conservative* by Barry Goldwater and who shares the conservative ideology of former California Governor Ronald Reagan. He actively campaigned for Reagan in his quest for the Republican presidential nomination in 1976. Although turnout was only about a tenth of the number that voted in the Democratic primary, the shift from nomination by convention to primary reflected the fact that the party nomination was now considered worth fighting for. Edwards, who was serving as a first-term state senator, was the insurgent candidate, and his victory in part reflected a revolt within the Republican ranks against Thurmond's ten-year domination of the party. Westmoreland, who had never voted and who refused to identify with the Republicans until he announced as a candidate, ran with Thurmond's blessing. The general had returned to South Carolina to work in the administration of Democratic Governor West, a fellow alumnus of the Citadel, the state military college in Charleston. Considerable emphasis at that institution is placed on leadership development, and its graduates also include Hollings, Representative James Mann, and Lieutenant Governor W. Brantley Harvey, Jr., who assumed the role of titular head of the Democratic Party after his election in 1974. As others before him, Harvey found that in communities throughout the state he could call on alumni of the Citadel for help in putting together a statewide political campaign.

If Thurmond was the most visible symbol around whom Republicans built their party, far less visible but perhaps equally important was Roger Milliken, probably the wealthiest man in South Carolina and Republican state finance chairman from 1959 to 1965. He is president of the family-owned Deering-Milliken textile empire, the third-largest textile firm in the world, a man who shuns publicity, possesses exceptional managerial ability, and is devoted to conservative causes. He was one of the leaders in the Goldwater movement, one of seven men who met shortly after the 1960 presidential election to begin plans to secure the 1964 nomination for Goldwater. Milliken played a leading role in the discussions.[5]

Milliken employees for years have played integral roles in the Republican Party structure in South Carolina. His personal lawyer, Robert Chapman, was appointed a U.S. district judge by President Nixon. After Edwards was elected governor, he selected a Deering-Milliken executive as administrative assistant. Democrats in the 1960s referred to Milliken as the "Daddy Warbucks" of the Republican Party in the state and attempted to exploit his antilabor image among blue-collar workers.

Milliken's attitude toward labor unions is reflected by the 1956 decision to close the company plant in Darlington, South Carolina, after a favorable union vote. Although the U.S. Supreme Court upheld a National Labor Relations Board finding that the plant was illegally closed to "chill" union activity, continued litigation almost 20 years later has blocked workers who had lost their jobs from receiving payments awarded by the NLRB. There are no unions in any Deering-Milliken plants.

One top South Carolina Republican official explained that Milliken "always figures prominently in high-level South Carolina Republican strategy because he has got tremendous economic power. If you get assurance from the Milliken interests in the party, you can go a long way politically, as far as funding of a campaign is concerned. . . . If you have a multi-million-dollar business empire and you need to raise money, you just put a bunch of people on telephones calling your accounts payable, and you just say, 'Look here, Charlie, we are trying to raise a little money for so and so, and certainly would appreciate it if you would buy two tickets.' Now that is not wrong and everybody does it, and of course it is a great big thing for us. . . . Thank God, he is a Republican when it comes to raising money." [6]

DEMOCRATS AND PROGRESS

Perhaps in recognition of the state's history in leading the South out of the Union, South Carolina was given a little more time in yielding to the forces of social change. The state fought to the end in the courts, but

5. Stephen Shadegg, *What Happened to Goldwater? The Inside Story of the 1964 Republican Campaign* (New York: Holt, Rinehart and Winston, 1965), pp. 30–38.

6. Interview with Arthur Ravenel, Jr., South Carolina Republican state finance chairman, February 19, 1974.

South Carolina rejected extremism. Once the state was forced to submit to an end of legal segregation, it did so with dignity.

The color line was not broken until January 1963. A week before Harvey Gantt entered Clemson University, Governor Hollings concluded his term of office by telling the legislature, "As we meet, South Carolina is running out of courts. If and when every legal remedy has been exhausted, this General Assembly must make clear South Carolina's choice, a government of laws rather than a government of men. As determined as we are, we of today must realize the lesson of 100 years ago, and move on for the good of South Carolina and our United States. It must be done with law and order."

The message was symbolically reinforced a few days later when incoming Governor Donald Russell staged as the major social event for his inaugural a barbecue on the grounds of the governor's mansion to which "all of the people in South Carolina" were invited. The mansion is located on the edge of a low-income black neighborhood in Columbia. Thousands turned out, ranging from Negro maids clad in housedresses to society matrons in furs. At the same time, at his first inaugural in Alabama, George Wallace was vowing "segregation today, segregation tomorrow, segregation forever."

The previous summer, South Carolina had in state Representative A. W. Red Bethea a gubernatorial candidate voicing the same rhetoric as Wallace, and he received 7 percent of the vote. Russell, a former University of South Carolina president and a man of first-rate intellect who became a federal appeals court judge, had given lip service to segregation, saying the state should select the best legal mind to deal with the problem.

Gantt quietly entered Clemson and later commented, "If you can't appeal to the morals of a South Carolinian, you can appeal to his manners."

The year 1968 marked the beginning of a new ten-year registration period, required by state law. Regular courthouse hours for the first time, provision for deputy registrars, and a provision that allowed a notary public to validate old registration certificates, which could then be exchanged by mail for new ones—all eased the burden of reregistration of blacks. The new law reflected unspoken recognition by the Democratic-controlled legislature of the legislators' growing dependence on the Democratic-oriented black vote. More than 200,000 black voters were reregistered or registered for the first time that year.

At the 1970 state Democratic convention, a black vice-chairman of the party was elected for the first time. About 200 of the approximately 900 delegates and alternates at the convention were black. The only major conflict occurred when blacks and liberal whites forced a change in a "freedom of choice" plank in the party platform. Added was the phrase "as interpreted within the framework of the laws of the land." The Supreme Court already had ruled that freedom-of-choice desegregation plans were, for all practical effect, unacceptable.

A. J. Whittenberg of Greenville, who had brought the original desegregation suit against Greenville schools, called the original plank a "slap in the face" to himself and other blacks. "They fought to be here," he told the convention, "They want to be here. Don't drive them away." After the compromise was accepted with little dissent, Whittenberg drew laughter and applause when he rose again and told the convention, "I can go back home showing my teeth. . . . Instead of working 12 hours a day for the Democratic Party, I'll work 14." [7]

Segregationist white politicians began to modify their positions in the process of campaigning for black votes, and they also began to change their attitudes. For example, in the period of massive resistance, state Senator L. Marion Gressette directed the legal effort to avoid desegregation, including not only court battles but removal from the state constitution of the mandate for a state system of public schools (restored more than a decade later). As chairman of what became known as the Gressette Committee, he symbolized resistance to desegregation. But in 1970 he attended the state Democratic convention and sat with the integrated delegation from Calhoun County. After the state Senate was reapportioned and he no longer represented just tiny Calhoun, Gressette campaigned actively in his heavily black new district. When he became president pro tem of the Senate in 1973, he hosted a cocktail party in the Wade Hampton Hotel across from the statehouse, and more than a score of blacks attended as invited guests. One of them commented, "If someone had asked me ten years ago if this could ever happen, I would have said it would never be possible."

During his years as chairman of the school committee, Gressette's number-one adversary was Matthew Perry, an exceptionally able black civil rights lawyer. In 1974, Perry ran for Congress, and the main speaker on his behalf at one fundraising dinner was Gressette. In unprepared remarks the two men spoke of each other with warmth and respect, and sat down as friends. (In 1976, Perry became the first black federal judge from the Deep South when he was appointed to the U.S. Court of Military Appeals. The appointment resulted from the bold initiative of Senator Thurmond, a move that enhanced his political standing among blacks.)

Gressette's enlarged constituency received material as well as symbolic rewards. After Orangeburg County became part of his senatorial district, Gressette soon became known as the legislative patron of long-neglected South Carolina State College, the only traditionally black state-supported institution of higher learning.

As governor, Robert McNair, a former rural legislator who was elevated from lieutenant governor and served six years in the statehouse,

7. Jack Bass, *Porgy Comes Home* (Columbia, S.C.: R. L. Bryan Co., 1972), pp. 42–43.

displayed impressive growth in office. He won a substantial tax increase that included a raise in both sales and corporate income taxes, and he moved on a broad front to expand educational and social programs, including statewide implementation of the federal food stamp program.

However, his record was marred by the slaying in February 1968 of three black college students at South Carolina State College at Orangeburg by state police gunfire, in what blacks tended to view as a "massacre" and whites as an "incident." After a student demonstration against a segregated bowling alley, McNair called in massive numbers of law enforcement officers, who were armed with shotguns loaded with lethal buckshot; they were authorized to shoot without an order if they felt their lives endangered.

The deadly confrontation at Orangeburg dramatized that the potential for racial violence always had existed in South Carolina, a reminder of the sometimes brutal economic reprisals and fear of physical threats that black South Carolinians had experienced in winning political rights in the 1950s and the early 1960s. I. DeQuincey Newman, who from 1958 to 1970 served as NAACP field secretary and as the state's foremost black political strategist, declared after the slayings at Orangeburg, "The fact that such a thing could happen and did happen is an indication that despite all that might be considered progress in terms of interracial cooperation, beneath the surface South Carolina is just about in the same boat as Alabama and Mississippi." [8]

In a contrasting display of leadership, McNair told a televised audience that South Carolina had "run out of courts, run out of time, and must adjust to new circumstances" in the midst of an emotional controversy early in 1970 when a midyear desegregation order involving extensive busing was implemented for the 58,000-pupil Greenville school system. McNair's leadership stood out in sharp contrast to the actions of governors in such states as Louisiana and Florida, who were espousing defiance of the latest mandate of the U.S. Supreme Court.

In 1968, McNair had vice-presidential ambitions and maneuvered to include six black delegates with a half vote each and an equal number of black alternates, in the first integrated South Carolina delegation to a National Democratic Convention. It was the only Deep South delegation that went unchallenged. At the state convention, blacks already were approaching proportional representation.

A black-oriented United Citizens Party was organized at the end of 1969. Its founders saw it as a vehicle for electing officials in majority black counties and channeling black dissatisfaction with the slowness shown in opening up state employment and in appointing blacks to policymaking boards and commissions. But many of the founders with-

8. Jack Nelson and Jack Bass, *The Orangeburg Massacre* (New York: World, 1970), p. 236.

drew when the UCP ran statewide candidates in 1970. "We had an agreement with people who helped us circulate petitions that we weren't organizing against Democrats on the state level," explained James Clyburn, the first UCP chairman, who later became a member of Governor West's staff. Although the UCP became an outlet for black frustrations and stimulated the Democrats to show greater responsiveness to black problems, the third party was unsuccessful in electing candidates.

Hollings, who had defeated Russell for governor in 1958, beat him again in the 1966 Senate primary. As governor, Russell resigned for appointment to the Senate after the death of Olin Johnston, in effect a political self-appointment that he was unable to successfully defend to the voters.

Hollings followed Thurmond's conservative voting line for two years, even voting against confirmation of Thurgood Marshall as the first black Supreme Court justice. But after his reelection in 1968 to a full Senate term, Hollings moved to the left, often supporting domestic social legislation in opposition to Thurmond. He attracted national attention in 1969 when he forced South Carolina to confront poverty in its midst. In a series of "poverty tours," Hollings accompanied Reverend Newman through littered city alleyways and dusty country roads. Inside weathered shacks, Hollings came face-to-face with hunger and malnutrition, children infested with intestinal parasites, parents who stayed up at night to protect their children from rats. Hollings returned to Washington to tell the disbelievers in a speech in the U.S. Senate, "There is substantial hunger in South Carolina. I have seen it with my own eyes." He acknowledged that as governor he had helped cover up the problem in order to present a better image to help attract industry.

Once acknowledged, the conditions could not be ignored. "South Carolina is undoubtedly being hurt by the publicity," declared Old Guard state Senate leader Rembert Dennis, "but the situation for action is so serious I think our junior senator should be commended for what he's doing."

Thurmond reacted differently. He suggested that it was all a politically motivated Democratic effort to win black votes. He said "friends" had told him there was no great problem, and added that there have always been those who didn't want to work.

"I would like to lose the argument and that there would be no problems," Hollings said the next week while walking through Negro slums in Anderson, a textile city of 35,000 that had not a single unit of public housing. "But here it is," he said as he stood on a street of unpainted shacks, wrecked cars, and littered yards, with black children scurrying around.

The 1970 campaign for governor provided a clear test of the politics of race. Lieutenant Governor West was a moderate who had actively fought the Ku Klux Klan as a state senator and who stood almost alone in the Senate against repeal of the compulsory school attendance law. As lieutenant governor he had taken an unprecedentedly bold step by delivering an address at a dinner in Clarendon County in honor of NAACP Executive Director Roy Wilkins. Nevertheless, 1970 was the year of massive school desegregation in the South, and West muted his campaign appeal to blacks and at one point even engaged in a bit of racial rhetoric by attacking the U.S. Department of Health, Education, and Welfare for "social experimentation."

In Representative Albert Watson the Republicans fielded a strong candidate with a gift for traditional southern political oratory that wrapped evangelical religiosity in a patriotic blanket. Watson wore a white tie to symbolize his outlook on race.

The crucial event of the year was an episode at Lamar, where a mob of angry and frustrated whites in Darlington County attacked school buses carrying Negro children. Nine days earlier, Watson had addressed a massive "freedom of choice" rally at Lamar that was protesting a mid-year court-ordered desegregation plan. West and McNair spurned invitations to appear.

Watson told them, "*Every section* of this state is in for it unless you stand up and use *every* means at your disposal to defend [against] what I consider an illegal order of the Circuit Court of the United States." He had drawn applause when he opened his remarks by declaring, "There are some people who said, 'Congressman, why are *you* coming over here this afternoon to speak to some of those hard-core rednecks over there?' You know my response to them? 'Those citizens are interested in their children, and I'll stand with them.' "

The violence at Lamar, although never mentioned directly by West in the campaign, was a crucial issue that hurt Watson with white racial moderates who had voted for Richard Nixon in 1968. Later, two Watson aides were linked to an attempt to stage a racial confrontation at a high school in Columbia. *The State*, the largest daily newspaper in South Carolina and one with an aristocratic tradition (dating back to its establishment in 1891 expressly to oppose Pitchfork Ben Tillman), endorsed West. The editor of the newspaper, Citadel graduate William D. Workman, Jr., had run for the U.S. Senate in 1962 as a Republican.

Watson got all-out support from the Nixon administration in a well-funded campaign. Vice-President Spiro Agnew and President Nixon's daughter Julie and son-in-law David Eisenhower made trips to South Carolina to join Thurmond in campaigning for Watson. But West pulled support from both Nixon and Wallace voters to add to his solid black majority and won by 28,000 votes, 53.2 percent of the major party total.

West lost to Watson 433–410 in the upper-middle-income Arcadia precinct in suburban Columbia, which in 1968 had voted 667 for Nixon,

132 for Humphrey, and 69 for Wallace. West won 10,532–5,362 in Anderson County, which Wallace had carried with a majority of 6,419 to a combined 5,043 for Nixon and Humphrey. West won ten of the 12 counties in which Wallace had received either a majority or plurality in 1968. In Columbia's Ward 9, where all but 24 of the 1,904 registered voters were black, West won by 1,006 to 19.

West drew support among Nixon voters, reacting to Watson's redneck appeal and the threat he posed to stability, and from Wallace voters, many of them traditional Democrats reacting against the Nixon administration's economic and school policies. Thurmond had promised in 1968 that there would be "freedom of choice" under Nixon, and in 1970 the Democrats literally played back, as "broken promises," tapes of Thurmond speaking on television and radio two years earlier. The schools had become integrated, "freedom of choice" was dead, and promised textile import legislation had not yet passed, resulting in layoffs and "short time" for textile workers.

In his inaugural address, West promised "a government that is totally color-blind." He declared: "The time has arrived when South Carolina for all time must break loose and break free of the vicious cycle of ignorance, illiteracy, and poverty which has retarded us throughout our history." He promised "new and innovative programs" to provide adequate housing and health care and eliminate hunger and malnutrition.

The West administration was marked by the creation of a State Housing Authority and authorization of state bonds to help finance low- and middle-income housing, an active effort to encourage expanded participation in the food stamp program, approval of a second medical school, a record level of industrial development, and creation of a Human Affairs Commission that required affirmative action programs on minority hiring by all state agencies and also possessed broad authority to handle discrimination complaints against state agencies. It is by far the strongest such state commission in the South. West considered the agency a key in defusing racial incidents that might otherwise escalate into major confrontations.

South Carolina is governed by well over a hundred semiautonomous boards and commissions. When state agency and department heads balked at submitting affirmative action plans to overcome past discrimination in hiring, West called them together, warned that the federal government had enforcement powers in such matters, and bluntly told them, "I don't like the idea of the federal government having to come down and tell us to do what we know is legally and morally right." [9]

In a 1974 veto message against capital punishment, West said, "Reinstitution of the death penalty in South Carolina would not, in my opinion, . . . serve as a deterrent to crime, but would rather be a return to

9. *New York Times*, May 27, 1973.

a barbaric, savage concept of vengeance which should not be accepted, condoned or permitted in a civilized society." The legislature, which has no tradition of yielding to the executive, easily overrode the veto.

Such bold action by West was unusual. Despite lagre surpluses while he was governor, no action was taken to provide the 20 percent state matching funds required to expand the federal Medicaid program to the roughly 200,000 medically needy or to increase the scandalously low support given welfare families with dependent children. James Clyburn, the top black aide on West's staff (he was appointed director of the Human Affairs Commission), said at the end of the West administration that the governor was committed "as a person, but the problem came with the people he surrounded himself with. The most conservative elements around the governor had the most influence with him." [10]

West had urged the legislature "to free the spirit of South Carolina from the bondage of limited expectations." The election of Edwards in 1974 brought in a different philosophy. "We will not embark on a careless adventure of change . . . because change for the sake of change defeats all good purpose," Edwards said in his inaugural address. "Our job is to direct change in a responsible and open way to help our people." He placed emphasis on combating crime and establishing a $50 million state reserve fund. Edwards later voiced support for expansion of the state kindergarten program, but only when "the economy dictates."

Perhaps nothing better illustrates Edwards's insensitivity to black poverty than a speech he made to a grassroots gathering of rural blacks several months after his inauguration. The meeting had been arranged by Reverend Newman, continuing his education program for white politicians that included the poverty tours for Hollings and West. The governor sought to explain that he could relate to poor people, that he had not always been a rich doctor, and said, "I guess I know as much about poverty as any of you." [11] He said his father and mother were schoolteachers and described how as a child he had kindled a fire on a cold morning. He apparently was unaware that among blacks in South Carolina a household with both parents working as schoolteachers would have been considered an upper-middle-class environment.

Edwards, who was attracted to politics by ideological concerns, expressed some of his political philosophy when he told the Republican State Executive Committee after they elected him to the Republican National Committee: "As the Democratic Party moves ahead with irresponsible ideas and plans, and they don't realize the American people are ready for a balanced budget, a strong national defense, and preparing ourselves so strongly that no nation would think of opposing us, it is time we lay aside party frictions and party battles and start to

10. *The State*, January 12, 1975, p. 6B.
11. *The State*, May 18, 1975, p. 15A.

realize who the true enemy is, and that's the irresponsible people in America who are trying to undermine us." [12]

Edwards first became active politically because he was "fed up with all of the things that were going on in America back in the early sixties. Things were going on that I was irritated by—the rioting, the campus riots, the street marches, the revolutionary-type stuff, the anarchy, the irresponsible government is the way I like to describe it, where there is no regard for the taxpayers' money and the experiment with all the great schemes that came out of Washington in the sixties. I just got to the point where I felt like why doesn't somebody do something, and then I realized I couldn't expect somebody else to do something unless I did it myself." [13]

DEMOCRATIC DISUNITY

After the election of Donald Russell as governor in 1962, the unopposed candidacies of McNair and West in the 1966 and 1970 Democratic primaries in part reflected a degree of unity among Democrats in response to the Republican challenge.

In addition to its solid base of black support, the Democratic Party developed into a loose coalition that included courthouse officials, a rather highly politicized and close-knit law enforcement establishment, academics and other liberals, and a basically weak organized labor movement. Financial support and its resulting influence came from the top levels of business and finance, which supported stability, "fiscal responsibility," and an emphasis on economic development—values in part shared by blacks who perceived that alliance with law enforcement agencies would mean fairer treatment and that economic development meant job opportunities. It was a delicately balanced assortment of competing philosophies and interests.

Disillusionment with the image and performance of Lieutenant Governor Earle E. Morris sent Democratic leaders looking elsewhere for a candidate in 1974. Once one of the bright, young, progressive leaders in the legislature and state Democratic chairman in 1966, Morris at 45 had been in state politics half his life and had gone stale. An unhappy domestic situation that resulted in divorce and his remarriage to a much younger woman created image problems.

Although Morris had a moderate record on race and enjoyed good

12. Ibid., July 18, 1975, p. 1A.
13. Interview with James B. Edwards, March 3, 1975.

rapport with blacks, his support eroded among established black leaders when he spoke of himself as a "John Connally Democrat" at a time when the former Texas governor's impending switch to the Republican Party was a topic of major political speculation.

Representative James Mann was approached by party leaders, but decided not to run. Had he chosen to make the race, Mann was confident there would have been no other major candidates to oppose him.[14] Mann later attracted national attention for his eloquence on the House Judiciary Committee during the Nixon impeachment inquiry. "It is not the presidency that is in jeopardy from us," Mann said at the end of the televised proceedings. "We would strive to strengthen and protect the presidency. But if there be no accountability, another president will feel free to do as he chooses. But the next time, there may be no watchman in the night."

After Mann said no, attention focused on Representative William Jennings Bryan Dorn, a 13-term congressman who for years had nurtured statewide ambitions, as the Democratic establishment's preferred alternative to Morris. One of the state's most prominent black political leaders, upset by Morris's flirtation with the Republicans, secured the blessings of Governor West and paid a visit to Dorn in his Washington office to encourage his candidacy and to pledge influence with the black vote.[15] Although Dorn had an image as a flag-waving ultraconservative, for a decade his voting record reflected a streak of progressive independence. He had supported most antipoverty programs, and in 1965 he had been the first of the state's political leaders to defend social change. He stood alone among Deep South congressmen in opposing antibusing legislation, all the while maintaining strong support from the congressional district that gave George Wallace his strongest support in South Carolina.

When Dorn and Morris both got into the race to split the establishment vote, it provided an opening for 36-year-old Charles D. (Pug) Ravenel. A politically ambitious Charleston native, he returned to the state after achieving a measure of fame and fortune as a scrambling quarterback who received All-American mention at Harvard and as a successful investment banker on Wall Street. He holds a graduate degree from Harvard Business School.

Ravenel appealed to the same sense of alienation from established institutions and leaders that George Wallace has exploited, but Ravenel used the politics of trust rather than the politics of fear. He combined an appeal to reform of institutions that reflected "politics as usual" with an appeal to a progressive spirit. He was the first successful candidate in the state to campaign openly as an opponent of capital punishment

14. Interview with James Mann, January 30, 1974.
15. Confidential interview.

266

and as a proponent of the right to collective bargaining by public employees.

A sample of what kind of governor Ravenel might have been is illustrated by three recommendations he made to West for appointment to the board of a newly created state consumer agency. West had solicited the recommendations shortly after Ravenel won the primary, and he followed them in appointing a black welfare mother of 11 children, a 22-year-old woman who had been the first female student body president at the University of South Carolina, and a high school tennis coach. Appointments to state boards and commissions traditionally had gone almost exclusively to people with business or professional backgrounds.

Ravenel generated excitement and captivated much of the press corps. He utilized the first sophisticated media campaign in the state, ran a poll that showed honesty and integrity to be the most important issues, broke precedent for South Carolina by making full financial disclosure of his assets and contributions, and (in the style of the 1970 successes of Reubin Askew in Florida and Dale Bumpers in Arkansas) campaigned aggressively as a progressive reformer. He attacked the state Senate establishment that had blocked legislation on ethics, home rule, and campaign reform.

The only legislative body in the South ruled by seniority, the Senate for decades had been controlled by a few men of considerable ability and political skill who believe in fiscal conservatism while serving as referees on decisions that affect the major economic interests that operate in the state. It is the politics of reward for favors and for friends and punishment for those who challenge the system.

The two most senior members of the Senate, personal friends and in most cases political allies, were Gressette and Dennis. Both enjoyed substantial law practices that included well-paid appearances before the Public Service Commission, the agency elected by the legislature to regulate public utilities and transportation companies. Such practices had come under fire, but attempts to prohibit it by law had been blocked in the Senate. Ravenel not only used Gressette and Dennis as whipping boys, but he also antagonized the Old Guard when he referred to the Senate in an unguarded moment as "a den of thieves."

In his final debate with Dorn just before the runoff primary, Ravenel said he would seek good relations with all members of the legislature, but added, "if you don't get the results you expect, I think you ought to take off the gloves, step into the ring, and bare-knuckle it out. Strength respects strength." [16] In his campaign, Ravenel spent roughly half a million dollars; what was unusual was not the amount but the fact that he reported it. According to federal campaign reports, Thurmond spent more than $600,000 two years earlier for a Senate race in which there

16. *The State,* July 26, 1974.

was no primary opposition. Although there were no reports, those who should know estimate that the West and Watson campaigns in 1970 cost not much less than that.

Ravenel's march to the governorship ended when the state Supreme Court ruled that he failed to meet the state's residency requirements. The South Carolina Constitution requires that a candidate for governor be "a citizen and resident . . . for five years next preceding the day of election." Ravenel had been back in Charleston for more than two years after a 17-year absence. There was ample evidence that he always had planned to return to South Carolina, and the legal definition of residency is an imprecise one in which intent weighs heavily. In a challenge suit before a lower court judge, Ravenel won a favorable ruling that he had never surrendered his residency despite voting and paying taxes in another state. It was sufficient for the Democratic Party to allow him to enter the primary.

However, *The State,* South Carolina's largest newspaper, editorialized early in May that "no less a body than the South Carolina Supreme Court should rule" on the residency question. An institutional defender of the status quo, the Supreme Court consisted of five justices, all of them former legislators who had been elected by the legislature.

With the primary less than three months away, Ravenel considered the matter sufficiently resolved to avoid the risk to his campaign that an appeal would entail by casting doubt about his eligibility. A full-fledged campaign could be delayed no longer. Besides, General Westmoreland, then the favorite in the Republican primary, had been away a longer time and after military retirement had returned to his native state even more recently than Ravenel.

The question of who was responsible for the suit that ultimately ruled Ravenel ineligible (the state Supreme Court ruled that the Constitution required "actual residence in the state" for the five-year period) is one that remains unanswered in South Carolina. The parties of record were a perennial candidate in the Democratic primary and a disgruntled country music disc jockey, but their lawyer was Eugene Griffith, a former Republican state senator who is a first cousin of W. J. B. Dorn. Griffith told reporters there were "several" other individuals involved in backing the challenge, and friends of Dorn's wife passed stories that she had at least given her approval to the idea of the suit. Griffith a few years earlier had nominated a Republican opponent against his congressman cousin, and there is a widely shared but unproved belief in the Democratic hierarchy that the suit had substantive Republican input. Polls showed Ravenel far ahead of Edwards at the time.

In a week of frenzied activity after the state Supreme Court ruling, Hollings endorsed a proposal for the governor to call a special session of the legislature to attempt to place a constitutional amendment on the ballot that would allow Ravenel to serve. West refused, in part because his poll of the legislature showed insufficient support in the Senate to approve the amendment and in part because of information that the state Supreme Court would invalidate any such effort.

Ravenel's campaign had been skillfully planned and executed by Marvin Chernoff, a native of Ohio who had worked in Democratic presidential campaigns. The decision to run was based on Chernoff's analysis of past election returns, which showed him that voters in the state were "uncontrolled" and that an independent candidate could win. Ravenel scored a stunning upset by leading Dorn in the first primary by 1,600 votes, with Morris trailing substantially. In the runoff, Ravenel won decisively, 186,000 to 155,000, and received more than 70 percent in each of the three large urban counties.

But when the state Democratic convention reconvened to choose a replacement candidate, Ravenel rejected Chernoff's advice to throw his support to an alternative reform candidate or behind Representative Mann, who had agreed to run as a compromise candidate acceptable to the Old Guard. Ravenel said it would be "wrong" for him to close the door on any candidate who was interested. On the third ballot he announced his support of Senator Richard W. Riley of Greenville, a reform leader in the state Senate. By then it was too late, and Dorn won the nomination with solid Old Guard support. The usually austere, 72-year-old Gressette "danced a jig in the aisle" when the final vote was announced, *The State* reported the next morning.

Forty-three of the 46 state senators were Democrats, but all but five at least covertly had pledged their support to Edwards after Ravenel won the nomination, Edwards said later as governor.[17] Once Dorn became the nominee, the Old Guard senators moved solidly behind him, and Edwards proclaimed himself a reform candidate and campaigned as the candidate of change.

One poll showed that a majority of South Carolinians considered themselves "conservative," but a majority also viewed Dorn as "more conservative than I am." Yet, at the end of the campaign, in response to hostile questioners at a public forum in Greenville, Dorn made one of the most forthright statements on race heard from an American politician in the 1970s, although the press barely mentioned it. It was in response to a question about "busing for racial balance" and came at a time when schools in Boston were in turmoil over a court-ordered busing plan and President Ford had expressed his personal opposition to the busing concept.

Dorn's response is worth recording:

Do you think we're going back to the days when the bus went around and picked up the black children and took them to school and came back and picked up the white children? Those days are gone forever. And to say that

17. Interview with James B. Edwards, March 3, 1975.

we ought to do away with federal funds for busing just to take cities like Boston and Detroit and Denver off the hook when our people in South Carolina are obeying court orders and obeying HEW guidelines—it's the most preposterous thing I've ever heard of! And President Ford, with the Ku Klux up there in Boston, and he's got the 82nd Airborne on "standby," and setting one policy for one part of the country and one for the other—it's wrong! My children ride the bus 10 miles each way to school, and they go to a good consolidated high school, and it's part of a child's education these days to go to school with children of different races and different color and learn it's one small world we live in and that we've got to get along with Chinese and Japanese and people from all countries. My father used to be school superintendent in Greenwood, and I remember when he consolidated the schools and it ended classism in Greenwood County, and busing might end another kind of "ism."

There was little difference between Ravenel and Dorn on programmatic issues such as tax reform, ethics legislation, or a commitment to expand the state kindergarten program, and Dorn had given full support to Ravenel after losing the Democratic primary. But news stories of Mrs. Dorn's alleged role in the suit and the fact that Dorn was embraced by the Old Guard that Ravenel opposed were factors in Ravenel's refusal to endorse Dorn. Ravenel said he would vote for Dorn by writing in his name, but that he could not endorse him.

After the election, Ravenel said, "It would have been hypocritical for me as the candidate for change to endorse the no-change candidate. The Democratic establishment being behind Dorn made it difficult for me to endorse him . . . my political integrity and intellectual integrity were involved—this man doesn't represent what I've been fighting for. I'm not a politician; it's political integrity that won in July [the primary]. Endorsing Dorn would have turned off tens of thousands of people by 'dealing.' The people voted against the Democratic establishment." [18]

Senator Hollings, the most ardent Ravenel supporter among the established political leaders in the state, had advised him "to pull back and join the team . . . He could run for governor four years from now and win in a cakewalk." [19]

Dorn's narrow loss (48.4 percent of the major party vote) and Ravenel's failure to "join the team" left many Democrats bitter and the party in a state of disunity. The perceptive state Democratic chairman, Donald Fowler, said the long-range impact of the Ravenel campaign "is still a matter of uncertainty. Only time will tell whether the people were responding to a uniquely attractive personality, the issues to which he addressed himself, or a combination of the two." [20]

When compared with the average county-by-county vote for Democratic candidates in the 1966 and 1970 races for governor and the 1968

18. Telephone interview with Charles D. Ravenel, November 21, 1974.
19. *The State*, October 1974.
20. *Columbia Record*, September 26, 1974, p. 10B.

U.S. Senate race, Dorn fared better than the average in only eight of the 46 counties, seven of them in the congressional district he had represented for 26 years. Dorn's performance was more than 10 percent below the Democratic average in 11 counties, including the four most populous ones—Richland (Columbia), Greenville, Charleston, and Spartanburg. Nine of the 11 were counties in which Ravenel had received more than 60 percent of the vote in the runoff primary against Dorn, which suggests that Ravenel's refusal to endorse was perceived by his followers as an anti-Dorn signal. (See maps, pp. 409–456, Appendix A)

BLACK POLITICS

Democratic loyalty among blacks was as great as ever in 1974. In 44 precincts in which registration was 90–100 percent black, Dorn received 94.6 percent of the vote. In 31 precincts with registration 80–89 percent black, Dorn received 85.3 percent of the vote.

Although Edwards had helped desegregate the county dental society in Charleston and openly sought black votes, he once had suggested that the South Carolina law to disfranchise paupers supported at public expense should be enforced against welfare recipients. Furthermore, in the Republican primary he had blamed inflation on the food stamp program. Such programs disproportionately benefit blacks because of the disproportionate number of blacks who are poor, and such insensitivity gave blacks little incentive to change their traditional allegiance to the Democrats. Edwards did best among blacks in his home county of Charleston, but even there he received only 9.2 percent of the vote in precincts with 90 percent or more black registration and 21.7 percent in precincts 80–89 percent black. Statewide he received only 5.4 and 14.6 percent, respectively, in all such precincts.

Governor Edwards's showing among blacks was weaker than Thurmond's in 1972. With a new "image" based on direct appeals for black support, Thurmond received 6.6 percent of the vote in precincts with 90 percent or greater black registration and 22.7 percent in precincts with 80–89 percent black registration. Much of the Republican vote no doubt came from the whites who were registered in those precincts. Thurmond in 1972 was far more open in seeking black votes than West had been in 1970, and Thurmond thus ended the traditional fear of open solicitation of black support.

Thurmond's new "image" was planned after the rejection of Watson in 1970. In an unusually candid interview with Thurmond's hometown newspaper in Aiken, his former top aide, Harry Dent—then a political operative in the White House—explained before the 1972 campaign, "We're going to get him on the high ground of fairness on the race question. We've got to get him in a position where he can't be attacked like Watson by liberals as being a racist."

A few weeks later, Thurmond announced the appointment to his staff of Thomas Moss, a black voter registration project director and onetime labor union organizer. Moss sought out needs in the black community, and Thurmond responded by announcing federal grants for various projects in black communities and made dedication speeches at several of the projects. The new image campaign also included building Thurmond into "South Carolina's indispensable man in Washington." Thurmond made scores of announcements of approvals of federal projects for South Carolina, many of them from programs he had voted against. It prompted his Democratic opponent, liberal state Senator E. N. (Nick) Zeigler, to call Thurmond "a scrooge in Washington and a Santa Claus in South Carolina."

Because of its central statewide computerized voter registration system, which includes information on age, race, sex, and occupation, South Carolina is the only state in which precise data are available on turnout by race. The system was developed in 1968 as part of an election reform package that liberalized registration laws.

Since voting participation is partly a function of income, the rate of black participation is less than that for whites. In 1970, blacks comprised 24.8 percent of the total registration but accounted for only 22.9 percent of the total vote in the general election. In 1972, black registration increased slightly to 25.2 percent of the total, but the voting percentage declined to 22.2. In 1974, black registration increased to 26.3 percent, and the black percentage of the total vote was 22.4.

In 1970, 50.3 percent of the registered blacks actually voted, compared with 55.8 percent of the whites, a difference of 5.5 percent. The difference increased in 1972 to 10.6 percent when 58.5 percent of the registered blacks and 69.1 percent of the registered whites voted. In 1974 the difference in turnout was 10.1 percent, with 56.3 percent of the registered whites and 46.2 percent of the registered blacks voting.

The increased gap between black and white participation rates from 1970 to 1974 indicates that blacks saw less difference between Dorn and Edwards than between West and Watson. The limited enthusiasm Dorn generated among blacks is reflected further by the Richland County turnout for black congressional candidate Matthew Perry. He received 854 more votes than Dorn, although there was only a six-vote difference in the vote totals received by their Republican opponents.

By 1975, there was a difference of only 0.5 percent in proportion of voting-age population registered: 60.8 percent of the blacks and 61.3

percent of the whites.[21] In North Carolina and Louisiana, the only other southern states covered by the Voting Rights Act that collect registration data by race, the differences in registration by race were 17.6 and 16 percent, respectively.

The level of registration is by no means uniform throughout the state, but the greatest difference between white and black levels of registration no longer occurs (as it did a decade earlier) in counties with the greatest percentage of black population. Of 12 majority black counties, ten in 1974 showed a higher rate of black registration as a percentage of voting-age population than the statewide average of 60.8 percent. The other two were less than 3 percentage points behind the statewide average. The lowest rates tended to occur in counties where the percentage of black population was too small to raise hopes of electing black candidates to local office. For example, the lowest rate of black registration was in Pickens County, whose 9.4 percent black population is the smallest in the state; only 30.6 percent of the black population of voting age was registered there. Of the five counties in which less than 40 percent of the black voting-age population was registered, four were among the 14 counties with less than 30 percent black population.

The exception was Newberry County, with 33 percent black population, and the explanation there may well be that county's historic record of an unusually high level of intimidation of blacks. Not only was the difference between black and white registration rates there 36.7 percent, greater than in any other county, but the difference in turnout among those who were registered also was greater than the state average in both 1970 and 1972. Newberry County was home of Coleman L. Blease, perhaps the most blatantly racist politician in the state's history, a man who as governor in 1911 said a few weeks after a lynching that when a Negro puts his hands on a white girl, "the sooner the Negro is put six feet under the ground the better."

A look at county data reveals, as expected, that the combination of heavy black population and high rate of black participation greatly stimulates white political participation. Whites in all 12 of the majority black counties were registered at a higher percentage than the state average of 61.3 percent. In ten of the counties the white registration rate was more than 15 points higher than the statewide rate. As a percentage of those registered, whites in the majority black counties voted at a slightly higher rate than the state average, and blacks in those counties at a rate about equal to the state average.

The combination of heavy black population and participation not only makes it possible to elect blacks, but it can also result in a different kind of white candidate or can change the attitude of a white incumbent. In 1966, when three blacks challenged three white legisla-

21. U.S. Commission on Civil Rights, *The Voting Rights Act: Ten Years After* (Washington: U.S. Government Printing Office, January 1975), p. 54.

tive candidates in majority black Williamsburg County, where whites still had an edge in registration, voting polarized strictly along racial lines. Two years later, the incumbent white sheriff and his white opponent both attended the organizational meeting of a new NAACP chapter; both promised to hire black deputies at the same pay as whites and to fully enforce the 1964 Civil Rights Act and its public accommodations section. After the county senator, a lawyer whose clients had included the local Ku Klux Klan, was reapportioned into a new district that had 38 percent black registration, he commented to a reporter that if you got the black vote, you only needed to get 12 percent of the white vote. The next week, he appointed the brother and campaign manager of his 1966 black opponent to the county voter registration board, promised to appoint blacks to county boards and commissions, introduced legislation to create a county housing authority, and joined his 1966 opponent on the board of an organization that worked primarily to help poor black farmers and was cited by the director for making significant contributions to the organization's progress.

By 1972 Williamsburg County had elected a biracial delegation to Columbia. The black member, the Reverend B. J. Gordon, was chairman of the state Welfare Rights Organization and a nephew of Reverend Newman, the civil rights leader.

Only urban counties use voting machines in South Carolina, and the use of paper ballots in rural counties still makes fraud a matter of concern in some rural areas. When George Hamilton, the black former executive director of the South Carolina Human Relations Commission, ran for the House in 1974 in a legislative district that included machine-dominated Hampton County, he reported being detained without cause by local law enforcement officials when he sought to investigate and obtain affidavits regarding possible election fraud.[22]

When South Carolina was forced in 1974 to reapportion the state House of Representatives into single-member districts by litigation brought under the Voting Rights Act, the result was to increase overall black representation from three to 13.

Black legislators report no overt or covert attempts to restrict their participation in any way. After organizing a black caucus in 1975, they easily persuaded the new speaker to appoint blacks to every standing committee. "The result is that there is black input into every policy decision in the legislature," explained Representative I. S. Leevy Johnson. He said there was some hesitation among the blacks about forming a separate caucus after their number increased, "but the whites expected us to do it. They would ask, 'When is the black caucus organizing?' "[23]

22. Ibid., p. 155.
23. Interview with I. S. Leevy Johnson, March 3, 1975.

Representative Ernest A. Finney of Sumter, an attorney elected in 1972 who became the first chairman of the black caucus, said of his first term in the legislature, "There has not been the pressure that I expected from people who were in positions of leadership. I found that if you do your job, and they know where you stand, they don't put any pressure on you. . . . My deskmate and I have philosophical differences that go back ten years, but by and large we get along fine. He respects me and I respect him, and we vote our convictions." [24]

The 13 black representatives elected in 1974—all but one of whom were college graduates, seven with postgraduate degrees—each contributed $300 of the $7,000 legislative salary to pay for administrative costs after they organized the Black Caucus. In addition, they held a series of regional meetings to get input on issues and problems from hundreds of local black political activists. They also worked quietly with the Congressional Black Caucus to lobby the South Carolina congressional delegation for support of the Voting Rights Act extension in 1975. All six Congressional Democrats—five representatives and Senator Hollings —voted for the extension. In the legislature, the Black Caucus won victories on such symbolic issues as commission of a portrait of black educator Mary McLeod Bethune to hang in the State House and official recognition by the state of Martin Luther King's birthday. On substantive issues, they won support for a $2.6 million expansion of public kindergartens, despite opposition by Governor Edwards.

Statewide black political leadership has included many people motivated by high ideals, a few venal brokers who sold and delivered to the highest bidder, and all gradations in between. By the time Ravenel ran in 1974, he said he was told it would cost $65,000 to "deliver" the black vote.[25] Such cash traditionally is distributed as "gasoline" money, an undetermined amount of which goes into legitimate expenses of arranging car pools, distributing literature, and other campaign expenses. It is a subject seldom discussed publicly, but the transfer of funds generally involves little or no accounting for expenditures and involves some understanding that the recipients will attempt to influence their followers in support of the donor. White candidates who speak in black churches traditionally place cash contributions in the collection plate, and in some counties a minister perceived as influential by white politicians may get a new set of tires for his car.

Ravenel condemned the "buying" of black votes, publicly rebuked one aide who passed money, and said that in the runoff his campaign spent $2,000 for gasoline money for which receipts were brought in.[26] Instead of the traditional approach that involved distributing cash to

24. Interview with Ernest A. Finney, February 12, 1974.
25. Interview with Charles D. Ravenel, August 30, 1974.
26. Ibid.

traditional "leaders," Ravenel hired ten blacks for his campaign staff of 33, which reflected his pledge that state employment should reflect the racial composition of the state.

"LEGISLATIVE GOVERNMENT"

Key observed that in South Carolina the governor was "little more than a ceremonial chief of state," [27] that the legislature "has grasped firm control of the critical sectors of state administration," [28] and that within the legislature "the Senate holds primacy." [29]

The Great Society measures of Lyndon Johnson, which gave the governor direction of new federal spending programs and provided a new source of patronage, did much to enhance the power of the governor in South Carolina. His appointment powers have also increased as state government has expanded. But to a great extent, what additional power there is depends directly on the governor's ability to persuade the legislature to do what he wants it to do.

When Edwards attempted to appoint a Republican magistrate in Richland County in 1975, the Senate refused under its "advise and consent" authority to confirm the appointment, and the Republican governor then appointed a Democrat. Although technically appointed by the governor, magistrates by tradition have run in the Democratic primary, which is treated as an advisory election. They serve as judges of limited jurisdiction and provide an important element of grassroots organizational support for the Democratic Party.

The legislature continues to elect the Highway Commission, the state board of education, the boards of trustees of the state universities and colleges (although the governor appoints a Higher Education Commission and other overlapping boards that result in a highly fragmented policymaking structure for higher education), the board for the Department of Social Services (welfare), and Supreme Court and Circuit Court judges.*

In addition, the chairmen of the Senate Finance Committee and the House Ways and Means Committee serve with the governor and two

27. Key, *Southern Politics*, p. 155.
28. Ibid., p. 151.
29. Ibid., p. 152.
* In 1975 only three of the 21 jurists were without legislative experience, and one of those three was the former law associate of Solomon Blatt, Sr., who had served 33 years as speaker of the House before stepping down in 1973.

other constitutional officers (comptroller general and treasurer) on the Budget and Control Board. The board not only writes the state budget but also has vast authority in the administration of state government that includes decisions on issuance of state bonds, construction of buildings, policy over public lands, control of the retirement system, direction of personnel practices, audit of state agencies, general supervision of data-processing systems, supervision of printing and central purchasing, and coordination of professional research and statistical services. Moreover, the board is empowered to approve the transfer of funds within agencies after the legislature passes an appropriations bill.

One of the most powerful men in state government is the state auditor, Patrick C. Smith. Technically he serves as secretary of the Budget and Control Board, but he functions as executive director and is treated with deference throughout state government as one who exerts considerable influence on the essential political question of who gets what. During the West administration, the state surplus averaged $50 million annually because of Smith's proclivity of making low revenue estimates. He sits in on all meetings of the two legislative committees that shape the appropriations bill, and his word is accepted as the highest authority. Although Smith keeps a low profile, he is not reticent in committee hearings to speak out against social legislation on grounds that it is to costly and that the state cannot afford it. Shortly after taking office, Edwards announced creation of a Governor's Committee on Long Range Priorities and named Smith the chairman.

Although governors came and went every four years, for almost three decades the chairman of the Senate Finance Committee was Edgar A. Brown of Barnwell—a lawyer, banker, and businessman who with fellow townsman Sol Blatt symbolized the "Barnwell Ring" that dominated the state. The Ring consisted of like-minded conservative rural legislators.

Blatt, by his policy of appointing no more than one member from any county to the Ways and Means Committee, which handles finance legislation in the House, ensured that the eight counties with half the population would have no more than one-third of the vote on the committee. For no apparent reason other than an unwillingness to depart from tradition, Blatt's successor, Rex Carter of urban Greenville, changed the policy only slightly when he made Ways and Means appointments in 1975 for the first time. Carter added a second member from Greenville County, a Republican who changed his residence to avoid running as an incumbent against Carter after the House was reapportioned into single-member districts in 1974.

One writer once characterized Brown and Blatt this way: "They act as though The Maker personally adds a gold star to their charts each time they bring South Carolina through with another balanced budget. No matter that the state ranks near the bottom of almost every scale of economic and social health; it has been limping along with change in its pocket, and for Brown and Blatt that is reward enough." [30]

When Brown retired in 1972 at the age of 83 after a half century in the legislature, he spoke of Depression years in the early 1930s when school teachers received $50 a month and were paid in scrip because the state was bankrupt; moneychangers would redeem the scrip in cash at a discount up to 20 percent. The state had no credit rating at that time, but Brown left with a Triple-A rating for South Carolina bonds on Wall Street. "I manage the state's money like I manage my own," Brown once said, "and that means I don't spend more than I have."

Brown and Blatt often feuded, but the man who always could bring them back together was the late John K. Cauthen, who as executive director of the South Carolina Textile Manufacturers Association was the state's most effective lobbyist and simultaneously a trusted adviser of both legislators, as well as whoever the governor happened to be. Working through Cauthen, the dominant textile industry traditionally maintained a low political profile and a degree of enlightened self-interest in matters of public policy.

After passage of the 1964 Civil Rights Act, the industry joined with the state attorney general and the Justice Department's top official in the state to sponsor a workshop for textile personnel managers on the full meaning of the equal employment section of the act. Subsequently, the act was explained to line foremen through a presentation over the state's closed-circuit educational television network. The textile industry, which had faced a shortage of workers at the time, made a smooth transition that solved the industry's labor supply problems and provided an entry for thousands of blacks into the manufacturing work force. When Governor McNair put through his major tax package, a key element in its passage was the assurance from Cauthen of the industry's acceptance of an increase in the corporate income tax rate that was included in a package otherwise dominated by consumer taxes. In the early 1970s, several of the state's top textile executives made a trip to the Orient with state officials and discovered that Japan was a lucrative market for many of their products, and not just a competitor with low-priced textile exports to the United States.

Despite the active Republicanism of Roger Milliken and a few others, most of the major textile operatives in the state tend to be quietly Democratic at the state level, and state government in turn adopts a generally protective attitude toward the industry, an attitude that was nurtured in the era dominated by Cauthen, Blatt, and Brown.

Brown was succeeded as Finance Committee Chairman by Dennis, his "trusted lieutenant" for many years, a man who had tended to many

30. Roger Williams, " 'Two Old Men'—In S.C., Brown and Blatt are the Senior Partners," *South Today* 2 (April 1971):4–5.

of the details and a master of parliamentary maneuver in his own right. Dennis, who was 57 when Brown retired, was serving his 30th year in the Senate. The more senior Gressette moved up to president pro tem.

The seniority system does more than vest power in the hands of a few men accountable only to their local constituencies. Because the Senate is controlled by a few, it is there that the state's financial interests center their attention. The three private electric power companies that operate in South Carolina were each paying $7,500 annual retainers to Senator Brown's Barnwell law firm when he retired. Carolina Power and Light showed sufficient appreciation for past services that it continued the payment after his retirement, although the other two did not.

Dennis, whose law office in low-country Berkeley County is far removed from the service area of Duke Power Co. in the Piedmont, was paid $20,000 in legal retainer fees by Duke in 1972. He received more than twice that amount from South Carolina Electric and Gas Co. for representing them in rate cases before the Public Service Commission. In addition, he served as assistant general counsel to the South Carolina Public Service Authority, a state-owned power-generating system commonly known as Santee-Cooper and headquartered in Berkeley County, the Dennis barony. With that background and his familiarity with electric power companies, it was perhaps natural that Dennis introduced and guided to passage in 1973 a bill that provides for joint financing and construction of a nuclear power plant by South Carolina Electric and Gas Co. and Santee-Cooper. The private utility will operate the plant, whose output will be proportionately divided, and taxes will be paid only on the portion financed by the private company. The plant will be located in Fairfield County, the home of another senator whose legal services were retained by South Carolina Electric and Gas Co.

When state Representative H. F. Bell of Chesterfield County was elected chairman of the influential House Judiciary Committee in 1971, the recognition of his legal ability by his peers was such that Carolina Power and Light Co. placed him on a $15,000 retainer. His Democratic primary opponent the next year made much of that fact—enough, it was said, to make that issue the key to the retirement of the incumbent. A neighboring state senator, faced with similar charges by an opponent, commented later that Bell "didn't know how to handle it. I said, 'Of course, I appear at rate hearings; I want to be sure that the people of my county are treated fairly.'"

As a result of the combination of press exposure of the practice, use of it by opponents as a political issue, and public outrage at the inflation-fueled, double-digit utility rate increases during the nation's energy crisis, the retainers became a less attractive way of doing business both for the lawyer legislators and the power companies, whose payment for such services by law must be filed as a public record.

The American Bank and Trust Co. collapse, in which a state-chartered bank folded in 1974 with a loss of roughly $40 million to its stockholders, suggests the cozy relationship between financial institutions and the Senate. The chairman of the Senate Banking Committee served as a director of the bank, and an investigation by the Federal Deposit Insurance Corporation disclosed that the bank loaned large sums to a number of real estate developers, apparently without adhering to standards set by state law. One development company was owned by another member of the Senate. It is not unusual to find even the so-called progressives in the Senate listed as directors of banks in their communities. The state showed almost no interest in investigating the bank collapse.

One of the reformers in the Senate said that when it comes to who does the work for insurance companies and the small loan industry, two of the most active special interest groups, "all you have to do is watch who speaks on the floor for their bills." He added that "business has just controlled this state." The influence of banks was such that when a freedom-of-information act was passed, it excluded the records of agencies that regulate the banking industry. When a senator suggested after the collapse of the American Bank and Trust Co. that someone besides banking industry representatives serve on the Board of Bank Control, industry protest squelched the proposal.

Lieutenant Governor Harvey shocked the Senate elders in 1975 when he attacked the seniority system and dared make some appointments to conference committees without first consulting with the senior members. An effort was made to take away his appointive power, but public reaction to so raw a display of power politics was such that the Senate retreated. Harvey reassured Gressette and Dennis that he never thought "it was proper for me to appoint committees without any consideration or consultation with other persons," but he also told them he believed "longevity should not be the criteria [sic] for leadership in the Senate." [31]

Harvey's open challenge and an attempt by reformers to weaken seniority suggest that the system may have begun to crumble beneath the forces of change. The Old Guard—a term which may include freshman senators who prefer to go along in order to get along—was sufficiently concerned in 1975 to write seniority into the Senate rules for the first time, no longer relying on tradition. They beat back every effort to weaken seniority, including a proposed amendment by the reformers to allow those senators not elected to either the Finance Committee or the Judiciary Committee (which together are assigned well over half of all bills) a seat on one standing committee of their own choosing, without respect to seniority.

When reform Senator Harry Chapman had the floor, a veteran chided him for opposing seniority and pointed out that he had stepped aside

31. *The State*, February 12, 1975, p. 1B.

from a committee chairmanship so that Chapman could assume it. "I want to thank you for the kindness you showed in stepping aside," Chapman replied, "but after serving as chairman for two years, I find that no legislation has been referred to the committee."

The seniority system, which rewards longevity rather than ability, discourages many able men from running for the Senate or remaining in it. With few exceptions, reform leaders in the House who move to the Senate tend within a few years either to get out or get along. One erstwhile reformer was in the Senate only a few months before he accepted a $3,000 retainer from a private electric utility company. Another, who decided that one term in the Senate was enough, called the atmosphere "psychologically and physically intimidating" for those who attempt to challenge the Old Guard power structure. "They'll cut you to pieces on the floor," he said. "They attack you personally, and it's not only the verbal abuse but there's an atmosphere of violence. No one will admit it, but it's there."

Not too many years ago, one senator whose background included experience as a professional boxer squared off against another senator and literally knocked him out on the floor of the Senate chamber. "The reformers get together and talk about that. They laugh, but the atmosphere of violence is there, and it's intimidating. Those fellows play rough." [32] Nevertheless, retaliation is more likely to come in the traditional form of political punishment, such as killing a bill sponsored by a reformer or taking away a choice assignment.

Reapportionment, which ended the old system of one senator to a county and a structure in which the senator controlled government within his county, failed to seriously shake the established order. Whether single-member districts will bring reform to the Senate, as some proponents hope, remains to be seen. If litigation to force single-member districts under the Voting Rights Act is successful, it is almost certain to result in blacks entering the Senate.

Senator Travis Medlock, who served in the state House of Representatives when the first blacks were elected, contends that election of even one black senator with ability "would be devastating. . . . It would give leverage to the progressives because these senators from the rural areas are very mindful of that black bloc vote, and it would be there looking at them every day, and that does make a change. I saw it happen in the House. If you had a black man or woman sitting in the Senate you have a different ball game because when he or she stands up there, it's the voice for that segment in every county in the state. I'd rather have the black on my side than all eight of the progressives. The emergence of black representation helped cast the House in a progressive stance." [33]

32. Confidential interview.
33. Interview with Travis Medlock, March 4, 1975.

CONGRESS

The death of House Armed Services Committee Chairman L. Mendel Rivers in 1970, the defeat of District of Columbia Committee Chairman John L. McMillan in 1972, and retirement of Veterans Affairs Committee Chairman W. J. B. Dorn and next-senior Representative Thomas S. Gettys in 1974 changed the image and reduced the power of the state's congressional delegation. In those four years, the average seniority among the six representatives dropped from 16.7 to 3.3 years. Representative Mann moved from junior member in 1970 to senior member in 1975. The average age fell by more than 15 years.

Representative Mendel Davis of Charleston, 28 when he was elected by a basically populist coalition of blue-collar whites, blacks, and rural followers of his patron and godfather, L. Mendel Rivers, reflects the mildly progressive outlook of the three Democratic freshmen elected in 1974. Davis represents the district in which organized labor is strongest in South Carolina. Significantly, all three Democratic newcomers in 1974 —Butler Derrick, Kenneth Holland, and John Jenrette—won with open support from organized labor, a reflection both of changing attitudes toward labor unions in the state and a growing appreciation of the campaign help labor can supply through volunteers and other contributions.

When Davis ran the first time, it is noteworthy that labor leaders in Charleston approached the secondary level of black leadership, since the older and more established black leaders had committed themselves to other candidates. Davis's success is also a reflection of the spread of political leadership among blacks and the growing independence of increasingly sophisticated black voters and their dwindling reliance on political guidance from established leaders.

OUTLOOK

South Carolina has yet to hold an election in which even a third of the voting-age population has gone to the polls. The low level of registration and participation outside the Black Belt counties suggest either that political awareness among the citizenry is undeveloped, or that few campaigns have exposed issues that might excite the mass of the population, or both.

Although Republicans have mounted a challenge to Democratic rule in South Carolina, possess in Strom Thurmond a solid base around which to build, and received a boost by winning the governor's office in 1974, the combination of their limited success in the legislature and the weakness of the governor's office leaves them in a less than competitive position. Except for Thurmond—who has also won elections as a Democrat, a Dixiecrat, and a write-in candidate—the GOP has failed to develop a cadre of candidates. Its future success may in part depend on whether Democrats overcome factional division that grew out of the 1974 campaign.

The 29 percent of the vote received by an obscure Republican candidate for secretary of state in 1974 can be considered the core Republican strength in the state. Yet Thurmond received 62 and 63 percent of the vote in his 1966 and 1972 elections. The average margin for Hollings in 1968 and 1974 was even larger. With a solid core vote for both parties, it is the ticket splitter who tends to vote for both Thurmond and Hollings and who decides the winners of statewide elections. Unless given a reason to do otherwise, he tends to vote Democratic.

Survey data on racial attitudes in South Carolina during late 1960s and early 1970s consistently showed that almost half of the whites and almost half of the blacks considered the rate of desegregation "about right." A slight majority of whites thought it "too fast," and a slight majority of blacks and less than 10 percent of the whites thought it "too slow."

In a state where the 1970 poverty rate was 23.9 percent and where black families were 4.3 times more likely to be poor than white families, major economic problems remain. A progressive spirit appears alive in the state, and the Democrats have a tradition of selecting candidates with proven ability and moderate outlook. How much the Edwards administration will slow the momentum of social progress developed under its four Democratic predecessors is a question that only future developments can answer.

Chapter

12

TENNESSEE

Genuine Two-Party Politics

> Both parties have to scrap for it. Neither
> gets fat and happy. They have to com-
> pete—and that way they stay clean and
> hungry.
>
> —Senator Howard H. Baker, Jr.[1]

THE TERM "two-party politics" is a frame of reference in almost every
southern state, but only in Tennessee is it a reality. There, the tradition
of the frontier and the pioneer spirit in the mountains of East Tennessee
and the tradition of the Old South that comes sweeping across Memphis
from the Arkansas and Mississippi Delta plantation country are joined
by the legacy of Middle Tennessee, where Jacksonian democracy took
root and populism flourished. Fundamentalist religions have instilled in
Tennesseans a respect for honesty and integrity but have also tended to
foster a narrowness of outlook and suspicion of change.

The interstate highways that link the state's metropolitan areas have
helped reduce the level of isolation. The four urban centers of Davidson
(Nashville), Shelby (Memphis), Knox (Knoxville) and Hamilton (Chattanooga) counties in 1970 contained 1.7 million people, 43.3 percent
of the total for the state. Together with the developing tri-cities metropolitan area of Bristol, Kingsport, and Johnson City in Sullivan and
Washington counties in the northeast, the six most urban counties cast

---

1. Howard H. Baker, Jr., quoted in Neal R. Peirce, *The Border South States*
(New York: W. W. Norton, 1975), p. 305.

47 percent of the vote in 1974. More than a sixth of the statewide vote comes out of Shelby County, the largest of the metropolitan areas.

The Tennessee Valley Authority, despite its occasional insensitivity, has produced a model of systematic regional development. Its cheap power, flood control, recreational facilities, fertilizer experiments, land use pioneering, and local government research give to Tennesseans an appreciation of government's social role that is unique in the South.

The political climate of Tennessee has spawned liberal and progressive leaders such as Estes Kefauver and Albert Gore, whose careers never reached full maturity, and the more tragic Frank Clement. But in times of alienation, Tennesseans tend to look for a third party, and George Wallace served as their most recent vehicle of protest. Wallace also drew many of the ultraright Goldwaterites from the Republican Party and left it less ideological, better organized, more moderate, and the most successful of any in the South.

The original Supreme Court reapportionment order, *Baker* v. *Carr*, came out of Tennessee, and it paved the way for Republicans to compete for domination in the state legislature—more so than in any state in the South. Not until after the 1970 elections left Republicans with both U.S. senators and the governor did the Democrats slowly begin to organize. But aided by Watergate and the recession, they united in 1974 to win back the governor's office and make other significant gains.

BACKGROUND

The politics of contemporary Tennessee have their roots in the Civil War. The state rejected the Confederacy until after the fall of Fort Sumter and after President Lincoln asked for 75,000 troops. For almost a century after the Civil War, Tennessee politics remained frozen by the state's division in that conflict. Unionists in East Tennessee joined the federal armies by the thousands. When Confederates were in control, Unionists and their families suffered. Later, reprisals followed against the secessionists.

Much of Middle Tennessee and most of West Tennessee was plantation country, but the mountainous East was dominated by small farmers who found slavery unprofitable and who rejected the notion that it was a divinely ordained institution. When Tennessee seceded in 1861, becoming the last state to join the Confederacy, the vote of Middle and West Tennessee was 87,392 to 14,315 in favor. But in East Tennessee the vote was 32,923 to 14,780 against secession. Six counties in the Highland Rim area of West Tennessee, an area with few slaveholders, also voted no.

The bitterness of the conflict left a brand of Republicanism and party loyalty that was passed on from generation to generation. Lamar Alexander, an East Tennessee native who won the 1974 Republican nomination for governor, recalled that his father had confided to him that he had once voted for a Democrat, a friend who was running for magistrate, and Alexander told the story as though revealing a skeleton in the family closet.[2]

Although reaction to the national Democratic Party began to change traditional voting patterns for president beginning in 1948 and for statewide offices more than a decade later, voter response in 1974 to Watergate and the recession bore a striking resemblance to the 1861 secession vote. It was a sharp reversal of the 25-year revolt against the Democratic Party.

Of the 24 counties carried by Lamar Alexander against Democrat Ray Blanton, only four had voted for secession—and Alexander failed to get as much as 52 percent in any of the four. Blanton carried 59 of the 63 counties that voted for secession. Three of the 12 antisecession counties that he carried were located in the Highland Rim area of the old congressional district he had represented, and his vote in six of the others was below his statewide average of 55.7 percent. As Key wrote in discussing Tennessee in 1948, "Social mechanisms for the transmission and perpetuation of partisan faiths have an effectiveness far more potent than the political issue of the day."[3]

Not until after the 1960s did the state Highway Department remove signs welcoming visitors to the "Three Great States of Tennessee." The Grand Divisions represent geographical as well as historical divisions. Although the 35 Appalachian counties that made up East Tennessee remain predominantly Republican, Democrats there tend to be more liberal than those in the west. The hilly farmland of Middle Tennessee, whose 39 counties fan out from the state capital of Nashville eastward to the ridge of the Cumberland Mountains and westward to the lower Tennessee River, have tended to be more moderate in racial outlook than West Tennessee, where there were more blacks and fewer white yeomen farmers.

With an established mountain base on which to build, Republicans gained support from rebellion in West Tennessee against the national Democratic Party drive for racial equality that began with Harry Truman in 1948. The emergence of a suburban middle class reaching against entrenched, unresponsive Democratic courthouse control and manipulation of elections helped the Republicans develop a leadership cadre

2. Interview with Lamar Alexander, August 1974.
3. V. O. Key, *Southern Politics in State and Nation* (New York: Vintage, 1949), p. 76.

that became visible in the Eisenhower years. The Goldwater movement swept in a wave of conservative ideologues. The deaths of the Old Guard Republican leaders, who viewed a party challenge at the state level as a threat to their dominance and control of federal patronage, left an opening for new leadership that wanted to challenge the Democrats at every level. Finally, *Baker* v. *Carr* provided impetus for party growth and resulted in substantial GOP gains in the reapportioned legislature. When Tennessee voted Republican in the 1952 presidential election for Dwight Eisenhower and again in 1956 (even though a native son, U.S. Senator Estes Kefauver, was on the Democratic ticket), perceptive observers understood that new Republican opportunities existed and political patterns frozen since the Civil War were breaking down.

In race-conscious West Tennessee, alienation at Democratic concern with racial equality was apparent when Memphis political boss Edward H. Crump joined the Dixiecrats in 1948. In addition to the social issue, growing affluence in the white suburbs was creating a political climate that made traditional Republican economic conservativism attractive to a developing middle and upper middle class.

Until the 1960s, Republicans controlled local government and the two congressional districts in the east, but they seldom made a serious effort at statewide office. During the heyday of Crump, who dominated Tennessee politics for more than two decades after coming to power in 1932, the Republican leadership participated in an "arrangement" under which the GOP fielded no serious challengers for statewide office. In return, GOP leaders received a share of patronage from Washington and maintained a limited, but safe, sphere of influence.

Crump dominated Tennessee politics for more than two decades. Memphis had "efficient government, a clean city, and other blessings, but all without freedom or liberty." [4] Retribution against political enemies was swift. Crump provided poll tax receipts for black voters, reportedly including many trucked in on election day from Mississippi and Arkansas, and provided paternalistic protection and a higher than usual level of public services in the black community. Those whose votes were controlled by Crump were by no means all black.

Statewide, Crump allied with one of two competing factions in each county. His ability to control a large majority of the Shelby County vote, combined with a split elsewhere, the low participation rate (about 300,000 of 1.6 million eligibles voted in the Democratic primary), and the voluntary self-exclusion of about 100,000 Republicans from meaningful political decision making through the Democratic Party, made Crump the dominant figure until his death in 1953. Through its usual control of the governor and the governor's dominance of the legislature, the Crump organization controlled patronage and the legislative process.

U.S. Senator Kenneth D. McKeller, who served 36 years in Washing-

4. Ibid., p. 63.

ton, was one who came under Crump's domination. McKeller was a patronage man who was proud that at one time he had more people on the federal payroll than any other member of Congress.

The case of Gordon Browning reflects Crump's control of Shelby County. Browning received 5,444 Shelby votes when he ran for the U.S. Senate in 1934. In 1936, in favor with Crump, Browning received 59,874 votes in Shelby County in a successful race for governor. Out of favor with Crump in 1938, Browning got only 9,315 Shelby votes when he ran again.

"I have said before, and I repeat it now," wrote Crump in an advertisement in 1948 that reflected his campaign style, "that in the art galleries of Paris there are twenty-seven pictures of Judas Iscariot—none look alike but all resemble Gordon Browning; that neither his head, heart nor hand can be trusted, that he would milk his neighbor's cow through a crack in the fence; that of the two hundred and six bones in his body there isn't one that is genuine; that his heart has beaten over two billion times without a sincere beat." Browning was again the opposition candidate for governor.

Crump was more temperate in speaking of Kefauver, then an anti-Crump challenger for the U.S. Senate. He likened Kefauver to a pet coon "that puts its foot in an open drawer in your room, but invariably turns its head while its foot is feeling around in the drawer. The coon hopes, through its cunning by turning its head, he will deceive any onlookers as to where his foot is and what it is into." The allegory introduced the campaign charge that Kefauver was in reality a "darling of the Communists" who was "desperately trying to cover up his very bad record." Kefauver put on a coonskin cap, honorable badge of the pioneer, and made political hay. He might be a pet coon, he conceded, but he was not Crump's pet coon.[5]

Under Tennessee election laws, which traditionally provided for no primary runoff, Kefauver won the nomination in 1948 with 42.2 percent of the vote, and Browning won by a majority. They won by 2–1 margins in the general election.

In 1952, the 82-year-old McKeller was defeated by populist Representative Albert Gore, and 32-year-old Frank Clement knocked off Browning for governor.

An oft cited story, perhaps apocryphal, is that after the 1952 election Clement and his campaign manager Buford Ellington paid a courtesy call on Crump, who reportedly told them, "If you two play it right, you can keep this going for 20 years." And indeed, for 18 years there was a "leapfrog" government, in which Clement and Ellington alternated in the governor's office. The other constitutional offices in Tennessee are

5. Ibid., p. 58.

elected by the legislature or the Supreme Court. As a result, there were no openings for new Democratic leadership to develop. As the governorship alternated between Clement and Ellington, the patronage-oriented Democratic Party operated as a stepchild out of their office.

For more than a decade, Kefauver, Gore, and Clement dominated Tennessee politics. They were a trio whose combined potential of personality, youth, and political talent was unmatched in the South in the 1950s, and perhaps in any state. All received consideration for a spot on the Democratic national ticket. By the end of 1970, the political careers of all three would be over.

Clement electrified the state when he first hit the political stump as a scripture-quoting, spellbinding orator. Clement rallies were more like evangelical crusades, and he would close speeches (which often ran an hour or more) by asking the audience to join hands and sing with him as a sound truck began his campaign theme song, "Precious Lord, Take My Hand." Governor Browning's comment in the 1952 campaign was, "I'm sure the Lord would like to, but Mister Crump has him by one hand and Daddy Clement has him by the other, and it's just a little difficult for the Lord to get very close to him." [6]

As governor, Clement hung a picture of Jesus in the governor's office. His political skills matched his religious fervor, and he exhibited some progressive tendencies. His administration produced reforms in mental health, provided free textbooks, and standardized methods of state purchasing. Although the Highway Department traditionally had been a source of patronage, a former associate says that in the last Clement administration, the governor refused pressure to rush contracts on interstate highways and insisted first on sound planning and engineering. Tennessee became one of the first states of its size to link all of its major cities by interstate highways. At Clinton, Clement became the first southern governor to mobilize the National Guard to preserve order in a racial crisis and to uphold a federal court order on school desegregation.

But Clement's career peaked when he keynoted the 1956 Democratic National Convention. Despite some good lines attacking the Eisenhower administration, his Tennessee stump style of oratory and repeated use of the line "How long, oh Lord, how long" came off as bombastic corn-pone to many of the delegates and to much of the country watching on television. New York sportswriter Red Smith, assigned to cover the convention, wrote as his lead, "The young governor of Tennessee, Frank G. Clement, slew the Republican party with the jawbone of an ass here last night. . . ."

6. David Halberstam, "The End of a Populist," *Harper's* (January 1971):38.

As a national political figure, Clement was finished. Although he served another term as governor, he was nominated with only 43 percent of the vote. His behavior became erratic, and there were problems with alcohol. After Kefauver's death, Clement lost the Democratic nomination for the U.S. Senate in 1964, halfway through his last term as governor. He won the nomination two years later, only to lose the general election. And two years after that, at age 50, with his wife suing for divorce, he drove his car across the center line and died in a head-on collision.

But the Clement legacy lives on. His oldest son Robert carried all 95 counties in the Democratic primary for a seat on the Public Service Commission in 1972 and attracted attention by challenging telephone rates. Another son, Frank, Jr., excited audiences with his oratory in 1974 in a few appearances as a 25-year-old campaign manager for one of the candidates for governor. His sister, Annabelle Clement O'Brien, won election to the legislature in 1974, beating an incumbent Republican in a GOP stronghold. Annabelle, as she is universally called, is a character out of a southern gothic novel, a tall, vivacious woman with country charm and one of the most politically astute minds in Tennessee. She served as an executive assistant for 18 years in the governor's office under both her brother and Buford Ellington. Her campaign style was to "get me some buttermilk and cheese and crackers in the morning and drive to the hollows and see folks."[7] The days of voting for the Clement clan appear far from over in Tennessee.

Ellington governed as a consolidator, rather than as an innovator, and he did almost nothing to build the Democratic Party organization during the years of Republican upsurge. Each of the major Democratic figures had his own personal following.

Unlike the governors, who basically represented the status quo, Kefauver put together a coalition supported by Negroes, labor, urban low-income whites, small farmers, and liberals generally. Kefauver was a man ahead of his time. As a member of the U.S. House of Representatives in the 1940s, he had written a book calling for an end to the seniority system. He understood the threat to the nation involved with the loss of personal liberties during the McCarthy era and was among the few who stood up to McCarthy. He battled McKeller to protect the Tennessee Valley Authority.

In 1950–1951 he helped expose in nationally televised hearings the role of organized crime, including the cozy relationships with the political structure in many of the nation's metropolitan cities. He and Gore both were deeply concerned about concentrations of wealth. In the 1950s, Kefauver was a consumer advocate; he investigated price fixing in drugs, steel, autos, and bread and exposed the dangers of monopoly control.

7. Interview with Annabelle Clement O'Brien, August 17, 1974.

In 1952 he violated the political protocol of the day by entering the New Hampshire presidential primary and defeating President Truman. Although he won 14 of 17 presidential primaries, he was denied the Democratic nomination; four years later, he was Adlai Stevenson's running mate. His biographer, Joseph Bruce Gorman, found in Kefauver "a very special quality, an attraction which won him the support of the mythical common man, who saw in Kefauver an honest, sincere and unique champion of ideals and values that seemed to be ignored or taken lightly by too many others in public life." [8]

Although he was an ambitious and socially enlightened Yale Law School graduate, Kefauver's image was that of the folksy campaigner in a coonskin cap, a style he adopted out of political necessity. In Tennessee, he was known as "old Estes." He had a style that excluded him from the social life of the more sophisticated circles in Washington and made him something of an outsider even in the liberal Kennedy administration.

With Gore, he refused to sign the 1956 Southern Manifesto, and he refused to compromise his liberal position on race. At home, in 1954 and 1960, he survived vicious campaigns heavy with racism and the message that he somehow was a Communist sympathizer because he believed in the United Nations. There were towns where people wouldn't shake his hand or escort him, but Kefauver survived with his patience, perseverance, and dignity and by speeches, whether in person or on radio and television, that gave people "credit for being interested in the twentieth-century world, for having intelligence." [9]

Halberstam relates a story from Kefauver's 1960 campaign against Tip Taylor, a conservative segregationist West Tennessee judge. Kefauver was in Washington voting, and Halberstam described the scene as the senator's campaign manager spoke for him in a hostile Middle Tennessee town:

> "I realize I'm a damn poor substitute for Estes Kefauver," he began, "but then so is Tip Taylor." Laughter. Heightened interest. "Now I'm just a country lawyer from Franklin, Tennessee, and my client is charged with voting for the 1957 Civil Rights Act, and I just want you to know that I'm here to plead him guilty. And I want you to know that if he hadn't voted for it, I wouldn't be here speaking for him." Those old farmers may not have known what the civil rights bill was, and they may have suspected that they didn't like it anyway, but they did know something about honesty and courage, and they began to cheer and applaud, and I never doubted from that day that Estes would win reelection, which he did, almost two-to-one.[10]

8. Joseph Bruce Gorman, *Kefauver: A Political Biography* (New York: Oxford University, 1971), p. vi (preface).

9. Wilma Dyckman, "Too Much Talent in Tennessee," *Harper's* (March 1955):51.

10. Halberstam, "End of a Populist," p. 38.

TWO-PARTY POLITICS

In 1963, Kefauver died at the age of 60, suspected of alcoholism and physically and emotionally drained from excessive political conflict just as he was accumulating the seniority that might have made him one of the giants in the Senate. By then, Tennessee had voted for three successive Republican presidential candidates, and reaction against the Democrats and a sense of alienation were setting in. Although it was not apparent at first, Kefauver's death marked the beginning of disintegration of the Tennessee Democrats.

Even more profound changes were taking place among Republicans, where the deaths of their two U.S. representatives, Carroll Reece in 1961 and Howard Baker, Sr. in 1964, left a leadership vacuum. Reece was a wealthy, articulate, effective Taft conservative grounded in the classical economics he once taught. An "arrangement" on federal patronage had been worked out between Reece and Kefauver, the senior senator. Despite the Republican gains in presidential voting, the GOP still made no serious challenges at the state level, because maintenance of the status quo allowed Reece to retain control of the party.

But insurgent movements were already developing in the cities, where new leadership was rising from those whose first political involvement came in the Eisenhower campaigns. William C. Carter, Jr. (known as "bald Bill" to differentiate him from William L. Carter, a beer distributor known as "beer Bill," after both were elected as Republican legislators from Hamilton County) recalls how he recruited William E. Brock III in 1956 to help run a poll watchers school. "Our biggest concern at that time was to get some sort of clean honest election," Carter said. Two years later, Brock won election to a top position with the Young Republicans. He and his friends attended leadership training schools conducted by the Republican National Committee and by 1962 had organized Hamilton County to the point of having a volunteer worker for every 100 voters in many precincts. It was a traditional, precinct-based voter identification and mobilization effort, following the steps outlined in a handbook prepared by the Republican Congressional Committee.

Brock, the heir to a candy manufacturing fortune and grandson of a onetime Democratic U.S. senator of the same name, was a logical GOP candidate for a congressional seat. When conservative Democratic incumbent James B. Frazier lost to liberal Wilkes Thrasher in a bitter primary in 1962, Republicans quietly encouraged support of the liberal challenger in order to improve Brock's chances. There is no registration by party in Tennessee, which makes such raiding quite legal. Brock then capitalized on the organizational base built by the Republicans and the support of Frazier's disappointed conservative Democratic supporters. A report that a $14,000 contribution from the state Democratic organization was made to Brock's headquarters gained wide currency.[11]

Brock won the election by 2,007 votes for a major Republican breakthrough—the first GOP congressman outside the traditional First and Second districts.

In 1964 there flowed into the Republican leadership vacuum a wave of Goldwater partisans centered in Memphis,

> prepared to exploit the older norms of white supremacy, laissez faire, antiunionism, and businessman Bourbonism. . . . Politically inexperienced, but deeply ideological and impatient with the supineness of the Old Guard, the New Guard proposed to bring to politics the hard sell, the grass roots drive, and the systematic organization which generated success in the business world. Their goal was the merging of the Democratic Party traditionalists, the West Tennessee planter belt, the white supremacists, the representatives of banking, finance, industry, and insurance, and ideological conservatives in general under the Republican banner.[12]

They controlled the state convention and sent Tennessee's first all-white delegation to the national convention, ignoring the plea by veteran black Republicans for inclusion.

Simultaneously, Howard Baker, Jr. emerged from East Tennessee as a candidate for the U.S. Senate. He was the heir of the traditional mountain wing of the party that his father had represented in Congress, but the younger Baker recognized the trend in presidential elections and was ready to lead a challenge to Democrats at the state level. Baker blended racial moderation and economic conservatism and attracted the anti-Goldwater elements of the party. Baker had more than the credentials he inherited from his father: Baker's father-in-law was Senate Minority Leader Everett Dirksen. Baker also shared the Kefauver attributes of a first-class intellect and personal honesty to go with his own boyish good looks and charm.

Goldwater became the first Republican since 1948 to lose Tennessee in a presidential election. Baker later recalled standing on a platform with Goldwater when he announced in Knoxville that he favored selling TVA. "I had an intense desire to sink into the dust, which I later did," Baker said.[13]

Meanwhile, Representative Ross Bass, a liberal whose voting record paralleled Kefauver's, had defeated Governor Clement in the Democratic primary for the nomination to fill the remaining two years of Kefauver's

11. Norman Parks, "Tennessee Politics Since Kefauver and Reece," *Journal of Politics* 28 (1966):150.
12. Ibid., p. 151.
13. Peirce, *The Border South States,* p. 306.

term. Although Bass later defeated Baker, 569,000 to 517,000, and Gore defeated conservative Republican Dan Kuykendall, 570,000 to 493,000, both of them ran behind Lyndon Johnson's 635,000–509,000 margin over Goldwater in the presidential vote. It was the first real challenge Republicans had made for the U.S. Senate this century, and the results showed they were competitive.

Two years later, Clement defeated Bass in the Democratic primary. Voting analysis supports the contention of liberal Democrats that Republicans, especially in Middle Tennessee, raided the primary to support Clement; votes by Bass on civil rights issues had alienated conservatives. The factional struggle in the Bass-Clement races further weakened the Democrats. Furthermore, Clement was no longer a fresh young face, and his personal problems had become political liabilities. Baker swept to a 100,000-vote victory over Clement and emerged as Tennessee's most popular Republican.

Also in 1966, Ellington won another term as governor without Republican opposition. He had won the primary against John Jay Hooker, a Nashville lawyer of uncommon ability who was compared in style and philosophy to his friends the Kennedys. Thus, support for liberal Democrats continued to dwindle. Ellington stayed out of the Senate race.

Brock and Baker view development of the Republican Party in Tennessee from different perspectives. Baker's view is one of building from the top down: "First one wins for President, then for the Senate, then for governor, and lastly adds more congressmen and comes close to winning the legislature." [14]

Brock believes that "the thing that is wrong with the Republican Party [in the South] is that it starts at the top." He recalls that in 1965 he sat down half a dozen friends and drew up a ten-year plan to "take over the state of Tennessee . . . We set up targets, the number of legislators by county, the number of state senators, the number of congressmen, and of course the governorship. We met all of those objectives on target, in fact were slightly ahead." [15]

He believes the Goldwater candidacy, by activating people who had never before been involved in politics, allowed Republicans to put together a cohesive network of people in West and Middle Tennessee that made Baker's 1966 campaign a runaway. Brock pointed out that he had already won the Chattanooga area congressional seat and that Republicans in Memphis were simultaneously building a strong organization. Dan Kuykendall ran a close Senate race in 1964 and won a Memphis area congressional seat in 1966, the same year Baker was elected.

In 1965, Brock was thinking of making a race for governor, and he

14. Ibid.
15. Interview with William Brock, February 1, 1974.

talked William C. Carter, Jr. into going to work full-time as organizer and then executive director of the Republican Party. The *Baker* v. *Carr* reapportionment order gave further impetus to the Republican effort. By 1966, Carter was directing a three-man staff in Nashville (plus three field men) and had developed a Republican organization in about 75 of the 95 counties, albeit with limited success in hard-core Democratic Middle Tennessee. The Republicans gained 16 seats in the state House of Representatives that year, giving them 41 of 99, and Kuykendall became the fourth Republican U.S. representative. Brock considered running for governor but backed out when former Governor Ellington entered the race.

For an attractive candidate like Howard Baker from East Tennessee, it was a case of the right man from the right place at the right time. That's the way the Brock wing of the Republican party sees it, and in part it explains the GOP factionalism centered around the two men. Many of the Brock people feel Baker never appreciated their organizational efforts, which many of them believe elected him.

In 1968 the Democratic falloff continued. George Wallace received 34 percent of the vote, a close second behind Richard Nixon's 38 percent and ahead of Hubert Humphrey's 28 percent. The protest against the national party continued in 1972 when Wallace swept a Democratic presidential primary with 68 percent of the vote.

The direction of the Tennessee voters seemed clear in 1970, and it wasn't the direction Albert Gore traveled. Gore was never a man to compromise principle.

It was Gore who had made a seven-hour speech in the Senate in the Eisenhower years that revealed the under-the-table Dixon-Yates scandal, an effort to force the TVA to buy power from private utilities to meet expanding demand. The clear intent was to create a precedent for reentry of the private utilities into the TVA market region. By the late 1960s, Gore was opposing the war in Vietnam, had voiced support for civil rights legislation, and had voted against the confirmation to the Supreme Court of Judges Clement F. Haynsworth and G. Harrold Carswell, whose rejections were proclaimed by Nixon as being based on an anti-South bias.

In Washington, Gore thought it enough that he voted his conscience and served as spokesman for the little man in pushing tax reform and supporting progressive social legislation—higher Social Security benefits, Medicare, Appalachia programs, the whole New Deal idea that government had a role in providing services to people, and the Great Society education, housing, and antipoverty programs. But he never developed a staff to serve his constituents' immediate problems. Patronage and political fence mending had come to bore him. The son of a dirt farmer,

Gore in his early campaigns played a fiddle in country towns, but he did not play the fiddle after he became a senator, and many of his admirers felt he had become too aloof.

A Memphis reporter once accompanied a regional spelling bee champion to Washington and joined the youth for lunch with Gore in the Senate dining room. Gore expressed admiration to the boy for his ability and confided, "I never was much good at spelling. For example, there are certain words I just have a real problem with, like 'pill.' I always wanted to spell it with one el." The reporter took notes and considered it a heartwarming story that would reveal an endearing human quality, but Gore took him aside and asked him please not to use the story. He got quite serious and said, "I just hate for anybody to know I can't spell. Please don't mention it."

In 1970, Gore received only 51 percent of the vote in the Democratic primary against Hudley Crockett, a television newscaster and former press secretary for Governor Ellington. Gore salvaged a majority only because he won over 63.9 percent support from East Tennessee Democrats; he trailed in all three congressional districts anchored in West Tennessee. Hooker won the Democratic nomination for governor with less than 45 percent of the vote. Neither Crockett nor Hooker's closest competitor, Stan Snodgrass, endorsed the winners of the primary, and Democratic unity was at an all-time low.

Hooker and his family had spent some $700,000 in the 1966 campaign, and he spent the next three years developing a fried chicken chain to compete with the Kentucky fried chicken of Colonel Harlan Sanders. Hooker had also branched into other business ventures. Many of Hooker's well-placed friends became wealthy by buying low and selling out when the Minnie Pearl Fried Chicken stock peaked.

But overexpansion and shoddy management created problems for the enterprise, the stock plummeted, and for Hooker and the Democrats the problems were greatly compounded when the Securities and Exchange Commission began an investigation whose timing could not have been better for the GOP. The traditionally Republican *Nashville Banner* carried story upon story about lawsuits and threatened lawsuits. As one Democrat put it, "The chicken feathers started flying, and that was it." The SEC investigation turned up no wrongdoing on the part of Hooker but did result in revised accounting procedures under SEC regulations.

Most Democrats in Tennessee will swear that the SEC action was politically timed to embarrass the Democratic Party leader and thus weakened Gore in his campaign against Brock. Vice-President Spiro Agnew proclaimed Gore the number-one target of the Nixon administration, and Gore responded by greeting Agnew at the airport when the vice-president came to Tennessee to attack him.

Halberstam, whose early years as a journalist were spent in Tennessee, gave this description of the Brock campaign:

> Though in debates and in personal confrontation and in his own speeches he stays away from the issues he has raised, this is in fact the most disreputable and scurrilous race I have ever covered in Tennessee. It is made all the more shabby by the fact that he injects this stuff into the atmosphere at one level and then acts the nice young man. His newspaper ads and television ads are hitting away daily at the most emotional issues they can touch. His media firm came down here a year and a half ago and found that the five most emotional issues were race, gun control, the war, busing, and prayer, and they are making this the campaign. Keep Gore answering false charges. It is not the old, sweaty, gallus-snapping racism that was once used against Claude Pepper: rather it is cool and modern. And while I have covered shabby racist campaigns in the past, there is something about this one which is distinctive. This is the first time that a campaign like this has been tied to the President, the Vice President, and the Attorney General of the United States.[16]

Gore fought back by citing Brock's votes in the House against Medicare and the Appalachia program. He solidified his support among blacks. Students and other volunteers were mobilized as Gore sought to organize the urban precincts, but the effort was late getting started and involved less than 70 precincts in Nashville, Knoxville, and Memphis. Subsequent analysis showed that the effort improved Gore's performance in those precincts between 2 and 5 percent.[17]

Before the Senate campaign, Gore wrote that the Nixon administration's "Southern Strategy" had placed him "in the eye of a storm, and from where I stand the gales and driving rains are both evident and destructive."[18] Actually, in the face of Brock's well-organized, well-financed campaign, the fact that Gore won 48 percent of the major party vote was rather remarkable.

In the governor's race, Republicans emerged with a moderate and attractive candidate in Winfield Dunn, who generated enthusiasm and a heavy turnout, particularly in his home area of Memphis. Dunn ran 13,000 votes ahead of Brock, winning 53 percent of the major party vote for governor.

Gore carried only four of the 21 West Tennessee counties, whose drift away from the Democrats began in 1948 when Strom Thurmond received 28.9 percent in West Tennessee, more than double his statewide average. Wallace in 1968 led in 17 of the West Tennessee counties in a three-way race for president, and he finished second in the other four.

16. Halberstam, "End of a Populist," p. 38.
17. David Price and Michael Lupfer, "Volunteers for Gore," *Journal of Politics* (May 1973):425–430.
18. Albert Gore, *The Eye of the Storm: A People's Politics for the Seventies* (New York: 1970), p. 189.

In 1972, West Tennessee Representative Ray Blanton, who had supported Wallace, received only 38 percent of the vote in a poorly-financial statewide Senate race against Baker and in West Tennessee trailed Gore's 1970 showing by 5 percent. Baker received a substantial minority of the black vote, which is concentrated in Memphis, both in reaction to Blanton and because Baker's vote for open housing legislation and his overall record reflected moderate attitudes on race.

Analysis of precinct returns in Memphis indicates that Republicans in statewide races made deep inroads among traditionally Democratic low- to moderate-income white voters and continued to receive strong support from upper-income whites. Blacks tended to vote almost solidly Democratic, and college students—many of them apparently reflecting upper-middle-class backgrounds—tended to vote Republican.

In Precinct 57, an upper income all-white area with average property value of $40,000, turnout was 79 percent in 1970, more than 15 percentage points higher than in any of the other precincts. Precinct 57 voters cast 80 percent of their votes for Baker in the 1966 Senate race, 78 percent for Richard Nixon (and only 9 percent for George Wallace) in 1968, 81 percent for Bill Brock in the 1972 Senate race, and 87 percent for losing GOP candidate Lamar Alexander for governor in 1974. In that year, partisan loyalty was demonstrated when 908 voters participated in the Republican primary, compared with 308 in the Democratic primary.

Working-class voters in Precincts 38–2, 52–2 and 52–3 (all 99 percent white neighborhoods with average property value of $15,000 and median educational attainment between 10.9 and 11.4 years) respectively voted 53 percent, 45 percent, and 73 percent for Wallace in 1968. Support for Baker ranged from 67 to 74 percent and for Brock from 64 to 72 percent. Both ran strongest in the precincts in which Wallace ran strongest. Alexander received 54 and 57 percent in the two precincts in which Wallace received a majority and 42 percent in Precinct 52–2, where Wallace received 45 percent. By a 2–1 margin, voters from these three precincts participated in the 1974 Democratic primary.

In Precinct 46–1, an area that contained a large number of college students, where property values averaged $15,000 but where voters had a median educational level of 14 years and voted on the campus of Memphis State University, Baker received 75 percent in 1966, Nixon 66 percent (and Wallace 16 percent) in 1968, Brock 67 percent, and Alexander 72 percent. More than 55 percent participated in the Republican primary in 1974.

In Precinct 35–2, 99 percent nonwhite and with an average property value of $10,000 and median educational level of 8.2 years, Baker received 3 percent, Nixon 1 percent (and Wallace 0.1 percent), Brock 1 percent, and Alexander 8 percent. Of 694 who voted in the 1974 primaries, only 5 participated with the Republicans.

DEMOCRATIC RESURGENCE

The resurgence of Tennessee Democrats in 1974 was more than a mere reaction to Watergate and the recession, and it is worth examining in some detail. Not only did they regain the governor's office, but they picked up 12 seats in the state House of Representatives, after holding a 50–49 margin, and added a Senate seat to increase their margin there to 20–12, with one independent. West Tennessee, despite its support for Republicans for national office, had continued to send rural conservative Democrats to the legislature, providing a bare Democratic majority.

The Tennessee Democrats traditionally had been divided into two roughly defined factions, with Crump and later Ellington basically representing traditional conservative business and planter interests and an insurgent faction that was more liberal and believed in an active role for government in providing services and regulating corporate influence. Kefauver and Gore emerged from that faction, and Clement managed to keep a foot in both camps. After a Republican administration took over the governor's office, the Democratic Party became virtually an abandoned child in the next two years. Because of its history of automatic general-election victories, combined with deep factionalism and conservative, courthouse-based leadership, the Democratic Party was the very antithesis of an efficient, effective, and disciplined organization.

Yet the Republican victories in 1970 and 1972 wiped out not only the established leadership of the Democratic Party but its factionalism as well. By 1974, the reality of being out of office for four years and facing a Republican Party that was better organized, better financed, and better disciplined unified the Democrats of Tennessee as never before. Leadership emanated from the speakers of the two houses of the legislature and from James Sasser, a young Nashville attorney and former Gore campaign aide who became party chairman in 1973. But there was no party headquarters, no staff, not even out-of-pocket expense money for the chairman. The only thing the Democratic Party could claim was a $65,000 debt.

In contrast, the Republicans ran a well-financed state headquarters that was the best in the South in recruiting candidates, providing research assistance, holding workshops on campaign and fundraising techniques, expanding its roll of dues-paying party members, sending out a party newspaper, building its cadre of dedicated workers, and strengthening county organizations.

House Speaker Ned McWherter and Lieutenant Governor John Wilder, who holds that position by virtue of his election by the Senate and its speaker, decided they had to act if the Democratic Party was going to survive. They began to impose party discipline, especially in the House.

They organized fundraising efforts and for the first time began an active recruitment of candidates, searching out people who had demonstrated ability and leadership potential in their communities.

McWherter, one of many Democrats who have become ambitious for higher office, made two trips across the state to help recruit quality Democratic candidates for the legislature, seeking out conservatives in rural areas and more liberal candidates in urban districts. "You've got to fit the candidates of our party to the kind of district they're running in," he said.[19] And he helped raise money that by 1975 enabled the Democrats to retire their entire party debt. With a Democrat in the governor's office, fundraising will no doubt become easier.

Although Democrats held bare majorities in the legislature in 1971, the concept of party discipline was not yet accepted in the Senate. When the Democratic caucus voted to elect a new comptroller, veteran incumbent William Snodgrass got solid Republican support and the defection of enough Democrats to win reelection. Although three veteran Senate Democrats who held committee chairmanships refused to support the caucus, Wilder took no punitive action, reappointing all three to their chairmanships. But when an effort was made to dump Wilder four years later, he stripped three chairmen of their assignments, warned Republicans against joining the Democratic insurgents, and survived with a tougher image.

A turning point came with the election of four new Democratic Supreme Court justices in the summer of 1974. A series of political blunders by Governor Dunn, a dentist whose approach to political matters was described by a Democratic state senator as "delightfully naïve," had resulted in a return to popular election of Supreme Court judgeships, but without provisions for a party primary.

Tennessee in 1970 had adopted a "modified Missouri plan" for appointing judges, in which the governor would select from three nominees chosen by a nonpartisan judicial review commission. Actually, no Supreme Court justices had been elected since 1910 because deaths or resignations always allowed the governor to fill a vacancy, but provision for election of Supreme Court judges remains in the state constitution. When a vacancy occurred, Dunn failed to make an appointment until after the constitutional filing deadline. For legal advice, Dunn had gone to the sitting chief justice, whose court would ultimately have to rule on the question, and the governor acted on that advice. Meanwhile, a Democratic candidate filed for the vacancy. When the legal issue became a widely publicized controversy, Dunn's nominee withdrew, and the legislature subsequently repealed the appointment procedure. By this time, three Supreme Court justices had indicated they planned to retire.

19. Interview with Ned McWherter, August 20, 1974.

The Democrats selected a broad-based nominating commission that included a law school dean and a former dean of another law school. The commission held publicized hearings in the state's major cities for potential candidates. They refused to renominate the incumbent chief justice, a onetime aide to Buford Ellington who had handled patronage and other matters in the governor's office and had gone to a YMCA law school at night. His appointment to the Supreme Court came from Ellington.

The Democratic Party not only came up with an impressive slate of four candidates with judicial experience, one an incumbent justice, and another who had been a president of the state bar, but they also helped finance the judges' campaign against a weak Republican ticket and swept to victory. The election was symbolically significant because it showed the Democrats were active as a party, that they picked good men, and that they were courageous in dumping the chief justice, an act that may have been unprecedented in any state.

As the first Republican governor elected in 50 years, Dunn proved to be a man of personal charm and honesty, as well as an effective campaigner. Although his father had served as a Democratic representative from Mississippi, Dunn had never held public office before he became governor. He put forward a progressive program that included a tax increase, development of a statewide kindergarten program, establishment of a housing authority to sell bonds to help finance housing for low- and middle-income families, took politics out of state police promotion practices, and pushed for prison decentralization. He hung a portrait of Abraham Lincoln in the governor's office.

But he proved inept in dealing with the legislature, including members of his own party, and his critics considered him naïve in his unquestioning trust of the business establishment. Not only did he lack political experience, but he also selected and usually listened to a staff with little political background or experience in government. As governor, he acquired a reputation for stubbornness and inflexibility.

As a result, Dunn ended up with a record number of vetoes overridden in his last year in office. His political ineptitude in handling the court situation not only cost him the opportunity to appoint a Republican majority to the Supreme Court but also cost Republicans the chance to select the next attorney general, an office filled in Tennessee by the Supreme Court. The attorney general also serves on the state Building Commission, a major source of patronage.

When a Veterans Administration–financed medical school was proposed for East Tennessee in the heart of safely entrenched Republican Jimmy Quillen's congressional district, Dunn yielded to opposition from the Memphis-based medical establishment and opposed the new school. Since the project was dear to Quillen and to the Republican-dominated

East, Democrats in the legislature made a deal, agreeing to support the second medical school in exchange for East Tennessee Republican support of the repeal action on court appointments and other measures.

The result was that Dunn both lost the right to appoint judges and failed to block the medical school. He also lost the leadership of his own party in the legislature which contributed to a decline in his image as an effective governor. In mid-1974, a statewide poll showed that although Dunn maintained a personally favorable image, especially high among older voters and regular churchgoers, his 54–33 approval rating showed a smaller favorable margin than either of the state's Republican senators. Howard Baker was the most popular political figure in the state, with a 64–15 rating; for Brock it was 50–20. When performance was measured, Dunn received a 43–51 rating, a majority unfavorable.

Nothing demonstrated better the leaderless nature of the Democratic Party than the 1974 primary for governor. A dozen candidates entered, and Blanton emerged as the nominee with only 22.7 percent of the vote. A few weeks after the primary, all the losing candidates joined Blanton at a unity luncheon and pledged him their support. Washington Butler, the only black in the race and a man whose ability impressed objective observers, volunteered, "I don't care who the candidate is, you're going to get more and better social programs with a Democratic administration." (Butler later was named to Blanton's cabinet.) The next day, former Senator Gore introduced Blanton at a statewide unity meeting of Democratic leaders. Jake Butcher and Franklin Haney, both wealthy young businessmen who each spent more than a million dollars in heavy media campaigns in the gubernatorial primary, actively supported Blanton, with Haney helping pay for several polls.

Blanton ran a methodical campaign sticking closely to bread-and-butter issues, playing heavily on the Democratic tide. He spoke out against higher interest rates and against Tennessee's fair trade laws that limited retail discount sales, and he made a populist pitch against banks and insurance companies. His polls showed that Lamar Alexander, a smoothly articulate lawyer who had managed campaigns for Dunn and Baker, was being hurt by the fact that he had worked for a while in the Nixon White House. Blanton took Democratic congressional candidates to Washington to meet with labor officials and later declared, "At least when I go to Washington I can see my friends; he [Alexander] has to go to the Lewistown prison" (where several former White House aides were serving Watergate-related sentences).

Blanton, who was viewed by progressives as a "redneck congressman from a redneck district" in his 1972 Senate race, met with black and labor leaders and made commitments that he lived up to after his election. Veteran Tennessee AFL–CIO President Matt Lynch, who had made a campaign contribution to Lamar Alexander in the Republican primary, later joined in a labor endorsement of Blanton. Lynch said later, "He doesn't make commitments until he understands an issue and has been thoroughly briefed, and his flexibility is a real strength."

Blanton campaigned with Democratic congressional candidates throughout the state, and he and black congressional candidate Harold Ford campaigned together in Memphis. Blanton learned that one no longer loses white votes by addressing the needs of the black community, and he helped Ford build the strength he needed in the white community to win in a district that was 40 percent black. Ford upset Kuykendall, and the Democrats picked up another congressional seat with the victory of Marilyn Lloyd, who replaced her husband on the ballot after he was killed in a plane crash. Her victory regained for Democrats the seat held by Republicans since Brock's first victory in 1962.

More than a decade of steady Republican gains in the legislature also ended in 1974. The GOP losses in Tennessee in part were attributed to a new reapportionment plan, drawn up by Democrats, that changed the boundaries of some urban districts to cluster Republican precincts together, thus shifting the balance toward the Democrats in marginal districts. For example, boundaries were redrawn in the Chattanooga area that resulted in one new district's containing the residences of three incumbent Republicans, two of whom were forced to move in order to run for reelection without facing an incumbent of their own party.

OUTLOOK

Whether 1974 was the beginning of a return to Democratic dominance or only a temporary setback for Republican development likely will depend on events outside the state's borders. A short-term test will be whether Brock can retain his Senate seat in 1976. The type of campaign he waged against Gore left deep bitterness among Democrats, and whoever is their nominee can expect unified party support. "Sort of the litmus test of whether you're a Democrat is whether you supported Bill Brock," Sasser explained, and "even some of the Democratic conservatives don't like Brock." [20]

Although rival Brock and Baker factions exist, it is clearly in neither's interest for their followers to become openly divided. The two senators have joint offices in a number of Tennessee cities, and Brock's home office workers give special emphasis to constituent service. "When someone calls about a problem with Social Security or veterans benefits and

20. Interview with James Sasser, August 21, 1974.

303

gets a return call the next day that action has been taken, the word gets around and people don't care about your voting record or anything else," an aide once explained.

A somewhat shy man who does not project the warmth of Baker, Brock has compiled a solidly conservative voting record in the Senate. But he has joined with a number of rather liberal Democratic newcomers in pushing for procedural reform in the Senate, and he refused to support President Ford's proposal to increase the price of food stamps during the 1975 recession. Bill Casteel, a political reporter for the *Chattanooga Times* who has followed Brock's career from the beginning, believes he has mellowed since going to the Senate and contends that Brock has developed a genuine sense of compassion for the unfortunate.

Brock himself has come to condemn the Republican Party in many areas in the South for having a "racial hangup. They either felt they had to outshop the Democrats on the racial issues, or at least take a similar stance, which I think is very short-sighted, and I think you are building your foundation on a footing of clay. Race is not the issue to build either a party or a state, and if the Republican Party has something to offer the state, it is in its ability to organize for economic growth, more jobs, more opportunity for some new ideas, more aggressive leadership. . . ." [21]

Nevertheless Brock remains stigmatized by judgments like that of the *Almanac of American Politics, 1974:* "probably more than any other sitting senator, [he] owes his place in the Senate to shrewd exploitation of racial fears and prejudices." [22]

In Tennessee, two-party competition has resulted in government that is more responsive, more open, and more reflective of a democratic republic. What Bill Brock says committed him to building a Republican Party was a vote fraud he witnessed when he first directed a GOP poll-watching effort in the 1950s, a situation that eventually resulted in statewide use of voting machines.

Although Tennessee does not approach Florida in government modernization, its legislature is the only other in the South that ranked in the nation's top half in the study by the Citizens Conference on State Legislatures.

It will take more elections to determine whether Tennessee will remain a genuinely competitive two-party state. But because of the strong Republican Party established on a historic base of strength, the future for two-party politics perhaps is brighter in Tennessee than anywhere else in the South.

21. Interview with William Brock, February 1, 1974.
22. Michael Barrone, Grant Ujifusa, and Douglas Matthews, *The Almanac of American Politics, 1974* (New York: E. P. Dutton, 1973), p. 938.

Chapter

13

TEXAS

Still the Politics of Economics

> Texas is the happy hunting ground of
> predatory wealth.
> —former Senator Ralph Yarborough [1]

TEXAS is different from the other states of the old Confederacy. The cultural blend of the South and the West, the presence of two substantial minority population groups, the prolonged frontier period, the massive deposits of oil and natural gas, the dramatic rate of urbanization in recent decades, and the massive size of the state (801 miles from north to south and 773 miles east to west—greater than the distance from Washington to Birmingham, New York to Chicago, or San Francisco to Phoenix) all combine to make Texas unique.

Historian Lawrence Goodwyn, a onetime participant-observer in Texas politics, has suggested that the unpredictable behavior of Texans results in part from an identity crisis, a cultural clash between the optimistic tradition of the expansive frontier as "a land of promise and possibility" and the pessimism of the South that grows out of "a sense of thwarted intentions and tragic history." [2]

Beginning with the leadership of Sam Houston during and after the days of the Texas Republic, a brand of liberalism has repeatedly manifested itself in the political life of the state. It peaked first in the Farmers

---

1. Interview with Ralph Yarborough, December 10, 1974.
2. Lawrence Goodwyn, *The South Central States* (New York: Time-Life Books, 1967), pp. 140, 142.

Alliance movement, which originated in Texas and became the basis for the People's Party in the 1890s, the high point of Populism in America. In every generation since, there has been at least one political figure to keep that spirit alive. Another peak came in support of the New Deal in the 1930s.

Nationally, the greatest impact came in the 1960s, with the Great Society programs of President Lyndon B. Johnson, a very shrewd, able, complex, and calculating politician who cut his political teeth under the New Deal of the 1930s and wanted to "out-Roosevelt Roosevelt." Texas also provided Johnson with the tradition of the Alamo and the legacy of the Jacksonian frontier spirit that respected physical combat when challenged, a cultural environment which helped shape his attitude toward the war in Vietnam that led to his political downfall.

It was the southern rather than the western heritage that gave Johnson his insights into the significance of the Civil Rights Act of 1964 and Voting Rights Act of 1965, two landmarks of his presidency. Although only one Texan in eight is black (the Mexican-American population is 18%, or slightly more than one in six), racial attitudes were shaped by the experience shared with other southern states in the Civil War and Reconstruction. It includes the legacy of legal racial segregation and oppression (551 lynchings were recorded in east Texas—where virtually all blacks in the state resided—between 1882 and 1943, compared with 596 in Mississippi and 571 in Georgia[3]), a restricted suffrage to keep blacks from participating in politics, and a tradition of one-party politics. It was a Texas case, *Smith* v. *Allwright*, in which the Supreme Court in 1944 held the white primary unconstitutional, opening the way for black political participation throughout the South, a central force in the region's political transformation during the next three decades.

Within the state, political disagreement over economic issues, beginning in the New Deal, had developed sufficiently for V. O. Key to note in 1948 that "the terms 'liberal' and 'conservative' have real meaning in the Democratic politics of Texas." They continue to have meaning. Although personalities dominate discussion of recent Texas politics, they symbolize the continued clash of relevant philosophical differences about the role of government, the services it provides, and who pays for those services.

3. Melvin J. Banks, "The Pursuit of Equality," quoted in Chandler Davidson, *Biracial Politics* (Baton Rouge: Louisiana State University Press, 1972), p. 15.

STATE OF THE STATE

Although Texas is unique in the South in having a sizable liberal movement with historical continuity, the dominant forces are conservative.
There has been no liberal governor since the 1930s, and the conservatives
have dominated Texas politics since World War II. Key found a class
that had built huge fortunes from oil, men "imbued with faith in individual self-reliance and unschooled in social responsibilities of wealth." [4] Neal
Peirce, an authority on all 50 states in the 1970s, wrote, "With few exceptions, the essential power in Texas has remained in the hands of an im-
mense oil-insurance-banking-construction axis so close to the ruling
political circles that the two have seemed virtually indistinguishable." [5]

But the dominance of the moneyed establishment has begun to
wane. The lifting of legal restraints designed to reduce political participation—barriers such as the poll tax and annual voter registration—have
increased political participation and stimulated a growing sense of political awareness among blacks and Mexican-Americans. Reapportionment
and creation of single-member legislative districts expanded opportunities in the 1970s for the election of minorities—blacks, Mexican-Americans, and Republicans. The Sharpstown Bank scandal in 1971 triggered a
wave of procedural reform and provoked at least a temporary revolt by
the voters, who elected a new group of state officials with an unaccus-
tomed willingness to confront long-neglected state issues. But the defeat
of U.S. Senator Ralph Yarborough in 1970 by Lloyd Bentsen removed
from public office the individual who for almost two decades personified
political liberalism in Texas and left the liberal movement at least temporarily without a recognized statewide leader. Bentsen, a man of considerable ability who grew up wealthy and developed a personal fortune
of his own, subsequently emerged as the dominant political personality
in Texas in the 1970s.

Ronnie Dugger, perceptive publisher of the *Texas Observer*, a twice-
monthly liberal journal whose investigative reporting since 1954 has
achieved national recognition, summarized the changes in the state since
the mid-1950s: "There has been subtle acceptance of the progressive environment, the change of milieu, the cultural change. There has been a
subtle change forward. I wouldn't say leftward. There has been a subtle
moderation of the harsh themes of the right. For example, 20 years ago,
federal aid to education was unthinkable; now it is accepted. Sympathy

4. V. O. Key, *Southern Politics in State and Nation* (New York: Vintage, 1949),
p. 255.
5. Neal Peirce, *The Great Plains States of America* (New York: W. W. Norton,
1973), p. 284.

for the poor was unthinkable, thought of as Communist, and now it is acceptable. Blacks have been integrated in most ostensible aspects; that was unthinkable 20 years ago. Generally, the state has moved with the country somewhat toward civility. But fundamentally, it has not changed; fundamentally, it is still governed by the principle of corporate interest."[6]

Key wrote that "the Lone Star State is concerned about money and how to make it, about oil and sulfur and gas, about cattle and dust storms and irrigation, about cotton and banking and Mexicans."[7] A contemporary study adds:

> These concerns doubtlessly continue, but as Texans crowd into the big cities such issues may well play a secondary role. Primary attention is shifting to the difficulties arising from the concentration of many people with radically different backgrounds into very limited, technologically developed, amounts of space. Problems of air and water pollution have assumed great importance because the cities produce more waste, refuse, and pollutants than they can dispose of easily. Problems of transportation, housing, and schools are taking on a different and more serious complexion. Perhaps even more important are the myriad problems associated with the existence, in the heart of the great urban centers, of poor black and Mexican-American minorities surrounded by affluent suburban whites.[8]

Texas ranks fourth in the nation in population and by 1980 will move ahead of Pennsylvania for third place behind New York and California. The 1970 census showed Texas 79.7 percent urban compared with 82.9 percent rural in 1900. Sixteen of the state's 24 Standard Metropolitan Statistical Areas contain more than 100,000 population, and Houston and Dallas are among the nation's ten largest cities. Two-thirds of the population resides in a triangle with the northern point just above the Dallas–Fort Worth urban complex, then descending in 300-mile legs of interstate highway southeast to Houston and southwest through Austin to San Antonio. A 200-mile east-west interstate highway connects the bottom corners.

Of the state's 254 counties, 146 lost population in the 1960s. In 1960 the 221 Texas counties with fewer than 50,000 people cast 33 percent of the state's votes; in 1972 they cast only 26 percent. Meanwhile, metropolitan areas of the big cities—Houston, Dallas, Fort Worth, and San Antonio—increased their share of the statewide vote from 36 percent in 1960 to 43 percent in 1972. The total vote in those 12 years increased from 2.2 million to 3.4 million.

Although the office of governor allows an individual with sufficient political astuteness, sense of timing, strength of personality, and other

6. Interview with Ronnie Dugger, December 11, 1974.
7. Key, *Southern Politics*, p. 254.
8. James Anderson, Richard Murray, and Edward Farley, *Texas Politics*, 2nd ed. (New York: Harper and Row, 1975), p. 28.

attributes to exert considerable influence in shaping policy, the office of governor in Texas institutionally is one of the weakest in the nation and by far the weakest for any of the largest states. More than 200 boards and commissions select agency and department heads, and the governor's authority to appoint board members is limited by overlapping six-year terms. The weakness of the office makes it difficult for Republicans to recruit really first-rate candidates, who realize that even if elected they would have limited authority to act and that Democrats would retain policy control through legislative dominance.

Although the governor develops a state budget, the budget that counts is the one prepared by the Legislative Budget Board. The story is told that when John Connally was governor, the chairman of the Senate Finance Committee remarked to him that his budget had received more consideration than that of any other governor.

"Fine," the governor is reported to have replied. "What did you think of it?"

"Oh, I didn't read it," the chairman answered. "I just used it as a doorstop."

The chairman of the Legislative Budget Board is the lieutenant governor, an office in which Texas concentrates more power than does any other state. The lieutenant governor controls the appointment of four of the other nine Budget Board members and he directs a large full-time staff. In addition to his direction of the budget, he appoints all committees and committee chairmen in the Senate, assigns bills, controls the flow of legislation, and decides who has the floor during debate. Although the governor has a line-item veto over the state appropriations bill, Lieutenant Governor William P. Hobby explained that "if it's something you think the governor might veto, you just lump it into a single appropriation of say $20 million for administration of the University of Texas." [9]

Candidates for governor and lieutenant governor do not run as a team in Texas, but if two able, like-minded progressives were to ally as candidates and win election with a well-defined program, it could accelerate the reform movement in the state.

DEMOCRATIC BACKGROUND

In 1952 a judge with populist inclinations decided to run for attorney general of Texas, declaring his intentions at a chance meeting with

9. Interview with William Hobby, December 17, 1974.

Governor Allan Shivers. The judge was Ralph Yarborough, and Shivers told him, "Ralph, we've got a man picked. You stay out of that race."

The arrogance of the remark and unavailability of funds for an insurgent candidate for attorney general stung Yarborough into running instead for governor against Shivers in the Democratic primary. Shivers won narrowly, and the same year he led most of the official Democratic hierarchy into public support of Republican presidential nominee Dwight Eisenhower, a native Texan and personal friend of Shivers from their service together in World War II.

The events of that year launched a bitter struggle within the Democratic Party that shaped the next two decades of Texas politics. Shivers became leader of the so-called Tory Democrats, a loose conservative coalition whose domination of state government diminished only after the Sharpstown Bank scandal in 1971. He later became president of the U.S. Chamber of Commerce and, as head of a major bank in Austin, remains quietly influential in Texas political matters.

Leadership of the conservative Democrats shifted in the 1960s to John Connally, like Shivers a dynamic personality who served three two-year terms as governor. Connally returned home after serving as secretary of the navy in the Kennedy administration. Lyndon Johnson, who in the Senate had trimmed his New Deal instincts, maintained close ties to the state's moneyed establishment and developed his own personal fortune. But he was a consensus politician who kept a leg in the liberal camp and never deviated on issues of Democratic Party loyalty. Although Johnson was actively involved in matters of political strategy at home and intervened in matters that affected his interests in Washington, he never activated his personal organization on behalf of other candidates, and he did not attempt to exert direct influence on questions of internal public policy within the state.

Like the conservatives, liberal Democrats in Texas basically are a loose coalition, but since 1950 they have tended to coalesce on issues involving racial moderation, support of the national party and its presidential nominees, expansion of state government in providing social services, shift of the tax burden from consumers, and opposition to domination by "special interests." The labels "liberal" and "conservative" are broad umbrella classifications, of course, and one might be "liberal" on race and "conservative" on economic issues, or vice versa. In the cities, how one voted on Ralph Yarborough was one means of dividing liberals and conservatives, but Yarborough's East Texas rustic image, slashing campaign style against "the interests," and his known abstinence from alcohol also made him popular with rural conservatives.

In 1954, Yarborough again challenged Shivers. As described two decades later by historian Goodwyn, "in terms of money spent, chicanery, corruption, demagoguery, and rhetorical violence, it was the nearest thing to a class struggle that the state has endured since Populism and

Reconstruction." Yarborough had the support of organized labor, and the central legend to emerge was the filming and distribution by the Shivers forces of what came to be known as the "Port Arthur Story." At the climax of the campaign, television screens across Texas projected a dramatic documentary that began in utter silence, with long seconds of panoramic sweeps of what seemed to be a deserted city. According to the legend, it took several days for film crews to gather the necessary footage of empty streets because of passing bread trucks and other early morning activity. A strike of retail clerks was in progress that summer in Port Arthur, and after 60 seconds or so of eerie silence, a narrator suddenly intoned, "This is Port Arthur, Texas. This is what happens when the CIO comes to a Texas city." [10]

Shivers won by a narrow margin, and the aftermath included the founding of the *Texas Observer,* a muckraking journal that has produced a list of nationally known writers, including Robert Sherrill, Willie Morris, Larry McMurtry, Bill Brammer, and Larry King, as well as historian Goodwyn. More importantly, the steady disclosure of unseemly conduct during the next two decades helped spur more aggressive reporting by the establishment press, served as a deterrent to unsavory political activities, and raised relevant political issues that might otherwise have remained submerged. Although its circulation never exceeded a few thousand, the paper remains well read within the inner world of Texas politics.

In 1956, Yarborough lost by 3,000 votes to Price Daniel, who was brought home from the U.S. Senate by the state's conservative establishment to run for governor. Yarborough maintained that the election was "stolen," a practice not unknown in Texas politics, and he subsequently won a special election for the Senate seat vacated by Daniel. A New Deal supporter as a young man, Yarborough denounced racism and advocated a liberal economic philosophy. In the Senate he voted for every civil rights measure, fathered the cold war G.I. Bill, backed measures designed to benefit organized labor, the small businessman, and the small farmer, and saved Padre Island as a national seashore. Despite his liberal position on race, Yarborough consistently ran well in low-income white precincts in the cities.

Yarborough also had a self-righteous quality that manifested itself in gratuitous, personal attacks on political opponents. When John Connally decided to retire without seeking a fourth two-year term as governor in 1968, Yarborough said Connally had seen "the handwriting on the wall" and that he had been popular "only because he was shot with President Kennedy."

It was the feud between Governor Connally and Senator Yarborough

10. Lawrence Goodwyn, paper delivered in November 1974 before the Southern Historical Association and published in 20th anniversary edition of the *Texas Observer* "Dugger's Observer," December 27, 1974, p. 5.

and their respective factions that had prompted Vice-President Lyndon Johnson to persuade President John F. Kennedy to come to Texas in November 1963 in an effort to unify the Democratic Party, the trip on which Kennedy was assassinated in Dallas. Johnson became president, and Connally achieved a level of political invulnerability. The wounding of Connally destroyed any chance for a major liberal breakthrough in state politics. He had narrowly defeated liberal Don Yarborough—no relation to Ralph—in the 1962 governor's race. In a 1964 rematch, Connally won easily.

Connally avoided racial rhetoric in campaigning, and in seeking re-election in 1964 he described his fundamental goal as an improvement in the state's educational system so that more Texans might "share in the economic fruits of the technological space age." Although Connally's efforts to strengthen funding of higher education were viewed as progressive, he had the support of moneyed interests who realized that a weak university system would hamper economic development. The improved system was financed by doubling the sales tax, thus placing the burden on those least able to pay in a state that has no corporate or personal income tax.

When the poll tax—a deterrent to voting by poor blacks, poor Mexican-Americans, and poor whites—was declared illegal, the conservatives won a battle to require annual registration, with a January 31 deadline that fell three months before the state primaries and at least nine months before the November elections. The objective, of course, was to keep the electorate small, and the Connally faction succeeded in getting early annual registration into the state constitution. But the registration system was successfully challenged in the courts, and since 1972 prospective voters have been able to register up to 30 days before an election. Registration is good for two years, and voting in an election automatically extends one's registration for another two years.

In 1964, Johnson personally intervened to dissuade Representative Joe Kilgore from offering a major conservative challenge to Yarborough in the Democratic primary. Those close to Johnson agree he was motivated in part by an expressed desire to avoid disunity in the Texas Democratic Party during his presidential campaign, but he was also influenced by his desire to "out-Roosevelt Roosevelt" in innovative domestic social legislation. Johnson knew that the hardworking Yarborough, as a key member of the Senate Labor and Public Welfare Committee and a champion of an increased federal role in health, education, and other fields, would prove a valuable ally in helping shape Great Society programs. Eighty percent of that legislation went through Yarborough's committee.

Although Johnson discouraged opposition to Yarborough again in 1970, he was no longer president, and his old ally Connally encouraged Bentsen to make the race and led efforts to raise ample funds. It was a bitter and vicious campaign. No longer a supporter of the war in Vietnam, Yarborough had become an outspoken critic and had supported a call for a peaceful "moratorium" against the war. In a tactic reminiscent of the "Port Arthur story," Bentsen throughout the spring of 1970 ran television film clips of the riots outside the 1968 Democratic National Convention in Chicago, implying that Yarborough somehow was responsible for these and other violent acts of civil disobedience that involved antiwar militants.

Yarborough, as usual, was poorly financed, and Bentsen had what seemed—even by Texas standards—to be an unlimited supply of money. Yarborough diligently attended to his Senate business, let his organization slip, and perhaps lost touch with his constituency. Bentsen won the primary with 54 percent of the vote. In 1972, Yarborough ran unsuccessfully for the Democratic nomination to oppose Republican Senator John Tower, a race that apparently ended Yarborough's political career.

Bentsen's ability to speak fluent Spanish and to use money effectively helped him win many Mexican-American votes against Yarborough, thus cutting into part of the liberal coalition. Bentsen then shifted to the center, made peace with the labor, Mexican-American, and black leaders who had supported Yarborough, and won in the fall by a 53–47 margin against Republican George Bush, one of the most attractive candidates the GOP in Texas has been able to offer.

In the Senate, Bentsen developed a moderate voting record and quickly established himself as an ambitious and skillful political pragmatist with unusual ability as a problem solver, a man knowledgeable in modern management techniques, with a first-rate mind and the willingness, discipline, and capacity for hard work. At home, his efforts to achieve good relations with all segments of the Democratic Party have been relatively successful, despite the continued bitterness of Yarborough and some of his supporters and a general attitude of distrust among liberals, who view him as a man who has little feeling for people and is too much a part of the moneyed establishment.

A bill passed by the 1975 legislature to establish a 1976 presidential primary designed to maximize Bentsen's chances to win delegates was headlined by the *Texas Observer* as "L.B. Jr.'s bill." When compared with Lyndon Johnson, Bentsen is viewed at home as more urbane and perhaps less compassionate, and he differs from Johnson in that Bentsen never experienced economic hardship as a youth. His inner circle includes the brother of Robert Strauss, the Texan whose chairmanship of the Democratic National Committee led the party toward the center after the McGovern disaster of 1972.

THE SHARPSTOWN BANK SCANDAL
AND DEMOCRATIC PROSPECTS

With pressure for change already building through such forces as legislative reapportionment and the removal of barriers to political participation by the poor, the event that ushered in a new era in Texas politics was the Sharpstown Bank scandal. It involved public revelations of
the influence over state affairs by special interests, touched off a wave
of legislative reform, destroyed or crippled several political careers, reduced the influence of "the lobby," spawned progressive new leadership
in the state, and created a political atmosphere in which such substantive
issues as a new state constitution, equalization of school financing, and
consumer and environmental protection could be dealt with.

In brief, the Sharpstown Bank scandal centered on efforts by Frank
Sharp, a wealthy and influential Houston banker and developer, to get
special legislation passed to establish a state equivalent of the Federal
Deposit Insurance Corporation (FDIC). The measure would have allowed his financially troubled Sharpstown State Bank to escape federal
regulation.

In July 1969, Sharp met in a hotel suite with state House of Representatives Speaker Gus Mutscher. After discussion of the proposed
legislation and a comment by Mutscher that he had lost money on a
stock investment with a Sharp-controlled company, Sharp suggested that
the loss might be recovered by investment in stock of another Sharp-
controlled company, the National Bankers Life Insurance Co. Subsequently, Mutscher invested $130,000 borrowed with Sharp's approval
from the Sharpstown Bank. The loan was secured only by the insurance
stock. Similar loans and purchases were made by Governor Preston
Smith, aides and relatives of Mutscher, and certain key legislators. After
two months they sold their stock at inflated prices arranged by Sharp,
resulting in apparent profits of $125,000 for Governor Smith and his
partner, state Democratic Executive Committee Chairman Elmer Baum,
$70,000 for Mutscher, and lesser amounts for others. The transactions
occurred while a special session of the legislature approved the two bills
sought by Sharp. Governor Smith vetoed the bills after objections from
other banks and the intervention of former Governor Shivers, who had
become head of a major bank in Austin.

After the transactions were disclosed, Sharp made a deal with the
Republican federal prosecutors, who allowed him to plead guilty to two
minor charges and receive a probated sentence in return for testifying
against Democratic officials involved in the scheme. Among the casualties was Lieutenant Governor Ben Barnes, who although never con-

nected directly with the bribery conspiracy, had on other occasions borrowed money from another Sharp-controlled bank for profitable investments and whose name was mentioned repeatedly in testimony. The Barnes-dominated Senate had given expeditious treatment in passing Sharp's bills. A protégé of both Lyndon Johnson and John Connally, Barnes had been elected House speaker at 26 and lieutenant governor at 29. Johnson had proclaimed him a potential future president, and he was heir apparent to Democratic leadership in the state.

A *Wall Street Journal* reporter wrote in 1969 of Barnes, "He's the hottest property in Texas politics and political observers wonder whether he's 'another LBJ.' . . . Here, where the liberal and conservative wings of the dominant Democratic Party still wage bitter, unrelenting warfare, Mr. Barnes currently enjoys support from both groups." [11] The *Texas Observer* had concluded in 1968 that Barnes had become, "perhaps in ways Lyndon Johnson never did, in Texas, the consummate consensus politician." But even before the first hint of the Sharpstown scandal, Barnes had made a major political blunder when he supported removal of the sales tax exemption on food in 1969. He directed passage of the bill through the Senate, winning by one vote, but a filibuster led by Senator Oscar Mauzy of Dallas, one of the most effective liberals in the legislature, allowed time for public reaction to mobilize. Opposition was so strong that the House voted unanimously against the food tax. Barnes was a hardworking young man of unquestioned ability, astute in both a political and business sense, and he had developed a degree of personal wealth through good credit, judicious investments, and an able business partner. The association with the Sharpstown Bank raised questions in the public mind as to whether his quick accumulation of wealth had resulted from the inside information that might accrue only to a man of his political prominence. His image tainted, Barnes ran a weak third in the Democratic gubernatorial primary for governor in 1972.

Another casualty in the Sharpstown fallout was Waggoner Carr, a conservative Democrat who after two terms as speaker of the House was elected attorney general—traditionally a stepping-stone position in Texas politics. When liberal Democrats deserted him in a 1966 U.S. Senate race, he lost by almost 200,000 votes to Republican incumbent John Tower. Carr later became president of National Bankers Life Insurance Co., the Sharp-controlled firm involved in the stock manipulation. He eventually was exonerated by a jury, but the cloud of scandal apparently ended his political career as well as Barnes's.

The Texas scandals developed from investigations by the Securities and Exchange Commission during the Nixon administration, and close associates of Barnes and Carr believe the agency was motivated politically—specifically, to remove potentially strong opposition to Senator

11. Quoted in Jimmy Banks, *Money, Marbles and Chalk* (Austin: Texas Publishing Co., 1971), p. 216.

Tower—a charge Texas Republicans vehemently deny. John Osorio, a former state insurance commissioner and later National Bankers Life president who was convicted in January 1973 on federal charges involving embezzlement of NBL pension funds for the purpose of manipulating stock prices, claimed after his conviction that the government obtained indictments against him only after he refused to say he had "bought off" Barnes in connection with the 1969 bank bills. The Texas disclosures by the SEC followed less than a year after the same agency apparently leaked information involving Tennessee Democratic gubernatorial nominee John J. Hooker (see Chapter 12).

Whatever the motivation, the result in Texas was that the Sharpstown revelations put into clear focus the domination by organized special interests of public policymaking and aroused a public outcry against corruption.

During the months in which the Sharpstown scandal was unfolding, while Mutscher (who was eventually convicted on charges of bribery and given a suspended sentence) was denying guilt, the issue was kept alive by a legislative coalition of Democratic liberals and a handful of Republicans, known collectively as the "Dirty Thirty." The name came from a scornful lobbyist after Mutscher's defenders defeated by a vote of 118–30 a resolution by Representative Frances Farenthold that proposed creation of a joint Senate-House committee to investigate fully the involvement of public officials in the stock scandal. That was in March 1971. Later, as the evolving scandal generated reform, the "Dirty Thirty" label became a badge of honor, and one of the 30, Price Daniel, Jr.—son of the former governor and U.S. senator who became a state Supreme Court justice—succeeded Mutscher as House speaker. (During his term, the 1973 legislature passed procedural reforms in campaign reporting, strong ethics legislation, laws requiring public access to meetings and to records of public agencies, and tough restrictions on lobbyists.)

In the fall of 1971, a Travis County (Austin) grand jury returned indictments against Mutscher, one of his aides, and Speaker Pro Tempore Tommy Shannon. The grand jury report declared, "Some Texas lawmakers . . . were too busy granting political favors and being influenced in exchange for 'turning a fast buck' to be concerned about good government for the people. There is dire need of reform so that good laws for the protection and well-being of our citizens might be passed."

Former colleagues report that although Barnes was receptive to the wishes of "the lobby," he remained in control and "knew when to sit down on them," but that Mutscher fell under their domination. "When you came to Mutscher to discuss a matter, he would say, 'I wonder what the third house would think,'" one former representative recalled. "That's how he referred to them." [12]

12. Interview with Land Commissioner Robert Armstrong, December 10, 1974.

"The lobby" is a term widely used in Texas and it includes collectively the lobbyists for the railroads, the chemicals, the Texas Manufacturers Association, the oil "majors"—Exxon, Mobil, Texaco, Arco, and Gulf—the Texas Independent Producers, the Texas Mid-Continent Oil and Producers Association, the home builders, the beer distributors, and others. Fallout from the Sharpstown scandal sent "the lobby" into mild retreat, and the old days of "booze and broads" lobbying have virtually ended. "What they do now is work to elect people who think like they do," commented several lobby watchers. Basically, the lobby promotes "conservatism," meaning probusiness positions opposing corporate taxes and social programs that would involve increased spending.

In 1972, "Sissy" Farenthold—a Vassar graduate, lawyer and key member of the "Dirty Thirty"—ran for governor as a liberal reformer and aroused statewide response with her calmly delivered attacks on special interests and their influence. Discredited Governor Smith received only 9 percent of the vote to finish fourth in the Democratic primary, and the tarnished Barnes received only 18 percent. Multimillionaire rancher-banker Dolph Briscoe, the largest individual landowner in Texas, emerged as the conservative front runner with 44 percent, and the liberal Farenthold was second with 28 percent.

Briscoe had run for governor in 1968 and had served in the legislature in the 1950s, where he at times opposed the tight fiscal policy of Shivers. His 165,000-acre Catarina ranch—part of his million-acre ranching empire—for years had served as a gathering place for the state's top Democratic politicians to hunt, fish, and plan political strategy.

In the 1972 runoff, Briscoe and Farenthold both ran as "reform" candidates. Briscoe's campaign was directed by the ubiquitous DeLoss Walker of Memphis. One Briscoe television spot flashed pictures of such Texas symbols as the Alamo, then focused on a shot of the state capitol while an announcer's voice said, "Texas has many things to be proud of—but state government is not one of them." Briscoe refused to debate Farenthold and seldom commented on the issues, and she described him as "a bowl of pablum."

Farenthold surprised most observers by finishing with 45 percent of the vote in the runoff. It was quite a showing for an urbane, Catholic feminist who advocated easing of abortion laws. She also favored abolition of the Texas Rangers, symbols of the western frontier heritage whose activities in south Texas had aroused antagonism among Mexican-Americans, especially aggressive younger Chicanos developing a sense of ethnic pride. However, she failed to hold Yarborough's rural followers. Compared with the 44.8 percent Yarborough received in his 1970 Senate race from voters in the 188 counties with populations below 25,000, Farenthold got only 32 percent. She received 52.2 percent in the eight counties with more than 200,000 population, counties that collectively cast slightly more than half of the total statewide vote.

In the general election, the heavily favored Briscoe won by 100,000 votes against ultraconservative state Senator Henry Grover. Briscoe won with only a plurality, as La Raza Unida candidate Ramsey Muniz attracted more than 200,000 votes. They came mostly from chicanos, but analysis showed that more than a third of his vote came from disaffected liberals.

The 1972 governor's race reveals much about Texas voting patterns. A clear pattern emerges of conservative voters who consistently vote for the most conservative Democrat in the May primary, then vote against him in the fall for a more conservative Republican. Meanwhile, liberal Democrats tend to back their party winner in the fall, after opposing him in the spring.

Professor Richard Murray has demonstrated clearly how precincts in Dallas and Houston that went strongly for Briscoe in the Democratic primary shifted away from him in the general election. In precincts that voted for Farenthold in the runoff, the shift in November was to Briscoe. Houston Precinct 164, a black area, gave Briscoe 4.7 percent of the vote in the runoff against Farenthold and 92 percent in the general election against Grover. Houston Precinct 129, a white upper-class area, voted 73.1 percent for Briscoe against Farenthold, but only 23 percent for him against Grover.

In the few nonurban areas of Republican strength—the Panhandle, the Permian Basin, and the hill country around San Antonio (populated by descendants of pre-Civil War German immigrants) conservatives traditionally run well in Democratic primaries. Republicans then carry these areas in November.[13]

Perhaps the most significant defeat in 1972 was that of John Connally's brother Wayne for lieutenant governor, a race in which he ran as the heir apparent for leadership of the traditional conservative faction, the group whose grip on Texas was loosened in 1972. (John Connally formally affiliated with the Republican Party the next year.)

The *Dallas Morning News*, the voice of the conservative Democratic establishment, for years has preached what its editor, Dick West, explained this way: "Look, the Democrats numerically are going to run Texas. Now you good people, you conservatives, stay in that party. Don't go off and vote Republican. Don't go in the Republican primary. Stay in the Democratic primary and nominate good people and support them, because the Democrats are going to win anyway." [14]

Surveys indicate that Texans continue to identify far more strongly with the Democratic Party than do voters in such border or peripheral southern states as Tennessee, Virginia, North Carolina, or Florida. The

13. Murray, *Texas Politics*, pp. 62–65.
14. Interview with Dick West, December 18, 1974.

Comparative State Elections Project found that only 10 percent of Texas voters identified with the Republican Party in 1968, compared with 22 percent for the border South and 27 percent for the United States. Identification with the Democratic Party was 58 percent in Texas, compared with 50 percent for the border South and 45 percent for the United States.[15] In terms of party identification, Texas was almost identical with the Deep South states of Alabama and Louisiana. Although survey data in the 1970s showed slight increases in Republican identification, the traditional ties with the Democratic Party remain a powerful force in Texas politics. Texas does not register voters by party.

In 1974 the state moved from two-year to four-year terms for the governor and other constitutional officers. In accordance with a strong two-term tradition for governors, Governor Briscoe was reelected easily in 1974 to another four years in office.

As he promised in his 1972 campaign, Briscoe had provided a scandal-free first administration, but it was also one that was barren of innovative programs. Briscoe tends to be characterized by veteran political observers as "the most liberal of the conservative governors" and one veteran state official called him "naïvely sincere" but ineffective. Close associates report that Briscoe's quest of the governorship resulted more from a pledge to his father to become governor than from specific ideas about the needs of Texas. Briscoe appears to be a transitional figure from a leadership that looked to the past for direction to new leaders whose focus is oriented toward present and future change.

The other statewide officials elected with Briscoe in 1972 and reelected in 1974 tend to be classified as "moderates" or "progressives." Such advocates of consumer and environmental issues as Attorney General John Hill and Land Commissioner Bob Armstrong, together with reform-minded Lieutenant Governor William Hobby, look suspiciously liberal to old-line conservative Democrats who always have viewed veteran Secretary of Agriculture John White as liberal. White, always a party loyalist, and Armstrong both campaigned actively for McGovern in 1972. The *Texas Observer* considers all of the new breed to be within the "moderate" spectrum and has characterized White as a "former liberal." Such labels are imprecise in Texas, but they are widely used in casual political conversation.

The next governor of Texas—and the smart money is either on Hill or Hobby—likely will project the "progressive" image associated with such "New South" governors of the 1970s as Dale Bumpers and David Pryor of Arkansas, Jimmy Carter of Georgia, John West of South Carolina,

15. David M. Kovenock, James W. Prothro, and Associates, *Explaining the Vote: Presidential Choices in the Nation and the States, 1968* (Chapel Hill: Institute for Research in Social Science, University of North Carolina, 1973), vol. 2, p. 428.

Linwood Holton of Virginia, and Reubin Askew of Florida—all of them moderates and mild reformers on social and economic issues in their states. Hobby is former editor of the family-owned *Houston Post*, grandson of a former governor, and son of Oveta Culp Hobby, secretary of health, education, and welfare under President Eisenhower. His newspaper provided strong editorial leadership during the school desegregation crisis in Houston. Hill is a more dynamic personality, a man whose wealth came as a plaintiffs' lawyer who sued corporations. Among his cases was a $3 million settlement from Texas-based Braniff Airlines in a civil action concerning a plane crash.

In addition to Hill and Hobby, Armstrong and Comptroller Bob Bullock are viewed as potential candidates for higher office. A reform leader while in the legislature, Armstrong as land commissioner increased state royalties from public lands that produce oil. Bullock, a onetime conservative segregationist, was elected in 1974 after campaigning on a pledge to recruit more minority employees and vigorously attacking special interests and promising to crack down on tax evaders. Immediately after his election, he hired for his staff the chief lobbyist for Common Cause in Austin.

Four years after the Sharpstown Bank revelations, a second major scandal resulted in 1975 legislative action to create a state Public Utilities Commission. Texas was the last of the 50 states to operate without state regulation of public utilities; interstate rates were set by local governing boards. The action followed the suicide of a top former executive of Southwestern Bell, the largest Texas affiliate of the American Telephone and Telegraph system. His widow released a lengthy report he had compiled alleging a pattern of payoffs to hundreds of local officials in the guise of campaign contributions and other payments. It was another revelation of the use of accumulated wealth to corrupt the political system in order to increase the public's costs and a company's profits.

Whoever is the next governor, he will have to deal with the problem of educational financing. Pressure for tax reform and school finance equalization followed a three-judge federal court decision at the end of 1971 in *Rodriquez* v. *San Antonio Independent School District*, which held that the state must overcome inequities in school financing based upon differences of resources in the property tax base among school districts. In 1973, however, the U.S. Supreme Court ruled 5–4 against the lower court order.

In the majority decision, in which Justice Potter Stewart joined the four Nixon appointees to the Supreme Court, Justice Lewis Powell concluded, "The need is apparent for reform in tax systems which may well have relied too long and too heavily on the local property tax. . . . But the ultimate solutions must come from the lawmakers and from the democratic pressures of those who elect them." In his dissent, Justice Thurgood Marshall acidly responded, "The Court's suggestions of legislative redress and experimentation will doubtless be a great comfort to the school children of Texas' disadvantaged districts, but considering the vested interests of wealthy school districts in the preservation of the status quo, they are worth little more."

Although debate and ferment set off by the original decision continued, pressure for immediate action waned. However, a $1.5 billion state surplus at the end of 1974—created by a state revenue windfall on skyrocketing prices on gas and oil, which are taxed in Texas on a percentage of the wellhead price—provided the basis for a school financing bill in 1975. The complicated formulas in the bill marked a first step toward equalization, immediately increased the basic salary for starting teachers from $6,600 to $8,000, but did nothing about the lack of even a pretense of uniformity in property tax assessment.

REPUBLICAN EMERGENCE

When John Tower won election to the Senate in 1961, it excited Texas Republicans about the prospect of becoming competitive, if not dominant, in Texas politics. Those hopes have not been fulfilled.

A Methodist minister's son who studied at the London School of Economics, Tower was a 35-year-old economics professor at Southwestern University in his native Wichita Falls when Republican leaders were searching for a candidate to run against Senator Lyndon Johnson in 1960, who by a special legislative act was allowed to run simultaneously for vice-president. Tower had switched to the GOP in 1951, following his conservative inclinations. "I'll tell you honestly," Tower later said, "there wasn't much of a struggle to get that nomination; the party felt a moral obligation to run a candidate against the Democratic Majority Leader, and after others had refused to run, they came to me and said, 'You can articulate the party philosophy; you do it.' " [16]

Tower made a respectable showing in 1960, and the following year he defeated conservative Democrat Bill Blakley, largest stockholder in Braniff Airlines, by 10,000 votes, winning with the help of liberals who wanted an ideological purge of the Democratic Party. The Republicans raised money and developed a professional staff, but they never were able to attract a sufficient number of conservative Democrats. Gold-

16. Stephen Hess and David S. Broder, *The Republican Establishment* (New York: Harper and Row, 1967), p. 346.

water in 1964 proved a disaster for Texas Republicans, who that year challenged every congressional race and ended up with no victories and loss of the two seats they had held.

Tower proved to be an able campaigner and won again in 1966, this time with 56 percent of the vote against conservative Waggoner Carr. Like voters elsewhere in the nation, many Texans saw an advantage of having a man from each major party in the Senate.

Although Republican presidential candidates generally run quite well in Texas and the GOP has proven competitive in races for the U.S. Senate, their success at other levels has been slight. Between 1950 and 1974, Republican presidential candidates averaged 50.7 percent of the two-party vote in four presidential elections and 48.5 percent in six contested senatorial elections. But in seven races for governor, the percentages fall to 37 percent.

Further down the ballot, the weakness is much more glaring. In 1972 and again in 1974, no Republican candidate ran for either lieutenant governor or attorney general, the second and third most powerful offices in state government. In 1972, Republicans challenged only 13 of 24 seats in the U.S. House of Representatives, 12 of 31 in the state Senate, and 74 of 150 in the state House of Representatives. Few Republicans sought local office outside metropolitan areas.

In 1974, the Republicans lost one of their four U.S. House seats and one of their 17 state House seats; their candidate for governor received only 31 percent of the vote after an intensive 18-month campaign. The Republican Party subsequently made a sharp reduction in its state headquarters staff in Austin. On the other hand, the election of Republican county judges—the key administrative office in Texas counties—in populous Harris and Dallas Counties proved Republicans can win against entrenched Democratic incumbents who fail to keep up with change.

Most of the black and Mexican-American vote in Texas goes to Democrats by default. As in other southern states, the battle in the Republican Party is between conservatives and ultraconservatives, and the ideological battles tend to keep the party's base narrow.

The 1974 reelection to Congress of youthful Republican incumbent Alan Steelman in a restructured district in Dallas suggests an alternative strategy to the fading dream of ideological realignment. Steelman had been elected in 1972 as an environmentalist after taking on the Dallas establishment by opposing the proposed $1.6 billion Trinity River Project. Opponents of the project, which would open Dallas to barge traffic and flood part of the Big Thicket area, attacked it as an ecologically unsound boondoggle.

"The only thing," said Steelman, "that will move significant numbers of Democrats into the Republican Party, in my judgment, will be when the statewide Texas Republican Party presents a platform and a slate of candidates that are broadly representative philosophically of the state. And so far the Republican Party has not done that. Our image is that of the country club, vested interests, big oil." Steelman, who is no liberal, is guided by the five basic principles of "fiscal responsibility, a free market economy, clean environment, human rights, and strong national defense." His basic criticism is that the Republicans in Texas tend to be oriented to ideology rather than to issues that affect "the average guy." [17]

Two narrow defeats for the Senate by George Bush, to Yarborough in 1964 and Bentsen in 1970, deprived Texas Republicans of one of their most attractive candidates. Bush was elected to the U.S. House in 1966 as a moderate against a conservative Democrat. He received an unusually high 34 percent of the black vote (the Republican candidate for governor received 10 percent) after he promised "to work with the Negro and white leadership to root out the causes" of civil disturbances and rioting and said he would "not appeal to the white backlash." The handsome son of former Connecticut Senator Prescott Bush, he later served as ambassador to the United Nations, Republican national chairman, ambassador to China, and director of the Central Intelligence Agency. He figured prominently in 1976 vice-presidential speculation until he was forced to remove himself from consideration during his CIA confirmation hearings.

Tower remains the dominant figure among Texas Republicans, and his judgment is decisive in strategy matters. Tower avoids tying himself to other party candidates in years he must run, and other Republicans grumbled that their candidate for governor could have been elected in 1972 if Tower had run with him as a team in the year of the Nixon landslide. Tower has discouraged Republicans from making across-the-board challenges, remembering 1964, when Republicans challenged Democrats at all levels; the Democrats then mobilized and wiped out the entire slate. Because loss of the Senate seat would remove the party's most significant symbol of success and source of power, Tower's supporters defend his strategy in terms of both party and personal political survival. But the strategy leaves the party without a pool of talent from which to develop candidates.

Republicans doubled to fourteen their number of legislative seats from the three largest counties when they were split into single-member districts in 1972, and they should gain a few more when that principle is applied to all urban counties. But creation of a relatively few Republican enclaves by a Democratic-controlled legislature will ensure Democratic dominance of both houses of the legislature for the foreseeable future.

When John Connally formally moved into the Republican Party in 1973, it raised Republican hopes of realignment that would bring in other

17. Interview with Alan Steelman, January 30, 1974.

conservative Democrats. A man of forceful and dynamic personality and of unquestioned ability and charm, the epitome of the tie between the moneyed interests and politics, Connally served as secretary of the treasury in the Nixon cabinet and in 1972 headed the national "Democrats for Nixon" effort. Connally saw no place for a Texan like himself in national Democratic Party leadership after the repudiation of Lyndon Johnson and his Vietnam policy. He also saw a leadership vacuum developing in the national Republican Party and made his move to fill it.

Democrats in Texas generally perceived Connally's action as motivated by personal ambition; Watergate already had become enough of an issue to tarnish the Republican image by the time of Connally's switch, and there was no following of other Democrats after Connally changed his party affiliation. In July 1974, he was indicted on bribery charges growing out of his 1972 presidential campaign involvement. After his acquittal the following April, Connally declared himself a "moderate conservative" and resumed speech making around the country, but it was clear that he had put behind him any major role in state politics.

Like Republican parties throughout the South, the events of Watergate dampened enthusiasm among party workers in Texas and exposed the weaknesses that already existed. Texas remains essentially a one-party state in which Republicans can play a useful watchdog function and offer a challenge, but for years to come there appears little chance that the GOP will become truly competitive.

LIBERALS AND CONSERVATIVES

Ideological liberals and conservative Republicans in Texas tend to argue that the election of either a Republican or a liberal Democrat as governor is necessary before Texas can become a true two-party state. Only then, they contend, would conservatives in sufficient numbers join the Republican Party to make it truly competitive.

There are fallacies in this argument. Although there are clear patterns of a liberal-conservative cleavage, the conservative Democrats never have existed as a well-oiled political machine; rather, they have always been a loose coalition supported by many interests. They include tradition-oriented rural party loyalists; urban conservatives who by habit vote Democratic in the primary and Republican in the general election; the financial elite, who want to back a winner and want that winner to be friendly to their interests; and many local elective officials at all levels. The lack of voter registration by party serves as an additional deterrent to development of a strong two-party system. In addition, the national trend toward ticket splitting is reflected in Texas elections.

Despite the development of a significant Republican Party that can offer a serious challenge in specific races, Democratic dominance remains a fact of political life in Texas. When the state moved to four-year terms for the governor and other constitutional officers, elections were set in nonpresidential years to remove the chance that a Republican at the state level could ride the coattails of a popular candidate for the White House, such as almost occurred in the 1972 race for governor.

Meanwhile, an expanded electorate has broadened the liberal base of blacks, Mexican-Americans, and blue-collar workers who tend to vote Democratic. In response, the Democratic Party at the state level has opened its doors wider; in recent years, it has moved gradually leftward on social issues, both absorbing much of the old forces of liberal coalition and holding onto many traditional conservatives. One no longer has to be a liberal in Texas to realize that failure to provide health care, economic opportunity, and education for the disadvantaged results in problems for society at large.

Men like Briscoe, Hill, Hobby, and Bentsen are all millionaires. The fact that they are beginning to address themselves and the state to long-standing inequities hardly makes them look dangerously liberal to the electorate at large. Although liberals in Texas have not won many elections, their campaigns have served to educate the public to dormant political issues, and the new political leadership is beginning to respond to that awareness. Furthermore, what Key called the "strident tone of irreconcilability" in Texas politics is waning as the old order changes. After more than two decades of fighting, many ideological liberals have grown tired, and basically they have won their fight to open the process to greater participation.

Although political combat in Texas has calmed down considerably, it is still far from dull. An exchange that occurred when Senator Birch Bayh of Indiana presided in 1969 over a Democratic Party task force hearing in Austin on proposed changes in party rules provides an example of liberal-conservative confrontation.

At the hearing, Frank C. Erwin, Jr., a conservative Austin lawyer whose years as chairman of the University of Texas Board of Regents were marked by his interposition of his philosophical outlook into matters of academic freedom (he was removed from the post by Briscoe), clashed with Albert Pena, a San Antonio liberal leader. The verbal battle began when Erwin, who had served as Democratic state chairman and national committeeman under John Connally, drew derisive laughter from the liberal audience.

"I've been losing public meetings like this and winning elections for years," he snapped.

"You've been *stealing* elections for years," said Pena.

"You're a liar!" Erwin retorted.

"And I say *you're* a liar," Pena shot back. "Like in 1956 at Fort Worth, when you had to call in Lyndon Johnson and Sam Rayburn to help you steal that convention!"

"I'm glad you finally admitted what you think of Lyndon Johnson," said Erwin. "You've taken advantage of him for years."

Author Jimmy Banks, who recorded the exchange, noted that while it may have shocked out-of-staters seeking methods to achieve party unity, "the only thing surprising about it to Texas observers was that it occurred during the summer of an 'off year' instead of during a typical campaign or convention." [18]

In Houston (Harris County) there is genuine two-party politics based on strong, competitive precinct organizations built by a moderate-to-liberal Democratic coalition and an energetic group of conservative Republicans. Under the direction of Billie Carr, the wife of a local labor union president, the Harris County Democrats—an organization independent of the official Democratic Party of Harris County—developed clubs in more than 200 precincts, and their well-developed organizational structure helped them elect liberal Democrats locally and become a significant factor in statewide politics. The two most liberal Texans in Congress, Barbara Jordan—who was the only black member of the state Senate in this century—and humanist lawyer Bob Eckhardt, both come from Harris County.

Billie Carr got started in 1953 after the official Democratic leadership followed Governor Shivers in support of Eisenhower and attempted to keep the name of Adlai Stevenson off the ballot in Texas. It was the arrogance of Shivers which got her going. She recalled that at a meeting in which she objected to a bill setting up a state loyalty review board, Governor Shivers told her, "Little lady, I hold Texas in the palm of my hand." [19]

The countervailing force to Billie Carr in Houston for years has been Nancy Palm, a surgeon's wife who as unpaid Harris County Republican chairman has developed among conservatives the same kind of precinct organization, a staffed full-time office, and a committee that recruits and supports candidates who must be philosophically right as well as personally clean. A dedicated and outspoken believer in individual self-reliance who considers Gerald Ford and Richard Nixon both too liberal on social issues, she often is referred to as "Napalm," a play on her name and a reflection of her personality. Almost half of the Republicans in the legislature usually come from Harris County.

18. Banks, *Money, Marbles and Chalk*, pp. 13–14.

19. *The Washington Post*, December 26, 1971. Quoted in *Practicing Texas Politics*, 2nd ed., Eugene W. Jones, et al., eds. (Boston: Houghton-Mifflin, 1974).

Outside of Houston, however, there are few precinct organizations and few signs of partisan party competitiveness.

In Dallas, the second-largest city in Texas, the conservative establishment that ruled the city for decades received its first setback when single-member legislative districts were created. The final blow came in 1975 when a federal judge ordered single-member districts for city council, thus bringing an end to handpicked government by the Citizens Charter Association, composed of top leaders of the Dallas business establishment. The creation of single-member legislative seats allowed Republicans and moderate-to-liberal Democrats to win seats for the first time, but whether the freer political climate will produce strong party organizations such as exist in Houston remains to be seen.

One obstacle to true interparty or ideological competition in Texas is the unusually high cost of campaigning, which tends to favor incumbents or the candidates of the moneyed interests. The $2.4 million that Senator Tower reported spending in his 1972 reelection campaign (as an incumbent without primary opposition) demonstrates how high that cost can be. In addition to the sheer physical size of the state, Texas has more commercial television stations and more radio stations than any state in the union. Altogether there are more than 475 broadcast stations, including 55 television outlets.

In 1971, Tower conducted a series of videotaped interviews with Washington officials which virtually every television station in Texas ran as news, granting widespread exposure to the senator without cost. Before his 1966 campaign, Tower made similar use of "free media" with a series of interviews in Vietnam with Texans in the armed forces, interviews made while Tower was visiting as a member of the Senate Armed Forces Committee. Considering the cost reported by Tower (in addition to the "free" perquisites of incumbency), the contention by Ralph Yarborough that Bentsen's campaign budget in 1970 was $6.7 million is worth noting, even though Bentsen campaign aides insist the figure is grossly exaggerated.

When Fred Hofheinz, another of the wealthy Democratic moderates, won election as mayor of Houston, the campaign cost reported was well in excess of a half million dollars, a further indication of the resources required for a candidate to make a serious run for a statewide office such as governor.

In any event, a major problem for any challenger to an incumbent senator in Texas will be the limit on campaign spending for communications media set by the Federal Election Campaign Act. Under a formula set by the act, the maximum allowed spending for Texas in 1974 was $890,604, of which no more than $543,000 could be spent on broadcast media.

MINORITIES AND POLITICS

Although the tradition of discrimination and high incidence of poverty among both blacks and Mexican-Americans (44 percent for blacks and 45.3 percent for Mexican-Americans in 1971, compared with 12.6 percent for white Texans [20]) suggest a natural political alliance, the two groups basically are separated both geographically and culturally. The 18.4 percent Spanish-surnamed population is concentrated in south and southwest Texas, an area where almost no blacks live. The 28 counties in which at least half of the people have Spanish surnames are located on or close to the Mexican border. By contrast, the black population, 12.6 percent of the total, is concentrated in an area east of a line drawn roughly north from Corpus Christi through San Antonio, Austin, and Fort Worth to the Oklahoma border. Basically, this is the area where Negro slaves first lived with their masters. Since 1950, the migration of blacks in Texas has largely been rural to urban, but within the state. In Harris County the black population increased from 150,000 in 1950 to 350,000 in 1970 (from 125,000 to 317,000 in the Houston city limits). For Dallas County the increase in that period was from 83,000 to 220,000.

Although it will be years before the barriers of language, color, and culture are overcome, black and Mexican-American political leaders speak openly of the need for alliance. Mexican-Americans in Texas are less cohesive politically than blacks, and the "brown Caucus" in the legislature does not include some of the more conservative legislators with Spanish surnames. But the fact that both black and brown caucuses exist is a recent development from which a significant future alliance may develop. As with the Republicans, creation of single-member legislative districts tends to help minorities. The number of black legislators increased immediately from two to eight after single-member districts were ordered in the three largest counties in 1972, and the number of Mexican-Americans in the legislature increased by three.

The traditional political role that emerged out of the 19th century for Spanish-surnamed people was one in which powerful "patrons" who owned large amounts of land controlled the votes of poor, uneducated Mexican-Americans living on their properties. The patrons tended to be conservative and paternalistic men whose control of votes gave them influence with Anglo politicians who shared their interests in retaining a supply of cheap farm and ranch labor. Lesser political bosses, called *jefes*, relied on traditional techniques of city ward leaders dealing with immigrant groups.

20. Ibid., p. 10.

The nonmilitant League of United Latin American Citizens (LULAC), organized in 1929, emphasized civic responsibility. After World War II the dominant organization was the G.I. Forum, founded in 1948 as a protest against discrimination after a funeral home refused to bury the body of a veteran for no other reason than that he was a Mexican-American.

The election in 1956 of Henry B. Gonzalez of San Antonio to the state Senate, where he was an outspoken liberal, was the next significant breakthrough, and Gonzalez received more than 250,000 votes as a candidate for governor in the 1958 Democratic primary. In 1961 he was elected as the state's first congressman of Mexican descent. His victory followed the formation of "Viva Kennedy" clubs. John F. Kennedy generated enthusiastic support among Mexican-Americans, both because he was a Catholic and because he expressed concern over the Mexican-Americans' living conditions. The clubs were consolidated into an organization known as the Political Association of Spanish-speaking Organizations (PASO) that attempted to develop political involvement among the most impoverished Mexican-Americans. However, factionalism and inability to agree on strategy weakened the organization after Kennedy was elected.

The state's second Mexican-American congressman is Eligio de la Garza, a conservative Democrat who has easily won reelection every two years since 1964, despite opposition from young militants.

Political awareness among Mexican-Americans was stimulated further in 1967–1968 when low-paid farm workers in the Lower Rio Grande Valley went on strike and marched to Austin to dramatize their demand for a state minimum-wage law. Governor Connally met the marchers on a highway south of Austin and declared he would neither support their demands for minimum wage legislation nor meet with them at the capitol. Imported strikebreakers from Mexico, arrests of strike leaders by the Texas Rangers, and court injunctions broke the strike, but the highly publicized movement further awakened political awareness among Mexican-Americans and a search for a Chicano cultural identity.

Stimulated in part by the example of black militancy, new organizations developed to make Mexican-Americans "masters of their own destiny." The most visible group was the Mexican-American Youth Organization (MAYO), founded in 1967 and supported with funds from the Ford Foundation to advance a program designed to fulfill "the destiny of La Raza (the people)." Goals included a third-party political movement, Chicano control of schools in predominantly Mexican-American communities, and an end of economic domination by Anglos. Revolutionary rhetoric and threats of violence followed in the wake of vocal opposition from Representative Gonzalez, who opposed the third-party idea and the development of a separate Chicano identity, arguing instead for integration and cooperation.

One of the MAYO founders, Jose Angel Guitierrez, a graduate student in political science, returned to his native Crystal City—where a PASO-backed slate had temporarily held control of the City Council—and helped organize a student strike to protest discrimination in school activities. That led to a take-over by Chicanos of the school board and city hall and to formation of La Raza Unida as a formal third party.[21] One of the goals outlined by Guitierrez was "direct confrontation with the gringo . . . to polarize the community over issues into Chicano versus gringo. . . . The attitude gringoes have of racial superiority, of paternalism, of divine right, of xenophobia, of bigotry, and of animalism is well-known to La Raza." [22] Guitierrez is a more gentle personality than such rhetoric suggests.

In 1972, when La Raza Unida ran a statewide candidate for governor, the party drew enough voters out of the Democratic primary to result in the defeat in San Antonio of state Senator Joe Bernal and County Commissioner Albert Pena, both men who sympathized with many of the goals of the Chicano activists.

La Raza credibility also was hurt by widely believed Democratic charges in 1972 that the new party was subsidized by Republican funds, a GOP tactic aimed at cutting votes away from Democrats. An analysis of 29 counties with substantial Mexican-American populations showed that Briscoe in 1972 ran almost 25,000 votes behind the total won by Preston Smith in 1968, despite a much heavier total vote in 1972 (Smith had carried all 29 counties). Although Briscoe led Republican Henry Grover in all 29 counties, La Raza candidate Ramsey Muniz led in three counties and was second in 11. Muniz clearly contributed to the decline in Democratic strength.[23] However, although Muniz received 214,118 votes for governor in 1972, or 6.3 percent, his vote was less than that of Henry Gonzalez in the 1958 Democratic primary for governor.

In 1974, the La Raza party blundered by opposing several liberal Democratic Chicano state legislative candidates, such as incumbent Representatives Ben Reyes in Houston and Gonzalo Barrientos in Austin, both young men who were elected after working as community organizers among fellow Mexican-Americans. Although Muniz ran again for governor in 1974, he received only 5.7 percent of the vote. La Raza clearly had failed to unite Mexican-Americans in its third-party movement.

Although the militant rhetoric and zealotry of La Raza repelled large

21. For a full discussion, see John Shockley, "Mexican-American Politics in Texas," in *Practicing Texas Politics,* pp. 113–117.

22. Ibid., p. 119.

23. James, et al., *Texas Politics,* p. 76.

numbers of Mexican-Americans, many of whom tend to be politically conservative, the party's activities stimulated political and cultural awareness of all Mexican-Americans in Texas, raised issues that had been dormant, and forced the Democratic Party to respond more assertively to attract Mexican-American voters. La Raza also provided a training ground for young activists. The election of Guitierrez as county judge, the top county official in Zavala County (Crystal City), suggests that La Raza could expand its base as a local party in other counties with majority Chicano populations.

Although no Mexican-American ever has been elected to statewide office in Texas, a candidate such as Houston Comptroller Leonel Castillo could emerge as a unifier among Chicanos. A trained social worker who moved from community organizing into elective politics and made the office of comptroller a power base in Houston, the 35-year-old Castillo ran an impressive race in 1974 as an insurgent candidate for Democratic state chairman.

In Houston, Castillo developed broad support with his crackdown on property tax inequities, including a successful attempt to force the elite River Oaks Country Club to pay higher taxes. He believes political unification among Mexican-Americans is necessary before an effective statewide alliance can be forged with blacks. "The Chicano community is not as liberal or as monolithic or as much a bloc vote as is the black vote," Castillo said. "The black vote tends to be pretty much solid, strong, and predictable." [24]

Although urban black politics varies from city to city, a look at Houston—the South's largest city—suggests some broad regional trends as well as developments with long-range implications for Texas.

The urban migration that accompanied removal of legal barriers to black political participation resulted in a class of newly enfranchised blacks which, if organized, could trade its bloc vote in exchange for policies beneficial to the black community. In the cities, where they were usually concentrated in segregated housing and less susceptible than in rural areas to implied or actual intimidation, most black voters were poorly equipped to deal with political issues. Moreover, white elites were ill prepared to interact with blacks.

Two basic problems developed as black political organizers emerged to broker with the white political establishment. The first was that benefits were not available to specific black voters, but only as a general betterment of social or economic conditions for blacks. The result was that it was often very difficult to persuade blacks to register and vote. Often, blacks could be mobilized only when clearly racial issues were

24. Interview with Leonel Castillo, December 15, 1974.

injected into the campaign. The second problem arose whenever the organization leadership accepted personal benefits from candidates less favorably disposed than others to the interests of the black community in general, which sometimes happened.

As in most of the South, early political organization among Houston blacks was based on the churches, the one traditional institution that blacks could call their own. Its ministers by tradition played a role of general community leadership and served as go-betweens with the white community. With their congregation as a base, ministers could organize the black vote with little cost.

Beginning in the 1920s, the Negro Baptist Ministers Association in Houston, organized and directed by the Rev. L. H. Simpson, dominated black politics. Simpson served as key black confidant of longtime Mayor Oscar Holcombe, received cash to distribute as he saw fit in order to get out the vote, and was an acknowledged community leader who got such benefits for his community as the paving of a major thoroughfare in the black Fifth Ward area.

At the end of the 1940s, as black registration and voting rose sharply, conservative Democrats made efforts to "buy" black votes, and rival black leaders accused the ministers of "selling out" black interests. The Harris County Council of Organizations (HCCO) emerged with the aim of unifying the black vote and making sure it was not sold out for personal gain. In stressing its commitment to community interests, HCCO provided for the expulsion of any council leader or official who accepted personal payoffs to influence the group's decision. Some 50 to 75 groups, many of them civic organizations, affiliated with the HCCO and paid nominal dues. A rotating screening committee reviewed potential candidates, and a final slate was selected at a full membership meeting. Its recommendations won the respect of the black community, and the group played a pivotal role in the 1950s.

In 1953 the establishment of the Harris County Democrats formally structured blacks into a coalition with a strong precinct organization that was to include organized labor, a Mexican-American group, and white liberal elements. The precinct work also stimulated political awareness among nonunion low-income whites. Much of the financial support for black organizational efforts came from labor and white liberal elements.

A black-supported liberal slate won six of eight seats in the state House of Representatives in 1958, and a liberal county judge was elected the same year. Candidates with HCCO endorsements received 80 to 90 percent of the vote in black precincts. HCCO's effectiveness is explained in part by its broad base and democratic form of organization, which attuned it to the interests and sentiments of the black community. And because it endorsed candidates who were known to be friendly to black aspirations, the council's role was not that of persuading people to vote for particular candidates but of letting them know who these candidates were. For roughly 15 years, from the early 1950s to the late 1960s, HCCO dominated black politics in Houston.

In addition to the liberal HCCO, there was also a United Political Organization dominated by wealthy, conservative black businessmen who supported John Connally and served as a major source of black appointments by him. One leader of the group remarked after Connally expressed opposition to a civil rights bill sponsored by President Kennedy, "Negroes are handicapped by always picking a loser. They are tied to the liberals, but the liberals usually lose. I think something is to be gained by aligning oneself with a man who wins office." [25]

Black registration climbed sharply in this period, and blacks began to feel they were giving more to the coalition than they were receiving. That feeling crystalized in 1963 and 1964 when Barbara Jordan, a young, articulate black attorney of unusual ability, twice was defeated as a legislative candidate while running on the countywide liberal slate. While all whites on the slate received 80 to 90 percent of the vote among blacks, she received only 30 percent of the vote in white areas where other liberal candidates were receiving 65 to 70 percent.

She won a state House seat in 1966 after the county was split into smaller districts, and her election in a newly created majority black state Senate district in 1968 coincided with a liberal split over presidential politics and a bitter break over the Vietnam war issue. Organized labor generally backed Hubert Humphrey and withdrew from the coalition after the Harris County Democrats endorsed Eugene McCarthy, who had entered the race as an antiwar candidate. The schism was widened by personal animosities.

Because much of the resources for HCCO came from the AFL–CIO support of the coalition, the Council decided to withdraw from the coalition in the face of disruption of outside financial support. The result was that HCCO was then forced to rely on the candidates it endorsed to provide the resources to get out the word and get out the vote. The candidates best able to provide the resources often were not those whose positions best reflected general black interests. Thus, HCCO committed itself early to Ben Barnes in the 1972 governor's race but finally agreed under liberal pressure to make a joint endorsement of Barnes and underfinanced liberal Sissy Farenthold, who received 55 percent of the black vote to 30 percent for Barnes. In 1974, HCCO's credibility suffered further when, after it endorsed Briscoe over Farenthold, she ended up with 60 percent of the black vote.

Meanwhile, in 1972, Barbara Jordan was elected to Congress from a newly created, predominantly black district, drawn in Austin simul-

25. Chandler Davidson, *Biracial Politics: Conflict and Coalition in the Metropolitan South* (Baton Rouge: Louisiana State University Press, 1972), p. 47.

taneously with the dissolution of her predominantly black state Senate district.

Her opening speech at the 1974 Judiciary Committee impeachment hearings—when she poignantly described how the Constitution, although not originally intended for people like her, now served, and governed, all Americans—helped make her a national figure.

In 1975 she led efforts in Congress to include Texas in an extension of the Voting Rights Act, a move that prompted State Comptroller Bullock—a former secretary of state and the chief election officer in Texas—to observe that the federal law "could reduce the likelihood of intimidation" at the polls. Texas was brought in under a provision to include states in which less than 50 percent of the eligible voters cast ballots in the 1972 presidential election and in which ballots had been printed only in the English language when more than 5 percent of the eligible voters were members of a language minority. Although the "trigger" that brought Texas in was the provision that applied to Mexican-Americans, inclusion under the Voting Rights Act will mean protection for both minorities in such matters as reapportionment plans and all other election law changes, which in the future must be reviewed by the Justice Department to ensure that they have no discriminatory effect.

The election of blacks from predominantly black areas greatly reduced the essential middleman role the council had played for years. The number of black state representatives from Houston increased from one to four when single-member districts were adopted in 1972. A black candidate endorsed by HCCO received only 24 percent of the vote in 1974 against incumbent state Representative Craig Washington, an articulate and independent-minded young black lawyer.

A cadre of elected black officials, neither controlled nor selected by whites and often not economically dependent on them, is emerging as a new elite of black political leadership. "Black voters are now beginning to feel insulted by groups telling them who to vote for," Washington said after his 1974 reelection. "In the old days they obediently took the HCCO slate cards. Now you meet people who get angry when they're offered a card. They say, 'I make my own decisions.' "[26] In statewide or national elections, the direct communication a candidate achieves primarily through television allows black as well as white voters to receive information and images on which to make an independent political choice.[27]

26. *Houston Chronicle*, July 28, 1974, sec. 2, p. 5.

27. For a full discussion of black political groups in Houston and Dallas, see Richard Murray and Arnold Vedlitz, "Political Organization in Deprived Communities," paper delivered at the 1974 annual meeting of the American Political Science Association.

Nevertheless, the church, civic, fraternal, and other organizations still serve as political forums among blacks. With the legislative black caucus as a base, a statewide association of elected black officials is likely to emerge in Texas and to serve as an unofficial screening committee for statewide political candidates. But such an organization will face problems of personal jealousies and factional rivalries. For example, rivalry exists among black legislators from Houston who view Barbara Jordan as a potential appointee to the U.S. Supreme Court and compete among themselves to determine who would be next in line for Congress if she received such an appointment.

The legislative black caucus demonstrated the power of a small, cohesive bloc in 1974 when the legislature, which meets only in odd-numbered years, sat as a constitutional convention. The document they produced failed by three votes to get the two-thirds majority required for a public referendum because the eight-member black caucus had united with a coalition of delegates formed by organized labor to block passage after a right-to-work provision was included. A new document was submitted in 1975, without the right-to-work provision.

State Representative G. J. Sutton of San Antonio, chairman of the black caucus and possessor of one of the most perceptive and experienced political minds of any black leader in the South, in 1974 rose on a point of personal privilege to criticize the proposed constitution as a document that basically protected the vested interests of organized wealth and failed to protect human rights.* In fact, there was nothing comparable in the proposed new constitution to the provisions for individual rights contained in a new constitution approved almost simultaneously in neighboring Louisiana. "I saw it as an antiblack constitution," said Sutton, an older brother of Percy Sutton, Manhattan Borough president in New York City.[28] Representative Sutton was 63 when elected to the Texas legislature in 1972, an election made possible by single-member House districts in Bexar County. He and five other blacks

---

* In 1975, Texas voters rejected the new constitution. Strong opposition developed that was funded by such business leaders as George Brown, head of the giant Brown & Root construction firm, but the death blow came when Governor Briscoe came out against the document a few weeks before the vote. Former Governors Shivers and Smith joined the opposition, who contended among other things that the provision for annual legislative sessions would be an unnecessary expense and might lead to higher taxes. Without the right-to-work provision, the modernizing features of the new constitution held little appeal for them. The new document would have removed many of the restrictions contained in the 1876 constitution that have hamstrung government efficiency in Texas and have delayed change in response to altered social and economic conditions. The 1876 constitution was written for a rural state in reaction both to alleged misrule under Reconstruction government and to economic conditions so depressed that the economy-obsessed delegates had refused to hire a stenographer or to print the proceedings because of the cost.

28. Interview with G. J. Sutton, December 13, 1974.

voted in 1975 against submitting the constitution to a referendum, even after removal of the right-to-work provision.

A secondary source of black leadership—and a primary source of training for the next wave of political leaders—is organized labor, which has eight A. Philip Randolph chapters in Texas. Organized labor has both the resources and the inclination to expand black voter registration and participation, in rural east Texas as well as the cities.

ORGANIZED LABOR

Organized labor in Texas exerts a significant influence, an influence which is likely to grow. Although the rate of union membership is little more than in most southern states, the much larger population base results in roughly 250,000 members affiliated with the state AFL–CIO, far more than in any other state in the region. Monthly dues of 25 cents provide a total annual budget of more than $700,000. The result is a physically impressive, well-staffed state headquarters in Austin and by far the best state labor newspaper in the South.

Although some Texas liberals accused labor of "selling out" after Briscoe's election, AFL–CIO President Harry Hubbard responded, "We went around for years butting our heads against a stone wall, and now we find there is a door open and we can walk through and get done some of the things we've been fighting for. I'm a liberal and I agree with the liberals on issues, but I think it's more effective to work from within." [29]

After Hubbard became AFL–CIO president and Briscoe became governor, the two sought common ground. They worked out an acceptable compromise for a larger role for labor within the Democratic Party structure. The accommodating Briscoe named a trade union official as commissioner of labor. Hubbard developed a screening committee to recommend lists of names to the governor, who began appointing union members to boards and commissions. Briscoe also supported some changes sought by the AFL–CIO in workmen's compensation and unemployment insurance. Finally, Hubbard and his staff worked with Briscoe's staff on legislation and provided lobbying support for measures on which they agreed.

Organized labor's role in campaigns became stronger after the 1973 reform legislature imposed limits on campaign financial contributions. The use of computerized voter registration lists, volunteer workers, and

29. Interview·with the authors, December 17, 1974.

telephone banks provided major campaign resources for labor-backed candidates, many of them people with limited financial means. In addition, the state AFL–CIO provided cash contributions up to several hundred dollars for legislative candidates they endorsed.

INFLUENCE IN WASHINGTON

The Texas influence in Washington, which peaked in the 1950s and 1960s with Sam Rayburn as speaker of the House and Lyndon Johnson as Senate majority leader and then president, diminished sharply in the 1970s. Although four House committees remained under chairmen from Texas, the revolt against seniority in 1974 toppled two Texans, Wright Patman on Banking and Currency and Bob Poage on Agriculture, from committee chairmanships. But Rayburn and Johnson left Texas a legacy of federal largesse. In 1974 the state ranked third in its share of federal outlays and only sixth in its share of the tax burden, and Texas outstripped all states in the South except Mississippi and Virginia in 1974 per capita federal spending.

Texas has yet to experience the pattern of retirements, defeats, and deaths of senior congressmen that has depleted most southern delegations of much of their seniority, especially in the House. After the death of Representative Patman in 1976, 14 of the state's 24 U.S. representatives —all of them Democrats—had been in Congress a decade or more. For decades Texans have explained their power in Congress with the aphorism, "We pick 'em good, we elect 'em young, and we keep 'em there." But the departure of Connally from the Nixon cabinet left Texas for the first time in decades without an individual symbol of the state's power in Washington.

Because of its size and the concentration of wealth that depends on federal policy toward oil and gas, national defense, interest rates, and computer contracts, Texas will remain influential in Washington. But barring success in the long-range presidential ambitions of Bentsen and Connally, the influence of Texas in the 1950s and 1960s in the nation's capital is unlikely to be matched for some time.

OUTLOOK

Despite the vast wealth in Texas, no state has more people who fall below the federal government's poverty guidelines. Removal of voting restrictions and heightened awareness by the black and Mexican-American minorities have increased the pressure on the state to provide more in the way of education, health care, and other social services.

At the same time, corporate interests also are becoming more important in Texas. The national leadership in the oil industry is concentrated in the state, including the headquarters of both Shell and Tenneco and most of the division headquarters for Exxon, Gulf, Texaco, and others. A well-documented report in the *Texas Observer* about power and money in Houston explained that city's interlocking directorships: three Houston banks with holding companies that in 1975 showed more than $9.6 billion in assets shared directors with Exxon, Texas Eastern Transmission, Brown & Root, El Paso Natural Gas, the Halliburton Co., Armco Steel, Southwestern Bell, International Telephone and Telegraph, Ethyl Corporation, the King Ranch, several insurance companies, and the law firm of Vinson, Elkins, Searls, Connally and Smith—the firm in which former Governor John Connally is a partner. Representatives of the Connally law firm sat on the board of more than one bank, as did executives of several corporations and insurance companies, creating a secondary interlock. A similar situation existed in Dallas, home of two of the nation's 25 largest banks.

Only Nevada makes less tax effort than Texas, a state that has wealth but has been little inclined to tax it. In the coming years, the central question in Texas will be whether recent procedural reforms will lead to substantive changes in what government provides, who receives it, and who pays for it.

Chapter

14

VIRGINIA

Out of the Byrd Cage

FRIENDS referred to the "Byrd organization" and enemies to the "Byrd machine," but regardless of the label, the apparatus put together by Harry Flood Byrd, Sr. in the 1920s dominated and controlled Virginia politics for more than 40 years. Whatever its virtues—and it had some— it succumbed to modern urban society and the disease of "massive resistance."

V. O. Key labeled Virginia a "political museum piece" and wrote of the Byrd organization:

Organization spokesmen in Congress look out for the interests of business, and the state government, although well managed, manifests a continuing interest in the well-being of the well-to-do. The quid pro quo for support of the organization is said to be taxation favorable to corporations, an anti-labor policy, and restraint in the expansion of services, such as education, public health, and welfare. The organization pursues a negative policy on public services; if there is an apparent demand it will grudgingly yield a bit here and there, but it dedicates its best efforts to the maintenance of low levels of public service. Yet it must be said that the organization gives good government; while the school system is inadequate it is about as good as the money appropriated will buy. The organization, however, has an "adding machine mentality"; attached to the fetish of a balanced budget, it takes a short-run view that almost invariably militates against the long-run interests of the state. Men with the minds of tradesmen do not become statesmen.[1]

1. V. O. Key, *Southern Politics in State and Nation* (New York: Vintage, 1949), p. 27.

The legacy of Byrd domination continues in the physical presence of Senator Harry F. Byrd, Jr., a congenial conservative who calls himself an "independent Democrat" and is considered more flexible than his father. Former Byrd Democrat Mills Godwin, now a Republican, presides as governor. The Byrd tradition continues in at least the expectation of high standards of fiscal and ethical integrity among officeholders. But as a cohesive, dominant, controlling force in the political life of Virginia, the Byrd machine is dead. Death came without honor, as the taint of racism left its mark upon the leader of a group of gentlemen otherwise known for their honor and integrity.

For many Virginia citizens, those who reside in or commute to or from the Richmond or Hampton Roads areas, the living legacy of the Byrd "pay-as-you-go" policies is confronted daily in the toll roads and toll bridges and tunnels that link cities like Norfolk, Portsmouth, Newport News, Hampton, Virginia Beach, Suffolk, and Chesapeake, which cluster around the state's great harbor. Virginia today is an urban-dominated state in which the *Washington Post* is the newspaper of greatest circulation, a state in which participatory democracy is only recent and in which the sudden rapid increase of the electorate has, as usual, resulted in political instability. The "urban corridor," a term widely used in Virginia political discussions, descends like a tail of the Boston-to-Washington megalopolis from the populous northern Virginia suburbs of Washington, down to Richmond, and curves eastward to Hampton Roads. The corridor cuts through the state in a band of 20 counties and 14 cities and contains roughly 60 percent of the state's population.

In Virginia the thrust of post–World War II political development has been the challenge to the Byrd organization from within the Democratic Party, and the challenge to the Democrats for control of state government by the Republicans. The Byrd organization's failure to endure basically reflected the inflexibility of Harry F. Byrd, Sr. and his inability to adjust to dynamic forces of change. An insistence on "pay-as-you-go" and a fixation against the state's using its credit to borrow for capital improvements resulted in the Byrd machine's failure to meet demands for public services. Relying on a controlled rural white electorate, the organization failed to recognize and adjust to the political realities of urban growth, the impact of reapportionment, and the development of black political participation. Its refusal to accommodate the bright "Young Turks," a name given by Virginia newspapers to a group of men who entered the legislature after World War II and sought modest reforms, ensured a challenge from within. Finally, the plunge into "massive resistance" as a means of meeting the challenge of the Supreme Court's school desegregation decisions proved a dead end, leading to disaster for the organization, embarrassment to the state, and a tragic failure of leadership for the region.

BACKGROUND

Harry F. Byrd, Sr. was descended from William Byrd, who laid out the city of Richmond in the early days of colonial Virginia. Harry Byrd's father was Richard Evelyn Byrd, who served as speaker of the House of Delegates during part of the period when U.S. Senator Thomas S. Martin dominated Virginia politics from 1893 until his death in 1919. An uncle, Henry D. (Hal) Flood, served in Congress and was right-hand man to Senator Martin.

Harry Byrd voluntarily quit school at 15 to work for his father's debt-ridden newspaper in Winchester. Young Byrd saved it from bankruptcy. Later, he helped develop the largest family-owned apple orchards and processing facility in the world. In part, it was personal experience that led to his obsession with debt as something to be avoided.

Political debate over debt had helped define the modern Democratic and Republican parties in Virginia after Reconstruction. Byrd, born in 1887, grew up in a household and among relatives deeply preoccupied with the great debate. The "Readjuster" movement of the 1880s won the initial battle, which was fought over the issue of "readjusting" the state's pre–Civil War debt or paying it in full. The Readjusters, under their leader William Mahone, became the Republican Party and formed a coalition with blacks. Mahone agreed to provide for free public education and to abolish the whipping post, which had been used primarily to punish blacks. (A sentence to the whipping post also resulted in disfranchisement.)

Full payment of the $45 million debt for prewar construction of railroads, turnpikes, and canals was fought for by a coalition of bankers, brokers, speculators, and railroads, who won the support of much of the conservative "better element" who desired to protect the "honor" of the commonwealth. An attempt was made to divert funds for public education into payment of the debt. The funding act was accompanied by another which would have sold to private interests the state's ownership in railroads, an act that threatened the future of Mahone's recently chartered railroad, which crossed southern Virginia. Earlier, conservative leaders had expressed opposition to free schools, and one governor in the 1870s had pronounced them "a luxury . . . to be paid for by the people who wish their benefits."

The Readjuster-dominated General Assembly increased funding for public schools, established a college for Negroes, abolished the $1 poll tax, increased taxes on corporations and reduced taxes on real estate, and issued new bonds to pay $21 million to settle the debt, a settlement upheld by the U.S. Supreme Court.* Blacks were appointed to a number of minor offices.

By 1883 the Bourbon Democrats had accepted Mahone-imposed tax reforms and other measures and had regained control by exploiting a race riot at Danville. They passed a new election law written "to perpetuate the rule of the white man in Virginia." [2] When the Populist revolt that swept the South in the next decade arrived in Virginia, it collapsed because of insufficient support. The Readjuster movement had spent too much energy too recently for another protest movement to succeed.

After Senator Martin rose to prominence, a constitutional convention in 1902 reinstituted the poll tax, which had the immediate effect of reducing the number of Negroes qualified to vote from 147,000 to 21,000. A small electorate was one of the hallmarks of the Byrd organization, whose regime into the 1940s was marked by elections in which less than 10 percent of the voting-age population participated. "By contrast," Key observed, "Mississippi is a hotbed of democracy."

As a young state senator, Harry Byrd attracted attention in 1923 when he led the fight that defeated a $50 million highway bond issue, a program that many other states in the South were adopting in the 1920s in order to "get out of the mud." Byrd viewed the bond issue as unwanted debt that would burden rural property owners. The death of Martin had left Virginia without an identifiable political leader, and Byrd emerged victorious over a competing faction to win the 1925 race for governor.

After his election as governor, Byrd demonstrated strong, shrewd leadership. His "program of progress" reorganized state government into a dozen departments, passed the strongest antilynching law in the South, engaged in a few battles with the oil and telephone companies, and shortened the ballot to provide for popular election of only three statewide officers—governor, lieutenant governor, and attorney general. His administration also demonstrated interest in industrial development.

As governor, he amended the Constitution to prohibit issuance of general obligation bonds for almost any purpose. "Pay-as-you-go" became an article of faith for four decades, years in which special regional authorities were created to build roads and bridges. Because their bonds did not carry the full faith and credit of the state, higher interest rates resulted in unnecessary costs estimated at more than $100 million.

Byrd's lieutenant was E. R. Combs, who served as clerk of the state Senate, as chairman of the state Compensation Board that set salaries

* West Virginia, which split off to remain in the Union, eventually paid $14 million as its share of the prewar Virginia debt.

2. *Richmond Dispatch,* quoted in Virginius Dabney, *Virginia: The New Dominion* (New York: Doubleday, 1971), p. 393.

for local officials in every county, and often as Democratic national committeeman. After Byrd was elected to the U.S. Senate, Combs served as genteel boss of the machine; he toured the courthouses for a little social politicking, kept the organization trim and conferred with Senator Byrd between courthouse tours to discuss upcoming elections, advised the governor on upcoming appointments, and kept everyone at home informed about what the senator was thinking.[3] Meanwhile, in Washington, Byrd fought the New Deal and voted as a Taft Republican, but as a member of the Democratic majority he accumulated power through seniority and closed his career as chairman of the Senate Finance Committee.

Virginia has more than its share of able political reporters, but few capture the flavor of the state's politics as well as Charles McDowell, a columnist for the *Richmond Times-Dispatch*. Here is his impressionistic picture of the legislature in the Byrd days after World War II:

> A terribly decorous place. It was a place where the members tended to be the leading citizens of their towns and counties. They came there as a great honor. They were aware every day, and it was perfectly obvious, that they were the heirs in their minds of Thomas Jefferson, George Mason, and Patrick Henry. They talked about it constantly. No day went by on the floor that it wasn't referred to as the oldest, continuous legislative body in the western world. They sat among pictures of Jefferson and Mason and all of those and talked about them like they were still there. Their observance of parliamentary procedure was the most devoted and precise that I have ever seen in any legislative body. Everybody was forever in his seat. Nobody was reading a newspaper in his seat. They were as attentive as school children. They were filled with good orators. They all agreed about everything. All votes in the House were 94 to 6, or 93 to 7, but everybody was there.
>
> They were extremely ethical people, and it stunned reporters from other states that saw it. It stunned lobbyists from other states. It stunned everybody. There was no man to see to get a highway contract. There was no man to see to get a bill through the committee. There was no money ever changing hands. Many an old Byrd politician would be insulted at the offer of a campaign contribution that was distasteful, over a hundred dollars or so. It was an almost unbelievably honest, formal and backward place, but a charming place.[4]

How was it backward?

There was an assumption that the poll tax was right. There was an assumption that a country school with four teachers teaching 60 kids apiece was just fine. There was an assumption that the state owed the citizens very little in the way of service. There was an assumption that their job was mostly to be terribly honest, good accountants, pay-as-you-go, build good

3. J. Harvie Wilkinson, III, *Harry Byrd and the Changing Face of Virginia Politics* (Charlottesville: University of Virginia Press, 1968), pp. 52–53.

4. Interview with Charles McDowell, October 30, 1973.

roads, and keep it clean. They felt no great obligation to do service. So, it was backward.[5]

In a sense it was the legacy of Reconstruction:

They associated Reconstruction with an all-powerful and arbitrary and arrogant government that did bad things to people, and they associated it more than that with debt, debt, debt. . . . So the government was to be not powerful and it was to be low taxing, and it was never to be run at a loss. That is what really mattered. Most of those old men that I knew in the Virginia General Assembly, in the early fifties even, understood that schools weren't very good, and that the hospitals needed help and all kinds of things. But they didn't think really there was anything much the Virginia government could do about it. They voted against all such things.[6]

As Virginia's cities and suburbs developed after World War II, the rural-oriented Byrd organization was slow in responding to new demands for schools, water and sewer lines, streets, and other public services. As early as 1949, anti-Byrd candidate Francis Pickens Miller charged: "We have inadequate services in many departments of government because of the backward-looking, unimaginative, and undemocratic leadership of the Byrd machine." He described Byrd himself as the "absentee landlord" of Virginia politics, who ran things through "overseers."

Miller had been a leader among liberal Democrats who campaigned for Harry Truman in 1948; Truman's victory in Virginia without the support of Byrd was considered an upset and something of a defeat for the organization. Byrd continued what he would call his "golden silence" in presidential elections, and the only Democrat to win Virginia in a presidential election since 1948 was Lyndon Johnson in 1964. Byrd's refusal to endorse Democratic presidential nominees was in reaction to the national party's growing concern with civil rights. Differences over the question of party loyalty added to the strains within the Byrd organization.

The Byrd organization also faced significant opposition from within its ranks in 1949. Horace Edwards, a recent mayor of Richmond and one of the few urban legislators to win favor with Byrd, challenged John Stewart Battle, the organization's candidate for governor. Edwards appealed for a 2 percent sales tax to finance schools and for an end to pay-as-you-go. He even won support from some key organization leaders, including a young delegate from Nansemond County, Mills E. Godwin. Battle had demonstrated ability and loyalty as a mildly progressive leader in the state Senate. He was well liked, intelligent, dignified, and a man of handsome appearance.

In the end, Edwards was caught between the whispered word of

5. Ibid.
6. Ibid.

Byrd leaders that "a vote for Edwards is a vote for Pickens Miller" and a countercharge from Miller to reform-minded Virginians that "a vote for Edwards is a vote for Battle." Some Republican leaders urged their party followers to enter the Democratic primary for Battle against the "radical" Miller. There was no runoff provision in the primary then, and Battle was elected with a plurality of only 42.8 percent of the vote. Miller finished second with 35 percent. Battle's victory margin, impartial analysts acknowledged, came from Republicans who entered the primary. There was only token GOP opposition in the general election.

In 1953, Republican state Senator Theodore Roosevelt (Ted) Dalton proved a tireless campaigner who aired all the issues—he called for election law reform, repeal of the poll tax, popular election of school boards (who were appointed by circuit judges elected by the legislature), higher pay for teachers, more funds for mental health, and greater emphasis on industrial development. But when Dalton proposed a $100 million highway revenue bond issue, Senator Byrd construed the proposal as a slap at his sacred pay-as-you-go philosophy, and entered the campaign without restraint. In the end it was Dalton vs. Byrd. The Byrd candidate, Democrat Thomas B. Stanley, won by an uncomfortably close margin (225,878 to 182,887).

In 1954 the organization took another blow in the legislature, this time from a dozen "Young Turks" in the House. They forced a compromise in which part of a surplus was appropriated for state services rather than returned as a tax rebate. Unlike previous antiorganization leaders, the Young Turks considered themselves part of the Byrd machine, as its progressive wing. In age they averaged less than 40; most were World War II veterans, and they were respectable men who had earned college and graduate law degrees. Rather than accept them as potential future leaders, however, the regular organization, where possible, imposed sanctions such as inferior committee assignments.

But the tough races for governor in 1949 and 1953 and the Young Turk revolt in the General Assembly were all clear signs that by 1954 the organization was in decline.

MASSIVE RESISTANCE

When the Supreme Court handed down its school desegregation decision in 1954, the initial reaction was mild. Governor Stanley on May 18, 1954 said, "I am confident the people of Virginia will receive the opinion of the Supreme Court calmly and take time to carefully and dispassionately consider the situation before coming to conclusions on steps which should be taken." He promised to seek the views of leaders of both races before deciding what the state should do.

In Southside Virginia, which included most of the 31 contiguous counties which in 1950 had 40 percent or greater black populations, there was a significant meeting on June 20. Twenty Southside legislators met in the Petersburg firehouse to express officially their "unalterable opposition to the principle of integration of the races in the schools."

It soon became clear that Senator Byrd also had disapproved Governor Stanley's initial reaction. On June 25, Stanley conceded that he had been "wrong" in his moderation and declared, "I shall use every legal means at my command to continue segregated schools in Virginia."

Twenty months later, Byrd proclaimed from his Washington office about the Supreme Court school segregation cases, "If we can organize the southern states for massive resistance to this order, I think that in time the rest of the country will realize that racial integration is not going to be accepted in the South." He joined Senator Strom Thurmond and other southerners in leading the drive in Congress to pass the Southern Manifesto.

"Massive resistance" became the battle cry in Virginia for those who wanted to fight even token compliance with the Supreme Court order. Moderate leadership in Virginia and throughout the South was placed on the defensive. Defiance was dressed in legalistic language and given a facade of respectability.

James Jackson Kilpatrick, then editor of the *Richmond News Leader*, used his considerable talents as a writer to develop an intellectual justification for defiance by unearthing the doctrine of "interposition," in which John C. Calhoun had argued that a state could interpose its sovereignty to resist and even nullify the effects of what it considered an unconstitutional and intolerable federal ruling. For two months, Kilpatrick devoted his editorial page to the interposition doctrine, and the editorials were reprinted throughout the South. Other southern legislatures followed the lead of Virginia in adopting interposition resolutions "to resist this illegal encroachment upon our sovereign powers. . . ."

The legal steps became more and more extreme, with Southside legislators and congressmen calling the shots. Directed and approved by Byrd, the legal charade continued. Local option was rejected. Any school that admitted black students was to be closed. Tuition grants were provided for private schools. The emotional debate developed an atmosphere of extremism in Virginia and throughout the South. For the poor whites in the Deep South who were being told by the most respected leaders of their region that the Supreme Court had acted illegally, there was surely nothing immoral about joining resistance to such wrongdoing, and the eventual outcome was violence.

When Dalton ran again for governor in 1957, he attacked massive resistance and found himself caught in the fallout of the violent confrontation at Little Rock, Arkansas, where President Eisenhower sent troops to enforce a federal court desegregation order. Attorney General Lindsay Almond, the Democratic candidate for governor, publicly supported massive resistance, promising to "dedicate our every capacity to preserve segregation in the schools," although Almond already had expressed private misgivings about the effort. Dalton, who had received 44.7 percent of the vote four years earlier, this time got only 36.5 percent. If massive resistance rejuvenated the Byrd organization, the effect was only temporary.

Once examined calmly, interposition was legal nonsense, since the matter had clearly been resolved by the Civil War. Leaders who stirred emotions with racist speeches later would claim they had bought needed time for the public to accept the change that was coming. But raising false hopes and intensifying the voters' emotions hardly fostered a climate for acceptance.

Through it all in Virginia, a diligent corps of capitol reporters covered in detail what was going on. The charade ended after schools were actually closed in Norfolk and Charlottesville, then later in Southside Prince Edward County. Moderates had been kept informed by the press, and they organized to keep the schools open. One of them was Henry Howell, who made a second attempt for the legislature and was elected in reaction to the school closings.

Byrd never yielded. But the tide of public opinion had turned, and business leaders realized the economic damage being done and the futility of pursuing an unworkable policy. A small group, including the publisher of the Richmond newspapers and his two editors, paid a visit to the senator. Kilpatrick already had called for a new policy. Pulitzer Prize-winning Editor Virginius Dabney of the *Times-Dispatch* had never supported massive resistance all along, but his views had been suppressed by the publisher. Now they all found Byrd adamant, insisting on "a last-ditch stand . . . and not give an inch until we're completely overwhelmed."[7] Dabney later recalled that Byrd's attitude was that "Virginia is the keystone to this whole fight, and as long as we hold out we can win."[8] Governor Almond also had found Byrd intractable, later recalling that Byrd had "expressed concern as to what his Southern colleagues in the Senate would think if Virginia gave up."[9]

It was Almond who eventually broke with Byrd after the closing of the schools and restored sanity to the situation. Although as a politician

7. Confidential interview.
8. Interview with Virginius Dabney, March 12, 1974.
9. *Norfolk Virginian-Pilot,* June 9, 1974.

he had supported massive resistance, as a lawyer and former attorney general he knew it would not work. When both a federal court and the Supreme Court of Virginia in January 1959 declared the school-closing statutes void because of the state constitutional mandate for free public schools, the next step was either acceptance of token integration or complete abandonment of the public school system. Almond refused to follow the latter course, but only after making a segregationist speech pledging that he would not yield "to those who defend or close their eyes to the livid stench of sadism, sex, immorality, and juvenile pregnancy infesting the mixed schools of the District of Columbia and elsewhere. . . ."

Almond said later, "I don't know why I made that damn speech. I saw the whole thing crumbling. I was tired and distraught. . . . My underlying thought and motivation was to show the people that we had done everything we could do." [10]

A week after his just-begun-to-fight speech, which Byrd commended, Almond calmly addressed the General Assembly and explained his plans to end massive resistance. He won a key 20–19 vote in the Senate, and the tide was turned. A week later, 21 Negro children entered formerly all-white schools in Norfolk and Arlington without incident.

TOWARD THE MODERN ERA

A background figure on the state scene during the massive resistance furor was Harry F. Byrd, Jr., who went to the state Senate in the late 1940s and promptly was appointed to four major committees. He supported massive resistance to the end, insisted on pay-as-you-go, and thwarted the attempt by Almond to impose a sales tax to finance large-scale improvements in the state.

Elsewhere in the South, politicians viewed the sales tax as a means of extracting money from the poor, especially from blacks. It is no accident that the sales tax originated in Mississippi and remains highest there, a 5 percent state levy that covers food and other essentials. Although the sales tax also is simple and relatively inexpensive to collect, that was a secondary consideration. The opposition of the Byrds to the sales tax resulted from its greater impact on rural areas, the heart of the organization's strength. Incomes were significantly lower in rural areas, and personal and corporate income taxes would place the burden on urban areas. The Byrds spoke of protecting the plain people from the

10. Ibid.

sales tax, and though they spoke with genuine feeling, the fact was that the organization did not like any tax which spread a greater part of the cost of government to its rural strongholds.

There was always a feeling among the Byrd people that progress was not necessarily bad, nor was spending some state money if it was done by the right people: the right people were the Byrd people, the country club people, the bankers, the power structure. Almond, who had split with the organization on massive resistance, had confirmed suspicions that he could not be "trusted."

The man who provided the leadership that brought Virginia into the modern era was courtly, austere Mills Godwin, who as a state senator from Southside played a major leadership role in the fight for massive resistance. But Godwin sensed the changing mood in Virginia and demonstrated the political skills and leadership ability to survive the shifting winds and changing currents of the state's politics. He grew up in Nansemond County, developed into a top debater at William and Mary, earned his law degree at the University of Virginia, spent three years with the FBI, returned home and ran for the House of Delegates in 1947 as a 33-year-old lawyer, and five years later was elected to fill a state Senate vacancy.

He not only supported massive resistance but also led the fight for the most extreme measures. He joined with young Byrd in the fight against the sales tax. He attacked organized labor. In the fight to prohibit local school districts from deciding whether they wanted to integrate, Godwin had declared in the Senate that "integration, however slight, anywhere in Virginia, would be a cancer eating at the very lifeblood of our public school system."

He won election as lieutenant governor in 1961 against Armistead Boothe, a leader of the Young Turks. Boothe called Godwin "a penny-pinching school closer," and Godwin retorted that Boothe was soft on integration and had tried to sink Virginia's right-to-work law. But Godwin recognized Virginia was in ferment, and as lieutenant governor he spent much of his time getting around the state, making innocuous speeches, and listening. Meanwhile, Governor Albertis Harrison emphasized industrial development and presided over a period of calm, in which forces for change continued to ferment.

In 1964, a year in which the senior Byrd himself was rebuffed when the state Democratic convention endorsed Lyndon Johnson for president despite Byrd's opposition, Godwin and Harrison both campaigned actively for the Democratic national ticket against Goldwater. Also in 1964, the poll tax was wiped out for presidential elections (and for all elections in 1966). The black vote in Virginia grew significantly larger.

With the poll tax gone, the presidential vote in 1964 surpassed 1 million for the first time, and 270,000 more voters went to the polls than

349

ever before in Virginia. Lyndon Johnson received 53.5 percent of the vote, including 99 percent of the black vote (Goldwater had opposed Johnson's 1964 Civil Rights Act). The solid black bloc provided Johnson's margin of victory. Typical of returns from black precincts were those from Richmond's Precinct 16, where Johnson won 2,138 to 14, and from Pembroke Precinct in Hampton, where Johnson won 1,238 to 8. In the Jefferson Park Precinct at Newport News, Johnson won 1,325 to zero.

Another development in 1964 was court-ordered reapportionment, which shifted 11 seats in the 140-member General Assembly from rural to urban areas, six of them to northern Virginia suburbs of Washington and five to the fast-growing Hampton Roads region. Since neither had ever been Byrd strongholds, rural dominance and the Byrd machine were further undercut.

Godwin not only expanded his political base with his support of Lyndon Johnson, but he also began to hint that the state might need a sales tax to meet public demands for services. Segregation was a dead issue, and Godwin's attention turned to better-financed education. Godwin developed a Democratic coalition similar to those in South Carolina and Georgia, combining courthouse and rural traditional Democrats, blacks, organized labor, and liberals, while retaining full support from a business and financial establishment that was ready for economic modernization and development. But in Virginia, the coalition did not endure.

Godwin won the Democratic nomination without opposition in 1965 and ran against progressive Republican Linwood Holton and Conservative Party candidate William J. Story, Jr., a proud member of the John Birch Society. Godwin campaigned on the theme of change, that "our people are ready for new and bolder steps to keep pace with the times." When questioned about his previous support for massive resistance, he replied that the issue had been "long since settled. The program . . . bought valuable time during which people were able to adjust for conditions that were inevitably to come."

Holton, a mountain Republican out of the tradition of Ted Dalton, was a Harvard Law graduate whose timetable was to make a respectable showing in 1965 in order to lay the groundwork for a successful race four years later.

The new Godwin retained the support of the organization, but he also got the endorsement of the state AFL–CIO and the two most influential Negro political groups in the state, Richmond's Crusade for Voters and the Independent Voters League in the Tidewater region. Even a moderate like Holton could not overcome the bad taste the Goldwater candidacy had left among blacks.

Godwin won with only a plurality of 47.9 percent. He received more than three-fourths of the black vote, which before the Goldwater candidacy had tended to support Republicans in Virginia, and black support provided the difference in his 57,000-vote margin over Holton. The

Republican candidate received only 37.7 percent of the vote, but he got 44 percent of the major party vote, enough to launch him into a four-year campaign that eventually met with success.

Virginia was poised for a wave of progress. Godwin sensed it and declared in his inaugural, "If there is a watchword for our time, it is to move, to strike out boldly, to reach for the heights."

His achievements were impressive. He skillfully maneuvered through the legislature a state sales tax to finance greatly expanded educational facilities and programs that included public kindergartens, and he ended "pay-as-you-go." He won support for an $81 million bond issue to finance capital improvements in mental health and higher education facilities, established a statewide community college system, accelerated Virginia's recruitment of new industry, promoted tourism, and created a blue-ribbon commission that wrote a modern new constitution and won acceptance for it in the state.

Significantly, the new constitution declared education a fundamental right and provided that the General Assembly maintain "an educational program of high quality." The constitution also provided for annual rather than biennial sessions of the legislature, modernized the state's judicial system, and turned the state's basic law away from the tradition of negative government.

Although Godwin eventually appointed 35 blacks to various boards and commissions, more than any previous governor, the number was hardly impressive in view of the more than 2,500 appointments a governor makes in Virginia. Few governors have as much appointive power, and blacks grumbled that those he made were late in coming.

Although Godwin helped Virginia's state government adjust to the demands of a modern society, he did nothing to alarm the banks, utilities, insurance companies, and other economic forces whose interests always had coincided with those of the Byrd organization.

After Godwin's election but before he took office, Harry F. Byrd, Sr., 78 and in failing health, resigned from the U.S. Senate, and Governor Harrison appointed Harry Byrd, Jr., a state senator for 18 years, as his father's successor.

Events the following year were to break the organization's hold on electoral politics, increase Republican strength, reflect the emergence of urban ticket splitters as a major force, and usher in an era of increasingly fluid political alignments that continues in Virginia.

A full-scale assault on the organization in 1966 toppled 79-year-old incumbent Senator A. Willis Robertson and 83-year-old Howard Smith (a 36-year House veteran), chairmen respectively of the Senate Banking and House Rules Committees. Harry Byrd, Jr. survived by less than 9,000 votes after a challenge from Armistead Boothe in the Democratic primary. Within a year, the Byrd organization had lost almost 100 years of seniority in Washington.

Smith lost to liberal Delegate George Rawlings and Robertson to moderate Young Turk state Senator William Spong, both by less than 700 votes. The right-wing ideologues of the Virginia Conservative Party, who urged their followers to stay out of the primary because Robertson and Smith had failed to resign from the "foul and filthy" Democratic Party, apparently were responsible for the defeat of two of the most influential conservatives in Congress, and they took pride in it.[11]

Although Spong and Byrd both won easily against Republicans in November, Conservative Party candidates received 8 percent in each race, down from more than 13 percent in the governor's race a year before. While Spong captured 58.6 percent of the popular vote, Byrd won only 53.3 percent; Spong pulled almost 41,000 more votes than Byrd did. Significantly, blacks voted overwhelmingly for Byrd's little-known Republican opponent. A study of 37 black precincts showed that Spong received 96 percent of the vote, but Byrd got only 13.5 percent. The turnout in those precincts was only half of what it had been in the 1964 presidential election, a factor that helped allow Byrd to win his narrow victory.

As often happens when veteran southern congressmen lose to liberal Democratic challengers in a primary, the conservative Democratic supporters of Judge Smith joined Republicans in electing an obscure former Department of Agriculture lawyer, archconservative William Scott, over Rawlings. The lesson of the 1966 primary was that the era of relatively easy victories for the Democratic organization was over, and future opposition would be serious.[12]

In 1968, Richard Nixon won Virginia with 43.4 percent of the vote, followed by Democrat Hubert Humphrey with 32.5 percent and George Wallace with 23.6 percent. Voting in the state's six metropolitan areas accounted for 55.9 percent of the total statewide vote. The table below[13] illustrates the contrast in voting behavior between city and suburb; the pattern generally reflects national patterns.

	CITY	SUBURBS
Nixon (R)	37.5%	48.8%
Humphrey (D)	40.6	29.0
Wallace (AIP)	21.4	21.6
Other	0.5	0.6

11. Dabney, *Virginia*, p. 559.

12. See Ralph Eisenberg, "1966 Politics in Virginia: The Elections for U.S. Senators," *University of Virginia Newsletter*, May 15, 1967, pp. 1–4.

13. Eisenberg, "The 1968 Election in Virginia: Voting Patterns and Party Competition," *Newsletter*, June 15, 1969, p. 3.

Wallace's proportion of the total vote was far greater than the previous high for a third-party candidate, 16 percent in 1912 for Theodore Roosevelt. His strength was centered in the conservative Southside, but he also drew heavily among the traditionally Democratic working class in the Tidewater cities. Although the overall vote increased 30.6 percent from 1964, to almost 1.4 million, the vote in black precincts was only 5 percent greater than in 1964.

In 1969 the Godwin coalition fell apart as Democrats divided bitterly into conservative, moderate, and liberal factions. The division helped elect Holton as Virginia's first Republican governor in this century.

The organization candidates were crushed in the Democratic primary. The conservative incumbent lieutenant governor received only 23 percent of the vote, to finish a weak third behind moderate William C. Battle, son of former governor John Battle, who led Howell by only 4,000 votes in the first primary. In the runoff, Governor Godwin endorsed Battle, predicted a Republican win if Howell won the Democratic nomination, and said he would not support Howell if he was the nominee. Battle won the runoff with 52 percent of the vote. Howell's major strength came in the cities, where he won 59.4 percent of the vote, including 95 percent of the urban black vote. Significantly, the turnout in the primary was relatively small, with only 433,613 votes cast for governor. The falloff was especially heavy in the suburbs.

Godwin's intervention in the runoff triggered mass defections by Howell supporters from Battle in the November election against the progressive Holton. After the runoff, there was a hectic meeting at which Howell and some of his supporters confronted Battle with a virtually impossible demand for control of a number of appointments roughly equal to Howell's share of the vote. Battle turned them down. Although Howell maintained personal party loyalty and said he would vote for Battle, he told his supporters they were "free spirits."

The Richmond-based Crusade for Voters and the state AFL–CIO subsequently endorsed Holton, giving him support unusual for a Republican from blacks and organized labor. AFL–CIO President Julian Carper said the decision was made before the runoff to support Holton if Howell lost, and that it resulted from Godwin's intervention.[14]

Battle had been a supporter of John F. Kennedy in 1960 and was campaign manager for Spong in 1966, but to Howell followers he was tied too much to the Byrd machine and too indebted to Godwin. In a newsletter to its members just before the election, the AFL–CIO explained that there was little difference in the platforms of Holton and Battle and that both "are very likable and both have undeniable qualifications to hold public office." The election of Holton, the newsletter continued, "will mean the end of machine politics in our state. . . . The strength of the political machine was plainly seen during the Demo-

14. Interview with Julian Carper, March 13, 1974.

cratic primary, when its influence definitely prevented Senator Howell from becoming the Democratic nominee for governor."

Although Howell had remained aloof, he accepted an invitation in October to attend a unity dinner in support of Battle. But Godwin and Watkins Abbitt, a conservative Southside congressman and state Democratic chairman, blocked efforts to seat Howell at the head table or even to recognize him when dignitaries were introduced. It was that snub which killed any chance of winning back support among Howell's followers, according to Joe Fitzpatrick, who had been Howell's campaign manager but who was a party loyalist and had gone to work for Battle in the general election.

Holton won by 65,000 votes. The Crusade for Voters endorsement brought significant results, as Holton received 57.5 percent of the vote in predominantly black precincts in Richmond. A statewide analysis of urban black voting showed Holton winning 37.2 percent, less than a majority everywhere except Richmond, but almost double his 1965 percentage against Godwin. Holton also diluted and in some cases eliminated the usual Democratic majorities in the Tidewater cities.

A significant feature in the November general election was the size of the turnout, more than double that of the Democratic primary. In November the suburban portion of the metropolitan vote was 57.5 percent, compared with 42.3 percent for the central cities, a significant reversal from the relative proportions in the Democratic primaries. In the suburbs, Holton ran almost 5 points ahead of his statewide percentage and received a plurality of almost 47,000 votes there.

Twenty-four Republicans were elected to the 100-member House of Delegates with Holton, more than doubling their representation there. Democrats Andrew Pickens Miller and J. Sargeant Reynolds were elected attorney general and lieutenant governor respectively, but Republican percentages for those offices (46 and 42 percent, respectively) for the first time exceeded 40 percent.

Even with Holton's election, the Democratic future appeared secure in the person of Reynolds, a former state senator and heir to a metals fortune who possessed charismatic appeal. "Sarge Reynolds was wealthy, liberal, and respected by business because he was knowledgeable about finances," recalled the late George Kelley, a veteran capitol reporter for Norfolk and Roanoke newspapers. "I remember hearing blacks point to him and saying, 'He's going to be president.' " [15]

But the 34-year-old Reynolds died unexpectedly and tragically of a brain tumor in 1971.

In 1970, Harry Byrd, Jr. declared himself a political independent and proceeded to win a majority of the vote against Democratic and Re-

15. Interview with George Kelley, November 2, 1973.

publican challengers. Byrd's official reason for leaving the party was a loyalty oath that would have bound him to support the 1972 presidential nominee. "I would rather be a free man than a captive Senator," he said in a lengthy prepared statement.

Veteran newsman James Latimer of the *Times-Dispatch*, the analytical dean of political writers in Virginia, reported in his story of Byrd's declaration of independence that the senator's statement "didn't mention what other, unofficial reports had hinted earlier: that a poll commissioned by Byrd had shown he would face considerably more trouble in a Democratic primary than he would running as an independent in the general election."

The Democratic loyalty oath was not new, but for more than 40 years Virginia had operated on the basis of an artful state attorney general's opinion that it did not apply in presidential elections. The change by the state Democratic Central Committee, later characterized by Byrd as an act of "complete political immaturity," [16] provided him with the opportunity to make a deft political move. The turnout in a three-way Democratic primary was only 129,000, the smallest since a not seriously contested Senate race in 1948. Byrd said later that the small turnout was the tipoff of his strength and that "when that fact sank into the political mind, I began to pick up a lot more political support." [17] Until then, many of his Democratic officeholding friends had held back.

In the Senate he caucused the next year with the Democrats, who accepted him as an independent Democrat and allowed him to keep his seniority and committee assignments.

After the death of Reynolds, and after the weak state of the Democratic Party had been demonstrated by Byrd, Howell ran for lieutenant governor as an independent and was elected.

Implementation of the national Democratic Party reforms in 1972 brought blacks and women and young people into the state Democratic convention in record and dominant numbers. After former Governor Godwin was denied a delegate's seat to the state convention from the Nansemond County convention, he then became a figurehead for the Committee to Reelect the President, the Nixon campaign effort in Virginia. He and Howell, longtime enemies, were heading for a clash in 1973, a factor that created organizational problems for Senator Spong, who was upset in his 1972 race for reelection. The Democrats ran no formal candidate for governor in 1973, backing Howell as an independent, but other events were pulling together a new Democratic coalition.

When Godwin formally switched to the Republican Party in 1973, it

16. Interview with Harry Byrd, Jr., March 8, 1974.
17. Ibid.

was "to save the state from Henry Howell," a description Howell used for Godwin's campaign. Godwin and Howell differ in background, political philosophy, and temperament, but many view the two as very much alike in one aspect. Former Senator Spong observed: "You can have this confirmed by anybody you talk to who is knowledgeable; neither Governor Godwin nor Howell can participate in anything without taking it over. I mean their personalities and their operation is such that they don't embrace you; they squeeze you to death." [18]

Howell grew up in a middle-class family in Norfolk. His father was a lumber salesman and considered himself a nominal Republican. The family lived a couple of years in New Jersey when Henry was a child, and he attended first grade with black children. Later, at the University of Virginia Law School, he was notable for the fact that he was not a fraternity man, did not come from an old Virginia family, and was not concerned with politics. He got a law clerk's job, but was not even aware at the time that it was the Byrd organization's local coordinator whom he asked to write a letter of recommendation. It was merely someone a friend had suggested might help.

After reading an article in Sunday *New York Times Magazine* about the undemocratic Byrd organization, Howell accepted a friend's invitation in 1949 to join the local campaign of Francis Pickens Miller, serving as precinct chairman. He then took on a larger local role when Miller challenged the senior Byrd for the Senate in 1952.

Howell subsequently found himself twice blackballed when put up for membership in the Kiwanis Club. He was not elevated to president in the customary manner after serving as vice-president of the local YMCA. After serving as Sunday School superintendent of his local Episcopal Church, he was never nominated to the church vestry. The reason, Howell said later, was "because I had opposed Harry Byrd. That was the sole reason, because I was white, Anglo-Saxon, Protestant, graduate of the University of Virginia, up-and-coming lawyer, and didn't have any noticeable halitosis or other communicable diseases. The idea was to ostracize." [19]

He ran for the House of Delegates in 1953, and the organization beat him. He lost interest in politics until the policy of massive resistance closed the Norfolk schools. But he had already developed the idea that the courts and public attention could be used to effect social change. In the mid-1950s he and another lawyer represented a black member of the Merchant Marine who had become mentally ill. The upshot was that Howell went into the segregated state mental hospital for blacks with a photographer and exposed primitive conditions at a court hearing. The presiding judge condemned the state for its failure to provide

18. Interview with William B. Spong, Jr., March 8, 1974.
19. Interview with Henry Howell, March 13, 1974.

adequate facilities, and the result was a sharp increase in legislative appropriations for the long-neglected institution.

Howell again ran for the House of Delegates in 1959 to fight the closing of the schools, and this time he won. Reporters found him a "bumptious, captivating sort of person," and one recalled his first impression of Howell was that he was the former Sunday School superintendent who was fighting for liquor-by-the-drink.

After Howell took the oath to uphold the constitution of Virginia, he went to his hotel room to read the document. He was struck by the language of George Mason, who ranks in Virginia with Jefferson and Madison and Patrick Henry, "that all power is vested in and consequently derived from the people. The magistrates are their trustees and servants, and at all times amenable to them." He later framed Mason's words and hung them on a wall in the lieutenant governor's office. To Howell, the words were the cornerstone of a democracy and meant "that politicians are going to listen to the people and run on specific issues, and they're going to work on the passage of what individuals can't do." [20] He also came to admire the political philosophy of Huey Long, but not Long's methods.

Howell considered himself a "people's candidate," but what he found in Richmond was a legislature of aristocrats who tended to talk to people like themselves and to represent their interests. Howell soon earned a reputation of being not just a liberal but a rather disruptive fellow. He filed the lawsuit that resulted in reapportionment of the Senate and then won election to one of the new seats awarded Norfolk. In Godwin's first term, Howell sued the governor, forcing the restoration of $11 million in federal funds that had been diverted from school districts "impacted" with the children of federal personnel.

He developed an antiestablishment and proconsumer image with a series of successful rate cases that won rebates from automobile insurance, electric power, and telephone companies. One suit resulted in rebates of $5 million to telephone customers. One of his major targets was the rate increase requests of Virginia Electric and Power Co. (VEPCO). He attacked the traditional policy, continued by Godwin, of placing millions in state funds in interest-free deposits with major banks.

Howell burst onto the state political scene when he ran for governor in 1969 with the slogan (borrowed from Senator Warren Magnuson of Washington) "Keep the Big Boys Honest." Leftover campaign buttons ordered for Magnuson were bought at a bargain price by Howell. To gain attention quickly, Howell ran a series of shouting, arm-waving television commercials attacking special interests. Opponents tagged him "Howling Henry," and ever since he has tried to tone down his

20. Ibid.

image among sedate northern Virginia liberals as something of a wild man. In both style and substance, few political figures could be more different from the traditional Byrd Democrats than Henry Howell. There are many in Virginia who believe—some with joy and some with fear—that he will be the next governor.

REPUBLICANS

As in Tennessee and North Carolina, the Republican Party in Virginia began the post–World War II period with a significant base of mountain Republicans, whose party ties date back to opposition to the Civil War. The Washington suburbs of northern Virginia mushroomed during the years of the Eisenhower administration, bringing Republican inmigrants from other states. Suburbs in other cities provided a base for the new recruits, younger families whose needs were not being met by a rural-dominated Democratic Party and economic conservatives who opposed the policies of the national Democratic Party. The "golden silences" of Harry Byrd, Sr. encouraged nominal Democrats to vote Republican in presidential elections, making it easier to break the habit of voting Democratic for lesser offices.

Republican strength centered in the Shenandoah Valley and in the Great Valley that extended into the mountainous southwest, home of the "Fighting Ninth" congressional district, a traditional antiorganization stronghold. For 12 years, from 1955 to 1967, the Fighting Ninth was represented by Democrat W. Pat Jennings, until 1975 the state's only liberal congressman. Jennings lost in 1966 to William Wampler, a conservative Republican he had defeated in 1954. Jennings went on to become clerk of the U.S. House, and Wampler—still only 40 when he went back to the House—secured an apparently safe seat.

It was Holton, the first Republican governor in this century, who set the tone in race relations that was reflected a year later in the inaugural addresses of "New South" Democratic governors in Georgia, South Carolina, Florida, and Arkansas. "No more must the slogan of 'states' rights' sound a recalcitrant and defensive note for the people of the South," Holton declared. "For the era of defiance is behind us. . . . Let our goal in Virginia be an aristocracy of ability, regardless of race, color, or creed."

Holton's words were followed with deeds. He appointed William Robertson, a former school principal from Roanoke, as the first black to serve on a governor's staff. Robertson met regularly with Holton as his adviser on minority problems, and the two worked together on innovative approaches in dealing with racial matters. Jobs, both in the public and private sector, were given priority, and *Washington Post* Virginia correspondent Helen Dewar wrote at the end of Holton's term that Robertson's successes were "not spectacular, but they were significant" in broadening employment opportunities for minorities in both state government and the private sector. When the two black members in the House of Delegates pushed for the South's first state open-housing law, Holton put his support behind the measure, and six of the seven Republican state senators voted for the bill, which passed.

The most dramatic incident in his administration came when Holton escorted his daughter to a 95 percent black high school during the midst of emotional turmoil over a Richmond desegregation order that involved provision for busing of some children to newly assigned schools. A photograph of Holton and his daughter made the front pages of newspapers throughout Virginia and the nation. Colgate Darden, Jr., who was World War II governor and, after retiring as president of the University of Virginia, became widely viewed as the wise old man of Virginia politics, wrote Holton to tell him that the event was "the most significant happening in this commonwealth during my lifetime."

Charley McDowell described Holton as a man "intolerant of nothing except intolerance." Although Holton grew up as a mountain Republican, his father bolted the party in 1928 to support Al Smith, a Democrat and Catholic who was being attacked for his religion. Holton's father called a gathering of the family clan to announce his decision and explained he was voting for Smith "because I can't stand bigotry."

Holton won praise for the quality of the people he appointed to office, and he proved to be a popular governor. At the end of his term, a statewide poll showed a 77 percent favorable job rating—an unusually high mark.

Holton had campaigned for President Nixon in 1968 and strongly supported his revenue-sharing and similar programs. But Holton's racial stand and his belief that if the GOP was to be successful in the South, it had to become moderate and broad based, clashed with the "Southern Strategy" of the Nixon administration. Holton, who like Winthrop Rockefeller in Arkansas and Howard Baker in Tennessee proved that moderate Republicans could attract substantial black support, believes the Nixon-type "Southern Strategy" has hindered Republican growth in the South.[21]

Because he believed it necessary in order to build the Republican Party, Holton insisted that the GOP field opposition to Byrd in 1970 and Howell in 1971, even though no strong candidates were available. It was an issue that split the party, and Republican candidates fared

21. Interview with Linwood Holton, September 25, 1973.

poorly. In 1972 conservatives won control of the party machinery, and the party moved at least temporarily to the right.

Holton believes that his policy of insisting on Republican candidates in major races resulted in Godwin's switching parties rather than running in 1973 as an independent, as Byrd had done. Richard Obenshain, the articulate young conservative GOP leader, contends that Godwin switched because of William Scott's 1972 victory.

Unlike the other states in the South, Virginia has moved away from nominating primaries. Voters do not register by party. Republicans tend to nominate their candidates by convention or mass meetings (caucuses) at which those who attend profess party affiliation, and Democrats in recent years have moved in that direction. The decision whether to hold a primary is made by the party organization, with local committees deciding the nominating method for local elections. The winning Republican candidates for governor, Holton and Godwin, were nominated at the state Republican convention, and Republican leaders tend to agree that the role of the party is to select the nominees and present them to the electorate. The divisiveness of the 1969 Democratic primary for governor and failure to nominate a party candidate in 1973 have left a negative feeling among Democratic officials about returning to statewide primaries. Thus, the tendency in Virginia is to return to the traditional role of political parties, thus strengthening two-party competition.

RECENT TRENDS

The race issue had revived in Virginia as a result of a U.S. district court order to merge predominantly black schools in Richmond with the predominantly white suburban districts in adjoining Henrico and Chesterfield counties. The court-ordered busing plan (which in many instances would have reduced travel distances) had been sought by the Richmond school district. The Fourth Circuit Court of Appeals rejected the district court order, and the Supreme Court upheld the Circuit Court with a 4–4 vote. Justice Lewis F. Powell, Jr., a former Richmond school board member, abstained.

Busing became an emotional issue, and the term "busing" became a racial code word. It was a key issue in 1972, when Republican U.S. Representative William Scott upset Senator Spong. One of the least well regarded men in the Senate, Scott indicated early in his term that he may not seek reelection in 1978.

Spong's defeat represented a retreat from reason in Virginia. An even-tempered, reflective man who believes he made a good senator but was perhaps "a failure as a politician," [22] Spong was the last of the Young Turks of the early 1950s to leave elective office. A *Texas Law Review* article about Spong in 1971 characterized him as "reason personified" and viewed his political success as "a victory for the force of reason in American life." The article, written before his 1972 defeat, warned, "There are long-term doubts about the prospects of a man like Spong as a Southern leader. It may be that as the wheel turns, the moderate men like Spong will be engulfed either by the forces of extreme radicalism or extreme conservatism." [23]

Spong once spoke of a Virginia of the future, "that would, by example, give leadership to the nation; a state that could retain the pride of its past without being blinded to the needs of the present and future; a society where people had attained an understanding of one another; a society of tolerance and goodwill."

In an interview, Spong reflected on the role the Young Turks had played in Virginia politics. They were young men from established families who had returned from World War II with "the perception that the nation is a much larger place than just the state of Virginia, and the world is a much larger place. . . . I realized when I came back from the war that those people shouldn't be made to sit in the rear of the bus, and I don't think that I had considered it in those terms." [24]

The other Young Turks already had become successful lawyers or judges and had dropped out of politics. "Most of them perhaps voluntarily decided that they couldn't accomplish what they had hoped that they could in the political process," Spong said.[25]

The race for governor in 1973 pitted Howell and reform against Godwin and the status quo. "Virginians are concerned that there are now some who would impose a radical change in the direction of the state," Godwin declared. "It takes a long time to thaw a watermelon if it's been frozen long enough," Howell asserted.

Godwin won with 50.7 percent of the vote, 525,075 to 510,103. Significantly, Howell carried a substantial segment of the 1968 Wallace vote despite Godwin's use of busing as a major issue and the subliminal appeal to racism in his advertising. Howell centered his campaign on repeal of the sales tax on food, which would be replaced by his "ABC plan" for additional taxes on alcohol, banks, and corporations.

Howell, Byrd, and Wallace share part of the same constituency—

22. Interview with William B. Spong, Jr., March 8, 1974.
23. John P. Frank, "Ruminations on Reason and Law: A Spong Song," *Texas Law Review*, December, 1971, Vol. 50, No. 1, pp. 35–58.
24. Interview with William B. Spong, Jr., March 8, 1974.
25. Ibid.

Howell the liberal with his fight against big business, Byrd the conservative with his fight against big government, and Wallace with his rhetorical attacks against both—in their appeal to a widespread sense of alienation in the 1970s against established institutions of authority. Byrd's feeling is "that the voters don't require that a candidate necessarily vote the way they want him to vote all the time, but I think they do want to have the feeling that he is sincere in his convictions." [26] (A 1973 poll showed a 60 percent approval rating for Byrd among Virginia voters, with only 12 percent disapproving of his performance and the remainder expressing no opinion.)

Precinct 16 in Richmond—a low-income, white working-class neighborhood that voted overwhelmingly for George Wallace in 1968, for Harry Byrd, Jr. in 1970, and for conservative Republican William Scott in 1972 also voted 145–68 for Howell. He carried the Southside Fourth Congressional District, traditionally a stronghold for Byrd and Wallace. Altogether, analysis indicated the Wallace vote split almost evenly between Howell and Godwin, who was endorsed by both Byrd and William Battle, the defeated Democratic candidate for governor in 1969.

Howell directly blamed his defeat on the NBC *Today* show, which at 8 A.M. on the morning of the election characterized him in a brief summary of the Virginia governor's race as "a populist who favors busing and who backed George McGovern a year ago." Howell had never advocated busing, but a year and a half earlier, in an interview with Washington television station WTOP, he had said that some busing *might* be required if the then pending Richmond decision (the court order to consolidate schools with adjoining counties) were sustained on appeal by the Supreme Court and if the principle were applied to Washington and its northern Virginia suburbs. Howell added that busing and consolidation were against the will of the people and "we can't invite revolution." The Supreme Court ruling came months before the election.

In response to protest from Howell headquarters, NBC ran a retraction on the "Howell . . . favors busing" report a few minutes before nine, but tens of thousands of Virginia voters already had gone to work by then. Howell said after losing that he would sue NBC. He probably would have, except for the death from cancer of *Today* commentator Frank McGee, who had given the erroneous report. In a memo to NBC before McGee's death, Howell asked for $10 million in damages and offered to settle for $2 million.

In the memo, he pointed out that McGee owned a farm in Rappahannock County which he visited an average of twice a month, that the local attorney who represented McGee was a man who had been Godwin's appointee as chairman of the State Board of Elections, and

26. Interview with Harry Byrd, Jr., March 8, 1974.

that the lawyer had served on a committee of "Byrd-machine Democrats" supporting Godwin and had signed a letter that "distorted Howell's
busing . . . position" by quoting out of context from the televised
interview.

Howell pointed out in his memo to NBC that the newsman who had
conducted the original WTOP interview wrote a week before the election that "both Howell and Godwin have taken firm public stands that
mass busing . . . should be opposed" and that much had been "represented and misrepresented" from the earlier interview. Howell's point
was that a simple call to the newsman would have clarified the issue.

The memo stated that Howell poll watchers reported that numerous
voters said they had heard the NBC report and had been influenced
by it, to Howell's detriment. The memo said that a retired police chief
in a small town and his wife voluntarily called Howell to say they
switched their votes because of the erroneous statement and didn't hear
the "retraction," stating that they discussed the remark they heard on the
Today show and concluded that "a national network can't be wrong."

In the last weeks of the campaign, Godwin had developed busing
into a major emotional issue. Howell pointed out he had never initiated
any statements on busing but had merely responded to news media
inquiries on the subject, and that NBC had interviewed him. His memo
to NBC concluded, "Whereas Godwin could only plant seeds of doubt
as to Howell's true position relative to busing, only a supposedly impartial newsgathering organization like NBC, with the apparent credibility of Moses, could convince the 'soft' Howell voters and the undecided voter that Howell had deceived them and intended to promote
busing."

In asking for damages, the memo said, "the clear inference to be
drawn from McGee's opportunity to be influential against Howell and
for Godwin is that McGee spoke with actual knowledge that the statement he made was false and with the intent to damage Howell." [27] NBC
had cited to Howell the usually authoritative *Congressional Quarterly*
as a source for its erroneous item, a bit of sloppy reporting that later
was the subject of a special staff meeting at the offices of the Washington periodical. A switch in less than 7,500 votes, or about four per
precinct, would have made the difference in the race.

The conventional political wisdom in Virginia is that Howell blundered by releasing in September a poll that showed him 13 points
ahead, thus stirring the Godwin forces out of lethargy, and that Howell
unnecessarily alienated those who would be affected by his tax proposals
by making those proposals unnecessarily specific.

27. The authors were allowed access to the memo during an interview with
Howell on March 13, 1974, before the death of McGee and while he was appearing
regularly on the *Today* show. The memo already had been sent to NBC officials.

At the same time, important events were occurring among Republicans of which the press and public, and perhaps even Godwin himself, were unaware. Godwin's campaign was viewed from Republican National Committee headquarters in Washington as a bumbling disaster. Norman Bishop, an Atlanta-based Republican field coordinator for the South who viewed Godwin's election as crucial to GOP progress in the region, moved into Virginia with as many experienced political field men as he could find. He worked with state Republican Chairman Obenshain to use emotional issues in a coordinated, hard-hitting attack on Howell and set up a telephone canvassing operation aimed at contacting 1 million voters in seven population centers.

"We put together a surrogate program to begin attacking Howell, because the Godwin people weren't effectively doing that," Bishop said. "They were putting out press releases that were six pages long. You know, that's too much crap. Also, they didn't mention busing . . . it just wasn't getting the job done." There was coordinated scheduling of Republican congressmen, especially Seventh District Representative J. Kenneth Robinson, and of some Democratic state senators who supported Godwin and were willing to attack Howell. "We wanted to make it not look like a giant conspiracy against Henry Howell," Bishop said, "so we kept the congressmen fairly localized."

They hit Howell on three issues: busing, the use of outside professional field men from organized labor, and his expenditures of money—"Virginia is not for sale." Actually, Howell and Godwin each spent more than $900,000 in the campaign, but Howell's public release of his expenditures, designed to reflect integrity, made his more visible.

"Obenshain became a hatchet man, and he really started hitting Howell with anything we could find," Bishop said, "We began putting together a series of throwaways and pamphlets on busing and everything else. Openly, blatantly prejudicial material. We referred to them as voter information documents. I think they're called smear sheets in some places. . . . I'm not talking about Segretti type stuff. I'm talking about factual material, but driving the point home. . . . Do one on gun control, which we had to use in the Ninth District area, but didn't want to use in northern Virginia. Busing we used, especially in Norfolk and Alexandria and Arlington and the Richmond suburbs. . . . We put the thing together totally separate from the Godwin campaign. The thing was, we couldn't get them to make a decision; so we were running our own show. If they don't like it, too damn bad. We were going to take it and go with it. And I don't think Godwin ever knew I was in there. He may have seen me around the headquarters some day, but I spent as little time in Godwin headquarters as possible."

The type of amoral political tactics described by Bishop, which had been introduced into Virginia politics in the Scott campaign for the

Senate against Spong in 1972, represents a change from the state's traditionally more genteel political code. "You have to be very careful up there, because they're such gentlemen, they don't even like to call the other side names," Bishop said.

In regard to the NBC *Today* show characterization of Howell, Bishop said, "I think what led NBC to have that impression was the fact that we sold that idea . . . we had it on tape. There was no doubt that Howell was probusing." [28]

Howell said he learned that the transcript of the interview had been purchased from WTOP by Attorney General Andrew Pickens Miller. "He is the one that bought the transcript and somehow he got it to Mills Godwin's people," Howell said.[29] With Howell's defeat and his own easy reelection as attorney general, Andy Miller became the top elected Democratic official in Virginia and a rival of Howell's for party leadership. Howell contended that Miller—whose father's efforts had first brought Howell into politics—represented a different party faction. The episode about the transcript helps to explain a personal antipathy between the two men that may affect future political developments in the state.[30]

Democrat Miller was reelected by more than 350,000 votes, and Republican John Dalton was elected lieutenant governor by 156,000 votes. Thus, the sons of both Francis Pickens Miller and Theodore Roosevelt Dalton—the two men who a generation earlier had begun the assault against the Byrd machine—were now top figures in the state's elected hierarchy. Each son had a reputation as somewhat more of a pragmatist and less of a fighter than his father. Dalton, the apparent Republican candidate for governor in 1977, will have to bridge the moderate and conservative factions in the party and seek support from the conservative Democrats.

Howell officially rejoined the Democrats in 1974, and a year later he made it clear he planned to run again for governor in 1977, in what apparently will be a head-on clash with Attorney General Miller. Soaring electricity rates—by 1975, electricity bills in some cases equaled house payments for Virginia residents—hold a special significance for Howell's prospects because of his long-established image as a battler against VEPCO. The *Richmond Times-Dispatch* quoted a disconsolate Godwin supporter: "I think a lot of us thought [the 1973 race was] Henry's last hurrah. We couldn't see him running again. But now with all the furor and emotionalism about electricity rates . . . I think Henry will run in 1977 and I think he can win." He complained that VEPCO

28. Interview with Norman Bishop, May 2, 1974.

29. Interview with Henry Howell, March 13, 1974.

30. Several attempts by the authors to secure an interview with Mr. Miller were unsuccessful.

would have nuclear power plants on line by the time the next governor came into office, that rates probably would drop, and that Howell would get the credit.[31]

However, Howell alienated some of his long-time political supporters in 1976 with what they viewed as unnecessarily dogmatic efforts by him on behalf of presidential candidate Jimmy Carter. For example, Howell personally initiated a move that resulted in Carter delegates running against an uncommitted slate backed by Joe Jordan, the black Vice Mayor of Norfolk and a veteran supporter of Howell, in Jordan's precinct. Such political effrontery caused some followers of Howell to threaten a switch in allegiance to Miller.

Godwin became the first man ever to twice win popular election as governor of Virginia. Unlike his dynamic first administration, which emphasized change, Godwin's second was marked by continuity. His major program concerned penal reform, an area where scandal was breaking when he took office. In the effort to build and strengthen the Republican Party, Godwin's efforts were little more than nominal.

James Latimer, an astute political writer for the *Richmond Times-Dispatch* for more than a quarter of a century, observed near the middle of Godwin's second term: "The first priority in Mills Godwin's mind is to keep the Virginia establishment in control . . . and to see if he can prevent the Republicans from nominating anyone against Young Harry." [32]

The grassroots take-over of the Democratic Party at the 1972 convention left the party in temporary disarray. Most of the old-line Byrd Democrats were swept out of party office. Although usually referred to in Virginia as "Howell's people" or "McGovernites," the new forces at the 1972 convention were basically national Democrats, many of them supporters of former Vice-President Hubert Humphrey. To men like Watt Abbitt, the Southside massive resister congressman and former state chairman, it was indeed a "radical" takeover, including the election of articulate and outspoken black women as national committee-woman and state vice-chairman ("chairperson" was not yet in vogue). The latter position went to Mrs. Jessie Rattley, who had earlier become the first black to win election to the Newport News City Council.

Howell watched the state convention from a deck above the floor at the Roanoke Coliseum and told reporters that the group that took over was too narrowly based to be effective. Joseph Fitzpatrick was elected state chairman and began the process of building for the first time what he called "a real Democratic Party in Virginia." In many counties, Democratic organizations had not met in years.

Yet by early 1973 the Democratic Party appeared to be collapsing.

31. *Richmond Times-Dispatch*, March 23, 1975, p. 1.
32. Interview with James Latimer, April 29, 1975.

Five senior committee chairmen in the House of Delegates led a group of ten Democrats who switched to "independent" status. Two others openly affiliated with the Republican Party. GOP leaders that spring were predicting they would add enough new members to their 25 incumbents to share control with the "independents" or perhaps even elect a Republican majority.

However, Democratic organizational efforts and recruitment of candidates combined in 1973 to crush Republican hopes of controlling the House of Delegates. The GOP actually lost five seats, and two veteran committee chairmen who switched to independent status also were defeated, one by a Republican and the other by a Howell Democrat. Another loser was incumbent Delegate William (Bullet Bill) Dudley, a onetime All-American halfback at the University of Virginia who had switched to the Republican Party.

In an unprecedented act of party discipline, the 1974 House Democratic caucus refused by a 31–29 vote to readmit two former members who had run for reelection as independents and defeated Democratic opponents. Independents who had faced no Democratic opposition were allowed admission to the caucus without penalty. The party sanction cost a popular 14-year veteran his chairmanship of the prestigious House Finance Committee.

Fitzpatrick, the Democratic chairman who gets along with all factions in the party, won election to the state Senate from Norfolk in 1975.

Party regularity was enhanced further when the Democratic caucus voted to ante up $100 each for a campaign fund. Roughly $6,000 would be available for such things as assisting Democratic candidates in special elections to fill vacancies which might occur in the House.

In 1974, two liberal Democrats defeated Republican incumbent congressmen in northern Virginia. One of the losers was 22-year veteran Joel T. Broyhill, the senior member of the Virginia delegation. The winners were Herbert E. Harris and Joseph L. Fisher, who quickly established themselves as the most liberal voting congressmen from Virginia since Pat Jennings lost in the Fighting Ninth in 1966.

The extent to which the Watergate scandal aided the Democratic resurgence is difficult to measure, but large numbers of traditionally Republican voters in the Washington suburbs apparently stayed home in the 1974 elections. There is no question that Watergate, combined with the new vigor shown by the state Democratic Party, put the brake on realignment. Senator Byrd said of Watergate, "Where it has had effect, and may continue to have effect, is among the Democratic politicians who because of the philosophy of the Democratic Party at the present time might prefer to move over to the Republican Party. I think it has stalled and perhaps will continue to stall some movement on the part of politicians toward the Republican Party."

Byrd viewed the effect as primarily on officeholders rather than the electorate. Concerning the traditional Byrd Democrats he said, "They are very independent-minded individuals. I think they will decide as time goes by which direction to go in. They may go back and forth for awhile. Neither party has really stabilized in its machinery and its direction. . . . The election of Governor Godwin has been helpful to the Republican Party." [33]

Whether Byrd himself would have switched to the Republican Party in 1970 if there had been no Republican opposition, a contention of former White House aide Harry Dent and others, is a question only Byrd can answer. When asked about it, he replied, "I wouldn't be prepared to comment on that." [34]

In 1975, state Democratic Chairman Fitzpatrick used Assistant U.S. Senate Majority Leader Robert Byrd of West Virginia as an intermediary to let Harry Byrd know he would be welcome to return to the fold, with the subtle hint that the Democratic caucus might be less gracious if he wins again in 1976 as an independent against Democratic opposition. Many of the Senate elders of 1970 who had been friends of his father are no longer around.

The decisions made by men named Harry Byrd for half a century have had enormous impact on Virginia politics, and the decision Senator Harry Byrd makes on running again for office in 1976 will be one of importance for the state. But no longer do such decisions shape the political direction and public policy of Virginia.

33. Interview with Harry Byrd, March 8, 1974.
34. Ibid.

Chapter

15

CONGRESS

The Fading Revolt

HISTORICALLY, Congress is where southern politics have exerted greatest national influence. The legacy of one-party politics allowed incumbent southern Democrats to accumulate seniority and rise to power as chairmen of major committees, for decades giving the South a dominance that greatly exceeded the region's share of membership in Congress. But the forces of change that have transformed state politics in the South are now being felt in Congress as well.

V. O. Key found that southerners in Congress on few occasions stood together against both northern Democrats and Republicans. "On the race question, and on that question alone," Key concluded, "does a genuine southern solidarity exist." [1] In his study of Congress from 1933 to 1945, Key detected an evolving southern disaffection with the national Democratic Party and the Roosevelt administration that would later emerge as a powerful conservative coalition in Congress. But at the time he wrote, Key found the importance of a "conservative coalition," a term already in use, to be exaggerated. On only 10 percent of the contested votes did a voting alliance form, in both the House and the Senate, between a majority of Republicans and a majority of southern Democrats against a majority of northern Democrats, and on many of those votes the southern Democrats were badly split.

But Key wrote a year after the Dixiecrat rebellion of 1948, just as the civil rights battles were beginning. In 1950, two leaders of southern liberalism, Frank Graham of North Carolina and Claude Pepper of Florida, were toppled from the Senate in emotional campaigns (see

1. V. O. Key, *Southern Politics in State and Nation* (New York: Vintage, 1949), p. 359.

Chapters 6 and 10) in which racism was combined with the smear of Communism. In the years after the 1954 Supreme Court decision that ruled school segregation unconstitutional, the cry went out from strident voices of reaction in the South that integration was a Communist plot. The word "liberal," already suspect, became an epithet. Two North Carolina congressmen who did not sign the 1956 "Southern Manifesto" attacking the Supreme Court for its desegregation decision were defeated, and that state's congressional delegation became one of the most conservative in the region for a decade and a half. Other southern moderates in the House, such as Carl Elliott of Alabama, Frank Smith of Mississippi, and Brooks Hayes of Arkansas, were defeated by conservative forces in the next few years.

Pepper returned to Congress in 1962 as a member of the House from a liberal district in the Miami area, which has regularly reelected him every two years. "Any liberal who honestly was a liberal and thereby indicated some appreciation of humanitarianism and exhibited concern for the people would find himself sooner or later taking a forward-looking—I think an American—position on civil rights," he said. "As soon as he did that, no matter what other virtues he had, he aroused an enormous amount of sometimes emotional opposition. . . . So you always have the problem as to whether you ever fight for anything. You know, if you are ever going to have a battle, you've got to have somebody that's got to be up in front. Now they may not last through the battle, but somebody has to be a part of the advance. And I reckon that I just had to pay the price of losing what could have been a long Senate career, because I did have some convictions and principles. Maybe I was foolish enough to try and stand by them, I don't know. But taking it all in all, I will let the record stand as it is. And I suspect that if I had it all to do over again, I would do exactly what I did before." Pepper said he could understand a southern congressman justifying a conservative position on race, but he added, "I just can't understand why southern representatives so often align themselves against progress and improvement on purely economic lines." [2]

THE DEMOCRATIC REVOLT

When Professor Wayne Shannon updated Key's study of the House through 1967, he found southern Democrats in a "full-scale revolt" that was:

2. Interview with Claude Pepper, February 1, 1974.

general, cutting across the most important policy dimensions that have characterized American national politics over the last 30 years. On three of these dimensions, domestic welfare and regulation, foreign policy, and civil liberties, many of the southerners have deviated sharply toward conservative positions that they have shared with a large group of House Republicans. On the other, civil rights, they have in recent years maintained their traditional conservative stance alone, deserted on roll calls by all but a handful of their former Republican allies.[3]

In the 20 years since Key's study, Shannon found a more than three-fold increase in conservative coalition voting, a low level of unity between southern Democrats and the northern members of the party, and a concentration of power through the control by southern congressmen of from one-half to almost two-thirds of the standing committee chairmanships since 1950.

But just as Key wrote at a turning point, so the revolt of southern Democrats documented by Shannon had reached its peak by 1967, the year his study concluded. By the mid-1970s, there had been four major departures from the pattern found by Shannon: (1) a steady and continuing loss of power in Congress by the South; (2) the election of Democrats more inclined to support the majority position of their party; (3) growth in southern Republican membership, whose conservatism was reflected by loyalty to party positions that exceeded the average for all Republicans in Congress; and (4) a gradual shift in position on civil rights issues, reflecting growing opposition among northern Republicans, strong opposition among southern Republicans, and weakening opposition among many newer southern Democrats.

The changes affecting Democrats began after the passage of the 1965 Voting Rights Act, with the 1966 elections. In the following analysis, the Republican trends are traced from the same year, for purposes of comparison and contrast, but the Republican pattern is consistent from 1964, the year Barry Goldwater attracted the support of former Dixiecrats to the Republican movement in the South. Senator Strom Thurmond of South Carolina switched to the Republican Party in 1964, and seven Goldwater followers were elected to the House as Republicans in 1964 from Alabama, Mississippi, and Georgia. A South Carolina Democrat switched the next year, giving the Republicans eight House seats from four of the states Goldwater carried. The voting records of Republicans elected in 1966 or later (see Table 15–3) reflect the voting patterns of those elected in 1964.*

3. W. Wayne Shannon, "Revolt in Washington: The South in Congress," in William C. Havard, *The Changing Politics of the South* (Baton Rouge: Louisiana State University Press, 1972), p. 662.

* Tables at the end of this chapter do not include voting records of interim senators who subsequently did not win elections.

Senator Harry F. Byrd, Jr. of Virginia represents a special situation. He was ap-

DEMOCRATIC TRENDS SINCE 1966

The most significant change in Congress has been the diminution of power through depletion of seniority by death, defeat, and retirement of southern Democratic congressmen in both the House and Senate, and from the assault on seniority in the House. In 1975 three senior southerners lost their chairmanships of major committees—Wright Patman of Texas on Banking and Currency, Bob Poage of Texas on Agriculture, and Edward Hebert of Louisiana on Armed Services. In the same year, the resignation of Wilbur Mills of Arkansas as chairman of the Ways and Means Committee took from the South perhaps the most powerful position in the House.

The number of House chairmen from the South in the 94th Congress (1975–1976) actually remained the same as for the 93rd, but the new chairmen headed such committees as Small Business, Post Office and Civil Service, Governmental Operations, and Public Works, with only the latter a committee that approaches major importance. (Table 15–1 at the end of this chapter shows the steady decline since the 84th Congress of southern domination of House committees, and also the decline in percentage of House Democrats from the South.)

In the Senate, the defeat of J. William Fulbright of Arkansas and retirement of Sam Ervin of North Carolina in 1974 also resulted in two fewer southerners serving as committee chairmen in the 94th Congress. The six Senate chairmanships held by southerners in the 94th Congress were fewer than in any Democratic-controlled Congress this century, and the number likely will continue to decline.

Herman Talmadge of Georgia is the last remaining southern Democratic senator to have been elected to the Senate between 1948 and 1966. Except for Agriculture Committee Chairman Talmadge and Finance Committee Chairman Russell Long of Louisiana, who was only 30 when

---

pointed in 1965 to the seat long held by his father, won a special election in 1966, was reelected to a full term in 1970 as an independent, then was readmitted to the Democratic caucus as an independent Democrat. For purposes of this study, Byrd is included as a Democrat who entered the Senate before 1966.

Tables on party unity or conservative coalition voting are based on scores compiled by *Congressional Quarterly*. For individuals, the scores represent the percentage of support on all roll calls and not the percentage of support given on roll call votes in which he participated. Thus, it is necessary to exercise caution in judging the record of an individual. For example, the party unity scores (see Table 15–3) of three Democratic congressmen elected in 1966—David Pryor of Arkansas, Ray Blanton of Tennessee, and Nick Galifianakis of North Carolina—all showed significant decreases in the 92nd Congress, a reflection of high absenteeism because of time spent campaigning in Senate races in 1972.

elected in 1948, the four remaining southern Democrats who held committee chairmanships in the 94th Congress—John Sparkman of Alabama on Foreign Relations, John McClellan of Arkansas on Appropriations, James Eastland of Mississippi on Judiciary, and John Stennis of Mississippi on Armed Services—all were over 70.

Although Professor Shannon's study dealt only with the House, an examination of voting records by new democrats in both the House and Senate for four Congresses from 1966 to 1972 reveals a trend toward greater party unity—or away from conservatism. The average scores of new southern Democrats on party unity—the frequency with which they voted with a majority of their party—steadily diverged from the average scores of pre-1966 Democrats in the Senate and the southern committee chairmen in the House, a group used by Professor Shannon to illustrate the southern revolt against the policies of the national party.

Although the trend began slowly, the rate of divergence grew steadily stronger (see Tables 15–2 and 15–3). Of the 22 new Democrats elected from the South between 1966 and 1970, only two—Bob Eckhardt of Texas and L. Richardson Preyer of North Carolina—could be rated as truly national Democrats. Eckhardt averaged 20 points higher and Preyer 4 points higher than the score for all House Democrats, a score which would be higher if limited to nonsouthern Democrats.

Significant change began with the class of 1972, which included six—Lindy Boggs and Gillis Long of Louisiana, William Lehman of Florida, Andrew Young of Georgia, and Barbara Jordan and Charles Wilson of Texas—whose voting records were clearly those of national Democrats, each with a party unity score higher than the average for all House Democrats. Young and Jordan, the first black members of Congress from the South in this century, both established themselves as individuals of unusual ability. Of the remaining eight members of the 1972 class, only Dale Milford of Texas recorded a party unity score lower than the average for the southern committee chairmen. The 1972 class voted with the Democratic majority on fifty-five percent of all roll call votes, a genuine emergence of moderation.

Of the 11 southern Democrats elected in 1966, three of them—David Pryor of Arkansas, Ray Blanton of Tennessee, and Nick Galifianakis of North Carolina—made unsuccessful races for the Senate in 1972. Pryor and Blanton subsequently were elected governors of their respective states in 1974. The only member of the 1966 class to lose a bid for re-election was the most conservative member, John Rarick of Louisiana, who was defeated in the 1974 Democratic primary.

The 13 new southern Democrats elected in 1974, with the exception of John Birch Society member Larry McDonald of Georgia, indicated in their 1975 voting that they would at least match the 1972 class in terms of national party unity. Collectively, the group voted with the Democratic majority on 57 percent of all roll call votes, with McDonald's 7 percent pulling the score down.

The demonstration by some of the newer members that they could vote for progressive legislation and survive also teaches more senior members that attitudes at home are changing. "I am the first member of the House of Representatives from South Carolina ever to vote for a higher minimum wage," said Representative Mendel Davis. "My colleagues said, 'Oh, that is the worst mistake you'll ever make; you are completely wrong.' I went home and campaigned on it, and most of my people appreciated it. . . . It is really an inborn fear that comes from the past of South Carolina's newspaper editorials against unions, against organized labor, etc. It scares them on a vote like this." [4] In 1974, three new Democrats were elected from South Carolina, each with the endorsement of organized labor in the state.

Representative Gillis Long, who was defeated in 1964 after one term in Congress, returned in 1972 and said, "The major trend is toward more progressive congressmen from the South, more national Democratic congressmen." [5] Long said that new attitudes were creating more and more districts in which the old populist dream of a coalition of blacks and working-class whites was emerging to elect progressives.

In the Senate, the constituency is statewide. Although a pattern of moderation emerges from the collective voting records of new Democratic senators elected in 1966 or later, none have achieved the party unity average for all Senate Democrats or come close to that of northern Democrats. But the average voting scores on party unity of post-1966 senators has differed from pre-1966 senators by increasing margins in each of four succeeding Congresses.

None of the seven Democrats elected between 1966 and 1972 could be rated as a liberal. This is true also for the three new Democratic senators elected in 1974—Dale Bumpers of Arkansas, Robert Morgan of North Carolina, and Richard Stone of Florida. But only one of the post-1966 group, Sen. James B. Allen of Alabama, was conservative enough to score below the party unity average of pre-1966 senators (Table 15-4). In contrast, the three most liberal members of the pre-1966 group of senators all suffered defeats in bids for reelection—Ralph Yarborough of Texas and Albert Gore of Tennessee in 1970 and J. William Fulbright of Arkansas in 1974.

Although the party unity scores of Yarborough, Gore, and Fulbright averaged well above those of the other pre-1966 senators, their liberalism was even more apparent in the low level of support they gave the "conservative coalition," the alliance formed when a majority of voting south-

4. Interview with Mendel J. Davis, January 30, 1974.
5. Interview with Gillis Long, January 24, 1974.

ern Democrats and a majority of voting Republicans oppose the stand taken by a majority of voting northern Democrats. Except for a 32 percent support of the coalition by Fulbright in the 90th Congress, none of the three ever supported the conservative position on as many as one-fourth of the votes (their pre-1966 Senate colleagues averaged more than 70 percent support for the coalition) between 1966 and 1972.

Although the post-1966 senators on the average gave somewhat less support to the conservative coalition than did the pre-1966 senators, the lowest level of support by any of the post-1966 group in the next four sessions of Congress was 45 percent support by Senator Lawton Chiles in the 93rd Congress (1973–1974). Chiles contended that most of the new southerners believe that race has been basically removed as a political issue, and this has provided a sense of liberation. And as a result, "we feel that freedom and are exercising it. We're not locked in as conservative or liberal at a time when issues that made up liberal or conservative are changing." [6]

On the other hand, Freshman Senator Sam Nunn of Georgia supported the coalition 86 percent of the time in the 93rd Congress, a figure exceeded among the post-1966 group only by Senator Allen's 87 percent.

Another change in the Senate is the demise of the southern caucus, once the center of opposition to civil rights legislation. The reason it died, said Senator Ernest F. (Fritz) Hollings of South Carolina, was "because the southern caucus took on the issue of racism." Hollings, elected in 1966 and the most senior of the newer southern senators, said the new members from the South "don't want to be identified as a southern group meeting on that basis. They don't want to be identified as racist. . . . When I first came up here, they had us all meeting around Dick Russell. Later on we met for awhile around Allen Ellender and decided what to do about a busing amendment. Those days are gone. We don't see our interest now as being any different from any other section of the country." [7]

Nevertheless, the defeats in the early 1970s of Gore, Yarborough, and Fulbright—all genuine progressives—suggest that no more than cautious moderation will emerge among the new southern Democrats in the Senate.

6. Interview with Lawton Chiles, January 30, 1974.
7. Interview with Ernest F. Hollings, January 28, 1974.

REPUBLICAN EMERGENCE

From 1960 to 1972, there were steady gains in the number of southern Republicans in Congress. Despite a setback in the 1974 election backlash of Watergate, in which Republicans in the South suffered a net loss of seven House seats and one in the Senate, the GOP held one-fourth of the old Confederacy's seats in the House and more than a fourth in the Senate in the 94th Congress (1975–76).

The most striking aspect of southern Republicanism in Congress is its solid conservatism. Of 29 Republicans elected to the House between 1966 and 1972, only one compiled a voting record less conservative on party unity than the average score for all House Republicans. That was Alan Steelman of Texas, who in the first session after his election in 1972 scored 57 on party unity, compared with 66 for all House Republicans in the 93rd Congress (see Table 15–5). The average party unity score was 78.4 for all southern Republicans elected in 1966 or later, 12.4 points higher—or more conservative—than for all House Republicans. The conservatism of Republicans covered the entire spectrum of issues: federal spending, civil rights, the war in Vietnam, defense, and foreign policy.

In the 92nd Congress, Representatives J. Kenneth Robinson of Virginia and Earl Ruth of North Carolina ranked second and third respectively among all House Republicans in their scores on party unity. In 1974, the second year of the 93rd Congress, Robinson ranked first in party unity among all House Republicans with a score of 93; William R. Archer of Texas was second with 92; and Representative Floyd D. Spence of South Carolina was third with 89. By coincidence, all three were elected in 1970.

Although there is little difference in voting patterns among southern House Republicans, they do differ in the intensity of their feelings about conservatism. Many Democratic "converts" tend to view conservatism as a moral crusade against the evil of liberalism. For example, David Treen of Louisiana, elected in 1972 as that state's first Republican congressman, had run unsuccessfully against the late Hale Boggs three times—in 1962, 1964, and 1968—and had run for governor in 1971. Treen said he ran against Boggs because of "his generally liberal philosophy" and that the way for the Republican Party "to build in the South is to field the conservative candidates." [8] Such intensity is rare among those who grew up in the Republican Party, either as mountain Republicans in the South or as migrants from outside the region.

In the Senate, a similar pattern emerges. The first Republican senator elected from the South was John G. Tower of Texas in a special election

8. Interview with David Treen, January 31, 1975.

in 1961. The most moderate of seven Republicans to serve in the Senate from the South is Howard H. Baker, Jr. of Tennessee, but his average score on party unity was still 7 points "more Republican" than the average for all Senate Republicans between 1967 and 1974 (see Table 15–6). In the 93rd Congress, the seven southern Republicans in the Senate averaged 79.1 in their party unity scores, 18.1 points higher than the average for all Senate Republicans.

An even more pronounced reflection of their devotion to conservatism is an average score of 86.4 in support of the conservative coalition in the 93rd Congress. Senator Jesse Helms scored 95 in support of the coalition, which means he was present and voted for support of the conservatives on 95 percent of all roll calls in which the coalition formed. Three of the other six southern Republicans—Thurmond (92), Tower (91), and William L. Scott of Virginia (91)—joined Helms with scores above 90.

During the four sessions of Congress studied, the average conservative coalition score among southern Republican senators was 12.1 points higher than that of southern Democrats and 10.8 points higher than that of the pre-1966 southern Democrats.

CIVIL RIGHTS

The most dramatic example of the change in attitudes on civil rights occurred when Congress in 1975 passed a seven-year extension of the Voting Rights Act. For the first time in this century, a majority of southern congressmen supported a civil rights measure.

The House vote was 341–70, and southern Democrats voted 52–26, or two-to-one, in support of the measure. Southern Republicans voted 17–10 in opposition to passage. The vote clearly reflects the divergence between southern Democrats and Republicans on this issue.

The 1974 class of southern Democrats voted 12–1 in support of the Voting Rights Act extension, the only negative vote coming from Mc-Donald of Georgia, and the 1972 class of southern Democrats voted 10–2 for the measure. In contrast, both of the two Republicans elected in 1974 from the South voted against the measure, and the 1972 class of southern Republicans voted 6–3 against passage.

During debate in the House on the Voting Rights Act extension, Walter Flowers of Alabama, speaking on behalf of an amendment to provide an escape clause for covered jurisdictions, said, "I doubt if a member who does not come from a covered jurisdiction can quite speak with the same tongue as we can." Andrew Young, a black congressman from Georgia, took the floor and responded, "Mr. Chairman, when my colleague, the gentleman from Alabama, spoke and said, 'You cannot know what it feels like to be under this act unless you come from one of the covered states,' I felt I had to stand before this House and tell the members how it feels to be covered by this act. It feels wonderful." [9] Flowers, the only one of the five southern Democrats on the Judiciary Committee to oppose the bill in committee, voted for it on final passage.

Since the bill extended coverage to certain jurisdictions with more than 5 percent Spanish-speaking population, the state of Texas was brought under the act for the first time, as were several counties in Florida. In addition, the act placed a permanent ban on use of literacy tests as a requirement for registration. A comparison of voting by representatives of districts previously exempt from coverage with voting by representatives whose districts were nonexempt shows that 80.5 percent of Democrats from exempt districts and 51.5 percent from nonexempt districts voted for the extension. In contrast, 64.3 percent of the Republicans from exempt districts voted to extend the act, but only 7.7 percent of the Republicans from nonexempt districts voted for the extension.[10] The lone favorable vote among 13 Republicans from nonexempt districts in Virginia, Louisiana, South Carolina, Alabama, and Mississippi (there were no House Republicans from Georgia in the 94th Congress) was John H. Buchanan of Alabama, a Baptist minister first elected in 1964.

In the Senate, which voted 77–12 to extend the Voting Rights Act, southern Democrats voted 9–6 for and Republicans 4–2 against it. The cleavage between pre-1966 and post-1966 Democrats was illustrated sharply. The pre-1966 Democrats voted 5–1 against the act, with Senator Eastland of Mississippi absent and Senator Long of Louisiana voting for it. The post-1966 group voted 8–1 for the act, with Senator Allen of Alabama the lone dissenter. The four Republicans from nonexempt jurisdictions voted against the act. Only the two Republican senators from Tennessee, an exempt state, voted for the measure. The 1975 Voting Rights Act vote represented a significant change among southern Democrats.

A study by Professor Merle Black of civil rights voting in the House between 1963 and 1972 reveals a shift by northern Republicans from the traditional position of the party of Lincoln into subtle and at times open opposition to civil rights measures.[11] And as the busing issue

9. *Congressional Record*, June 3, 1975, pp. H4816–4817.

10. Unpublished research by Merle Black, Department of Political Science, University of North Carolina at Chapel Hill.

11. Merle Black, "The Changing Regional and Partisan Bases of Congressional Support for Civil Rights Legislation: the U.S. House of Representatives, 1963–1972." Paper delivered at the 1975 meeting of the Southern Political Science Association, Nashville.

moved into the north, support for civil rights fell among northern Democrats as well as northern Republicans, another example of the political axiom that how one votes often depends upon whose ox is being gored.

Black broke down a series of votes related to civil rights in five categories—voting rights, equal employment, open housing, federal funds involving school desegregation, and busing. A major finding was the existence of a hidden northern Republican "southern strategy" of giving aid and comfort to the South in attempts to weaken civil rights measures through amendments or substitute bills, but then upholding the image of the party of Lincoln by voting for the bills on final passage.

For example, on a series of votes involving voting rights, northern Democrats voted 94.9 percent for final passage of such measures and 82.3 percent for the liberal position on amendments. The performance for northern Republicans was strikingly different. Although they voted 66.8 percent for final passage on voting rights legislation, they gave only 20.4 percent support for the liberal position on amendments.

Southern Democrats voted 28.6 percent for such measures on final passage and 15.3 percent for the liberal position on amendments. Southern Republicans voted 10.4 percent for final passage and zero percent for the liberal position on amendments.

Black found even sharper differences among northern Republicans between their degree of support for final passage and for liberal amendments on equal employment issues, and smaller but still significant differences on votes that involved open housing and school desegregation funds. The following tables show the percentage of support Black found on votes to strengthen civil rights:

	EQUAL EMPLOYMENT	
	FINAL PASSAGE	AMENDMENTS
Democrats		
Northern	96.7	93.7
Southern	27.8	18.3
Difference	68.9	75.4
Republicans		
Northern	83.3	21.7
Southern	1.9	0.0
Difference	81.4	21.7

| | OPEN HOUSING | |
	FINAL PASSAGE	AMENDMENTS
Democrats		
Northern	87.7	82.1
Southern	12.5	12.3
Difference	75.2	69.8
Republicans		
Northern	62.0	47.1
Southern	2.2	14.7
Difference	59.8	32.4

| | SCHOOL DESEGREGATION FUNDS | |
	FINAL PASSAGE	AMENDMENTS
Democrats		
Northern	73.8	85.4
Southern	12.1	18.8
Difference	61.7	66.6
Republicans		
Northern	62.0	47.1
Southern	2.2	14.7
Difference	59.8	32.4

What emerges is a pattern in which the northern and southern wings of the Democrats remained roughly equally divided on civil rights, whether on final passage or on amendments, while the northern and southern wings of the Republican Party differed as much as the Democrats on final passage but differed far less on amendments that would weaken or strengthen the legislation.

On busing, the results were more complex. On votes that affected only the South, support among northern Democrats was significantly stronger than when the result had national application, and northern Republicans openly deserted the party's traditional stance on civil rights legislation when they voted on busing measures that affected both the South and non-South, either as parts of civil rights bills or as riders to other legislation, giving only 20.5 percent support to such measures.

| | BUSING | |
	FINAL PASSAGE	AMENDMENTS
Democrats		
Northern	82.7	60.6
Southern	6.3	10.8
Difference	76.4	49.8
Republicans		
Northern	56.9	20.5
Southern	3.2	3.6
Difference	53.7	16.9

A study of voting on issues considered important by the Congressional Black Caucus in 1973 revealed striking differences between southern Republicans and southern Democrats from districts with at least 25 percent black population (see Table 15–7 at the end of the chapter). The 41 votes in the study covered a variety of issues, ranging from funding for the Office of Economic Opportunity and the Emergency Employment Act to support of the school lunch program and minimum wage amendments.

As Table 15–7 shows seven of eight southern Republicans from districts with at least 25 percent black population gave less than 10 percent support to the position of the Congressional Black Caucus. The lone exception was Representative Buchanan of Alabama, who voted 24 percent for the Black Caucus position and was the only one of the Republicans to vote against an amendment to reduce funding for the Office of Economic Opportunity, an issue of particular importance to blacks.

In contrast, only one Democrat from a district with at least 25 percent black population, David Satterfield of Virginia, voted less than 10 percent of the time for the Black Caucus. Only eight of the 30 Democrats —three of them from Virginia—voted less than 25 percent of the time with the Black Caucus position.

The average support from Republicans was 6.5 percent, compared with 38.1 percent, or nearly six times as much, from Democrats. Although southern Democrats from such districts are decidedly less conservative than Republicans, only rarely do they consistently represent the interests of blacks. Only seven of the 28 white Democrats supported the Black Caucus position as much or more than they opposed it.

CONSERVATIVE COALITION

The conservative coalition, which is formed when a majority of voting southern Democrats and a majority of voting Republicans oppose the stand taken by a majority of voting northern Democrats, operated at high levels of strength from 1967 to 1974. The coalition formed on at least 22 percent of the recorded votes for both houses of Congress in each of those eight years, and it achieved victories at least 59 percent of the time, as Table 15–8 illustrates.

The coalition operated as a major force in shaping national policy during this period, forming to oppose many of the programs of President Johnson and to support those of Presidents Nixon and Ford. For example, the coalition defeated efforts in 1968 to enact gun registration and licensing proposals, and its biggest victory that year was to defeat President Johnson's nomination of Abe Fortas to be chief justice of the Supreme Court. That defeat subsequently allowed President Nixon to name Warren Burger as chief justice, a move that turned the Court in a conservative direction.

The coalition opposed President Johnson's wishes on 55 votes in 1968, agreeing with his position in 16. The coalition disagreed with President Nixon's stated position only nine times in 1969 and only three times in 1970. In 1974 the coalition was in agreement with President Nixon on 48 of the 53 issues on which it formed, and it was in agreement with President Ford that year on 20 of 24 occasions.

Among the coalition victories in the first Nixon administration were its defeat of efforts to strengthen the enforcement powers of the Equal Employment Opportunity Commission, defeat of the Family Assistance Program, defeat of the Cooper-Church Amendment in 1970 that would have limited U.S. military involvement in Cambodia, and blocking of a bill creating a federal consumer agency. As Table 15–8 shows, the coalition began a downward trend after its peak in 1971, exhibiting a decrease both in the percentage of votes on which it formed and in its percentage of victories.

Table 15–4, reflecting a definite trend toward greater party unity by post-1966 southern Democrats in the Senate, also shows that there was less difference between the post-1966 and pre-1966 groups in the degree of support given the conservative coalition when it did form. But the trend toward greater party unity suggests a continued decline in the frequency with which the conservative coalition will appear.

CONCLUSIONS

If the voting records of the 1972 and 1974 classes of southern Democrats, especially in the House, are the beginning of a long-range trend, the impact of the conservative coalition will continue to gradually weaken.

The power of the South in Congress will continue to weaken in the short term, and the era in which the region played a major obstructionist role against social legislation appears to be ending. The emerging South in Congress increasingly demonstrates a pattern of party realignment, with southern Republicans voting more conservatively than even old southern Democrats, and recently elected Democrats voting more like national Democrats. Thus, the South in Congress reflects the trends within the region: a nationalization of outlook and perhaps a loss of regional distinctiveness. The revolt is fading.

TABLE 15–1

Southern Influence in the U.S. House of Representatives,
1951–1976

	SOUTHERN CHAIRMEN	HOUSE DEMOCRATS FROM SOUTH	HOUSE MEMBERS FROM SOUTH
82nd Congress (1951–1952)	52.6%	44.6%	24.1%
84th Congress (1955–1956)	63.2	42.9	24.4
86th Congress (1959–1960)	60.0	35.0	24.3
88th Congress (1963–1964)	55.0	30.2	24.4
90th Congress (1967–1968)	50.0	33.2	24.4
92nd Congress (1971–1972)	40.0	29.0	24.4
94th Congress (1975–1976)	38.1	28.0	24.8

TABLE 15–2

Average Scores on Party Unity for Southern Democrats in the U.S. House of Representatives, 1967–1974

	90TH CONGRESS (1967–1968)	91ST CONGRESS (1969–1970)	92ND CONGRESS (1971–1972)	93RD CONGRESS (1973–1974)
Average for 1966 Class of House Democrats	38	43	39	43
Average for 1968 Class	—	39	34	43
Average for 1970 Class	—	—	33	43
Average for 1972 Class	—	—	—	55
Average for All Post-1966 New Democrats from South	38	41	36	49
Average for Southern Committee Chairmen	40	38	28	32
Percentage by Which All Post-1966 Democrats Exceeded Average of Southern Committee Chairmen	(–2)	3	8	17
Percentage by Which 1966 Class Exceeded Average of Southern Committee Chairmen	(–2)	5	11	11
Percentage by Which 1968 Class Exceeded Average of Southern Committee Chairmen	—	1	6	11
Percentage by Which 1970 Class Exceeded Average of Southern Committee Chairmen	—	—	5	11
Percentage by Which 1972 Class Exceeded Average of Southern Committee Chairmen	—	—	—	23
Average Scores for All House Democrats	63	59	60	66

Source: Compiled from *Congressional Quarterly Almanacs* for 1968, 1970, 1972, and 1974.

TABLE 15-3

Party Unity Scores for All Southern Democrats Elected to the U.S. House of Representatives, 1966-1972

	90TH CONGRESS (1967–1968)	91ST CONGRESS (1969–1970)	92ND CONGRESS (1971–1972)	93RD CONGRESS (1973–1974)
CLASS OF 1966:				
Tom Bevill, Alabama	33	41	44	47
William Nichols, Alabama	26	34	28	33
a David Pryor, Arkansas	58	61	49	—
William Stuckey, Georgia	28	42	35	49
Jack Brinkley, Georgia	32	32	38	41
b John R. Rarick, Louisiana	8	20	22	22
G. V. Montgomery, Mississippi	23	20	17	22
a Nick Galifianakis, North Carolina	44	60	45	—
Walter B. Jones, North Carolina	29	39	34	41
a L. Ray Blanton, Tennessee	49	48	33	—
Bob Eckhardt, Texas	88	80	82	90
Average for Class of 1966	38	43.4	38.8	43.1
CLASS OF 1968:				
Walter Flowers, Alabama	—	34	28	44
William V. Alexander, Arkansas	—	46	47	57
William V. Chappell, Florida	—	28	23	38
c Patrick Caffery, Louisiana	—	34	37	—
c Charles H. Griffin, Mississippi	—	34	29	—
L. Richardson Preyer, North Carolina	—	65	67	65
James R. Mann, South Carolina	—	39	20	39
d Ed Jones, Tennessee	—	50	30	42
W. C. (Dan) Daniel, Virginia	—	22	21	18
Average for Class of 1968		39.1	33.6	43.3
CLASS OF 1970:				
M. Dawson Mathis, Georgia	—	—	28	34
e Mendel J. Davis, South Carolina	—	—	37	51
Average for Class of 1970			32.5	42.5
CLASS OF 1972:				
Ray Thornton, Arkansas	—	—	—	60
Bill Gunter, Florida	—	—	—	48
William Lehman, Florida	—	—	—	83
Ronald (Bo) Ginn, Georgia	—	—	—	54
Andrew Young, Georgia	—	—	—	85
f Lindy Boggs, Louisiana	—	—	—	71
John Breaux, Louisiana	—	—	—	47
Gillis Long, Louisiana	—	—	—	71
David Bowen, Mississippi	—	—	—	42
Ike F. Andrews, North Carolina	—	—	—	47

TABLE 15–3 (*continued*)

	90TH CONGRESS (1967–1968)	91ST CONGRESS (1969–1970)	92ND CONGRESS (1971–1972)	93RD CONGRESS (1973–1974)
Charles G. Rose, III, North Carolina	—	—	—	58
Charles Wilson, Texas	—	—	—	68
Barbara Jordan, Texas	—	—	—	88
Dale Milford, Texas	—	—	—	29
Average for Class of 1972				54.7
Average for All Post-1966 Southern Democrats in House	38	41.4	36.1	49.2
Average for Southern Committee Chairmen	40	38.1	27.6	32.1
Average for all House Democrats	63	59	60	66

a. Did not seek reelection in 1972.
b. Defeated for reelection in Democratic primary in 1974.
c. Did not seek reelection in 1974.
d. Elected in special election in 1969.
e. Elected in special election in 1971.
f. Elected in special election in 1973.

TABLE 15–4

Party Unity and Conservative Coalition Scores of All Southern Democrats in the U.S. Senate

SENATORS	PARTY UNITY 90TH	91ST	*92ND	93RD	CONSERVATIVE COALITI 90TH	91ST	*92ND	9
Lister Hill, Alabama	58	—	—	—	80	—	—	
John Sparkman, Alabama	52	30	26	34	63	66	69	
# James B. Allen, Alabama	—	28	35	30	—	83	91	
J. William Fulbright, Arkansas	38	56	70	42	32	23	21	
John J. McClellan, Arkansas	36	28	35	30	91	83	70	
Spessard Holland, Florida	52	34	—	—	76	91	—	
George Smathers, Florida	29	—	—	—	42	—	—	
# Lawton M. Chiles, Florida	—	—	53	63	—	—	49	
Richard B. Russell, Georgia	23	19	—	—	67	44	—	
Herman E. Talmadge, Georgia	31	36	42	38	64	88	89	
# Sam Nunn, Georgia	—	—	—	41	—	—	—	
Russell B. Long, Louisiana	56	37	41	43	60	69	69	
Allen Ellender, Louisiana	46	42	—	—	73	76	—	
# J. Bennett Johnston, Louisiana	—	—	—	47	—	—	—	

TABLE 15–4 (*continued*)

SENATORS	PARTY UNITY				CONSERVATIVE COALITION			
	90TH	91ST	*92ND	93RD	90TH	91ST	*92ND	93RD
James O. Eastland, Mississippi	30	29	25	23	77	70	80	84
John C. Stennis, Mississippi	41	33	28	18	95	83	94	61
Sam J. Ervin, North Carolina	37	36	34	32	75	87	83	79
B. Everett Jordan, North Carolina	45	37	37	—	71	72	64	—
# Ernest F. Hollings, South Carolina	44	51	57	53	53	57	54	54
Albert Gore, Tennessee	55	50	—	—	23	18	—	—
Ralph Yarborough, Texas	71	62	—	—	17	17	—	—
# Lloyd M. Bentsen, Texas	—	—	56	53	—	—	64	49
** Harry F. Byrd, Jr., Virginia	33	37	31	24	83	82	90	91
# William B. Spong, Jr., Virginia	54	60	57	—	68	62	60	—
Average for All Southern Democrats	44	39	42	38	64	65	70	68

	90TH CONGRESS (1967–1968)	91ST CONGRESS (1969–1970)	92ND CONGRESS (1971–1972)	93RD CONGRESS (1973–1974)
Party Unity Scores				
Average for All Democrats	57%	58%	60%	66%
Average for Post-1966 Group	49	46	52	48
Average for Pre-1966 Group	43	38	37	32
Difference by Which Post-1966 Group Voted More Often in Agreement with Democrats on Issues in Which Democratic and Republican Majorities Split	6	9	15	16
Conservative Coalition Scores				
Average for Post-1966 Group	61	67	64	64
Average for Pre-1966 Group	64	65	73	70
Difference by Which Post-1966 Group Voted Less Often in Support of Conservative Coalition	3	–2	9	6

* Voting of two interim Democratic appointees not included.
** Senator Byrd was reelected in 1970 as an independent but was admitted into the Senate Democratic caucus after the election.
# Elected to Senate in 1966 or later.
Source: Compiled from *Congressional Quarterly Almanacs* for 1968, 1970, 1972, and 1974.

TABLE 15–5
Party Unity Scores for All Southern Republicans Elected to the U.S. House of Representatives, 1966–1972

	90TH CONGRESS (1967–1968)	91ST CONGRESS (1969–1970)	92ND CONGRESS (1971–1972)	93RD CONGRESS (1973–1974)
CLASS OF 1966				
John Paul Hammerschmidt, Arkansas	84	78	74	74
J. Herbert Burke, Florida	84	71	76	66
a Ben B. Blackburn, Georgia	76	66	68	66
b Fletcher Thompson, Georgia	81	69	70	—
a Dan H. Kuykendall, Tennessee	75	56	65	71
a Robert D. Price, Texas	94	66	81	73
b William L. Scott, Virginia	88	80	81	—
William C. Wampler, Virginia	78	70	73	77
Average for Class of 1966	82.5	69.5	73.5	71.2
CLASS OF 1968				
Lou Frey, Florida	—	79	77	75
a Wilmer D. Mizell, North Carolina	—	82	85	78
a Earl B. Ruth, North Carolina	—	76	88	86
James R. Collins, Texas	—	78	81	88
G. William Whitehurst, Virginia	—	63	78	77
Average for Class of 1968		75.6	81.8	80.8
CLASS OF 1970				
Hill Young, Florida	—	—	82	79
Floyd D. Spence, South Carolina	—	—	78	88
a Lamar Baker, Tennessee	—	—	67	78
William R. Archer, Texas	—	—	87	88
J. Kenneth Robinson, Virginia	—	—	91	93
Average for Class of 1970			81.0	85.2
CLASS OF 1972				
Louis A. Bafalis, Florida	—	—	—	76
David Treen, Louisiana	—	—	—	83
W. Thad Cochran, Mississippi	—	—	—	76
C. Trent Lott, Mississippi	—	—	—	80
James G. Martin, North Carolina	—	—	—	82
a Edward L. Young, South Carolina	—	—	—	78
Robin L. Beard, Tennessee	—	—	—	80
Alan W. Steelman, Texas	—	—	—	57
Robert W. Daniel, Jr., Virginia	—	—	—	87
M. Caldwell Butler, Virginia	—	—	—	85
a Stanford E. Parris, Virginia	—	—	—	76
Average for Class of 1972				78.2

TABLE 15–5 (continued)

	90TH CONGRESS (1967–1968)	91ST CONGRESS (1969–1970)	92ND CONGRESS (1971–1972)	93RD CONGRESS (1973–1974)
Average for All Post-1966 Southern Republicans in House	82.5	71.8	77.9	78.4
Average for All House Republicans	70	61	67	66
Percentage by Which All Post-1966 Southern Republicans Exceeded Average of All House Republicans	12.5	10.8	10.9	12.4

a. Defeated for reelection in 1974.
b. Did not seek reelection to the House in 1972.

TABLE 15–6
Party Unity Scores of All Southern Republicans in the U.S. Senate, 1967–1974
(scores on support of conservative coalition in parentheses)

	90TH CONGRESS (1967–1968)	91ST CONGRESS (1969–1970)	92ND CONGRESS (1971–1972)	93RD CONGRESS (1973–1974)
a# Edward J. Gurney, Florida	—	83 (82)	85 (94)	74 (80)
# Jesse Helms, North Carolina	—	—	—	86 (95)
b J. Strom Thurmond, South Carolina	80 (91)	79 (86)	79 (83)	91 (92)
# Howard H. Baker, Jr., Tennessee	68 (73)	73 (76)	65 (65)	65 (69)
# William E. Brock, III, Tennessee	—	—	70 (75)	78 (87)
John G. Tower, Texas	48 (56)	63 (67)	70 (72)	86 (91)
# William L. Scott, Virginia	—	—	—	74 (91)
Average for All Southern Republicans	65.3	74.5	73.8	79.1
Average for All Senate Republicans	60	59	62	61
Percentage by Which Southern Republicans Senators Voted More Often in Agreement with Republicans Than Did All Republicans on Issues in Which Democratic and Republican Majorities Split	5.3	14.5	11.8	18.1

a Did not seek reelection in 1974.
b Switched from the Democratic Party in 1964.
Elected in 1966 or later.

TABLE 15–7

Votes of Southern Members of Congress from Districts with More Than 25 Percent Black Population on Issues Important to Blacks, 93rd Congress, First Session (1973)

	SUPPORT OF CONGRESSIONAL BLACK CAUCUS	OPPOSITION TO CONGRESSIONAL BLACK CAUCUS	NOT VOTING	BLACK POPULATION IN DISTRICT
DEMOCRATS				
William Nichols, Alabama	27%	66%	7%	31.3%
Walter Flowers, Alabama	37	51	12	37.9
Ray Thornton, Arkansas	71	29	0	31.3
Don Fuqua, Florida	37	51	12	28.0
Charles E. Bennett, Florida	30	71	0	26.0
Ronald (Bo) Ginn, Georgia	49	51	0	33.6
Dawson Mathis, Georgia	20	56	24	36.8
Jack Brinkley, Georgia	27	73	0	32.0
* Andrew Young, Georgia	98	0	2	44.2
William S. Stuckey, Georgia	44	44	12	31.0
Robert Stephens, Georgia	51	39	10	32.8
F. Edward Hebert, Louisiana	32	39	30	31.2
Lindy Boggs, Louisiana	81	11	8	39.7
Joe Waggoner, Louisiana	17	78	5	31.2
Otto E. Passman, Louisiana	39	46	15	34.5
John Rarick, Louisiana	12	66	22	29.7
Gillis W. Long, Louisiana	78	17	5	36.2
Jamie L. Whitten, Mississippi	27	73	0	35.5
David Bowen, Mississippi	32	66	2	45.9
G. V. (Sonny) Montgomery, Miss.	12	88	0	40.4
Walter B. Jones, North Carolina	27	71	2	35.8
L. H. Fountain, North Carolina	22	76	2	40.1
David N. Henderson, North Carolina	27	66	7	26.7
Charles G. Rose, No. Carolina	49	49	2	25.6
Mendel J. Davis, South Carolina	41	37	22	34.0
Tom Gettys, South Carolina	34	61	5	31.6
* Barbara Jordan, Texas	93	0	7	41.6
Thomas Downing, Virginia	17	73	10	30.1
David Satterfield, Virginia	2	93	5	26.2
W. C. (Dan) Daniel, Virginia	10	90	0	29.0
Averages	38.1	54.3	7.6	33.7
REPUBLICANS				
W. Jack Edwards, Alabama	5	88	7	32.7
William L. Dickinson, Alabama	5	93	2	29.8
John Buchanan, Alabama	24	73	2	30.0
W. Thad Cochran, Mississippi	2	88	10	43.1
Floyd Spence, South Carolina	5	93	2	33.8
Edward Young, South Carolina	7	88	5	42.2

TABLE 15–7 (*continued*)

	SUPPORT OF CONGRES- SIONAL BLACK CAUCUS	OPPOSITION TO CONGRES- SIONAL BLACK CAUCUS	NOT VOTING	BLACK POPU- LATION IN DISTRICT
Dan Kuykendall, Tennessee	2	90	7	47.5
Robert Daniel, Virginia	2	93	5	37.1
Averages	6.5	88.3	5.0	37.0

° Member of Congressional Black Caucus.
Source: Compiled from *Congressional Votes on Important Issues for Blacks* (Washington, D.C.: Joint Center for Political Studies, 1974).

TABLE 15–8
Impact of the Conservative Coalition

Column 1 represents the percentage of the recorded votes for both houses of Congress on which the coalition appeared. Column 2 represents the percentage of victories in both houses.

YEAR	(1) APPEARANCES	(2) VICTORIES	(3) IMPACT SCORE
1961	28	55	83
1962	14	62	76
1963	17	50	67
1964	15	51	66
1965	24	33	57
1966	25	45	70
1967	25	63	88
1968	24	73	97
1969	27	68	95
1970	22	66	88
1971	30	83	113
1972	27	69	96
1973	23	61	84
1974	24	59	83
1975	28	50	78

Source: The figures in columns 1 and 2 are derived from tables in *Congressional Quarterly Weekly Reports* (January 24, 1976): 170. The records include Kentucky and Oklahoma as well as the South. The authors created an "impact score" by combining the percentage of times the coalition formed with the percentage of victories.

Chapter

16

ORGANIZED LABOR

Unrealized Potential

BEGINNING with Operation Dixie after World War II, organized labor has viewed the South as a major target for organization, and southern liberals have hoped that labor's efforts would educate southern workers to vote their economic interests rather than their racial biases. But Operation Dixie was terminated several years before the American Federation of Labor and the Congress of Industrial Organizations merged in 1956. The operation represented a massive organizing effort, but it yielded meager results. Since the AFL–CIO merger, there have been no regionwide efforts, in terms of commitment of funds and manpower, on the scale of Operation Dixie.

During the roughest periods of resistance to social change in the late 1950s and early 1960s, AFL–CIO presidents in every southern state—many of whom are still around—stood with blacks on civil rights issues. Many of those labor leaders experienced threats of physical intimidation and in some cases actual bombings, but a result of that policy was the emergence of solid alliances between blacks and organized labor. By the mid-1970s, A. Philip Randolph Institutes financed by the AFL–CIO were operating in every southern state and training a new wave of black political leadership.

In the late 1960s, Professor F. Ray Marshall summarized trends which favor union growth in the South: (1) the reduction of the labor supply by migration of workers out of agriculture; (2) a changing southern ideology because of industrialization and the decline of agriculture, the most antiunion segment of the southern population; (3) increasing political power of the unions, in part because of a trend toward organizing the increasing number of government employees; (4) changing attitudes of southern workers; (5) pressure from unions in the non-South who need to protect their own state economies against the growing industrialization of the South; and (6) a slow trend toward unionization of white-collar workers.[1]

Another factor is the entry into southern industrial jobs by blacks, whose more receptive attitudes toward unions show up consistently on survey data. The changed racial climate also limits the exploitation of racial fears by southern plant managers, who for years had warned white workers that unionization would lead to integrated work forces.

The history of organized labor in the South is full of examples of workers seeking out unions in times of trouble and then being abandoned by them after strikes, despite great sacrifices on the part of the workers. Such experiences, even ones that occurred decades ago, can alienate workers and cause tremendous psychological problems for unions that still persist in some locales.[2] In addition, the history of union activities in the South includes many occasions in which resistance by employers was supported by state and local officials, sometimes by force.

Despite more favorable conditions, there was almost no growth in the rate of unionization in the South during the region's period of greatest change. None of the 11 states showed a steady increase both in numbers of union members and in unionized percentage of nonagricultural employees between 1964 and 1974 (see Table 16–1).

The rush of nonunion industry to the South in recent years did not occur in a vacuum but often resulted from conscious efforts, usually covert, of many state and local industry hunters to discourage plants with union contracts, in part to protect the labor supply for low-wage industries already in the region. The result is a perpetuation of predominantly low-wage industries. For example, union workers in the South in 1970 received median annual earnings of $8,053, compared with $5,839 for nonunion workers, according to a study by the Bureau of Labor Statistics of the U.S. Department of Labor.

Marshall and others have documented the efforts by some officials in the South to keep out union industry, and the authors heard confirmation from candid officials in some states. But those attitudes may be changing. Despite the sluggishness of union growth reflected in Table 16–1, the authors heard consistent comments from Democratic politicians in every southern state on the growing political importance of organized labor. Repeatedly, they spoke of attitudes that had changed only in the last few years, of welcoming labor endorsements many said

1. F. Ray Marshall, *Labor in the South* (Cambridge: Harvard University Press, 1967), pp. 345–351.
2. Ibid., pp. 332–333.

TABLE 16–1

Union Membership in the South, 1964–1974

	MEMBERSHIP (IN THOUSANDS)			PERCENTAGE OF NONAGRI-CULTURAL EMPLOYEES		
	1964	1970	1974	1964	1970	1974
Alabama	151	204	223	18.0	20.3	19.1
Arkansas	73	95	108	17.0	17.9	16.8
Florida	201	299	354	13.1	13.9	12.5
Georgia	150	251	264	12.7	16.2	14.5
Louisiana	147	193	194	17.1	18.4	16.3
Mississippi	53	76	84	11.6	13.2	12.0
North Carolina	89	137	140	6.7	7.8	6.9
South Carolina	52	81	82	7.9	9.6	8.0
Tennessee	184	274	295	17.6	20.6	18.7
Texas	370	523	567	13.3	14.4	13.0
Virginia	179	245	247	15.4	16.1	13.8
South	1,688	2,378	2,558	13.8	15.0	14.1
Non-South	15,500	17,379	18,008	29.3	31.6	29.9
United States	17,188	19,757	20,566	26.3	27.9	26.2

Source: U.S. Department of Labor, Bureau of Labor Statistics.

they would have shunned a few years earlier. In part, the welcome mat is out because of the threat of the Republican challenge; to seek labor support is a part of the new Democratic coalition politics. But Democratic candidates have also recognized the manpower and other valuable resources that unions can provide during campaigns, which become even more valuable as more and more restrictions are placed on campaign spending.

Interviews with state AFL–CIO presidents throughout the South confirmed the changing attitudes of politicians. One AFL–CIO official in Alabama spoke of the shift by George Wallace after the 1970 gubernatorial election in Alabama, in which Wallace ran second in the first primary after opposition from organized labor. Wallace subsequently sent emissaries to see Barney Weeks, the state AFL–CIO president. The governor then agreed to establish a labor school at a state university and acceded to a number of other requests from labor. One AFL–CIO official there declared, "We don't know how long he'll be working with us, but as long as he is, we plan to milk him for everything we can."

When Jimmy Carter was governor of Georgia, he breakfasted weekly with Herb Mabry, the state AFL–CIO president. When Dolph Briscoe became governor of Texas, where conservative Democratic governors long had fought organized labor, he sought input from state AFL–CIO

President Harry Hubbard on appointments to state boards and commissions and on other matters.

Louisiana is a special case because of the dynamism and political skill of AFL–CIO President Victor Bussie, whose political influence is substantially greater than that of any other labor official in the South (see Chapter 8).

The importance of cooperation with blacks, a policy strongly maintained by labor leaders, has begun to seep down to the rank-and-file. The Charleston Hospital Strike in 1969, in which a few carloads of white International Ladies Garment Workers Union members from other South Carolina communities joined the all-black hospital workers in protest marches, marked a joining of the civil rights and labor movements, with significant long-range implications. The Charleston strikers received support from the United Auto Workers, International Longshoremen's Association, and other union giants. It was a strike by garbage collectors in Memphis that attracted Martin Luther King to that city, where he was assassinated; later, it was Andrew Young, not yet a congressman from Atlanta, who was the chief tactician for the Southern Christian Leadership Conference in the Charleston Hospital Strike. At the end of 1974, Young got an enthusiastic reception from white and black textile workers at Roanoke Rapids, N.C., after a speech he made there a few days before a successful union vote. When Charles Evers ran as an independent black candidate for governor of Mississippi in 1971, he likewise stirred enthusiasm from a group of striking white and black woodworkers.

Similar signs of ferment are evident throughout the South in flirtations with unions by public employees and teachers. The gains made by blacks through organization during the civil rights movement have not gone unnoticed by white wage earners in the region.

But union influence remains limited with unorganized workers, and even among union members the effort at political education has been weak. With the exception of Texas, where the state AFL–CIO publishes a newspaper that meets acceptable standards of journalism, the labor press in every other southern state either is nonexistent or terribly weak. Because a good labor press can play a significant role in educating the rank-and-file on political matters, the absence of such means of communication results in a continued serious deficiency in the political education of workers in the South.

Marshall predicted that "the most important determinants of union membership [in the South] are likely to be dramatic and unpredictable events that could cause general increases in union membership throughout the region."[3] Massive unionization has yet to come to the South,

3. Ibid., p. 351.

but conditions appear more ripe for it than ever before. If it occurs, it will be followed by intensification of the trend toward realignment of political parties in the South to reflect the makeup of the parties nationally. But until membership grows and political education among working-class whites is strengthened, organized labor in most of the southern states will continue to represent more future potential than past or present impact.

Chapter

17

TOWARD THE FUTURE

A Cautious Optimism

THE ONLY CONSTANT in southern politics since World War II has been change. The political change has been accompanied by social and economic change more rapid than elsewhere in the country, and the result is a South in transition.

By no means have all southerners accepted the change, but the flamboyant, demagogic candidates and racist rhetoric of the past have all but disappeared. Appeals to race remain, but the code words hardly differ from those elsewhere in the country—"busing," "welfare chiselers," "crime in the streets." A hard core of resistance remains, as reflected in the 35 to 40 percent of the vote received by such candidates as Orval Faubus in Arkansas and Lester Maddox in Georgia in the 1974 Democratic gubernatorial primaries. But survey data show the greatest support for such candidates comes from those over 60 and those with less than an eighth-grade education.

"Personalism" remains a dominant characteristic of the southerner. It may manifest itself by good manners and solicitude in one-to-one human relations, as well as by an apparent blindness often displayed toward the dehumanizing aspects of racial discrimination. Politically, southern personalism appears in the barber shop discussions in which any politician who has truly arrived is referred to by his first name—"Big Jim" for Senator Eastland in Mississippi, "Ol' Strom" or "Fritz" for Senators Thurmond and Hollings in South Carolina, or "Young Harry" for Senator Harry Byrd, Jr. in Virginia.

The complexity and diversity of southern politics is reflected by the unique way each state has experienced a nearly universal political

397

transformation. The phenomenon was first evident in Florida and Arkansas, where election of Republican governors in 1966 led to a period of upheaval and finally ushered in a new period of political modernization and moderation. The result was a purging of the Democratic Old Guard and the revitalization of the Democratic Party in the face of a second-party challenge. The development of progressive Democratic leadership and election of Dale Bumpers in Arkansas in 1970 was accompanied by Republican collapse. In Florida the Democrats regained a position of dominance in 1970 with the election of Governor Reubin Askew and Senator Lawton Chiles.

In Georgia, where Republican Howard (Bo) Callaway narrowly failed to win the governor's office in 1966, the antiestablishment figure of Lester Maddox personified the transition period. The election of moderate Democrats Jimmy Carter in 1970 and George Busbee in 1974 restored clear one-party dominance in Georgia, a state where bright Republican hopes of the late 1960s had faded by the mid-1970s.

In Tennessee, the election in 1970 of Republican Governor Winfield Dunn and William E. Brock III as the state's second Republican senator finally forced Democrats to organize as a genuine political party. They took advantage of the Watergate atmosphere in 1974 to recapture the statehouse and won back two congressional seats after a decade of steady Republican advances. In this process, Ray Blanton, the successful Democratic candidate for governor, shed the Wallaceite image he had adopted in a losing 1972 race for the Senate. Instead, he projected the neopopulism of the new breed of southern Democratic governors in defeating Lamar Alexander, one of the more attractive Republican candidates in the South.

In North Carolina, Republicans captured the statehouse in 1972, setting into motion the forces that might allow an unknown Democrat to win, if the pattern elsewhere is followed.

In South Carolina, insurgent Charles (Pug) Ravenel defeated the Democratic Old Guard candidates in the 1974 primary, but was declared ineligible on a residency technicality. That led to the fluke victory of Republican James B. Edwards, the only ideological conservative Republican to win an election for governor in the South. The turmoil of the 1974 election in that state makes the future unpredictable.

In Virginia, the election of Republican Linwood Holton in 1969 marked the collapse of the Democratic Byrd organization. Virginia became the only southern state in which one Republican governor succeeded another, but the man who replaced Holton was the same man who had defeated him for governor in 1965 as a Democrat, Mills Godwin. The narrowness of his 1973 victory over Henry Howell, perhaps the most genuinely populist politician in the South in the 1970s, and the rebuilding of the Democratic Party suggest a move to progressive government in Virginia if the regional pattern prevails. Two Howell-type Democrats defeated incumbent Republican congressmen in 1974.

In Texas, the Old Guard went down in 1972, when Frances (Sissy) Farenthold ran as a liberal insurgent to beat out incumbent Governor Preston Smith and Lieutenant Governor Ben Barnes for second place in the Democratic primary. She lost in the runoff to Dolph Briscoe, "the most liberal of the conservative governors" as they say in Texas, whose transitional role likely will be followed by a successor in the mold of the "New South" governors elected elsewhere in the South in the 1970s.

In Mississippi, William Waller was elected in 1971 by running against the "establishment," but he also ran with the support of the Eastland organization against Lieutenant Governor Charles Sullivan, for whom Eastland felt personal animosity. The "Old Guard" was defeated in 1975 when Cliff Finch, a political unknown, won by more than 100,000 votes in a Democratic primary runoff against Lieutenant Governor William Winter, a onetime liberal hope who had faded after two decades in state politics.

In Alabama, the dominance of George Wallace has frozen political development, but the pattern elsewhere suggests possible trends for the future. Whether the demoralized Republican Party there, which peaked just before a calamitous loss in 1966, can seize the initiative remains to be seen.

In Louisiana, the Republican Party has yet to develop the leadership and organizational strength to really challenge the Democrats. Even so, the fact that even relatively weak Republican candidates can attract 40 percent of the vote in statewide contests confirms a high level of disenchantment with the old politics. The complete rejection of such old faces as that of former Governor Jimmie Davis in a 1971 comeback attempt marked an end to the politics of race in Louisiana. Democrats there are cast in the progressive, moderate mold that reflects overall party leadership of the region in the 1970s, notwithstanding the preoccupation of the national media with George Wallace.

The emergence of Frances Farenthold into national prominence in the women's movement reflects the ferment occurring within the region among women. Although the mythology built around southern womanhood persists and remains a psychological barrier to political participation, the early 1970s were marked by a gradual increase in women legislators and the first focusing of attention on the discrimination which women faced. Although the women's success, like that of the Republican Party, varied from state to state, the political role of women is part of the overall change transforming the region. The election of Evelyn Gandy as lieutenant governor in Mississippi in 1975 demonstrated that voters even in that most southern of states are willing to accept women for nontraditional offices.

399

Since 1950, all but a handful of the states in the South have either adopted new state constitutions or made substantial revisions. Many states have enacted provisions for judicial and local government reform, fewer restrictions on state financing, strong guarantees of a public school system (in jeopardy during the days of "massive resistance"), and occasionally, additional guarantees of personal liberty.

Several states have strengthened the role of the executive, but except for Tennessee, Alabama, Louisiana, and Virginia—all of which have moderately strong institutional power in the governor's office—the other states in the South vest limited authority with the state's chief executive, who in North Carolina even lacks a veto. A trend toward reorganization of state government into fewer departments has begun, but in states like South Carolina, Mississippi, Louisiana, and Texas, well over a hundred state agencies exist, many with semiautonomous boards or commissions. The power of state legislatures tends to be stronger in the South than in the rest of the country.

TABLE 17-1
*Percent of Voting-Age Population Casting Votes
in Presidential Elections, 1960–1972*

	1960	1964	1968	1972[a]
United States	63.1	61.8	60.7	55.7
Alabama	30.8	35.9	52.7	44.2
Arkansas	40.8	50.6	53.3	49.7
Florida	48.6	51.2	53.0	50.6
Georgia	29.2[a]	43.3[a]	43.4[a]	37.8
Louisiana	44.6	47.3	54.8	45.0
Mississippi	25.3	33.9	53.2	46.0
North Carolina	52.9	52.8	54.3	43.9
South Carolina	30.4	39.4	46.7	39.5
Tennessee	49.8	51.7	53.7	44.3
Texas	41.2	44.6	48.7	45.2
Virginia	32.8	41.1	50.1	45.6
Average for South	38.8	44.7	51.3	44.7
Difference Between South and U.S.	24.3	17.1	9.4	11.0

[a] Population 18 years old and over.
Source: U.S. Bureau of the Census, *Statistical Abstract of the United States, 1974,* Table no. 704, p. 438.

Increased levels of voter participation have served as a modernizing political force in the region, although voting turnout remains relatively low in the South. Table 17–1 shows that the percentage of the voting-age population which cast votes in presidential elections increased by 5.9 percent for the region between 1960 and 1972, in contrast to a 7.4 percent decrease for the country as a whole. In only two of the 11 southern states, North Carolina and Tennessee, did the percentage decrease between 1960 and 1972, and only in North Carolina was the falloff of 9 percent greater than that for the country as a whole. The difference in turnout between the South and the nation in 1960 was 24.3 percent; the difference was only 11 percent in 1972.

CONGRESSIONAL CHANGES

Despite the ascendancy of conservative forces after the defeat of the Populist movement in the 1890s and the disfranchising laws that followed, the strain of agrarian radicalism never disappeared from the politics of the South. William Havard contends that the Populist movement "may well have exercised a more lasting influence on the South and especially on factional forms of opposition in the South than it did in the Midwest, where it was more widely noticed in its early stages." [1] Wilsonian progressivism received both leadership and votes from southerners on such congressional issues as the tariff, regulation of finance and industrial capitalism, increase in income taxation, and many acts respecting easy credit and agricultural improvement. Even on labor issues and efforts to regulate wages and hours, where the record is less impressive, the southern role in Congress was not all negative. Although the early New Deal received opposition from some southerners in Congress, it also received considerable support from southern Democrats.[2]

Key's study was written as the southerners in Congress were beginning to turn sharply toward reaction. Twenty years later, Wayne Shannon found that conservative coalition voting had more than tripled, that low levels of unity with the northern members of the party existed among southern Democrats, and that the South had achieved a high concentration of power through control of from one-half to almost two-thirds of the standing committee chairmanships. But just as Key wrote at a turning point, so did Shannon, and the southern revolt which he documented reached its peak in 1967, the year his study concluded.

Since then, southern power in Congress has waned, and gone is the day when civil rights served as an issue which held southern members of Congress together. The most dramatic example of this change was the seven-year extension of the Voting Rights Act in 1975, on which a ma-

1. William C. Havard, *The Changing Politics of the South* (Baton Rouge: Louisiana State University Press, 1972), p. 706.

2. Ibid., pp. 704–705. See also George Brown Tindall, *The Emergence of the New South* (Baton Rouge: Louisiana State University Press, 1967), chaps. 1, 18.

jority of southern congressmen—including two-thirds of the southern Democrats—for the first time in this century supported a civil rights measure.

The tendency of the new Democrats to vote more frequently with the party majority will reduce the frequency with which the conservative coalition of Republicans and southern Democrats will form. The power of the South will weaken even further over the short term, as aged committee chairmen fade from the scene. And finally, the region's obstructionist role against social legislation appears to be ending. The emerging South in Congress is developing a pattern of party realignment, with southern Republicans voting more conservatively than even the old southern Democrats, and recently elected Democrats voting more like national Democrats.

REPUBLICAN OUTLOOK

Not until the Dixiecrat protest of 1948 was there a clear break that marked the end of the Democratic one-party "solid south." Republican party growth began in the 1950s, accelerated during the 1960s, and peaked in 1972. The development of southern Republican strength generally has been from the top down, with the greatest strength at the presidential level. The peak GOP strength was in 1972, when it held 31 percent of southern seats in Congress and 17 percent of the legislative seats. Republicans' losses were substantial in the Watergate reaction in 1974: one-fifth of their southern seats in Congress and more than one-fourth of their legislative seats in the South.

Beginning in 1952, Republicans received a slight majority of the total vote cast in presidential elections in the South through 1972. But the level of Republican identification among southerners has not increased since 1960, although Democratic identification has declined.

Although southerners have withdrawn from habitual allegiance to the Democratic Party, a number of serious students of the region's politics have questioned whether the reaction reflected in presidential voting may not primarily be one of protest and transitional confusion. In the three-way presidential election in 1968, the Republican share of the vote was less in every southern state than it was in 1960, and less than the 1964 level in all states but Texas. The explanation there is that the 1964 Democratic candidate was a Texan, and native-son loyalty inflated the Democratic vote.

Although the Republican Party carried five of the eleven states of the

South in both 1964 and 1968, only South Carolina went Republican in both of those elections. Elsewhere in the Deep South, the Goldwater vote shifted to Wallace in 1968 and represented a protest vote. The same thing occurred in the Outer South, but in smaller proportions, as Table 17–2 shows. In 1972, the Wallace vote shifted solidly to Nixon in near-total rejection of Democrat George McGovern.

TABLE 17–2

*Republican Percentage of Presidential Vote
in the South, 1960–1972*

	1960	1964	1968	1972
Alabama	42.1	69.5	14.1	73.9
Arkansas	46.3	43.4	31.0	69.2
Florida	51.5	48.9	40.5	72.1
Georgia	37.4	54.1	30.4	75.3
Louisiana	28.6	56.8	23.5	69.7
Mississippi	40.5	87.1	13.5	79.9
North Carolina	47.9	43.8	39.5	70.6
South Carolina	48.8	58.9	38.1	71.9
Tennessee	53.6	44.5	37.8	69.5
Texas	48.5	36.5	39.9	66.6
Virginia	52.4	46.2	43.4	69.3

Statistical indices utilizing the Ranney model (as illustrated in Appendix E) show that in the period from 1946 to 1963 there were eight Democratic one-party states in the South and three modified one-party, with only Virginia, Tennessee, and North Carolina in the latter category. When updated for 1964 to 1974, the model shows that only Mississippi, Louisiana, and Alabama remained one-party states, and Alabama moved into the modified one-party category when congressional elections were taken into account. All 11 states had moved in the direction of two-party competition, but only Tennessee had achieved genuine two-party status.

Republican identification as measured by the Gallup Poll was 22 percent in the South in 1960 and 19 percent in 1969. The 1974 De Vries survey found a Republican identification of only 16 percent in the South, but national Republican identification at the time had sunk to 23 percent, an unusually low level because of reaction to the Watergate affair.

Key identified three types of Republicans in the South: presidential Republicans, mountain Republicans, and Negro Republicans. But Key's presidential Republicans were voters with Republican leanings who had nothing besides Democrats to choose from at the state or local level. Thus, they differed from the presidential protest voters who subsequently reacted against the national Democratic Party but who opted for George

Wallace when given an alternative means of expressing their protest. The Negro Republicans of Key's day are virtually gone, but in some Deep South states, such as Mississippi and South Carolina, the Republican Party in recent years has actively sought black professionals and businessmen who might be attracted to an economically conservative philosophy.

Traditional mountain Republicans, who have furnished moderate party leadership in North Carolina, Virginia, and Tennessee, remain a source of GOP strength in regions where they have been strong historically, despite the party's move to more conservative positions. To this core the GOP has added migrants from other regions, usually business and professional families who moved into the region as part of the industrialization and economic expansion; urban and suburban middle- and upper-class migrants from farms and small towns; a smaller group who tend to be reformers and are interested primarily in building a two-party system; and a large group of conservative ideologues attracted by the Goldwater candidacy in 1964.

The Goldwater brand of conservatism made 1964 a key year in the development of the GOP in the South and is best reflected by the southern Republicans elected to Congress. They vote consistently against domestic social programs, give unquestioning support to defense spending, and generally display little grasp of the region's lingering problems of poverty and underdevelopment. Goldwater's strategy killed the chance for the Republican Party to assume a role of reform in the one-party South and attracted the most reactionary elements into the party.

Maturing Republican leadership in the region has begun to recognize that the "southern strategy" initiated by Goldwater, which includes subtle and not-so-subtle racial appeals, does not work. Not only has it driven the mass of black voters—who now number more than 3.5 million in the South—to the Democrats, but it also turns off many whites who perceive the arousal of racial emotions as a threat to stability. In addition, even some of the most conservative Republican leaders in the South have matured in their attitudes. For example, Clarke Reed, the veteran Mississippi Republican state chairman who emerged from the Goldwater movement, talks in terms of "enlightened self-interest" in attitudes toward blacks and their problems. "Enlightened self-interest says you should . . . go an extra mile. If they get more political participation, better education, make more money, pay more taxes, we'll all be better off." [3] Except for Governor Edwards in South Carolina, Republican governors who have been elected have tended to be moderates. The conservative wing has been more successful in statewide races for the U.S. Senate.

Republican growth can be expected to come primarily from the

3. Interview with Clarke Reed, April 2, 1974.

migrant newcomers and the suburban middle- and upper-middle classes, but the latter group also is the major source for growth of ticket splitters. Although Republican identification has shown no growth in recent years in the South, Democratic identification has fallen, and there has been a corresponding increase in the number of people who identify as politically independent. This is part of a national trend, but survey data suggest the trend is even stronger in the South, and it is the independent ticket splitter who likely will emerge as a major force in determining the outcome of southern elections.

Despite the 1974 Republican setbacks, the forces of social and economic change that have stirred political trends in the South will continue to exert pressure toward two-party political competition. But the potential for two-party growth will be achieved only if dynamic and skillful leadership develops within the Republican Party and only if the GOP can offer candidates of ability with solutions to problems.

BLACK POLITICS

It remains true, as it was when Key wrote, that an understanding of the political process in the South inevitably leads to the Negro. But the difference is that blacks have changed their status from political object to political participant, and it was the reaction by white southerners to that change that shaped contemporary politics in the region.

Although southern blacks basically have won the right to equality in political participation, the ultimate battle for economic justice remains to be won. By the mid-1970s the civil rights movement had moved off the streets and through the ballot box into a slowly growing presence in city halls, legislative chambers, and finally the halls of Congress. The increased black vote and the pursuit of it has resulted in a change in both the rhetoric and the attitudes of white politicians. Direct references to race have all but disappeared from southern political campaigns, and personal contact with black voters has sensitized the feelings of many white politicians.

The progress in black political development suggested by statistics can blind the unwary to the problems that remain. Despite the tripling of elected black officials in the region between 1970 and 1975, blacks still comprise barely 2 percent of all elected officials in the region, although they constitute almost one-fifth of the voting-age population. And despite huge increases in registration, the levels of black registration and participation remained significantly below those for whites. In addition, failure to develop common goals or to translate political gains into tangible economic benefits leave southern black elected officials facing problems that plagued their Reconstruction Era counterparts.

provide their own sources of political funds. If they are likely to develop such resources and their independence and influence should grow accordingly.

CONSOLIDATION OF CHANGE

A state official in Mississippi, who requested anonymity, said in 1974 that the burning of black churches and killing of three civil rights workers in the 1960s "were repulsive to people. . . . On the surface they were saying, 'Hell, they didn't have no business being down there,' but inside, people didn't like it. It hurt a lot of people inside." He added that many whites in the state retain segregationist sentiments, "but their children are going to school with blacks. They don't want any more explosive situations because their children are right in the middle of it now."

Former Governor Jimmy Carter of Georgia spoke of the "pride" of white southerners in accommodating to the change. "Once we had to confront the fact that we were right or wrong in the eyes of God, we said we're wrong, and if we can find a way to make this change without losing face, we'll do it. And the Supreme Court and other court orders were the things that permitted us to do it without losing face. And in many instances we did it with a great sense of relief." [4] Carter's victories over George Wallace in 1976 southern presidential primaries reflected the accommodation to change that he spoke about.

Andrew Young, whose congressional district included the governor's mansion in Atlanta, expressed some of the same views as Carter and also articulated a point made by white and black southerners: the importance of personal relationships between the races.

"In the South," said Young, "a lot of people in leadership positions had been cared for by black women, where there was not just a servant relationship, but where it was somebody that worked with the family through long years, and they were probably more mother to the people than their own parents were. And you had a complicated set of personal relationships in the white community in the South that made southern whites very, very guilty about the racial situation. And it seems to me that Martin Luther King's death was something of a turning point, of white people suddenly being willing to come around. I think a lot happened in white

4. Interview with Jimmy Carter, November 20, 1973.

America that's never been recorded, in the wake of the death of Martin Luther King and Robert Kennedy. . . . I sensed then that whites wanted to help, but didn't know how. And, of course, that was also the period when blacks began to express their hostility, and it was even more difficult. . . . With the slightest invitation the white community in the South was ready to move toward a new relationship with blacks."

Young felt that it could have gone either way. "The news media were not publicizing people like me. I mean, they were publicizing the folks that were saying, 'Burn.' You know, John Lewis was around, talking nonviolence even back then, but nobody was listening to John. It was the Black Panther types, you know, the rhetorical revolutionaries, that had the mass media. And that's the impression most whites had of blacks. At the same time, the Richard Nixons and the Lester Maddoxes were playing to the fears of this same white southerner and white American. And nobody was giving them a vehicle to get out of their racist heritage. And one of the reasons I ran was that it seemed to me that if I could win, it would put an end to the Nixon 'Southern Strategy.' Because I saw that Southern Strategy as really damaging everything I had been working for. And instead of a New South, you'd get the old Dixicrat South in Republican dress. . . ." [5]

The political liberation of southern blacks, important as it is, may be of less significance than the liberation of southern whites. "I'll tell you who's really free in Mississippi for the first time," Greenville editor Hodding Carter III declared. "It's not the black man, who still is economically about as much in bondage as he ever was. By God, the white Mississippian is free. . . . That's the hardest thing for me to remember now—how tiny a thing you could do ten years ago and be in desperate difficulty. You know, what few dissenting remarks could destroy you politically. Or make you fear for your job, or get you run the hell out of the state if you were a minister—as an awful lot of young ministers discovered in the early '60s. That just doesn't happen anymore." [6]

The South retains some distinctive regional qualities, but it has joined the nation's political mainstream. The speed with which that change was accomplished is at least partly attributable to the presidency of Lyndon B. Johnson, who guided the passage of the landmark 1964 Civil Rights Act and 1965 Voting Rights Act. Although Eric Goldman found much about Johnson that was not admirable, he concluded that his presidency was of major consequence in bringing the South back into the Union. "In considerable measure this resulted from long-running trends," Goldman wrote, "yet the fact that it was a Southern President who put through the tough civil rights laws made an enormous amount of difference. So too

5. Interview with Andrew Young, January 31, 1974.
6. Interview with Hodding Carter III, April 1, 1974.

did Lyndon Johnson's skillful exploitation of this fact, the general thrust of his domestic policies, and his persistent, patient message to the South—delivered publicly and still more often privately—to let up on 'nigra, nigra' and concentrate on economic and social advancement." [7]

V. O. Key concluded in 1949 that "the race issue broadly defined . . . must be considered the number one problem on the southern agenda. Lacking a solution for it, all else fails." [8] Race remains a problem in the South, but it is also a national problem, and it is the changing South where the solution may emerge from among people whose children "are right in the middle of it," or perhaps from that generation of children.

There remain the lingering problems of poverty in all its manifestations, residual racist attitudes, unequal standards of justice, a regressive tax structure, and a rate of political participation less than that outside the region. In addition, there are newer problems, such as threats to the environment and the perils of unregulated growth. But the South is shedding the sense of guilt and shame and pessimism that so recently prevailed. Within the region, southerners take pride in their ability to adapt to an era of traumatic change and hold to a spirit of cautious optimism that may make solutions possible.

When he was governor of Georgia, Jimmy Carter expressed the opinion that southerners are "very accurate mirrors of the average American voter. They are basically progressive, deeply patriotic, moderate to conservative in political orientation . . . They have a faith in a religious ethic. They also, politically speaking, have a faith in the basic institutions of our country. And we look on the vicissitudes and the failures and the embarrassments [such as] might be associated with Watergate as a temporary abberation and not as a permanent circumstance. I think we have a feeling that we can overcome it." [9]

The ability of Carter, as a representative of the emerging South, to appeal to voters outside as well as within the region as a presidential campaigner in 1976 reflects the transformation that has occurred in southern politics.

7. Eric F. Goldman, *The Tragedy of Lyndon Johnson* (New York: Alfred A. Knopf, 1969), p. 515.

8. V. O. Key, *Southern Politics in State and Nation* (New York: Vintage, 1949), p. 675.

9. Interview with Jimmy Carter, November 20, 1973.

APPENDIX A

Maps, Regional and State:
Demographic and Voting Patterns

ALABAMA

ARKANSAS

FLORIDA

GEORGIA

LOUISIANA

MISSISSIPPI

NORTH CAROLINA

SOUTH CAROLINA

TENNESSEE

TEXAS

REPUBLICAN PRESIDENTIAL VOTING,

1944, 1964, 1968

DISTRIBUTION OF BLACK POPULATION, 1970

Alabama

Maps 1 and 2 show the new political face of the Alabama black belt. V. O. Key noted that this region of the state was politically the most conservative. The planters of the black belt in league with the Birmingham industrialists exerted a strong influence on the state.

The enfranchisement of Alabama's blacks has turned that situation around. Map 1 shows the distribution of black people in the state. Map 2 shows counties of consistently anti-conservative voting. The correspondence between the two is striking. The black belt with its complete citizenry now enjoying the suffrage has become the most "liberal" area in the state. The final irony is that Birmingham (Jefferson County) has joined the black belt in this new situation as well, a reflection of the large urban black population in the state's largest city.

ALABAMA

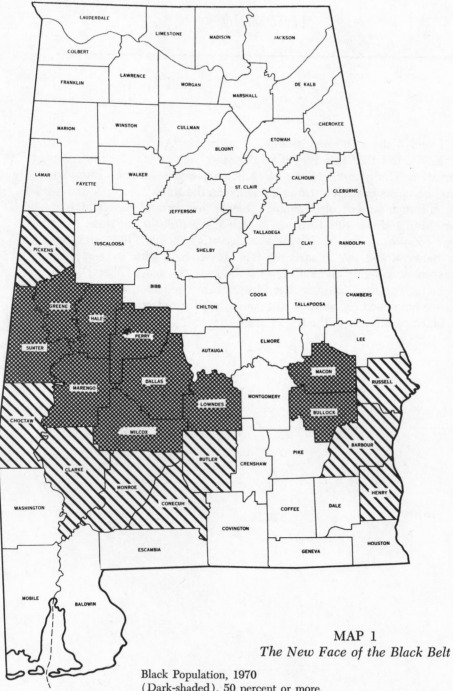

MAP 1

The New Face of the Black Belt

Black Population, 1970
(Dark-shaded), 50 percent or more.
(Light-shaded), 40 percent to 49.9 percent.

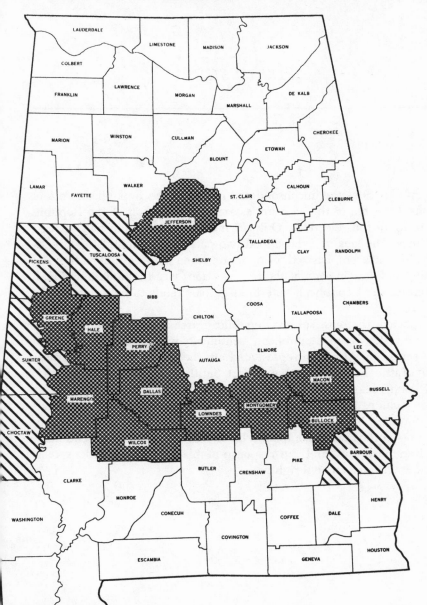

MAP 2
The New Face of the Black Belt

Anti-Conservative Counties: The criteria used are (1) a vote of 15 percent or more for the National Democratic Party of Alabama (NDPA) candidate in the 1970 gubernatorial election (22 counties), (2) 25 percent or more for McGovern in the 1972 presidential election (25 counties), (3) 20 percent or more for Humphrey in the 1968 presidential election (19 counties), and (4) less than 65 percent for Wallace in the 1974 gubernatorial primary (23 counties).

(Dark-shaded), meeting all four of the above criteria.

(Light-shaded), meeting three of the above criteria.

Arkansas

This map illustrates the unconsolidated nature of the Republican vote in Arkansas. Only ten of the 75 counties are in the top half of the Republican vote in all four elections. Only 12 more are in the top half at least three times. The lack of a developed two-party tradition and the attendant loyalties are emphasized even more when one considers the Republican candidate in each of the four elections was the same individual. In Arkansas, the Republican vote in large part tends to be a vote of the moment.

As expected, the most solidly Republican area is the Ozark section in the northwest, where Republican sentiment is traced to opposition against secession. Also well represented are the more populous counties: Pulaski (Little Rock), Sebastian (Fort Smith), Jefferson (Pine Bluff), and Miller (Texarkana). All are shaded. A third group of Rockefeller counties includes those with the larger percentage of blacks in the population, counties such as Mississippi, Lee, Phillips, and Chicot. Rockefeller's appeal thus was a compound of traditional Republican sentiment, urban Republicanism, and the response of blacks to Rockefeller's relatively liberal stance on civil rights.

ARKANSAS

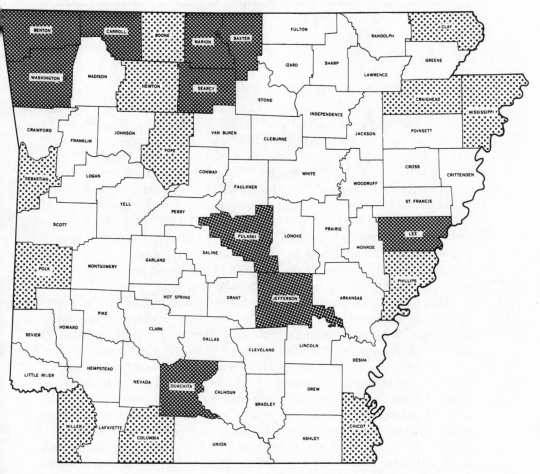

Ephemeral Pattern of Republican Strength

This map shows the counties in the top half of all Arkansas counties in voting for
Winthrop Rockefeller in the gubernatorial general elections of 1964, 1966, 1968, and
1970.
(Shaded dark), top half in all four elections.
(Shaded light), top half in three of the four elections.

Florida

Maps 1 and 2 demonstrate the relationship between immigration and partisanship in Florida. Much of Florida's Republicanism is imported. The amount of migration to Florida from Republican areas outside the South has been substantial in recent decades. Map 1 shows the percentage of inhabitants reporting their place of birth as outside the 16-state census South as of the 1970 census. The greatest areas of concentration of nonsouthern immigrants are the coasts of the peninsula. Southerners make up the great bulk of the population in the state north of Ocala and in inland Florida west and northwest of Lake Okeechobee. It should be noted that immigrants from the Northeast are concentrated on the eastern coast, while Midwesterners are predominant on the western coast. In addition, the southern tip of the peninsula includes Dade County, which has large Cuban, Jewish, and black populations.

Map 2 shows the Republican voter registration in 1974. The correspondence between Maps 1 and 2 is very close. Those seven counties with Republican registrations in excess of 40 percent report less than 50 percent of their populations as Southern born. Of the remaining four counties with less than 50 percent Southern born, three have Republican registrations between 30 percent and 40 percent. The fourth county is Dade. Of the 26 counties with more than 80 percent Southern born, 25 show Republican registrants comprising less than 10 percent of all registrants. In the remaining county, Putnam, 13.9 percent are Republican registrants. In only five other counties did Republican registration fall below 10 percent. In these five counties at least 70 percent are southern born.

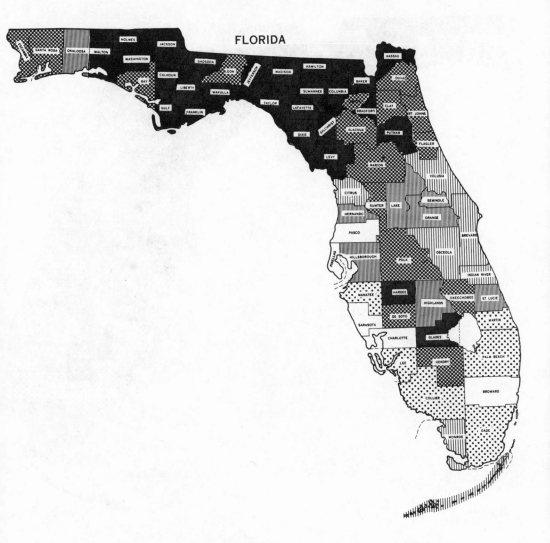

FLORIDA

MAP 1
Immigrant Republicanism

Percentage of population reporting birth in South, 1970. (Based on Bureau of the Census definition of the South, which includes 16 states and the District of Columbia.)

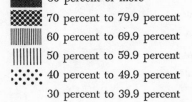

80 percent or more

70 percent to 79.9 percent

60 percent to 69.9 percent

50 percent to 59.9 percent

40 percent to 49.9 percent

30 percent to 39.9 percent

417

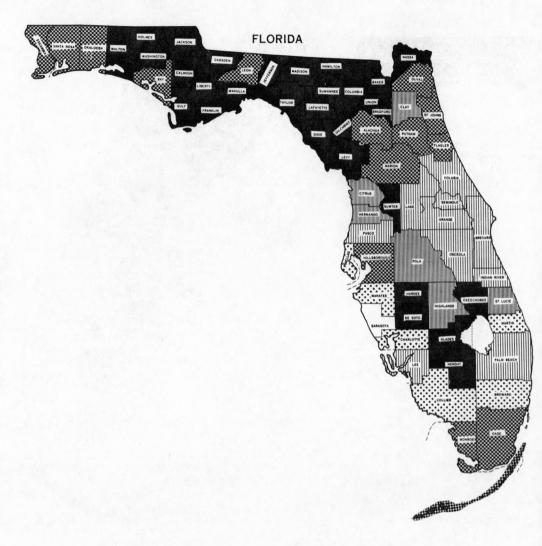

MAP 2
Immigrant Republicanism

Percentage of voters registered as Republicans, September, 1974.

50 percent or more

40 percent to 49.9 percent

30 percent to 39.9 percent

20 percent to 29.9 percent

10 percent to 19.9 percent

Less than 10 percent

Maps 3, 4, and 5 illustrate the tenuousness of party ties in Florida. Map 3 shows the Republican vote for governor in 1970. Reubin Askew, the Democrat, defeated the more politically conservative and socially flamboyant Claude Kirk with 57 percent of the vote. A comparison of Maps 2 and 3 shows that traditional partisan ties as expressed by voter registration were largely translated into ballots for the two parties. In other words, the conventional wisdom that northern immigrants to Florida register Republican and vote conservatively and for Republicans is given substantial support by the 1970 gubernatorial returns. An inspection of Map 4, however, leads to a different conclusion. Askew, running again in 1974, was faced by Jerry Thomas, a conservative Democrat turned Republican who ran very strong in the Panhandle, while Askew cleaned up in supposedly Republican areas of the peninsula. Not only were the 1970 returns a completely inaccurate predictor of the 1974 race, but partisan registration was just as bad. Askew carried the fifteen most Republican counties in the state, including Sarasota with 57 percent Republican registration, receiving 58 percent of the vote there. The supposedly conservative Republicans of the peninsula rejected Thomas, who was, however, warmly embraced by the Democrats of the Panhandle.

If Map 4 shows little correspondence with either party identification or behavior, what is the explanation for the distribution of the vote in the 1974 governor's race? A comparison of Maps 4 and 5 is very instructive. All but three of the 20 counties in which George Wallace received more than 60 percent of the vote in 1968 cast majorities for Republican Jerry Thomas, who in 1974 sought to capitalize on the busing issue. Fourteen of the counties gave Thomas 55 percent or more. Conversely, Thomas carried only one (Lake County) of the twenty-five counties in which Wallace received less than 40 percent. Clearly it is not party, but ideology, that counts in Florida, and the immigrant Republicans are a breed apart from the converts which Goldwater and Nixon have made in other parts of the South with their southern strategy.

FLORIDA

MAP 3
Ideology Is Stronger Than Party

Percentage of Republican vote for governor in 1970.
55 percent or more
50 percent to 54.9 percent
45 percent to 49.9 percent
Less than 45 percent

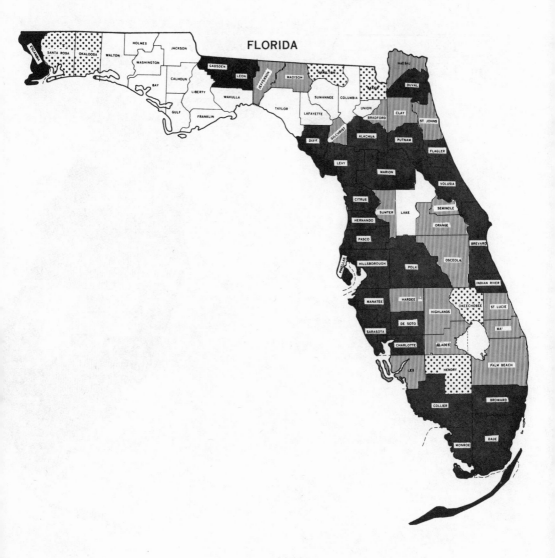

MAP 4
Ideology Is Stronger Than Party

Percentage of Republican vote for governor, 1974.

55 percent or more

 50 percent to 54.9 percent

45 percent to 49.9 percent

Less than 45 percent

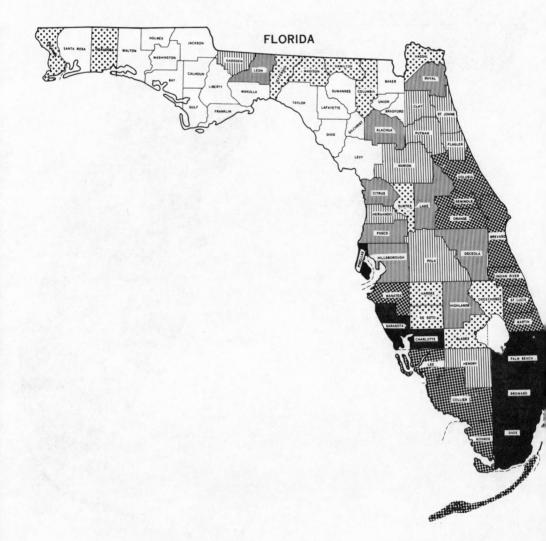

MAP 5
Ideology Is Stronger Than Party

Percentage of vote for Wallace for president in 1968.

60 percent or more

50 percent to 59.9 percent

40 percent to 49.9 percent

30 percent to 39.9 percent

20 percent to 29.9 percent

less than 20 percent

422

Georgia

Map 1 shows that Maddox's appeal was a compound of ruralism, racial conservatism, and populism. All three appeals are evident from Maddox's core support in southeast Georgia. These are all rural counties with few blacks and less money. Of the 21 strongest Maddox counties below the fall line, 14 were Talmadge counties, according to Key. Only one was an anti-Talmadge county. The Talmadgist strain augments the ruralist-racial-populist argument. Maddox also was strong in five counties within the outer reaches of the Atlanta SMSA (Paulding, Douglas, Cherokee, Forsyth, and Walton). The conservative element may be important here as well as some localism. Maddox is from Atlanta. The group of Maddox counties in northeastern Georgia comprise something known as the Tugaloo Cluster. Politics in this rural, hill area has a decided populist slant. Six of the counties were Talmadge bailiwicks. Along with a four-county cluster centered on Cherokee and Dawson Counties (these two are also Maddox counties), the Tugaloo Cluster was the only area of consistent Talmadgism in north Georgia. Even more interesting is that the Tugaloo Cluster was the area of greatest support for Lyndon Johnson in 1964 in the state.

Areas of Maddox weakness tend to be black belt and urban areas. The counties containing Atlanta, Columbus, Albany, Macon and Savannah (five of the six Georgia cities with populations in excess of 50,000) all showed anti-Maddox strength in all five elections between 1966 and 1974 in which he ran as a statewide candidate in the Democratic primary.

Of the 31 counties containing cities of more than 10,000 population, 19 were in the bottom half of Maddox support all 5 times. Six others were in the lower half 4 times. None of the remaining 7 showed consistent pro-Maddox tendencies. Therefore, of the 32 counties in which Maddox was weak each time, 19 are "urban" counties. Of the remaining 13, all but one have black populations in excess of 45 percent. The concentration of anti-Maddox strength in the black belt is notable. Race and ruralism remain potent factors in Georgia politics, although increasingly dwarfed by the growth of urbanism.

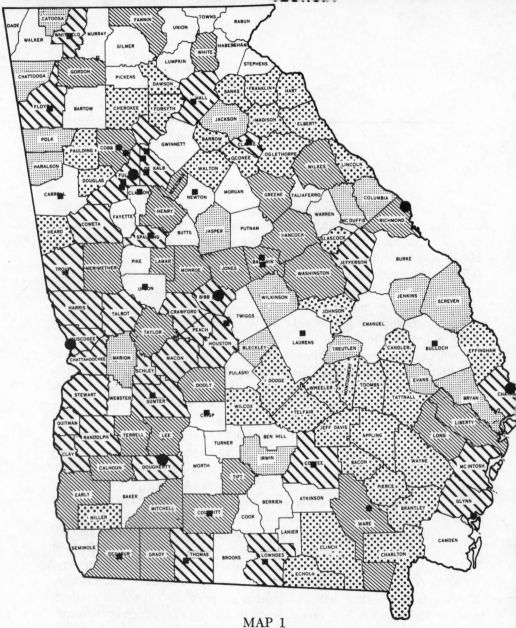

MAP 1
"Maddox" and "Anti-Maddox" Counties

Support for, and opposition to, Lester Maddox in five Democratic primaries, 1966–1974.

:·:·: In top half of counties for Maddox all five times.

▒▒ In top half for Maddox four times.

||||||| In bottom half for Maddox four times.

◣ In bottom half for Maddox five times.
Cities of more than 50,000 population, 1970.
Towns of between 10,000 and 50,000 population, 1970.

Maps 2, 3, and 4 show the lack of enduring attachments to the Republican Party in Georgia. Note the virtual absence of overlap among the three maps. Only one county, Fannin, is shaded in all three. Fourteen other counties are shaded twice. One of these is Towns, which like Fannin is a traditional Republican county. Eight others cluster within the Atlanta metropolitan area. The other five are the counties which contain Augusta, Athens, Macon, Warner-Robbins, and Rome, all towns of 20,000 or more (four are 30,000 or more). Apart from this reflection of an urban Republicanism, support for the Republican gubernatorial candidate fluctuates wildly.

In 1966, Republican support was found in counties which had strongly opposed Maddox, the Democratic candidate in the Democratic primary. Yet in 1974, it was the counties that strongly supported Maddox in that year's Democratic primary which voted Republican after Maddox lost the Democratic nomination. Although it has become legitimate to vote Republican in Georgia, exercising that option has a very different meaning there than in a traditionally two-party state. Georgia Republicans are not perceived as distinct from Democrats, but rather as a Democratic faction. If a voter's candidate is defeated in the Democratic primary, he still retains an alternative, albeit a negative one. He can vote against the primary winner in the general election. And that seems to be what has happened. In 1970, without the catalytic Maddox in the governor's race, the Republican vote took on what is probably a more "normal" form, with an urban and hill country base.

GEORGIA

MAP 2
Diffused Republicanism

Shaded areas show Republican strength in gubernatorial elections: 50 percent or more Republican in 1966 (Map 2), 40 percent or more Republican in 1970 (Map 3), and 40 percent or more Republican in 1974 (Map 4).

GEORGIA

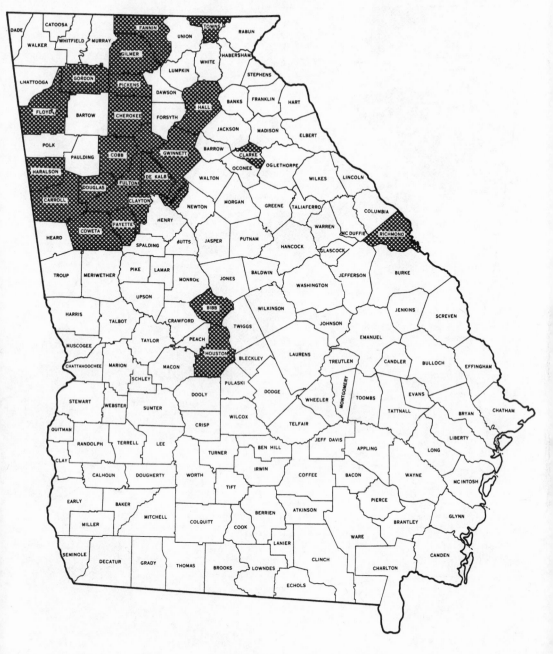

MAP 3
Diffused Republicanism

Shaded areas show Republican strength in gubernatorial elections: 50 percent or more Republican in 1966 (Map 2), 40 percent or more Republican in 1970 (Map 3), and 40 percent or more Republican in 1974 (Map 4).

GEORGIA

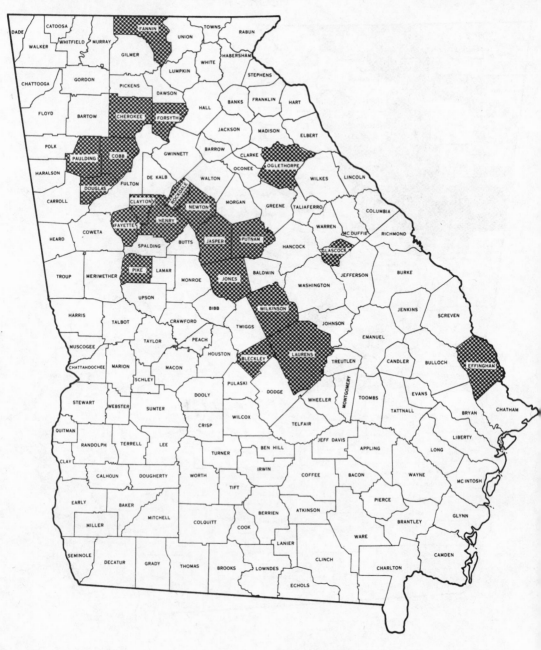

MAP 4
Diffused Republicanism

Shaded areas show Republican strength in gubernatorial elections: 50 percent or more Republican in 1966 (Map 2), 40 percent or more Republican in 1970 (Map 3), and 40 percent or more Republican in 1974 (Map 4).

Louisiana

Maps 1, 2, 3, and 4 illustrate the extent and character of regionalism in Louisiana politics. Twenty-six south Louisiana parishes have populations which are majority Catholic. Nearly all of these Catholics are French-speaking Cajuns. The politics of this region is distinct from that of Anglo-Saxon, Protestant, north Louisiana, in the relative lack of support for racist rhetoric, its comparative economic liberalism, and its ethnic cohesiveness. Three of these maps show the clarity of that distinctiveness.

The career of John McKeithen, twice governor of the state, illustrates the political nature of the Catholic parishes, called Acadiana. In his bid for the governorship in the 1963 primary, McKeithen displayed all the characteristics likely to lose him votes in Acadiana. He was a north Louisiana Protestant who ran as a segregationist and appeared distinctly to the right of his opponent, New Orleans Mayor deLesseps Morrison, a "liberal" Catholic. Consequently, McKeithen did his worst in Acadiana. In the 1964 general election, McKeithen faced Charleton Lyons, no less conservative and just as north Louisiana Protestant. Without the cues of either ethnicity or ideological diversity, Acadiana split. The distribution of the vote in Map 1 is rather haphazard.

By 1967, McKeithen had acquired a moderate image, which was highlighted by primary opposition from racist Congressman John Rarick. Acadiana, having rejected McKeithen four years earlier, solidly backed him in 1967 against the more conservative Rarick (see Map 2). Quite clearly McKeithen's strength had shifted to Acadiana.

The 1971 gubernatorial primary was similar to the 1963 race in that Acadiana solidly backed the liberal candidate, who this time was also a Cajun, Edwin Edwards (see Map 3). Bennett Johnston, a moderate, but to the right of Edwards, was a north Louisiana Protestant.

In the February, 1972 general election, support for Edwards was even more solid in Acadiana (see Map 4). His Republican opponent, David Treen, was very conservative and Protestant, but not from north Louisiana. He resided in suburban New Orleans. That the distribution of the Edwards vote was not really a product of party identification can be seen by comparing Maps 1 and 4.

In conclusion, Louisiana regionalism is distinct and persistent. It is determined largely by the tendency of the Cajun parishes to support more liberal, Catholic candidates and is not a factor of either factional or partisan identification.

LOUISIANA

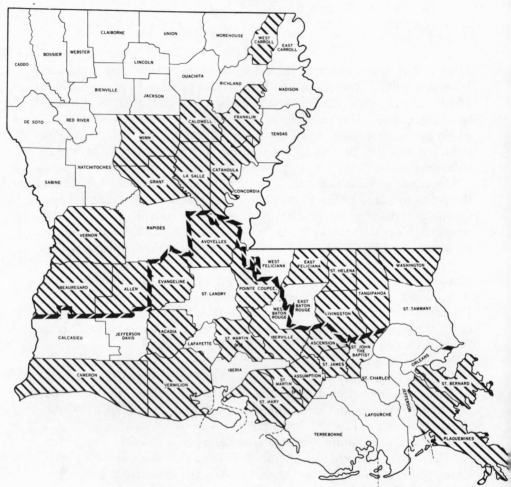

MAP 1
Regionalism in Louisiana Politics

Catholic parishes are located south of broken line. Shaded area represents parishes in which McKeithen received 70 percent or more of the vote in 1964 general election for governor against Republican Lyons.

430

LOUISIANA

MAP 2
Regionalism in Louisiana Politics

Catholic parishes are located south of broken line. Shaded area represents parishes in which McKeithen received 80 percent or more of the vote in 1967 Democratic primary against Rarick.

LOUISIANA

MAP 3
Regionalism in Louisiana Politics

Catholic parishes are located south of broken line. Shaded area represents parishes in which Edwards received 50 percent or more of the vote in 1971 Democratic primary runoff for governor against Johnston.

432

LOUISIANA

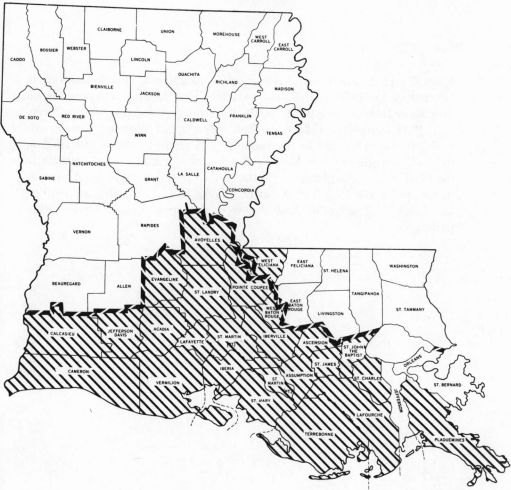

MAP 4
Regionalism in Louisiana Politics

Catholic parishes are located south of broken line. Shaded area represents parishes in which Edwards received 65 percent or more of the vote in 1972 general election for governor against Republican Treen.

Mississippi .

Maps 1 and 2, which respectively show the majority black counties in Mississippi for 1970 and the counties in which Democratic presidential candidate Hubert Humphrey made his strongest showing in the three-way 1968 campaign, reflect the concentration of national Democratic strength that is located in the black belt. A similar pattern prevailed in the 1972 presidential election, a reflection of changed voting patterns in the black belts throughout the South. Before the removal of legal barriers in the mid-1960s that had thwarted blacks from political participation, the black belt counties had reflected the most conservative voting patterns.

MISSISSIPPI

MAP 1
The New Face of the Black Belt in Mississippi

Shaded area represents counties with majority black population in 1970.

MISSISSIPPI

MAP 2
The New Face of the Black Belt in Mississippi

Shaded area represents counties in which Humphrey received 30 percent or more of the vote in 1968 presidential election.

North Carolina

Map 1 demonstrates the sharpness of the factional cleavage in the Republican Party as of 1972. The overlaying of results from two different primaries in 1972 illustrates the mutual exclusiveness of Helms and Holshouser support. Holshouser's votes came from the traditionally Republican areas of the mountains and urbanized piedmont. Helms was disproportionately strong in the traditionally Democratic areas of the coastal plain and the eastern piedmont. The eastern Helms voters are generally not converted Democrats, since the closed primary system restricts participants to party registrants. In the Democratic areas, Republican registration is generally exercised only by the staunchest Republican stalwarts. The Helms-Holshouser division, while obviously possessed of regional tones (Holshouser was from the mountains, while his opponent, James Gardner, and Helms were easterners), also embodies an ideological division. Holshouser represents a more moderate mountain and urban Republicanism, while Helms expresses a conservative reactionism on social issues. A similar division was seen in the 1968 gubernatorial primary.

Map 2 illustrates the importance of race-oriented voting in North Carolina. Goldwater, Helms, Lake, and Wallace all represent appeals to racial conservatism from the explicit segregationism of Lake to the opposition to federally-forced integration of the other three.

The phenomenon demonstrated is not the result of party orientation, as two of the individuals are Republicans, one is a Democrat, and the other was running as an independent. In addition, two of the elections used are primaries.

Neither can this pattern result from economic ideologies. Goldwater and Helms are economic conservatives. Lake and Wallace project populist images.

Nor is ruralism the key. Raleigh and Durham are both shaded, and the rural counties of the west are not.

Race is the key. The fact is that the black population is concentrated in those areas which are the most darkly shaded, and the reaction of the white voter in those areas has been distinctly racist.

Map 3 shows the existence of significant partisan change in North Carolina. Although Robert Morgan received 62.1 percent of the vote in 1974 and did best in traditionally Democratic areas of the east, below this veneer of a return to normalcy, substantial partisan change was persisting.

Although his showing was only 3.8 percentage points less than that of Kerr Scott in 1954, Morgan's proportion was 15 percentage points or less than Scott's in 18 counties. Thirty-nine counties experienced Democratic losses of 10 points or more. These counties are almost all in the eastern part of the state, where Democratic strength was traditionally the greatest.

The similarity of Maps 2 and 3 is striking. Twenty-four of the 39 counties with significant falloff meet at least three of the criteria of Map 2. Of those meeting all four of the criteria of Map 2, only four counties did not experience Democratic losses of 10.0 points or more. Two of these (Northampton and Bertie) have populations which are majority black, which would serve to enhance the Democratic percentage in 1974. Another one (Harnett) is Morgan's home.

It appears, then, that opposition to integration has prompted substantial defection from the Democratic Party and that this defection (or some of it) is enduring. Substantial numbers of the defectors did not return to the Democratic Party even to vote for a candidate whose racial credentials were conservative, who was from the same region of the state, and who was running in a decidedly Democratic year.

NORTH CAROLINA

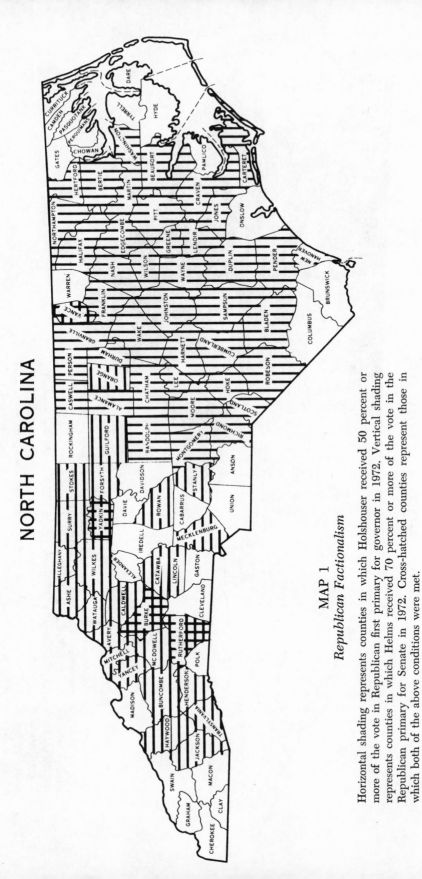

MAP 1
Republican Factionalism

Horizontal shading represents counties in which Holshouser received 50 percent or more of the vote in Republican first primary for governor in 1972. Vertical shading represents counties in which Helms received 70 percent or more of the vote in the Republican primary for Senate in 1972. Cross-hatched counties represent those in which both of the above conditions were met.

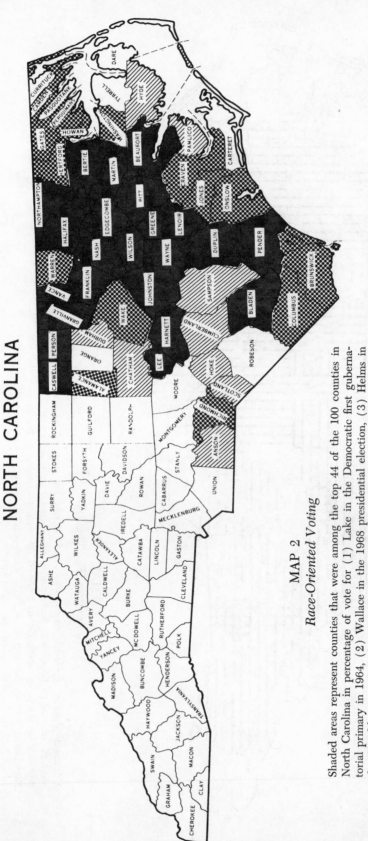

NORTH CAROLINA

MAP 2
Race-Oriented Voting

Shaded areas represent counties that were among the top 44 of the 100 counties in North Carolina in percentage of vote for (1) Lake in the Democratic first gubernatorial primary in 1964, (2) Wallace in the 1968 presidential election, (3) Helms in the Republican senatorial primary in 1972, and (4) in which Goldwater received a larger share of the 1964 presidential vote than did Nixon in 1960. Darkest-shaded areas represent 23 counties in which all four criteria were met. Medium-shaded areas represent 18 counties in which three of the criteria were met. Light-shaded areas represent nine counties in which two of the criteria were met.

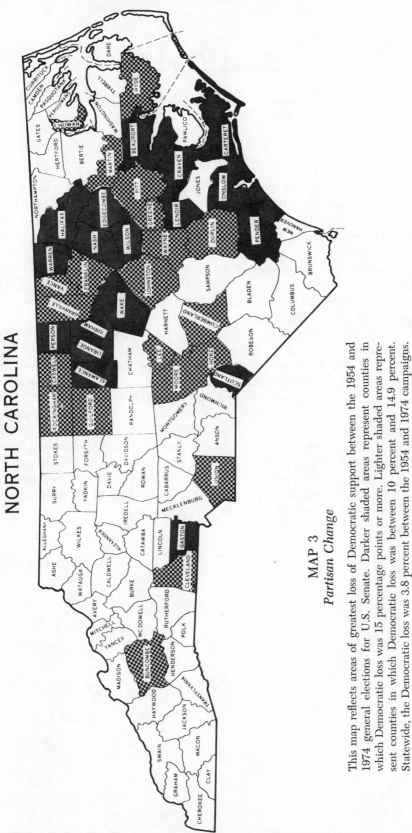

NORTH CAROLINA

MAP 3
Partisan Change

This map reflects areas of greatest loss of Democratic support between the 1954 and 1974 general elections for U.S. Senate. Darker shaded areas represent counties in which Democratic loss was 15 percentage points or more. Lighter shaded areas represent counties in which Democratic loss was between 10 percent and 14.9 percent. Statewide, the Democratic loss was 3.8 percent between the 1954 and 1974 campaigns.

South Carolina

Map 1 shows the distribution of counties casting 60 percent or more of their votes for either W. J. Bryan Dorn or Charles (Pug) Ravenel in the Democratic runoff primary in 1974. Dorn's vote is concentrated within his old congressional district and in a southern extension of that district in and around Barnwell County, the epitome of the traditional Democracy which Dorn represented. Ravenel's strength was urban and black belt based. Four of the six largest cities (Columbia, Charleston, Greenville, and Florence) are in counties which supported Ravenel with 70 percent or more of their vote.

The general election for governor in 1974 is analyzed in Map 2. Once again, Dorn's best showing was in his old district and in adjacent Barnwell County. Dorn's greatest fall-off from the normal Democratic vote was in those counties in which Ravenel had done his best. Of the eleven counties in which Dorn received 10 percentage points or less than the normal Democratic vote, five were counties that had given Ravenel 70 percent or more, and four were counties where Ravenel's percentage had been between 60 and 70. Many supporters of Ravenel apparently interpreted his refusal to endorse Dorn as a signal to vote Republican.

The Dorn fall-off in these areas seems to be a direct reaction to the Dorn-Ravenel contest as the base here is the normal Democratic vote, not the absolute percentage of the vote received.

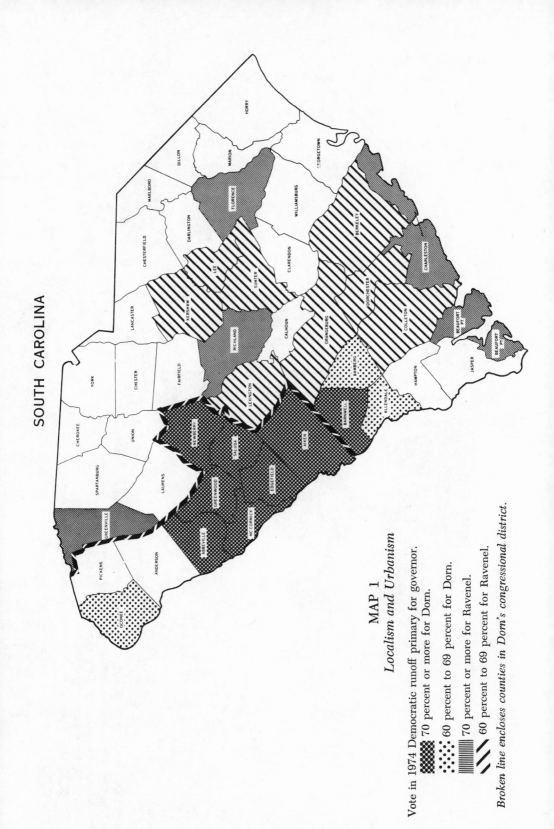

SOUTH CAROLINA

MAP 1
Localism and Urbanism

Vote in 1974 Democratic runoff primary for governor.

70 percent or more for Dorn.

60 percent to 69 percent for Dorn.

70 percent or more for Ravenel.

60 percent to 69 percent for Ravenel.

Broken line encloses counties in Dorn's congressional district.

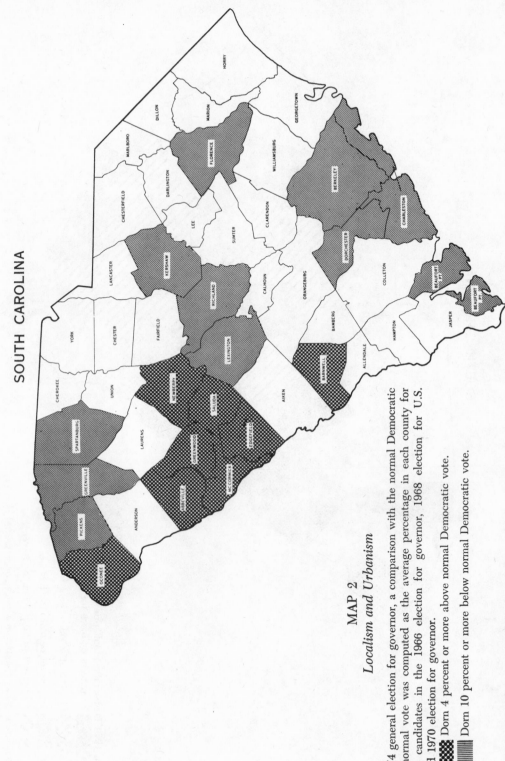

SOUTH CAROLINA

MAP 2

Localism and Urbanism

Vote in 1974 general election for governor, a comparison with the normal Democratic
vote. The normal vote was computed as the average percentage in each county for
Democratic candidates in the 1966 election for governor, 1968 election for U.S.
senator, and 1970 election for governor.

Dorn 4 percent or more above normal Democratic vote.

Dorn 10 percent or more below normal Democratic vote.

Tennessee

Maps 1 and 2 show the persistence of partisan loyalties more than a century after they were forged by the Civil War. Anti-secessionist sentiment in 1861 still correlates remarkably well with Republicanism, well over a century later. Of the 32 counties which opposed secession, 29 cast 40 percent or more of their ballots for a Republican governor in 1974, and 20 of them voted majority Republican. Fourteen other counties not opposing secession were comparatively Republican. Nine of these are on the fringes or within the confines of the eastern unionist core, and only 5 of the 14 voted majority Republican.

Although Maps 1 and 2 illustrate the persistence of partisan loyalties, Map 3 shows that severe strains, nevertheless, have occurred. In the 1970 senatorial election, faced by the choice between a liberal Democrat and a conservative Republican, west Tennessee voters chose the ideology of their fathers over the party of their fathers. Middle Tennessee Democrats remained loyal, and the break is severe. Republican Brock received as much as 40 percent of the vote in only 7 of the 42 counties he lost.

Map 4 demonstrates the death of machine control in the Democratic Party. No longer does a Mr. Crump hold the reins, clustering east and west Tennessee Democrats into a winning coalition. Localism is now the key. Only Blanton's support had any statewide character, undoubtedly due to his greater statewide exposure because of his 1972 Senate race. Butcher picked up five counties in the west, but his real strength was around his Knoxville home. Wiseman ran well around Tullahoma, his home. Crockett carried his home of Nashville, and vicinity. Haney's friends and neighbors around Chattanooga supported him. The folks in Waverly liked favorite son Powers.

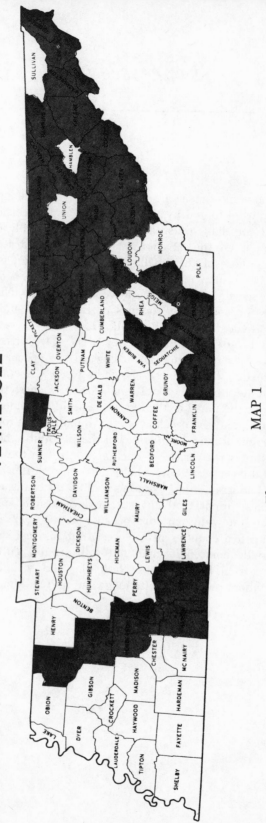

TENNESSEE

MAP 1
The Persistence of the Civil War

Shaded area represents counties in which a majority voted against secession in June, 1861.

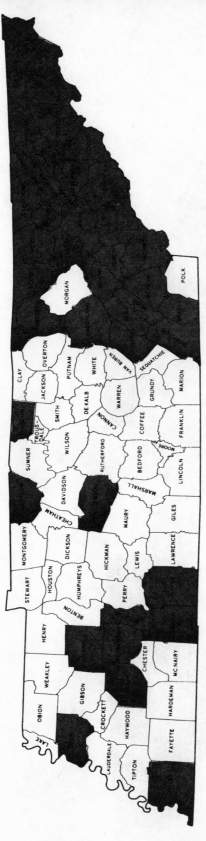

TENNESSEE

MAP 2
The Persistence of the Civil War

Shaded area represents counties in which the Republican candidate for governor in 1974 received 40 percent or more of the vote.

TENNESSEE

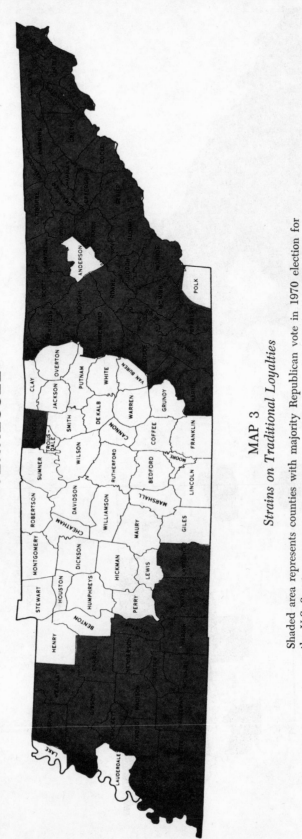

MAP 3

Strains on Traditional Loyalties

Shaded area represents counties with majority Republican vote in 1970 election for the U.S. Senate.

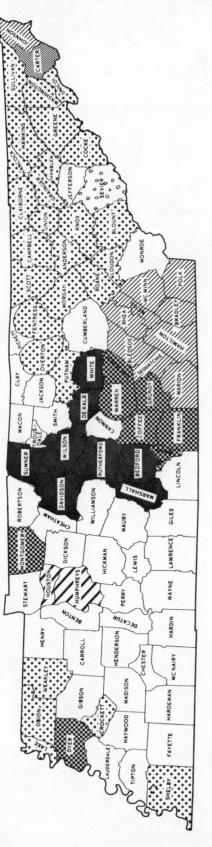

TENNESSEE

MAP 4
"Mr. Crump Is Dead"

Plurality counties for candidates in the 12-man field for governor in 1974 Democratic primary. Ray Blanton won the nomination with 22.7 percent of the vote. Tennessee law does not provide for a runoff. Percentages reflect each candidate's statewide total.

Blanton 22.7 percent

Butcher 20.2 percent

Wiseman 13.7 percent

Crockett 13.3 percent

Haney 12.9 percent

Butler 2.4 percent

Powers 2.1 percent

Pack 2.1 percent

(Four candidates who shared 10.7 percent of the statewide vote failed to win a plurality in any county.)

Texas

This map shows the distribution of the two minority population groups in Texas, Negroes and Mexican-Americans. It illustrates clearly that the heaviest concentrations of both groups are located in different parts of the state, a result of the plantation tradition of east Texas and the proximity of southwest Texas to the Mexican border.

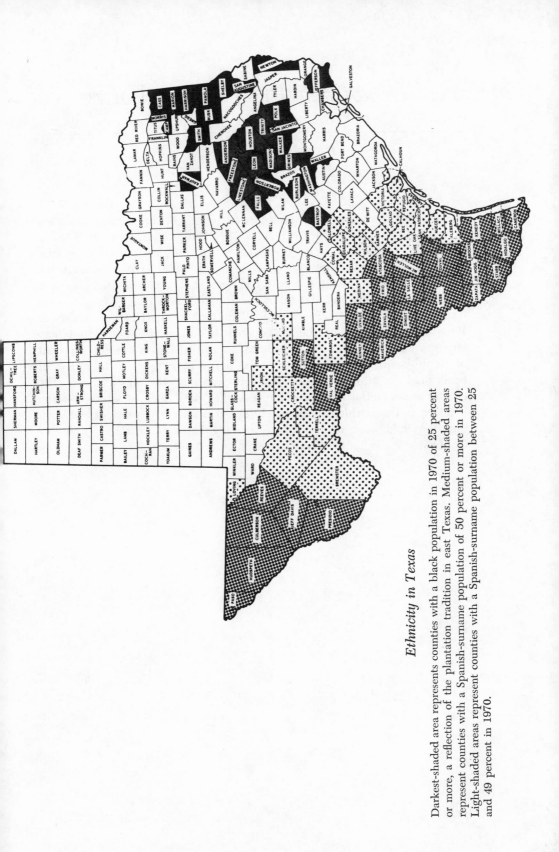

Ethnicity in Texas

Darkest-shaded area represents counties with a black population in 1970 of 25 percent or more, a reflection of the plantation tradition in east Texas. Medium-shaded areas represent counties with a Spanish-surname population of 50 percent or more in 1970. Light-shaded areas represent counties with a Spanish-surname population between 25 and 49 percent in 1970.

Republican Presidential Voting

These maps show areas of Republican strength in the presidential elections of 1944, 1964, and 1968. The 1944 map reflects the traditional pockets of Republican strength in the South, primarily in counties that were anti-secessionist before the Civil War. The 1964 map reflects the appeal of Barry Goldwater, who voted against the 1964 Civil Rights Act, in the Deep South and the falloff of Republican strength in the most traditional areas of GOP strength. The 1968 map shows a return of Republican strength to the areas of strongest traditional Republican strength and the spread from those areas. It also shows the development of Republican strongholds in Florida, a result in part of migration of traditional Republicans from the midwest and the northeast to the coastal areas of the Florida peninsula. The 1968 race, in which George Wallace ran as a third party candidate and attracted most of the support that had gone to Goldwater in 1964, indicates that the vote for Goldwater in the South was primarily a protest vote.

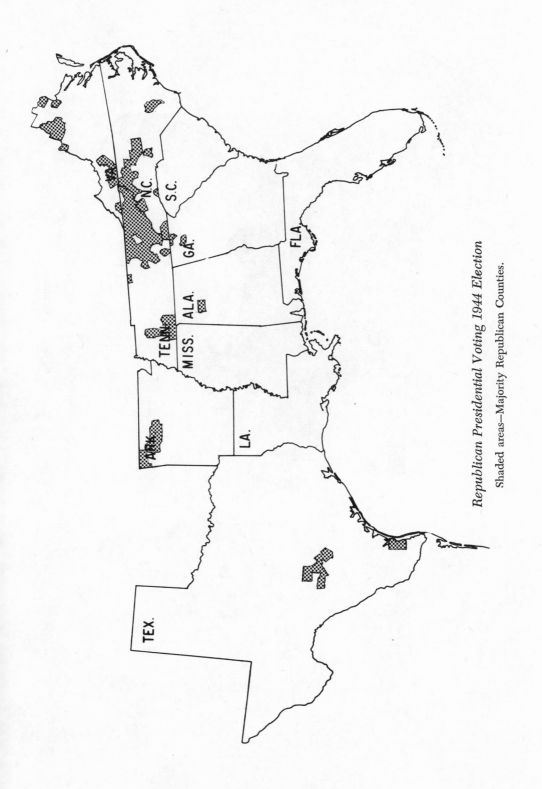

Republican Presidential Voting 1944 Election

Shaded areas—Majority Republican Counties.

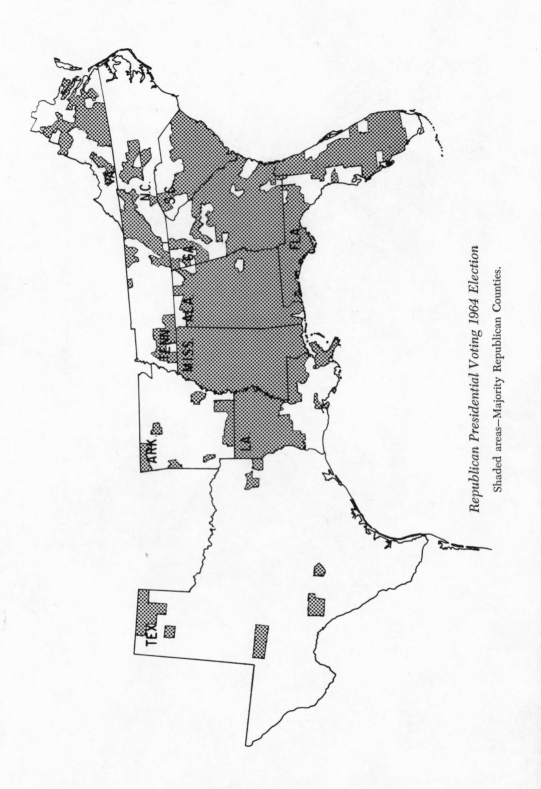

Republican Presidential Voting 1964 Election

Shaded areas—Majority Republican Counties.

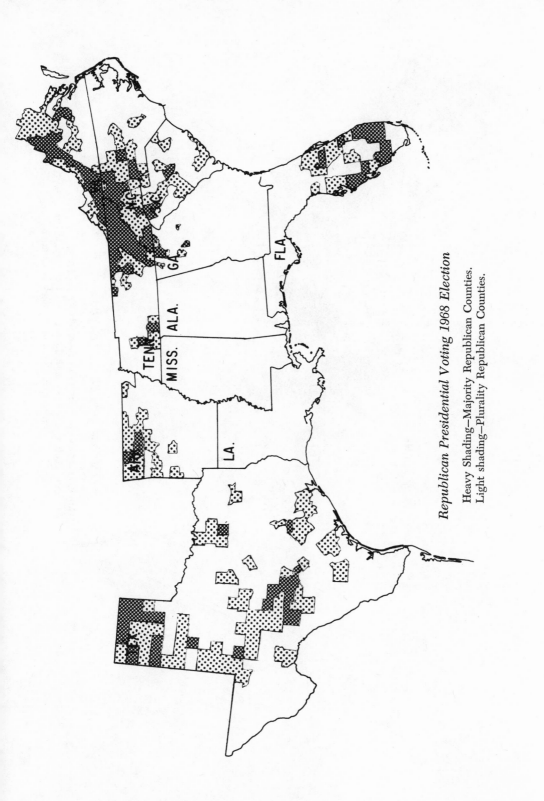

Republican Presidential Voting 1968 Election

Heavy Shading—Majority Republican Counties.
Light shading—Plurality Republican Counties.

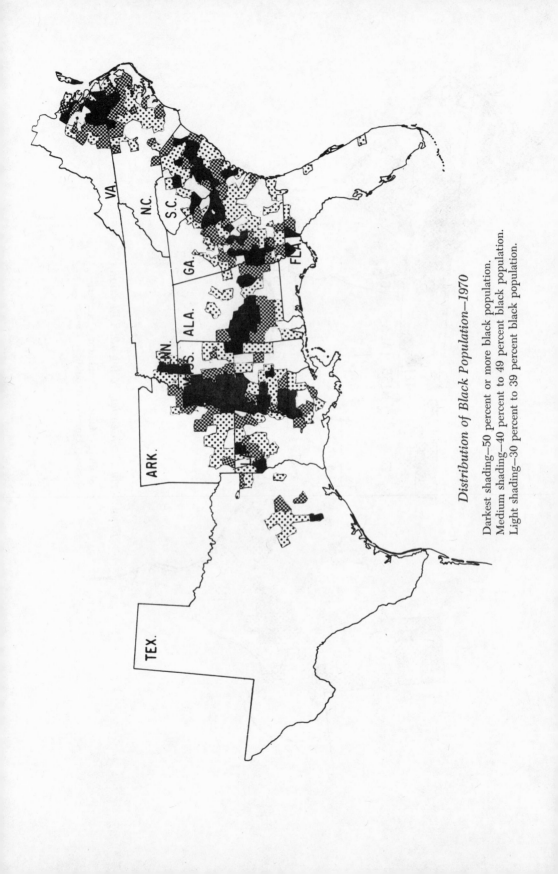

Distribution of Black Population—1970

Darkest shading—50 percent or more black population.
Medium shading—40 percent to 49 percent black population.
Light shading—30 percent to 39 percent black population.

APPENDIX B

Graphs: Voting Trends in States of the South

ALABAMA

ARKANSAS

FLORIDA

GEORGIA

LOUISIANA

MISSISSIPPI

NORTH CAROLINA

SOUTH CAROLINA

TENNESSEE

TEXAS

VIRGINIA

Four Facets of Alabama Politics

(1) National political parties are virtually irrelevant to Alabama. Strom Thurmond received Alabama's electoral votes in 1948 and his electors were listed on the ballot as Democrats. Walter Jones received one electoral vote in 1956 from an elector listed as a Democrat. Six of the eleven electors (also listed as Democrats) cast ballots for Harry Byrd in 1960. In 1964 the Democratic electors were unpledged. In 1968 the Alabama Democratic Party electors were pledged to George Wallace. Hubert Humphrey was the candidate of the Alabama Independent Democrats and of the National Democratic Party of Alabama (NDPA). The NDPA also was pledged to George McGovern in 1972, and, for a change, so were the regular Democratic electors. Republican presidential electors have done fewer contortions, but the Republican Party has failed to field a candidate in two gubernatorial elections since 1950, in 1962 and in 1970.

(2) Republican presidential candidates have carried the state twice, in 1964 and in 1972. But the new Republican vote is fickle, most of it going to Wallace in 1968. The best gubernatorial showing was James Martin's 31 percent against Lurleen Wallace in 1966. Martin had done much better in his senatorial race against Lister Hill in 1962, receiving 49 percent of the vote. Apart from these flurries, Republican success on the statewide level has been miniscule.

(3) The NDPA polled 125,000 votes in 1970 for governor. This 15 percent of the vote for a black candidate represented substantial change for Alabama, but basically represented a high level of anti-Wallace sentiment among blacks.

(4) The 1,050,000 votes cast for president in 1968 represented a 388 percent increase over the number twenty years before. Presidential ballots doubled between 1948 and 1952 and nearly doubled again from 1960 to 1968. The off-year gubernatorial elections drew less well, but the middle Wallace races (1966 and 1970) each drew about 850,000 voters, only 200,000 less than did the intervening presidential campaign. The 1974 turnout was only about 600,000, reflecting the lackluster nature of still another plebiscite on George Wallace.

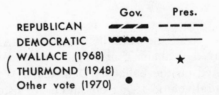

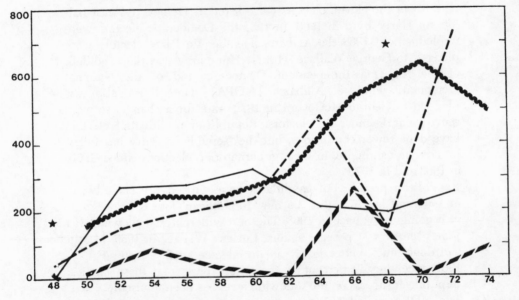

ALABAMA VOTES, 1948–1974
Votes in thousands

Democratic presidential vote shown is that for the candidates of the national Democratic Party, irrespective of the party label under which their electors appear on the ballot. An exception is 1964, a year in which there were no electors pledged to national Democratic Party candidates. The same situation occurred in 1948, when the Democratic electors were pledged to Thurmond.

Arkansas

Since 1952, Republican presidential candidates have run close, but did not carry the state until 1972. From 1952 until 1968 the Republican vote was constant, and it was constantly second best.

In gubernatorial elections until 1964, the Republican Party was less competitive, the best showing being 38 percent against Orval Faubus in his first campaign. Winthrop Rockefeller turned the party around. The Republican vote tripled between 1962 and 1964, when Rockefeller outpolled Goldwater by 11,000 votes, although losing. In 1966 Rockefeller gained 52,000 votes, while the Democrats lost 80,000, to walk away with 54 percent of the vote. In 1968 he had 52 percent. But by 1970 a new and appealing personality had appeared. Dale Bumpers added 83,000 votes to the Democratic tally, while Rockefeller lost 125,000, and Bumpers won with a landslide 62 percent. The Republican party was back where it had been before Rockefeller.

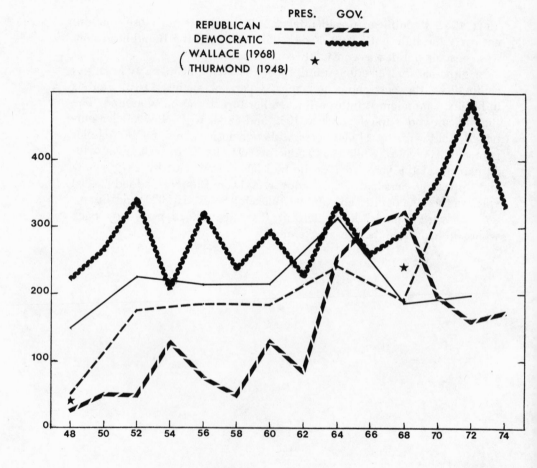

PRES. GOV.
REPUBLICAN
DEMOCRATIC
(WALLACE (1968)
(THURMOND (1948)   ★

ARKANSAS VOTES, 1948–1974
Votes in thousands

Two Facets of Florida Politics

(1) Florida appeared to be a state going Republican in the 1950s. Only once since 1948 has a Republican presidential candidate not carried the state. In 1964, Lyndon Johnson barely edged Barry Goldwater by 2.2 percentage points. In a three-way race, Richard Nixon carried the state with 40 percent in 1968 and a plurality of 210,000 over the second-place Hubert Humphrey. But other state-wide gains have been less impressive. One governorship, an impressive 55 percent for Claude Kirk in 1966, and one senatorial victory, that of Edward Gurney in 1968 with 56 percent, were sandwiched between solid Democratic victories. Reuben Askew's reelection victory in 1974 with 61 percent of the vote could only dim Republican hopes, although Richard Stone barely eked out a Democratic victory in the same year in a three-way Senate race.

(2) The 1966 gubernatorial election, the first of the off-year elections designed in part to divorce Republican state contenders from presidential coat-tails, resulted in the only Republican victory. Republican gains were 135,000 votes over 1964, while Democratic losses were 265,000. A decreased level of participation has followed the move to off-year elections. The 1974 turnout was 700,000 less than in 1972.

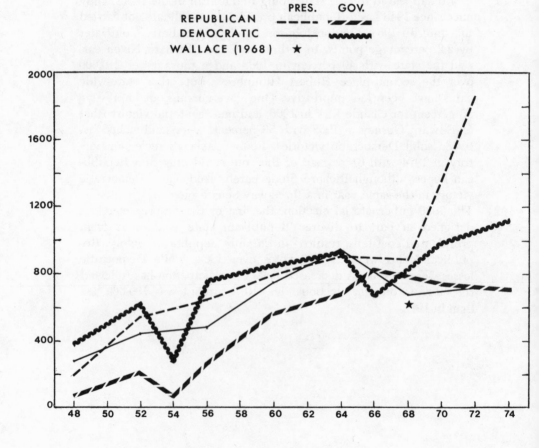

PRES. GOV.
REPUBLICAN
DEMOCRATIC
WALLACE (1968) ★

FLORIDA VOTES, 1948–1974
Votes in thousands

The 1954 election was held to fill a vacancy in the governor's office. In 1966, Florida shifted its gubernatorial elections from presidential to off-years.

Georgia

The Goldwater candidacy was the beginning of Republicanism in Georgia. Goldwater carried the state, relying on a presidential Republican base that had been slowly increasing but had not yet attained competitiveness. He received an increase of 125 percent in the Republican vote over 1960. This increase of 342,000 was attained while Democratic votes were increasing as well, by 64,000. The 1964 campaign brought in large numbers of Georgians, both black and white, who had not habitually voted previously.

Two years after Goldwater carried Georgia, the state had its first Republican gubernatorial candidate, Howard (Bo) Callaway, and he gained a plurality of the vote by 3,039 over Lester Maddox. The write-in candidacy of Ellis Arnall prevented Callaway from winning a majority, and the legislature elected Maddox. Republican gubernatorial votes have been declining since 1966.

Wallace carried the state in 1968, with a plurality of 43 percent. Thurmond, denied the Democratic place on the ballot in 1948, did his worst in a Deep South state with 20 percent in Georgia.

About 200,000 more voters cast ballots in presidential elections than in the off-year gubernatorial contests, not a massive difference considering the size of the presidential vote, about 1,200,000.

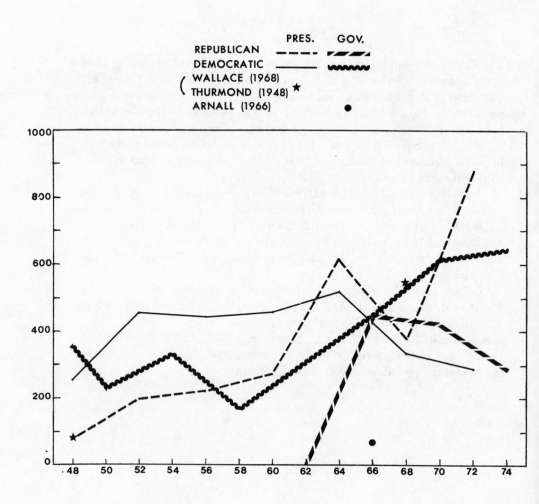

GEORGIA VOTES, 1948–1974

Votes in thousands

The 1948 gubernatorial election was called to fill a vacancy.

Louisiana

Louisiana epitomizes the nature of presidential Republicanism. Dwight Eisenhower carried the state in 1956. The Republicans fielded no gubernatorial candidate that year. Eisenhower had received 47 percent of the vote in 1952. That year the Republican gubernatorial candidate took 4 percent of the votes. Goldwater carried the state in 1964, and 38 percent voted for the party's man for governor. The state Republicans did better in 1972, David Treen receiving 480,000 votes for governor, more than the Democratic presidential candidate attracted (by 182,000); the first time that had ever happened. Still, Treen received only 43 percent. There was no Republican name on the gubernatorial ballot in 1968 nor in 1948 nor in the above-mentioned 1956.

On the other hand, Louisiana only went Republican in presidential elections three times out of the seven. Twice the Democrats carried the state. Adlai Stevenson barely won in 1952. In 1960, John Kennedy, aided by a heavy Catholic vote, received 407,000, far more than George McGovern's 298,000 in 1972. Still, Kennedy barely won a majority with 50.4 percent, but a slate of unpledged Independent electors received 170,000 votes that year. Democrats have done much better for governor. Edwin Edwards's 641,000 votes in 1972 was only 46,000 short of the Nixon total in that year. Gubernatorial balloting was in February, not November. Democratic candidates for governor have never been seriously endangered. Nor have the party's senatorial nominees, although Bennett Johnston received only 55 percent in 1972 in a three-way race in which former Democratic governor John McKeithen received 23 percent.

In the other two presidential elections, third parties won—Thurmond in 1948 with 49 percent and Wallace in 1968 with 48 percent. In 1956 an unpledged States's Rights slate drew 7 percent, and John Schmitz of the American Independent Party received 6 percent in 1972.

Louisiana's peculiar scheduling of gubernatorial elections in February of presidential years normally restricts the electorate, but when there is a credible Republican gubernatorial candidate the difference in turnout from presidential elections is minor. In 1964 gubernatorial turnout was an impressive 86 percent of presidential, and in 1972 the heated-up governor's race actually attracted 70,000 more ballots than the uninteresting presidential campaign. The increase in presidential voting has been substantial throughout the period, though not massive by southern standards. In the gubernatorial elections, however, the appearance of believable Republican contenders caused 1,365 percent more people to vote in 1972 than in 1948, compared to an increase of 126 percent in presidential ballots.

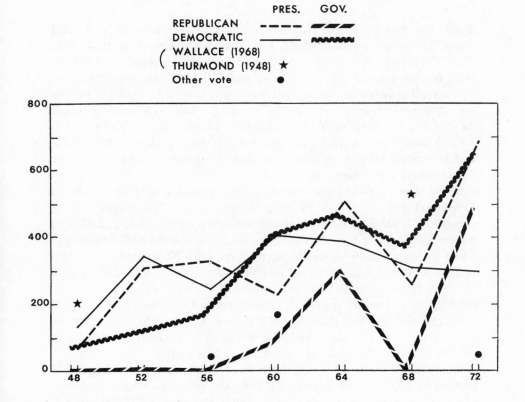

	PRES.	GOV.
REPUBLICAN	– – – –	/////
DEMOCRATIC	———	∿∿∿∿
WALLACE (1968)		
THURMOND (1948) ★		
Other vote ●		

LOUISIANA VOTES, 1948–1972

Votes in thousands

Gubernatorial elections are held in February of presidential years.

Mississippi

There are two kinds of Mississippi elections—uncontested .and land-slides. There was no Republican candidate for governor in 1947, 1951, 1955, 1959, and 1971. Thus as few as 40,707 citizens voted. In 1963 and 1967, the presence of a Republican on the ballot brought out eight times the normal number of voters and the Democrat won with 62 percent and 70 percent respectively. In 1971, though there was no Republican there was a black Independent candidate, Charles Evers. The threat of a black candidate aroused even greater fear than that of a Republican and Democrat William Waller won with 77 percent. Mississippi voters seem to move only when they have to.

A few more cases in point—this time from presidential elections. Strom Thurmond and native son Fielding Wright carried Mississippi with 87 percent in 1948. Thomas Dewey received only 5,043 votes, and that required two separate tickets of electors. Barry Goldwater took Mississippi, a first for Republicans since Reconstruction, with 87 percent of the vote in 1964. George Wallace in 1968 received 64 percent in a three-way race. In 1972 Nixon—with whom the Mississippi electorate had not been particularly impressed previously (he received 14 percent of the vote in 1968 and had finished third in 1960 behind a Byrd Democrat slate of electors and another slate for John Kennedy)—received 78 percent, a modest figure by the landslide standards of Mississippi.

Stevenson did carry the state both times, with sizable showings of 60 percent in 1952 and 58 percent in 1956, the latter year in a three-way race with an unpledged states' rights slate. Stevenson's 173,000 votes in 1952 is still the most ever received by a Democratic presidential candidate. On the other hand, Waller received 601,000 votes for the governorship in 1971.

There were 236 percent more ballots cast for president in 1972 than in 1948. But the gubernatorial race of 1971 outdid the 1972 presidential contest by 135,000 votes. One should never underestimate the racial insecurity of the white Mississippian. In 1971 Evers received only 13,000 votes less than were cast in the 1948 presidential contest.

Not until the 1975 race for governor, which is not included on this graph, did Mississippi have a close general election this century.

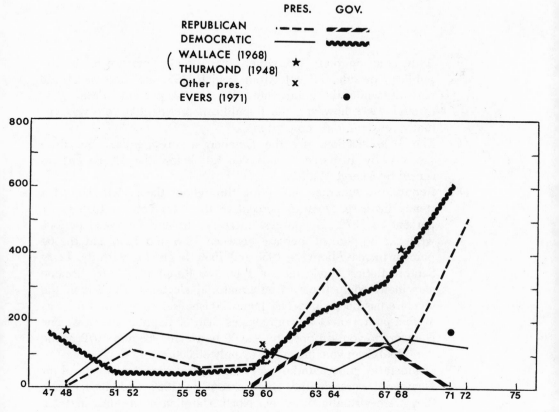

PRES.   GOV.

REPUBLICAN
DEMOCRATIC
(WALLACE (1968)
THURMOND (1948)   ★
Other pres.   ✕
EVERS (1971)   ●

MISSISSIPPI VOTES, 1947–1975
Votes in thousands

471

Four Facets of North Carolina Politics

(1) As in other Southern states there was a major increase in the Republican presidential vote from 1948 to 1952—an increase of 116 percent—while the total vote rose by 53 percent. From 1952 through 1968, however, the Republican presidential vote was virtually constant and competitive.

(2) The 1968 election saw the Democratic presidential vote drop severely—by 42 percent—and even fall below the 31 percent received by George Wallace.

(3) Republican gubernatorial voting throughout the period showed a steady increase, from 26 percent of the total vote in 1948 to 51 percent in 1972. The largest increases in any four-year periods were the 86 percent increase between 1948 and 1952 and the 64 percent increase between 1956 and 1960. Beginning with the Terry Sanford-Robert Gavin race of 1960, the Republican Party became marginally competitive in gubernatorial elections. Since then the increase has been slow. The James Holshouser victory of 1972 was more a matter of Democratic losses than of Republican gains. The Democratic vote dropped by 92,000 between 1968 and 1972, while the Republican vote increased by only 30,000.

(4) Democratic gubernatorial votes have run consistently ahead of Democratic presidential votes except in 1960 and 1964, when they were virtually the same. North Carolina is the only state in the South with four-year terms for governor, in which the gubernatorial election is held in presidential election years.

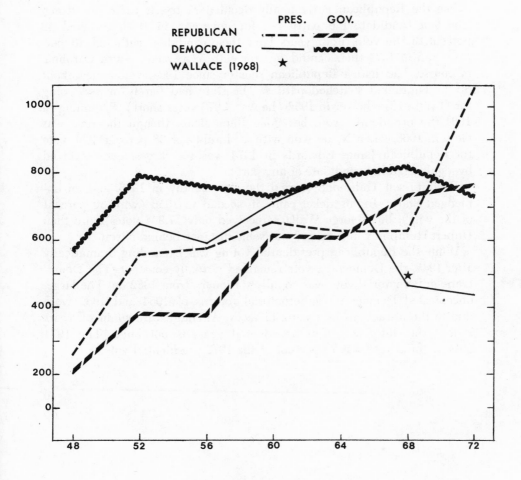

	PRES.	GOV.
REPUBLICAN	‑‑‑‑‑	/////
DEMOCRATIC	———	∿∿∿∿
WALLACE (1968)	★	

NORTH CAROLINA VOTES, 1948–1972
Votes in thousands

South Carolina

When the Republican Party finally decided to try, it came on strong. The first candidate the party ran for governor, in 1966, received 42 percent of the vote. Four years later their candidate gathered 46 percent, and in 1974 their candidate won with 52 percent. South Carolina, of course, had had a Republican senator since 1964, when incumbent Strom Thurmond switched parties. The state had barely missed going for Dwight Eisenhower in 1952 (he was 4,973 votes short). Beginning in 1964 the presidential vote has gone Republican, though the race was close in 1968, when Nixon won with a plurality of 38 percent. The vote for Republican James Edwards in 1974 was the largest ever received by a gubernatorial candidate of any party.

Favorite son Thurmond carried the state solidly in 1948, and an unpledged States' Rights ticket came in second in 1956 (with 30 percent of the vote), but George Wallace received only 17,944 votes more than Hubert Humphrey in 1968 and was some distance behind Nixon.

While the Republican presidential voting was expanding dramatically after 1948, the Democratic vote remained virtually constant. The Democratic gubernatorial vote was equally stationary from 1962 on. The large, uncontested Democratic gubernatorial returns of 1954 and 1962 were due to the attractions of senatorial races. Although turnout in off-years is less, the difference from presidential years is not huge. The 1974 gubernatorial vote was 75 percent of the 1972 presidential vote.

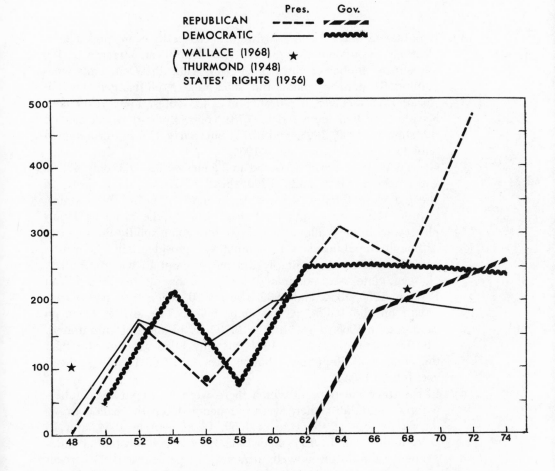

SOUTH CAROLINA VOTES, 1948–1974
Votes in thousands

Five Facets of Tennessee Politics

(1) Republicans have been consistently competitive in presidential elections throughout this period. The Republican increase of 120 percent in number of votes since 1948, while the Democrats were gaining 64 percent, made the 1952 race a cliffhanger. Dwight Eisenhower received a plurality of 2,437 votes. Four years later his plurality had increased to 5,781 votes. Richard Nixon carried the state in 1960, 1968, and 1972, but Barry Goldwater retained only 44 percent of the vote in 1964.

(2) George Wallace finished second in Tennessee in 1968, only 47,800 votes behind Nixon and 73,600 ahead of Hubert Humphrey, in effect a close three-way race. As in most other southern states, George McGovern's vote total was virtually the same as Humphrey's, with the Wallace vote apparently going solidly Republican.

(3) Although Republicans were competitive presidentially, in gubernatorial elections they simply did not attempt to win until 1970. No candidate was nominated for governor by the Republican Party in 1950, 1954, and 1966. Until 1970, when they had a candidate on the ballot, it was only token. The switch from no candidate in 1966 to a winner in 1970 was an amazing turnaround. The Democratic victory in 1974 was only 1,056 votes greater than the number of Republican ballots cast in 1970. The Republican vote fell by 120,000.

(4) In the three elections in which there were no Republican gubernatorial candidates, there were independents on the ballot, drawing 22 percent of the vote in 1950, 13 percent in 1954, and 19 percent in 1966. In 1958 and 1962 there were substantial independent candidacies as well, attracting 34 percent and 23 percent of the voters respectively and far outpolling the token Republican candidates. The popularity of these independents reflected a desire for an alternative to the Democrats, which Winfield Dunn finally capitalized on in 1970.

(5) The off-year gubernatorial elections, which began in 1954, attracted no more than 40 percent of the turnout of presidential elections, until 1970. With voter interest aroused by a vigorous senatorial race, the 1970 turnout for governor was only 93,000

short of the 1972 presidential vote. Without the pull of a close Senate race the 1974 gubernatorial election was still only 160,000 votes shy of the 1972 turnout. The fielding of credible Republicans has apparently pulled many previously gubernatorial non-voters into the voting booths.

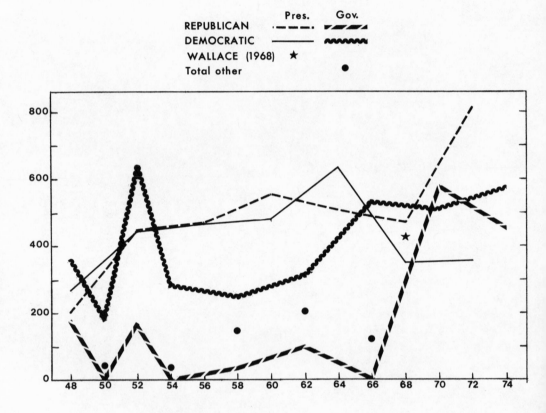

	Pres.	Gov.
REPUBLICAN	‑‑‑‑	▨▨▨
DEMOCRATIC	———	〰〰〰
WALLACE (1968)	★	
Total other		●

TENNESSEE VOTES, 1948–1974

Votes in thousands

Texas

Though the Democratic gubernatorial trend line shown would make a snake envious, a more intelligible pattern emerges if presidential on-year and off-year elections are considered separately. The off-year Democratic vote shows an amazingly consistent increase from 1950 to 1970, an increase of 237 percent, whereas the on-year Democratic trend is much less regular. The positions are reversed, however, when total votes cast are considered instead. Except for an unusually large turnout in 1952, the on-year increase is very regular while the off-year varies irregularly. The total gubernatorial vote doubled between 1958 and 1962 as the Republican Party mounted its first significant gubernatorial challenge. In 1974, the contest for governor a foregone conclusion, the vote fell off sharply.

Republican inroads were first made in 1952 when Dwight Eisenhower received 53 percent of the vote and 263 percent more ballots than had Thomas Dewey in 1948. From 1952 until 1968, the Republican presidential vote was virtually constant, winning by a substantial margin in 1956 as the Democratic vote dropped, and barely losing in 1960 and 1968 (by pluralities of 46,000 and 39,000, respectively). In 1960 a Republican gubernatorial candidate first drew more than 300,000 votes, although he was soundly defeated. The same year John Tower received 41 percent in a senatorial bid against Lyndon Johnson. In a special election the next year Tower squeaked through to win that seat, and the Republican Party suddenly became legitimate at the state level. The Republican gubernatorial candidate received 46 percent in 1962, but did not do as well again until 1970. In a three-way race in 1972, Dolph Briscoe retained Democratic control of the governor's chair by a close 100,000 votes (and only 48 percent of the total vote). The Republican candidate for governor received only 32 percent of the vote in 1974, when gubernatorial elections were changed to four-year terms in nonpresidential election years.

Neither George Wallace in 1968 nor Strom Thurmond in 1948 did particularly well in Texas, receiving 19 percent and 10 percent of the vote respectively. Wallace received fewer votes than did the Republican gubernatorial candidate in 1960. Showman Lee (Pappy) O'Daniel, a figure out of the Texas past, pulled 122,103 votes in a write-in campaign for governor in 1956, 228 more than Thurmond did eight years earlier.

La Raza Unida candidate Ramsey Muniz mounted third party gubernatorial bids in 1972 and 1974, collecting 242,000 and 89,000 votes respectively, and never more than 7.1 percent of the vote. Although his candidacy made the 1972 race a close one, the La Raza Unida's impact has been negligible in state politics.

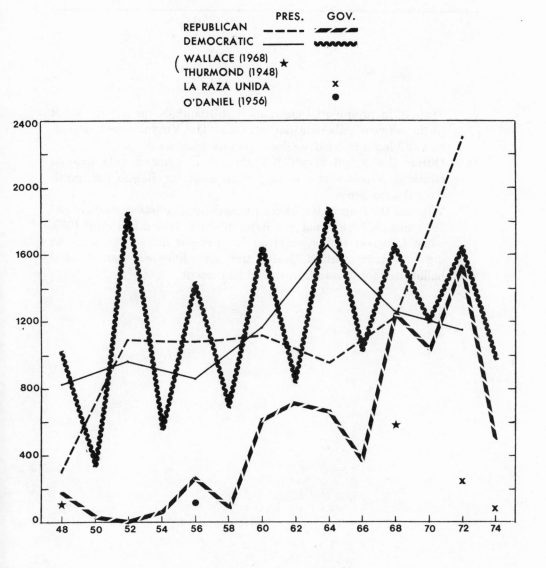

	PRES.	GOV.
REPUBLICAN	- - - -	/////
DEMOCRATIC	———	~~~~~
(WALLACE (1968)	★	
(THURMOND (1948)	★	
LA RAZA UNIDA	x	
O'DANIEL (1956)	●	

TEXAS VOTES, 1948–1974
Votes in thousands

Three Facets of Virginia Politics

(1) Turnout in presidential elections is substantially greater than that in the off-year gubernatorial elections. The Virginia electoral system still has a restrictive effect upon the electorate.

(2) During the period in which Democrats dominated gubernatorial elections, Virginia was voting consistently for Republican presidential candidates.

(3) Whereas the leap in Republican presidential ballots came between 1948 and 1952, gubernatorial Republicanism languished until 1969, when Linwood Holton received 127 percent more votes than he did four years earlier. During the same four-year period, total ballots cast for governor increased 63 percent.

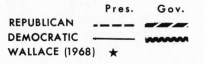

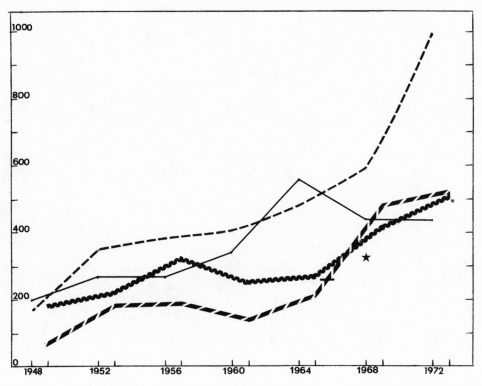

VIRGINIA VOTES, 1948–1973
Votes in thousands

Howell vote for governor is plotted as Democratic although he was on the ballot as an independent. There was no Democratic candidate.

APPENDIX C

*Survey of Attitudes Among White
Southerners, Black Southerners,
and Nonsoutherners*

The data in the following tables are taken from a national in-depth survey of 4,004 Americans who were 18 years of age or older in November and December of 1974. The study was conducted by De Vries and Associates for a private client who agreed to release the data for publication in this book.

The "South" in this study consisted of the 11 states of the old Confederacy. The sample for the "South" consisted of 961 respondents, 25 percent of whom were black. In accordance with standard survey techniques, interviews were proportioned to each state within the South. The primary sampling unit within each state was the county.

Urbanized areas were sampled by a systematic process using a sampling traction, which, with a random starting point, would determine a sampling block at a specific interval. In rural areas for which population data were not available, small townships were randomly chosen. At each sample point, interviews were grouped in clusters of five interviews.

Narrative reference to these tables is made in Chapter 1.

RELIGION AND CHURCH ATTENDANCE

Southerners were more than three times as likely as nonsoutherners to be Baptist, and nonsoutherners almost three times as likely to be Catholic as residents of the South. Within the region, blacks were more than twice as likely as whites to be Baptists.

TABLE C-1

RELIGION	SOUTH	NON-SOUTH	TOTAL	SOUTH WHITE	SOUTH BLACK
Catholic	11.4%	29.2%	25.0%	12.4%	1.8%
Baptist	44.7	12.9	20.5	34.3	78.0
Methodist	13.2	10.9	11.4	14.4	10.8
Lutheran	2.4	7.8	6.5	3.1	0.6
Episcopalian	1.9	2.5	2.3	2.6	—
Other Protestant	14.4	19.4	18.2	17.9	5.1
Jewish	1.3	3.6	3.0	1.8	—
Other	5.7	6.2	6.1	7.1	2.3
No religion	4.0	6.8	6.1	4.8	1.3
Refused	1.0	0.7	0.9	1.6	0.1

The respondents in the 1974 national study were asked how often they attended church.

TABLE C-2

CHURCH ATTENDANCE	SOUTH	NON-SOUTH	TOTAL	SOUTH WHITE	SOUTH BLACK
Weekly (or almost weekly)	49.6%	38.6%	41.2%	46.7%	58.1%
At least once/month	22.2	16.9	18.2	20.0	27.8
At least once/year	18.8	23.3	22.2	22.1	9.7
Never	7.4	18.6	16.0	8.8	3.4
Not sure	2.0	2.6	2.4	2.4	1.0

PUBLIC ISSUES

TABLE C-3

Gun Control: *"Guns should be treated like cars. The guns should be registered and the user should be required to pass a test in order to get a license to use the gun."*

	SOUTH	NON-SOUTH	TOTAL	SOUTH WHITE	SOUTH BLACK
Strongly agree	59.7%	65.5%	64.1%	57.5%	65.1%
Mildly agree	17.9	14.9	15.7	17.7	18.5
TOTAL AGREE	77.6	80.4	79.8	75.2	83.6
Mildly disagree	8.6	5.9	6.6	9.0	6.9
Strongly disagree	12.0	11.3	11.5	13.7	8.8
TOTAL DISAGREE	20.6	17.2	18.1	22.7	15.7
Not sure	1.8	2.4	2.1	2.1	0.7

TABLE C-4

Question: *"In general, which level of government—federal, state or local—does the best job of handling its own responsibilities?"*

LEVEL OF GOVERNMENT	SOUTH	NON-SOUTH	TOTAL	SOUTH WHITE	SOUTH BLACK
Federal	18.2%	13.6%	14.7%	10.9%	39.1%
State	30.2	27.0	27.8	32.4	24.6
Local	32.6	37.9	36.7	38.5	16.4
None/not sure	19.0	21.5	20.8	18.2	19.9

TABLE C-5

To examine levels of confidence in major American governmental, religious, social, and occupational groups and institutions, respondents were given a list and asked to tell whether they had a great deal of confidence in that item.

	SOUTH	NON-SOUTH	TOTAL	SOUTH WHITE	SOUTH BLACK
Governmental Institutions					
Supreme Court	44.2%	43.4%	43.6%	42.6%	49.1%
Military	54.5	39.3	42.9	54.7	54.1
Presidency	34.6	31.6	32.3	38.5	23.5
Congress	30.0	28.5	28.8	28.2	33.9
State legislatures	27.8	24.9	25.6	28.2	26.0
Religious Institutions					
Baptist Church	50.2%	28.0%	33.3%	47.4%	61.2%
Methodist Church	37.4	26.8	29.4	39.6	31.9
Catholic Church	24.5	27.9	27.1	23.2	25.5
Social and Economic Institutions					
Public elementary and high schools	44.0%	41.7%	42.2%	39.7%	53.7%
Parochial elementary and high schools	32.9	33.4	33.3	33.1	32.9
National Association for the Advancement of Colored People (NAACP)	27.3	19.1	21.1	13.7	67.1
AFL–CIO	19.8	15.4	16.4	15.1	34.5
National Organization for Women (NOW)	18.5	13.6	14.8	15.1	27.6
Major oil companies	11.7	6.2	7.5	11.3	11.9

TABLE C-6
Disaffection Index °

	SOUTH	NON-SOUTH	TOTAL	SOUTH WHITE	SOUTH BLACK
"Special interests get more from the government than the people do."	76.4	74.6	75.0	75.6	79.6
"The tax laws are written to help the rich, not the average man."	73.2	77.4	76.5	72.4	75.4
"Most elective officials are in politics for all they personally can get out of it for themselves."	66.1	62.1	63.1	64.9	69.8
"What you think doesn't count much anymore."	63.4	63.7	63.7	63.6	64.5
"The people running the country don't tell us the truth."	77.6	78.8	78.5	77.5	78.3
Average disaffection score	71.3	71.3	71.4	68.2	73.5

° Disaffection index is a composite score based on a scoring system that measures the degree of disaffection. Answers to questions that measure disaffection were scored as follows:
   Strongly agree—100 points
   Mildly agree—75 points
   Not sure—50 points
   Mildly disagree—25 points
   Strongly disagree—0 points
The percentage of total respondents in each category was multiplied by the appropriate scores, and the sum of these scores expressed the disaffection index for each group of respondents. A score of 50 would reflect a neutral attitude of disaffection.

The disaffection index provides a more refined method of measuring disaffection than would be achieved simply by combining the "strongly agree" and "mildly agree" levels of agreement. The disaffection index reveals that the identical level of alienation between the South and non-South masks significant differences in the level of disaffection between white southerners (68.2) and black southerners (73.5).

RELIABILITY OF INFORMATION SOURCES

The respondents were asked to study a list of information sources that might influence the way they made up their minds about important issues, and then to evaluate the reliability of each source.*

TABLE C-7

(MEAN SCORES) INFORMATION SOURCES	SOUTH	NON-SOUTH	TOTAL	SOUTH WHITE	SOUTH BLACK
Spouse	8.04	8.37	8.29	8.08	7.86
Doctors	7.86	7.58	7.65	7.64	8.39
Church	7.93	7.51	7.61	7.67	8.63
Priests/ministers	7.51	7.04	7.15	7.28	8.08
Television news	7.19	7.06	7.09	6.77	8.28
Radio news	7.12	6.94	6.98	6.75	8.14
Teachers	7.03	6.92	6.95	6.88	7.37
Books	6.53	6.81	6.74	6.33	6.93
Friends/neighbors	6.77	6.62	6.65	6.69	6.84
Newspaper articles	6.71	6.54	6.58	6.38	7.58
Newspaper editorials	6.44	6.35	6.37	6.14	7.14
Magazine articles	6.22	6.21	6.21	5.98	6.86
Work associates	6.21	5.97	6.03	6.15	6.35
Political party	6.00	5.80	5.84	5.60	6.93
Television talk shows	5.70	5.74	5.73	5.25	6.90
Radio talk shows	5.59	5.72	5.69	5.16	6.69
Civil rights movement	5.31	5.35	5.34	4.23	8.21
Labor unions	5.14	5.19	5.18	4.58	6.74
Government officials	5.48	5.08	5.18	5.12	6.44
Newspaper advertisements	5.25	4.94	5.02	4.83	6.37
Political candidates	5.07	4.86	4.91	4.60	6.29
Women's movement	5.10	4.79	4.86	4.63	6.44
Television advertisements	4.87	4.29	4.43	4.31	6.41

* Question: "Please look at this card while I read a list of information sources that may or may not influence the way you make up your mind about important issues. Using this scale that runs from 1 to 10, I'd like you to tell me how reliable you feel these information sources are. A score of 9 or 10 means that you feel the information source is very reliable; a score of 1 or 2 means that you feel the information source is not very reliable. Scores in between mean the information source falls somewhere between reliable and not reliable at all."

NOTE: Subsample mean scores varying by 0.5 or more from the total sample mean scores are considered statistically significant differences.

TABLE C-8

INFORMATION SOURCES	SOUTH	NON-SOUTH	TOTAL	SOUTH WHITE	SOUTH BLACK
(1st mention)					
Television news	19.4%	17.0%	17.5%	17.3%	24.7%
(1st and 2nd mentions combined)					
Television news	19.0%	18.2%	18.4%	17.4%	21.9%
Newspaper articles	13.3	16.4	15.7	14.7	8.0
Radio news	5.4	6.3	6.1	4.2	8.1
Political candidates	5.5	4.9	5.0	5.6	6.0
Newspaper editorials	4.0	5.3	5.0	5.0	1.5
Political party	3.1	3.8	3.6	2.9	4.0
Not sure	30.4	23.3	25.0	31.3	28.9

Note: All other information sources were mentioned by less than 4 percent of the respondents.

Inside and outside the South, television news was mentioned most frequently as the most influential source of information on politics. Newspaper articles were mentioned almost as frequently as television news by southern whites (14.7%) and respondents outside the South (16.4%), but far less frequently by southern blacks (8.0%). Differences in perceptions between southern whites and nonsoutherners were insignificant.

The respondents studied the same list of information sources and were asked: "Which of these sources do you think supplies you with the most reliable information about politics? Which is second?"

TABLE C-9

INFORMATION SOURCES	SOUTH	NON-SOUTH	TOTAL	SOUTH WHITE	SOUTH BLACK
(1st mention)					
Television news	41.5%	34.7%	36.4%	37.6%	53.2%
(1st and 2nd mentions combined)					
Television news	29.7%	26.5%	27.3%	28.8%	31.8%
Newspaper articles	15.4	19.3	18.4	16.8	11.8
Radio news	10.9	9.3	9.7	10.0	13.7
Newspaper editorials	6.7	8.2	7.9	7.9	3.3
Magazine articles	4.4	6.0	5.6	5.3	2.2
Television talk shows	3.4	4.9	4.6	3.3	3.8
Not sure	1.5	1.5	1.5	1.4	2.0

Note: All other information sources were mentioned by less than 4 percent of the respondents. "Church" was mentioned by 4.5 percent of the southern black sample.

As a first-mentioned information source, television news was significantly more important to southern black respondents than to white southerners and to nonsoutherners. Newspaper articles and editorials were mentioned more often by southern whites than blacks.

PARTY SELF-IDENTIFICATION

The respondents were asked: "When you think about political parties, do you generally consider yourself to be a Democrat or a Republican?

TABLE C-10

POLITICAL PARTY SELF-IDENTIFICATION	SOUTH	NON-SOUTH	TOTAL	SOUTH WHITE	SOUTH BLACK
Democrat	56.5%	48.3%	50.3%	47.3%	82.6%
Republican	16.2	23.0	21.4	20.5	5.8
Independent (volunteered)	19.2	21.4	20.9	24.1	6.2
Other (volunteered)	2.0	2.6	2.5	2.8	—
Not sure	6.1	4.7	4.9	5.3	5.4

Although Democratic identification was far higher among southern blacks (82.6%) than among either southern whites (47.3%) or non-southerners (48.3%), there was little difference between the two latter groups, with the non-South slightly more Republican in identification and the white South slightly more "independent."

APPENDIX D

*Selected Demographic Characteristics
of Southern States*

The data in the following tables were provided by the Bureau of the Census, U.S. Department of Commerce. The "South" in these tables consisted of the 11 states of the old Confederacy.

The Bureau of the Census made special computations and computer runs in order to obtain some of the data, which in most cases cover the 20-year period from 1950 to 1970. Narrative reference to these tables is made in Chapter 1 and in individual state chapters.

TABLE D-1

Population 25 Years Old and Over
Who Completed Four Years in High School,
1950–1970

1950		1970	
Non-South	35.7%	Non-South	54.8%
Florida	34.8	Florida	52.6
United States	33.3	United States	52.3
Texas	29.9	Texas	47.4
Virginia	28.2		
		South	44.4
South	24.9	Virginia	44.2
Tennessee	24.3	Louisiana	42.2
Louisiana	21.6	Tennessee	41.8
Mississippi	21.5	Alabama	41.3
Arkansas	21.2	Mississippi	41.0
Alabama	21.1	Georgia	40.6
North Carolina	20.5	Arkansas	39.9
Georgia	20.4	North Carolina	38.5
South Carolina	18.6	South Carolina	37.8

497

TABLE D-2
Total Population, 1950–1970 and 1970–1974

	UNITED STATES	NON-SOUTH	SOUTH (11-STATE)	ALABAMA	ARKANSAS
1950	151,325,798	114,775,683	36,550,115	3,061,743	1,909,511
1970	203,211,926	153,165,744	50,046,182	3,444,165	1,923,295
1974	211,390,000	157,457,000	53,933,000	3,577,000	2,062,000
% Increase, 1950–1970	34.2	33.4	36.9	12.5	0.7
% Increase, 1970–1974	4.0	2.8	7.7	3.9	7.2

	FLORIDA	GEORGIA	LOUISIANA	MISSISSIPPI	NORTH CAROLINA
1950	2,771,305	3,444,578	2,683,516	2,178,914	4,061,929
1970	6,789,443	4,589,575	3,641,306	2,216,912	5,082,059
1974	8,090,000	4,882,000	3,764,000	2,324,000	5,363,000
% Increase, 1950–1970	245.0	33.2	36.0	1.7	25.1
% Increase, 1970–1974	19.2	6.4	3.4	4.8	5.5

	SOUTH CAROLINA	TENNESSEE	TEXAS	VIRGINIA	
1950	2,117,027	3,291,718	7,711,194	3,318,680	
1970	2,590,516	3,923,687	11,196,730	4,648,494	
1974	2,784,000	4,129,000	12,050,000	4,908,000	
% Increase, 1950–1970	22.4	19.2	45.2	40.1	
% Increase, 1970–1974	7.5	5.2	7.6	5.3	

TABLE D-3
Number of Persons Living in Metropolitan Areas, 1950–1970
(and percentage of total population)

	UNITED STATES	NON-SOUTH	SOUTH (11-STATE)
1950	84,853,700 56.1%	72,241,963 62.9%	12,611,737 34.5%
1970	139,418,811 68.6	111,783,914 73.0	27,634,897 55.2
Numerical Increase	54,565,111	39,541,951	15,023,160
% Increase	12.5	10.1	20.7

	ALABAMA	ARKANSAS	FLORIDA
1950	1,063,254 34.7%	196,685 10.3%	1,323,206 47.7%
1970	1,801,095 52.3	595,030 30.9	4,656,993 68.6
Numerical Increase	737,841	398,345	3,333,787
% Increase	17.6	20.6	20.9

	GEORGIA	LOUISIANA	MISSISSIPPI
1950	1,235,572 35.9%	1,020,188 38.0%	142,164 6.5%
1970	2,280,230 49.7	1,996,197 54.8	393,488 17.7
Numerical Increase	1,044,658	976,009	251,324
% Increase	13.8	16.8	11.2

	NORTH CAROLINA	SOUTH CAROLINA	TENNESSEE
1950	896,736 22.1%	528,710 25.0%	1,349,511 41.0%
1970	1,896,423 37.3	1,017,254 39.3	1,917,695 48.9
Numerical Increase	999,687	488,544	568,184
% Increase	15.2	14.3	7.9

	TEXAS	VIRGINIA	
1950	3,644,726 47.3%	1,210,985 36.5%	
1970	8,234,458 73.5	2,846,034 61.2	
Numerical Increase	4,589,732	1,635,049	
% Increase	26.2	24.7	

TABLE D-4
Nonurban Population: Percentage of Total Population, 1950–1970

	UNITED STATES	NON-SOUTH	SOUTH (11-STATE)
1950	54,478,981 36.0%	35,349,388 30.8%	19,129,593 52.3%
1970	53,886,996 26.5	36,121,080 23.6	17,765,916 35.5
Numerical Change	−591,985	771,692	−1,363,677
Amount of Decline in % of Population	9.5	7.2	16.8

	ALABAMA	ARKANSAS	FLORIDA
1950	1,720,806 56.2%	1,278,920 70.0%	957,415 34.5%
1970	1,432,224 41.5	962,430 50.0	1,321,306 19.4
Numerical Change	−288,582	−316,490	363,891
Amount of Decline in % of Population	14.7	20.0	15.1

	GEORGIA	LOUISIANA	MISSISSIPPI
1950	1,885,131 54.7%	1,211,820 45.2%	1,571,752 72.1%
1970	1,821,501 39.6	1,235,156 33.9	1,230,270 55.4
Numerical Change	−63,630	23,336	−341,482
Amount of Decline in % of Population	15.1	11.3	16.7

	NORTH CAROLINA	SOUTH CAROLINA	TENNESSEE
1950	2,693,828 66.3%	1,339,106 63.3%	1,839,116 55.9%
1970	2,796,891 55.0	1,358,321 52.4	1,618,380 41.2
Numerical Change	103,063	19,215	−220,736
Amount of Decline in % of Population	11.3	10.9	14.7

	TEXAS	VIRGINIA
1950	2,873,134 37.3%	1,758,565 53.0%
1970	2,275,784 20.3	1,713,653 36.8
Numerical Change	−597,350	−44,912
Amount of Decline in % of Population	17.0	16.2

TABLE D-5
Migration, 1950–1970

	YEAR	UNITED STATES	SOUTH (11-STATE)	ALABAMA	ARKANSAS	FLORIDA
White	1940–1950	1,522,000	157,000	−140,000	−259,000	564,000
	1950–1960	2,668,000	903,000	−145,000	−283,000	1,516,000
	1960–1970	2,284,000	2,021,000	− 5,000	+ 38,000	1,340,000
	Change	6,474,000	3,091,000	−290,000	−504,000	3,420,000
Black	1940–1950	−180,000	−1,622,000	−204,000	−158,000	12,000
	1950–1960	−131,000	−1,487,000	−224,000	−150,000	96,000
	1960–1970	− 85,000	−1,477,000	−231,000	−112,000	−32,000
	Change	−396,000	−4,586,000	−659,000	−420,000	76,000

	YEAR	GEORGIA	LOUISIANA	MISSISSIPPI	NORTH CAROLINA	SOUTH CAROLINA
White	1940–1950	− 49,000	− 2,000	−108,000	− 95,000	− 24,000
	1950–1960	− 8,000	43,000	−110,000	−121,000	− 4,000
	1960–1970	198,000	26,000	10,000	81,000	44,000
	Change	141,000	67,000	−208,000	−135,000	16,000
Black	1940–1950	−243,000	−147,000	−326,000	−164,000	−208,000
	1950–1960	−205,000	− 93,000	−323,000	−204,000	−218,000
	1960–1970	−154,000	−163,000	−279,000	−175,000	−197,000
	Change	−602,000	−403,000	−928,000	−543,000	−623,000

	YEAR	TENNESSEE	TEXAS	VIRGINIA
White	1940–1950	− 97,000	173,000	194,000
	1950–1960	−217,000	147,000	85,000
	1960–1970	1,000	92,000	206,000
	Change	−313,000	412,000	485,000
Black	1940–1950	− 48,000	−107,000	− 29,000
	1950–1960	− 59,000	− 33,000	− 74,000
	1960–1970	− 51,000	− 4,000	− 79,000
	Change	−158,000	−144,000	−182,000

TABLE D-6
Nonnative Population in the South, 1950–1970

	SOUTH (11-STATE)	ALABAMA	ARKANSAS	FLORIDA	GEORGIA
1950	3,237,475	93,020	199,465	715,120	145,635
1970	9,388,196	330,479	335,552	2,733,004	603,145
Increase	6,150,721	237,459	136,087	2,017,884	457,510
Increase in % of total population	9.9	6.5	7.0	14.4	8.9

	LOUISIANA	MISSISSIPPI	NORTH CAROLINA	SOUTH CAROLINA	TENNESSEE
1950	122,540	67,630	168,350	72,405	219,365
1970	419,980	203,150	587,870	317,016	528,439
Increase	297,440	135,520	419,520	244,611	309,074
Increase in % of total population	6.9	6.0	7.4	8.8	6.7

	TEXAS	VIRGINIA
1950	935,830	498,115
1970	2,118,007	1,211,554
Increase	1,182,177	713,439
Increase in % of total population	6.8	11.0

TABLE D-7
Number of Farms, 1950–1969

	UNITED STATES	NON-SOUTH	SOUTH (11-STATE)	ALABAMA	ARKANSAS
1950	5,388,437	3,221,753	2,166,684	211,512	182,429
1969	2,730,250	1,820,990	909,260	72,491	60,433
Numerical decrease	2,658,187	1,400,763	1,251,424	139,021	121,996
% decrease	49.3	43.5	58.0	65.7	66.9

	FLORIDA	GEORGIA	LOUISIANA	MISSISSIPPI	NORTH CAROLINA
1950	56,921	198,191	124,181	251,383	288,508
1969	35,586	67,431	42,269	72,577	119,386
Numerical decrease	21,335	130,760	81,912	178,806	169,122
% decrease	37.5	66.0	66.0	71.1	58.6

	SOUTH CAROLINA	TENNESSEE	TEXAS	VIRGINIA
1950	139,364	231,631	331,567	150,997
1969	39,559	121,406	213,550	64,572
Numerical decrease	99,805	110,225	118,017	86,425
% decrease	71.6	47.6	35.6	57.2

TABLE D-8
Number Employed in Agriculture, 1950–1970

	UNITED STATES	NON-SOUTH	SOUTH (11-STATE)	ALABAMA	ARKANSAS
1950	7,215,380	4,436,214	2,779,166	253,477	217,595
1970	2,840,488	1,993,779	846,709	46,299	54,588
Numerical decrease	4,374,892	2,442,435	1,932,457	207,178	163,007
% decrease	60.6	55.1	69.5	81.7	74.9

	FLORIDA	GEORGIA	LOUISIANA	MISSISSIPPI	NORTH CAROLINA
1950	134,074	277,204	160,595	305,052	363,998
1970	110,994	75,521	47,999	53,714	103,805
Numerical decrease	23,080	201,683	112,596	251,338	260,193
% decrease	17.2	72.8	70.1	82.4	71.5

	SOUTH CAROLINA	TENNESSEE	TEXAS	VIRGINIA
1950	198,268	248,805	445,939	174,159
1970	39,778	62,114	194,635	57,262
Numerical decrease	158,490	186,691	251,304	116,897
% decrease	79.9	75.0	56.4	67.1

TABLE D-9
Per Capita Income, 1950–1970

YEAR	UNITED STATES	NON-SOUTH	SOUTH (11-STATE)	ALABAMA	ARKANSAS	FLORIDA
1950	$1,496	$1,624	$1,091	$ 880	$ 825	$1,281
1970	3,119	3,282	2,620	2,317	2,142	3,058

YEAR	GEORGIA	LOUISIANA	MISSISSIPPI	NORTH CAROLINA	SOUTH CAROLINA	TENNESSEE
1950	$1,034	$1,120	$ 755	$1,037	$ 893	$ 994
1970	2,640	2,330	1,925	2,474	2,303	2,464

YEAR	TEXAS	VIRGINIA
1950	$1,349	$1,228
1970	2,792	2,996

APPENDIX E

Measurements of Interparty Competition

Ranney Scale Formula, Graphs, and Tables

Levels of Interparty Competition for the South on the Ranney Scale*

Austin Ranney measured interparty competition for all states from 1946 to 1963 by averaging: (1) the mean percentage of the two-party vote for governor cast for the Democratic candidate, (2) the average percentage of seats in the state senate held by Democrats, (3) the average percentage of seats in the state house of representatives held by the Democrats, and (4) the percentage of terms for governor, state senator, and state representative held by Democrats. His scores varied from .000, which is perfect Republican domination, to 1.000, which is absolute Democratic domination. Ideal competition thus would be .500. For this book, the same methodology was used to create scores for the 1964 to 1974 period for the eleven states in the South.

Graph One represents an update of the Ranney formula. Graph Two represents a modification of the Ranney formula by the addition of two other averages that reflect party competition. Added to Ranney's four measures were (1) an average of the mean Democratic vote for U.S. Senate and the percentage of terms won by Democrats, and (2) an average of the mean Democratic vote for the U.S. House of Representatives and the percentage of terms won by Democrats.

The House vote for a state was calculated by totaling the votes received by party candidates within the state as a whole. In the case of Arkansas, which does not report vote totals in uncontested elections, the means of the separate district races were used.

The order of the states has changed since 1964. South Carolina, for example, has moved from most Democratic state to seventh place. Although there still remain two distinct clusters, they tend to break up somewhat in Graph Two, which adds the effect of party competition in congressional elections. In three states—Louisiana, Arkansas, and Georgia —the level of congressional competition was insignificantly different from

---

* Adaptation and updating from Austin Ranney, "Parties in State Politics," Herbert Jacob and Kenneth Vines (eds.), *Politics in the American States* (Boston: Little, Brown, 1967).

that at other levels; but in the other eight states, the additional factors reflected a higher degree of party competition within the state than found at other levels.

Ranney characterized states with scores of .900 or more as Democratic one-party states, those between .700 and .900 as modified one-party, and those between .300 and .700 as two-party. In the period from 1964 to 1974, only Tennessee among the states in the South achieved two-party status, and the score for that state on the modified Ranney formula strengthened the two-party designation for Tennessee.

The Ranney findings for 1946–1963 showed eight one-party states and three modified one-party states in the South—with only Virginia, North Carolina, and Tennessee in the latter category. When updated from 1964–1974, only Mississippi, Louisiana, and Alabama remained one-party Democratic states, and Alabama moved into the modified one-party category in Graph Two, a result of greater Republican successes in congressional campaigns.

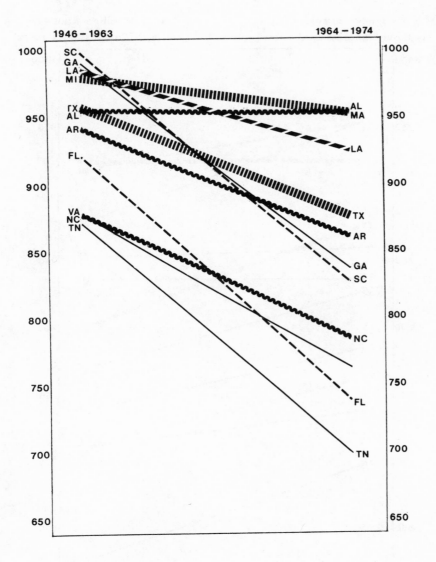

GRAPH ONE

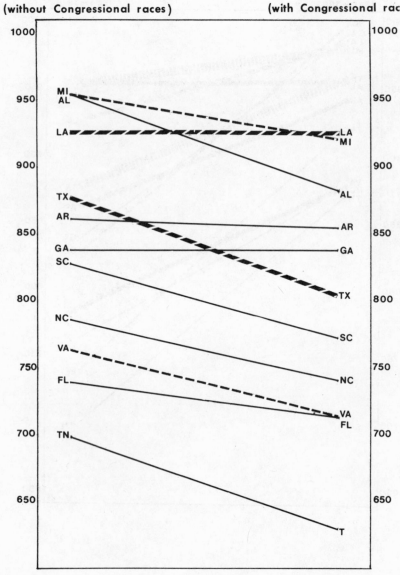

1964—1974
Ranney Formula
(without Congressional races)

1964—1974
Modified Ranney
(with Congressional races)

GRAPH TWO

The following tables show the scores compiled for the graphs in this Appendix illustrating the level of interparty competition within each of the states of the South.

TABLE E-1

	SCORES 1946–1963	SCORES 1964–1974	WITH CONGRESSIONAL RACES INCLUDED, 1964–74
Alabama	.957	.954	.882
Arkansas	.943	.861	.854
Florida	.922	.739	.712
Georgia	.992	.838	.838
Louisiana	.987	.925	.925
Mississippi	.981	.954	.921
North Carolina	.879	.786	.740
South Carolina	1.000	.828	.772
Tennessee	.872	.699	.630
Texas	.959	.977	.804
Virginia	.880	.764	.714

TABLE E-2

1964–1974 DEMOCRATIC OF 2-PARTY	STATE	% VOTE GOVERNOR	% STATE SENATE SEATS	% STATE HOUSE SEATS	% GOVERNOR, SENATE, HOUSE TERMS IN CONTROL	1964–1974 RANNEY FORMULA SCORE	1946–1963 RANNEY FORMULA SCORE
.0025	Alabama	84.0 (3)	98.6	99.0	100.0	.954	.957
.0817	Arkansas	59.5 (6)	98.1	97.8	88.9	.861	.943
.1830	Florida	55.2 (4)	73.6	72.9	93.8	.739	.922
.1535	Georgia	59.4 (3)	87.2	88.7	100.0	.838	.992
.0617	Louisiana	72.8 (3)	99.1	98.1	100.0	.925	.987
.0265	Mississippi	85.2 (2)	97.5	99.0	100.0	.954	.981
.0933	North Carolina	52.7 (3)	87.3	87.0	93.3	.786	.879
.1720	South Carolina	53.1 (3)	94.4	90.5	93.3	.828	1.000
.1725	Tennessee	67.6 (3)	65.6	59.8	86.7	.699	.872
.1155	Virginia	50.5 (3)	86.7	81.8	86.7	.764	.880

NOTE: With one exception, all figures used in updating the Ranney scores are percentages of the two-party vote. The exception was in the 1973 gubernatorial race in Virginia, where Democratic Lieutenant Governor Henry Howell, on the ballot as an independent, was counted as a Democrat, there being no official Democratic Party candidate.

TABLE E-3

STATE	% VOTE SENATOR	% VICTORIES SENATOR	MEAN	% VOTE HOUSE	% VICTORIES HOUSE	MEAN	GRAND MEAN	1974 MODIFIED RANNEY FORMULA SCORE
Alabama	75.5 (4)	100.0	87.8	62.8	56.5	59.7	73.8	.882
Arkansas	76.2 (4)	100.0	88.1	80.1	79.2	79.7	83.9	.854
Florida	53.4 (4)	75.0	64.2	61.8	74.4	67.6	65.9	.712
Georgia	75.8 (4)	100.0	87.9	72.0	86.7	79.4	83.7	.838
Louisiana	93.6 (4)	100.0	96.8	82.1	93.8	88.0	92.4	.925
Mississippi	78.5 (4)	100.0	89.3	79.6	83.3	81.5	85.4	.921
North Carolina	56.2 (4)	75.0	65.6	57.1	71.2	64.2	64.9	.740
South Carolina	51.7 (5)	60.0	55.9	68.4	83.3	75.9	65.9	.772
Tennessee	47.3 (5)	40.0	43.7	53.4	55.8	54.6	49.2	.630
Texas	49.6 (4)	50.0	49.8	74.2	89.3	81.8	65.8	.804
Virginia	62.8 (5)	75.0	68.9	55.9	51.7	53.8	61.4	.714

Bibliographical Essay

The following essay is designed as an evaluation of secondary sources that the authors found most helpful. For those interested in a more complete bibliography of materials about the South and its politics, comprehensive bibliographical essays can be found in Monroe Lee Billington, *The Political South in the Twentieth Century* (New York: Scribner's, 1975—available in paperback); Numan V. Bartley and Hugh Davis Graham, *Southern Politics and the Second Reconstruction* (Baltimore: The Johns Hopkins Press, 1975); and Neal R. Peirce, *The Deep South States of America* and *The Border South States* (New York: W. W. Norton and Co., Inc., 1974, 1975).

V. O. Key, Jr., *Southern Politics in State and Nation* (New York: Knopf, 1949), remains the classic beginning for any study of southern politics since World War II. It provided the foundation on which this study was based.

William C. Havard, editor, *The Changing Politics of the South* (Baton Rouge: Louisiana State University Press, 1972) includes insightful and perceptive introductory and concluding chapters by Havard and an excellent chapter on the South and Congress by Wayne Shannon. The state chapters, each written by a different author, are of very uneven quality.

Far more useful for insight into the politics of the respective states are the books by Neal R. Peirce. *The Deep South States of America* include Alabama, Arkansas, Florida, Georgia, Louisiana, Mississippi and South Carolina. *The Border South States* include North Carolina, Virginia and Tennessee. Texas is included in *The Great Plains States of America*. Peirce's books provide basic profiles on each of the states that go beyond politics and include sections on major cities.

C. Vann Woodward, *Origins of the New South, 1877–1913* (Baton Rouge: Louisiana State University Press, 1951) and George B. Tindall, *The Emergence of the New South* (Baton Rouge: Louisiana State University Press, 1967) are excellent surveys of southern history and provide valuable political background.

Alexander Heard, *A Two-Party South?* (Chapel Hill: University of North Carolina Press, 1952) provides a solid starting point for the study of two-party development in the region.

Monroe Lee Billington, *The Political South in the Twentieth Century*

(New York: Scribner's, 1975) provides a well-written overview of the major themes of regional political development. His chapter, "White Politicians and Black Civil Rights," is an excellent summary of the role played by the demand for equality under the law for Negroes as a force in shattering the one-party political system in the region.

J. Harvie Wilkinson, III, *Harry Byrd and the Changing Face of Virginia Politics, 1945–1966* (Charlottesville: University of Virginia Press, 1968) is perhaps the best of a number of useful books on contemporary state political developments. An excellent balance between textual material by the authors and selected readings is found in Eugene W. Jones, Joe E. Ericson, Lyle C. Brown, and Robert S. Trotter, Jr., *Practicing Texas Politics* (Boston: Houghton Mifflin, 1974).

Other useful books about the states include Bruce Galphin, *The Riddle of Lester Maddox* (Atlanta: Camelot, 1968), James Anderson, Richard Murray, and Edward Farley, *Texas Politics*, Second Edition (New York: Harper & Row, 1975); William D. Barnard, *Dixiecrats and Democrats: Alabama Politics 1942–50* (Tuscaloosa: University of Alabama Press, 1974), which provided valuable background on Alabama politics during the early period of this study; Nunan V. Bartley, *From Thurmond to Wallace: Political Tendencies in Georgia 1948–1968* (Baltimore: Johns Hopkins Press, 1970); Jack Bass, *Porgy Comes Home: South Carolina After 300 Years* (Columbia: The R. L. Bryan Co., 1972), which contains useful chapters on politics; Walter Lord, *The Past That Would Not Die* (New York: Harper & Row, 1965), which provides an excellent analysis of the forces of resistance in Mississippi; Jim Ranchino, *Faubus to Bumpers* (Arkadelphia, Arkansas: Action Research, Inc., 1972), a valuable analysis of recent political development in Arkansas; Virginius Dabney, *Virginia: The New Dominion* (New York: Doubleday, 1971); Thad Beyle and Merle Black, editors, *Politics and Policy in North Carolina* (New York: MMS Press, 1975).

Pat Watters and Reese Cleghorn, *Climbing Jacob's Ladder: The Arrival of Negroes in Southern Politics* (New York: Harcourt, Brace, Jovanovich, 1967) is perhaps the best of a number of useful books on black political development in the South. Chandler Davidson, *Biracial Politics: Conflict and Coalition in the Metropolitan South* (Baton Rouge: Louisiana State University Press, 1972) provides insights into the developments of maturing black political participation and suggests a trend toward populist-based coalitions between blacks and working class whites. The report of the U.S. Commission on Civil Rights, *The Voting Rights Act: Ten Years After* (1975) provided valuable background and analysis of the impact of the Voting Rights Act.

F. Ray Marshall, *Labor in the South* (Cambridge: Harvard University Press, 1967) is an excellent study.

Valuable background and insights on Republican development in the

South in the 1950s are contained in chapters in Samuel Lubell, *The Future of American Politics* (New York: Harper & Row, 1952) and *Revolt of the Moderates* (New York: Harper & Row, 1956). For the 1960s, see Bernard Cosman and Robert Huckshorn, editors, *Republican Politics: The 1964 Campaign and Its Aftermath for the Party* (New York: Praeger, 1968) and Stephen Hess and David S. Broder, *The Republican Establishment: The Present and Future of the GOP* (New York: Harper & Row, 1967).

J. Morgan Kousser, *The Shaping of Southern Politics* (New Haven: Yale University Press, 1974) carefully documents the use of suffrage restrictions from 1880 to 1910 and their effect in disenfranchising blacks and poor whites and creating the one-party system that persisted for almost half a century in southern politics. However, a close reading of V. O. Key's *Southern Politics* suggests that Kousser overstates the difference between his findings and Key's analysis.

For insights into southern voting behavior, see David M. Kovenock, James W. Prothro, and Associates, *Explaining the Vote: Presidential Choices in the Nation and the States, 1968* (Chapel Hill: Comparative State Elections Project, Institute for Research, University of North Carolina, 1974).

Index

Index

Index

Index

Index

Index